T0329469

SHERLOCK HOLMES

SHERLOCK HOLMES

A SECRET HISTORY

JOHN V. HENNESSY

Algora Publishing
New York

Library of Congress Cataloging-in-Publication Data —

Names: Hennessy, John V., author.
Title: Sherlock Holmes: a secret history / John V. Hennessy.
Description: New York: Algora Publishing, 2017. | Includes bibliographical
    references.
Identifiers: LCCN 2017029558 (print) | LCCN 2017035697 (ebook) | ISBN
    9781628942903 (pdf) | ISBN 9781628942880 (soft cover: alk. paper) | ISBN
    9781628942897 (hard cover: alk. paper)
Subjects: LCSH: Doyle, Arthur Conan, 1859-1930—Characters—Sherlock Holmes.
    | Doyle, Arthur Conan, 1859-1930—Criticism and interpretation. | Holmes,
    Sherlock. | Detective and mystery stories, English—History and criticism.
    | Private investigators in literature.
Classification: LCC PR4624 (ebook) | LCC PR4624 .H46 2017 (print) | DDC
    823/.8—dc23
LC record available at https://lccn.loc.gov/2017029558

Printed in the United States

To my wife
Ellen McLaughlin

"There is, perhaps, in everything of any consequence, a secret history which it would be amusing to know, could we have it authentically communicated."
— James Boswell

"Everything comes in circles." "The old wheel turns, and the same spoke comes up. It's all been done before, and will be again."
— Sherlock Holmes

"There was something very strange in all this."
— John H. Watson

TABLE OF CONTENTS

i

Introduction

The aspiration of this work is to analyze the origins and ambitions of the Sherlock Holmes stories, and the individuals involved in them, and to build a foundation of conditions of possibility regarding Arthur Conan Doyle's intentions for creating these stories and these people in the forms we have them in. In an effort to find the design behind Sherlock Holmes' animation, what amounts to an industry has sprung up, involving writers of every bent and description in each country in which the stories are read. Holmes puts me in mind of the observation G. K. Chesterton made about one of his own characters in his short story "A Picture of Tuesday": "But, like all the works of God, you have to see him twenty times before you see him for the first time." This study hopes to provide new insights, quite a few actually, for seeing this work of God, and his creator, at least fractionally, for the first time. The Holmes Canon and the absorbing life of their author have been so thoroughly investigated already as to make many other justifications for such a project untenable.

Past writers have approached the hyper-complex nature of the Holmes stories but none seems to have fully grasped them in their entirety, and I realize I have not done so myself. Every year Holmes' imprint on fiction literature grows deeper and wider, like a footprint in the melting snow, and imitation is still the greatest compliment. Doyle's writings in general, and these stories in particular, have gained the distinction of being the most pirated works of modern fiction. Even Hamlet, whose influences colored the greater part of European literature and led it indirectly to the modern "anti-hero," which Sherlock himself epitomizes from time to time, left no such widespread emotional impression. The drama of Hamlet reaches psychological levels Holmes readers would not feel to be completely unfamiliar ground, a testimonial in itself to the fact that these stories possess unexplored depths. I doubt if any other character, real or unreal, has had so many films made of his exploits, and there are even modern dance dramas, plays, and ballets, dealing with his adventures. Only religious leaders such as

Jesus or Buddha have more written about them. It's fitting that Holmes has such celebrity among so many different peoples, and this critique hopes to be able to show some reasons for it.

An effort has been made to avoid covering those areas others have surveyed. It's mandatory to bring into such an inquiry those boldly distinguishable connections such as Dr. Joseph Bell and Wilkie Collins, but I attempt to deal with them in a less apparent manner. When the characters, themes, or situations found in other Doyle writings overlap with those of the Canon, and I realize their use will enhance the focus of my picture or support my claims, I don't hesitate to mention them, but the center of gravity always remains Baker Street. This presented a difficulty to this undertaking, for the themes of almost all of Doyle's fiction are analogous, hence the choice of what to exclude was more problematic than what to include. Overlap of intentions and interests plays a major role in the development of all our author's work. The Holmes stories are actually only a small part of their author's entire output, and a number of theories I put forward find clearer expression in some other works, but the compass of this book does not allow their inclusion. Often exotic and bizarre personalities serve as surrogate fathers to characters; consequently the project got more formidable and convoluted the longer I kept at it, like a snowball rolling downhill.

A survey of Doyle's work reveals an extremely aggressive mental life, with concepts, often eccentric and singular, restlessly being unfolded and modified: the sign of a prolific reader coupled to a susceptible personality. What we will primarily be looking at here is the evolution of his thoughts — for one's thoughts, like the other habits one picks up in life, never stop changing.

CHAPTER ONE. DOYLE'S RATIONALE

The world that Sherlock Holmes was born into was a generation in revolution with partisans in rampant search of the "modern," attempting to overthrow the "old," without always being aware of what either might be. This deficiency of a precise definition, however, was only a bottleneck, not a blockade, which in no way disheartened the seekers, for they knew that the modern existed and that it could be discovered. Artists and writers in various countries were aspiring desperately to be present at the birth of the dewy avant-garde movement and assist in the delivery if possible. It was not an easy birth, for not everyone was enthusiastic to see these new ideas greet the light of day, but the advance troops never gave up.

In Doyle's day this entire concept and everything it epitomized, especially the new freedom of choice it offered the artist, was both novel and fresh. "In the England of the Nineties, for example, the minor poets and aesthetes claimed to be 'modern' because they broke with Victorian tradition, imitated the French Symbolists, and defied middle-class bourgeois morality. In the same England of the late Nineties a much stronger claim to be 'modern' was being made by very different writers, notably Shaw, with his Socialism and epigrams about rates and taxes, H. G. Wells, in his science fiction, and Rudyard Kipling, with his empire-building and steam engines," J. B. Priestley tells us in his *Literature and Western Man*, adding, "So it was elsewhere, throughout Western Europe: the ambitious writers, not the elderly and academic, and not those who were content to be easy public entertainers, were all 'modern.'"

Up until now Doyle had written several novels in a traditional style, and although he undoubtedly realized such works were no longer contemporary, he persevered in them anyway, believing they were somehow sufficient to his efforts. Although we are hardly alert to it today, Doyle operated under a great deal of risk with the first Holmes story and the initial reaction to it was cool enough to frighten any young writer. Indifference can be daunting, and according to Priestley at any rate, the English are the most indifferent people in the world when it comes to literature.

In 1886, while Doyle is working on *A Study in Scarlet*, another young doctor, Sigmund Freud of Vienna, was setting up practice as a specialist in nervous disorders, while in Germany the philosopher Friedrich Nietzsche was seeing through the press an impressive study of modern morals — *Beyond Good and Evil*. A year prior he had published *Thus Spake Zarathustra*, and a year later he would bring out his *The Genealogy of Morals*: works dilating the edges of modern philosophical thought. This eminent year also saw, printed in Paris, *The Symbolist Manifesto*, whose author, the poet Jean Moréas, was considered an unofficial leader of this most advanced school of writing.

Symbolism itself is far more than the name implies. The more various symbols you utilized in your writing, the more legitimate it was considered as a work of art — and the greater the number of sources and references your symbols covered, thereby leading the reader's mind by association into the theme of your piece of writing, the more potent the whole effect was.

Association, a vehicle of symbolism, has always been a foundational part of human consciousness and, as Freud realized, of the human unconsciousness as well. Orientals believe that eating the ginseng plant will somehow aid human longevity simply because the plant itself takes so long to mature. When English and American sailors were caught in a calm and could not fill their sails, they would sit around on the deck and whistle tunes, hoping to "whistle up the wind."

Symbolist writing and painting had been around for a number of years but the *Manifesto* did much to give the movement definition, scope, and acceptance. Stéphane Mallarmé believed you could create literature out of a few evocative, mysterious phrases with one thought drawing the mind to another thought or group of thoughts or feelings, often in a circuitous route but reaching the goal nevertheless. Subtlety plays its part here, and subtlety and innuendo were looked upon as goals in themselves. Overlap of intentions and references also plays a role, with the power of suggestion carrying the greatest force. Something is constantly being aimed at in Symbolist writing, although the target itself may be elusive.

Doyle realized that various aspects of the theories of association were borrowings from the early French philosopher Denis Diderot, whose writings contain the nucleus of the thought, if not all the atoms, and only elaborated upon by Mallarmé and the others. Diderot used the example of the vibrating string which causes other strings around it to vibrate by association. Doyle's writings include general thoughts about the French Symbolist poets as well as particular thoughts about Mallarmé, who, along with Paul Verlaine, struck him as odd but interesting writers.

The influence of all this on art and writing was immediate and widespread with Doyle, despite his offhand comments, acutely conscious of the implications of the *Manifesto* and of the crusade it championed. It was now understood that a truly contemporary writer, hoping to express himself in terms of modernity, could not ignore the connotations of this development or they in turn would be ignored by an aristocracy of intellectuals who were confident they were leading the people from ignorance to enlightenment. The character of Sherlock Holmes finds definition within the bounds of these circumstances, for he was designed to be the world's first modern detective.

The American Edgar Allan Poe, some of whose work was translated by Baudelaire and studied by Mallarmé, is credited by the French with having inspired the Symbolist movement. They felt that Poe had showed them the way with his poetic attempts at capturing not just the outer world of man but the inner as well. Poe's theory and practice of what he called "a suggestive indefiniteness" — his belief that poetry should be evocative rather than descriptive, seems to have made the deepest impression. He was an original innovator in two different kinds of shorter fiction: the scientific wonder tale and the detective story, and Doyle picked up on both. Through symbolic fantasy, Poe attempted to express a psych-pathological condition within his characters; an attempt that Baudelaire for one did not back down from emulating. Doyle himself utilized visionary symbolism in such diverse works as *The Poison Belt* and *The Lost World*, among others. Behavior both criminal and non-criminal that is governed by a compulsion, in some cases accompanied by a disease or deformity, either mental or physical, is a common denominator in much of Doyle's and Poe's work, as it is in that of the American master Nathaniel Hawthorne. In his short stories "The Murders in the Rue Morgue" and "The Mystery of Marie Rogêt," Poe puts into the mind and mouth of his famous detective Dupin associative thoughts dealing with the case in hand, examples of which can be found in other writers on Holmes. Poe demonstrated how one thought leads, however circuitously, to a manifold thought, and also how a shrewd thinker can follow and explain the stepped reasoning behind the mental shifting, with these passages considered by the French to be the arch examples of associative writing. Doyle was cognizant of Poe's work and even went so far as to have Holmes offer criticism of Dupin's line of reasoning in *A Study in Scarlet*. One important aspect of Symbolism we must keep in mind is that the artist must never for any reason tell of his borrowings or references, although he may hint at them.

That which is modern is not necessarily that which is contemporary. Some writers no longer impress us as being innovative because of our familiarity with their works, but in their day they were recognized as cutting-edge and novel. Doyle appreciated the value of their ingenious donations and the new insights their novelty helped bring to light.

In the middle of the eighteenth century, the young, enthusiastic Scotsman James Boswell journeyed to London cherishing the hope of meeting and befriending the celebrated writer Samuel Johnson. From what he tells us, the thought of writing a biography of Johnson had germinated in Boswell's mind years before the two met in their adopted city of London, a city destined to play a major role in both their lives.

Doyle's favorite historian, Lord Macaulay, has said of Boswell's *The Life of Samuel Johnson LL.D.* that it is "the most interesting biographical work in the world." Johnson himself was an accomplished biographer, evidenced by his numerous books and shorter pieces on such men as Richard Savage and Sir

Francis Drake; still useful works, in addition of course to his *The Lives of the Most Eminent English Poets.*

In his Introduction, Boswell compares himself to Francis Bacon; one he considers to have understood what was genuinely important in the life of an historical figure, in this case Julius Caesar. Not only will Boswell display to us the agreeable aspects of his subject, but he will treat us to the "shade as well as the light": the dark side of the man, including his "faults or failings," claiming "that my mode of biography, which gives not only a *History* of Johnson's *visible* progress through the world, and of his publications, but a *view* of his mind in his letters and conversations, is the most perfect that can be conceived, and will be more of a Life than any work that has ever yet appeared." This seemingly arbitrary advance finds justification, for his work is an impressive creation that revolutionized the entire technique of biographical writing. Like Doyle himself, Boswell was born in Edinburgh, and like Watson, was a stranger to London with neither family nor friends there. Watson was wounded out of the Army, while Boswell was turned down for a commission in the foot-guards. He opted to become a lawyer, and after studying law in Utrecht returned to Britain, dividing his time between Scotland, where he was a Laird, and London. One reason Watson came to London was to economize on his half-pay, and as Boswell expressed it, "there is no place where economy can be so well practiced as in London: more can be had here for the money."

Having arrived, Boswell meets Johnson, and for the rest of their lives both men are linked intellectually and emotionally. Johnson was born and raised in Litchfield yet prefers to live in London, for he tells us of the city, "the intellectual man is struck with it, as comprehending the whole of human life in all its variety, the contemplation of which is inexhaustible."

Boswell is a lawyer who is known primarily for his writings, just as Doyle and Watson are physicians famous for their writings. Boswell and Watson are married, while their subjects are single. Watson is called by Holmes "Boswell" a number of times, as in "I am lost without my Boswell," found in "A Scandal in Bohemia," while in "The Man with the Twisted Lip" Doyle goes so far as to have Watson's wife address him as "James." In fact, "Boswell" had become a kind of nickname for an exceptionally observant companion.

The character of Johnson can be separated from that of Boswell, for there is no shortage of other works written on him, but it was not just the life of Johnson that Doyle was recreating but rather the relationship and the interaction between the two men.

The fact that we are told so little of the early life of Holmes is a borrowing from Boswell's work in which Johnson divulged little of his early life. Boswell had to question him repeatedly for what information he got pertaining to his boyhood, which is covered in a page or two of what was originally an eight-volume work.

Johnson said of biography that it is rarely well executed since "they only who live with a man can write his life with any genuine exactness and discrimination; and few people who have lived with a man know what to remark about him." These two positive features are blended in Watson, who not only lives with Holmes but knows what to remark about him as well. A room at Johnson's house was at Boswell's disposal, which he often availed himself of while in London, and Johnson in turn spent some time at Boswell's estate, plus they traveled together, so in a sense Boswell can be said to have lived with his subject. Boswell tells us of his bold, energetic plan of using narrative to analyze the poet's life but also "wherever it is in my power, his own minutes, letters, or conversation, being convinced that this mode is more lively, and will make my readers better acquainted with him, than even most of those were who actually knew him, but could know him only partially; whereas there is here an accumulation of intelligence from various points, by which his character is more fully understood and illustrated." A survey of the Canon asserts compliance with this scheme, for in the aggregate there is a huge volume of written correspondence utilized to reveal plot and character, and the stories are famous for their record of private dialogue, especially between the two main characters.

The irascible Johnson is difficult to get along with, and he, like Holmes, has a nasty habit of making negative comments about the writing style of his historian. A few of the detective's adventures are the product of his own pen, for Johnson offers the advice "that every man's life may be best written by himself."

Born the son of an itinerant bookseller in 1709 in Staffordshire, Samuel Johnson, from the beginning "a king of men," according to Boswell, was obviously one of the most fascinating, intelligent, and original men that ever lived. Apparently there were almost no bounds to his learning; he wrote essays on and reviewed books covering subjects as diverse as tea, Church history, America, distilling, politics of all stripes, etymology, dead languages, etc. "That superiority over his fellows, which he maintained with so much dignity in his march through life, was not assumed from vanity and ostentation," Boswell tells us, "but was the natural and constant effect of those extraordinary powers of mind, of which he could not but be conscious by comparison; the intellectual difference, which in other cases of comparison of characters, is often a matter of undecided contest, being as clear in his case as the superiority of stature in some men above others." Although he could not be considered as the master of any one field, "he had accumulated a vast and various collection of learning and knowledge, which was so arranged in his mind, as to be ever in readiness to be brought forth." His superiority rested in what Boswell called "the art of thinking, the art of using his mind; a certain continual power of seizing the useful substance of all that he knew, and exhibiting it in a clear and forcible manner." Johnson was so hungry for knowledge in any and all fields he even learned to knit from a woman, in an age when no Englishman would have been caught doing such a thing. Doyle himself emulates this attitude for both men studied in some depth philosophy, biography, etymology, and history, among other fields.

Johnson knew more of human life, which he studied constantly and intensely, from a great variety of angles, than his contemporaries. Observing everything around him, he seemed to be able to read the character and interests from the dress and manners of those he came in contact with almost immediately. "No man was a more attentive and nice observer of behaviour in those in whose company he happened to be," we are told. The speech patterns of different people, Johnson tell us, informs us of where they are from. Of peoples' dress Johnson tells us, "there is no man who works at any particular trade, but you may know him from his appearance to do so. One part or the other of his body being more used than the rest, he is in some degree deformed." In Mrs. Thrale's memoir *Thraliana*, we are told that in spite of the fact that he appeared "sometimes so absent and always so near-sighted, he scrutinizes into every part of almost everybody's appearance"; and Boswell enforces this: "the force of his attention and perceptive quickness made him see and distinguish all manner of objects, whether of nature or of art, with a nicety that is rarely to be found."

The thought process, work habits, and mental cast of Johnson and Holmes are similar. We are told by Boswell, "by reading and meditation, and a very close inspection of life, he had accumulated a great fund of miscellaneous knowledge, which, by a peculiar promptitude of mind, was ever ready at his call, and which he had constantly accustomed himself to clothe in the most apt and energetick expression." William Strahan tells us, "He is capable of the greatest application, and can undergo any degree of labour, where he sees it necessary, and where his heart and affections are strongly engaged." In his essay on *The Life of Samuel Johnson*, Macaulay tells us he had "great muscular strength," with "great quickness of parts," but this was accompanied by "a morbid propensity to sloth and procrastination; a kind and generous heart, with a gloomy and irritable temper." Johnson worked by fits and starts and often sat around doing nothing but thinking for days or weeks at a time, himself admitting that he wrote, "in my usual way, dilatorily and hastily, unwilling to work, and working with vigour and haste." Johnson often "talked for victory," as Boswell calls it; he took any side or championed any opinion — provided he talked well — but Holmes never permits himself to engage in this disagreeable posture.

The poet is aware of his powers of observation and occasionally chides his friend, as Holmes does Watson, for not being as eagle-eyed as himself. Holmes once remarked to Watson, "You see, but you do not observe," and one day when Johnson and Boswell were riding in a coach, the Scot tells us, "He expressed some displeasure at me, for not observing sufficiently the various objects upon the road." The poet laments that he himself can see out of only one eye, and then not very clearly.

Being a "profoundly superstitious man, obsessed with the idea of numbers," Johnson often did things like count the steps that it took to reach a room, including the steps on the stairs leading to different floors. Watson is amazed to learn that Holmes has indeed counted the steps leading to their apartment, and Holmes shows disappointment with him for not having done so himself. Now, these next few quotes are of great interest to students of Holmes. Johnson believed that "nothing is little to him that feels it with great sensibility, a mind able to see common incidents in their real state, is disposed by very common incidents to very serious contemplations," elaborating, in a dedication of a book on draughts, "Triflers may find or make any thing a trifle: but since it is the great characteristick of a wise man to see events in their causes, to obviate consequences, and ascertain contingencies, your Lordship will think nothing a trifle by which the mind is inured to caution, foresight, and circumspection."

The mode of speech of both subjects is analogous for Johnson spoke with "deliberate and strong utterance," with Macaulay saying, "He uttered his short, weighty, and pointed sentences with a power of voice, and a justness and energy of emphasis," adding that he spoke "in language so exact and so forcible that it might have been printed without the alteration of a word." This thought is reinforced by Boswell, who tells us that his "attention to precision and clearness in expression was very remarkable," being "always most perfectly clear and perspicuous; and his language was so accurate, and his sentences so neatly constructed, that his conversation might have been all printed without any correction." As far as we know, Watson never had to correct Holmes' speech.

These two celebrated men, Holmes and Johnson, did not live in actual poverty, but they had very little when how they lived is compared to the value of the benefits they bestowed upon their society and their nation. Neither had actual incomes to speak of, although Johnson later in life was awarded a modest pension, yet both were famous in their own country and even throughout much of the rest of the world, while still living.

Johnson himself was a bit of a private detective who could often be found at the police station gathering information about criminals and criminal activity. He was friendly with a "Mr. Welch, who succeeded the celebrated Henry Fielding as one of his Majesty's Justices of the Peace for Westminster; kept a regular office for the police of that great district; and discharged his important trust, for many years, faithfully and ably." In his "eager and unceasing curiosity to know human life in all its variety," Johnson "attended Mr. Welsh in his office for a whole winter, to hear the examinations of the culprits". Welch had to go to Italy for his failing health or Johnson would have spent more time with him. In 1763 the poet helped debunk an infamous fraud known as "the Ghost in Cock-lane," going through as much trouble and applying as much thought to the case as Holmes himself devoted to his problems. Johnson even got himself involved in a murder case when a friend of his, a Mr. Baretti, an Italian writer living in London, got into a fight in an alley with a pimp and stabbed him to death. Along with a number of other acquaintances of Baretti's, including the actor David Garrick and the artist Joshua Reynolds, Johnson testified upon the character of the man, who, because of this testimony, was acquitted.

Among the plethora of influences on Doyle's art, none stands out more than the Irish writer Joseph Sheridan Le Fanu. Born in Dublin in 1814 and dying there, a recluse, in 1873, Le Fanu, a generation older than Doyle, was in the ranks of those writers he learned from. His middle name, which he always used, advertises he was related, on his mother's side, to the playwright Richard Sheridan.

Although educated for the law at Dublin University and called to the bar in 1839, Le Fanu turned instead to a career in literature, producing fourteen novels and a great number of short stories. A three-volume collection of his varied tales was published in 1880, seven years after his death, by Bentley and Son of London, and that was probably how Doyle was introduced to him. He enjoyed a great reputation among writers such as V. S. Pritchett, Montague Rhodes James, and Elizabeth Bowen, all of whom wrote introductions to editions of his work in later years, and Le Fanu even influenced some of James Joyce's work, as Joyce himself tells us. Doyle paid the greatest compliment imaginable when he recycled the bizarre plot of Le Fanu's *Uncle Silas* for his own early novel *The Firm of Girdlestone*. Although subject and style make it difficult for us to take Le Fanu seriously today, he must actually have been something of a household word in the recent past, judging by his enormous influence on other artists as well as the vast number of times he was published. Charles Dickens utilized Le Fanu for his book *A Christmas Carol* — at least two of his capsule tales are expressly based on the older writer's work; and Bram Stoker, author of *Dracula*, mined him for much of his own riches.

In his short stories in particular the Irishman makes great use of the miraculous and the spine tingling. Horace Walpole and Edgar Allan Poe are among his artistic ancestors and, much in the manner of Poe, Le Fanu's tales oscillate between the poles of supernatural horror and suspenseful detection. Le Fanu never became drawn into questions of logic and deduction. Stories such as "The Murdered Cousin" and "The Evil Guest" are fundamentally preoccupied with the unraveling of mysteries, but nowhere, as far as I can discover, does he create a true detective, and the police are never called into it. Often Le Fanu can be vivid and moving, showing considerable skill, but he is a Gothic writer with all the faults of the species, foremost among them being his plots' uncompromising predictability. Emotional responses that are exaggerated and calculated make for wooden, stilted, conventionally Gothic characters as well. If an individual, usually an aged and loyal servant, warns the newly arrived young relative that a spirit has been known to frequent the halls of the manor at midnight, the Greenwich Observatory would not go wrong setting their clocks by the spook's appearance, for no one does a more accurate job of keeping time than a Victorian apparition. Dickens might have had Le Fanu in mind when he said, "Ghosts have little originality," and they "'walk' in a beaten track." Nevertheless, in these dark tales we have located solid prototypes for both the character of Holmes and the form, plots, settings, details, and themes, for any number of the Holmes stories, as well as for a generous balance of Doyle's other works.

"Green Tea: A Case Reported by Martin Hesselius, the German Physician," a short story published by Le Fanu in 1869, is undoubtedly the single most eminent influence on the Sherlock Holmes stories. A masterpiece by any standard, "Green Tea" is perhaps the most insightful short piece of writing in any language. Pritchett regarded Le Fanu as having great psychological insight into human nature, and "Green Tea" best exemplifies his blend of primitive mental terror with modern psychodrama.

The story deals with a Rev. Jennings, an English clergyman living in London with an avocation for studying pagan and pre-Christian metaphysics.

While engaged in the writing of a book on this subject, Mr. Jennings begins to be visited by a shaggy, grinning monkey, invisible to others, who distracts the man with such antics as following him about the streets, talking to him, squatting on his bible while he preaches, singing blasphemies into his head to interrupt his prayers, and eventually driving his victim to self-destruction. The ape is what the Irish call a "pookah"; an animal that only one person in the world can see.

An invasion from the subconscious region has taken on an objective persona, and horror is on a very personal level in all of Le Fanu's work. Instigated by the imagination, preternatural creatures or ghosts assume the forms of animals such as birds, bears, monkeys, and especially dogs and cats in his writings. In his alarm of the haunting ape, the Rev. Jennings turns to a Dr. Harley for help, but he proves to be a "materialistic man" who is incapable of ministering to the soul, wherein the real sickness lies. Our attention is drawn to Harley Street: the London thoroughfare housing the offices of England's greatest specialists, warning us that all the physicians in the world cannot alleviate the sufferings of Jennings.

Harley arranges for Jennings to meet a Dr. Hesselius at a party. Dr. Hesselius, a medical practitioner and a student of metaphysics, acknowledges the high reputation of Harley and his colleagues while admitting respect for Emanuel Swedenborg, the Swedish religious philosopher and mystic whose writings heavily influenced European and all Western thought. Hesselius alternates between describing his role in the events and his understanding of them, both as a doctor and as an "intelligent layman." Doyle also writes many of his stories, usually through the medium of Dr. Watson, both from the frame of reference of a physician, which Doyle himself was, and from the perspective of a knowledgeable layman. It is Hesselius who outlines for us the awesome details of Mr. Jennings' evil times, and the tale will conclude with his thoughts, but what we are reading is actually the chronicle of an anonymous English doctor working from Dr. Hesselius' own notes.

A number of parallels between Hesselius and Holmes come to light, such as the fact that both are published writers in their fields. Hesselius has published a work entitled *Essays on Metaphysical Medicine*, and a tract, *The Cardinal Functions of the Brain*. The affiliation between the two is evidenced in the conversation between Lady Mary, hostess of the gathering at which Jennings and Hesselius have been introduced, and the doctor. After the Reverend departs the party, Hesselius confronts the hostess and informs her of his having been favorably impressed with the clergyman, and she in turn speaks of her own high regard for the man. What follows puts us in mind of someone we know, and we don't even have to squint to see it. Hesselius tells Lady Mary, "It is pleasant to hear so good an account of his neighbourly virtues. I can only testify to his being an agreeable and gentle companion, and in addition to what you have told me, I think I can tell you two or three things about him."

"Really!"

"Yes, to begin with, he's unmarried."

"Yes, that's right — go on."

"He has been writing, that is he *was*, but for two or three years perhaps, he has not gone on with his work, and the book was upon some rather abstract subject — perhaps theology."

"Well, he was writing a book, as you say; I'm not quite sure what it was about, but only that it was nothing that I cared for; very likely you are right, and he certainly did stop — yes."

"And although he only drank a little coffee here to-night, he likes tea, at least, did like it, extravagantly."

"Yes, that's *quite* true."

"'He drank green tea, a good deal, didn't he?' I pursued."

"Well, that's very odd! Green tea was a subject on which we used almost to quarrel."

"'But he has quite given that up,' said I."

"So he has."

"And, now, one more fact. His mother or his father, did you know them?"

"'Yes, both; his father is only ten years dead, and their place is near Dawlbridge. We knew them very well,' she answered."

"'Well, either his mother or his father — I should rather think his father, saw a ghost,' said I."

"Well, you really are a conjurer, Doctor Hesselius."

"'Conjurer or no, haven't I said right?' I answered merrily."

"You certainly have, and it *was* his father..." Lady Mary is forced to admit. When the perplexed hostess asks, "But how *did* you find it out?" Hesselius cryptically answers, "By the planets, of course, as the gipsies do."

That answer will have to do for us as well, since Dr. Hesselius never does explain his reasoning in gathering such detailed intelligence regarding a man he exchanged only a few sentences with.

In the brief but penetrating analysis of Holmes offered to us by Dr. Joseph Bell, Doyle's former medical teacher at Edinburgh, as a preface to the first edition of *A Study in Scarlet*, Bell observes that the author has "created a shrewd, quick-sighted, inquisitive man, half doctor, half virtuoso, with plenty of spare time, a retentive memory, and perhaps with the best gift of all — the power of unloading the mind of all the burden of trying to remember unnecessary details." Bell has already told us, "There is nothing new under the sun. Voltaire taught us the method of Zadig, and every good teacher of medicine and surgery exemplifies every day in his teaching and practice the method and its results. The precise and intelligent recognition and appreciation of minor differences is the real essential factor in all successful medical diagnosis. Carried into ordinary life, granted the presence of an insatiable curiosity and fairly acute senses, you have Sherlock Holmes as he astonishes his somewhat dense friend Watson; carried out in a specialized training, you have Sherlock Holmes the skilled detective."

He has obliquely alluded to Holmes as being a medical doctor a number of times, as in the use of the modifier "skilled," a term almost always used to modify "physician." In some of the stories the division between medical and criminal detection is more a question of preference than role.

Dr. Hesselius assures Harley he will look into the Jennings case in an unofficial capacity, the relative position Holmes adopts in the field of police work. A few days later Dr. Hesselius pays a pseudo-social visit to the clergy's apartment and upon being told that he was engaged, opts to wait in the library. The entire third chapter of "Green Tea" is devoted to a description of the Jennings library, followed by a lengthy rumination by Hesselius upon a set of Swedenborg's *Arcana Caelestia,* in the Latin, found open upon the table.

In 1716 Swedenborg was appointed assessor with the Royal College of Mines in his native Sweden, but in 1747 he resigned this post, abandoned science, and turned wholly to theocentric studies. Dr. Hesselius himself comes to mind, and so in fact does Holmes, for when we are initially introduced to him it is as a scientist working in the laboratory of St. Bartholomew's Hospital. He remains throughout his life a scientist studying primarily chemistry and criminology, while always entertaining a strong propensity toward the metaphysical. Holmes himself is an assessor for the mining industry. He tells us in "The Adventure of the Empty House" that while absent from London for three years, he spent some of that time "in a research into the coal-tar derivatives, which I conducted in a laboratory in Montpellier, in the South of France." Since coal tar is derived from coal, you could never research it unless you knew how to analyze the coal itself.

Swedenborg believed the Scriptures revealed a certain law of correspondence, that every natural object is an expression of a spiritual cause; and I can't help finding a parallel in this to Holmes' system of detection if we regard an object as a clue to the meaning of an act. Several experiences of divine revelation convinced Swedenborg that he was a direct "instrument of God"; the very words Dr. Hesselius uses to describe himself in the last chapter of "Green Tea," entitled "A Word for Those Who Suffer." Hesselius is convinced that God, working with him and through him, strives to ease the suffering of mankind. The ideals and guise of Jesus, as well as the spiritual posture of the Hindu yoga, come to mind for essentially this is their function in the world. Speaking of a patient whom he has cured, the doctor asks, "Who, under God, cured you? Your humble servant, Martin Hesselius. Let me rather adopt the more emphasized piety of a certain good old French surgeon of three hundred years ago: 'I treated, and God cured you.'"

Swedenborg had no intention of founding a new sect, but following his death his followers organized "The Church of the New Jerusalem," with the first congregation meeting in London, by the way.

Doyle is an avid reader of this mystic, acknowledging his supernatural debt to him in his work *The History of Spiritualism* asserting that modern Spiritualism started with Swedenborg, and his own conversion to this practice was made easier by his reading of the theologian. A Swedenborgian minister is featured in his story "The Great Keinplatz Experiment," technically a ghost story since it involves the separation of body and soul.

We rejoin Dr. Hesselius waiting patiently in the library of Mr. Jennings, where he finds markers in several of the Swedenborg volumes directing his attention to certain passages dealing with the nature of evil spirits and their intentions towards mankind, which are not good, as we can imagine. In this paralleling of themes, we are being shown that Jennings is not the first victim to experience whatever it is he is now going through, for Swedenborg has been there himself. Doyle will adopt this applicability of title or contents of a book, indirectly, by association, to presage or correlate a thematic development quite often; we shall examine a few examples eventually.

This monkey in "Green Tea" was appropriated from Nathaniel Hawthorne's *The House of the Seven Gables*; one of the few psychodramas strong enough to compete with Le Fanu's work. This story of revenge, and by implication, ghostly retaliation, is instigated by a wrong committed generations previous by a Colonel Pyncheon, initial yet wrongful owner and inhabitant of the namesake house. The curse of Matthew Maule, swindled owner of the land upon which the house is built: "God will give you blood to drink," is fulfilled on the day the Colonel opens his new home and is found dead in his study, his beard saturated with his blood. The Colonel has died of apoplexy, Doyle's favorite vehicle of natural death. The Colonel's descendants still own and occupy the house, however. During the course of the story, a monkey, an organ grinder's pet, is brought to perform for the residents of the house. The ape beams covetousness and animal lust, especially avariciousness, by virtue of his constant begging for coins while the creature's tail, sticking out from between his legs beneath his gabardine jacket, creates a phallic symbol advertising his carnality. "Doubtless, more than one New-Englander — or, let him be of what country he might, it is as likely to be the case — passed by, and threw a look at the monkey, and went on, without imagining how nearly his own moral condition was here exemplified," Hawthorne tells us, adding that the animal personifies "horrible ugliness, spiritual as well as physical."

Maule's grandson, his agent of retribution against the Pyncheon family, earns control over the mind of Alice Pyncheon as surely as Le Fanu's demon acquires sway over Jennings. Both victims slowly forfeit their self-control and dignity under the onslaught of mental malevolence. The evil power of Maule eventually kills Alice in an indirect form of suicide, for she catches a lethal cold while doing his bidding. The monkey comes back into the narrative with the death of the victim, as if to leer at the pathetic humans who felt so superior to it.

Doyle wrote a story whose very title amounts to a pun on Hawthorne's work, entitled, "The Adventure of the Three Gables." In it Holmes receives a letter from a Mary Maberley soliciting his help investigating "a succession of strange incidents [that] occur to me in connection with this house." The house itself, The Three Gables, in addition to having gables, is as poorly kept and depressing as its American model, yet this doesn't stop two different parties from struggling over ownership. One group is hoping to buy the place from Mrs. Maberley, but they also demand ownership of absolutely everything in it: furniture, fixtures, and all the personal items of the family. It is obvious to Holmes they are after something of great value to them and will stick at nothing to get it, for they go so far as to break into The Three Gables and search the house. The burglars break open a shipping trunk of Mrs. Maberley's recently deceased son and seem to have escaped with all but the last page of a novel in manuscript form that the son wrote in Italy. The novel, if published, would have exposed a certain notorious lady for what she really is, rendering her upcoming marriage to a young English lord impossible. She hires thugs to get the novel back at all costs and by any means. This brings the whole thing back to *The House of the Seven Gables*, in which the restitution of the home to its rightful owners is brought into being with the finding of a deed; a manuscript. In both tales it is the piece of writing that is the target of the struggle.

As unlikely as it may sound, the story of "Green Tea" is possibly derived from a true incident that occurred to a member of the James family, America's most prominent literary family, which included Henry James Senior; Henry Junior; and his brother William. Henry, the father, born in Albany, New York in 1811, was a writer of insightful psychology centering upon religious questions, and although better known in Doyle's day, is still read today. His son Henry wrote short stories, essays, and travel pieces as well as criticism, and is regarded by many as America's greatest novelist. He lived much of his life in England, becoming a citizen in 1915 in sympathy with the war effort, and died there a year later. The younger brother William, born in New York City in 1843, was a physician like Doyle, having received his degree from Harvard in 1869, and like Holmes, concentrated on chemistry as well as fabricating some of history's most important contributions to modern philosophy. Doyle fashioned much of his own life on that of William, whose sympathy with believers in the spirit world led James to years of dedicated psychic research. Henry wrote ghost stories, William believed in them, and Arthur did both.

In 1844, the James family was living in London where Henry the elder was immersed in a painstaking study of *The Book of Genesis*. Late one chilly afternoon, seated alone in his apartment contemplating the dying embers, he suddenly experienced a frightening apparition as a feeling of great terror gripped him. It seemed to him there was an almost invisible shape, neither animal nor human, squatting in the corner "raying out from his fetid personality influences fatal to life." The horror lasted only about ten seconds, but James felt himself "reduced from a state of firm, vigorous, joyful manhood to one of almost helpless infancy," adding that he wanted to "appeal to the public to protect me." His life was now filled with chronic unrest and apprehension similar to, if somewhat less devastating than, the Rev. Jennings' own sorrows. He consulted doctors in London (Harley Street, most assuredly), but they told him he was simply overworked, recommending rest and outdoor activities. Nothing helped. Of importance to us is the fact that James tells us he lost all interest in studying the Scriptures and this in turn caused feelings of guilt.

One day while taking a water-cure, James met a local lady named Sophia Chichester, who tells him he has experienced what Swedenborg called a "vastation"; a sign of his going through a regenerative process of awakening, purgation, and illumination on the spiritual level. This naturally created interest for the theologian in James, who henceforth followed Swedenborg's teachings for the rest of his life, claiming to have found happiness in his works, and eventually overcoming any doubts he may have entertained regarding his faith. The correlations, if not the ultimate outcome of the two cases are obvious.

This eccentric adventure was found in Henry James Senior's autobiography, published in 1869, the same year as "Green Tea." Putting together this information Doyle must understandably have been impressed by how quickly and efficiently Le Fanu had transformed this story of an encounter with evil to compose his own fantastic vision.

William James, in a tip of the hat to the American writer James Fenimore Cooper, compares the true philosopher to a "pathfinder," and James himself was a real pioneer. He believed that one should not study philosophy for its own sake but rather use it in an effort to solve some specific problem in life such as God, free will, immortality, and so forth. We know he considered the question of crime within the realm of the philosophical thinker, for he makes use of a contemporary murder case in Massachusetts to win a point in his writings on morals and belief. We'll come back to this later. The main criteria James used for considering whether a problem in life was valid to be an object of quest utilizing philosophy is its "seriousness," and crime, always a worriment for mankind, and a sub-division, more or less, of the study of morals and ethics, is certainly serious enough, especially to its victims. The question of morals forms a large part of William James' work, taken as a whole.

If specific concepts are found to have positive experiential operations in life, pragmatic insight can then be used further to explore their meanings. James believed a connection between psychology and the natural sciences such as biology and chemistry had to be established. He hoped to help transform psychology itself into a genuine science, and to him some share of the credit must be given for creating a "new" psychology, allied with science and combining "the methods of observation with those of speculation and reflection."

"From man's total personality emerges a philosophy which is humanistic, pragmatic, and experiential, vindicating man's faith in his highest ideals and encouraging his noblest efforts for the well-being of himself and his fellow men," James tells us. Sherlock is what he called "an examiner of the sensible world," and Sherlock uses psychology and the methods of this field more than any other detective in fiction, and until recently, in real life as well. It was James who brought into being, in 1875, the first American courses in experimental psychology and the "psychological laboratory," believing the highest aim of psychology must be "practical."

Holmes' posture while thinking, sitting perfectly still with closed eyes is a borrowing from William James who often did just this even while teaching a class at Harvard. It would be fascinating to know if James read Doyle's stories as we know his friend Oliver Wendell Holmes did, and if so, what he thought of them.

The American Pragmatists, of which James was a leader, built a philosophy on their respect for the richness of being, rejecting the intellectual's awe for logic and consistency, and he realized it is completely irrational to have a belief in the existence of ready-made truths for such things do not exist, believing instead that truth is a completely indispensable, "practical" element in the maintenance of life.

In *The Principles of Psychology*, James discussed what he called "necessary truths." Elsewhere he says, "To me, 'truth,' if there be any truth, would seem to exist for this kind of thing [the professional philosophy-shop with all of its pretensions], and to reveal itself in whispers to the meek lovers of the Good, in their solitude, the Darwins, the Lockes, etc. and to be expressly incompatible with officialdom. 'Officials' are products of no deep stratum of experience." It is often these shallow thinking "officials" who give the Great Detective almost as much trouble as the criminals themselves.

The real philosophers are constantly seeking clues to the nature of knowledge, and the search takes them to wherever such clues may be found, even in the most primitive of settings and the most mundane and practical of situations. In the case of William James, his clues originated in the biology and psychology of his time, in the teleological interpretation of mind. Those philosophers who have contributed to an understanding of truths, James believed, include all who attempted to bring truth into a dynamic relationship with existence. Such thinkers have tried to have truths respect the dynamic ever changing, concrete nature of reality; and they have never failed to attempt to understand mankind's role in that changing reality. They realized as well that man can take an active part in the real shaping of the as yet unfinished future, and James believed that a man such as Holmes could change that future.

We have scratched the surface of William James' mind, but we must hesitate this study somewhat and return to Le Fanu; another scratched mind.

"Green Tea" is the first story of a collection entitled *In A Glass Darkly*. "The Familiar" is the second. In this tale a Captain Barton has returned to England after a life spent in the Royal Navy only to find himself stalked at night by an elusive being whose footsteps only he can hear, and he is naturally filled with dread. In desperation he visits a minister for advice telling the Doctor of Theology he is sure there is "a dreadful God" who distributes retribution to the guilty, for he is suffering the torments of the damned and claims to be haunted by "a DEMON!"

One evening a shot is fired at Barton but misses, and later that night the Captain encounters a grotesque little man who snarls at him and, expressing disappointment at the fact that he is still alive, sidles away. The following evening the Captain again meets the small man who is described as a monkey-like individual "short in stature," a foreigner who wears a fur cap and walks fast and vehemently, presenting to the world "a singularly evil countenance, agitated, as it seemed, with the excitement of madness."

Barton takes to locking himself in his flat after receiving written messages regarding his life by one who signs himself "THE WATCHER." The tormented man comes to believe that an owl he keeps is infecting his dreams and harbors evil intentions toward him connected with the ape-like man. The owl is known in demonology as a "familiar"; an animal that helps a witch or demon commit acts of terror. Eventually Barton is frightened to death in his own bed through the agency of the bird and his own imagination. At the close of this tale Le Fanu tells us, "The whole circumstance was, in his own mind, vaguely and instinctively connected with certain passages in his past life, which, of all others, he hated to remember." We learn that the Captain, when in command at sea, had one of his men whipped and the man died in the hospital; hence Barton's sense of guilt. Earlier Barton had asked a physician if there was a disease that could shrink a man, or if a man could still be alive after having apparently died of lockjaw.

"The Familiar" is a "vengeance tale," as are all the stories in this collection. It is simply "Green Tea" with a human fiend, and as in the initial story we ourselves are being asked to decide what is real. The work is not as satisfying as the first piece, for there we had the thrill of discovery whereas in "The Familiar" we obviously have a writer repeating himself. Doyle learned a useful lesson from the fact that the Irish writer so adroitly adopted the same general theme and plot into yet another piece of good fiction.

The Canon is lopsided in the measure that each individual tale divulges to us regarding Doyle's intentions. This must be kept in mind, for some stories, though absorbing as mysteries, will be only brushed in quickly, or not even approached, while alternate pieces will be alluded to chronically in this appreciation. I'm placing considerable accent upon the office of *A Study in Scarlet* for this innovational short novel uncovers more available and convincing data about Holmes than any other work, for my present purposes. Doyle mistakenly concluded this was to be not just the first, but also the last effort utilizing the detective and thus packed far more intelligence regarding some of his archetypes into this work than was necessary if he had contemplated the opportunity of carrying the performance further.

The physical formats of "Green Tea" and *A Study in Scarlet* are surprisingly similar starting with the titles: *A Study in Scarlet, Reminiscences of John W. Watson, M.D., Late of the Army Medical Department*, in one case, and "Green Tea: A Case Reported by Martin Hesselius, the German Physician," in the other. Each title mentions a color, the kind of association that can be quite important in symbolism. The word "Case" in Le Fanu's piece, a word found in one of the earliest Holmes stories, "A Case of Identity," is also used in the name of a collection: *The Case Book of Sherlock Holmes*, and is a direct borrowing from the field of medicine. The Irish piece is a 27-page story bordered by a preface and conclusion, and in between ten chapters, each with a heading. It's an unusual format and is best suited to a novel. *A Study in Scarlet* is divided into two separate parts, necessary since two different tales are being told: the story of the relationship between Holmes and Watson and their involvement in this case, plus the story of the misadventures of Jefferson Hope. "Green Tea" does the same thing in its development in a more condensed form. The initial speaker, an anonymous English physician, causes us to understand that the story to follow is not an account of his own experience but rather that of the physician whom he served as secretary — Doctor Hesselius, a German who could be considered a medical investigator. The Englishman has rendered a translation and fictionalizing of Hesselius' notebooks on the case.

The English doctor informs us that he himself can no longer practice medicine because of an infection he received that cost him two fingers and "the more painful loss of my health." Watson, in roughly two pages of self-introduction, gives us what little autobiographical details he wants us to know. Watson tells us he joined the Army, was immediately sent to the Afghan Wars where he was wounded out of the service, gave up practicing medicine, returned to England, and settled in London: scene of "Green Tea," and most of *A Study in Scarlet.*

The influence of Doyle's fellow Scot and personal friend Robert Louis Stevenson on his writing can be glimpsed on the opening page of this initial Holmes story, and we will breach that impact briefly and fill in the blanks later. Listen to the first paragraph of Stevenson's short story, "The Adventure of the Hansom Cab." "Lieutenant Brackenbury Rich had greatly distinguished himself in one of the lesser Indian hill wars. He it was who took the chieftain prisoner with one hand; his gallantry was universally applauded; and when he came home, prostrated by an ugly sabre cut and a protracted jungle fever, society was prepared to welcome the Lieutenant as a celebrity of minor luster. But his was a character remarkable for unaffected modesty; adventure was dear to his heart, but he cared little for adulation; and he waited at foreign watering-places and in Algiers until the fame of his exploits had run through its nine days' vitality and begun to be forgotten. He arrived in London at last, in the early season, with as little observation as he could desire; and as he was an orphan and had none but distant relatives who lived in the provinces, it was almost as a foreigner that he installed himself in the capital of the country for which he had shed his blood." Both Watson and Rich have been wounded in action, then weakened by fever while serving as officers in the British Army. Both then gyrate to London, although they have no relatives there, and each eventually falls in with a former comrade in arms in a bar or club. Doyle does not ignore Lt. Rich's act of valor, but he transfers it to Murray, Watson's orderly who succeeded in bringing the wounded Captain safely through enemy lines to his own side. Keep in mind that in all three stories we are discussing we are talking about their opening sentences and thoughts.

Holmes is related spiritually to a creation of Stevenson's, utilized in a number of his short pieces: Prince Florizel, a Bohemian nobleman living in London who "was not without a taste for ways of life more adventurous and eccentric than that to which he was destined by his birth." The Prince and his confidant Colonel Geraldine, like a medieval knight and his squire, prowl London, and sometimes further afield, searching out adventure, and seeking, through their generosity, intelligence, and shrewdness, to right wrongs and fight evil.

"The civil authorities were never taken into the secret of these adventures; the imperturbable courage of the one and the ready invention and chivalrous devotion of the other had brought them through a score of dangerous passes; and they grew in confidence as time went on," Stevenson tells us of the intrepid pair.

In an exotic tribute to Stevenson, Prince Florizel is featured in Doyle's novel of London's sporting life *Rodney Stone* as though he were a real historic figure. This aristocrat who goes incognito about his business also foreshadowed the King of Bohemia who showed up at Baker Street wearing a mask in "A Scandal in Bohemia."

Incidents, characters, and even the format found in Wilkie Collins' 1868 novel *The Moonstone* served as models for an abundance of developments found in Doyle's writing. The history of the theft in England of a large yellow diamond that had previously been stolen from a Hindu religious idol by a British officer, a situation obliquely echoed in Doyle's novel *The Sign of the Four* is the plot of Collins' work. Rachel Verinder has been gifted the gem as part of her inheritance on her eighteenth birthday only to have it stolen from her room that very night. Many are suspected with the plot taking numerous baroque twists and dead-ends before the real culprit is identified. As in *A Study in Scarlet* the work is divided into a number of sections each loosely corresponding to a different character's version of the affair; the total adding up to a novel. This multiple narrative device sets a precedent in which individuals such as Watson, Holmes, Lestrade, Hope, and numerous others, give their redaction of the events. A survey of the Canon in its entirety would reveal that though Watson is the primary narrator, a nose count would affirm there are many others involved in the telling. The additional maneuver Doyle uses of introducing a newspaper article containing relevant information into the record is a direct borrowing from *The Moonstone* where it can be found a number of times.

The story itself is a tale of vengeance: the vengeance of the evil Colonel John Herncastle, embittered by his sister's refusal to talk with him, and the retribution of the Hindus who have vowed to retrieve their stolen gem and revenge the sacrilege to their idol.

Sergeant Cuff, the police detective attempting to solve the case is one of Holmes' many archetypes with Watson's role taken by Betteredge, the family butler, who acts as assistant to the sergeant during his investigations. Betteredge relates valuable installments of the plot himself while rounding out the character of Cuff: impressing upon us the man's mental abilities, which are prodigious, and supplying a physical description of him, who could stand in for the thin, eagle-nosed Holmes easily.

Interestingly enough Cuff fails to solve the case; it just comes to an end on its own, as it were. "It's only in books that the officers of the detective force are superior to the weakness of making a mistake," he ruminates philosophically. In turn, Doyle adopts this attitude, for in a number of cases Holmes' failure to bring about a successful conclusion results in the detective's lament upon the uncertainty of human endeavor.

With Doyle, as with Collins, a distance is maintained between the readers and the event, for everything is related in a very calm and cool manner. We view crime and sin in a detached, deductive way, as a puzzle, which the investigators may or may not solve, as a purely intellectual exercise, but not as something that affects them or us very much. Dr. Joseph Bell, in the essay already quoted, makes an insightful observation about Holmes when he points out there is something "almost inhuman," about the man.

The writings of Arthur Doyle in general, and the characterization of Holmes in particular, owes a great debt to one of the most interesting and talented, yet eccentric writers in history: the American, James Fenimore Cooper.

Cooper was born in 1789, the same year the United States Constitution went into effect; a dynamic determinant in his future I believe for he went on to become an authority on matters dealing with the Constitution. Cooper had a justified reputation for cranky capriciousness and sharp legal squabbles. His later years were wasted in convoluted judicial battles regarding his vast tracts of land in Upstate New York. If Cooper received a negative review on one of his books from a newspaper critic he thought nothing of suing the paper. The argumentative, litigious Frankland in *The Hound of the Baskervilles* is based principally upon Cooper's personality.

He started writing in 1820 with a weak novel *Precaution*, followed by two novels of the American Revolution, *The Spy* and *The Pilot*. Like Doyle he wrote fiction that included stories of the sea and of the middle ages, in addition to travel books, histories, and essays, but it was not until the five amazing novels that came to be known as "The Leather-Stocking Tales" appeared that he achieved recognition. The first writer from the New World to gain fame in Europe, Cooper was known as "the American Walter Scott," and Walter Scott, as we know, was Doyle's favorite novelist.

His repetition of plots, themes, characters, and speech is often so heavy as to mar some of his work but beyond doubt Cooper was one of the most influential writers that ever lived.

The five Leather-Stocking tales: *The Pioneers*, *The Last of the Mohicans*, *The Prairie*, *The Pathfinder*, and *The Deerslayer*, center upon the character of Hawkeye at various stages of his life, from youth to old age — and what is most interesting for us, not in chronological order. Hawkeye dies of old age in the third work, *The Prairie*, only to be brought back to life as a younger man thirteen years later in *The Pathfinder*; a curious development not lost on Doyle.

Arthur Conan Doyle brought into being a detective who could aid his people in fighting evil in London and in the country. Cooper developed the woodsman Hawkeye: the end product of the vicious strife he was born into. Hawkeye is a man of many names, his real name being Nathaniel Bumppo, often shortened to Natty Bumppo; a reference to the fact that he is at one and the same time a mixture of a highly sophisticated individual (Natty) and a country bumpkin (Bumppo). He is also known by sobriquets the Indians have given him such as Hawkeye, Pathfinder, Deerslayer, and Leather-Stocking, not to mention others he does not bother to use.

A work of art is always an outward manifestation of the mind that made it. This strange system of names is not normal for anyone, and Cooper is far from normal. There is no question but that he had a mental problem and I am not the only observer to record it.

Hawkeye, the epitome of unfettered individualism and natural aristocracy, was as popular in Doyle's day as Holmes is today. He has extended practical skills and physical endurance matched to distinguished courage and one way or another lives by a strict moral code, although his bearings are determined by the constant warfare in which he lives. In *The Prairie*, Cooper takes a moment out of the action and endeavors to explain what it is he was attempting to create with this unique individual. "The man, I speak of, was of great simplicity of mind, but of sterling worth. Unlike most of those who live a border life, he united the better, instead of the worst qualities of the two people." Cooper is speaking of the whites and Indians. "He was a man, endowed with the choicest and perhaps rarest gift of nature, that of distinguishing, good from evil. His virtues were those of simplicity, because such were the fruits of his habits, as were indeed his very prejudices. In courage he was the equal of his red associates; in warlike skill, being better instructed, their superior. In short, he was a noble shoot from the stock of human nature, which never could attain its proper elevation and importance, for no other reason, than because it grew in the forest."

Here, probably, is the single most isolated influential paragraph from another's writings on the expansion of the character of Sherlock Holmes. What the young doctor waiting serenely for patients in Portsmouth is actually going to undertake is to demonstrate a literary experiment; to picture what "proper elevation and importance," such a hero as the scout might conceivably attain if he lived not in the forest primeval but in the equally dangerous element of Victorian London. Doyle even physically transfers Holmes from the country to the city, for we know he was born on a farm. Cooper wrote later in his life that he had sought to portray in Hawkeye "a being removed from the every-day inducements to err, which abound in civilized life, while he retains the best and simplest of his early impressions; who sees God in the forest; hears him in the winds;" adding, "in a word, a being who finds the impress of the Deity in all the works of nature, without any of the blots produced by the expedients, and passion, and mistakes of man."

Sherlock Holmes is Hawkeye. He is even constitutionally fashioned upon the scout, for Hawkeye is portrayed as tall and thin with sharp features set in an alert, intelligent face. Watson, upon first meeting Holmes, observes: "In height he was rather over six feet, and so excessively lean that he seemed to be considerably taller. His eyes were sharp and piercing, save during those intervals of torpor to which I have alluded; and his thin, hawk-like nose gave his whole expression an air of alertness and decision. His chin, too, had the prominence and squareness which mark the man of determination."

Watson tells us elsewhere that Holmes has not just a hawk-like nose but "clear-cut, hawk-like features." In his nonfiction Doyle added to the imagery, for when questioned about the detective in later years he said, "He had, as I imagined him, a thin, razor-like face, with a great hawks-bill of a nose, and two small eyes set close together on either side of it. Such was my conception."

The more personable embodiment of the detective that has come down to us is the result, according to his creator, of the illustrator Sidney Paget, using his brother Walter as a model. Doyle tells us, "The handsome Walter took the place of the more powerful, but uglier Sherlock; and perhaps from the point of view of my lady readers, it is as well." Hawkeye himself is never described as handsome, only lean and powerful looking. Even the dress of Holmes is influenced by the American, for in the December 1893 issue of *The Strand*, containing "The Final Problem," Doyle had Paget depict Holmes wearing a deerstalker cap, the headgear we associate him most often with. Watson tells us that Holmes "loathed every form of society with his whole Bohemian soul," and the scout as well prefers to either be alone or with his Indian allies, shunning "the developments" the townsmen have built in the forest.

Hawkeye is a scout and hunter, first for the British and their allies in the wars against the French and their allies, and later with the Americans and their allies against the British and their allies. He is called "an irregular" in the service of God and the King, and sometimes the chief of the irregulars, holding no official rank in any army. In "The Adventure of the Missing Three-Quarter" Holmes says, "You may look upon me simply as an irregular pioneer, who goes in front of the regular forces of the country."

Hawkeye, like Holmes, is something of a superman for he can go days without food and still fight his enemies, and he will go just as long without sleep if necessary. Also like Holmes, he is often at odds with the people, even the law, in his society. His offenses and discontent often stem from the fact that he has more integrity, instinctual honesty, and humanity than those who oppose him. This is often regarded as the sign of an individual who "sees more and is more thoughtful" than his community in general.

Cooper, born in New Jersey and moving with his family to New York almost immediately, was raised in a world that had experienced, and would continue to experience, during his lifetime and for years to follow, some of the most vicious warfare in the history of mankind. New York was the stage of constant bloody conflict between Europeans and Indians, or between the whites and Indians with each other. That part of the Seven Years' War that was fought between France and England included many battles in northeastern America, where it is called the French and Indian War. Samuel Johnson made an observation on this state of affairs in an article published in 1756 declaring that the dispute between the French and English in America was so atrocious and barbarous as to be "only the quarrel of two robbers for the spoils of a passenger," adding, "Such is the contest, that no honest man can heartily wish success to either party." It finally merged into the American Revolution. The British regiments did not abandon their strongholds in the Upstate New York area until after 1800, although the Revolution had ended some twenty years earlier. This in turn helped bring about the War of 1812, with much of the fighting taking place on or around the New York lakes; Cooper played a role while serving in the new American Navy. This war ended with the determining battles at Fort McHenry and Niagara Falls, both in New York. To this must be added the Anti-Rent Wars fought between tenants and large landowners or "patroons," as they are called in New York, as well as the conflicts between the different "empires," after which "the Empire State" is named. New Yorkers even mustered an army and attacked

Canada in an effort to bring down the British Empire. As Hawthorne tells us of this period, "it was a time in which every man in America was a soldier." Nameless clashes were a way of life when the Indians were "on the warpath," or when the French decided to move down from Canada to do some fighting for a while and then go home. The scalps of humans were bought, sold, and traded just like beaver pelts, with the scalp of a woman or child having the same value (one gold coin) as that of a fighter. The situation became so vicious during the "Cherry Valley Massacres" in Central New York that the British decided to stop paying "scalp-bounty" after realizing they had been buying some of their own people's scalps from the Mohawks. Cooper lived in the Cherry Valley.

Ambush and treachery were a way of life and to be tortured to death was actually regarded as a rather normal way to die. "We do whatever we have to do in order to win the war," is a sentiment and assertion we hear spoken by different characters in different ways in just about all of Cooper's tales. Cooper knew well the effect of constant warfare on susceptible human nature, and Doyle as well is aware of the intensity of this atrocious course of action and shows it in his non-Holmes story, "The Silver Hatchet." One weapon used by all sides, and always kept within instant reach, was the tomahawk, which could be thrown or used hand-to-hand. In "The Silver Hatchet," a tomahawk, a museum piece, exudes an evil influence on any and all who hold it. To simply have the weapon in your possession enflamed your desire to kill someone with it.

Intelligence, courage, and especially the ability to deceive your enemies were the most valuable merits a man could have in the New York wars. "Hate is very strong, but cunning has a longer arm," is a shibboleth the Indians lived by. In wars primarily between whites, such as the Revolution, Cooper affirmed, "similarity of language, appearance, and customs, rendered prudence doubly necessary," for "Great numbers ... wore masks." Such statements often come from his novel *The Spy*, and as we know, Holmes never hesitates to play the spy, or to wear a mask, if it becomes necessary "to win the war."

Throughout much of his long life of warfare Hawkeye's main enemy is the Mohawks, who form part of the Iroquois Confederacy, called (in his day) the Six Nations. The word "Iroquois" is important for it means "real adders," a reference to this tribe's preference to ambushing like a snake. For their cunning, cruelty, and bloodthirstiness Hawkeye calls them "miscreants" and "reptiles." Mohawk means "cannibal," with the scene in *The Last of the Mohicans* in which the Mohawks fall on all fours and lap up the blood of the dead and dying women and children exposing their ferociousness quite accurately. The Indians themselves are proud of these classifiers and the qualities they show. Sherlock employs the word "miscreant" a number of times and repeatedly compares his antagonists to reptiles. Doyle uses the word miscreant in his pamphlet "The Case of Mr. George Edalji" in talking of one who would attack and maim a horse.

The work by Doyle in which the most graphic scenes of torture and murder take place is one set in New York State. *The Refugees: A Tale of Two*

Continents, although opening in France, closes in New York, with its style, themes, and high adventure, as well as incidents and scenes, being so close in spirit to the works of Cooper, especially *The Pathfinder*, that it is difficult to tell them apart. Amos Green, the American frontiersman in Doyle's novel, is pure Hawkeye.

On one of his tours of America, Doyle traveled up the Hudson to Ossining, ostensibly to visit Sing Sing Penitentiary but also to see the Hudson Valley, scene of Cooper's best novels as well as the setting of *The Refugees*. The worst of the fighting had taken place in the Hudson Valley, and we find that Sherlock Holmes lives in Mrs. Hudson's house. Some of *A Study in Scarlet* even takes place in New York City, the city washed by the waters of the Hudson, and where Cooper spent so much of his life, and where he died. In *Three of Them, A Reminiscence*, a non-fiction piece designed to emphasize Doyle's close relationship and love for his three children, he calls his kids "the Leather-skin Tribe," and describes a scene of them playing at being Indians on the warpath, complete with tomahawks. He employs the word "danger," in what is a very ominous way to give an account of a child's game. This seemingly insignificant gesture is a conspicuous link to Cooper, showing his influence on all of Doyle's work, for the word "danger" seems to appear on every page of the American's fiction; danger in many forms; a natural result of his environment. Doyle named one of his shorter pieces "Danger!" written to instigate his country to adopt protective measures against an enemy who could blockade England with submarines during a war.

"We depend entirely on your experience, honest old man, to discover the means to apprise our friends of their danger," one character tells Hawkeye in *The Prairie*. In the war between good and evil, it is the function of the good man to warn his friends of danger; this is Cooper's teaching, and this becomes a primary function for Holmes as it was for Hawkeye.

Cooper viewed the situation in his state as a coming into being of Thomas Hobbes' human condition in which the bonds of "the civic state," once broken, result in what Hobbes called a state of "war of every man against every man" or, perhaps more to the point, as Hobbes also called it, "a war of all against all." Hobbes believed that every social whole could be seen on analysis to be no more than a stabilized system of competing parts. In a tribute to Hobbes, Cooper utilized his philosophy as the backbone of his novel *The Crater*.

This setting of scene and place is important here for we are shown by Doyle, right from the very beginning, the second page of *A Study in Scarlet*, that the locale of his tale to come, London, has become "that great cesspool into which all the loungers and idlers of the empire are irresistibly drained." Lounger and idler were euphemisms for the criminal and the potentially criminal in this era. A sentence that impressed Doyle was an observation of Lieutenant Rich's in regard to London: "They talk of war, but this is the great battlefield of mankind." In one of his many comments in regard to his adopted city, Johnson referred to it as "Babylon." More indirectly he observed, "A great city is, to be sure, the school for studying life." In the Holmes stories we have London, or often "the country," described as scenes of great evil, with the country perhaps the more evil of the two. Denis Diderot tells us that the isolation of the homes in the country, as opposed to the closeness of the city, makes crime more difficult to detect or solve. Watson, in speaking of London, called it "the great wilderness."

In *A Study in Scarlet*, certain members of Scotland Yard request Holmes' help solving a mystery involving a body found in an empty house, and before this can be solved, another related murder takes place in a London hotel. An American, Jefferson Hope, arrested for the killings, tells a story of pursuing both victims around the world for vengeance, claiming they well deserved to die, being culpable of rape and murder under the guise of religious prerogative while living as Mormons in America. Hope secured a job as janitor in a college in New York where he stole the poison he used in his vengeance killings in London.

Hawkeye is distinguished by his acuteness and penetrating observations in dealing with the forest and its inhabitants, especially with his enemies. From studying the simplest of tracks and other clues he can recount exactly what has taken place in the woods. Cooper tells us he "saw, and noted with a degree of minuteness that would have done credit to the habitual observation of his friends the Delawares." After one example of his skills we learn, "From such undeniable testimony did the practised woodsman arrive at the truth, with nearly as much certainty and precision as if he had been a witness of all those events which his ingenuity so easily elucidated." Listen to this monologue delivered by the scout when a naïve newcomer, finding a moccasin print, dismisses it as unimportant in following a trail, claiming one print to be much like another. Hawkeye stares at him in amazement, and then gives him a lesson in keeping his scalp. "One moccasin like another! you may as well say that one foot is like another; though we all know that some are long, and others short; some broad, and others narrow; some with high, and some with low insteps; some in-toed, and some out. One moccasin is no more like another than one book is like another; though they who can read in one are seldom able to tell the marks of the other." Then Hawkeye adds, "You are right, boy; here is the patch we saw so often in the other chase. And the fellow will drink when he can get an opportunity: your drinking Indian always learns to walk with a wider toe than the natural savage, it being the gift of a drunkard to straddle, whether of white or red skin."

Holmes too practices this "habitual observation," and also "with a degree of minuteness," as we see in such stories as "The Adventure of the Bruce-Partington Plans" in which he studies a broken laurel branch with a magnifying glass searching for clues. Holmes maintains there is no branch of detection so important, yet so neglected, as the art of tracing footprints. He even penned a monograph on the subject entitled "Upon the Tracing of Footsteps," a piece Hawkeye could have written, if he could have written at all. Holmes argued that so long as a criminal remains on two legs he must leave behind some indention, some abrasion, and some "trifling displacement," which can be detected by the expert, scientific observer. Footprints are the first thing Holmes centers on in all cases where they could have been left, and examples of studying prints appear in an amazingly large number of tales. In "The Adventure of the Devil's Foot," Sterndale's prints lead to the killer while in "Silver Blaze" tracks lead to the stolen race horse. In "The Crooked Man" Holmes knows the tracks he has found belong to an animal of the weasel family, so he is obviously something of a ranger or hunter himself. We are told of Hawkeye that he has "stores of experimental knowledge," "obtained by so long a sojourn in the wilds," and he is advised to "return to your countrymen to deliver up some of those" stores of knowledge. Well, Doyle is now delivering up some of this experience to his countrymen with the assistance of his detective. Watson as well fits into the role of hunter and tracker for he has "coursed" (a word meaning "hunted and tracked, usually with hounds") "many creatures in many countries."

Hawkeye lives among the Indians and resembles them in thought, attitude, skills, and composure. This is quite an achievement, as Cooper tells us of the Indians, "for so practiced and acute do the senses of the savage become, more especially when he is on the war-path, that trifles apparently of the most insignificant sort, often prove to be clues to lead him to his object." Holmes is said to also have the equanimity and immobility of countenance of the Indian. In "The Crooked Man" Watson tells us, "His eyes kindled and a slight flush sprang into his thin cheeks. For an instant the veil had lifted upon his keen, intense nature, but for an instant only. When I glanced again his face had resumed that red-Indian composure which had made so many regard him as a machine rather than a man." In "The Naval Treaty" a similar comparison is made: "He had, when he so willed it, the utter immobility of countenance of a red-Indian, and I could not gather from his appearance whether he was satisfied or not with the position of the case."

The Great Detective leads a life of lounging about his Baker Street flat in his dressing gown fighting boredom, but when a problem presents itself that interests him, he suddenly bursts forth with electrified enterprise and energy until the case is resolved. Cooper tells us of the Native American that he is indolent, even lazy, except when at war when he then becomes fierce with unspent energy.

Hawkeye, like the Indian, speaks rarely, and when doing so keeps it as brief as possible. If any one word could be employed to describe the scout it would be "sagacious," meaning to be wise and foreseeing, to perceive accurately and to have sound judgment. His sagacity is what distinguishes him from the ordinary run of men, and this word and this thought is repeated in reference to him constantly. The Indians, whose own sagacity is emphasized by Cooper, say of a wise man that he has "long ears" and sees with "his eyes opened," and they say this quite often of their great friend and enemy Hawkeye. Doyle tries to avoid using the word sagacious in reference to Holmes, but we do hear it every now and then.

CHAPTER TWO. GREEN GOLD

When Dr. Hesselius finally gets to interview Jennings, he learns the strange nature of his illness and the unfortunate fact that the little ape's appearances are becoming progressively more numerous, and its behavior more outrageous. Jennings fears the imp is attempting to drive him to suicide, recounting a recent close call in which he nearly threw himself into the abyss of a well shaft. "May God deliver me!" the harassed man cries. Hesselius offers encouragement, promising he will do his best to help, and as a start tells Jennings, "I'll give to-night to the careful consideration of the whole case." We think of Holmes immediately, for it is he who devotes entire days and nights to the quiet contemplation of problems. Leaving Jennings in the hands of his servant, the doctor sets off "for an inn about two miles out of town, called 'The Horns,' a very quiet and comfortable house, with good thick walls. And there I resolved, without the possibility of intrusion or distraction, to devote some hours of the night, in my comfortable sitting-room, to Mr. Jennings' case, and so much of the morning as it might require." "The Horns" is an associative reference to the word "dilemma," which originally meant "to be caught between two horns," as of a bull, for there is no real favorable way out of this situation for its victim.

Holmes' use of tobacco as a mental stimulant can be traced back, at least in part, to "Green Tea," in which the Reverend, describing his work habits, tells us he used tea as a stimulant, adding that everyone who writes, and therefore thinks, does so *on something* — tea, or coffee, or tobacco." One evening Watson returns from a day at his club to find their flat so choked with smoke he thinks the place is on fire. "All afternoon and late into the evening he sat lost in tobacco and thought," is how Watson describes another such episode. The chiefs of the Plains tribes, before a council meeting, smoked tobacco in pipes, believing their thoughts were deeper and clearer after having done so, Cooper tells us.

The climax of "Green Tea" takes place in the period of time in which Dr. Hesselius spends the night in the village inn thinking. The thoughts of the man, which he does not share with us, have undoubtedly led him to accept certain truths, which must be too unbelievable for him to communicate. He himself admits the case involves "more than I have set down," and the English doctor as well, taking his information from the journals of Hesselius, also warns us he is withholding information. We are given enough counsel to convince us to apprehend there is a mystery in this story "Green Tea" that may focus upon deeper consequences and interweaving interpretations.

In the course of this fateful night, the Rev. Jennings destroys himself in his bed by cutting his throat with a razor. Le Fanu has learned that it is human actions and thoughts that create spirits and fiends, and that it is the soul which must be cleansed. He offers no solutions here, or anywhere else in his writings, but he at least tries to locate the center of the problem. If he sounds like a stern moralist, that is, at one level, what he wishes to be, for the plot of "Green Tea" and "The Familiar" are both borrowed from Plato's *Laws*, an early attempt at the systemization of ethics and morals, and the punishment of wrongdoers. Plato warns us that the gods will send an omen and a demon to wreak retribution on any who are guilty of impiety; the worst crime you can commit. We are reminded a number of times that Jennings is a minister and has a "sacred calling," and it may be the willful neglect of his duties and the turning away of his thoughts from God that makes him culpable, instigating "a strange shame and horror." Mental evil, Le Fanu is saying, is far more horrible and terrifying than anything from beyond the grave, and surely more forceful in the abnormal changes it can work upon an individual. "Green Tea" is pure psychodrama; possibly the strongest in literature, with its chief strength lying in the thought that it is open to so many interpretations.

In "The Familiar," Barton's sin is brought to light by one who calls himself "The Watcher," this being the title Plato bestows on he who should be chosen to maintain the morals, and the laws, of his people. Barton, as captain, has had a foreigner whipped, which was permissible in Plato's Greece, and on board a British ship as well; but his mangling and the near-death of the man as a result of this was a breaking of the code of justice for which Barton is made to pay with his body.

Dr. Hesselius claims he was not called into the case in time to do anything. By his own admission Holmes is also unsuccessful in resolving a number of cases: a client is murdered in "The Five Orange Pips" that he should have saved, and he fails to get back the photo from Irene Adler, and there are others, but this in no way diminishes his self-confidence and determination to fight evil.

Two others, René Descartes and Swedenborg, also made startling discoveries while sitting before a fire at a village inn and were eager to share their thoughts about it with mankind. Much of Descartes' writings — all of them, if you really want to stretch a point, are autobiographical. The Frenchman has shown by good example the enclosure in the supposedly non-fiction world of philosophy the thought that autobiography as a genre provides, in his own words, "an ideal medium for the communication of the philosophical subject." Descartes didn't invent this of course, he found it, but he showed the world its new potential currency by employing autobiography to bring mankind to a novel level of reality; a reality based solely on a purely inner light. The stories of Sherlock Holmes must be considered part biography and part autobiography. Any character built on thoughts, your own or those of others, is as real, perhaps more real, than a simple figure of flesh and blood. There are really no fictitious characters in literature. Doyle makes mention of Descartes, along with Bacon, Baruch Spinoza, and Immanuel Kant, in the short story "The Man From Archangel" where he lists them as being among "those who have pried into what is unknowable."

René Descartes was born in 1596 into the landed gentry of his France much as Holmes was born into the landed gentry of England. His father entrusted the son's education to the Jesuits; thus, at age eight the boy was sent to the college of La Flèche in Anjou, where he remained for eight years. Like Doyle himself he received a strict, formal Jesuit education from which he benefited greatly but ultimately rebelled against.

Although often at odds with the Church, and for a while placed on the Index of Forbidden Books, Descartes remained devout in spirit and so loyal to the Church he made it the first of his maxims of conduct "to abide by the old law and religion." He seems to have kept this maxim all his life in spite of some startling revelations in his writings. Holmes also has his religious side for in "The 'Gloria Scott,'" which touches upon his university days, we learn he went to chapel. Johnson was devoutly religious all his life, and a regular churchgoer, as was Boswell.

After finishing at La Flèche the young man headed for Paris to taste the pleasures of this world, but after a year or so his mind got caught up in scientific, mathematical, and philosophical investigations, and stayed caught for the rest of his life. Until gas was used in the First World War, the military was considered a noble calling and our philosopher spent most of his life as a mercenary soldier. He died in Sweden in 1650, where he had been called by the young Queen Christiana, who in her ambition to adorn her reign with the luster of learning obtained the tutelage of the by now famous philosopher. Doyle comes across the interesting information that Descartes named himself after the estate he had been born on, *Les Cartes*, a word meaning cards, as in the game of cards. Swedenborg, who admired Descartes and admittedly borrowed from him freely, no doubt got the inspiration of naming himself after his nation from the Frenchman. His real name was Swedberg, but he changed it to Swedenborg, a word encapsulating the English name of his country.

Only six works, some of which are not much more than lengthy pamphlets, make up Descartes' contribution to philosophy, with his *Discourse on Method* of 1637, the most influential, especially when viewed through the lens of modern scientific thought. The repeated use of the word "method," or sometimes "methods," to epitomize Holmes' process of detection is a link, not only to René Descartes but, as we shall see, to other philosophical developments. In a letter to his friend Dr. Isaac Beeckman, the philosopher says he intended "to give to the public a completely new science for solving uniformly any arithmetical and geometrical problem whatever." It wasn't actually a new science he had in mind, but rather a new method, and he hoped to apply its broad plan to successfully solve the problems of the other sciences as he had used it to unravel puzzles he had encountered in algebra.

Descartes believed philosophy to be the basis for all other sciences, and since there was nothing certain in philosophy, it was up to him to find something certain, and that method rather than curiosity should guide the inquiry. He realized there were more difficult sciences than math and wondered whether his methods could be extended to "disciplines in which greater obstacles tend to stifle progress." What he realized was that many answerable problems in science could seem unanswerable because of the way they have been formulated. Believing he had found a method for solving any question concerning number and figure, he made much of a procedure for translating scientific problems that were not ostensibly about number and figure into ones that were.

Descartes believed he had discovered, or invented, a new logic, based primarily upon the fact that we should never accept anything as true if we did not possess evident knowledge of its truth, emphasizing he would be careful "to avoid precipitate conclusions and preconceptions, and to include nothing more in my judgments than what presented itself to my mind so clearly and distinctly that I had no occasion to doubt it." Another facet of this logic he called his "method of doubt," stressing the taking as positively false anything that seems in the least uncertain to the enquiring mind. Whatever commanded assent in the face of the strongest efforts at rejecting its truth would have the best possibility of being true. The main aspect of this, that in order to find the truth about something we must eliminate everything which cannot be true, and that whatever is left, no matter how improbable, must be the truth, is in a simplified way, the heart of the scientific method, as it was formulated by René Descartes. Holmes puts it well himself: "That process starts upon the supposition that when you have eliminated all which is impossible, then whatever remains, however improbable, must be the truth. It may well be that several explanations remain, in which case one tries test after test until one or other of them has a convincing amount of support." What Doyle did was to condense the principal rules of the method found in the chapter of that name, from Descartes' *Discourse*, into one or two sentences. Holmes' methods would not exist without the scientific method, its foundation, but patience will show there is far more to it than this. The scientific method has become so much a part of the thought of modern man that we take its existence for granted, but it was René Descartes who gave it birth, and the very phrase is associated with him. His original title for the method was "The Plan of a Universal Science which is Capable of Raising Our Nature to its Highest Degree of Perfection," and in Sherlock Holmes we have a noble effort to bring this perfection into being. Holmes' methods represent an aggressive break with traditional police procedures up until this time, just as Descartes' philosophy symbolized a sudden parting of the way with accustomed thought. The typically obtuse official detective Inspector Lestrade is emblematic, not exceptional, in his crude rejection of anything resembling intellectual reasoning or smacking of scientific method.

The usual police detective of the time was a man of little education, a thief-taker who relied upon his knowledge of underworld habits and characters for success.

In "The 'Gloria Scott,'" which involved Holmes' first efforts at detection, he outlines briefly his life style at the university: "I was never a very sociable fellow, Watson, always rather fond of moping in my rooms and working out my own little methods of thought, so that I never mixed much with the men of my year." And in "The Musgrave Ritual," we learn that "during my last years at the university there was a good deal of talk there about myself and my methods." Here are efforts at drawing analogies between Holmes and Descartes; the latter being a loner who drew constant debate and controversy wherever he went. Holmes conducts his life and directs his thoughts in the scientific spirit and objective nature of the French philosopher, and from his initial story Doyle is aligning this with a complex process of association — for even the title *A Study in Scarlet* is symbolic. The phrase implies a work involving blood, and there is blood enough spilled, but there is also the experience that when we first encounter the philosopher/detective he is found in a laboratory experimenting with human blood. A large portion of *Discourse on Method*, a fourth of the entire book, consists of Descartes' famous essay on the heart and the circulation of the blood in the human body; written to draw the world's attention to a practical application of the method. Holmes tells us the hemoglobin process he has just brought to light "is the most practical medico-legal discovery for years," an example of theory being put to the test. Descartes believed one should be demonstrative; one should make the demonstration themselves. Doyle himself was a student of blood and in 1882 had an article published in the British journal *Good Words* entitled "Life and Death in the Blood." He had an entire series of articles on blood planned but never carried out the project.

How one thinks, and how one can arrive at "correct reasoning," fascinated the French philosopher all his life, as it does any real philosopher. In "The Resident Patient" Holmes tells Watson, "some little time ago...I read you the passage in one of Poe's sketches, in which a close reasoner follows the unspoken thoughts of his companion," while a similar thought on Edgar Allan Poe appears in *A Study in Scarlet*. At this juncture in *A Study in Scarlet* Holmes gives his opinion on the mind of Lecoq, the creation of the French writer Emile Gaboriau. Such ancillary scenes, reinforced by numerous examples of Holmes' own mind at work (the signature of the man), puts one in mind of Descartes' autobiographical writings, causing us to realize that the detective, no less than the philosopher, is constantly examining the functions of the human mind.

In *Discourse on Method* the Philosopher insists he must, like Holmes and Hesselius, seek out some sanctuary where he might have "plenty of leisure to examine my ideas." One of the most interesting passages in all of Descartes' writings is when he describes how he goes about the process of thinking. The soldier stayed at quite a few inns since he traveled a good deal, and while passing through Germany one year "at the onset of winter," he took a room at a country inn. "There was no conversation to occupy me, and being untroubled by any cares or passions, I remained all day alone in a warm room." The room would have to be warmed by a fire, that being the only means of heat at the time. It was on this particular day that Descartes first speculated upon his great theory of the mind; sitting in front of a fire playing with a lump of wax. Since Dr. Hesselius is a German we may assume much of his work on the mind and its function was performed in his native country. Descartes does not hesitate to let us know that thinking for him is not an easy and prompt process, comparing himself to "a man who walks alone in the darkness," telling us his thoughts "go so slowly and circumspectly that if I did not get ahead very rapidly I was at least safe from falling." Thinking is also arduous for Sherlock Holmes. Watson describes the process of Holmes' thinking when working on a case: "I knew that seclusion and solitude were very necessary for my friend in those hours of intense mental concentration during which he weighed every particle of evidence, constructed alternative theories, balanced one against the other, and made up his mind as to which points were essential and which immaterial."

René Descartes and Holmes must affect conditions such as quiet, solitude, and warmth to force original thoughts to surface. When we draw up a mental picture of Holmes and Watson it is often in just this occupation, sitting in a fire-warmed room talking, thinking, and ruminating on the details of the proceedings of the mind. Holmes, by his own definition, was entirely cerebral, his body merely an "appendix" to his brain. This is pure Descartes. Swedenborg's conversion to a life devoted to God occurred under circumstances analogous to these conditions. While sitting in the parlor of a London inn following dinner, a mist surrounded him, and when it cleared he saw before him a man radiant with light. Interpreting this as a message from God, he devoted the rest of his life to theological study. Walt Whitman, whose work was better recognized in England than America at the time, tells us this historic event marked the emergence of the individual consciousness in modern religious thought. In "Green Tea" the recreation of the conditions of the enlightenment of Descartes and Swedenborg by Dr. Hesselius is not simply a reinterpretation of an event for its own sake but rather it is direct links being explored, for it was Descartes who first realized that the things that are inside the mind of man are more real than the things that are outside the mind. That's the importance of all this. The French philosopher used the famous example of the wax that changes its physical properties so readily and completely that obviously the only real "wax" that we can know exists in each individual mind. He even went so far as to assert that God, if he has existence at all, must exist solely in the mind in order for him to be real. Easy to see, from this and other statements Descartes made, how he could arrive at the ultimate conclusion, "I think, therefore I am." If after eliminating all the improbabilities, then whatever is left, no matter how improbable, translates to the fact that the monster persecuting the Rev. Jennings is real. It exists, since whatever it is it exists in the mind of the Rev. Jennings. If the monkey was simply of flesh and blood, Jennings could deliver it a kick and send it flying, but because the creature finds its reality in the mind it is truly dangerous. The shadow of René Descartes as well as of Plato falls on much of Le Fanu's writings.

In developing for us the mental texture of his new roommate, Watson announces a series of truly amazing as well as incongruous facts. Remarking upon Holmes' compass of learning Watson tells us, "His ignorance was as remarkable as his knowledge," adding, "Of contemporary literature, philosophy, and politics he appeared to know next to nothing." The word "contemporary" was used to modify the range of these fields, so we can assume Holmes is not altogether lacking in understanding of these studies, but this knowledge is limited to the non-contemporary. Watson continues: "Upon my quoting Thomas Carlyle, he inquired in the naivest way who he might be and what he had done. My surprise reached a climax, however, when I found incidentally that he was ignorant of the Copernican theory and of the composition of the solar system. That any civilized human being in this nineteenth century should not be aware that the earth traveled round the sun appeared to be to me such an extraordinary fact that I could hardly realize it."

Holmes is affirming to us the mind of ancient and medieval man, the belief that the earth was the center of the universe with the sun in orbit around it. Descartes himself had rejected the Copernican heliocentric theory — at least in name — as many believe, out of fear of religious opinion. Actually he may have been simply telling the truth, not believing in it at all; most people didn't at the time. Descartes did maintain the Copernican theory in substance in his idea that the earth was being carried around the sun in a great solar vortex. He had to be careful of what he said, following what he had written about the existence of God.

When Dr. Hesselius returns home the next morning after his night of meditation at The Horns, a message from Jennings begs of him to come immediately, for the ape has returned with a vengeance. Arriving at the victim's house, the Doctor hears from the servant Jones that his master has killed himself in the night by cutting his throat. Committing suicide is the great and final blasphemy; the most outrageous sacrilege against God, for it leaves no room for forgiveness and shows that one has given up hope. The demon in the mind has succeeded in forcing out whatever was good in the Rev. Jennings. And all this takes place "within the depressing stillness of an invalid bachelor's house." Suicide is brought into at least one story, "The Problem of Thor Bridge," but in general Doyle stays away from it.

"Green Tea" concludes with Hesselius telling a third party he has never failed to effect a cure in cases of the nature related to him by Jennings and he does not consider this case to be a failure either for he had not even commenced to treat the victim.

Jennings was engaged in writing a book "upon the religious metaphysics of the ancients," that had cost him much labor and thought, when he first encountered the apparition. When Dr. Hesselius is first told this fact, he answers with, "the actual religion of educated and thinking paganism, quite apart from symbolic worship? A wide and very interesting field." He seems to have realized all this without needing to be told. Jennings is one who has taken religion seriously enough to become one of its priests. Apart from the outward symbols of worship, the mythology of the pagans differs little from one group to another, or from the modern creeds that are based squarely upon them. A mind educated in too literal or too narrow a religious compass would understandably find itself on dangerous ground if such studies were pursued to their inevitable conclusions. Religious beliefs and practices play a direct and forceful role in the operation of "Green Tea," as well as guiding the conduct of the characters in *A Study in Scarlet*.

One interpretation placed on the reality of the glaring ape is that it could personify aspects of the development of life on earth as forwarded by the theory of organic evolution advanced by Charles Darwin in his 1859 work, *On the Origin of Species*. Did Jennings kill himself because he could not accept the thought of being descended from Darwin's ancestral ape? In Le Fanu's day, as in Doyle's, evolutionary theories and their implications were constantly under discussion, being the source of heated debate, so much so that the contemporary reader would recognize the association immediately. In *A Study in Scarlet*, Holmes carries forward a discussion of Darwin's opinions on music, but who is really interested in Darwin's opinions on music? I didn't even know he had any thoughts on music. When we think of the man, we automatically think of his writings on evolution.

The actual mystery in *A Study in Scarlet* begins when Holmes receives a message from Tobias Gregson, a Scotland Yard man, informing him of the finding of a man's body in an empty house in a place called Lauriston Gardens. The use of an empty house or apartment as a setting in a story is a borrowing from Stevenson, who employed this device in a number of his stories including "The Adventure of the Hansom Cab." The police cannot determine how the man died, or why, and Holmes and Watson go to the scene with Inspectors Gregson and Lestrade to investigate. The dead man's possessions include, among other things, a woman's wedding ring and two letters, one addressed to an E. J. Drebber and one to a Joseph Stangerson; items which tentatively identify the deceased as an American. On the wall of the room in which the body was found the word "*Rache*" is written in blood. Holmes determines the man was poisoned and that *Rache* is the German for revenge or vengeance. From examining the footprints around the house, he also realizes the victim was accompanied to the room by a second man, probably his murderer, and both had arrived in a cab.

Holmes attaches great importance to the wedding ring and places an advertisement in the newspapers to the effect that it had been found elsewhere and will be returned to the owner if they will call for it at Baker Street. Disguised as an elderly woman, a man shows up and claims the ring. He is followed by the detective upon leaving but eludes him.

The next day we learn the body was that of the American, E. J. Drebber. We are now introduced to the Baker Street irregulars, described by Watson as "half a dozen of the dirtiest and most ragged street arabs that ever I clapped eyes on." These rag-a-muffins are a loosely connected bunch of boys Holmes makes use of as scouts from time to time. In the early days of Scotland Yard the police often used children to help in a case. Children draw little suspicion from people who ordinarily have reason to worry about who might be watching them. There was the famous case in Birmingham in which a Yard man had his own children play on the street of the home of an Irish Fenian suspected of making bombs, in order to report on his activities. The strategy proved successful and led to an arrest. A lad was used to help make the arrest of the infamous murderer Daniel Good. The boy was acquainted with Good and not only led the police to his house, but rang his bell in order to draw him out in the open where capture would be easier. Again the plan worked. Stevenson, in his novel *David Balfour*, tells us a stranger, finding himself in the great teaming city of Edinburgh, would have little chance of finding an address without assistance. "It was, indeed, a place where no stranger had a chance to find a friend, let be another stranger. Suppose him even to hit on the right close, people dwelt so thronged in these tall houses, he might very well seek a day before he chanced on the right door."

A close is Scottish for court or alley, and from early photos we know them to be indeed very congested, unfriendly places. But the streets are full of boys who can be paid to assist the stranger. Stevenson tells us: "The ordinary course was to hire a lad they called a *caddie*, who was like a guide or pilot, led you where you had occasion, and (your errands being done) brought you again where you were lodging. But these caddies, being always employed in the same sort of services, and having it for obligation to be well informed of every house and person in the city, had grown to form a brotherhood of spies; and I knew from tales of Mr. Campbell's how they communicated one with another, what a rage of curiosity they conceived as to their employer's business, and how they were like eyes and fingers to the police." London had its own ragged army of children willing to do anything to relieve their hunger and they were ever on the lookout for a bit of adventure. Holmes is in charge of this gang of irregulars just as Hawkeye was the leader of the American irregulars. The youngsters set out in search of the cab that conveyed Drebber and his killer to the crime scene, while Gregson brings us up to date on the case. Drebber has been traced to a boarding house where he and Stangerson had checked out a few days previous, the pair being ordered to leave due to Drebber's aggressive sexual advances toward the landlady's daughter. He tried to force the girl Alice to leave with him, only to be stopped by her brother Arthur. Doyle uses his own name for this protector of womanhood. In attacking Drebber, Arthur has compromised himself for he is now the prime suspect in his murder.

Drebber's fellow American, Joseph Stangerson, has been found stabbed to death while a small box containing two pills, also found in the murdered man's room, presents to the Great Detective an opportunity to show himself in the light of a pragmatic man of experiments. Hoping to prove something, Holmes dissolves one pill in milk and gives it to an elderly dog. Nothing happens. The remaining pill is also given to the dog that now keels over and dies. Although one pill was harmless, the other contained the same poison used to kill Drebber.

Wiggins, leader of the irregulars, arrives with the hack driver he was sent in search of. Holmes feigns a request for assistance with his portmanteau and when the cabbie is off-guard, throws the cuffs on him and announces the arrest of the murderer. This device of using a cab and its driver to play a pivotal role in the story is an obvious borrowing from Stevenson's "The Adventure of the Hansom Cab." The records of Scotland Yard show that cabbies were of great assistance to them with information they provided being used in any number of cases.

Jefferson Hope's story, which now follows, is as pure a vengeance tale as is "Green Tea" itself. On the Fourth of May 1847, John Ferrier and an orphan girl Lucy, sole survivors of an ill-fated wagon train crossing the American desert, are rescued by a large group of Mormons trekking to Utah. This incident of a wagon train being lost in the American West and many of its members perishing is a borrowing from the true account of the Donner party, a group of travelers heading for California who in the winter of 1846-47 became trapped by snowstorms in the Sierra Nevada Mountains. About half of the group died of starvation with the rest surviving by eating their bodies. Doyle picked May of 1847 for the rescue of his pair of castaways, this being the time the Donner Party found deliverance. The account was spoken of throughout the world for years and was the focus of articles and books.

The Mormons are a people who style themselves as Chosen People of God, and act accordingly, with their religion encompassing the Hebrews' happy faculty for oversimplification. The mentality of these people, especially the "elders," is depicted by the fact that they would have abandoned the two stragglers to die on the desert if they had refused to submit to conversion to Mormonism. The Mormons are a study in intolerance whose elders speak with the authority of God, expecting blind adherence from their followers. "Everywhere a God is admitted, there is a cult; wherever there is a cult, the natural order of duties is reversed and morals corrupted," Diderot claims. He adds that Christianity is the most dangerous of religions for it was "the most subject to divisions," which is what Mormonism is; a division from the main branch. Diderot himself was estranged from his own Catholicism, formed by his Jesuit education, which he considered unyielding, as did Doyle, and no doubt we have something of a reflection of this adamantine attitude in the inflexibility of Doyle's Mormons. Henry James, Senior called Mormonism "downright deviltry, which reasonable people will some day be forced to sweep bodily from the earth." Doyle fashioned his Mormons primarily upon the English Puritans, a people driven out of their homeland by those who could no longer abide their narrow and overbearing religious attitudes and practices. A tally of Doyle's work shows us he had quite a lot to say about the Puritans and their troubled history with his novel *The Refugees*, dealing with the hardships and privations of the French Puritans, both in Europe and America, the paramount example. Doyle obviously harbored sympathy for them, which is surprising since Carlyle had little love for these religious fanatics as a group.

At one point in *A Study in Scarlet* Watson expresses surprise at his roommate's ignorance of who Thomas Carlyle was, and well he should — but I don't understand why Watson doesn't experience absolute amazement when in the next story, *The Sign of Four*, the following scene takes place. A conversation between the two, dealing with the nature of man, opens with Holmes asking, "Are you well up in your Jean Paul?" Johann Paul Friedrich Richter, the German philosopher, is always referred to by his first two names, and often as Jean Paul or John Paul. Watson answers: "Fairly so. I worked back to him through Carlyle." In spite of the fact that a relatively short period of time would separate the two cases, Holmes, rather than asking who Carlyle is, says, "That was like following the brook to the parent lake." Holmes is familiar enough with the writings of both Jean Paul and his translator and intellectual continuator Carlyle to offer comparative criticism on how their connection should best be approached. Are we to believe Holmes has been pulling the good doctor's leg in claiming he never heard of Carlyle, or was it just a confused oversight on the author's part?

The very fact that Carlyle has been commented upon in the first two stories gives us some indication of his distinct influence on Doyle's life. Carlyle, like Doyle, and so many others, had left his native Scotland searching for a cool spot on the pillow of England. Both had graduated from Edinburgh University, with Carlyle being a rector of the school when Arthur was a boy in the city. The lad would have admired this world famous personality and certainly was familiar with his commencement speech of April 1866. Carlyle's topics in this speech included subjects he had talked of and written about many times in the past, such as work, religion, history, and heroic men, but a responsive chord was struck at this particular occasion and his words where acclaimed and reported with enthusiasm from one end of the country to the other.

Like Doctor Doyle with his empty waiting room, Carlyle eked out a precarious living, chiefly as a teacher and tutor, until his writing found an audience. Carlyle was a trenchant critic of society, both his own and those of foreign lands, and he expressed his views in a sort of spiritual fictional autobiography, *Sartor Resartus*, and in his interpretative rather than historical *The French Revolution, A History*. His collection of six lectures published in 1841 under the title *On Heroes, Hero-Worship, and the Heroic in History* set forth his social discontent, as well as his belief that mankind, specifically the British, could be saved, spiritually and physically, by great men; the "heroes" that society produced, often in spite of itself. Each of the six lectures emphasizes a different and seemingly unrelated aspect of human existence having complex links rooted in the theory that each facet of being had its birth with a human agency who is to be regarded primarily as a "hero." The division includes the hero as Divinity, Prophet, Poet, Priest, Man of Letters, and King, with individual examples of personalities from each category plus a philosophical interpretation of that society each hero was born into, and which he in some way strove to change. The shadow of the hero falls over the whole history of his people, and of the world at large, Carlyle seems to be saying. With a few exceptions, the aim of his writings is moral instruction, and the medium through which he presents his lessons is biography; the story of a "great man" who has "a divine relation," "which in all times unites a Great Man to other men," adding that even the gods were only men of flesh and blood, but of the race of heroes.

The divine meaning of virtue and the infinite nature of duty and morality have been overwhelmed by greed, Carlyle believed, and the great evil in society was the fact that the pursuit of happiness had become an end in itself. Men, individually and in the mass, care only for material prosperity and outward success and power. His writings are a reaction against the materialism and indifference to human suffering experienced by modern man as a result of the Industrial Revolution which brought with it poverty, sickness, including mental ill-health, crippling inequality, overcrowding, crime, etc. Carlyle seemed to believe that in religion only was man to find the meaning of life: "For if we will think of it, no Time need have gone to ruin, could it have *found* a man great enough, a man wise and good enough: wisdom to discern truly what the Time wanted, valor to lead it on the right road thither; these are the salvation of any Time." The key word here is "salvation."

Carlyle's hero is one who can perceive the force that activates the universe and separates it from its visible appearance with which it clothes itself; he can tell reality from appearance. The clarity with which a man can make this distinction establishes his status as a hero, and the sureness with which his fellow men can grasp and accept his feat determines their status as hero worshippers; almost as important as the hero himself.

The story of the hero Holmes and biographer Watson continues now, with this new knowledge and more of the same to come, forming a component of the weave. Carlyle tried to admire the Puritans for being such pious and religious men, but "At bottom, I found that it would not do."

"They are very noble men these; step along in their stately way, with their measured euphemisms, philosophies, parliamentary eloquences, Ship-monies, *Monarchies of Man*; a most constitutional, unblameable, dignified set of men." Notice how Carlyle has managed to present the Puritans to our mind as constituting a sort of procession of men on the move, just as Doyle's Mormons are on the move, stepping along as in a procession. Carlyle continues, "But the heart remains cold before them; the fancy alone endeavours to get up some worship of them. What man's heart does, in reality, break forth into any fire of brotherly love for these men? They are become dreadfully dull men!" Both Carlyle and Doyle have made their religious communities consist of men only, with no women ever being mentioned; a comment perhaps on the absolute male dominance of the group with the sour, boorish nature of the Mormons brought home to us by their stern reluctance to find humor in the witty remarks of John Ferrier.

The use of the name John Ferrier, by the way, strengthens the link to René Descartes, who, while in Paris around 1628 befriended an optical instrument maker, Jean Ferrier, and two years later, when the philosopher was living in Holland, tried to persuade Ferrier, still in Paris, to join him in work on a machine for cutting telescopic lenses. He would not leave Paris, however, and the project was abandoned. Doyle often employs names he is familiar with in his stories, usually but not always with a specific reference in mind. Perhaps he means to tell us John Ferrier has clearer "vision" than the Mormons.

"The Country of the Saints," Jefferson Hope's account of his American misadventures, and Cooper's *The Prairie*, open in much the same way with a group of travelers from the East trekking by wagon across the endless American Plains in search of a new life. It is indicated that these people have also been forced to leave the East because of differences with the law; differences that find a basis in their religious convictions, the situation of the Mormons in America at the time. Some of Cooper's men are also entitled "elders" with the term carrying hierarchical religious connotations. Fleeing from what they perceived to be unjust persecution, the Church of the Latter Day Saints hoped to find freedom in the undeveloped west where there were no laws to hinder them.

We are in the land of the Pawnees, a tribe of vicious Indians, and a place of "arid wastes," as both Cooper and Doyle describe it. The American writer tells us his ill-fated group, led by the Bush family, included "both sexes, and every age, the number of the party exceeded twenty." And therefore Doyle, in a clever and complimentary move, tells us his migrants consist of a group of twenty-one. Doyle obviously writes with the books of other authors open before him. Cooper's pilgrims, as sanctimonious as the Mormons themselves, also take their names and mentalities from the *Old Testament*.

Hawkeye, upon meeting Ellen Wade, one of the Bush party, asks, "Did you not know that, when you crossed the big river, you left a friend behind you that is always bound to look to the young and feeble, like yourself."

"Of whom do you speak?" Ellen asks. "The law," Hawkeye answers. West of the Mississippi all must live by "Prairie law," as he calls it.

The Bush party is holding captive a young woman whose general description, including "curling tresses of hair," matches Lucy Ferrier, whom they hope to sell in California. In addition to the crime of kidnapping *The Prairie* actually develops into a murder mystery with Hawkeye being accused of killing one of the squatter's sons.

Lucy, adopted by John Ferrier, grows up to be a beauty sought by many. However, she falls in love with her most ardent suitor, a hunter and non-Mormon, Jefferson Hope. The character of Hope is fashioned primarily after Paul Hover, the young bee hunter in *The Prairie* who holds a forbidden love for Ellen Wade, a traveler with the Bush group out of indebtedness rather than choice. She is not really one of them and will flee with Hover, just as Lucy and Jefferson run from the Mormons. The noble and determined nature of Hope is linked to the moral qualities and simple virtues of Hawkeye and he too is a tracker and hunter who must interrupt his normal livelihood to rescue a woman and ultimately seek revenge against their enemies. Hope practices the code of the Indians; like them and like Hawkeye, he will venture anywhere and endure any privation to extract revenge upon his enemies. Of Hope we are told, "Year passed into year, his black hair turned to grizzled, but still he wandered on, a human bloodhound, with his mind wholly set upon the one object to which he had devoted his life." That one object is the killing of Drebber and Stangerson, responsible for the death of Lucy Ferrier. Doyle manages to include the word "prairie" into his description by telling us "prairie training had given Jefferson Hope the ears of a lynx."

Jefferson Hope's name is an articulation of the man. In America "Jefferson" is always associated with Thomas Jefferson, one of the founding fathers, who included among his principles for the new republic a hope for the complete division of religion and politics; the separation of Church and State. Early American leaders such as Jefferson, Washington, and Franklin were deists of one sort or another who viewed religion's power with suspicion. Thomas Jefferson advocated the dignity of the individual, putting great faith in "the common man," especially as he might come into being in America. This common man was what Jefferson actually believed in, not religion or even government. He was thought to have wild Republican ideas, sympathy with French Jacobinism, and an outspoken distrust of what his followers dubbed "privilege and aristocracy." Jefferson and his supporters did not believe in John Calvin's doctrine of the total depravity of man, regarding it as injurious to man's freedom. The Jeffersonian ideal of individualism and opportunity for all refused to jibe with the notion that mankind was born wicked, doomed forever, and "the rights of man" is hardly consistent with a religious conviction of total depravity and everlasting damnation. "The Country of the Saints" can be read as a re-enactment of the struggles between Thomas Jefferson and his many and vocal opponents who believed religion came before either politics or the rights of the common man.

The wedding of Church and State into a single unit is one of the goals of Mormonism, and it has been a source of confrontation, often violent, between followers of this hybrid religion and the authorities. There have been disputes, even gun battles, between Mormons and police in America. In Doyle's day conflicts between Mormons and government, often involving the use of Federal troops, were even more frequent. Mormon Elders had up to one hundred wives each, and such practices, illegal in the United States, were responsible for much of the bloodshed. The magazine *Punch* enjoyed reporting on the more humorous side of the Mormon polygamy issue to the British public.

Thomas Jefferson is President during the action of *The Prairie* and is mentioned numerous times during the course of the tale. We are even told that it is Jefferson's Louisiana Purchase that served as catalyst instigating the Bush party to push across the Plains toward the West. The name "Hope" speaks for itself; it was Thomas Jefferson's hope that America and its common people would live up to their potential. The name Jefferson Hope may have occurred to Doyle after seeing Collins' *The Moonstone*, where he names his hero Franklin Blake. The two men have much in common besides being named after famous American idealists and both are absolutely loyal to those they love.

Forming themselves into armed secret societies with names like Danite Band or the Avenging Angels, Doyle's Mormons raid farms and wagon trains for plunder and the kidnapping of women for polygamous marriages. Secret organizations of all kinds will play a distinctive role in many future Holmes stories, the precedent being set right from the beginning.

Lucy and her father, led by Hope, attempt to flee from Utah, for the marriage of a Mormon to an outsider is forbidden in the eyes of this church, and also, the Elders want such a beautiful woman for themselves. Their escape is thwarted in the foothills by the persistent avengers who overtake them while Hope is away hunting for food. John Ferrier is killed outright, shot to death by Joseph Stangerson in what they call "blood atonement," for disloyalty to the Church. Lucy is brought back, is forced to marry a powerful and wealthy farmer, and dies of sorrow within a month.

Both *A Study in Scarlet* and *The Prairie* are essentially love stories; romances, if you wish, full of beautiful young women and dashing men who love them. Cooper wrote some of the most honest and powerful romantic dialogue in literature, although it's the last thing in the world he's noted for. True enough, Holmes and Hawkeye are not often paired with women; but many other characters in the stories are. Both Cooper's and Doyle's tales deal with the kidnapping of young women, this practice being an American tradition dating back to before the invention of apple pie. The Indians in *The Leather-Stocking Tales*, awestruck by the beauty of white women, took advantage of every opportunity that presented itself to capture them, in a natural continuation of their traditional routine of stealing each other's females. Cooper equates the lust of the Indians for females to the greed of the whites for money, emphasizing the unscrupulous nature of both tribes in getting what they want. In *The Deerslayer*, a group of whites and Indians pull a raid on a small Iroquois encampment. The Mohican, Chingachgook, hopes to rescue his young wife, previously stolen by his enemies, while the whites see this as a good opportunity to kill a few women and children in order to sell their scalps to the government. Ishmael Bush, patriarch of the band of refugees in *The Prairie*, has kidnapped the new bride of an American Army officer and hopes to sell her as a slave, while the Indians they encounter plot in turn to steal her from him in order to make of her a "sister-wife" in the harem of their chief. An efficient warrior was expected to have a number of wives and at least a few children. Doyle equates his gangs of Mormons to groups of warring Indians, commonly called "bands" in America.

The personality of the two Mormon miscreants: Enoch Drebber and Joseph Stangerson is reflected in their names, for "stang" is a Scottish-British dialect variant of the verb "to sting," perhaps like a venomous scorpion, and "Drebber" is echoic of his comical, boorish nature. Enoch is the name of a Hebrew prophet whose writings, *The Book of Enoch*, stand out as a study in religious obsession and bigotry. The prophet Enoch believed in physically punishing any who would not follow his religion. One of Bush's sons is named Enoch, perhaps for the same reason. The *Book of Enoch* is found in those sections of the *Old Testament* known as the Apocrypha and Pseudepigrapha, words meaning "things falsely ascribed," for many doubt this fanatical bigot could actually be transmitting the word of God.

Hope establishes a plan of revenge on Drebber and Stangerson but before he can carry it out, the two realize his intentions and flee Utah without leaving a clue to their destinations. Jefferson Hope now becomes the nemesis of these two as surely as the monkey was the agent of retribution on the Rev. Jennings. Following years of tedious searching and repeatedly just missing the two, Hope finally overtakes them in Sherlock Holmes' London where, employed as a hack-driver, he gives Drebber a one-way ride. A few days later Hope succeeds in bringing about the death of Stangerson. Hope forced Drebber to swallow a pill that might, or might not, contain poison. It did. He had to stab Stangerson to death when the latter attacked him in a fit of rage. Holmes and Hope have played the tracker and the trapper, of animals and man — two maneuvers practiced by Hawkeye.

The two criminals have paid for their evil with their lives, and Hope himself, the day following his arrest, dies of an aneurysm: a stroke. Just about all the deaths in Doyle's novel are brought about by the self-imposed actions of the individuals who expired, although the circumstances of their deaths were initiated by outside forces. The murderer of Bush's son, when caught, is stood upon a boulder with a noose around his neck, the end of which is secured to a tree limb above him. "We leave you to your God," the avengers say as they turn and walk away, leaving him to fall off the rock from sheer exhaustion. The felon will be "sent before the judgment seat of the Lord." Watson tells us, "A higher Judge had taken the matter in hand, and Jefferson Hope had been summoned before a tribunal where strict justice would be meted out to him."

Fascination with all aspects of law and man's capacity to keep it and to break it is a hallmark of the mind of both Cooper and Doyle. One cannot help correlating the vengeance tale of Hope to the medieval tales of the knights of King Arthur, whose exploits are efforts to bring justice to the world, a comparison Doyle wanted us to make. The knights, personifications of the conscience of their society, are always called upon to bring justifiable punishment to those who have committed a wrong, usually against a lady, often with implied sexual overtones, as in the person of Lucy, or uncalled-for insult and sometimes violence against a man too old or weak to defend himself, as in the person of her father. Often it is society itself that has been wronged by a powerful but evil personality. Doyle was captivated with these medieval vengeance legends, using them as thematic material and background in historical novels such as *The White Company* and *Sir Nigel*; works their author considered his finest effort, even believing them to be superior to the Holmes stories. This offering of protection to the weak is also the prerogative of Hawkeye, among several others in Cooper's writings. Almost every work of Cooper's deals with the protection of women from danger, usually, but not limited to the threat offered them by the Indians. In *The Pathfinder* Hawkeye tells us he regards women as "so many feeble ones I was bound to protect and defend."

"Scarlet" is an unusual word, and taking it and thinking about it as a Symbolist furnished me with the reasoning appropriate for discovering the connection between *A Study in Scarlet* and the American tale of religious intolerance *The Scarlet Letter* by Nathaniel Hawthorne. Hawthorne tells us that in Massachusetts, before America became independent, there was "a people amongst whom religion and law were almost identical, and in whose character both were so thoroughly interfused, that the mildest and the severest acts of public discipline were alike made venerable and awful." What is being depicted is a Puritanical society ruled by "bearded men, in sad-colored garments," with "gray, steeple-crowned hats," who rule with both unyielding religious as well as secular authority; exactly what Thomas Jefferson hoped to avoid in the new nation. Hawthorne's "New England brethren" regard themselves as living in "the sanctity of Enoch" and share with Doyle's Mormons a hypersensitive ecclesiastical fanaticism. The desperate urgency and the rich mental texture of the moral gravity of the early American writer can be found in every page of "The Country of the Saints."

In *The Scarlet Letter*, a young woman Hester Prynne, is married to and then deserted by her older husband Roger Chillingworth: his very name an allusion to his cold, austere nature She has a brief passion with the young pastor Arthur Dimmesdale, resulting in the birth of an illegitimate child, Pearl. When Hester refuses to name Pearl's father, the unforgiving community demands atonement for her sin and for her silence. Dimmesdale, the classic example of a divided man, moralistically condemns his own passion yet disavows both Hester and their child. Hester, ostracized and forced to wear the letter "A" for adulteress on her bodice, lives both physically and spiritually on the margins of society where she and her daughter come to exemplify the silent suffering bred by misunderstanding and intolerance, as well as becoming a symbol of the great Christian virtue of patience. Hester does not consider simply walking away from her people any more than Ellen Wade, or Lucy Ferrier, or even the Rev. Jennings would, for all have a claim on their religious and social roots that itself accounts for ambiguous emotions, divided loyalties, and great anguish. Chillingworth resurfaces to torment Hester and Dimmesdale, and it lies in their reaction to the older man's evil that the divergent characters of the former lovers reveal themselves. All of Hawthorne's work deals with secret sin; that which we would hide from those nearest and dearest, and from the world in general — as well as asking what is real sin, and who the true sinner? Chillingworth is brimming with what he regards as righteous revenge but is himself guilty of having "violated, in cold blood, the sanctity of a human heart."

The physical description of little Pearl reads like a portrait of young Lucy, and spiritually both children are the victims of the sacerdotal zealots comprising the society in which they are reared. In *A Study in Scarlet* the idea of finding the word "Rache," assumed initially to be the name of a woman, written in blood on a wall, came from the practice in New England, as described in Hawthorne's work, of witches writing their names in their own blood in the devil's book.

The living arrangements of Holmes and Watson bears a strong relationship to the plans of the Rev. Arthur Dimmesdale and Dr. Roger Chillingworth, who rent rooms in the house of a "good widow." The American doctor sets up a small study and laboratory complete "with a distilling apparatus and the means of compounding drugs and chemicals." Like Holmes he is a chemist, and like Watson, a physician.

Hawthorne's is a tale of retribution: the reprisal of the community against Hester and her child, and the vendetta of Chillingworth for the father of Pearl, who he believes has wronged him. The novels of early American life now under discussion are replete with characters: often people in authority both religious and civil, who are unmalleable and unbendingly stubborn in all matters of life. This refusal to yield to others is instigated essentially by inflexible doctrinal sentiments and anxieties. Doyle read the connection between Hawthorne's clouded tragedy of the pathological retribution of one man for another and Le Fanu's stories written twenty years later. Instead of the foul ape haunting the Rev. Dimmesdale, we have the animalistic Chillingworth preying upon the social and sacred dread of one whose soul is burdened with the "low, dark, and misshapen figure" of guilt. Rather than one demon grinning and mocking at a hapless victim, in the American story we have "a herd of diabolic shapes that grinned and mocked at the pale minister, and beckoned him away with them." In an effort to expiate his sin Dimmesdale fasts and persecutes himself in acts of atonement while thoughts of insanity and suicide float just beneath the surface of the mind, as they do in any number of Hawthorne's people. Dimmesdale's fierce guilt, likened to "an influence dwelling always upon him like a curse," drives him to a point where "he stood on the verge of lunacy"; an emotion the Rev. Jennings would have understood. A number of other points of similarity exist between *The Scarlet Letter* and "Green Tea" such as the detail that the haunted one in each case holds back information from their doctors. We also have the uncomfortable truth that the plight of the victims cannot be cured— not, at any rate, by "an earthly physician," as Hawthorne puts it. Pearl is referred to as an "imp" and her impish ways are emphasized to us as she relentlessly follows her mother everywhere like a guilty curse, with her own mother admitting her inhuman behavior. When Dimmesdale finally determines to flee the conformity of the Puritan community his personality adopts unto itself a bizarre attitude that proves to be not very different from that of both the incubus and victim in "Green Tea." In his heart he now experiences something akin to loathing for his former brethren. While talking to a member of his congregation he has difficulty refraining from "uttering certain blasphemous suggestions that rose into his mind, respecting the communion-supper," and "he could hardly avoid laughing," when thinking of how a fellow deacon "would have been petrified by his minister's impiety!" He has become "this lost and desperate man" who is forced to admit to himself that he now doubts the very immortality of the human soul. The climax of Hawthorne's novel is congruous to both Le Fanu's and Doyle's works for the culpable self-judgment and mental agitation of the Rev. Dimmesdale kills him with heart failure; a species of self-willed suicide. With the death of the minister, Chillingworth, like the monkey in "Green Tea" ceases to have reality, for we are told "he positively withered up, shrivelled away, and almost vanished from mortal sight, like an uprooted weed that lies wilting in the sun." Having worked his evil his presence is no longer necessary, so he disappears, much as a pookah might when confronted by one who does not believe in it.

"A Study in Scarlet" also bears an affinity with Hawthorne's short story "The Gentle Boy," a work dealing with the persecution of the New England Quakers by the Puritans. Like all of Hawthorne's writing, the story is a blend of fact and fiction. A good-natured Puritan, Tobias Pearson comes upon a Quaker boy weeping over the murdered body of his father, a casualty of the Puritan effort to drive this sect, which they consider dangerous and outlandish, from New England. The Puritan adopts the orphan into his home just as John Ferrier did with Lucy, with the plot revolving around his efforts to raise the lad among a people who obviously fear and despise him. We are "holier than thou" is the message being sent by the Puritans, as it is by the Mormons. The boy "was like a domesticated sunbeam, brightening moody countenances, and chasing away the gloom from the dark corners of the cottage," and like Lucy has a great deal of personal beauty. Just as Lucy is termed "the flower of Utah," Ilbrahim is "a plant that would twine beautifully round something stronger than itself" for support in this cruel life. The Pearsons become targets of outrageous harassment among their own people, and due to this persecution the gentle Quaker Ilbrahim sickens and dies while still a child. Insensitivity has killed him as surely as it has Lucy. During the course of the action, Hawthorne introduces an old Quaker who describes how the Puritans drove his daughter to death, and from this Doyle takes the hint.

Yet another work by Hawthorne that influenced *A Study in Scarlet* is the short piece "The Canterbury Pilgrims," in which a young couple, Josiah and "pretty Miriam," flee the restricted life of their Shaker village without telling the Elders, in an effort to achieve a happier life in the outside world. The Shakers are a sect of Quakers once quite common in New England. We are told that the Elder of the village is an old man lacking any understanding of the problems of the young. The Shakers are not as formidable as many sects, for they permit those who really wish to leave their community to do so. The couple meets a group of travelers, pilgrims who are themselves seeking the comfort of Shaker life and who consequently try to warn the naïve refugees of just how pitiless existence can be in the real world. Doyle may have taken the idea for the wagon train of the Mormons from "The Canterbury Pilgrims," for one character mentions having gone on "the Oregon expedition," which was a famous wagon trek. A life full of travail and misery is what you shall find, the disillusioned travelers warn the fledglings, once you abandon the shelter of your religious brotherhood, but like Jefferson Hope and Lucy, they maintain their decision to desert their creed, determined to face the perils of life. The pilgrims themselves head towards the Shaker center, for "They sought a home where all former ties of nature or society would be sundered, and all distinctions levelled, and a cold and passionless security be substituted for human hope and fear, as in that other refuge of the world's weary outcasts, the grave." The Shaker hamlet is a sanctuary for those for whom the weight of eternity is far heavier than the burdens of this world.

Chapter Three. Another Cup of Tea?

Before I get ahead of myself I'll try to make good my claim that "Green Tea" is the single most influential piece of writing for the Holmes Canon. Much of what I have to say can be applied to "The Familiar" as well, but the first work is the superior of the two pieces as a work of art and this consideration would go a long way with an artist such as Doyle.

It might be instructive to deal somewhat with a non-Doyle story that emphasizes the authority of "Green Tea." Stevenson's 1886 work, *The Strange Case of Dr. Jekyll and Mr. Hyde,* is a shibboleth for the fact that people are often composed of two separate natures: one good, one evil, and these duel dispositions are not only opponent to each other, they are thoroughly irreconcilable.

The luckless Dr. Jekyll, a respected medical man, unthinkingly experiments with strange drugs; researches that force him to repeatedly mutate into his evil half, a smallish, ape-like monstrosity he names Edward Hyde. Jekyll's malefic fifty percent proves uncontrollable, violent, and loathsome, even to his creator, yet in spite of this he persists with the ill-favored investigations. If Jekyll is Jennings, then Hyde plays the role of the avenging fiend, a monster of one's own making. The animalistic Hyde is described as "particularly small and particularly wicked-looking," a "thing like a monkey," with "an ape-like fury." Playing the imp with Jekyll, he pulls tricks on the doctor, scrawling blasphemes on the pages of his books, just as the nemesis of Jennings shouted irreverences at him as he prayed. Stevenson interprets the demon of "Green Tea" to be that part of our human nature that personifies lust and violence, for Hyde commits atrocity after atrocity, climaxing in the murder of a Member of Parliament. The deformed alter ego becomes a permanent fixture, altogether replacing the doctor.

Books play an enlightening role in character revelation. Utterson, a lawyer friend of Jekyll's, a weak individual who has no interest in helping his fellow man ("I let my brother go to the devil in his quaintly 'own way.'") has a Sunday habit of reading "a volume of some dry divinity." Jekyll, even in his manifestation as Hyde, spends time reading "a pious work," but in a bow to Le Fanu, the book is "annotated, in his own hand, with startling blasphemies." Stevenson obviously believed blasphemy to have been the sin of the Rev. Jennings.

It may seem a bit unusual for me to be spending so much time on a Stevenson work but the whole idea of using "Green Tea" and "The Familiar" as the backbone for a more contemporary work of fiction may have occurred to Doyle following his reading of *Dr. Jekyll and Mr. Hyde*. A date of 1886 for Stevenson's novella means Doyle is thinking about, and actually in the process of writing, *A Study in Scarlet* as he analyzes the potential of how he could recycle "Green Tea." Stevenson was a successful member of that generation of artists who were at work just as the young writer was starting his own efforts, and these are the people you learn from.

In his vivid description of Hyde, the lawyer Utterson, disgusted by what he has seen, tells us he regarded the being with "loathing, and fear," adding, "There is something more, if I could find a name for it. God bless me, the man seems hardly human! Something troglodytic, shall we say?" Well, we shall say it, but first we better know what it means. I had to look up this strange word, a word as bizarre as Hyde himself, and I don't doubt Doyle had to as well. When he found it he learned it means "to creep," and that it comes from the Greek, "one who creeps into holes," and hence we have the story "The Adventure of the Creeping Man." He could hardly have called it "The Adventure of the Troglodytic Man." Who would have read it?

"Come at once if convenient — if inconvenient come all the same," reads an urgent message to Watson asking him to attend to Holmes, who obviously has need of assistance. No doubt sitting in front of the fire, Watson has been thinking over past experiences he has shared with Holmes, these ruminations being similar to the introspection we are party to of the English doctor in the opening pages of "Green Tea." Once at Baker Street, Watson finds his old friend pondering a letter bearing the information that a certain Professor Presbury, a physiologist and philosopher, has been turned upon by his pet wolfhound. The religious connotations of the name "Presbury" allies him to "Green Tea" for the word has something devotional about it, vaguely Protestant, bringing to mind the status of the Rev. Jennings. "Presbyter," for instance, was a synonym for "priest" in early England. We see that the Professor, like Jekyll and Jennings, is also unmarried.

"The Creeping Man" is basically a medical or scientific mystery so Doyle draws a comparison between Holmes' threshold presentation of the case to that of "the pathologist who presents a rare specimen." A Mr. Bennett, the Professor's assistant, arrives at Baker Street elaborating his employer's unprecedented antics. Like Watson, Bennett is also a physician so that makes two doctors in on the case, just as two physicians, Harley and Hesselius are involved in the problem of the Rev. Jennings. Bennett has surprised Mr. Presbury "crawling, Mr. Holmes — crawling!" along the hallway of his home. Not only that, but the Professor's daughter Edith, who has conveniently just burst into Holmes' flat, claims her father has taken to climbing up the side of the house during the night.

Agreeing to investigate the behavior of this fantastic person the pair of detectives scheme to somehow interview the man incognito at his home. The meeting does not go well for the professor suspects a plot and "His face was convulsed, and he grinned and gibbered at us in his senseless rage," throwing them out of the house with an over-the-shoulder glimpse showing him "leaning forward, his hands swinging straight before him, his head turning from side to side." In *Dr. Jekyll and Mr. Hyde*, Utterson, attempting to solve the puzzle, meets Hyde once at the beginning of the tale and like the encounter between Holmes and Presbury the interview is brief and unwelcome by Hyde. At the village inn where they are staying the two investigators, along with Bennett, plan to return to the house that evening to observe the scene at night. The business of staking out the house from across the street or hidden in the bushes is taken from the scenes of Enfield and Utterson prowling around Jekyll's place looking for evidence of his connection to Hyde. Bennett takes the place of Enfield for it was he who divulges to his cousin Utterson his encounter with the sinister Hyde, just as Bennett relates to Holmes his initial confrontation with the strange conduct of the professor.

The solution to the case comes into the mind of Holmes as the trio hides in the shrub opposite the house awaiting developments. The Great Detective sounds exactly like a medical man at this point as he relates that the symptom he found the most remarkable was to be located in the victim's knuckles. He points out that the knuckles are "thick and horny," adding this "can only be explained by the mode of progression observed by — " Enlightened revelation of so ghastly a nature forces him to pause and clap his hand to his forehead in amazement. The discovery Holmes is making is the incredible fact that Presbury, for some reason, has turned Darwin upside down and is slowly evolving into an ape. The subject of their observations emerges from the building and creeping around on all fours goes to the rear of the house and climbs up the face of it with the agility of a monkey. Tiring of this he brachiates down and amuses himself with provoking and tormenting his chained wolfhound, throwing handfuls of pebbles at him and prodding him with a stick. This freakish little scene is lifted right out of "Green Tea" with the role of the dog being played by the tormented Jennings. The hound slips his collar and goes right for the monkeyish professor's throat. A servant, the coachman Macphail, who lives above the stables and has witnessed the scene, rushes out and helps separate man and dog, but not before Presbury's throat has been ripped open. Just as it was with Jennings, there is a great deal of blood, but in this case Bennett and Watson manage to pull Presbury through and he will live. Had he died, his death could easily be regarded as a suicide similar to that of Jennings, complete with lacerated throat, and Dr. Jekyll, in his role of the ape-like Hyde, destroyed himself as well. The denouement of the case continues with the discovery of a letter from a colleague in Prague who has sold the old man a youth serum concocted from the fluids of a langur, a large monkey that crawls and climbs rather than walks erect. Presbury, like Jekyll, communicates by written messages with those who supply them with the drugs that have caused their altered conditions. The black-faced langur of South Asia incorporates a pun on the professor's name, for it is of the genus "Presbytis."

It appears the older man was in love with, and hoped to marry, a young lady many years his junior, Alice Morphy, daughter of a colleague, Professor Morphy, and we are told the girl "seemed to like the professor in spite of his eccentricities. It was only age which stood in the way." The professor had lost control of his ability to handle the side effects of the drug, becoming his own ape as it were, the situation of Jekyll and Jennings. Holmes tells those present what his philosophical mentality came up with regarding why this retribution befell Presbury. The real cause is that the victim believed "he could only gain his wish by turning himself into a younger man. When one tries to rise above Nature one is liable to fall below it. The highest type of man may revert to the animal if he leaves the straight road of destiny." Doyle is thinking both of Presbury and Jennings with these words, and it is no doubt the kind of precautionary advice Dr. Hesselius would have given the tormented clergyman had he been in time to prevent his tragic death. Dr. Hesselius' native country comes into it, for all of Presbury's troubles seem to have begun upon his returning from a trip to the Continent with drugs that he carried in a carved box "which one associates with Germany."

Doyle enjoys playing word games with his sources, such as "Green Tea," so in the last sentence of "The Creeping Man" we hear Holmes urging they take the early train back to London, "but I think we shall just have time for a cup of tea at the Chequers before we catch it." The two detectives stay at an inn named Chequers in both this story and "The Adventure of the Sussex Vampire." *Chequers* and *cartes* are both French table games and if this word chequers makes you think of René Descartes, as it did me, Doyle has scored an amazing piece of symbolist writing.

This piece of writing is based, as are almost all of Doyle's works, on historical incidents, and much of that history had unfolded in America. Alice Gibbons Howe, a young woman of Boston who eventually became the wife of William James, made the acquaintance of the Quaker poet John Greenleaf Whittier in 1867, when he was in his late sixties and she was about a third his age. The two became quite friendly, exchanging letters, visits, and gifts. "I am very thankful for the good Providence that brought about our acquaintance," he wrote to "my dear friend Alice Gibbons," on Christmas Day of 1875, "it has become a comfort and a refreshing to me." In one letter Whittier tells her he has enjoyed their talk about "eternal hope and suffering," and we all know where that kind of talk leads. He even wrote poetry for Alice.

The close relationship between Edith Presbury and Alice Morphy is based upon the friendship that grew between Alice Gibbons and Alice James, William's younger sister. Note the associative irony of the name "Gibbons," for a gibbon is an Old World anthropoid ape that lives in trees, a fact that may have presented to Doyle the idea for the story in the first place.

In his student days, or perhaps while waiting for the rare patient as a young and not very busy doctor at Battlesea, our author came across the works of the American Oliver Wendell Holmes, Senior. Known generally as Dr. Holmes (to distinguish him from his equally famous son of the same name), he was a prolific writer in the fields of fiction and non-fiction, including much scientific matter, and is best known today for his *The Autocrat of the Breakfast-Table*, which was one of three such collections of related essays, the other two being *The Professor at the Breakfast-Table* and *The Poet at the Breakfast-Table*. The breakfast table at 221B Baker Street is quite often the arena of thought, for it is there we experience the power of Holmes' deductive reasoning unfolding during the course of numerous cases.

Dr. Holmes is a lot like both Doyle and Sherlock, armed as he is with the sort of mind that took all knowledge for its province: versed in such diverse fields as law, chemistry, physiology, history, music, and naturally medicine. He was that type who had a book to his credit entitled *Mechanism in Thought and Morals*, but also a man of scientific experiments who invented the best stethoscope of his day. Henry James, Sr. said to him, "You are intellectually the most alive man I ever knew." Like Doyle he was a physician, a specialist in the problems of vision and eyesight. Arthur attempted to specialize in this field but made the mistake of attending a medical school in Heidelberg; although he spoke and read the language, he could not follow the technical German closely enough. Of his admiration of Dr. Holmes, Doyle said, "Never have I so known and loved a man whom I had never seen. It was one of the ambitions of my lifetime to look upon his face, but by the irony of Fate I arrived in his native city just in time to lay a wreath upon his newly-turned grave."

Close and careful observation of those around him seemed to be a natural preoccupation of the man, spilling over into the following fictional account taken from *The Autocrat of the Breakfast-Table* in which Dr. Holmes mentally regards a frail woman he's just met: "How long will school-keeping take to kill you? Is it possible the poor thing works with her needle, too? I don't like those marks on the side of her forefinger."

"The Creeping Man" was inspired by Dr. Holmes' essay "Professor Jeffries Wyman," which had appeared in *The Atlantic Monthly* for November 1874. The work was a memorial piece such as Dr. Holmes was often called upon to write (he seems to have known just about every prominent American literary and scientific personality of his day). Doyle probably read it in any of the many collections of Dr. Holmes' writings, which were, and still are, quite popular. Wyman of Harvard was one of the scientists, along with such professionals as Louis Agassiz (mentioned in at least one of the stories), who were responsible for bringing together vast collections of natural history specimens of their own and others, to form the Museum of Comparative Zoology at Cambridge, Mass. William James studied under Wyman in the fields of Physiology and Anatomy, and he considered Prof. Wyman the greatest teacher he ever met. Both James and Agassiz had taken part in a biological expedition to Brazil in 1865 while connected to Wyman at Harvard. Jeffries Wyman was born in the village of Chelmsford, Massachusetts, and taught in the town of Cambridge, so Doyle, searching for a suitable location for Prof. Presbury to live, merges the two names and comes up with Camford.

Oliver Holmes chooses to memorialize Wyman primarily through his gift of specimens to the Cambridge Museum and structures his eulogy to read as rumination during a visit to that institution. He notes the various cases containing the skeletons of animals in one room. "Most interesting of all are the skull and other bones of a mighty gorilla. His head and pelvis are far from human in their aspect, but his arm bone is so like that of his cousin Darwinian, that it looks as if it might have belonged to Goliath of Goth, or Og, king of Basham. The skeleton of a young chimpanzee, by the side of that of a child, has a strongly marked effect of similar significance. There are also whole series of special preparations to show the parts of the skeleton concerned in locomotion in different classes of animals." Doyle goes out of his way to draw attention to differences in locomotion of various apes in "The Creeping Man," fictionalizing Dr. Holmes' account of Wyman's collection for his quasi-scientific short story. In the fashion typical of his time Dr. Holmes goes on to moralize upon the display material by comparing ancient man to his modern counterpart — modern man as best exemplified by Prof. Wyman himself — for Dr. Holmes imagines that mankind "has developed at length into a being of that luminous intelligence, those commanding powers, those benign graces, those far-reaching aspirations, that empire over the instincts and passions, which show him, in his best estate, as but a little lower than the angels." This, he is sure, is what man should be. "Before us are the relics of the troglodyte's unhallowed feast; what a mental and moral space between him who left his tooth-mark on the bone and him who wrote its label." The unhallowed feast is a reference to the case before him containing evidence that the cavemen ate their dead, even cracking open the bones for marrow. Presbury has returned to his earlier troglodyte state and in so doing has become not an ape but rather an ape-man. Wyman gave "his time chiefly to the study of human and comparative anatomy," and this is the field of interest of Presbury. The memorial essay goes on to add that Wyman often performed "curious experiments bearing on different points of interest," and wrote papers on "the habits of animals." "He has given an admirable description of the arrangement of the spicula of bone in the neck of the human femur, and contrasted this arrangement with that observed in other animals not destined for the erect posture." He also experimented with "the great question of biogenesis, and the birth and development of living organisms." The Professor attempted to find the formula for why life existed in its present form and his eulogizer tells us that reading some of his writings "was like being taken into the workshop of the sovereign Artificer, engaged in the last and greatest of his creative efforts," calling this particular piece of writing "this remarkable paper." Wyman has been trying to alter, or even create life, perhaps human life, all this adding up to something like the fix Presbury got himself into, and I wouldn't be a bit surprised to learn the Englishman had been reading some of Wyman's stuff. Wyman and Presbury have played God, and like Jennings and Jekyll have dabbled into matters whose depths they should never have attempted to sound.

Dr. Holmes was a man who lived for admiration, and admitted so with engaging frankness. So indeed was Sherlock Holmes. We offer as evidence the reaction to his discovery of the "Sherlock Holmes test" for determining the different aspects of bloodstains. "His eyes fairly glittered as he spoke, and he put his hand over his heart and bowed as if to some applauding crowd conjured up by his imagination," is how Watson describes it. This sort of thing is replete throughout the Canon.

In one way or another all the pieces found in *The Case Book* reveal the fact that their author borrowed from, not just "Green Tea," but from Le Fanu in general, in addition to his own novel, *A Study in Scarlet*. This heavy renting from these medical mysteries induced Doyle to entitle the collection *The Case Book of Sherlock Holmes*, casebook being a term usually associated with medicine. I don't doubt Doyle grew to regard "Green Tea" as something of his own invention since he was so fond of rereading and lifting ideas from it.

In "The Problem of Thor Bridge" a Mrs. Gibson has been found in the middle of a stone bridge with a bullet through her brain. Miss Dunbar, the poor but attractive governess is accused of killing the wife thereby gaining the husband and his wealth. Holmes rebuffs his client Mr. Gibson for holding back data relevant to the case prompting the millionaire to compare him to "a surgeon who wants every symptom before he can give his diagnosis." Holmes counters with, "it is only a patient who has an object in deceiving his surgeon who would conceal the facts of his case." As we know, Dr. Hesselius suspects Jennings of screening important particulars dealing with religious doubts, terrors, and sexual depravation the man must be cultivating, but of which we are never told.

The two investigators room at the village inn during the progress of this case. They could stay at Thor Place but Doyle deliberately does not have Gibson extend an invitation to them. This will eventually give Holmes the opportunity of divulging his solution to the mystery "as we sat together smoking our pipes in the village inn." In "The Creeping Man," the epiphany scene in which the detective realizes Presbury is advancing towards apehood should theoretically have been enacted at the village inn as well, but like any good artist Doyle avoids predictability. Secrecy was part of the mystique of being a symbolist writer, and Doyle kept his secrets. "The Problem of Thor Bridge" is the only story in which the word "Problem" is used in the title and also the only one I can think of in which an actual suicide takes place. Like Le Fanu's tale, "Thor Bridge" deals with the situation of an individual being driven to self-destruction by the suspicions lodged within their minds: Jennings by theological alarms, Mrs. Gibson by her belief in the unfaithfulness of her husband and her hatred for the suspected object of his affections, Miss Dunbar.

The other collections make use of Le Fanu, including *The Memoirs of Sherlock Holmes*, which incorporated "The Crooked Man," whose very title is evocative of "The Creeping Man" and also bears a strong resemblance to *Jekyll and Hyde*. A Colonel Barclay, retired from the army in India is found dead of a head injury following a heated argument with his wife, now suspected of having killed him. Mrs. Barclay had gone out earlier that evening and upon returning home orders tea to be served ("which was quite contrary to her usual habits") in the morning-room where her husband joins her and the drama unfolds. His body was found by the coachman who entered the locked room through the French windows opening out upon the lawn. Major

Murphy, friend of the Barclays believes her innocent and calls upon Holmes to supplement the efforts of the local police. The dead man's face had twisted itself "into the most dreadful expression of fear and horror which a human countenance is capable of assuming," so obviously something horrendous passed through the mind at the moment of death. Holmes finds footprints indicating an unknown man had crossed the lawn either during or following the argument between husband and wife and entered the room. He was not alone for he had with him a small, agile animal that climbed the curtains and left small, five-toed prints. Watson suspects a monkey but Holmes, playing Hawkeye, realizes the tracks do not match those of a primate. Murphy admits the Colonel was capable of sudden violence and vindictiveness, as well as suffering from a singular form of depression, which came upon him unexpectedly at times, often lasting for days. He is victim of "a certain tinge of superstition" and appears to be haunted by an entity only he apprehends and dreads, much like the doomed Captain Barton of "The Familiar." Note the similarity of the names Barton and Barclay.

The thickening plot takes us back to India where as a young officer during the Mutiny, Barclay had sent his rival for his future wife's hand out through enemy lines, ostensibly in an effort to reach a distant British column. But Barclay had sold out his competitor, Henry Wood, to the enemy and they capture, torture, and sell him into slavery. Later, Barclay holds a position in society surrounded by success and respect while Wood suffers years of misery. Eventually escaping, Wood returns to England a spiritually as well as physically deformed man, warped from years of ill-usage, who "carried his head low and walked with his knees bent." He no longer has a straight back, crawling about with the aid of "a stick like a chimpanzee," a grotesque hybrid of the monkey of "Green Tea," the smallish man of "The Familiar" and Mr. Hyde. It is this poor creature that personifies the guilty conscience of Barclay and when confronted face to face with Wood — for it is he and his pet mongoose who have entered the room in which the argument had taken place — the man suffers a fit of apoplexy and drops dead, hitting his head on the way down. Remember the mongoose is used in India to kill poisonous reptiles.

The vividness of the man's own haunted thoughts and the consequences those thoughts evoke are what killed Barclay, for Wood tells us, "The bare sight of me was like a bullet through his guilty heart." The culpable mind of James Barclay brought about his death; he paid with his life in a form of suicide, if you wish to call it that. We are informed that "a just Providence" instigated a personal vengeance upon him. The Bible is introduced at the very end, giving it a religious twist, in the form of a comparison between this story of deception and treachery and the account of David, Uriah, and Bathsheba.

Much of this story of betrayal and slavery is borrowed from an incident found in Charles Kingsley's novel *Westward Ho!* The ordeal of the agonized and battered seaman Salvation Yeo, who sailed to the New World with John Oxenham, answers almost word for word the misadventures of Henry Wood. It's obvious to Doyle that Kingsley utilized Cooper's *The Prairie* for a large chunk of the tale, for the ingredients of a Spanish girl, slavery, warfare, and vengeance in Yeo's account, even to the giving of money for having told the story, is modeled upon events found within an eccentric account in *The Prairie*.

In Cooper's story, Middleton, a young captain in the American Army stationed in the Deep South, falls in love with and marries a Mexican-American girl named Inez. Having been married only one hour, the couple part to pack for a wedding trip, making arrangements to meet later. The bride, however, does not arrive as planned and is nowhere to be found. "Day succeeded day, and still no tidings rewarded the search that was immediately instituted, until she was finally given over by most of her relatives and friends as irretrievably lost." Cooper tells us, "Middleton was nearly crushed by the weight of the unexpected and terrible blow." One evening the Captain is out walking on the parade ground when he spots a stranger "meanly dress'd, with every appearance, about his person and countenance, of squalid poverty and of the most dissolute habits." The "crouching form of the intruder" tells Middleton he will tell him a secret dealing with his lost wife in exchange for money. The wretch had at one time been a kidnapper for the slave trade. The miscreant divulges a strong suspicion the girl has been stolen by slavers and is now being taken west to be sold. Middleton pays the man and returns home, but finding sleep impossible returns to the parade grounds only to find the body of his informant, "fallen a victim to his intemperance," having died of a fit, evident by "his obtruding eye-balls."

In Cooper's *The Crater; Or, Vulcan's Peak: A Tale of the Pacific* we find the situation of a sailor returning from the past to plague one who had done him a wrong. In his little known novel *The Wept of Wish-Ton-Wish*, as in a number of other works of the American, a mysterious stranger, a Nemesis from the past, disrupts the peace of a family. There is a comparable plot found in Sherlock's initial case "The 'Gloria Scott,'" among others.

In "The Adventure of the Golden Prince-Nez" we also see a debt to "Green Tea" with the role of Jennings being acted out by a Professor Coram. Instead of using tea to stimulate his mind to heightened mental effort, Coram consumes tobacco in the form of cigarettes, of which he smokes about seventy-five a day. The man is a recluse who rarely leaves the house, devoting his energy to analyzing documents found in the Coptic monasteries of Syria and Egypt, a work, he warns us, "will cut deep at the very foundation of revealed religion." As in "Green Tea," the sin of blasphemy is implied. A young assistant who lived in the household, Willoughby Smith, was found stabbed in the neck in the downstairs study, and in a manner similar to that of Jennings, bled to death. The mystery is not just who done it, but why, and how did they elude being seen entering and leaving the estate. The situation is bewildering, even for Holmes, but by surreptitiously depositing cigarette ash at suspect areas of the professor's bedroom floor he comes to the realization that someone is hiding behind the bookcases. Upon making the revelation public, sure enough the bookcase opens and out steps a woman, the murderess. It turns out that in his youth Coram, a Russian by birth, had been a revolutionary fighter who sold out, for his own advantage, a number of his comrades, including his wife Anna, the woman in the closet. Since then, "the Brotherhood" has been searching for him to extract revenge. Anna, having discovered his whereabouts, was surprised by Smith while going through the professor's study for evidence of his treachery, and killed him in a flurry of confusion. She kills herself with poison after telling Holmes to take the papers to the Russian Embassy. Like "Green Tea," this story concludes with a suicide, and true enough this seems to contradict what I said about the singularity of the suicide in "Thor Bridge," but this latest example was simply a matter of convenience on Anna's part, saving her from a trial and possibly the gallows.

"The 'Gloria Scott,'" already mentioned briefly, is based both on "Green Tea" and "The Familiar." This is critical information for Doyle emphasizes the fact of this being Holmes' initial venture in utilizing his gifts of deduction and methods of thought. Descartes provided the possibilities of existence while Le Fanu furnished themes and examples. Holmes and Watson sitting before their fire on a winter's night summon up the features of the *Gloria Scott* affair, a problem that had occurred years earlier. Holmes shows his friend a seemingly meaningless coded letter that had been sent to a Justice Trevor, "a fine, robust old man," who eventually died of horror having read its enigmatical message. Sherlock was attending university at the time and describes briefly his academic life in which he was "always rather fond of moping in my rooms and working out my own little methods of thought" which were quite distinct from those of the other fellows. No single sentence could more accurately portray Descartes' own way of life as a young man, for he often sought out a sanctuary where he might have "plenty of leisure to examine my ideas." The detective adds that he was fond of fencing and boxing, and it is understood that René, being a professional soldier, would constantly be practicing martial arts since his very life depended upon them. A subtle analogy is drawn linking the pious nature of the philosopher and the detective: we are shown Holmes' adherence to his religion by having him relate how he first met Victor Trevor, son of the Justice, at college, when the boy's bull terrier bit him "one morning as I went down to chapel." Holmes vacations at the Trevors' and makes the observation that the father is living under a cloud of fear. A man named Hudson, "a little wizened fellow with a cringing manner and a shambling style of walking," whose face is "thin and brown and crafty," with "an irregular line of yellow teeth," has paid an unscheduled call on the Justice, said visit having a devastating effect on the man's equanimity. His holidays over, Sherlock returns to school to work on a few experiments in organic chemistry but is summoned back by Victor who tells him of his father suffering a fit of apoplexy resulting from Hudson's visit. This vile drunk has, at Justice Trevor's orders, been made head of the household, and much to the discomfort of all is slowly taking over the place. He does this behind "a sneering, leering, insolent face," in which "two venomous eyes" stare out at the world. Young Victor calls him an animal and indeed, the devil himself. Like Jennings, Presbury, and Jekyll before him, Justice Trevor spends night after night pacing his room in mental agitation. Hudson suddenly leaves as unexpectedly as he came, and normalcy is slowly returning when the coded letter is delivered. The Justice dies soon after reading it. It was the older Trevor's enthusiastic confidence in the mental prowess of young Sherlock that encouraged him to take up detective work, and he begins with this problem before him. Realizing the importance of the letter, Holmes devotes himself to the task of deciphering its message, learning from it that Hudson has told some secret affecting the Justice who is being advised to flee for his life. Fearing his father has died of dread at being exposed for some previous "sin and shame," the son now produces papers dealing with the wreck of the bark *Gloria Scott*, a prison ship on which the Justice, then a young man, had been transported for bank fraud. Hudson was among the convicts, as was a felon named Jack Prendergast. A mutiny and escape is planned and carried out in scenes lifted from Cooper's novel of the sea *The Red Rover: A Tale*. The ship sinks but some convicts, including Hudson, Prendergast, and Trevor, survive and go on to Australia. There Trevor, a free but wanted man, makes a fortune in gold mining. He returns to England amid prosperity and respectability, only to be found, twenty years later, by Hudson, who could ruin him if he wishes. In dying of a stroke Trevor has paid with his body for his sins. Holmes did not arrive in time to prevent the death, just as Hesselius did not arrive in time. Like his archetype, Holmes has actually effected nothing towards preventing a death but rather performs the function of explaining a series of related extraordinary events to the reader. Watson, the initial narrator, has nothing to do with it except to bring it to the reader's attention, just as did the English doctor in "Green Tea." As usual Holmes has the last word on the matter, telling us the *Gloria Scott* was originally built for the China tea trade and Victor, devastated by the evil that has befallen his family, "was heartbroken at it, and went out to the Terai tea planting, where I hear that he is doing well."

"The Resident Patient" owes a great deal to Le Fanu's two stories, even opening with a lengthy soliloquy by Watson as he shares with us a resume of his friend's methods. Both cases chronicled in *A Study in Scarlet* and "The 'Gloria Scott'" are now mentioned as examples of instances in which Holmes feels he had not been involved enough to facilitate his solving of the mysteries. Both cases are linked to "Green Tea" for a considerable installment of this story centers on Hesselius' disappointment in his degree of involvement in the solving of the problem, and Watson is suggesting that the tale of the resident patient may fall into this category as well. An entire two and a half pages follow in "The Resident Patient" in which the Great Detective displays his ability to construe, from the expressions crossing Watson's facial features, the syntactical construction of the man's thoughts, echoing and emphasizing Dr. Hesselius' own abilities. Poe's associative reasoning also surfaces, further linking "The Resident Patient" to *A Study in Scarlet*, where the American writer is introduced. Holmes is once again obligated to play the physician for the action opens with a visit by a Dr. Percy Trevelyan whom Holmes deduces as having "Come to consult us." Trevor and Trevelyan are basically the same name, coming from the root "trier," meaning "a person who tries." This specialist in nervous disorders has been approached by a Mr. Blessington with the proposition that he will set up the doctor in practice if he receives a portion of the earnings and is allowed to become a resident heart patient living in the physician's home. Blessington is a man living in mortal dread of something; following the discovery that a pair of unknowns, posing as patients, have clandestinely entered his rooms for some reason, he sends Dr. Trevelyan to seek the assistance of Sherlock Holmes. Escorting the doctor to his house, Holmes talks to Blessington but, realizing the client is not giving full disclosure, walks out on the case. The next morning an urgent message begs Holmes to come at once, for when the maid took up a cup of tea to Mr. Blessington, she found him hanging from the ceiling in an apparent suicide. Feeling sure he is dealing with an act of revenge, Holmes investigates further, unearthing evidence that this man some years previous had been one of a gang of five thieves who had turned informant against the other four to save himself. One felon was hanged, three went to prison, and Blessington was let off. The three, released from prison after long sentences, search out their informant and in the night murder him in his own bed, just as Jennings had died in his own bed. There are religious connotations to the name Blessington for the original essence of "bless" is "a rite of consecration by sprinkling the altar with blood," with a blood sacrifice, possibly human, being implied. Blood atonement being paid with one's body for past treachery is the message, with the three killers meeting similar fates — for we learn that a steamer carrying them to safety sank in the Atlantic with the loss of all souls. Once again neither a doctor nor a detective could prevent death. "Wherever Fear can fly revenge can follow," Johnson tells us.

"The Adventure of Black Peter" inaugurates some interesting new American archetypes while maintaining a connection to Le Fanu. A former sea captain, Peter Carey, called Black Peter in tribute to his foul, violent nature has been found murdered in an isolated cabin he built on his property. This silent, gloomy man, regarded as "a perfect fiend" by his neighbors, seems constantly to be brooding over something in his past. His name Carey is an allusion to the large seabird, the Stormy Petrel, called by the sailors "Mother Carey's chickens." The bird is believed to fly before a storm so when spotted at sea it is assumed there will soon be rough weather. Carey's cabin has been constructed to resemble the interior of a captain's cabin on an English whaling vessel. "There was a bunk at one end, a sea-chest, maps and charts, a picture of the *Sea Unicorn*, a line of logbooks on a shelf, all exactly as one would expect to find it in a captain's room." He has been found nailed to the wall of this cabin with his own harpoon. Stanley Hopkins, the young police inspector from Sussex asks Holmes and Watson for help with the case and the three set out for the scene of the crime. Notice how many of the mysteries take place in the country rather than London or some other city. Remember, the French philosopher Diderot believed more crimes were committed in the country simply because there are more people in the cities to interfere with criminal acts.

The rendering of the individual Carey finds an exemplar in Cooper's novel *The Two Admirals: A Tale*, a story of those who live on the sea or its shores. Much of Cooper's story is built around the Dutton family, living on the English coast in a home very like a ship's cabin, even to having been constructed of the debris of wrecked shipping. This cabin is located in a remote, out of the way strip overlooking the ocean a few miles from town. Frank Dutton, a disgraced shipping-master, after being lowered in rank for drunkenness, is finally cashiered out of the navy for both his drinking and violent temper. His wife Martha and their daughter Mildred, both of whom "had so long been the subjects of his brutality and tyranny," still live with him. Dutton is obviously not as barbarous as Black Peter, but he comes close, especially in regard to the mental suffering inflicted upon his wife and daughter, warning them he shall have their "respect and love, if I break both your hearts in order to get at them." He just about does it, too.

Another American influence is Herman Melville's great novel of the sea, *Moby-Dick*. There actually was a real whale, called "Mocha Dick," who gained infamy by attacking and sinking a large English ship, the *Essex*. Doyle knew Melville had this particular whale in mind as a model for his own murderous animal and Sussex is a word play on Essex. Mocha is a color, a light brown. *Moby-Dick* is subtitled *The Search for the White Whale*, thus bringing a color into the title. "Green Tea" and *A Study in Scarlet* both come to mind for their titles also incorporate the names of colors.

Peter Carey was at one time captain of the whaler *Sea Unicorn*, linking the story to *Moby-Dick* for the creature being named is a narwhal, a white whale with a single horn sticking out of the front of its head, and in his novel Melville calls narwhales "sea unicorns."

In the chapter "The Mast-Head," Melville tells of Captain Sleet, one time master of the *Glacier*, who might be a real historical figure. Melville credits Sleet with inventing the crow's-nest and claims Sleet was in the habit of sitting in his invention and shooting at sea unicorns with a rifle. Like Carey and Dutton he got drunk on duty.

Captain Carey is based squarely upon Captain Ahab as well as a number of other creations of the American writer. Like his prototype Ahab, Carey spends much of his time pacing about his cabin brooding upon invisible enemies. Like Ahab and the owners of the *Pequod*, Carey is a Puritan, and as such would dress in black and wear a beard, and he is always in a sulking mood. His reputation for savage violence, nerve, and impetuosity is equal to his American counterpart and the two men are legends rather than real human beings. People would point out Carey's lodging to each other and wonder what he was doing in there; and the same is wondered of Ahab brooding in his cabin. Black Peter's drunkenness and violence is a sin against his religious beliefs, just as Ahab's lust for revenge against an animal offends the sensibility of some of his crew, especially the first-mate Starbuck. We are told of Carey, "He has been known to drive his wife and daughter out of doors in the middle of the night and flog them through the park until the whole village outside the gates was aroused by their screams." This character is built upon a real encounter Doyle had as a young doctor in July of 1882 in the city of Portsmouth. While out for a stroll in his new neighborhood, he came across a burly, red-faced drunk, kicking his wife and child around the streets, screaming abuse at them and at the gathering crowd. Arthur intervened on the woman's behalf, getting into a fistfight with the drunk. When a passing sailor got involved, Doyle, to avoid the obvious embarrassment of getting arrested, walked quickly away. He never forgot the incident or the belligerence of his antagonist.

Among the crew of the *Pequod* is the blacksmith Perth, an Englishman who has lost some of his toes to frostbite and, like Ahab and Carey, walks with a limp. At one time he was happy and prosperous, surrounded by a good family. "But one night, under cover of darkness, and further concealed in a most cunning disguisement, a desperate burglar slid into his happy home, and robbed them all of everything." The thief is alcoholism and Perth's character degenerates to that of a violent lush threatening and abusing his wife and children, some of whom actually die as a result of his violence and neglect. In desperation Perth takes to the sea. Seeing the pathetic note of the blacksmith, Ahab wonders aloud why the man simply does not go mad and relieve his mind of its burden of horror. Calling upon the smith with work, Ahab, studying the sparks of his fire, asks, "Are these thy Mother Carey's chickens, Perth? they are always flying in thy wake; birds of good omen, too, but not to all; — look here, they burn; but thou — thou liv'st among them without a scorch." He continues, "I, too, want a harpoon made; one that a thousand yoke of fiends could not part, Perth; something that will stick in a whale like his own fin-bone." This harpoon is to be made of a collection of stubs taken from the steel shoes of racehorses, the strongest steel made. Ahab claims, "these stubbs will weld together like glue from the melted bones of murderers. Quick! forge me the harpoon." Carey is transfixed by his own harpoon and pinned to the wall of his cabin, just as Ahab becomes attached by the whale lines to the back of his enemy, the white whale, and dragged to his death. We are not given the reason for Carey's desperate unhappiness, this being the key to his murder, but we assume that like the American captain he rages at fate itself. The ostensible argument for Ahab's monomaniacal hatred for, and need to kill, Moby Dick is because it had ripped off his leg on a previous voyage. *Moby-Dick* is a vengeance tale. Carey's malignant past came to haunt him for he was murdered by a sailor who had sailed under him on the *Sea Unicorn* and witnessed the Captain's own murder of a passenger during a storm at sea. The carnage in the Sussex cabin is compared to that of a slaughterhouse; a scene reminiscent of the episodes of flensing the dead animals in Melville's novel.

Holmes, Watson, and Hopkins lie in ambush for the suspected killer. "It was a long and melancholy vigil, and yet brought with it something of the thrill which the hunter feels when he lies beside the water-pool, and waits for the coming of the thirsty beast of prey." In *Moby-Dick* we have a great deal of this suspenseful waiting, both in the *Pequod* and in the long boats for the whales to show themselves. "What savage creature was it which might steal upon us out of the darkness?" Watson asks. More than an earthly creature is here implied, but the wait is rewarded only by the capture of the son of a banker who had vanished years earlier under charges of defrauding his clients. Dough-Boy, the steward on the *Pequod*, is described as follows, "He was naturally a very nervous, shuddering sort of little fellow, this bread-faced steward; the progeny of a bankrupt baker and a hospital nurse." Here you have Neligan, the bankrupt banker's son. Holmes realizes Neligan is innocent and sets a trap to catch the real murderer. In a strange turn of events, the Great Detective assumes the disguise of Captain Basil of an exploring vessel, soon to set out collecting specimens and in need of a harpooner. Holmes has taken upon himself the role of Ahab, a man on the trail of some miscreant he must capture, for the word basil means "king" or "royal," and in the Old Testament Ahab was indeed a king. After a few dead-ends he tricks the killer, a harpooner, into coming to the Baker Street flat with the lure of employment. This ploy brings in Patrick Cairns, an individual much like Carey himself, who had witnessed the murder of the banker Neligan. Cairns possesses something of the aspects of the revengeful monkey, or in this case gorilla, of "Green Tea," for he has "a fierce bull-dog face," "framed in a tangle of hair and beard," with "two bold, dark eyes," beneath "thick, tufted, overhung eyebrows." Following the accusation of Cairns as the killer, a tremendous battle ensues in which three men are needed to subdue the harpooner for he is as strong as the ape he resembles. Peter Carey met his match only in Patrick Cairns, just as Ahab found his equal only in Moby Dick. Doyle must have deliberately intended to depict two Irishmen, since both Carey and Cairns are Irish names. Perhaps the brute he came across at Portsmouth was Irish. Cairns relates how Black Peter killed the banker Neligan for the box of ill-gotten securities found with him after being picked up at sea following the sinking of his own ship in a storm. Hoping to cut himself in on the wealth, Cairns journeys to Sussex to blackmail Carey. The argument between the former shipmates is a rendering of the desperate conversations almost leading to violence between Ahab and Starbuck. Following one such verbal battle, Starbuck confesses he considered killing his obsessed captain while Ahab, in the fever of yet another altercation, this one in his cabin, pulls a gun on Starbuck, but the mate walks away unharmed. Carey and Cairns start drinking, a fight erupts, Carey goes for his knife, Cairns grabs a harpoon kept as a memento, and pins his opponent to the wall. Two members of the Pequod's crew, Radney and Steelkilt, with matching irritable, frantic natures, end up going at each other like two pit bulls. The harpooner Radney goads Steelkilt into attacking him to satisfy his unmerited hatred of the man, but the crew break up the struggle. The next time out in the long boats Radney is himself attacked and killed by Moby Dick — his death a foreshadowing of the impending death of Ahab and a warning that vengeance shall meet vengeance.

Some details of the ferocious murder scene in "Black Peter" are adopted from Cooper's novel The Pilot, which deals with the warfare between British and American ships during the Revolution. Cooper had been an officer in the new American Navy during the War of 1812 and had taken part in engagements similar to those he writes about. During the action between the English frigate and the American Ariel, found in The Pilot, the Ariel's coxswain Long Tom pins an Englishman to his own mast with a harpoon. Cooper owned part interest in a New York whaling vessel and that must have interested Doyle, who was a harpooner in the Artic trade when young. He was so accurate with the weapon that the captain of the Hope offered double pay if he would sail on another voyage as harpooner and surgeon, but Arthur turned him down, hoping to get on with his schooling.

"Let us walk in these beautiful woods, Watson, and give a few hours to the birds and the flowers," Holmes eulogizes as he gazes at the fields and forests of Sussex, giving in a nutshell much of the theme of Henry David Thoreau's *Walden*. The book is Thoreau's account of the year he lived in the woods of Massachusetts in a cabin on the shore of Walden Pond, not far from Boston. He built his lodging in 1845 and Hopkins tells us Carey was born in that year. Thoreau buys the shanty of an Irishman, James Collins, to get the roof and boards. A tobacco-pouch is found at the crime scene with the initials P. C. on it. Doyle has used the confusion offered by the initials "P. C." standing for both Peter Carey and Patrick Cairns as ingredients to thicken the plot; and Collins' initials can be thought of as P.C. for all the Irish in America at the time were called "Pattys" or "Pats"; and Thoreau uses the expression himself when he tells us he met "a young Patrick" in the woods. It was understood Patrick need not have been the boy's real name. Thoreau mentions another Irishman he came across who tells him he too would like to live in a small cabin in the middle of the forest, and in the course of his wandering Thoreau comes across a hut similar to his own on another pond occupied by an Irishman named John Field. The former inhabitant of the woods around Walden, the American writer tells us, was an Irishman with a colorful past, having fought at Waterloo. He was a heavy drinker who wore a head cover all year long, as well as being subject to "delirium, and his face was the color of carmine." The village people considered his cabin "an unlucky castle" and, as with the neighbors of Black Peter, avoided his place and his person. The cabins of Thoreau and Carey are both described at some length: Carey's by Hopkins, Thoreau's by himself. Carey's hut is 16 by 10 feet, a foot longer than the American's, which is 15 by 10, and both places have two windows and a center fireplace.

Holmes reaches the village of Woodman's Lee by railroad while Thoreau's link with the world is the railroad as well, for he walks the tracks to town. Woodman's Lee is a phrase that could describe either place, for lee means "shelter or protected place." Thoreau tells us that in the woods, when snow or darkness makes the landscape features difficult to see, we must steer "like pilots," using "certain well-known beacons and headlands." In the chapter "The Village," Thoreau equates his shack to "my snug harbor in the woods," and he a "man at the helm," "with a merry crew of thoughts," to keep him company. "I had many a genial thought by the cabin fire as I sailed," he adds.

As surprising as it sounds, Peter Carey is modeled somewhat after Thoreau himself, for in his thoughts this solitary writer "found in myself, and still find, an instinct toward a higher, or, as it is named, spiritual life, as do most men, and another toward a primitive, rank, and savage one, and I reverence them both," adding "I love the wild not less than the good." He even compares his way of life to that of an animal, for "We are conscious of an animal in us, which awakens in proportion as our higher nature slumbers." Mediating on what he considers wrong with the human condition he draws a few conclusions that find mention in Doyle's story. One former family in the area fell victim to the alcoholism of the father. "Bankruptcy and repudiation are the spring-boards from which much of our civilization vaults and turns its somersets," he claims, and bankruptcy, repudiation, and alcoholism are the springboards for the saga of "Black Peter." Young Neligan had sought out Carey in an effort to exonerate his father, unjustly accused of bank-fraud. Thoreau tells us the business failures who will not "fulfill their engagements because it is inconvenient," as Neligan's partner Dawson has done, "are perchance bankrupt in a worse sense than they who fail honestly." Neligan has failed honestly and his son is attempting to prove so.

With this convolution of so many disparate sources of material for a seemingly simple tale, we are catching sight of evidence that interlacement is the key to understanding Doyle's thinking. I cannot possibly have identified all the sources he availed himself of. Associative thoughts are brought about often by the introduction of one or two words, building to some of the most complicated yet fascinating stories in literature.

Sussex is the setting for yet another work, proving the impact of Le Fanu on Doyle. "The Adventure of the Sussex Vampire" is so close is spirit to the Irish writer's vampire pieces that should you withdraw the character of Holmes it could conceivably have been written by him.

Baker Street draws a disturbing plea for assistance from Robert Ferguson, a tea broker by trade who suspects his wife of practicing vampirism upon their infant son. As in the case of Dr. Hesselius, Holmes has been proposed by another party to the distressed victim as one who might be able to help. Holmes plays the surgeon when, on the cusp of divulging the reasons all these strange events are going forth, he tells us he will be brief for "The swiftest surgery is the least painful."

Ferguson dissembles by attempting to pass off his problem as someone else's, but the detective sees through the ruse. We have a splendid example of Doyle's dry sense of humor when Ferguson, relating suspicions of his wife's vampirism, groping for an answer to it asks, "Is it madness, Mr. Holmes? Is it something in the blood?" All the gothic ingredients are here, for the bizarre mystery is acted out in a house that carries "An odour of age and decay," whose "ceilings were corrugated with heavy oaken beams," and whose "uneven floors sagged into sharp curves." Ferguson is married to a Peruvian woman and has one son by her as well as an older, crippled boy by a previous marriage.

One compelling aspect of this drama that brings us back, not to the elaborate melodramas of Le Fanu, but rather to *A Study in Scarlet*, is the experiment with poison carried out on the spaniel of the Ferguson household. It seems that the older sibling was methodically poisoning the infant son out of jealous hatred when the baby's mother, realizing this, attempted to suck out the drug, not the blood, as it appeared.

"Sussex Vampire" is a correspondence with Bram Stoker's highly successful novel *Dracula*. In this piece Stoker metamorphosed the monkey of "Green Tea" into a vampire, a truly haunting presence who emerges in London in his quest for victims. Holmes' index contains references to vampirism in both Hungary and Transylvania, both countries having been haunts of the historical Count Dracula.

In Henry James' short story "The Author of Beltraffio," an English author, Mark Ambient, and his wife Beatrice, invite a young American admirer of Ambient's work to spend a weekend at their ancient manor house. The couple is engaged in an emotional struggle for the love of their seven-year-old son Dolcino; this competition is eroding the harmony of their marriage, a situation corresponding to the conflict in "Sussex Vampire." The Ambients do not merely fail to get along with each other, their relationship seems built on distrust and hate. At one point Mark, turning to the American says, "As for my small son, you know, we shall probably kill him between us before we've done with him!"

In desperation, Mrs. Ferguson barricades herself in her room, and Mrs. Ambient locks her husband out of their child's room, fearing he will poison the boy's affection for her. At one point in the narrative we learn Mark regards his wife as "almost a sinister personage" when the question comes up as to the possibility of her doing personal injury to Dolcino. The child becomes feverish, as does the Sussex infant, and Mrs. Ambient refuses to let even the family doctor examine him, just as Mrs. Ferguson denies permission to all but Watson to enter her room. Mrs. Ferguson's maid and confidant Dolores plays the role of Miss Ambient, the author's sister, who appears throughout the drama.

"The Author of Beltraffio" almost turns into a murder mystery when we realize Beatrice has allowed Dolcino to perish of fever, having denied him access to medical assistance. When he is told the boy is actually dead Mark asks, "Has she killed him?" Doyle constructs a story pivoting on this comment; mixing up the details a bit, for, as in all intricate borrowings, we have a fair amount of admixture and scrambling of characters and their roles.

In "The Sussex Vampire" Jack, the older son, hated the younger boy because of his health and beauty, which he lacked. In James' dark tale it is not a rival sibling who is resentful of beauty but rather the wife who despises and fears the eloquent artistry of her husband's writings. She actually fears all beauty, always on her guard against its influence; believing one must not "enjoy it without extraordinary precautions and reserves." Poison is even mentioned in "The Author of Beltraffio" as a metaphor for the malevolent sway Beatrice Ambient believes her husband's art exercised upon their son's mind.

CHAPTER FOUR. A LITTLE BROWN BOOK

Returning to *A Study in Scarlet* we find ourselves at Lauriston Gardens, scene of the murder of the American, Drebber, upon whose body a wedding ring is found. Hoping this object may be of sentimental value to the killer, Holmes inserts an advertisement in the newspapers to the effect that it was found in another location by someone the unknown suspect might not believe has any knowledge of its provenience. So certain is the Great Detective that someone will fall for the ploy that he has Watson clean and load his service revolver. While awaiting developments, Holmes fiddles with his violin, and then broaches a conversation regarding an antique book purchased the day before. Dr. Holmes of Boston also played the violin, though he was never skilled at it.

Not unlike the ruminations of Dr. Hesselius upon the books of Swedenborg, we are about to gain insight, by subtle association, into something of the themes, psychological motivations, source materials, and moral purpose, not only for *A Study in Scarlet*, but for almost all the Sherlock Holmes stories, here, at the very beginning of the whole business. The medium for this block of thoughts is a book or set of books whose parallel concepts enter the consciousness of the characters, and the readers, as though by accident or chance. The following paragraph in which the two investigators discuss Holmes' new book is my personal candidate for the finest piece of associative writing in literary history. The conversation passes for a rather casual exchange between two informed men. Further from that it could not be, for in it Doyle is divulging some of the most obliging and invaluable clues to instruments of influence upon the stories and upon his own personality as well.

An observation by Holmes opens the discourse. "This is a queer old book I picked up at a stall yesterday — '*De Jure inter Gentes*' — published in Latin at Liege in the Lowlands, in 1642. Charles' head was still firm on his shoulders when this little brown-backed volume was struck off." Watson asks, "Who is the printer?" Holmes answers, "Philippe de Croy, whoever he may have been. On the fly-leaf, in very faded ink, is written 'Ex libris Guliolmi Whyte.' I wonder who William Whyte was? Some pragmatical seventeenth century lawyer, I suppose. His writing has a legal twist about it." The answerer of the newspaper ad interrupts the discourse at this point and it is never continued.

Holmes does not translate the Latin title of his new book, for neither did Dr. Hesselius translate Swedenborg's title, *Arcana Caelestia.* We should first dispel any questions as to whether or not any such actual volume as Holmes' new acquisition exists, or, I should say, exists in this form, for there are a few works that come close. William White was an English divine born in 1604 who wrote several interesting Latin works published under the pseudonym Gulielmus Phalerius. But he wrote nothing whose title approaches the book under discussion. Boswell tells us about another William White, also a divine, from Pennsylvania, who visited London in 1771, becoming friends with Johnson and his circle. Upon returning to America, White came across a copy of Johnson's *Rasselas* that had been printed in America and sent him the book as a gift, and Johnson's letter of thanks is reprinted in Boswell's *Life.* The plot thickens for "Ex libris" doesn't mean "author," it means "from the library of," and is followed by the name of the owner of the book, so we are not being told the name of the author of Holmes' book at all. Doyle would have us believe Holmes does not understand what the elementary Latin phrase "Ex libris" means, yet Holmes is reading a work we know to be in that language, and he even understands the language well enough to offer stylistic criticism of the writer. In addition, we know Holmes to be a recognized authority on the motets of Lazarus, which are salutes to the Virgin Mary written in Latin. Watson speaks Latin as well since he is a physician; and he would have studied it in school anyway, even if he weren't — yet he fails to correct Holmes' mistake. Doyle, I believe, is suggesting there is a puzzle here the reader, without the aid of Holmes, is being called upon to solve. In *The Autocrat of the Breakfast-Table*, Oliver Holmes, Sr., facilitating a point he hopes to make to his audience of imaginary fellow boarders, sends for a book to support his argument. He describes this book as "the precious little black, ribbed-backed, clean-typed, vellum-papered 32 mo. 'DESIDERII ERASMI COLLOQUIA. Amstelodami. Typis Ludovici Elzevirii. 1650.' Various names written on title-page. Most conspicuous this: Gul. Cookeson: E. Coll. Omn. Anim. 1725. Oxon." Now that "Gul." on the title page is short for Guliolmi. Holmes continues, "O William Cookeson, of All-Souls College, Oxford, — then writing as I now write, — now in the dust, where I shall lie, — is this line all that remains to thee of earthly remembrance?" Dr. Holmes' statement "then writing as I now write," could be interpreted to suggest Cookeson wrote the entire book, not just his name and address, although Dr. Holmes knows better, the book being the work of Erasmus of Rotterdam. Dr. Holmes adds that Erasmus "laid the egg of the Reformation which Luther hatched." Carlyle had much to say about Luther, Charles I, and the wars centered on European religious conflicts, with the beheading of Charles being the product of one such dispute. Doyle's claim that Charles' head was still on his shoulders when this book was "struck off" is both a freakish bit of humor and a cleaver pun, always good form in associative writing. Watson asks who the printer was, yet the natural question when one is told the title of an unfamiliar book would always be in regard to the writer. Holmes tells him the printer was Philippe de Croy. The author is never mentioned; thus we could say the writer was anonymous, since neither detective really believes Whyte to be the author. The initial readers of René Descartes' works, since they were published anonymously because of fear of retaliation by the Church on some positions, were also left wondering, like us, who the author was. Philippe de Croy is a name meaning, by association, "a lover of thought," since Philip comes from *"philos"* (the Greek "to love" and *de croy* from the French *"croyant,"* meaning "believing" or "thinking"). A more apt description of Descartes I cannot imagine for he believed that thought and introspection could lead to knowledge, even to knowledge of external things, the basis of his philosophy of thought.

Doyle undoubtedly took the idea of utilizing foreign languages in this manner from the Irish philosopher Bishop George Berkeley. In Berkeley's important work of 1713, *Three Dialogues Between Hylas and Philonous*, he stages a Socratic confrontation between two disputants holding opposing views as to the ultimate reality of life. In one corner is Hylas, supporter of the theory that matter or material substance is the real basis of the universe, while his opponent Philonous would have it that the spiritual world represents "the reality and truth of things." Appropriately enough *hylas* is an ancient Greek word for "matter" while *philonous* is that language's word for "lover of the mind." Berkeley's book and its dialogues centered upon such questions as what is the ultimate source of our knowledge of reality, what we see when we perceive, and why, as well as other equally important issues, and is directly related to the thoughts of Descartes, and to what it is we are now discussing utilizing those thoughts, and to all the Holmes stories in general. It is Sherlock who perceives more than the others, so it is he who somehow knows the more accurate way to interpret the "sensible thing," the thing immediately perceived by the others around him, but he can then add something to that sensible thing to understand both what it is and why it is.

The Lowlands, where Holmes' antique book is from, specifically Leyden and Amsterdam, was where important works of Descartes first saw light. The book by Erasmus used by Dr. Holmes may have been published in the city of Amstel (Amsterdam) judging from the *Amstelodami* in the title. In 1642, Descartes' seminal *Meditations on First Philosophy* was published in Amsterdam, in Latin, while the first edition of his complete works was published there in 1644, also in Latin. The publishing of early books was a rough and tumble affair involving lawsuits, trials, bribes, and so forth, and Descartes' work was not exempt from this state of affairs. The first printing of *Meditations* was brought out in Paris in 1641, in Latin, so why didn't Doyle use this date instead of 1642? When this edition was struck off the author was living in Holland and exercised little or no control over the business. The second, Lowlands edition of 1642 is regarded as the best source we have of Descartes' intentions, for it is from his own manuscripts and published under his personal supervision. Descartes never wrote the book in French, although he helped others translate from the Latin — which seems amazing today, since French was his own language. He obviously felt more at home writing in the scholarly Latin, which gives some indication of his rich mental texture.

In *Meditations*, which is more or less a recapitulation of *Discourse on Method*, written some four years prior, the thinker attempts to lay the groundwork for a new philosophy and to outline his hopes for the future of mankind on the development of science and of mathematics in particular. He was attempting to bring philosophy into the world of science and is regarded as not only the father of modern philosophy, but of the sciences of math, physics, optics, and meteorology. He is often thought of as the father of all modern science. Watson at one point refers to Holmes' test tubes and other chemical equipment as "philosophical instruments" and this is exactly what the French thinker would have regarded them. What Darwin was to science Descartes was to philosophy, a leap into the modern world; the bringing forth of a "first philosophy," and it is this aspect of "first" that Doyle is centering upon. Before Descartes, intellectual activity was confined to methodizing and demonstrating the truths furnished to the mind by the Church and the ancients, especially Aristotle. The year 1642 is also the generally accepted date given to two great hard-won discoveries: the rotation of the planets (in the form of ellipses) by Johannes Kepler, and the circulation of the blood by William Harvey, and this date could be regarded as the year of mankind's recension of the classical world-picture of Aristotle. "You have brought detection as near an exact science as it ever will be brought in this world," Watson compliments Holmes as he observes the detective use a tape measure at the crime scene in Lauriston Gardens. Re-expressed in the ways of his method, with mathematics as the focal point, Descartes believed problems could be reduced to a form in which relations between magnitudes could be easily observed or mechanically calculated. Reduce your problem to a math equation if possible, and it will solve itself, he seems to be saying. Holmes is in the habit of calling his suspects "unknowns," a math term used extensively, and quite possibly initially, by the Frenchman, for the answer to any problem he is attempting to solve. In *Meditations*, Descartes also gave to the world the mechanical theory of the universe, to be discussed later.

As to the title of Holmes' book, *De Jure inter Gentes*, we are told the writing has a legal twist to it and could possibly be the work of "some pragmatical seventeenth century lawyer." This statement touches a lot of bases including the fact that Descartes' father and brother were both seventeenth century lawyers. The name of the book, which may be translated as "the laws between peoples," suggests a piece of legalese dealing with the laws or rules between peoples or tribes and the implications of breaking those laws, and so it is, for the title is taken directly from historical Roman laws known as "*Ius Gentium*," those laws whose protection extended to all people living in ancient Rome. The ancient city was teeming with people of different castes, patricians and plebeians, freemen and bondsmen, as well as foreigners, cohorts, aliens, etc. Each group and sub-group had complicated and often conflicting laws governing their actions: whom they were responsible to, what court had jurisdiction over them, and so forth. The *Ius Gentium* was the only aspect of the laws that was available to all who lived within the state and consequently was regarded as "the law of all people," but is generally known today by the designation it has come down to us as, "the common law." The actual work Doyle has in mind with this convoluted reference is *The Common Law*, written by the greatest of American jurists, Oliver Wendell Holmes. Written in the late 1870's, some of the book was derived from previously published essays and lectures delivered while the author was a teacher at Harvard. In reference to the fictionalizing of his case histories, Holmes chides Watson with degrading "what should have been a course of lectures into a series of tales." Here is a direct allusion to a rich assortment of influences on Doyle's work, men such as William James, Carlyle, and Justice Holmes, all of whose distinctive works were originally lectures delivered in institutions. The mention of a British monarch (Charles I) at this point in Holmes and Watson's exchange even refers back to *The Common Law*, for it was in the yearbooks of the British kings that the American lawyer found many of the cases he extrapolates. A case that occurred during Charles' reign is discussed in the chapter "Contract — I. History." Watson tells us Holmes keeps a "long row of year-books which fill a shelf," and these yearbooks are mentioned in at least five stories. Holmes describes his new book as "this little brown-backed volume," for it was the Boston publishing firm of Little Brown and Company that brought out the first edition of *The Common Law*, in 1881, and they remained its publisher until quite recently. The color of the hardback was brown, either in leather or buckram, and remained so until recent editions. Doyle draws our attention to the color of a book a number of times, as in the short story "The Doctors of Hoyland." In *Micah Clarke* a character resorts to checking a book to settle a question of law as it applies to the art of warfare among knights. The work is "the brown volume," having been written by a Fleming who goes unnamed, while earlier in the novel we had been told the volume was in Latin and had been printed at Liege in the Lowlands. This mysterious book is brought up and quoted a number of times in *Micah Clarke*, so Doyle seems to be trying to spell out something he regards as quite important to his work.

The personality of the author of *De Jure inter Gentes* has been modified with the absorbing noun "pragmatical," which denotes an aspect of philosophy, a system, in which it is held that the truth of a proposition, or anything actually, must be measured by its correspondence with experimental results and by its practical outcome. In pragmatism any metaphysical significance of thought is discarded, and all methods supposedly leading to truth through deduction from *a priori* grounds are rejected. Pragmatists hold that truth is modified as new discoveries are made and that truth evolves, being relative to time, place, purpose, and need. A theory becomes an instrument leading to an experiment and not an answer in itself. These principles are generally said to have been initially developed by the Americans Chauncey Wright and Charles Sanders Peirce, and advanced by William James and John Dewey. They rejected obscurantism, arrogance, and the view that the mind of man should bow down before mysteries it can never understand. This system included elements formerly considered too every day, too practical, too emotional, or even too irrational to be fully part of the intellect, holding that if philosophy is man's most comprehensive view of life, it suffers correspondingly when it leaves any field untouched. And this inclusion must be attempted while remaining true to the spirit of science and philosophy. Josiah Royce, an early American pragmatist, had written that his age needed a philosophy that would "give form to the spiritual interests of humanity," denying that sharp lines could be drawn between matter and mind, science and morals, reason and experience. Pragmatism asserted, on the contrary, that human ideas and ideals must be studied from a biological and social point of view, and they must be judged as instruments by which human beings bring some order into the buzzing confusion of their experience. An idea or ideal must be judged in terms of the specific context in which it arises, and its worth must be measured by its capacity to solve the particular problems that call it forth. We must find out what our ideas mean by tracing their consequences in our actual experience. This pragmatic method was a technique for criticizing abstraction, for pruning thinking down and making it responsible by testing it in the face of observable facts, and if used in fields such as law, philosophy, and sociology, was an attempt to combine realism with moral idealism. The pragmatic method is the method Sherlock regards as his own, but keep in mind that his flexible mind always thinks of the word in the plural.

Some pragmatists regarded themselves as "investigators," and Peirce for one used the title a number of times. The whole general concept raised a foundation for the new scientific information being inaugurated, and in actual human experience, with such pioneer developments as fingerprinting and blood tests. A pragmatist was one who valued ideas for their power to lead to still further generalizations, and "concrete reasonableness" in human thought and action according to Peirce. In its practical context lies the true fruitfulness of an idea, and in its ability to lead to observations that human beings would not otherwise make, and in giving an order to human experience it would not otherwise have.

There was reluctance among these thinkers to believe mankind could possibly settle moral problems by evoking some general definition of "the good," and Sherlock would agree, as he shall show us in any number of cases. They held that in ethics, knowledge that contributes to human values is real and that values live in the means as much as in the end. Absolute certainty has no place, nor the notion that men can solve their moral dilemmas by turning to a ready-made hierarchy of abstract values for all such judgments are made in some particular context, and before we can make that judgment we must first find out what the concrete problems are, what definitions and assumptions have been made, what goals and values are taken for granted, and what procedures are available.

These ideas, always considered so American, are not necessarily that, for they can be traced back to David Hume and the British empiricist, as well as to almost any lawyer, doctor, scientist, etc., who made even a small contribution to their field. It can even be considered as an outgrowth of Descartes since it attaches such reliance upon scientific method, the procreator of objective thought. If you wish to think of it as such, pragmatism is the philosophical and theoretical side of the scientific method, those aspects that cannot limit themselves to science, giving as an example the solving of a crime that could never be solved just with science. During his reading of an essay on Herbert Spencer by Wright, Doyle came across the following: "A theory which is utilized receives the highest possible certificate of truth. Navigation by the aid of astronomical tables, the magnetic telegraph, the innumerable utilities of mechanical and chemical science, and constant and perfect tests of scientific theories." They become "the standard of certitude, which science has been able to apply so extensively in its interpretations of natural phenomena." Wright adds, "Scientific investigations promise to throw a flood of light on subjects which have interested mankind since the beginning of speculation, — subjects related to universal human interests. History, society, laws, and morality — all claimed as topics with which scientific methods are competent to deal." He calls this "flood of light," in the next sentence, "scientific illumination." John Locke has already told us, "It is only light and evidence that can work a change in men's opinions."

We are going to see Sherlock Holmes move under the sponsorship of this mental condition in all his actions, a "flood of light" could be thought of as the trademark of the man. Wright believed a true philosopher should conduct a number of "original investigations in some department of empirical science," to test and develop his powers. By doing so, "he learns how to make knowledge profitable to the ascertainment of new truths — an act in which the modern natural philosopher excels." And Peirce believed philosophy itself "will be a series of problems capable of investigation by the observational methods of the true sciences." This is exactly what Holmes will be doing when he is first introduced to the world, performing an experiment at St. Bart's Hospital in a search of practical results.

The Scotch-American, Alexander Graham Bell must have personified for Doyle the perfect example of a pragmatic philosopher for he was one of the most celebrated of these "men of experiments." Bell was a prolific inventor whose work included the development of the telephone, the phonograph, and the records to play on it, recording techniques, the audiometer, new teaching methods for the deaf, the transmission of speech by light waves, and much else. Doyle himself urged improved oral teaching for the deaf and dumb, delivering a brilliant lecture on the subject at the Carlton Rooms in London in July of 1912. This was done with Bell in mind, as well as Denis Diderot, who published essays on teaching the handicapped. Bell and his assistant Thomas Watson made their great breakthrough on the invention of the telephone after years of investigations and experiments as Watson waited in an adjacent room listening for any sound from his receiver, until Bell accidentally spilled a chemical catalyst over his trousers and onto the telephone apparatus he was struggling to get some results from, uttering the famous, "Mr. Watson! Come here, I want you," which thus became the first words ever spoken over the phone. This tense, terse, historical scene between Bell and Watson is reenacted, almost word for word upon the occasion of the sudden success of Holmes' experiment on blood at the hospital lab. Holmes is introduced to Watson as he labors on a chemical analysis, for, like Bell he is primarily a chemist, such work forming a large part of the lives of both men. Holmes actually makes a discovery right in front of us and turns to John Watson for confirmation and possible assistance. "No doubt you see the significance of this discovery of mine?" he asks. Watson does not, and tells him so. Holmes claims his finding is an infallible test for blood-stains, and in an effort to draw Watson closer to the work says, "Come over here, now!" And in so doing he creates a situational duplicate to the successful telephone experiment. Doyle recreates as well, the emotional exchange that occurred between Bell and his assistant when they realized they had just invented the first real telephone. John Watson tells us, "Had he discovered a gold mine, greater delight could not have shone upon his features." Holmes shouts with pleasure, then calms down and goes through the analysis once again, for Watson's benefit, making of him an active participant and critical observer, which is the relationship of Thomas Watson to Alexander Bell. This scene also sets the relative position of Holmes and Watson in their affiliation to each other; Watson will always remain an auxiliary to the Great Detective, more than anything else. Holmes has the genius but Watson embellishes and sets off that brilliance like a chemical catalyst.

Professor Bell was in London in 1878 and paid a much-publicized visit to Queen Victoria at Windsor to demonstrate his invention. This particular date is noteworthy for the first Holmes story opens in 1878. By the next year telephone service was underway in London and the same year saw Edison open the first telephone exchange. Sherlock has also served the Queen and although he waved aside any question of knighthood he was not adverse to accepting a trinket as a reward as in the case of a "remarkably fine emerald tie-pin," presented to him at Windsor by "a certain gracious lady in whose interests he had once been fortunate enough to carry out a small commission." The reason Holmes uses the phone only three times in all the stories is because Doyle did not want people guessing at these associations to Bell, who was a world celebrity at the time. Watson tells us Holmes never wrote if he could telegraph, so the detective obviously realized the importance of saving time.

The name Bell is important, for Doyle never denied it was a Dr. Bell, his medical teacher at Edinburgh, who had served as prototype for Sherlock. Alexander Bell was born in Scotland and he too had been connected to Edinburgh University, not as a teacher, but for a year and a half as a student, so when John Watson first sees Holmes in the lab, he tells us, "There was only one student in the room." Doyle had a congenial sense of humor and we can picture him at a party acquiescing to questions with, "Yes, they are quite right. Holmes is indeed based on Bell." Bell and Bell is association transmitted fully, for it is a pun on both real life and art at the same time, and could be appreciated only by the artist himself, which actually augments its aesthetic worth.

None could be more modern in his thoughts than Charles Sanders Peirce, who believed that the Aristotelian philosophy is responsible for perhaps the greater part of modern Western civilization, but no longer met the requirements of new knowledge and advancing practice. "The old structure will not do for modern needs," was his creed. Peirce comes close to sounding like a police detective at times. "Doubt is an uneasy and dissatisfied state from which we struggle to free ourselves and pass into the state of belief; while the latter is a calm and satisfactory state which we do not wish to avoid, or to change to a belief in anything else." He refused to accept intuition, regarding the struggle, which he termed "Inquiry," to be the only sure way to get rid of doubt. The official police that Holmes is constantly at odds with over detection procedure emphasize intuition when they say they "feel" a suspect is guilty of a crime on little or no evidence while Holmes stresses experimentation, careful scientific observation, and most important, and therefore hardest of all, objective reasoning. Much of this is standard practice today for when the police visit a serious crime scene the first thing they do is call in the "lab men," the forensic people. This was not true in Holmes' day any more than the scientific method was used for problem solving in Descartes' time. When we hear Holmes speak of being practical we can substitute the word pragmatic for they are almost the same word having the identical Greek root, as does the word practice, although I realize there is far more to pragmatism than this. Right from the beginning Doyle wishes us to be witness to the fact that his creation is a practical man with useful purposes. After finishing his blood experiment and explaining it, rather superficially I admit, to Watson, he asks him if he understands the value of it. "It is interesting, chemically, no doubt," Watson admits, "but practically — " Holmes cannot let this go unchallenged, "Why, man, it is the most practical medico-legal discovery for years." In seeking Watson's help with this experiment Holmes is endorsing Peirce's position that scientific investigation is a communal process of settling beliefs; it takes a number of people working together. A hypothesis may be called true and yet be subject to refinement or adjustment, for beliefs are relative to confirmation, so as our method of uncovering new evidence grows, our viewpoints are corrected and restated, for all knowledge is fallible and open to rectification. Hence we now have Holmes emphasizing to Watson that assuredly some historical murder cases would have had different conclusions if the previous investigators had access to his blood test. Its importance is in its future effect on human behavior, what Peirce called, "that form in which the proposition becomes applicable to human conduct." Contrary to what many believe, neither pragmatists in general, nor Peirce, in particular, believed action to be more important than thought. "Reality is an affair of meditation," he asserts, but also urges the importance of applying Alexander Bain's definition of belief, as "that upon which a man is prepared to act." The pragmatists held that thought should be a stimulus to activity, this being the main function of thought, but here we have simply a restatement of Aristotle's "There is no passive knowledge." One's thoughts are not complete until they have found an outlet in action.

The pragmatists hoped to be more accurate than the philosophers that preceded them and they anticipated achieving this with the aid of science. Almost all of them were chemists of one sort or another with the early exponents such as Wright and James calling themselves "laboratory men." In his *Harvard Class Book* Peirce advises us to take up chemistry as an antidote to being hopelessly in love, and he must have been very much in love himself for in 1863 he was awarded one of the first Master's degree in chemistry given by Harvard, and he tells us he wrote a book entitled *History of Chemistry*. By 1864 he was lecturing regarding the agreements between philosophy and science, using the term "philosophy of science," but I don't think he coined this term. Together with Ralph Waldo Emerson he lectured on such subjects as British logicians with these programs being favorably commented upon by William James, who said of Peirce, "I never saw a man go into things so intensely and thoroughly." All of philosophy was based, Peirce believed, not on metaphysics, or ontology, or psychology, or any other field except logic, this being the key to the man's thoughts. In his magazine article "The Book of Life," Sherlock Holmes refers to himself as a logician. Their methods are simply logic, but this is significant for logic has everything to do with truth and in reality there is nothing simple about logic. The idea of a basic classification of the sciences as a kind of map of the fields of knowledge was a pursuit of the pragmatists, especially Peirce. He studied his method of classifying the sciences with Prof. Agassiz of Harvard.

Along with a few associates Peirce published some essays in 1883 as part of a book, *Studies in Logic: By Members of the John Hopkins University*, and helped form the John Hopkins Metaphysical Club. G. Stanley Hall was a brilliant philosopher who also taught at Hopkins, beating out Peirce for a permanent teaching position there. Stanley Hopkins is a young police detective whose mind Sherlock had a good deal of respect for.

Pragmatism emphasized the importance of the understanding of language and symbols with Peirce being a great student of semantics, and signs in general, with his writing going into such depths and detail on the semantic aspect of logic that in the reading one finds oneself breathing rare air indeed. Johnson was a student of etymology, having almost single-handedly written a dictionary of the English language. Boswell calls him "our great philologist."

Doyle seems to be one of the first to have recognized Peirce for the dynamic innovator he was. During most of his life Peirce was neglected and nearly unknown, the situation Sherlock finds himself in initially as we watch his reputation grow slowly over the years. Both men remained in the background letting others get much of the credit and notoriety they actually deserved. Doyle will mention all these American philosophers, directly or in puns, throughout his writings.

From the start, American thought has been an overseas branch of British thinking and is overwhelmingly British in tradition. The early English thinker John Locke realized careful observation and active experimentation within a scientific attitude, such as was practiced by the Royal Society of his day, must be given precedence over authority, or the knowledge garnered from books, in one's search for real knowledge. It is the quality of the observer that ultimately leads to truth. "Let us put the ideas of our mind, just as we put the things of the laboratory, to the test of experience," Locke tells us in *An Essay Concerning Human Understanding*. He believed in acquiring knowledge through what he called the "historical, plain method," of observation and experimentation, but this may be a good example of his sarcasm, for the historical method was prone to rely upon unquestioned authority rather than upon tests, at least in most fields. Locke doubted any aspect of life could easily, perhaps even possibly, be put into a general category simply because it happened to have some similarities to other aspects of life; everything must be carefully studied as an individual entity in order to learn its true nature. This seems to stem from his unusual belief that we can have knowledge only of "particulars," rather than of that which is "general." He regarded all life as being linked together by a "chain of life" that eluded the use of general categories since the general did not seem to regard all the links. Watson picks up a magazine in their rooms and comes across the pencil-marked article, "The Book of Life" that turns out to have been penned by none other than his roommate. This magazine, I'm sure, is either *Popular Science Monthly* or *The Monist*, both outlets for the Americans being discussed. Monism is the belief that everything in the universe is basically one, there being no independent parts; everything is but a part of a great chain of events. If you wish to stretch your imagination a bit you could say monism is the fundamental building block of the theory of association. In 1887, the year *A Study in Scarlet* was being written, Doyle must have come across William James' essay "Habit," in an issue of *Popular Science Monthly* in which he read, "Already at the age of twenty-five you see the professional mannerism settling down on the young commercial traveller, on the young doctor, on the young minister, on the young counsellor-at-law. You see the little lines of cleavage running through the character, the tricks of thought, the prejudices, the ways of the 'shop,' in a word, from which the man can by-and-by no more escape than his coat-sleeve can suddenly fall into a new set of folds." In a reference to his own article Holmes tells us of the chain of life that brings all events and facts together, "Let him, on meeting a fellow-mortal, learn at a glance to distinguish the history of the man, and the trade or profession to which he belongs. Puerile as such an exercise may seem, it sharpens the faculties of observation and teaches one where to look and what to look for. By a man's finger-nails, by his coat-sleeve, by his boots, by his trouser-knees, by the callosities on his forefinger and thumb, by his expression, by his shirt-cuffs — by each of these things a man's calling is plainly revealed." Obviously these two articles cover the same bases. Holmes now explains to Watson, in order to emphasize his point, how it is he knew, upon meeting, that Watson had just come from Afghanistan. "From long habit the train of thought ran so swiftly through my mind that I arrived at the conclusion without being conscious of intermediate steps. There were such steps, however. The train of reasoning ran: 'Here is a gentleman of a medical type, but with the air of a military man. Clearly an army doctor, then. He has just come from the tropics, for his face is dark, and that is not the natural tint of his skin, for his wrists are fair. He has undergone hardship and sickness, as his haggard face says clearly. His left arm has been injured. He holds it in a stiff and unnatural manner. Where in the tropics could an English army doctor have seen much hardship and got his arm wounded. Clearly in Afghanistan.' The whole train of thought did not occupy a second." "The first result," James tells us in this article on the exercise of habit on the nervous system, "is that *habit simplifies the movements required to achieve a given result, makes them more accurate and diminishes fatigue.*" He goes on, "The next result is that *habit diminishes the conscious attention with which our acts are preformed.* One may state this abstractly thus: If an act requires for its execution a chain, *A, B, C, D, E, F, G*, etc., of successive nervous events, then in the first performances of the action the conscious will must choose each of these events from a number of wrong alternatives that tend to present themselves; but habit soon brings it about that each event calls up its own appropriate successor without any alternative offering itself, and without any reference to the conscious will, until at last the whole chain, *A, B, C, D, E, F, G*, rattles itself off as soon as *A* occurs, just as if *A* and the rest of the chain were fused into a continuous stream." This is exactly the way a computer works by the way, making quick choices between yes and no. If we count from A to G, we realize James has stated in his explanation that seven steps are necessary to form a habit of thought and although he implies more may be used if necessary, we see that Holmes has constructed seven explanatory sentences divulging his mind's calisthenics before arriving at his "Clearly in Afghanistan." He has simply applied James' semi-abstract concepts to a concrete application. The American also used a military man as an example of long-standing, automatic habit. He tells a story borrowed from Thomas H. Huxley's *Lessons in Elementary Physiology* about a practical joker, who upon seeing a discharged veteran carrying home his dinner yelled out "Attention!" causing the veteran, trained over long years to execute the command, to drop his food and snap to Attention.

The philosophy of the pragmatists has been labeled "concatenism," meaning the world is a chain of interlocking links and James in particular stressed this sort of joint overlapping. "From a drop of water," we learn from Holmes' magazine article, "a logician could infer the possibility of an Atlantic or a Niagara without having seen or heard of one or the other. So all life is a great chain, the nature of which is known whenever we are shown a single link of it." In Diderot's work *D'Alembert's Dream*, we come across the following as part of a Socratic dialogue: "Don't you agree that everything in nature is linked together and that it is impossible for there to be a break in the chain?" In the next Holmes story, *The Sign of the Four* we find a chapter entitled "A Break in the Chain." In the same book just mentioned, Diderot, in praising the mind of the English philosopher Needham, tells us the man was so perceptive "He saw the history of the world in a drop of water."

Samuel Johnson believed that any knowledge that did not have roots in human experience, no matter how elegant or systematic, was valueless. He considered metaphysics to be a mere game of paradoxes and held a low opinion of Hume, Berkeley, and even Descartes, regarding all three as being too abstract to be true. His dislike of the metaphysicians hardly arose from a rationalization of his own intellectual inferiority however, rather he believed that the farthest one could go in philosophy was not far enough to penetrate ultimate obscurities or make any practical difference to the life of man. Philosophical systems existed in a vacuum Johnson believed, while the tremendous mysteries of life and death beat, inexorably at man's door, and Sherlock Holmes' door in particular is subject to a great many of these desperate beats. Johnson, like Holmes, seems to take men as they are. It is from quotes such as the following that gave to Johnson the title of "Father of American Philosophy." "Human experience, which is constantly contradicting theory, is the great test of truth. A system, built upon the discoveries of a great many minds, is always of more strength, than what is produced by the mere workings of any one mind, which, of itself, can do little. There is not so poor a book in the world that would not be a prodigious effort were it wrought out entirely by a single mind, without the aid of prior investigators," is a famous quote of his.

Chemistry fascinated and occupied the man all his life, so much so that his friends the Thrales installed a small laboratory at their home in Streatham where he would enlighten and entertain himself and guests with experiments. Johnson was a man of experiments who, even in old age, just before his death in 1784, gave money for a test balloon flight being carried out. He believed in being practical in all matters, and like Holmes is reluctant to accept extraordinary causes for events, preferring instead to believe most problems to have simple, natural explanations.

Darwin is the great embodiment of English pragmatism, a perfect man of experiments. The only form of reasoning that contributes new ideas in science, Peirce advocated, is "abduction," studying facts and "devising a theory to explain them." No doubt he was thinking of Darwin, and Peirce, along with Wright, made the chance variations of Darwin's biology central to their whole systems of thought. The belief that life is an unbroken chain is the basis of Darwin's theory of evolution, as it is expressed in his *Origin of Species*, and as it would have to be for any theory of evolution. Holmes, as he is being presented to us, is the end product of human evolution, both the physical, and more to the point, mental.

Closer to Doyle's own time the Scotch philosopher Alexander Bain, a man constantly being quoted by the Americans, especially James, had in 1873 published a work *The Emotions and the Will* that is often touted as a forerunner of pragmatism.

I'm not now dismissing or downplaying the length of the shadow cast by Descartes on the mind of Holmes, but rather placing it side by side with the more modern, more distilled method of pragmatism.

All this history of pragmatism carries us back to that tangible exponent of the viewpoint, *The Common Law*. The book established Oliver Wendell Holmes as a legal thinker of the first rank, a philosopher/judge still regarded by many as the greatest modern jurist in history. Immediately after the work came out it was accorded the status of a classic by many within the field and many without. Accolades came from both sides of the Atlantic for the legal judgments in it reflect the British as well as the American influences. *The London Spectator* called it "the most original work of legal speculation which has appeared in English since the publication of Sir Henry Maine's *Ancient Law*." In America, until recently, the law of the land was referred to as British common law, or often, English common law. Frederic W. Maitland said of

Wendell Holmes' book that it would "leave its mark wide and deep on all the best thoughts of Americans and Englishmen about the history of their common law." Watson tells us Holmes "Has a good practical knowledge of British law," a phrase that amounts to a definition of the book itself. Anglo-American legal principles and justice undergo analysis in *A Study in Scarlet*, whose setting is both countries, as in a number of the stories. The author may be attempting to notify us that Justice Holmes' book influenced his decision to create his detective initially, for as we know, it was the influence of Justice of the Peace Trevor that turned the young student Holmes' mind to the direction of criminology, convincing him to become a detective. In rural England a J. P. often served the same function as a judge. Doyle had no problem motivating the actions of his detective with the thoughts of an American lawyer and philosopher for both he and Judge Holmes believed fully in reciprocity of legal ideas between both countries since nothing in their judicial systems, each man realized, would prevent such a merger, and Doyle even went one step further suggesting Britain and the United States become one great country. Imagine what fun that would be.

The Common Law, composed for the most part of closely reasoned analysis of certain aspects of legal history, is difficult to categorize and has been mined by thinkers in many fields, even, as we are now seeing, fiction. These numerous archival references are being worked to give definition to the evolution of modern legal practice and social life in general. Wendell Holmes was known as the man who could turn law into literature and this is exactly what Sir Arthur is doing.

Oliver Holmes, Sr. was a scientist and man of experiments and this scientific attitude was planted in and blossomed fully in his son who believed the law, like every aspect of life, human and nonhuman, was subject to the principles of change and evolution. He tells us, "The life of the law has not been logic, but experience," and in keeping with this somewhat tricky bearing, or perhaps to rationalize it, adds, "all life is an experiment." The question Sherlock presents to his own mind is how best to take the guesswork out of criminal detection, and this desire for certainty in legal proceedings pervades the first four chapters of *The Common Law*. Wendell realized the legal code should make some adjustments to the orders of reason and reality and we find this constant search duplicated in the thoughts of Sherlock. The idealistic American hoped to bring scientific ingenuity into the judiciary thereby replacing a complacent imposing of the code. In a letter to William James he said, "Law as well as any other series of facts in the world may be approached in the interest of science." Justice Holmes even published an essay "Law in Science and Science in Law" dealing with this argument. The belief that law "scientifically conceived would bring in its wake not simply intellectual clarity but increased professional competence," is a hope fully endorsed by Sherlock, as was Wendell's anticipation of merging law and philosophy, with a definite empirical, practical, scientific leaning.

The Common Law is far more than a work of legal history; it is a philosophical and speculative endeavor in which the author attempted to seek out in the materials of legal historical data that which would support a new interpretation of the entire legal code. This approach to the field, which becomes Sherlock's own, is the main factor in the obvious estrangements in his relations with other agents of the law. The extrapolations found within the book represent a bringing into the modern world a re-interpretation of that which is ancient, that which you could call, as many have, "the old law." Realizing laws reflected the history of a people and the needs of those people Wendell approached his subject from the historical viewpoint with his writing showing a skillful capacity to blend account and principle into a forceful argument. The work deals heavily with the etymology of many legal and common words applied to law, this etymology being an integral ingredient of the record of the institutions themselves. Sherlock is a criminal historian as Wendell is a legal historian, with the former planning to write a book that would "focus the whole art of detection into one volume," and his friend Stamford suggests he write a work entitled *Police News of the Past*. These volumes were to be an answer to Wendell Holmes as well as Thomas Carlyle. The solution of a crime is rooted in the fact that you must have a complete knowledge of the history of your field, the overall theme of *The Common Law*.

In 1924, when Sir Arthur was a world-famous and much sought after author who could pick any publisher he wished, he went to Little, Brown and Co., publishers of Judge Holmes' *The Common Law*, to bring out his *Memories and Adventures*, hoping to pay back an old debt with this poetic gesture.

The title *Police News of the Past* amounts to a pun, for the nature of justice is the subject of much of Thomas Carlyle's discourse in his work *Past and Present*, of 1843. "Let us search more and more into the Past," he tells us in *Essays*, "let all men explore it, as the true fountain of knowledge; by whose light alone, consciously or unconsciously employed, can the Present and the Future be interpreted or guessed at." In *Past and Present* we also read, "If you do not know eternal Justice from momentary Expediency, and understand in your heart of hearts how Justice, radiant, beneficent, as the all-victorious, Light-element, is also in essence, if need be, an all-victorious *Fire*-element, and melts all manner of vested interests, and the hardest iron cannon, as if they were soft wax, and does ever in the long-run rule and reign, and allows nothing else to rule and reign, — you would also talk of impossibility! But it is only difficult, it is not impossible. Possible? It is, with whatever difficulty, very clearly inevitable."

Wendell Holmes believed the goal of the law could be toward a larger achievement, not just the individual and traditional success of the professional. The American thinks and speaks as a lawyer, but the work and goals of a detective could be thought of, especially if he happened to be Sherlock Holmes. Others are interested in maintaining the law, but he is interested in maintaining justice, and they are not the same.

Both Wendell and Sherlock found it natural to combine extensive learning and the study and application of law to an active concern with public affairs and the needs of government. Throughout his life Thomas Carlyle tried to prove history is the struggle of a people to reduce infernal chaos to divine order with the passion and integrity of the quest representing the common denominator for all great moralists. He equates order with goodness, claiming that the further the hero can proceed beyond the vanquishing of personal chaos to the creation of political, artistic, or spiritual order, the greater the man he is. "Of higher nature than the man who can attain the ordering of his own life is the man who can bring order to the lives of others." There are varying degrees of this ability, but it can be divided into two main divisions. There are men who can create order in government, and those who can create order in ideas. Carlyle devoted much of his thoughts to those who bring order to government believing that better government was the great need of his day. Doyle agrees with this therefore many Holmes stories deal with the preserving of the true mission of one's government. The active role of Wendell Holmes in his government goes without saying; he spent most of his very long life as a judge on state and federal courts, living a good deal of his time in Washington surrounded by the machinery of government. Johnson, like Doyle, had political ambitions and wanted to get into the House of Commons. Doyle ran but lost. Johnson did not actually make the attempt but talked about it a good deal. He served, in a legal capacity, many in government, including the Attorney General and the Solicitor-General of London, as we know from a letter to Boswell. He often served the Royal Family and other aristocrats by writing dedications and such for them. Boswell was active in politics since he was a Laird or Lord, in his native Scotland.

Anyone connected with the law knows it is not enough to suspect, or even to know that a crime has been committed; you must be able to rationally present your suspicions or evidence to the police and courts. *The Common Law*, in part, deals with "presentment," that aspect of the legal system that determines if a criminal act has been committed, and if so, what category of crime it falls under. The presentment is the claim of some agent, individual, or government, for legal revenge, which is of the opinion that he, or it, is entitled to that revenge. "The desire for vengeance imports an opinion that its object is actually and personally to blame. It takes an internal standard, not an objective or external one, and condemns its victim by that." The opinion is based on a purely subjective standard, and the presentment will determine if this standard is objective or external enough to warrant intervention by the legal system. The treatment of criminal law in Wendell's study commenced by contending that presentment was "the child of vengeance," and Doyle displays an uncanny understanding of the dramatic and emotional opportunity offered by the necessity of presentment, far more than any other writer in the field. This performance usually takes place at Baker Street, but can occur anywhere, and is usually directed at Holmes and Watson, though it may have a wider audience, and can even take the form of writing. It is a procedure so common in these tales as to be taken for granted. In many, possibly most narratives, this demonstration of the need for retribution occupies the bulk of the account, far more space than the solving of the crime. In *The Sign of the Four* the all-important second chapter in which Miss Morstan annotates the history of the disappearance of her father and the curious gift of pearls to herself is actually entitled "The Statement of the Case," this being a paraphrase of presentment familiar to the law courts. This will be followed by Jonathan Small's account as to why he behaved as he did, a perfect example of an application by one who firmly believes he is entitled to his vengeance. Jefferson Hope calculates his reasons for restitution in the largest section of *A Study in Scarlet*, the American section, while the conclusion takes only a few pages. It's interesting that there are no "trial scenes" in the tales, although court cases are constantly being mentioned. Doyle shows us the "internal standard," of Hope and countless others, and explores their natures, but only far enough for these people to give justification to their actions.

Revenge is the oldest motivation for murder known to mankind, but revenge has many definitions and intentions. Judge Holmes tells us, "a sound body of law is, that it should correspond with the actual feelings and demands of the community, whether right or wrong. If people would gratify the passion of revenge outside of the law, if the law did not help them, the law has no choice but to satisfy the craving itself, and thus avoid the greater evil of private retribution." Numerous stories show us the consequences of this situation in which the law as we know it, and possibly as it must exist when dealing with mankind in "common," simply does not have the compass to help each and every individual. Private reprisal becomes a matter of necessity under these circumstances and Wendell recognized the compromises that were constantly being made between moral theory and social practice. His object was to establish a relationship between morality and necessity and to formulate a workable basis for human conduct with full knowledge that the various forms of liability known to modern law spring from the common grounds for revenge.

This pivot upon which turns the plot and theme of the Holmes collection is as well the backbone of Le Fanu's ghost tales, for those who are haunted deserve to be haunted. "Green Tea" is a "curse" story in the sense of a curse being something that follows you, something you cannot get rid of. The Irish were famous for their curses, and just about all of Le Fanu's tales deal with vengeance or curse, as do ghost stories in general, with the evil personality being an affliction the cursed one justifiably deserves.

Justice Holmes understood that the chief function of legislation was to exercise a form of controlled retort, giving it legal definition and beneficial intentions; two wrongs do not make a right unless it is society that curbs and sanctions the second action. The Justice tells us this goes back to the earliest forms of legal procedure. "Modern writers have thought that the Roman law started from the blood feud, and all the authorities agree that the German law began in that way. The feud led to the composition, at first optional, then compulsory, by which the feud was bought off. The gradual encroachment of the composition may be traced in the Anglo-Saxon laws, and the feud was pretty well broken up, though not extinguished." The German word for revenge "*Rache,*" written in blood near the body of the murdered man in *A Study in Scarlet*, is a reference to these Teutonic tribal feuds, and it is of course the Anglo-Saxon laws that are now being broken. The term Anglo-Saxon brings us back to the early German quarrels for Saxon means "German." The soldier in *Micah Clarke* who is so fond of quoting from his law book is named

Decimus Saxon. *Decimus* is a Latin word meaning "one-tenth," Doyle's way of showing that at least one-tenth of the early Saxon legal code came directly from Rome. It's doubtful if the name of any character created by Sir Arthur is without meaning or association to something else. The investigation of the interaction between Roman law and that of other nations, which occupies so much of Wendell Holmes' work, motivated Doyle's short story "The Last of the Legions," in which he deals with differences between Roman and Old English law.

Jefferson Hope plans to marry Lucy, so in accord with written Roman law, he will be her owner, in fact strict Roman law already makes him her owner with the engagement. She is being dealt with here as an object but that was the case in Roman law, and still is in many societies. Intention is present in the understanding they are planning marriage following a lapse of time. "Here the prevailing view of the Roman law comes in to fortify principle with precedent." The Judge adds, "We are told that, of the many who might have the actual charge or custody of a thing, the Roman law recognized as possessor only the owner, or one holding as owner and on his way to become one by lapse of time." If a man stands in "a certain physical relation to the object and to the rest of the world," and has the intention of being owner, he is the owner. Hope is given the right to kill any who would steal his property, since there is no other law in Utah at the time except "the law of the Prairie," or as it was commonly called in America, "the law of the gun." Under the circumstances it was understood that any primitive means could be used to bring about justice for, as Wendell tells us, "a wrong has been done," and it should be avenged. Lucy has been deprived of her liberty and of her life while Jefferson Hope is hypothetically deprived of his life, for the Mormons would kill him if they could, and have attempted to do so a number of times, and both have lost their happiness; so we have a case of their being disinherited of the "inherent and inalienable rights" of "life, liberty, and the pursuit of happiness," the dream and hope of Thomas Jefferson. Lucy Ferrier's tragedy begins with the fact that she was an individual held against her will, a form of slavery. Both Wendell Holmes and Arthur Doyle were deeply involved in the war against slavery, Holmes in America, Doyle in Africa.

A Study in Scarlet invites our contemplation of man in his natural state, a condition in which the individual is not only unprotected but subject to the will of the strongest, and the brutality of the religious fanatic, without recourse to law, other than the law of the gun and the rope, or what Hawkeye calls, "frontier punishment," which he adds, is based on "eye for eye." Hawkeye tells us judgment and power is the only real law, and Wendell Holmes echoes this when he says, "the foundation of jurisdiction is physical power." This is as well the reasoning behind the institutions of chivalry and knighthood for they were a direct extension of the earlier similar Roman system and consequently could not function without physical power. The later knights became both the law keepers and lawmakers of their day. The tales of the knights are often referred to as "vengeance tales," and the modern police, especially the detective, are the ones who must practice retribution in the name of "the folk," against the perpetrators of crime.

Much of Wendell Holmes and William James is based, albeit indirectly, on David Hume's belief that in some areas of life, morals and ethics, for example, "sentiment," generated by experience, played a far more important role than reason. Moral judgments or valuations are distinct from conclusions of reasoning, and values are not the same sort of thing in the actual life of man as established facts. Hume believed "There is no synthetic *a priori*" rule of justice, that right and wrong do come into being, as it were, from something antecedent to them in human experience and "common interest and utility," set the standard, and they "beget infallibly."

A term Wendell found regularly cropping up in the old legal documents was "body for body," which first found vitality, he believes, in that early epoch when duels were legal and frequently engaged in to settle questions of law. I find that even Shakespeare used this, for in *The Merchant of Venice* we find one seeking vengeance by demanding "a pound of flesh" from the body of another who cannot fulfill a civil contract, at a time when it was quite within the scope of the law to cut off a person's hand or arm. Judge Holmes questioned whether such a standard was still appropriate in contemporary society while admitting that any form of punishment satisfied a thirst for vengeance in some way, and was a need that must be answered. Even the modern view of criminal regulation must include punishment meted out to protect society from actions harmful to it and its members. Punishment is not intended to reform the criminal but to deter crime, so if the criminal pays with his body, society benefits. "The prisoner pays with his body," is the method jurisprudence allows one convicted of a crime in the modern world to atone for that wrong, and deals both with imprisonment as well as causing physical suffering or death. The Holmes fictions are reactions and attempts at elucidations to uncertainties raised by *The Common Law* with this judicial controversy becoming a mastering factor in the philosophical expansion of the themes and characters. Who, if anyone is to benefit from punishment meted out to a particular offender? What crime should be punished? What crime should not? And what indeed is the very nature of crime and punishment itself? This is but a sampling of the interrogatory temperament of Doyle's writings. The problem of who has the right to extract reprisal becomes an armature around which the narratives of a number of the accounts are woven. The Rev. Jennings has paid with his body for his arrogance in questioning the mind of God, and Jefferson Hope, after confessing his culpability to the murder of his fellow countrymen, dies of a stroke, before he can be brought to trial. Hope has compensated for his acts with his body, Drebber and Stangerson have made amends with their deaths, and we shall witness many others do so in the Canon. In no other writer's work do we find such a large number of characters dying so conveniently and persistently of such ailments as strokes, heart attacks, accidents, etc., as we do in the Holmes mysteries. Barclay in "The Crooked Man," and Trevor in "The 'Gloria Scott,'" and the three retribution seeking bank robbers who died during a shipwreck in "The Resident Patient," come to mind, just to mention a few cases we have already discussed. All this is a bit of a bend of the meaning of the letter of the law, but it is what Doyle meant to show nevertheless, and bear in mind that it represents only a distortion of the image, like a crack in the mirror, not a complete reinterpretation of legal regress. The implication is that Hope, and so many others, will now be in a position of judgment before God, and it's even spelled out for us with Watson's already furnished observation on Hope's sudden death. Some questions are so complicated that only God can make such august decisions, not man. Divine intervention is even implied when in a story such as "The Resident Patient," those who, like the Worthingdon bank gang, would cheat justice by fleeing England find themselves at the bottom of the sea. Other felons are caught and sent to jail, or killed by Holmes or the police, and this will be included in my study, as will those important instances in which Holmes lets certain wrongdoers go free. "Once or twice in my career I feel that I have done more real harm by my discovery of the criminal than ever he had done by his crime. I have learned caution now, and I had rather play tricks with the law of England than with my own conscience," Sherlock tells us, reflecting the hope that sentiment would influence at least some legal decisions. True enough all Sherlock's problems do not answer strictly to the cases found within Judge Holmes' book, but then neither does Judge Holmes' book deal exclusively with the common law.

Either Sherlock Holmes himself was a lawyer, or he put so much reading and thought into legal subjects as to cause confusion in the matter. In "The Adventure of the Norwood Builder" Watson brings up the memory of Bert Stevens, "that terrible murderer," who wanted to hire Holmes to get him off, which sounds like a lawyer's activity, as does his interest in a case involving a lost will, alluded to in *The Sign of the Four*. Holmes was recommended to a troubled Robert Ferguson by a law firm he was associated with somewhat loosely, as attorneys often are, for Holmes worked with them on a case of maritime law regarding the ship *Matilda Briggs*, which was connected somehow "with the giant rat of Sumatra, a story for which the world is not yet prepared," and hopefully never will be.

Various cases Watson introduces by name alone, and which become the focus of some speculation, much of it humorous, refers back to when Wendell Holmes speaks of cases in his book without additional discussion, realizing that if anyone is interested in pursuing them further, they can look them up in the law books.

Johnson was such an expert in litigation that a professional lawyer such as Boswell felt no embarrassment in consulting him. In 1765, having heard of his interest in the subject, Trinity College, Dublin, surprised Johnson with a compliment by bestowing on him Honorary Doctor of Laws. He was so proud of this he used the initials LL.D., after his name in such places as the title pages of his books. "The end of law is protection as well as vengeance. Indeed, vengeance is never used but to strengthen protection. That society only is well governed, where life is freed from danger, and from suspicion; where possession is so sheltered by salutary prohibitions, that violation is prevented more frequently than punished." Here was Johnson's opinion of punishment, and both Holmeses may have had it in mind for their judgments.

Doyle is forced to exercise selectivity in his borrowings from the American jurist's manual, not just because of the volume of cases presented, but also since many, perhaps most of the litigation covered deals with civil and business torts the nature of which would strike strangely on present day ears or would assuredly not be suspenseful enough for fans of the Great Detective. Rather than *The Hound of the Baskervilles* we could have a mystery built around "The Case of the Dog That Killed the Neighbor's Sheep," an actual case from *The Common Law*. However, Doyle must have had the book in mind while working on *The Hound of the Baskervilles* since what is known as "dog law," the responsibility of the owner of a dog to the rest of society, is discussed. How about an adventure built around the goods that were delivered thirty days later than the contract specified, or a case of ownership centered upon a purse of gold that was left on the desk of a bank, not dropped on the floor. That last one might have interested Holmes. The violence of "Silver Blaze" could be replaced by the more placid proceedings involving the possessor of a horse who knowingly let said horse eat grass in his neighbor's field without the express permission of the field's owner. A real challenge to Doyle's creative genius might involve litigation Oliver Wendell Holmes introduces dealing with the consequences of a covenant to keep a parcel of land properly manured being broken. Evil comes in all manner of guises. We could have a thriller involving the crop of corn laid claim to by two different Yankee farmers, or one focusing on the barrel of salt being delivered instead of the barrel of mackerel. This last incident is pursued at some length in *The Common Law* and Doyle actually mentions the case in "The Adventure of the Noble Bachelor" when we learn Holmes' morning mail contained letters "from a fish-monger and a tide-waiter." I am told a tidewaiter is a person who has something to do with shipping goods by boat, and he may be the one getting blamed for the mix-up. Doyle sees the oddity in these cases of course, and even adds one of his own. In "A Case of Identity" Holmes tells of working on the "Dudas separation case" in which the wife complained of her husband's conduct in "winding up every meal by taking out his false teeth and hurling them" at her. This only strengthens my contention that Sherlock is an attorney himself, for the questions such problems give rise to fall squarely under civil jurisdiction and would be handled in the civil courts or by a lawyer.

The mental texture of Hawkeye, Wendell, and Sherlock, is as lean and free of self-deception as their spare, hard bodies. Any photo of the tall, thin, hawk-like, unsmiling face of Wendell shows us a plastic reproduction of the verbal descriptions of Sherlock. For Wendell Holmes, man was alone in the cosmos and had no choice but to make the best of his situation. Commentators tell us this pessimistic cast of mind was in part caused by the impact on his early life, in which he had seen some very bloody action in the Civil War and was wounded three times. The determining factor in the psychological make-up of Sherlock also appears to be the acceptance of a constant state of warfare as the norm for human life. The two Holmeses, Hawkeye, and Doyle, all shared respect for strength, especially moral fortitude, and had a tough suspicion of weakness. They believed that whatever law it is that exists must be upheld by the strong for the good of all. Dr. Holmes as well believed in the use of physical force against the criminal class, telling us, "But hard treatment often proves the most useful kind of discipline," in regard to felons.

Wendell, like Sherlock and his creator, are essentially patriotic in nature, and this attitude, if you fully regard your country as a correct moral entity, can be very strong. Wendell believed that truth itself was "the majority vote of that nation which can lick all others." Locke stated that "all Government in the World is the product only of Force and Violence, and that Men live together by no other Rules but that of Beasts, where the strongest carries it." Every human activity, Johnson maintained, could be traced back to some selfish motive. In Carlyle's mind power was not brute strength, it was the beautiful, the mysterious, the divine, and heroes of any age are figures of divine power whatever their differences: "Understanding the nature of the universe, recognizing that the power within themselves has the same source as the power found within all things, they affirm, rather than struggle with the divine will."

In a consistently wise use of the law Wendell Holmes had found a route out of perplexity; man had developed legal codes and they must be honored or all is chaos. Doyle sends his alter ego Holmes into the world to uphold the law of his people, to defend the rights of all within the Empire, and some without. Sherlock attempts to bring into existence harmony between man and man, and between man and society, and nothing unstabilizes that social order like crime. And Chief Justice Holmes lurks in the background to render decisions and expound the fine points of the law, when necessary. Wendell came to value the law not as an abstruse exercise but as a living vital aspect of civilization, just as Sherlock valued the detection of wrong and the overthrowing of evil as a vital endeavor of the good man in society.

For all these men the basic reality of life could not be separated from a necessary amount of cruelty and vicious struggle. If the value of the law was to be weighed properly, Wendell realized it must be according to empirical criteria, beginning with the harsh reality that some men are truly evil, however much this thought might offend the weak and sentimental. Belief in the law itself became for him what he called "a can't help," or, as he often referred to them, "self-evident truths," or that which cannot be denied, and thus a means to a wider truth. Listen to David Burton's adroit description of Wendell Holmes: "Aristocratic, yet democratic; detached, but involved; stoic yet passionate; callous, though tender; convinced of life as a quaint adventure of the protoplasm without losing sight of man's innate dignity," and this brilliance, he adds, "only thinly masked a complex, paradoxical, restless mind, original, individualistic." We must pause and ask ourselves, which Holmes is he talking about? One often gets the feeling that Sherlock is motivated by an aristocratic sense of responsibility that was inbred rather than deliberated, and one definitely does sense this in Wendell's case. The more one studies these two men the more difficult it becomes to tell them apart. Wendell was a man who had a wide range of interests; at one and the same time he might be studying art, making woodcuts, reading philosophy, acting as Massachusetts Supreme Court Judge, reading novels and short stories, and studying bimetallism, not to mention writing articles and speeches on the law. Walter Scott was his favorite novelist, as he was for Doyle, while both men's preferred historian was Thomas Macaulay. Sir Arthur introduced a character based squarely upon Wendell Holmes into at least one story, which we shall deal with later. One bizarre piece of irony I discovered was the fact that Judge Holmes was dubbed with the sobriquet "the Great Dissenter," in token of his practice of differing with the legal opinions and renderings of his fellow justices while a member of the U. S. Supreme Court, and as we know Sherlock came to be known as "the Great Detective." I don't know exactly when either title was first used, but they were both common currency while Doyle and Wendell Holmes were still alive.

Wendell, like his father before him, was not inclined to take a back seat to any of his contemporaries in estimating his own importance, for he did not, as he emphatically explained, count modesty among the virtues. Hence he conscientiously abstained from it, feeling this so-called virtue was inimical to objectivity and hence to truth itself. Both father and son were regarded by those who found them overbearing as "selfish, vain, and thoughtless of others," a description that could easily be applied to Sherlock on occasion, but only if you did not need his help. Hawkeye as well is justifiably proud of himself, "a man's gifts are his gifts," he enlightens us in regard to his own abilities, "and it's flying in the face of Providence to deny them." "Praise, in general, was pleasing to him," Boswell tells us of Johnson, "but by praise from a man of rank and elegant accomplishments, he was peculiarly gratified." Such men do not hide their light under a bushel, thus inviting many to wish to put it out.

According to letters and library records we know Wendell Holmes loved reading detective and mystery stories, being especially fond of the Sherlock Holmes pieces. Did he have any idea that Doyle had utilized his and his father's writings and lives as material for his great creations? I really think he did. A mind as keen as his could not have failed to realize these works of fiction were related to his accomplishments. Wendell was a prolific letter writer who, in his correspondences with the English writer and teacher Harold Laski, a former student of his at Harvard, and Sir Frederick Pollock, another English jurist and author, brought up the subject of Sherlock and his creator numerous times. In the Laski correspondence alone, which started around 1916 and lasted until Holmes' death in 1935, the two between them talked about Sherlock seven times, and Doyle twice. Here's a letter from Laski to Holmes dated June 6, 1924. "What else have I read? In bed at night — you will smile — the whole series of Sherlock Holmes, which I liked and was mystified by as much as ever. I found some inconsistencies, which amused me, I mean different biographical details in different stories and I surmise from the account of S. H.'s school days (people used to hit him over the shin with a wicket) that he went to Eton — a fact, previously unpublished." I don't know if Wendell smiled at this but I know he wrote back on August 16, asking Laski to let him know of any other inconsistencies he found, obviously very attentive to ideas others held of this character. In one letter Laski belittles Sherlock Holmes as a literary character; the Judge does not even answer the charges — he ignores them, which is unusual in this correspondence. In the letter of April 9, 1932, Holmes writes Laski that no murder mysteries following the Doyle efforts are as good, adding however that he liked *The Moonstone* by Collins. Also in 1932, just before he went on summer vacation with his family, he wrote Judge Pollock that he must have been getting cultivated as he read "Spengler, and John Dewey, Salter and Belloc and McDougall and C. D. Broad — sweetened by rereading all of S. H." One has to wonder how many times he had read these stories already, and why, since he used the word "sweetened," those thoughts of S. H. were so pleasant to him. The Judge was ninety-one years old at this time and still rereading Doyle, so he was obviously fascinated by the stories. Did the Great Dissenter see his own thoughts and labors materialized in the Great Detective? Keep in mind this represents a small selection of the numerous correspondences Wendell carried on, and I could hardly research all of it. I probably read about one percent of Wendell Holmes' communications.

Let's pause here and deal with some concrete examples emphasizing the influence of Wendell Holmes on his namesake. One work that could stand as the supreme example of the Englishman's use of *The Common Law* is "The Adventure of the Six Napoleons." The Italian word for vengeance is *vendetta*, and such a vendetta, in a form unchanged since the days of Rome suggested the plot of "The Six Napoleons." What brings Holmes into it, strangely enough, is the stealing, and then smashing, of cheap plaster of Paris busts of the Emperor Napoleon. At the scene of one of these robberies however, an unknown man has been found with his throat cut and the details point to an Italian connection. A number of times the Mafia is mentioned by Lestrade as being mixed up in it but this fear proves unjustified. The introduction of this organization is not without associative significance however, for the Mafia was originally formed as an instrument of revenge against injustices perpetrated by Italian landlords upon poor and ordinarily defenseless tenants. The personality of the German blood feuds is brought into the picture for the manager of Gelder and Company, the workshop where the plaster busts were manufactured, is "a big blond German," who at one point becomes "flushed with anger, and his brows knotted over his blue Teutonic eyes," the very personification of an individual who feels a wrong has been perpetrated upon him, especially when we remember the face becomes flushed with blood pressure. "*Geld*," the German word for money was the media used by early Germanic tribes to buy off a feud, and the word was used in Early England to mean "payment."

The eventual culprit of both the robberies and the murder turns out to be an Italian emigrant named Beppo. While a worker at the Gelder factory, Beppo hid the stolen famous black pearl of the Borgias in one of six identical busts of the Emperor immediately before being apprehended by the police for an unrelated felony. The historical Italian family of the Borgias was infamous for its capacity to exact vengeance upon their enemies. While he is in jail, the statues are sold to various owners; hence Beppo, upon being released, must acquire the busts somehow, and break them open to find the swiped treasure. The true nature of the Italian vendetta emerges upon learning that the murdered man, Pietro Venucci was brother to Lucretia Venucci, chambermaid to the Prince of Colonna, from whom the pearl was stolen. Lucretia was also the name of one of the more bloodthirsty of the Borgia women. Beppo took the prize from Lucretia Venucci, no doubt also by theft, and her brother was subsequently killed in a failed attempt to carry out a vendetta for this trespass against his sister.

Like his name, Beppo is primitive, being a "sharp-featured simian man, with thick eyebrows and a very peculiar projection of the lower part of the face, like the muzzle of a baboon." It is even brought to our attention that he moves like an ape, Doyle's recognition of his role of "bringer of vengeance," as is both the malicious monkey of "Green Tea," and the twisted "foreigner," of "The Familiar." The old laws, laws as primitive as Beppo himself ("the earliest appearance of law was as a substitute for the private feuds between families or clans") have been given preference over the common law. Beppo is breaking statues of plaster but in reality it is the statutes of the law that are being broken. Etymologically speaking both words are close enough for if you look up "statute," you will be referred to "statue," from which it is derived. Burton, Oliver Wendell Holmes' famous biographer tells us of *The Common Law*, "His purpose was to show that legislation was not the product of sovereign authority but of social customs, essentially instable, which were cast in the form of statutes to be used for a while." The cast statues of Napoleon have been useful temporarily and now must be broken. Morse Hudson, one of the purveyors of the busts declared, "No one but an anarchist would go about breaking statues," and we now realize to what he was referring.

Beppo is finally caught by Holmes at Laburnum Villa, in the Chiswick section of London. *Laburnum* is Latin for any of the genera of small poisonous trees or shrubs of the legume family, the reference being to the Italian practice of poisoning one's enemies. This Italian revenge is a major theme in a number of Doyle's writings, and Stevenson explored it in "The Pavilion on the Links."

An amazing phenomenon takes place in "The Six Napoleons" for the very book *The Common Law*, in its notebook form, makes an appearance by association. Watson tells us that while questioning Mr. Harding, who owns one of the shops that sold the busts, "Holmes had taken several notes." He is using a notebook just as Wendell always carried a notebook, writing his thoughts for his book into it, even while sitting at his own table eating. Keep in mind that a notebook being used by the detective is mentioned only a few other times.

In "The Adventure of Charles Augustus Milverton" and "The Adventure of the Abbey Grange," among several other cases, Holmes lets murderers go free by simply keeping quiet about what he has learned, something Wendell would have understood, although he never advocated the practice.

Lord Brackenstall, owner of Abbey Grange, has allegedly been murdered by thieves who broke into the house, tied up his wife Mary, killed him when he surprised them while stealing the silver, and got away. Lady Brackenstall admits she did not love her husband, a drunken brute who often mistreated her, with His Lordship's predatory and ferocious nature underscored by depicting his slain body lying upon a tiger skin rug. Holmes comes to the realization that it was not burglars that committed this deed but a ship's officer whom Lady Brackenstall had met while sailing back to her native Australia. Once again we have a narrative appraising the letter and intention of the common law, for although Australia, like America, is a foreign country, it too adheres to the practices of English common law, and the crime as well was committed in England. Interestingly enough, Detective Hopkins, who called Holmes into the case, tells us the chief suspect, a burglar well known to the police by the name of Randall, was believed to be in America, and as the account progresses, we learn that he had already been arrested in New York and therefore could not have committed the crime. The common laws of three continents are being analyzed and compared in this case, with emphasis on their flexibility and reciprocal nature. The identification of the killer as a Captain Crocker uncovers the circumstances surrounding the brutal treatment of Mary Brackenstall by her husband, and the details of the killing. This is followed by a presentation of her case by Lady Brackenstall and a mock trial by jury. In Cooper's stories a number of legal issues, including a case of murder, are decided by those involved in the crimes, without recourse to outside, higher authority. In reference to a murder that could be regarded as justifiable, Hawkeye tells us, "when we live beyond the law, we must be our own judges and executioners." Holmes designates Crocker as the prisoner and tells Watson, "you are a British jury," then adds rather sarcastically, "and I never met a man who was more eminently fitted to represent one." He then adds, "I am the judge." This amounts to a pun on Wendell Holmes' persona for he had just been made a Justice of the U. S. Supreme Court the year before the story was published, and was so popular by now he was known as "the Judge," just as George Washington is often called simply "the General." Wendell tells us, "A judge who has long sat at *nisi prius* ought gradually to acquire a fund of experience which enables him to represent the common sense of the community in ordinary instances far better than an average jury." Sherlock claims he will handle the case "in due form of law," which is another reference to Wendell, whose effort for legal exactness was legendary.

Marriage laws and their consequences are being discussed in "The Abbey Grange" in the guise of fiction. Sherlock deals in all sorts of cases, as his namesake Wendell handled all types of problems as lawyer and judge. Doyle also studied and wrote about the British marriage laws, which he hoped to see amended toward more fairness to the wife. The Great Detective, after learning the facts of the case, decides not to go to Detective Hopkins with his evidence, justifying his decision by claiming, "You must look at it this way: what I know is unofficial, what he knows is official. I have the right to private judgment, but he has none." No other possibility is really open; the situation is at a "stalemate," a word taken from stall and mate, as in the name Brackenstall. When Watson finds the defendant not guilty Holmes shouts "*Vox populi, vox Dei*," in effect confirming that the law of the folk, which is the law of God, has been carried out. Doyle took this phrase "*Vox populi, vox Dei*," from Cooper's novel *The Crater*, where we find it used in exactly the same way. Self-defense justifies killing one's fellow man, Sherlock realized, even to God.

"The Abbey Grange" takes us back to early English history, upon which it is based. In Early England the law was often administered by Danes, foreigners against whom the natives often banded together in Robin Hood fashion. Later the law was carried out by Norman officials, also foreigners, who quickly turned themselves into agencies for raising money by fines, while the English overlords proved little better. A number of Lords, realizing the danger inherent in the state of affairs, approached the King and obtained his consent to their setting up a court within their manors. This put the administration of law and justice on a local footing, and negated the Norman attempt to centralize justice, as we read in *The Common Law*. This scene of litigation being carried out in a manor that is as old as we can assume Abbey Grange to be is based squarely upon historical precedent.

Here is a partial explanation for much of the thoughtful ambiguity found throughout the stories. Are the people in any number of these accounts justified in their deeds, even if those deeds are illegal, and is Sherlock correct in letting them off, or in not letting them off, and by whose standards is he acting? Perhaps Doyle regards Sherlock as the final adjutant of justice, one close in spiritual nature to the absolute judge himself. In the last sentence of this story Holmes admonishes the couple whose innocence he has just reestablished: "may her future and yours justify us in the judgment which we have pronounced this night!" That sounds pretty lofty, especially speaking in the plural like that.

"While we were alone, I endeavoured as well as I could to apologize for a lady who had been divorced from her husband by act of Parliament." Boswell is telling us here of a conversation with Johnson, referring to a famous scandal of the day, involving Lady Diana Beauclerk. "I said, that he had used her very ill, had behaved brutally to her, and that she could not continue to live with him without having her delicacy contaminated; that all affection for him was thus destroyed; that the essence of conjugal union being gone, there remained only a cold form, a mere civil obligation; that she was in the prime of life, with qualities to produce happiness; that these ought not to be lost; and, that the gentleman on whose account she was divorced had gained her heart while thus unhappily situated." Minus the murder itself we have here the gist of "Abbey Grange." A student of British history such as Doyle realizes that Lady Diana will from now on be treated as little better than a criminal by society. Johnson, however, is not sympathetic to the woman's problems, believing her to be in the wrong in this particular case, but Boswell knows him to be a fair, if stern, judge. A number of times Boswell calls his friend "the Judge," as when he defends him against charges of being of a satirical and rough nature. "I admit that the beadle within him was often so eager to apply the lash, that the Judge had not time to consider the case with sufficient deliberation." Boswell adds that "Johnson's benevolence to the unfortunate was, I am confident, as steady and active as that of any of those who have been most eminently distinguished for that virtue. Innumerable proofs of it I have no doubt will be for ever concealed from mortal eyes." Concealed, as is Sherlock's charity to Lady Brackenstall.

Somewhere in his writings Aristotle tells us he regards blackmail to be the most reprehensible of crimes, for it is not only a heinous evil in itself, but it is being used to cover up another wrong. It is a form of double jeopardy, if you wish. This is important since Aristotle is the first philosopher whose morals we recognize as our own. True enough, our needs have changed over the years, but those years number in the thousands, and for most of that time the moral and ethical judgments of Western man were the judgments of Aristotle. Doyle realizes that if this thoughtful observation is true, this makes of the blackmailer the foulest of miscreants. Blackmail is the focus or is suspected in any number of narratives such as "The Boscombe Valley Mystery," where extortion covers up earlier murders, and itself leads to murder, as it also does in "Black Peter." Moriarty, the most dangerous transgressor Holmes challenges, is a leader of blackmailers.

In "Charles Augustus Milverton" a situation arises where a victimized individual murders a notoriously vicious extortionist, determined to either bleed money out of her or ruin her. Upon returning from "our evening rambles" (right out of Boswell), Holmes and Watson find the card of Milverton with a note adding he will return shortly. Sherlock considers him "one of the most dangerous men in London," as well as "The worst man in London." Holmes compares this "king of all the blackmailers" to "slithery, gliding, venomous creatures, with their deadly eyes and wicked, flattened faces," that we see "in the Zoo." "*Augustus*," is a Roman title often used for a ruler, many of whom were infamous for their cruelty, while his last name epitomizes his evil calling, for a mill grinds down grains, as this reptile, with his "smiling face and a heart of marble," with the ruthless regularity of a millstone, pulverizes any whose sad secrets fall into his vile clutches.

Holmes was expecting this visit from the blackmailer. One of his victims has previously called upon the detective with a plea for assistance in recovering "several imprudent letters" penned while young. Attempting to retrieve the documents Milverton has been invited to visit Holmes, whose efforts to reason with the cad fail. The prey is a Lady Eva, an obvious enough pun on "the Lady Eve," a sometime title of the primordial mother of *The Book of Genesis*, making of Milverton the devil himself, come to pollute mankind by degrading innocence. Like her namesake, our victim is threatened with the loss of paradise for, to the average Englishwoman of the time, marrying a man with money, or a title, or both, was the most successful accomplishment she could hope for in life, and this devil's exposure of the letters would render that unlikely.

We are treated to a display of Holmes' prodigious acting capacity in handling this crisis, as well as his competency in the application of makeup and disguise. As Watson gets to know him better, he is forced to admit the stage lost a great actor in Sherlock Holmes, a sentiment echoed by one character, who admits, the night before he is hanged, that in Holmes the law has gained what the stage has lost. Aware that he cannot buy off nor intimidate the predator, the investigator disguises himself as a plumber, "a rakish young workman, with a goatee beard and a swagger," gains access to the Milverton home, and walks out with his housemaid, even becoming engaged to her, all in a few days.

Neither Hawkeye nor anyone else in *The Leather-Stocking Tales* hesitates to play any deception they deem necessary to survive, and to win the unending wars. We even find Hawkeye and the Indians disguising themselves as animals to fool their enemies. In order to effect a rescue in an Indian camp, Hawkeye dresses in the bear costume of an Indian jester and walks right into their midst. Holmes adopts the disguise of a variety of characters to facilitate the solving of a mystery, or for any other purpose. A similar situation recorded in "A Scandal in Bohemia," discovers him appropriating the persona of a clergyman to fool a woman into admitting him into her home. Once again he is successful. "It was not merely that Holmes changed his costume," Watson tells us, "His expression, his manner, his very soul seemed to vary with every fresh part that he assumed." This is the caliber of praise reserved for Johnson's friend David Garrick, considered by many to have been the nonpareil actor the stage has ever seen. Garrick was raised in Lichfield, having been one of Johnson's pupils in his short-lived private school for boys there, and when the two settled in London they became close friends. As a rule Johnson did not care for actors, at the time regarded as morally loose and licentious. He never hesitated to defend Garrick against attacks upon his character for he saw close-up the actor's generosity toward the needy and his fine integrity. Praise of Garrick's powers was universal; even Boswell, rather indifferent to the theater, spoke of his performances in terms similar to Watson's appreciation of Holmes.

Watson however is outraged by the trick of deceiving Milverton's maid, yet Holmes suffers no compunction at all. This is a comment on Diderot's essay "The Paradox of Acting," one of his most famous and debated pieces of writing in which he assures us the last thing a great actor should wish for is feeling. "Great genius is scarcely ever accomplished by any great degree of feeling. A genius will love justice, but he will exercise that virtue without tasting its sweetness. It is not his heart, it is his head that does everything. Whereas the emotional man loses his head at the slightest occurrence; he will never be a great king, a great minister, a great general, a great lawyer, or a great doctor." Sherlock's cold, unemotional disposition generates an opportunity for a far more pronounced acting capacity than any simply involved individual could hope to achieve. "You can fill the auditorium with such moist-eyed creatures," the philosopher tells us of the emotional ones, "but don't put any of them onto the stage." The celebrated artist's tears are always false or else he is not a skilled performer. The truly gifted can imitate "tones of voice, conformity of action, speech, facial expression, voice, movements and gestures perfectly." All these qualities are brought forward by Holmes' Thespian efforts. His concentration is on his art, not his emotions, which have nothing to do with it. Diderot goes on, "His tears are like those of an agnostic priest preaching the Passion, of a seducer at the feet of a woman, he does not love but wants to deceive. This is why the actor on the stage and the actor in real life are such two different people that it is difficult to recognize the one in the other." Here are even listed some of the roles the detective is found to play: priest, minister, and admirer of women.

Having gained access to Milverton's villa, Holmes learns the floor plan and decides to burgle the place, with the assistance of Watson. "I suppose," Holmes puts to his reluctant friend, "that you will admit that the action is morally justifiable, though technically criminal." This ambivalent consideration reveals to us the sophisticated level of thematic adoption from *The Common Law* going on in this fiction.

It's time to be introduced to a new influence on Doyle's writing in the form of a personal friend. Robert Barr was born in Glasgow, Scotland in 1850, but his family moved to Ontario in 1854, and a Canadian he was raised. He became a teacher and writer in Canada and for a while lived just across the border in Detroit, Michigan. He was published in newspapers and magazines, mostly in the States, for some reason known only to himself, under the pseudonym of Luke Sharp. Having settled in London he achieved some measure of fame as a novelist, and as editor of *The Idler*, an influential but short-lived magazine he helped found. He died in Italy in 1912.

Doyle and Barr lived near each other and became good friends. Barr lived in a log cabin in Canada when young, grew up among the Indians, knew their customs and language, and had actually accompanied the U. S. Minister of the Interior on a mission to conclude a treaty with the Iroquois (Hawkeye's old enemies) in 1881. Doyle must have looked upon his friend Barr as a living link between himself, Cooper, and Hawkeye, and they must have talked of America often. A "correspondence" grew between Barr and Doyle as they borrowed from each other's writings over the course of their friendship. Barr wrote detective stories satirizing Sherlock Holmes with his character Sherlaw Kombs. Professor Challenger, a Doyle creation we cannot deal with here, is fashioned in part upon Barr himself.

Barr's novel *The Measure of the Rule* is a heavily autobiographical account of his education at an Ontario teachers college where the rules governing the students' behavior is so strict as to be unbearably oppressive. Male and female pupils cannot talk to each other, and must view the works in the school art gallery on separate days so as to avoid contact, are just a few examples of these regulations. This puritanical authoritarian harshness, this "measure of the rule," and its baneful effects on the characters in the narrative represents the main focus of the work.

The school is under the direction of Headmaster John Brent, an inflexible disciplinarian who does not hesitate to persecute his charges unmercifully for the sake of upholding draconian rules of conduct. He is malevolent towards all, but seems to be especially vindictive toward the young women for reasons of his own, reasons never gone into. Brent ostensibly exercises such strictness from a distorted analysis of the spirit of the regulations, but there lurks in the background an unmistakable love of revenge governed by a willful spitefulness in his psychological makeup. He is vicious.

John Brent preys upon the guilt of the young caused by their indiscretions, just as Milverton exploits the guilt of indiscretion itself. Both enjoy what they do, are adroit at it, and neither would conceive of himself as being evil.

It's simply the way they make their living. Having the capacity to cause misery, they will cause it when they can. The London blackmailer refuses to sell back the gauche letters at a reduced sum for the identical reason the Canadian headmaster will never overlook the slightest fumble on the part of those in his charge, to make examples of them to the others.

Under cover of darkness Holmes and Watson enter Milverton's villa, locate his study and open the safe, but as they are about to grab the letters someone enters the room and the two burglars hide behind the window curtains. The interruption is caused by the miscreant himself, who, failing to notice his safe has been forced, sits at his desk and proceeds to read a legal document. The two detectives in desperation are about to make an attempt at escaping when a tap at the veranda door tells us Milverton has a visitor. A heavily veiled woman that was obviously expected by Milverton enters and the two begin discussing yet another collection of letters Milverton shows an interest in. Suddenly the man realizes he has been deceived, for his nocturnal guest is another, quite unexpected party. A young victim of past business has come with revengeful intentions and the frightened blackmailer tries to reason with her: "I wouldn't hurt a fly of my own accord, but every man has his business, and what was I to do?" This is just the kind of thing Brent would tell one of his indiscrete students and, interestingly enough, the scene is taken from Barr's *The Measure of the Rule*. The book's protagonist, the student Thomas Prentiss, fractures the code one evening on a whim by unexpectedly paying a house call on a female student, Aline Arbuthnot. He finds her home, and the two talk in her sitting room — knowing it is forbidden behavior — when suddenly the maid warns them none other than their Nemesis, the headmaster, is coming up the walk. The pair is trapped, and in desperation Prentiss hides behind the window drapes where he eavesdrops on the conversation between Arbuthnot and Brent, in which Brent explains how necessary it is to enforce the rules of the institution, and never give in to any weakness he may personally feel. This particular incident ends well, for Brent leaves no wiser than when he came; but in the long run he gets his way by finding opportunity to wreak vengeance on the pair.

While hidden behind the drapes Holmes and Watson overhear evidence that indeed Milverton had ruthlessly ruined his present visitor's life. These pleasantries over, the woman whips out a revolver and shoots him repeatedly until he is dead. The crime of blackmail, one immorality used to cover up another, has led to murder, and the blackmailer has paid. Watson wishes to offer assistance to him but Holmes physically restrains his friend, who tells us, "I understood the whole argument of that firm, restraining grip — that it was no affair of ours, that justice had overtaken a villain." With his restraint on the impulsive Watson, Holmes maintains his moral position as judge and jury, in effect condoning the slaying of that "villainous character." The murderess escapes into the night followed by Holmes and Watson, who just about make their getaway. Though actually witnessing the slaying, the investigators have no intention of revealing their knowledge to the authorities and offer them no assistance. Upon learning the identity of the killer from a photo in a shop window, Holmes enjoins silence for once and for all with the rationalization that "there are certain crimes which the law cannot touch, and which therefore, to some extent, justify private revenge." This crime may be a crime, but this criminal is no criminal, he seems to be saying.

One contention of Wendell Holmes, an oft repeated one, is that the actual law, for good or for ill, is what the judge in a case says it is. This in effect affirms Sherlock's stance in acting as the epitome of the law in this and in any number of other cases. The American believed that "not the nature of the crime, but the dangerousness of the criminal, constitutes the only reasonable legal criterion to guide the inevitable social reaction against the criminal." Obviously an ample number of the *populi* would administer a judgment analogous to Holmes' in regard to the end of this nefarious extortionist.

Doyle has the famous true case of Madeleine Smith in mind as he writes. In 1857, Smith, a woman of Glasgow, was indicted for murder for poisoning a foreigner, Pierre Emile L'Angelier, whom she had been intimate with. She was presented the chance to marry well, but the Frenchman had love letters and threatened to use them unless he was paid off. He ended up getting poisoned, Smith was arrested and tried, and the Scotch jury returned a "Not Proven" verdict and she walked away. Public opinion showed most people believed her guilty, but that it was right she had not been found guilty in a court, for was she not after all only protecting herself? The trial had been held in Doyle's own city of Edinburgh and proved to be one of the most famous affairs in British legal history.

In "The Adventure of the Blue Carbuncle" we come across James Ryder, a first time thief so abject and contrite over his thoughtless stealing of a gemstone that, accepting his promise never to do it again, Holmes lets him off without even a warning. Truth in some fixed form, whether in life or law, does not exist, Wendell believed, and judges who sought it or claimed to have found it he dismissed as naïve, going so far as to say, "for my part, I think it a less evil that some criminals should escape than that the Government should play an ignoble part." In *The Common Law* we read, "The truth is, that the law is always approaching, and never reaching, consistency, ... it will become entirely consistent only when it ceases to grow." He realized the law would never cease to grow.

We are always forced to admit that Sherlock Holmes knows the realities of life, and as such is often almost overwhelmed by the inscrutable and often incompatible nature of truth. Synthetic judgment based on *a priori* knowledge is how Immanuel Kant believed we know something, but it is not the position of Wendell or Sherlock. Wendell felt the judge must weigh his judgments and contrast them with the needs of historical truth, society, justice, and his own individual regard and the needs of the code. The law is based on frail human decisions, and new experiences and imaginative insights, not only *a priori* or predetermined patterns, or even precedents. And both Holmeses realized that judgment could take many forms.

Chapter Five. Law of the Brahmans

Just as the Holmes stories bring into being a display of the evolution of philosophy and science, as exemplified by, among other facets of thought, René Descartes' discoveries, and Charles Darwin's theory of evolution, they additionally focus upon the history of religion. Doyle quite possibly borrowed this idea from Melville's Moby-Dick after realizing that the growth of man's religious consciousness is the ultimate theme of the novel.

On the second page of *The Sign of the Four* we learn that Holmes is the world's "only unofficial consulting detective," the first to hold that position for he has "created it." The term consulting is on loan from the field of medicine with "consulting surgeon," to the Royal Infirmary of Edinburgh being a position held by Dr. Joseph Bell. Hesselius is one who is being consulted as well. Holmes may presently be the world's only consulting detective, but Doyle knows he is not the first, for that honor belongs to Zarathustra of the ancient Aryans.

Doyle has introduced himself to that famous series *The Sacred Books of the East*, published by the Clarendon Press of London over a number of years spanning the last quarter of the nineteenth century. This collection gave to the original ancient sources a readership and popularity they still enjoy. Not only did Sir Arthur absorb vast quantities of crime fiction and non-fiction, but being a closet lawyer and legal historian, he devours anything pertinent to the law he comes across. London was the center of Eastern studies with such companies as Truber publishing translations of the Indian law books. *The Sacred Laws of the Aryans*, printed by Clarendon in 1879, was possibly the work that first attracted our author to this field. The study of the Aryan laws was considered essential by many, among them Henry Adams, Wendell Holmes' close friend, critic, and advisor, who said, "no really thorough historical acquaintance with this subject [scientific legal history] is possible without tracing the stream of legal institutions back through the German hundred, as well as through the Roman city, to its Aryan source."

The land of the Aryans was first limited to a large region in Northern India, but by the time the law texts were committed to writing, their lands included all of India and then some. The early Aryans were agricultural people who led a settled life, keeping cattle, while their Semitic and Asiatic neighbors, many of them nomads, pirates, and raiders, moved about in tents and kept sheep and goats but not cattle. These laws could be regarded as the legal codes of the farming and cattle herding people. The texts had their source in the ancient Vedic schools of the Aryan Hindus and were originally to be committed to memory by the young students to teach them their civil and religious duties — concepts that cannot be separated in Indian life.

The influence of these rules over the lives of Holmes and Watson is often obvious enough. Doyle's imagination regarded Holmes, and possibly Watson, to be of the caste of the Brahmans, the priestly, educated caste from which leaders are drawn. I have to say "possibly Watson," for I am really not that sure of Doyle's intentions in this regard. The two men are both very conscious of the caste system, as we see in "The Adventure of the Second Stain," when Holmes tells his friend, "Now, Watson, the fair sex is your department," following the departure of an excitable female client. The Brahman does not yield to or regard the emotions of any woman. Holmes questions her true motives, calling our attention to her attempted efforts to hide her excitement, but adds, "Remember that she comes of a caste who do not lightly show emotion."

Studentship for the good Hindu should continue for forty-eight years, or just about all one's life, for learning is considered sacred and should never be abandoned. "Education never ends," Holmes tells Watson one day, "It is a series of lessons with the greatest for the last." "Let him be untiring in fulfilling his duties," and be "possessed of self-command and energetic," we are told of the Brahman and in "The Yellow Face," we are told Holmes was indeed "absolutely untiring." A diligent Brahman or student is never caught napping and if possible is never even seen to sleep, and it must be said of him "that he does not sleep." Holmes has an unsleeping will, for so indeed does his enemy the untiring will of evil. His ability to do without the normal amount of sleep or rest other men would find necessary is legend. The Aryan law keeper can remain awake all night long, especially on certain important ritual nights, and not sleeping is a ritual in itself for the Great Detective. A law student "shall not touch a woman with his face, in order to inhale the fragrance of her body," "nor shall he touch her at all without a particular reason." He should not even talk with them except for a particular purpose. "Nor shall he desire her in his heart." Like the Aryans, Holmes has "kept his organs in subjection," for among this caste those keeping the vows of chastity, "are declared the most excellent of men." This accounts well enough for Holmes' behavior, but not Watson's, since he marries, although it is not forbidden for a Brahman to wed.

There are injunctions against laughing, or even smiling, and Watson tells us Holmes rarely laughs, and that his laughter "always boded ill to somebody." Watson himself is never known to laugh or smile. These are hardly rules for humans as we in the West know them, they seem better suited to robots, which accounts for some of Holmes' stiffness, but keep in mind that many devout societies such as Quakers, Puritans, some priests and monks, and so-forth, are not very different.

Self-praise is to be avoided, but as we know the detective ignores this attitude completely. From time to time he seems conscious of the fact that he is breaking a sacred law and offers justification as in "The Greek Interpreter," when he tells us, "To the logician all things should be seen exactly as they are, and to underestimate one's self is as much a departure from truth as to exaggerate one's own powers." Holmes seeks simply for balance and truth, as he should, and echoes Wendell Holmes at the same time.

To acquire knowledge of such disciples as math, grammar, etymology, astronomy, and phonetics, is a religious act to the Aryans and will help you in the afterlife. Notice the mention of etymology, a subject we find the detective displaying some learning in, as does his creator.

"A king and a Brahmana, deeply versed in the Vedas, these two, uphold the moral order in the world," for "On them depends the existence of the fourfold human race, of internally conscious beings, of those which move on feet, and on wings, and of those which creep." It is up to them to prevent confusion, and "to protect the young (offspring) and to uphold the sacred law." Holmes is called upon to protect the young in "The Adventure of the Illustrious Client" when an incognito member of the aristocracy, perhaps an agent of the king, as is implied, joins forces with him to protect the life of a foolish young girl.

Does not Sherlock Holmes epitomize "the eight good qualities of the soul: compassion on all creatures, forbearance, freedom from anger, purity, quietism, auspiciousness, freedom from avarice, and freedom from covetousness." As we know, he is a generous man, often charging nothing to those who cannot afford his services, while from others he gets very little compared to the valuable assistance he renders. Another facet of the law informs us that the "qualities by which a true Brahmana may be recognized are, the concentration of the mind, austerities, the subjection of the senses, liberality, truthfulness, purity, sacred learning, compassion, worldly learning, intelligence, and the belief (in the existence of the deity and of a future life)." We are reminded that reasoning is a means of arriving at the truth and that coming to a conclusion through reasoning will help the student to decide properly. The keeper of the law will conduct himself as an Aryan, and "He shall always speak the truth." Here is Nietzsche's rationale, in part, for saying that the first Persian virtue is to tell the truth and shoot straight. Holmes can shoot straight, even engaging in pistol practice in his apartment, drawing the queen's initials in the wall with bullet holes.

Holmes plays tricks on unsuspecting people but that is permitted among the Aryans if the eventual purpose is self-defense, or for the protection of your people, or of your land and herds. During the course of his adventures the Great Detective assumes thirteen disguises to facilitate the solving of a mystery but this is permissible for they are assumed with the keeping of the Sacred Laws in mind.

The Brahmana of the texts is a mixture of priest, sheriff, and judge, and here we have Sherlock Holmes, as we know him. He has the right to take the law into his own hands when necessary to "restrain those who do not restrain themselves." This scripture is most important for it seems to be the basis for the justification for all law. "Men continue to prosecute their own advantages by the nearest way; and the utmost severity of the civil law is necessary to restrain individuals from plundering each other," Johnson told Boswell one day. The ancient texts tell us people such as "robbers and bandits," are to be fought against by the upholder of the Word, "the righteous man," who follows the law. A righteous man who does not rescue a weak man from injury incurs as much guilt as he who injures the other. Here we have the reasoning behind Holmes' self-contempt when in "The Five Orange Pips" he fails to protect John Openshaw, making light of his fears for his life, telling Openshaw to go home and not worry for he will take care of it tomorrow. But tomorrow never comes, for Openshaw is murdered on his way home and Watson tells us Holmes was "more depressed and shaken than I had ever seen him."

In a real sense Holmes takes on the character of a yogi, an ascetic. Because of his holiness, he can "promise safety from injury to all people," the yogi's function. He is single and has no children. Holmes finds all emotions "abhorrent to his cold, precise but admirably balanced mind," for an ascetic is "wholly indifferent to pleasure and pain." "Through the practice of Yoga true knowledge is obtained, Yoga is the sum of the sacred law, the practice of Yoga is the highest and eternal austerity; therefore let him always be absorbed in the practice of Yoga." There is no such creature as a fat yogi, and Holmes is extremely thin: the physical build we always associate with the ascetic. The perfect yogi would be one who conceivably exists on air alone, as our investigator appears to do. Johnson loved good food, but nevertheless fasted whenever from time to time, often for lack of money, occasionally forgetting to eat, and sometimes as a religious exercise. "He had resolved not to dine at all this day, I know not for what reason," Boswell remembers, while Johnson himself tells us he often fasted for two days at a time simply because he does not feel hunger as others do. Sitting with crossed legs is a position of the meditating yogi, and this attitude Holmes often assumes while thinking, "settling himself down in his armchair and closing his eyes," or sometimes he "sat upon the floor like some strange Buddha, with crossed legs." Yoga is a custom shared by both the Hindu and Buddhist faithful, so there is no conflict here. The word Buddha means "the Enlightened One." As regards *The Sacred Laws of the Aryans*, I have been selective in my choices, as was our author.

Some of these injunctions are bizarre to modern ears. I wonder what Doyle made of the rule forbidding a righteous one to eat of the food offered him by a professional physician, for swift disaster was sure to follow. One of the most hideous mistakes a man can commit is to urinate on his own shadow. The whole village is in trouble then.

The *Zend-Avesta* is the sacred writings of the Parsis, the Aryan followers of the ancient religion Zoroastrianism, who inhabited Persia until the

Mohammedans killed them, converted them, or drove them out. The great three-volume translation of the *Zend* by James Darmesteter was published by Oxford University Press in 1880, and incorporated into the sacred book series shortly thereafter. The *Zend* is a compilation of religious laws, tales, histories, litanies for rituals, and hymns.

The religion is called Dualism, or Mazdaism, or Magism, or Zoroastrianism, or Fire Worship, according to whether its main tenet, or its supreme God, Ahura Mazda, or its priests, or its supposed founder, or its apparent object of worship, has been most kept in mind. The religion itself is still practiced, as it was in Doyle's day, principally in Bombay and London. Zoroastrianism is a common spring out of which a number of religions: Hinduism, Mohammedanism, even a little of Christianity, flowed, being much older than any of them. Zoroaster, translated into Greek as Zarathustra, and known to the Roman world as Zorro, the compiler of the *Zend*, is regarded as its founder. The historical question of Zarathustra is still open; none seem to know exactly when he lived although all agree he was a real man. In one of the books he complains about finding enough money to pay for his three daughters' weddings, and you can't get more real than that. One is "a worshipper of Mazda, a follower of Zarathustra." Mazda is a God while Zarathustra is a lawgiver with some attributes of a god; a sort of demigod, a designation found in the Persian religion. Zarathustra, the writer and transmitter of "this fiend-destroying law of Mazda," declared himself to be a prophet after having compiled the *Zend-Avesta*. He is called, "an unequivocal one, a man of perfect honesty, a vessel of wisdom, a saint of knowledge, a great man," who is also entitled "the lawgiver," and I believe Doyle liked to regard Wendell Holmes as a reincarnation of the ancient Persian sage; one who is born, "to think according to the law, to work according to the law, to speak according to the law." Wendell had read Zoroaster by the time he was eighteen years old he tells us in an essay he had published in *The Harvard Magazine* while he was still a sophomore.

The main feature of Mazdean belief is the existence of two principles, a good one, Ormazd, and an evil one, Ahriman. They were created by the two supreme powers with the division of all beings in nature into two corresponding classes; the end of the struggle between Ormazd and Ahriman by the defeat and destruction of the evil principle; the resurrection of the dead and everlasting life, are all established in the *Zend*. Ormazd or Mazda is all light, truth, goodness, and knowledge, while Mainyu, or Ahriman, is all darkness, falsehood, wickedness, and ignorance. His title, Prince of Darkness, an epithet for Satan, is a borrowing from this older doctrine. The world is twofold, being the work of two hostile beings, Ahura Mazda, the good principle, or Angra Mainyu, the evil one. All that is good comes from the former, all that is evil emanates from the latter. The history of the world is the story of their conflict, how Mainyu invaded the world of Mazda and marred it, and how he shall be expelled from it at last. It's believed that imperfection and suffering are properties of the original world and permanently so, and Mainyu the evil one was their author. Mazda fights Mainyu and all expect him to eventually defeat evil, but it is also understood he does not possess the power to restrain him or his realm permanently. This God of the Parsis is a great expounder of the laws, for we are told Mazda is so intelligent he discerns "what things are lawful or unlawful," "with his wonder-working thoughts of Righteousness."

The followers of Zarathustra are "the enlightened ones," and he himself is "the enlightened one," but the works of this good god and these good men is arrested by the evil one, "the offspring of the Evil Mind," and his hoard of minions who have destroyed the hopes of mankind for a happy life on earth, and for immortality in heaven. Fighting the evil one is especially difficult, for like the Christian devil he can assume any form he wishes.

These sacred Canons not only dictate episodic narrative in the Holmes stories guiding the behavior of the personalities, but also actually compose interludes of scene and setting. Fire, water, and earth are sacrosanct and worthy of worship to the Aryans, with fire lighting and the keeping of a fire regarded as both a religious act and an art. A priest is called literally a "fire-man," for his chief function deals with the holy fire and its kindling, "and their works are productive of rewards." Holmes and Watson almost always maintain a fire, weather permitting. The main tenet of the faith, the struggle between good or light, and evil or darkness, is symbolized by the light of the blaze, therefore many of the laws involved deal with the performance offerings of the domestic fire, which is holy, and who tends it, who does not, etc. Within Judaism and Christianity, lights and fires are lit on holidays as symbols of this unending war between light and dark. Our two investigators live in the warm, dry, light filled world of Baker Street, while their enemies inhabit the dark, damp, foggy world of the city and the even more sinister country. Sleep seems to be a denotation of evil influences for it brings personal darkness and a holy man, a bringer of light, has the assignment "to withstand the darkness, to withstand the Daevas (devils) born of darkness." Zarathustra tells us he cannot sleep while there is evil in the world and Sraosha, "the master of holiness," an angel-god, is described as one who never sleeps. Zarathustra "wakefully guards the creation of Mazda" and "protects all the material world with his club uplifted, from the hour when the sun is down," fighting everlastingly with the Daevas. The Christians adopted this stance, for the followers of the Lord Jesus must expect to lose some sleep as we read in Thessalonians: "For all you are the children of light, and children of the day: we are not of the night, nor of darkness. Therefore let us not sleep, as others do: but let us watch and be sober. For they who sleep, sleep in the night: and they who are drunk, are drunk in the night."

This godlike champion Zarathustra is "the first of saints," but there are others, assistants, forms of archangels, regarded as god's faithful adherents upon earth, and at the same time conceived of as persons of flesh and blood for man is active in the conflict, his duty in it being laid before him in the laws and rituals. Another demigod, Rashnu, is "the uninjured, the best killer, smiter, destroyer of thieves and bandits, in whatever part of the world thou art watching the doings of men and making account." The evil one is a being "full of crime," which will lead mankind to "the destruction, which awaits him." Zarathustra is "to the wicked, in very truth, a strong tormentor and avenger, but to the righteous he is a mighty help and joy." The king's army and the police helped this holy man protect the people just as Holmes relies from time to time upon advice and assistance from police officers. Holmes in turn offers what help he can, often "without any active interference, to give some hint of suggestion drawn from his own vast knowledge and experience." It was not only the English police who turned to Holmes for help, for his knowledge of criminology was not limited by national boundaries, and he was able to quote "parallel cases," from crimes that had been committed abroad. "He appears to know every detail of every horror perpetrated in the century." The gods can travel over the world to bring thieves to justice and along with the gods, the good Mazidan worships "those of the saints within the Province, and those of the saints without the Province." Holmes offers assistance to and answers the call for help from police departments and princes of foreign lands such as the Pope and the Paris Sûreté. "My practice has extended recently to the Continent," he tells Watson, somewhat proudly. America and Australia, which Holmes never visits, is the setting for a good portion of some tales, and would be "one of the settlements," of the holy people, and must be protected as such, for any colony which "furthers the settlements of the Aryans is to be offered protection."

This prophet is appointed by his god to be "a cattle-chief, who was both skilled and like-wise energetic," one "who might hurl back the fury of the wicked." Not a member of the army or police force that we know of, he may not have taken part in the fighting itself, but we are given enough information to realize that Zarathustra Spitama, not Sherlock Holmes, was the world's first unofficial consulting detective, hired to help his people against the predators. The ascetic is an unofficial personage as well, for we are told, "let him not wear any visible mark of his order, nor follow any visible rule of conduct." The regular forces, like the regular armies of the Aryans, are simply not effective enough to deal with all the problems themselves. Doyle paints a sad enough picture of the London police in the person of John Rance, the constable who let a murderer pretending to be drunk, slip through his hands. Holmes recognizes him as a "blundering fool," interested only in his gin and his retirement with the name Rance being a pun on "rancid." Holmes explains that he is an "irregular pioneer, who goes in front of the regular forces of the country," while thinking here also of Hawkeye, the quintessential irregular protecting "the settlements." The helpers of the detective, called "street Arabs," or "the Baker Street irregulars," appear in the very first story. In his capacity of "unofficial personage," Holmes realizes he has more freedom than those who, like Stanley Hopkins of Scotland Yard, "must disclose all, or he is a traitor to his service."

Evil does not fight alone either for Mainyu has his servants, among them Aeshma, the personification of invasion and rapine, the chief scourge of the Aryans, plus the malicious Daevas. The Daeva-Worshippers are the enemies of the holy man, and it is they "who live in sin." They are known as the men of Mainyu and destroying them is a benefit to the whole world.

There is also a presence that is difficult to place into any category, a sort of evil angel called "the Drug," described as "that most powerful, fiendish

Drug that Angra Mainyu created against the material world," with its ultimate goal being "to destroy the world of the good principle." This word Drug is used in all the translations of the ancient texts but the translators do not tell us much about its meaning. I believe the English word drug was substituted for an ancient Eastern word for "stupefies," or for the name of something that causes one to think incorrectly, or possibly not at all. The French word *"stupéfiant"* is used in exactly the way the English use "illegal drug." The Drug seems to be anything that dazes the mind, leading to wrong thinking. In our historic case the word may also apply to actual narcotics such as cocaine, heroin, or hemp, or to any of the drugs the people of the East have always used. Soma, a hallucinogen, has always been in common use, and still is, among the Zoroastrians. A variety of such narcotics are mentioned in the Holmes stories including bhang, cocaine, morphine, and opium, along with just about anything a person could drink or smoke. Doyle seems quite anxious to reveal Holmes' drug addiction, for a reference to it appears on the first page of *The Sign of the Four*. Johnson took opium for his many crippling sicknesses and depression. Holmes says his cocaine is "transcendently stimulating and clarifying to the mind." This is just what the Zoroastrians tell us of their soma. But by taking a drug such as cocaine Holmes is violating the Aryan laws for he is giving up the right to exercise full control over himself. For one such as him, the addiction to any narcotic would be described by the holy people as "self-pollution," and something to be feared, for it is unforgivable. Because of his heavy use of tobacco and cocaine Watson calls his friend a "self-poisoner," and it is Watson who convinces him to give up the drug. The detective's life is an act of opposition between "the drowsiness of the drug, and the fierce energy of his own keen nature." When the doctor saw Holmes at Cambridge holding his tiny syringe he at once "feared the worst," but the detective was able to reassure him that "It is not upon this occasion the instrument of evil." Drug is used as a verb and as a noun in the Persian texts, assuming the role as a personification of evil, especially the wickedness of deceit, their reasoning probably being that a mind subject to drugs is easily deceived. The Aryans realized that "hidden evil," was the real thing to be feared in life. "I assure you that the most winning woman I ever knew was hanged for poisoning three little children for their insurance money," Holmes warns us in an example of hidden agenda. In his Preface to *The Red Rover*, Cooper says, "It was also believed it might be useful to show that crime can be committed under a fair exterior." The word can also be described as "fraud and malice," since deceit is an element found in both, and is often their motive. Zarathustra is one who can detect malice for he knows "those things which are not to be known by beings such as us." Sir Arthur has a great deal to say about deceit, its consequences amounting to a major theme of his output. The Drug is also simply "a lie," and in the pronoun form often used in place of "lie." To the early Christians the devil was the Father of Lies.

Other prophets, equal to Zarathustra, and regarded as his sons, will appear in the future, when he himself is gone, to fight for the protection of his people. When the appointed time has come, a son of the holy one, still unborn, named Saoshyant (the Beneficent One) will appear, men will rise from the dead, and everlasting happiness will reign over the world. It is Holmes we are told who is "a benefactor of the race." Saoshyant will profit the whole world "by fighting the Drug, by withstanding the Drug." This being will be born at the end of time; will bring eternal light and life to mankind as his father brought them the law and the truth; will destroy Ahriman and his evil horde; and will also bring about the end of the world.

This war in nature involves powers that work for evil and powers that work for good; there are such beings that injure man, and such beings that benefit man, called angels and friends. Mythra is one of the creatures of Mazda; his name means "friend" and his title is "light of heaven," for he is the light that is friendly to mankind. Watson is meant to be the demigod Mythra with the name Watson derived from the name of the Scotch engineer James Watt, one of the leading developers of electricity, a true bringer of light to mankind. James Watt is mentioned by Carlyle at least twice as an example of a "Scotch Hero," in this case as an exponent of Scotch industry. When Sir Arthur became successful as a writer and could pick any agent he chooses, he went to A. P. Watt. "It may be that you are not yourself luminous," Holmes tells Watson, "but you are a conductor of light. Some people without possessing genius have a remarkable power of stimulating it." The followers of Mythra addressed each other as friend, and this word appears in many forms various times in the relationship between the two detectives, as in "The Adventure of the Dancing Men," when Holmes uses the expression, "friend Watson."

Land and cattle represented to the Aryans their most valuable property, and whatever threatened these, such as the wandering tribes who struggle with them for control of the territory, and whom they came to regard as devil-worshippers, were the worst of all things and to be dreaded. The cattle of the people, called the "Kine" in the translations, become personifications of the people themselves, and symbols of the struggle, and one of the people's occupations was "to keep the cows in health." Zarathustra, the individual entrusted with the redemption of the people and the kine, makes a pledge to the holy ones, "And I choose Piety, the bounteous and the good, mine may she be. And therefore I loudly deprecate all robbery and violence against the (sacred) Kine and all droughts to the wasting of the Mazdaynasnian villages." The Hindus still regard their cattle as being so important to their livelihood as to regard them as objects of worship and therefore sacred.

We are dealing with the history of mankind here, the efforts of the farmers to protect themselves and their livestock from the predatory cattle thieves with an actual farm being named at least once in the texts. The whole idea behind all this was the basic protection of the home, and therefore the farm, since almost everyone in the Aryan world was a farmer with the "Prosperous home-life," so sought after as to be an object of worship in some prayers and hymns. The Good God is one who through his Good Mind, "bestows upon them the peaceful amenities of home and quiet happiness (as against the fearful ravages which they suffer)" and add to this the love of the sacred fire of the hearth and you have the crux of the religion. Watson gives us a strong hint of this purpose when he describes the home of Mrs. Forrester. "It was soothing to catch even the passing glimpse of a tranquil English home in the midst of the wild, dark business which had absorbed us." This business is nothing less than murder. The word Aryan probably comes from the root "ar," meaning, "to plow," as in "arable," for the Aryans plowed their lands while the nomads did not. They prided themselves on their settled life and industry, but their prosperity made of them targets of the tribes always lurking on the horizon. Sherlock has an older brother named Mycroft. Croft is a word used throughout Britain; in England it usually means a cottage, but in Ireland it means both a cottage and often an entire farm, while in both countries the word was in the past commonly used for a small family farm. This gives to the phrase Mycroft Holmes the rough meaning of "my farm and home," since holme is an old form of "home." Holmes and homes amount to a perfect pun, for both words are pronounced the same. Another writer in the field tells us she sees the phrase "sure-locked homes" in the detective's name. This would mean the home secure from attack and shock, and is a good piece of thought. Mycroft is obligated to protect the kine also, but we shall see that he falls down on the job, unlike his younger brother. We know the Holmes family "were country squires, who appear to have led much the same life as is natural to their class." That would mean they were farmers and no doubt kept a small herd of cows.

When Holmes himself retires from the active business of investigations, he buys "a small farm" in Sussex, on which to raise bees. Sherlock Holmes is born on a farm and he dies on a farm. During his retirement he wants to give himself up "entirely to that soothing life of Nature for which I had so often yearned during the long years spent amid the gloom of London." In one story Holmes mentions off the top of his head that there was a fall in agricultural prices, and he believes this may have something to do with the case in hand, so obviously he has farming and farm prices on his mind, and knows what such information can mean. In another story, "The Adventure of the Three Garridebs," a constructor of agricultural machinery, who also has a brother who is a farmer and cattle herder, needs Holmes' help, and when John Openshaw in "The Five Orange Pips" is murdered by "cunning devils," we see just how upset Holmes became. We are told both Openshaw's father and his uncle had been killed by the same gang, so the problem has been handed down from generation to generation. Openshaw is a word that also eventually means farmer for it denotes a cleared or open piece of land such as a farm. Holmes is simply a farmer who has been forced to put aside his own work and take up arms to protect his own welfare and the welfare of his people, exactly as the *Zend-Avesta* tells us Zarathustra was called from his farm by the persecuted to aid them in their hour of peril. Holmes' powers of observation relate him to the Aryans for in the *Zend* we learn that "the most right ones," the angels of good possess, and can give to man, to use to fight evil, "the swiftness of the feet, the quick hearing of the ears, the health of the whole body, and the eye-sight of the male horse, that in the night, through the rain, the snow, or the sleet, from as far as nine districts, can perceive a horse's hair, mingled with the earth, and knows whether it is from the head or from the tail." This reads like a scene from "Silver Blaze," and what is the theme of that story if not "they're stealing our livestock"? Watson comes into it as well, for Mythra is "Lord of the Wide Pastures," a reference to his position as protector of cattle.

The predators are called "the thieving nomads" by the Aryans. One of the most reprehensible characters found in the Canon is Dr. Grimesby Roylott, the villain of "The Adventure of the Speckled Band," one so detestable as to attempt murder on his own stepchildren to gain their inheritance. In her presentation of the case, Helen Stoner, his intended victim, emphasizing the vicious nature of the man, tells us, "He had no friends at all save the wandering gypsies, and he would give these vagabonds leave to encamp upon the few acres of bramble-covered land which represent the family estate, and would accept in return the hospitality of their tents, wandering away with them sometimes for weeks on end." To let wanderers who might steal cattle and property live on your estate is as perverse as a man can get, and to actually live among them in their tents is to show yourself as being no better than them. Notice Roylott has let his farm go to ruin. In *The Hound of the Baskervilles*, a gypsy named Murphy (the Irish word for foreigner) is one of a band whose presence on the moor is used to establish its wild nature. Gypsies are mentioned in about a half-dozen other stories, always with undesirable connotations. In *The Sign of the Four*, contrasting the personality of Jonathan Small, a man guilty of theft and murder, to the upright family he came from, we are told of his people, "They were all steady, chapel-going folk, small farmers, well known and respected over the country side, while I was always a bit of a rover."

The English and the Scots were constantly making raids on each other's camps for the purpose of stealing cows, and cattle theft is a habitual theme in Scotch Literature. In "The Adventure of the Priory School," Holmes solves the case after realizing horses wearing "shoes which counterfeited the tracks of cows" made the hoof prints. These shoes were "supposed to have belonged to some of the marauding Barons of Holdernesse in the Middle Ages" and were used in cattle raids. Doyle finds another modern counterpart to the nomads in that breed of men called pirates who still trouble much of the world. In his pirate tales the desperate and vicious pirates are compared time and again to tigers and lions, predatory animals feared by all herdsmen. Doyle calls these predators "the enemies" of mankind, which is what the Aryans would have considered, and no doubt did call, somewhere in the texts, their own foes. To illustrate their true temperaments Sir Arthur called his pirates "rovers." Cooper wrote a novel named *The Red Rover* after the pirate of that name. Stevenson had much to say about these cutthroats with novels such as *Treasure Island* and *Kidnapped*, and even brought them into stories that take place on land, such as *The Master of Ballantrae: A Winter's Tale*. The worst of Doyle's pirates, the infamous Capt. Sharkey is even thought by his own crew to be "the devil himself." These stories are pure vengeance tales, the best example being "How Copley Banks Slew Captain Sharkey." Following the murder of Bank's wife and his two sons by Sharkey, who has sunk so many innocent ships he proudly tells us he cannot "bear their names in mind,"

Banks plays Sharkey's game by rigging himself out as a pirate to trap the fiend. Any trick was acceptable to the holy people. The ploy succeeds and Banks exercises justifiable vengeance upon the miscreant by blowing him to pieces with gunpowder, a borrowing from one of Cooper's stories. Banks has had to be a fiend to the fiend for the regular forces were helpless, not being able to catch the pirate.

Zarathustra, we are led to believe, is sometimes given gifts by those people or governments he helps. "Yea, he who will propitiate Zarathustra Spitama with gifts midst men, this man is fitted for the proclamation, and to him Ahura Mazda will give the (prospered) life." It would be wrong of the holy one not to accept gifts under such circumstances. Holmes does not hesitate to accept gifts from some people, such as the enormous fee charged the Duke of Holdernesse for the finding of his son, or the emerald tiepin given perhaps by the Queen, and he takes a thousand pounds from the King of Bohemia. He probably takes a fee whenever he can get it, telling Watson that when people come to see him, "I listen to their story, they listen to my comments, and then I pocket my fee." The early members of Scotland Yard were often given gifts of money by people they had helped and were also entitled to share in rewards for the recovery of stolen property or the apprehension of criminals. Johnson accepts gifts for his writings and Boswell tells us Joshua Reynolds, an artist whose portrait of one of Henry Baskerville's ancestors hangs in Baskerville Hall, was given a gold snuffbox by an empress.

Bear in mind I am condensing the thoughts of about twenty-five sacred books into a few pages, and must leave out much information that would serve to reinforce the theme I am now developing.

Chapter Six. The Great-Souled Man

No philosopher since Immanuel Kant has left such an undeniably original imprint on modern thought, from art to politics, as Friedrich Nietzsche, and for a mind like Doyle's, seeking out the latest philosophical considerations on which to base the characterizations of the world's first modern detective, nothing could have been more apt, for who could be more state-of-the-art than a living contemporary. Nietzsche presented philosophy to his own mind, and to the mind of the world, as an aspect of mythological reasoning, a true challenge, and suitably enough, much of his observations were based upon the imagination of the ancients.

Nietzsche himself approaches mythological proportions. Born in the Prussian province of Saxony in 1844, his brilliance became apparent quite early and he was offered the post of Professor of Classical Philology at Basel in 1869, at the age of twenty-five. He was also a bit of a professional soldier, or would have been, had not injuries and illness kept him from remaining in uniform for any lengthy period of time. Like Walt Whitman, he drove an army ambulance during a major war, perhaps an important development in Whitman's thought. During the Boer War, Doyle will become involved in the Medical Corps, which included the ambulances.

Ecce Homo is Nietzsche's attempt at an intellectual autobiography, and a very successful one at that. One early work to be dealt with in more detail later is *The Birth of Tragedy from the Spirit of Music* of 1872. His best-known work *Thus Spake Zarathustra*, finished in 1883, was preceded by *The Joyful Wisdom*, which is considered a prelude to *Zarathustra*. *Beyond Good and Evil*, regarded as both an explanation and an elucidation of *Zarathustra* and a preparatory work for *The Will to Power* was begun in the summer of 1885, and finished the following winter. The book included a chapter entitled "The Natural History of Morals" which puts us in mind of Holmes' assertion of his vast "knowledge of the history of crime." In 1887, the German wrote an entire book on morals entitled *On the Genealogy of Morals*, a historical/philosophical approach to such subjects as good and evil, good and bad, guilt, conscience, and so forth, including a history of law, especially early German law, reminiscent of Wendell Holmes' *The Common Law*, which I am sure Nietzsche read. Like the American, he was interested in harmonizing ancient moral codes with the needs of contemporary existence. Law is revenge systematized and made public, a reaction against those who would take their own vengeance against wrongs. "The creed of revenge has run through all my works and endeavors like the red thread of justice," he tells us. In this fascinating statement we cannot help reading the mind of Jefferson Hope with the red thread of justice, carrying its "creed of revenge," becoming a scarlet thread of reprisal in *A Study in Scarlet*. The purpose of the law is to dam and keep within bounds this effervescence of hysterical reactivity on the part of the injured party, the renouncing of "the vendetta" by people who "gave the law power over themselves!" Nietzsche assures us.

Philosophy was Nietzsche's paramount field of study but etymology and philology was his avocation, as it was for Sherlock and Sir Arthur. I don't know how many languages Sherlock spoke, although we see him employing Latin and German in *A Study in Scarlet*. At one time, while on holiday "He had received a consignment of books upon philology and was settling down" with them when they were interrupted by their next case. I wonder if Nietzsche's "We Philologists," a small but important work that found light in Germany in 1875, was among them. Holmes underlines his role as thinker when he delves into the study of etymology and philology, for the study of language in great depth is but one remove from the actuality of pure thought itself.

The study of etymology, the origin of language, was a special favorite of Diderot. Holmes' probing into the ancient languages could be a search for evidence that all languages sprang from one common root, a continuation of a quest that occupied Diderot for years. It was his plan to determine "experimentally" the natural history of language, believing words do not merely convey ideas; they have intangible picturesque and sonorous effects and have the power of creating specific physiological reactions that go beyond the mere sum of rational and usual content. This is their "emblematic value," involving what we would call a process of association with the total effect of a word far surpassing its literal meaning. Through the power of words language is enabled to overcome the limits of its analytical function. Because of this, different things are portrayed at the same time by the reader, a psychological phenomenon, involving the mechanism of man's reaction to the world around him and his mode of thought. A word is far more than the sum of its parts is what Diderot is saying, and adds something Doyle must have found motivating, for he claims that great writing is often obscure. We are dealing here with an early effort at developing a theory of association, and can draw a line from it straight to the French Symbolists, and from them to the convoluted mind of Arthur Conan Doyle.

Carlyle also utilized etymology in his work with some early-published pieces being translations from the German, such as Johann Wolfgang von Goethe's *Wilhelm Meister's Wanderings* as well as explanations of German culture in his *Life of Schiller*. It may well have been this aspect of the Scot that first attracted the attention of Nietzsche. Carlyle's *Heroes* so influenced

Nietzsche as to become the basis of much of his writings, including his theory of the superman. The German philosopher affirms that the rearing of superior people should be the main function of the state. "How can one praise and glorify a nation as a whole? — Even among the Greeks, it was the *individuals* that counted," adding, "The Greeks are interesting and extremely important because they reared such a vast number of great individuals." They did this "not by any means owing to the goodness of the people, but because of the struggles of their evil instincts." In his battle against evil the noble man finds his greatness. Nietzsche probably also has in mind Aristotle's "great-souled man," with the intelligence to see what others cannot, and "speaks loudly," of his knowledge. Over the years Nietzsche will alter his thoughts on this subject reflecting a form of evolution in his thoughts, but it still remains, in spite of much else he wrote of equal importance, his signature contribution to philosophy. Complicated and misunderstood by many, often deliberately, it is hardly the breed of concept that sits easily on all minds, and like Diderot and Whitman, he did not hesitate to contradict himself when he saw fit. They are quite right in doing so I think, for real knowledge is full of contradiction.

As far as Nietzsche is concerned, moral distinctions and simple human values are mere distractions, never to be considered when determining who the superman is, for his actions are those of one who is a law unto himself; he is beyond good and evil. A transvaluation of all values is understood to be necessary since Christianity and the society it advances is the product of the resentment of the botched, weak, and sickly. All that is beautiful, strong, proud, and powerful, all qualities resulting from strength, all forces that tend to promote or elevate life, have been seriously undermined. A new table of values, the values of "the strong, mighty, and magnificent man," must be brought into existence. He then goes on to pick a few possible examples of that handful of historical individuals he considers to be exemplifiers of his ideal.

Nietzsche's sister tells us he regarded the teachings of Jesus as "our noblest ideal," as did Carlyle. "And now if worship even of a star had some meaning in it, how much more might that of a Hero! Worship of a Hero is transcendent admiration of a Great Man. I say great men are still admirable; I say there is, at bottom, nothing else admirable! No nobler feeling than this of admiration for one higher than himself dwells in the breast of man. It is to this hour, and at all hours, the vivifying influence in man's life. Religion I find stand upon it; not Paganism only, but far higher and truer religions, — all religion hitherto known. Hero-worship, heartfelt prostrate admiration, submission, burning, boundless, for a noblest godlike Form of Man, — is not that the germ of Christianity itself? The greatest of all Heroes is One — whom we do not name here! Let sacred silence meditate that sacred matter; you will find it the ultimate perfection of a principle extant throughout man's whole history on earth," Carlyle assures us. Nietzsche, as far as I know, did not write anything about Jesus. Both thinkers however, had much to say about Napoleon, as did Arthur Doyle. A collection of non-Holmes stories, those featuring the adventures of Brigadier Gerard, deal indirectly with Napoleon, under whom Gerard served. Mention is made of Napoleon in the Canon as well.

The highest praise Nietzsche can pay to any man is to compare him to the French Emperor; the closer the comparison, the more perfect you became. Carlyle had quite a low opinion of Napoleon, while admitting his great feeling for reality. Napoleon, the Scot claims, was infamous for his lies and falsehoods, especially pertaining to his military achievements, and despite his rationale for these falsehoods, no man has the right to tell such lies. For Carlyle, sincerity is absolutely necessary for the true hero and one outstanding aspect of Holmes is his obvious sincerity. "The Great Man's sincerity is of the kind he cannot speak of, is not conscious of," Carlyle says, adding, "his sincerity does not depend on himself; he cannot help being sincere!" Here's something very interesting. Carlyle goes on to say, in the great man's sincerity he would just as soon be a farmer, like Cromwell, or George Washington, or as "A simple Diocletian prefers planting of cabbages." At the conclusion of his great study Boswell tells us Johnson had "inflexible integrity," and "cannot be charged with any offence, indicating badness of *heart*, any thing dishonest, base, or malignant."

Richard Wagner, one of Germany's paramount men of music is included among the supermen for his music, intensity, and passionate life, with Nietzsche claiming he could not have survived his own youth without Wagner's music. The two men became good friends with the philosopher insisting his friend produced a sort of super-music suitable for the superman. At one point we learn he so identifies with the composer that if you wish when reading his essay "Richard Wagner in Bayreuth," "you need not hesitate to substitute my name or that of 'Zarathustra' whenever the text gives the name of 'Wagner.'" Nietzsche adds that the significant traits of his own nature all belong to the composer, that both of them possess "a Will to Power such as no man has yet possessed, reckless spiritual courage, an unlimited capacity to learn without any corresponding diminution of capacity for action." By will to power, I think he meant, in this case, to achieve greatness in art, but the phrase has other meanings.

Holmes is fond of music, German music in particular, and in "The Adventure of the Red Circle" we learn Wagner is his favorite composer. The detective has always displayed an eloquent understanding, and an almost mystical need for music, like some other great artists. He and Watson would take a break from their labors and enjoy performances by such as Wilma Norman-Neruda, a famous violinist who afterwards became Lady Hallé. They also enjoyed the Spanish violinist Pablo Sarasate, who possibly played some of his own pieces at St. James Hall when they went to see him. As they are going out the door to hear Sarasate, Holmes says, "I observe that there is a good deal of German music on the programme, which is rather more to my taste than Italian or French. It is introspective, and I want to introspect." Holmes' own playing aids him in thinking, he tells us a number of times. Just as the German philosopher had before him the image of Wagner as an example of greatness, Sherlock had Nicolò Paganini, the celebrated Italian violinist generally considered the greatest master of technique who ever lived. He told Watson "anecdote after anecdote of that extraordinary man." Holmes' monograph on the polyphonic motets of Lassus is said by experts to be the last word on the subject. A good deal of the ideas for all this may have come about from the fact that an accomplished violinist in Doyle's day was an Alfred Sherlock, who specialized in German music.

This theme of the superman was not handled in fiction solely by Doyle, for George Bernard Shaw worked out the motif in play form in *Man and Superman*, which premiered at the Royal Court Theatre, London, on May 21, 1905. Ironically enough, Shaw, in his lengthy dedication mentions both Doyle and Napoleon as contributors to the development of the characters found in the comedy. Shaw's work is based so squarely upon Nietzsche there is even a convenient "Revolutionist's Handbook" appended to it that could have been penned by the philosopher himself. Elsewhere Shaw admits he stole the character of the brigand/poetaster from Doyle, a reference to Brigadier Gerard. In the play, Holmes is mentioned by name and reputation, with his uncanny detection abilities, in keeping with Shaw's disruptive style, allocated to a brilliant young lady. I wonder if GBS drew conclusions based on similarities between Holmes and Nietzsche, and it would be interesting to learn his thoughts on Doyle's work in general. Shaw felt the new superman would be godlike, and we shall see he comes quite close to Doyle's intentions.

And yet none of these individuals whom Nietzsche examples seem to be worthy of being called the superman, for he tells us, "Never yet hath there been a Superman." The superman is yet to come but some few have approached close to this goal, for reasons that have no dependency upon the existing moral code of lesser beings.

Nietzsche's most remarkable accomplishment is unquestionably *Thus Spake Zarathustra* finished a year prior to *A Study in Scarlet*, and a work he regarded as a new *Zend-Avesta*. The philosopher's mind found such nourishment in the legend of the ancient Persian that the seer became his unabashed alter ego, much as the personality of Holmes merged with the mind of Arthur Doyle. One reason Zarathustra was picked to convey his own thoughts of good and evil, the German tells us, was because he "was the first to see in the struggle between good and evil the essential wheel in the working of things." It was in his teachings that we first "meet with truthfulness upheld as the highest virtue." The philosopher's sister Elizabeth informs us he considered himself a new Zarathustra, a prophet whose thoughts would rule for a thousand years. Now in spite of this it must be understood the ancient Persian is not to be regarded as a superman, but rather as one who had unwittingly led mankind astray by being merely a successful man, "a higher man." The old Zarathustra had erred in his defense of the weak, and Nietzsche's new personification is an attempt at soliciting the ancient warrior's help in making restitution for his error. This distinction plays an important part in the Holmes theme. "One day Zarathustra severely determines his life-task — and it is also mine. Let no one misunderstand its meaning. It is a yea-saying to the point of justifying, to the point of redeeming all past things." The philosopher seems to look upon the new poet/warrior of his book as the first example of the superman, for he lives by pure enlightened self-interest and is called "The soul most self-loving," who will act for "the tremendous purification and consecration of mankind."

The ancient Persians divided existence into periods of time called a generation, or periods of one thousand years. Both the ancient Zarathustra and Nietzsche's newer model, believed another being would come after him and be as great as him. These beings, called "a son," will appear in a time that is distant. Nietzsche echoes the *Zend* when he declares this event is all part of the "Eternal Recurrence," the Persian belief that everything comes in cycles.

In *Beyond Good and Evil* he modifies his thoughts somewhat, referring more to what he calls "the philosopher of the future," than to the superman or even the higher man. Watson claims Holmes was "a man whose knowledge was not that of other mortals." Aside from the reference in this to the status of demigod, it amounts to a description of Nietzsche's true philosopher to come.

Nietzsche seems to be encompassing Holmes as he outlines his ideas of the new philosopher, "He shall be the greatest who can be the most solitary, the most concealed, the most divergent, the man beyond good and evil, the master of his virtues, and of super-abundance of will; precisely this shall be called *greatness*: as diversified as can be entire, as ample as can be full." His true philosopher never marries, a regarding of the man in the light of the religious ascetic. The philosophers of the future "will be men of experiments," and each will be "one of the scientific workers of philosophy," and among other things, "critic, historian, riddle-reader, moralist, seer, and free-spirit." In *Human, All-Too-Human: A Book for Free Spirits* Nietzsche offers a definition of this last term, namely "the thinking man, the intellectual aristocrat, the philosopher and ruler." He is not the superman but rather a bridge, used to reach the concept of superman, although Doyle makes no distinction between the two. The reference to critics is a thought borrowed from Carlyle's acidic criticism of his society and also an apt designator of Holmes' and Doyle's analytical, often censorious audit of their own communities. At one point the German actually calls this new breed of men investigators, whose function it was "to make whatever has happened and been esteemed hitherto, conspicuous, conceivable, intelligible, and manageable, to shorten everything long, even "time" itself, and to *subjugate* the entire past: an immense and wonderful task, in the carrying out of which all refined pride, all tenacious will, can surely find satisfaction." The historian with the ability "to subjugate the entire past," would have knowledge of, and the power to write about this past in such books as a history of law or crime, it is implied. Nietzsche offers definitions of people like Watson, Lestrade, and Gregson, and all others who cannot reach the heights of Sherlock Holmes. Real philosophy, real investigation, is not for everyone. It is not for people who have simply "nimble, everyday intellects, or clumsy, honest mechanics and empiricists," even though they may be "close to such problems." Such are often merely "gregarious," meaning "to be fond of the company of others, or wishing to be one of the herd," and Tobias Gregson's last name becomes a pun on the word. True virtue, as opposed to the conventional sort, is not for all, but should remain the characteristic of an aristocratic minority who were born and bred for it.

In speaking of the greatness of the individual the philosopher says, "Terrible is aloneness with the judge and avenger of one's own law," adding that this judge and this avenger of the law is close to the superman. The avenger of the law in particular is as alone as "a star projected into desert space." I could go on with this but it would only prove that Nietzsche repeats himself, as do all philosophers, and that his versions of these personas are of a very complex nature.

Facets of the German philosopher's life were used as building blocks for the characterization of Holmes. Nietzsche had a drug problem in the form of excessive use of chloral hydrate, first used to control insomnia, an affliction he shared with the Great Detective. The drug quickly became habit forming in spite of repeated efforts to rid him of it and is considered one of the factors in his eventual nervous breakdown.

Nietzsche believed there is a type of man in society so ignorant and lawless they can understand only brute force, and such men, when they injure society, should be beat, not with a whip, which should only be used on women, but with a stick or club. Holmes usually takes a club rather than a gun on his excursions against darkness, for Watson tells us his loaded riding crop was his favorite weapon and it is mentioned in at least three cases. In another case, while posing as a seaman, he carried a thick oaken cudgel. One of Mazda's demigods, Sraosha, who never sleeps, carries a club in his war with evil. When Johnson felt threatened he carried what Boswell describes as an oak stick, and adds that he carried it often, for his London was no place for the faint hearted. There was one special occasion when the poet/translator James Macpherson, angered at Johnson's refusal to acknowledge his *The Works of Ossian, the Son of Fingal*, as a genuine translation from the Old Scot. vowed physical violence upon him. Boswell tells us, "He feared death, but he feared nothing else, not even what might occasion death." Boswell believed that Johnson feared the "unknown state of being" that follows death.

Upon his retirement, as I mentioned, Holmes started an apiary, a bee farm "where his time is divided between philosophy and agriculture." This is a bow to the German who would have us accept his truths as a "form of honey" offered to the world. "It is the *honey* in my veins that maketh my blood thicker, and also my soul stiller." He uses such metaphors a number of times. His alter ego as well will accomplish this when "moons and years" have passed over Zarathustra's soul, and "his hair, however, became white." Zarathustra will become a honey farmer. Nietzsche may have had a theory, or even knowledge that the ancient Persian was in fact a beekeeper. Nietzsche may even have regarded mankind to be like unto a race of bees and he their keeper.

Doyle did not agree with everything Nietzsche said, he did admire it though. It's impossible not to. Much of what the philosopher wrote would be in opposition to Doyle's way of thinking, for instance, his contempt for the common man, and his loathing for democracy, which he called "the folly of the 'greatest number,'" being two examples. Holmes, and others with noble intentions in the adventures, are either in fact or practice, aristocrats, but both Holmes and his creator believed in democracy in theory. True enough, Doyle did not believe in giving women the vote, but Nietzsche, who despised anything — such as the vote — that defeminized women, anything that made them, in his estimation, less of a woman, had formed his attitude towards this question. Nietzsche believed in mingling with people but only to learn from them, not to love them, which he found impossible. Doyle enjoyed mixing with all sorts and never despised them. Holmes used people to learn from, but after all that was his life's work; it was for their own good.

While enjoying a recuperative vacation on the Cornish coast, the two investigators are sought out by Mortimer Tregennis and the village vicar to investigate what will become, in Holmes' words, the "strangest case I have handled" and known to the world as "The Adventure of the Devil's Foot." The preceding evening, Mortimer had been playing cards with his sister Brenda and brothers George and Owen at the family cottage, leaving around ten to return to his home. The following morning Mrs. Porter discovered the sister dead and the two brothers raving mad, with no explanation for the event. A cousin, Dr. Leon Sterndale, a lion hunter and explorer, upon learning of the tragedy, hurries from Plymouth, where he had been set to return to Africa.

That night Mortimer dies of symptoms akin to those affecting the rest of the family. After examining the room in which the event occurred, Holmes decides to make a few tests. "One experiment served to show me the line of his investigation," Watson explains, as the detective lights an oil lamp similar to the one Tregennis had in his room when he died. The experiment, he tells us, is one he is not likely ever to forget, as they begin an ordeal that almost costs them their lives. Speculating that a substance that upon combustion released a toxic gas into the atmosphere caused all the injuries, Holmes places some residue powder he found in Mortimer's room above a lit lamp and awaits any developments. A foul odor almost immediately fills the closed room. "At the very first whiff of it," Watson says, "my brain and my imagination were beyond all control." All sorts of horrors enter their minds, and Holmes passes out while the half dead Watson, with great effort, drags both out of the room to safety.

"In their passion for knowledge, will they have to go further in daring and painful attempts than the sensitive and pampered taste of a democratic century can approve of?" Nietzsche asks of the new philosophers. For him, there was only one answer. One daring man of experiments was Dr. William Morton, a nineteenth-century American dentist of Boston who became interested in tests centered upon the use of ether to produce insensibility in a patient. Although aware irreversible dangers such as madness or death could be suffered by one inhaling too much ether, Morton sealed himself in a room and filled the atmosphere with ether gas. He fell unconscious but survived intact. In September of 1846, Dr. Morton successfully employed ether to deaden a patient's nerves while pulling a tooth, and news of the experiment spread quickly. Dr. Oliver Holmes had undertaken early trials of the application of ether, using himself as a subject and published the records of the tests. He wrote to Morton with the suggestion of using the words "anesthesia" and "anesthetic" to describe the employment of the gas, and the terms were universally adopted. Doyle learned of these experiments in medical school and used ether on his own patients as well.

Nietzsche had a tremendous appreciation of science, considering it second only to art, which he regarded as the most significant aspect of life. Holmes has reenacted Dr. Morton's trial on himself, just as he had recreated Dr. Bell's laboratory undertaking leading to the invention of the telephone. The new philosophers "will love to make use of experiments in a new, and perhaps wider and more dangerous sense," so our two investigators have saturated their brains with a novel and dangerous gas, a truly daring thing to do.

Holmes' research convinces him that although Mortimer was the perpetrator of the first crime, he was the victim of the last. Mortimer is described as physically something of a dwarf, for he "was a thin, dark, spectacled man, with a stoop which gave the impression of actual, physical deformity," while in his personality he was "strangely reticent, a sad-faced, introspective man, sitting with averted eyes, brooding apparently upon his own affairs." A sick, weak, cripple who spends his time nursing resentment and hate for his fellow man, his spite reaching out even to his own family. He has executed his sister and driven his brothers mad — but who, in turn, killed this malignant one remains a mystery.

Holmes goes on to prove it was Leon Sterndale who killed Mortimer for his having killed his secret love Brenda. Sterndale was aware of Mortimer's guilt for it was his own botany specimen, the poisonous devil's foot plant of West Africa, that Mortimer stole and used in such a manner. Like Jefferson Hope, Sterndale has lived in parts of the world, in this case Africa, where men must make their own law, admitting he has "spent much of my life outside the law, and that I have come at last to be a law to myself." Sterndale killed Mortimer, making him pay for his treachery with his body, after informing Mortimer that he "had come both as judge and executioner." This avenger of the law heated a powder extracted from the deadly plant, forced Tregennis to inhale its fumes, and watched as he died a terror ridden death, but no pity was shown, for "my heart was flint." From Nietzsche we learn that the true critics and investigators must have "a certain considerate cruelty" in their dealings with the world "even when the heart bleeds." He emphasized these philosophers "will be *sterner* (and perhaps not always towards themselves only) than humane people may desire." The sterner ones will have a genuine disgust for all that is "idealistic, feminine, and hermaphroditic." Sterndale (a sterner one) is surely counted among the new, bold investigators, for his search in the name of justice could cost him everything, even his life. Fearing no jury would believe such a far-fetched yet true account of Mortimer Tregennis' guilt, the lion hunter showed great courage and resolve in his decision to kill the man himself. Holmes does not turn him over to the police and Watson seconds the decision.

Sterndale's explanation of what thoughts prompted his actions is a textbook example of the use of presentment in law as it is outlined in *The Common Law*. In a society such as tribal Africa, or even rural England of the time, where there is confusion on the part of legislation in the governing of many unusual situations, Sherlock's view of jurisdiction is as valid as any other, Doyle is emphasizing. His decision to let Sterndale go free is nothing less than a legal judgment not to indict, thereby negating the need for the case to go before a court.

Sterndale is described as something of a lion himself with his "huge body, the craggy and deeply seamed face," featuring "fierce eyes" and "grizzled hair." The God of the *Old Testament*, when faced with a false prophet who refused to obey him, sent out a lion to tear him to pieces. Leon is the Gaelic word for "lion," so once again all types of justice have been administered.

We catch a glimpse here of Holmes cultivating his avocation etymology, studying the ancient Chaldean language as part of the process of recuperation and our author as well decides to amuse himself with words and their history. We saw what he did with the first part of Sterndale. The last half, "dale," is a corruption of "dyal," which is Cornish (scene of the action) for "revenge," giving us "stern revenge." Morton and Mortimer are essentially the same name since both are based on "mort," meaning a swamp or moor. The word also means "death," and in the obsolete form was a note sounded on a hunting horn to announce the killing of the quarry. The Tregennises call their home Tredannick Wartha in the English fashion of giving rural residences names since they have no numbers. "Tredan" is Old English for "to walk upon, as in to tread," and also used in the rare form to mean a footprint. The word "nick" is old slang for the Devil, as in "Old Nick." "Wartha" is from the Middle English "warte" meaning "a raised place" and we get the word wart from it. A raised grave is on Doyle's mind for this devil of a place.

Watson, acting as spokesman for his creator, gives his opinion of the Harley Street specialists when he states that "Dr. Moore Agar, of Harley Street, whose dramatic introduction to Holmes I may some day recount," was responsible for ordering the great investigator to put aside his work and go on holiday. Agar, usually written in the form agar agar, but also in the singular form, is a product made from seaweed and is employed as a laxative. Moore (more) Agar means "more laxative," or something very like it.

The poison used has a number of relatives in real life. Doyle was probably familiar with an herb they call in France *Le Thé du Diable* (the Devil's Tea). This hallucinogenic can kill if taken improperly and was responsible for two deaths in France in 1992, following which it was taken off the market. There is a drug called *Radix Pedis Diaboli* or Devil's Foot Root, a poison from West Africa. The original idea for this poisoning of a suspect in "The Devil's Foot," as well as the death by poison pill of a suspected criminal in *A Study in Scarlet*, can be traced to the practice in West Africa of a drink being made of various ingredients, some of which are lethal, and one of which is probably the one we are discussing, that is often forced upon an indicted defendant by the tribal witch doctors. If he drinks the potion, as he must, and lives, he is considered innocent and set free. If he dies he is regarded as having been guilty and no harm was done anyway. I have seen a film of a West African being given this drink as a test of his guilt or innocence, and he dies right in front of the camera in distress and pain. This sort of thing is practiced in various parts of the world, but is very common in West Africa, where Sterndale and Doyle both visited.

Sounding like it will be Holmes' last case, "The Adventure of the Dying Detective" is anything but. A summons by Mrs. Hudson fetches Watson to the bedside of his friend, wasting away of a rare oriental disease. Raving like one insane, Holmes refuses to let the doctor treat his illness, instead insisting Watson, following strict instructions, seek out a Mr. Culverton Smith, a planter of Sumatra who has acquaintance with the malady from previous experience on his plantation, charging him to come to Holmes' assistance. Holmes admits suspecting Smith of foul play in regard to the planter's nephew who died horribly of the same ailment. Watson proceeds to Smith's house, but not before running into Inspector Morton, a Scotland Yard man who for some reason seems quite amused by news of the detective's terminal illness. When he is refused admission the intrepid doctor barges in on Smith and delivers his request for aid. The ex-planter is obviously acquainted with the detective and appears morbidly interested upon learning of the dire straits of his health. Culverton Smith owes more to Nietzsche for his mental and physical makeup than he does to his parents. Upon first seeing the man Watson is amazed at his "great yellow face, coarse-grained and greasy, with heavy, double-chin," this enormous skull set on a body "small and frail, twisted in the shoulders and back like one who has suffered from rickets in his childhood." This character epitomizes the evil of deceit, at one point being called by Holmes a monster. He is a malignant dwarf twisted and diseased with evil intentions, oozing hate and resentfully nursing secret thoughts of vengeance all hidden behind his "malicious and abominable smile." Nietzsche says of those who are crooked and misshapen, "there is no smith in the world that could hammer you straight and right for me." That's where we get the name Smith, while in English a Culverton means a medieval musket or cannon, coming to us from the Latin through the French and eventually means "an adder, or serpent." Watson returns to Baker Street with expectations Smith will soon follow.

Upon hearing Smith's approach the detective insists Watson conceal his presence in a hiding place and "listen with all your ears," a borrowing from Cooper who tells us the Indians used the expression "listen with both your ears." The conversation that follows, overheard by Watson, gives strong evidence the planter did indeed poison his nephew, and Holmes as well, by mailing both men a small box equipped with a spring loaded finger piercing needle carrying the dreaded disease. In rushes Morton to arrest Smith with the doctor having overheard enough to act as witness in the case. The whole charade has been one elaborate experiment on the part of Holmes and Morton. Johnson's religious practices, as well as the attitude of the Hindu ascetic compliment Holmes' own nature for at the end of this three day fast to make himself appear wane and sick he tells us, "my habits are irregular, and such a feat means less to me than to most men," as he ends his fast with a glass of claret and a few biscuits.

When Watson first encounters his friend, he is overwhelmed by Holmes' sense of exhaustion, finding him feeble and wasted. The detective asks a scientific question, "I am somewhat exhausted; I wonder how a battery feels when it pours electricity into a nonconductor?" Being a thinking machine is not enough of a challenge for this great investigator, he would metamorphose into a piece of electrical equipment if he could, to satisfy his sense of wonder.

At one point Watson moves closer to the ailing man to diagnose his symptoms but what follows for almost two pages is Holmes' successful attempt at keeping his friend from getting close to him. When we realize the entire story is only sixteen pages this seemingly irrational conflict between the two men is all together out of proportion to the narrative's overall length. There must be a good reason for it and the artist's intentions can be found in *Thus Spake Zarathustra*, under the chapter "The Pitiful," which opens with the words, "MY FRIENDS, there hath arisen a satire on your friend: 'Behold Zarathustra!'" And behold him we do, for the first two pages of the narrative are lengthy descriptions by Mrs. Hudson and Watson regarding the condition of Holmes, now reduced in health by the infection, making of him a satire of his vigorous, strong, former self. To satire is to attack, and the detective has indeed been attacked by a vicious enemy using an equally vicious weapon.

Nietzsche says the merciful ones, by which he means those who act out of pity for others, he cannot help holding in contempt for their "bliss is in their pity." "If I must be pitiful, I dislike to be called so; and if I be so, it is preferably at a distance." Holmes tells Watson that if he comes any closer he will order him out of the house. When asked why, he answers, "Because it is my desire."

Much of mankind's problems are the fault of "sinners and bad consciences," that "one should entirely do away with," to achieve health, Nietzsche claims. When the sinner that is Smith is gotten rid of by being exposed, Holmes' health miraculously returns. "Like a boil is the evil deed: it itcheth and irritateth and breaketh forth — it speaketh honourably." It is easy to act one way and speak another Nietzsche reminds us, exactly what Smith has performed in this tale of an undetected, festering, evil deed. "'Behold, I am disease,' saith the evil deed: that is its honourableness. But like infection is the petty thought: it creepeth and hideth, and wanteth to be nowhere — until the whole body is decayed and withered by the petty infection." Smith and Tregennis have murdered members of their own family for money, something Nietzsche would unquestionably have regarded as infection.

"And if a friend doeth thee wrong, then say: 'I forgive thee what thou hast done unto me.'" It is understood Watson and Mrs. Hudson will forgive Holmes his deception on them. "Thus speaketh all great love: it surpasseth even forgiveness and pity."

Doyle recycled the name Morton in this drama to remind himself of the experimental nature of the case and the word also contains the root word "mort," meaning death, so it is a double pun for Holmes has approached death in both tales.

In Oscar Wilde's short story "Lord Arthur Savile's Crime," a young aristocrat plots to kill an aging relative in answer to a palm-reader's prophecy, believing such a foretelling must come true. In his initial effort Lord Arthur strives to murder his aunt with a poison capsule enclosed in a small box of candy. He fails, and in his second attempt delivers to an uncle a clock attached to an explosive device. The miniature bomb fails to ignite, just as Smith's little trick on Holmes came to naught. During the course of the plot Lord Arthur, needing to visit an anarchist incognito, calls himself Robert Smith.

On the surface "A Scandal in Bohemia" seems simple enough and involves neither murder nor theft, nor any other crime, although one is suspected. A nobleman, the next hereditary King of Bohemia, calls at Baker Street requesting Holmes' talents in getting back a compromising photo of him with the New Jersey born opera contralto Irene Adler. The Duke is to be married to a Scandinavian princess whose family would call off the match should the photograph be made public, thus Holmes, like the ancient Zarathustra, is being called upon to aid the nobility. Adopting the disguise of a groom, he visits Adler's London villa to scout the place, only to arrive in time to see the singer and a young man suddenly rush out of the house, hail a hansom, and make for a church, where Holmes unintentionally becomes the legal witness to their wedding. Returning to Irene's home the next day, Holmes succeeds in gaining entry; he discovers the photo is hidden in a space in the wall of the living room, but he cannot retrieve it at this time. Leaving, he hopes to return the next morning and with a hearty "Ah Ha!" reach into the hiding place and yank out the photo. The following morning however reveals that Irene and her new husband have fled, a letter and portrait photo of Irene being all that remains. The note states that she does not plan to blackmail the Duke and the affair, at least for him, is considered closed.

The ultimate plot relies heavily upon Samuel Johnson's play *Irene, A Tragedy*, produced by his friend Garrick. As far as I know it was Johnson's only effort for the stage and it was not well received. The story itself was the subject of a novel by Bandello published in 1554. George Peele also wrote a play based on this novel but the work has been lost. Johnson may have borrowed from Peele's drama as well as from Richard Knolles' *The Generall Historie of the Turks*. Knolles tells how Mahomet the Second of Turkey was so infatuated with his Greek slave Irene he neglects his duties as ruler. Irene is "of such incomparable beautie and rare perfection, both of body and mind, as if nature had in her to the admiration of the world, laboured to have showne her greatest skill." The ministers and soldiers grow rebellious, complaining that the Sultan can no longer rule his passions. Mahomet calls together his detractors and in their presence cuts Irene's head off to display to them what kind of a ruler he actually is. It's obvious Knolles disapproves of the tyrant, just as Holmes keeps his distance from the nobleman of Bohemia. Gilbert Swinhoe penned a work called *The Tragedy of the Unhappy Fair Irene* in 1658, in which Irene acquires a husband to whom she is devoted, and the interest turns on whether or not she will be able to keep Mahomet off by delays and complaisance, until her husband can rescue her. This woman of nobility, loyalty, and passion, in spite of her efforts, also ends up getting her head cut off. There was also an anonymous play of 1664, *Irena, a Tragedy*, in which she is being held captive by Mahomet but has a Greek lover who hopes to rescue her and flee on a vessel to a foreign land. Irena has a very strong personality in this work and even the Sultan, this time the picture of politeness and magnanimity, stands in awe of her.

How much of all this Johnson or Doyle were familiar with we have no way of knowing, but they were obviously knowledgeable of some of it. The theme of Johnson's piece, as in all the other versions, is Love vs. Honor. These noblemen are torn between the interests of the state and the interest of the heart, and it is the interests of the state, and therefore their own self-interest, that triumphs.

In Johnson's *Irene* we have the entire plot and development of "A Scandal in Bohemia." Transference of affection takes place, for Mahomet was at first in love with another before meeting the slave Irene, while in Doyle's drama the Bohemian nobleman has found a new love in the aristocrat he has become engaged to. Mahomet turns against Irene, whom he had previously loved, out of a belief she intends treachery against him, suspecting her to be part of an assassination plot. Disguise comes into Johnson's production, for characters wear masks to hide identities, as the Duke wore a mask to fool Holmes. The letters and messages sent back and forth in Doyle's piece are borrowed from all these plays in which messages are exchanged and read aloud to advance the plot. Johnson's work carries a religious interest for the question of Irene giving up her Christian faith to please the Sultan emerges, and different religions also play a part in "A Scandal in Bohemia," as we shall see. At least one critic tells us the theme of Johnson's labor is the struggle between glory and religion.

One character that is completely Johnson's own is Aspasia, a female friend of Irene's and like her a slave. She, more than Irene seems to serve as model for Adler, for she comes close to being, at least for Johnson, a perfect woman. Aspasia is remarkably beautiful and attractive to all types of men, and possesses a deep Christian piety that disallows her from altering her religious convictions at any price, even if she were to be made queen. We are told Aspasia has acquired a masculine intellect, supported by masculine learning that puts us in mind of Irene Adler's tomboyish trick of dressing up as a man. In a snub at nobility and wealth that finds echo in Doyle's theme, Aspasia says she wants neither riches nor titles, but rather, "Love be my wealth, and my distinction virtue."

Demetrius, a Greek nobleman versed in philosophy and literature, is her male counterpart, as Adler is a sort of female Holmes, with each pair admiring the other's spiritual and intellectual values. Johnson's wife Elizabeth died young, as did Irene Adler, and it is understood he is trying to read the profile of her and himself into these two noble people. Aspasia became for Johnson a sort of ideal, with qualities he sought for in women all his life: intellect, common sense, literary taste, and a certain masculine attitude towards life.

"A Scandal in Bohemia" is a counterpoint to Poe's "The Purloined Letter" and Collins' "A Stolen Letter," each of which traces the efforts of a detective to retrieve a blackmail document. The theme of all three pieces is analogous, with the exception that in Doyle's search for the modern he uses a photograph as the boodle, making his production probably the first piece of fiction to employ a "blackmail photo." At least one incident is borrowed from that great well of creativity, *The Moonstone* by Collins. When Holmes needs to gain unwelcomed access to the Adler villa he arranges to create a disturbance in the form of a street brawl following which he will pretend to be injured, hoping to be taken into the house out of sympathy. In *The Moonstone* Mr. Septimus Luker tells a journalist he fears burglary by a gang of Hindus. "It might be their object to collect a crowd, and create a disturbance in the street, and, in the confusion thus caused, to obtain access to the house."

Again we broach the subject of blackmail and where blackmail is concerned Holmes, as we know, never balks at playing deceitful tricks or to commit theft if necessary. We saw him play a trick on Milverton's housemaid hoping to obtain information, adding he could not like the woman anyway, for she was ignorant. The model for this thought is found in Boswell when he chronicles Johnson's disgust with the maid of a mutual friend because the girl was thickheaded. The biographer says it was the first time he heard a woman referred to as a blockhead.

We are also dealing here with the making and breaking of marriage contracts, actually one of the most written about facets of law in the world. Three out of the first five Holmes narratives: *A Study in Scarlet*, "A Scandal in Bohemia," and "A Case of Identity," pivot on the marriage contract, referring us back to *The Common Law*, which discusses numerous cases involved in the breaking of such a bond. Marriage was far more decisive in Doyle's day when such commitments were always expected to be for the duration of one's life. The mutual interrelationship brought about by the agreement to marry, called in the English speaking world "the engagement," was as important as the ceremony itself for questions of honor came up since the pact was usually a verbal accord. In "A Scandal in Bohemia," the nobleman fears Irene will send the photo to his future in-laws, not on the day of his marriage, but rather, "on the day when the betrothal was publicly proclaimed." In Poland, where Irene lived and where she met this man, engaged couples are considered as good as married and can even live together with the blessings of their families. The forced marriage of Lucy Ferrier is as much an occasion for blood revenge as was her ultimate death for she was already planning to wed another.

In such a puzzle as we are now unraveling we are being introduced to one of "those mysteries," that either cannot be solved by the official police, or are of too delicate and personal a matter for the authorities. The aristocrat seeks out Holmes in abject despair, for here lies his last hope of averting what Watson calls "a great scandal," possibly affecting European stability.

The *Bible* has much to say about scandal: "God is great; and when a scandal is to end, brings some devoted man to take charge of it in hope, not in despair!" This is from Jeremiah, and was quoted by Carlyle in *Latter-Day Pamphlets* of 1850. Surprisingly enough Jesus tells us one of his functions is to prevent scandal. "The Son of man shall send his angels, and they shall gather out of his kingdom all scandals, and them that work iniquity." "Woe to the world because of scandals. For it must needs be that scandals come: nevertheless woe to that man by whom the scandal cometh." Woe indeed, for elsewhere in the *New Testament* we learn that those who cause scandal go straight into "the furnace of fire." For the purpose of gaining admittance to Adler's villa Holmes poses as a Nonconformist clergyman, for the priest is the descendant of Jesus and Jesus was clearly a nonconformist as well as a member of the clergy. Watson has second thoughts about being deceitful with Irene, and it is only his fear of displaying treachery to his friend that prevents him from giving the show away. Watson seconds his apologia by assuring himself that they are not injuring her but rather, "We are but preventing her from injuring another." Her immortal soul can be dammed, thus the Biblical justification for tricking her is here answered.

Scandal, its circumvention and the inflection of punitive measures upon its workers, is the preeminent theme in any number of Holmes' cases, as in "The Adventure of the Three Students," when Hilton Soames, Greek lecturer at St. Luke's College asks the man for help in solving the theft of examination papers, or else "there will ensue a hideous scandal." Lestrade in "The Adventure of the Norwood Builder" thanks the detective for preventing "a very grave scandal, which would have ruined my reputation in the Force." A detractor tells Holmes he dislikes his profession because it instigates one to "pry into the secrets of private individuals, when you rake up family matters which are better hidden." Holmes corrects the man, assuring him the private detective, on the contrary, is "doing the reverse of what you very justly blame, and that we are endeavouring to prevent anything like public exposure of private matters which must necessarily follow when once the case is fairly in the hands of the official police." Even in cases not covered in the Canon we find scandal, for Watson informs us Holmes has a bunch of dispatch-cases filled with documents, not just of criminal matters, "but of the social and official scandals of the late Victorian era." Those who fret over gossip because of Holmes' data can allay their fears for "no confidence will be abused." In "The Speckled Band" Holmes emphasizes he will not tell the real truth behind the case until Helen Stoner's death, for after all Roylott was her mother's husband, and remember, Irene Adler is dead before the unfolding of her story.

Right from the beginning we sense Holmes does not care for this masked nobleman hunting for assistance, but ignoring his personal feelings he devotes himself completely to the task, for some things are more important than oneself. When the detective informs the future king that Irene has married, the arrogant lout claims she could not possibly love her new husband, the implication being she could not prefer another to him. The man is a small-minded individual who thinks solely of his own plans and advantages, his own happiness.

In his essay "The Bedwarfing Virtue," from *Thus Spake Zarathustra*, we are told that for people with small minds, especially among the aristocrats, small virtues are necessary. The motivation of the nobleman is to come out of this looking as clean as possible, no matter what he may have done. Of the nobility Zarathustra informs us, of "this hypocrisy found I worst among them, that even those who command feign the virtues of those who serve." The hypocrisy of the rulers is what is at question, "Round, fair, and considerate are they to one another, as grains of sand are round, fair, and considerate to grains of sand." For the rulers want their small happiness, even while "they peer modestly after a new small happiness," but, "In their hearts they want simply one thing most of all: that no one hurt them." Instead of taking more active roles in life these parasites are among that class of people who wait much as "toll-gatherers and land keepers and shop keepers," wait for people to come to them, always with money or favors for them. He is not finished with the aristocrats quite yet. "There are actors without knowing it amongst them, and actors without intending it — , the genuine ones are always rare, especially the genuine actors." The nobleman wears a mask, as did the ancient Greek actors, and the Greek word for actor is hypocrite. Holmes as well plays a number of roles in the case, hoping to overcome the actors. Adler tell us she has been trained as an actress and shows us her skill by passing herself off as a man in what used to be called "a trouser role" in the theater.

Holmes turned down a knighthood, but Doyle accepted the honor in 1902, after much hesitation for reasons unrelated to the award itself. Holmes was always a knight in the true sense of the word; he did not need the title. Doyle tells us that Conan is the name of an aristocratic French family that included a number of famous knights, so he has lived up to his name.

Doyle, however, is well aware of the low side of the nobility, as we may see in any number of stories such as "The Red-Headed League," where the villain turns out to be a card-carrying member of the aristocracy, as is the so-called nobleman of "The Noble Bachelor," whose name, St. Simon, refers to "simony," meaning, by association, someone who will do anything for money.

These writings, no matter how heavily influenced by Nietzsche, reflect, but do not necessarily endorse the German's views. It's more complicated than that. Doyle partially blamed Nietzsche for the First World War, contending he had "inoculated the German spirit with a most mischievous philosophy," yet Doyle painstakingly studies and utilizes this philosophy, and what a weak word "mischievous" is when thinking of the death of millions.

Johnson never tired of attacking the arrogance and pompousness of the nobles, though he believed in the system itself. Birth, not merit, should come first in man's estimation, but merit and morals will always sway men's minds in the right direction. The entire moral fabric of society was dependent upon the subjection of one man to another, and the system of aristocracy was the fairest way to apply and practice this subjection. Without this order Johnson believed we would have a "perpetual struggle for precedence," that would do more harm than good. Passive acquiescence to authority that was not based on personal merit and morals however was not the true nature of the aristocratic structure, and the King of Bohemia is not a natural nobleman. If Johnson insisted on the need of deference to rank, he realized a compatible obligation was owing to the other side: "I would behave to a nobleman as I should expect he would behave to me, were I a nobleman and he Sam. Johnson." When Johnson sees what he regards as duplicity committed by an important member of the nobility he speaks out. As was common practice the poet had asked a member of the privileged class to be associated with his enterprise of publishing his huge undertaking the *Dictionary of the English Language,* and it appears it was understood by Johnson, and others, that Lord Chesterfield would endorse and contribute financially towards the endeavor. But Boswell tells us Chesterfield "had behaved to him in such a manner as to excite his contempt and indignation." There was a continued neglect of sponsorship on Chesterfield's part, and without a royal patron, an author, no matter how talented, could achieve little. Johnson went to see Lord Chesterfield but the meeting did not go well for his lordship kept him waiting claiming he had company. This company turned out to be Colley Cibber, a cheap poetaster and talentless rival of Johnson's on the literary scene. Walking out of the house Johnson never returned, claiming it was no loss since he never received any real support anyway. It looks like Chesterfield was waiting to see if the book was going to be a success before becoming involved, which was a shabby trick under the circumstances. The Lord tried to make up for it after the *Dictionary* came out and was praised by all, but the author only became enraged at Lord Chesterfield's audacity.

Holmes is almost as arrogant as the King of Bohemia himself, even refusing to shake hands with the man. A short while following the incident just related, Johnson was talking with a Dr. Adams about it and Adams defended Chesterfield by saying the whole thing was just a terrible mistake on Johnson's part. Defending himself, Johnson said Lord Chesterfield "is the proudest man this day existing." Dr. Adams tells him "there is one person, at least, as proud; I think, by your own account you are the prouder man of the two." "But mine (replied Johnson instantly) was *defensive* pride." Holmes is arrogant in defense, and out of sympathy and understanding for all those people a man such as the King of Bohemia, and Lord Chesterfield perhaps, have damaged with their God-given, but misused nobility. I can see much of Boswell's *Life* in Nietzsche, and so did Doyle.

In "A Scandal in Bohemia" we are given a lesson in natural selection, as it exists according to Darwin's theories, and as Charles Sanders Peirce interprets those themes in his essay "Evolutionary Love" of 1893. "A Scandal in Bohemia" saw light in book form one year prior to this which creates a problem for me, but not a serious one since as is standard with many philosophers, Peirce would write something, then circulate it among friends and enemies testing their reactions and measuring their criticism, before publishing. He was an eccentric man who never had any of his philosophy published in book form until after his death, in spite of his notable reputation. Sensitive to evaluation he often addressed it quite personally, as in his essay "Concerning the Author."

"A Scandal in Bohemia" has religious overtones to it, as does "Evolutionary Love," with the opening section offering us a brief history of the variety of love, the focal point of which is the writer's own belief in God's love. He claims the great evolutionary agent of the universe is love and hate, with passionate love and hate being the co-ordinate powers, and the "One Supreme Being, by whom all things have been made out of nothing, to be cherishing-love." The apostle John he tells us, preached "God is light and in him is no darkness at all," and that "God is love." Peirce also quotes John's message that the world should be saved through the Son of God who will judge the world. But, "He that believeth in him is not judged: he that believeth not hath been judged already." Peirce translates this last part to mean "God visits no punishment on them; they punish themselves, by their natural affinity for the defective." This reinforces Doyle's belief that the evil ones reap their own rewards in paying with their bodies, and possibly their souls as well. The lesson we draw from John's gospel, Peirce tells us, is that this is the way the mind develops, and that it is "capable of further evolution." I'm not sure what he means by this; perhaps he wants to show the light of revelation overcoming the darkness of doubt. Irene sends a note to Holmes that Watson calls "this epistle," in which she describes her suspicions of the detective and how by following him to his home she overcame those doubts, replacing them with the truth. In this endeavor her servant "John, the coachman," aided her. This is also the name of a coachman engaged by Holmes as a confident in "The Man with the Twisted Lip," another religious story. Perhaps they are the same man. Irene also lives in St. John's Wood, a direct reference to the evangelist.

"Love is not directed to abstractions, but to persons," Peirce tells us, adding "growth comes only from love," and now he is talking of selection, such as Darwin had in mind. He will attempt "to define the logical affinities of the different theories of evolution," but realizes the theorists may have overlooked something. Those who believe only in taking a cold, analytical approach to evolution, excluding such things as love and sentiment are mistaken. "I willingly confess to having some tincture of sentimentalism in me," for this sentimentalism represents only "the doctrine that great respect should be paid to the natural judgments of the sensible heart." Holmes is much like Peirce, for has he not also taken a sentimental approach in his feelings for Irene. "In natural selection, strictly so called, it is the crowding out of the weak" while in "sexual selection, it is the attraction of beauty, mainly." The King is not only a powerful giant of a man but rich enough to hire the intelligence he needs, such as Holmes, to assist his efforts. Irene's new husband, Godfrey Norton has no such clout but is "a remarkably handsome man, dark, aquiline, and moustached."

The second half of the essay, "Second Thoughts. Irenica" contains a play on the name of the Greek goddess of peace, Irene, which is also a Greek word meaning "peace." Irenica is a word the philosopher made up from the word Irenic, which means "promoting peace, or peaceful." Peirce invented many words from already existing ones if he felt the new word better encompassed his intentions. The plural, Irenics, is a noun used to denote the practice or doctrine of promoting peace among Christian churches in relation to theological differences, often referred to as Irenic Theology. Doyle's Irene lives up to her name for when the case is drawing to a close she informs Holmes, "your client may rest in peace," for there will be no scandal.

Holmes tells us Irene "was a lovely woman, with a face that a man might die for." These are serious words coming from a man often regarded as a machine, and we can believe his appreciation. She has chosen a handsome mate in Norton, with a good mind, just like herself, for they are two of a kind and meant for each other by birth and natural selection. Peirce says the process that brought these two together is "evolution by creative love," and they follow what he termed "the law of love." They even have the same name for Godfrey, as we already know, means "God's peace." Godfrey looking aquiline links them in biological symbolism, for aquiline means "of or like an eagle," and Adler is the German for eagle. They represent what the philosopher terms, when alluding to the *Origin of Species* as "those exquisite and marvelous adaptations of nature." They would propagate the best of the species in their children, thus personifying the struggle for existence.

The name Norton refers us to Charles Eliot Norton, editor of a collection of Chauncey Wright's works entitled *Philosophical Discussions* published in 1877, dealing with interpretations of Alfred Russel Wallace's and Charles Darwin's speculations and their impact on mankind. Norton was professor of art history at Harvard, a translator of Dante Alighieri, editor of a collection of John Donne's poems, as well as collections of the letters of Emerson, Lowell, Ruskin, and Carlyle. He had lived in London off and on, had been friendly with both the Holmes and James families, and kept up a correspondence with Henry James, Jr. Godfrey Norton is a lawyer and therefore part of "evolutionary law," as Peirce called it, for law is a result of evolution, as Wendell Holmes taught us. Here is one of the most important statements in my book. Sherlock Holmes is the naturally selected end product of this evolutionary creation, since he is the ultimate upholder of the law, the personification of pragmatism applied to criminal investigation, law procedure, and all importantly, justice. I said Wendell Holmes made an appearance in the fiction and here he is, for Wendell is the prototype for Godfrey Norton. The physical description matches and both think alike for during the marriage ceremony, when Godfrey acts to convince Sherlock to be quick and decisive regarding his role as witness, he yells out "Come, man, come, only three minutes, or it won't be legal." Wendell insisted upon everything being according to the strict letter of the law, for legality was all.

The religious nature of the story is reinforced by the fact that Norton is of the Inner Temple, a statement carrying religious overtones. Norton plays Wendell Holmes, the advocator of a scientific resolution of the law, while Adler is an opera star, an artist. Peirce tells us, "Where there is a motion, where history is a-making, there is the focus of mental activity, and it has been said that the arts and sciences reside within the temple of Janus, waking when that is open, but slumbering when it is closed." Both art and science seem to be necessary for a truly historical event to take place.

The King of Bohemia is a prime example of what C. S. Peirce called the late nineteenth century love of greed, meaning, in this story, for social position and more power, since he is already rich. His greed is manifested by three loves: love of self, love of a limited class having common interests and feelings with one's self, the love of mankind at large. That last love is not "that deep, subconscious passion that is properly so-called, but merely public spirit," Peirce tells us. The nobleman wishes to embrace the power to graft his thoughts on to other people, with such a man conveniently regarding his motives as acting purely in the public spirit, but he is interested only in what Peirce calls his own "sustenance and enjoyment."

Dr. Sloper, Catherine Sloper's father from Henry James' novel *Washington Square* works as a model for the Bohemian nobleman with their shared faculty of demanding their own way. Even Sherlock shows an affinity with Sloper for the man does indeed love his daughter Catherine as surely as Holmes loves Irene, and Holmes' reaction to her marriage is not unlike a father whose daughter has married without his blessing or approval. The same feeling of betrayal is there. At one point Dr. Sloper hopes to carry off his daughter to Europe just as Norton takes Irene to the Continent. Morris Townsend is regarded as handsome, almost beautiful, a feature he shares with Norton. Elopement is talked of in *Washington Square* and the marriage of Irene and Godfrey could be thought of as an elopement in spirit with all the characteristics of such. Disguises of a sort come into the American novel for Catherine's aunt, in her clandestine meeting with Townsend to discuss future stratagems adopts deceptive attire, even once wearing a veil completely covering her face. A meeting in a church also occurs in James' work.

In James' *The Portrait of a Lady*, a young woman born and raised in New York (within view of Irene's New Jersey) travels to Europe where she encounters those whose morals and goals are quite different from her own. Bohemia is the country of Holmes' client, but also a reference to the bohemian lifestyle of Irene Adler, as well as that of Isabel Archer, and her friend Henrietta Stackpole, with the appellation being employed a number of times by James. Miss Stackpole is a newspaper columnist, in her day considered strictly a man's domain, with this reversal of gender being displayed when Irene disguises herself as a man in order to gather information. The personal independence of the artist is actively sought after by all three ladies listed above. Lord Warburton could play the part of the King for he wishes to marry Isabel but she refuses him and then successfully avoids him. Blackmail does not enter into this story however.

The Bostonians is James' novel of worthy and noble enemies, Verena Tarrant, a young Bostonian heavily involved in the woman's movement of her day, and Basil Ransom, a Southern lawyer who harbors no sympathy or support for the crusade. In spite of this they fall in love. The use of the Inner Temple may have occurred to Doyle from James' repeated mention of Tremont Temple, a Boston Baptist church hall having a long association with radical causes, such as the woman's movement. On its stage Verena has performed for her cause so well we are told, "she might easily have a big career, like that of a distinguished actress or singer." Basil regards her work with the suffragettes as an obstacle to their love and during an argument with him as to whether or not she should give up her work to marry him Verena compares herself to "a singer with a beautiful voice who has accepted some decree of never raising a note." She regards herself as being silenced, bringing in overtones of emotional blackmail. The important scene in which Godfrey rushes Irene out of the house to the church and marriage is echoed in the episode where

Basil hastens Verena from the hall where she planned to speak, to the nearest church to marry her.

The heavy in *The Bostonians* is played by a rich suitor to Verena named Henry Burrage, not by any means in the same league as the King, but nevertheless a thoroughly odious individual too eager to employ his wealth, position, and contacts, to get his own way, especially with women. As calculating as Baron Gruner of "The Illustrious Client," yet not as evil, Burrage makes up for it in his contempt for the feelings of others. To illustrate his nature, one character's thoughts run thus: "She had a theory that he proposed to almost any girl who was not likely to accept him — did it because he was making a collection of such episodes — a mental album of declarations, blushes, hesitations, refusals that just missed imposing themselves as acceptances, quite as he collected enamels and Cremona violins." Like the Baron, he is a collector of artifacts and women, and he catalogues his acquisitions — if only mentally.

In her childish trust Miss Tarrant is not very different from Miss de Merville, another who refuses to admit of evil, and just as Violet cannot deduce the grasping character of the Baron, Verena fails to apprehend the complex and maneuvering essence of Olive Chancellor, an older woman responsible for instigating Verena's involvement in the feminist movement and convincing the girl to move in with her for reasons of her own, reasons only darkly hinted at. The family of Verena, as naïve in the aggregate as she is in the singular, symbolically rent her out like a horse, for a certain amount of money is gifted to them by Olive for as long as the strange relationship lasts.

If one word were to be used to describe the tone of "A Scandal in Bohemia," it would have to be irony, and with Henry James, a rich sense of irony flowers in all his fiction.

Never once are we told that Hawkeye loves Alice Munro, the beautiful young heroine of *The Last of the Mohicans*, but through Cooper's sophisticated style we understand without being told. At the conclusion of the adventure Alice returns to England, where she marries an aristocrat. Some years later she returns to New York and is watched clandestinely from a distance by Hawkeye, who does not approach her — the equivalent of Holmes' studying the photo of Irene. He not only talks on occasion of Irene but also "refers to her photograph," which holds great importance for him. Hawkeye and Holmes love from a distance, and in their minds only, and must be content with this. Cooper's tales are full of women the scout comes into contact with but the situation never goes beyond friendship.

Among Irene Adler's many incarnations we come across Molly Aston, a real-life celebrated beauty Johnson met a number of times and fell in love with. That's easy to understand as we study her portrait by an unknown artist reproduced in Peter Quennell's book on Johnson. One thing noticeable, which Quennell commented upon, is, as he put it, "her large aquiline nose." In Mrs. Thrale's *Anecdotes of the Late Samuel Johnson, LL.D.*, she tells us that "when Mr. Thrale once asked him which had been the happiest period of his past life? he replied, 'It was that year in which he spent one whole evening with Molly Aston.'" "That, indeed, was not happiness," Johnson said, "it was rapture." "Molly was a beauty and a scholar, and a wit and a Whig; and she talked all in praise of liberty: and so I made this epigram upon her — She was the loveliest creature I ever saw!!!" Johnson adds the epigram, in Latin, that Mrs. Thrale translates.

> Persuasions to freedom fall oddly from you;
> If freedom we seek — fair Maria, adieu!

Obviously Molly longed for a new sense of freedom in her life and enlisted Johnson's sympathy, and he now likes to fancy that this freedom she seeks would cause him to lose her. In another book Mrs. Thrale, commenting on all this romantic daydreaming, tells us this epigram was borrowed from an earlier French version celebrating a young lady who, in order to express her yearning for independence of expression, attended a masquerade dressed as a Jesuit priest. In the gloating note Irene sends Holmes after bolting, she admits to often dressing in men's clothes to "take advantage of the freedom which it gives." Mrs. Thrale includes information that Molly actually gave speeches on liberty and ended up marrying Lord Lyttelton, of whom Boswell tells us, "Johnson seems to have been not favourably disposed towards that nobleman." Mrs. Thrale suggests that he was offended by Molly Aston's preference for his Lordship over him.

Queen Victoria's uncle Prince Leopold was a potential king, if not of England then of some other European state. He was later to rule Belgium. In London he maintained a German actress, Karoline Bauer, in a villa overlooking Regent's Park. It was understood that if he was placed on a throne he would have to give her up, but such things could be difficult and costly, especially if letters or photos were involved.

Doyle also has in mind "Skittles," as she was known, a true beauty of his day, whose real name was Catherine Watters and who owned a villa in St. John's Wood. One has only to see a photo of her to see what I mean. She has been linked with Albert Edward, Prince of Wales, by a number of historians.

The reader is advised to also dig up a photo of Lillie Langtry, regarded in Doyle's era as the most beautiful woman in the world. Known as "the Jersey Lily," she was for years rumored to be intimate with the Prince of Wales. While Oscar Wilde was living on Salisbury St., London, he met Lily, and so he tells us, fell violently in love with her. It was for her he wrote his poem, "The New Helen," and when the first volume was struck he presented her with it, inscribed on the flyleaf, "To Helen, formerly of Troy, but now of London." Wilde could be thought of as a model for the nobleman in Doyle's tale, for was he not "King of the bohemians"? His mother, Jane Francesca Elgee, born in 1826 in Wexford, Ireland, was an ardent Irish patriot publishing articles and poems under various names including Speranza. Famous for outlandish costumes, as was her son Oscar, she occasionally dressed as a man. Like Irene Adler, she was a foreigner in England and interestingly enough was often heard to say she had been an eagle in a previous life.

Speaking of Wilde, this photo of Irene, like the portrait of Dorian Gray, is all Holmes will ever have of her since she has died. She has lost life, but her photo has captured her beauty, as have the haunting pictures of Molly, Lily, and Skittles. Lord Henry, infatuated with Dorian's charms, actually owned seventeen photographs of the man. Godfrey Norton is a recreation of Dorian, what with his physical attractiveness, and his flight with Irene is modeled upon a similar incident when Dorian's father eloped with his future mother, a woman described as "one of the loveliest creatures I ever saw" by a male in the novel. Dorian's mother, like Irene, died young.

Gray falls in love with an actress, Sibyl Vane, "the loveliest thing I had ever seen in my life." She is pictured for us a number of times dressed in men's or boy's clothing, for her roles demand it. They become engaged, but the agreement is a secret, as was that of Irene and Godfrey. Sibyl dreams of fleeing from her life in the theater into something new and wonderful with Dorian, if she can succeed in getting out of the hands of her fat manager to whom she is bound for three years. Like the King of Bohemia, the manager is an oily character with a sort of pompous humility and a ring on every finger. The people at the theater, including his intended, nickname Dorian "Prince Charming," and he affects a certain attempt at incognito, never revealing his true name. We can imagine the young Irene Adler being fascinated with a real prince showering her with attention, gifts, and compliments. But remember, as Dorian's portrait transforms, bringing to light the moral decay of the subject, he realizes he has been wearing a mask, concealing his true age and ethical character. For this reason he rejects Sibyl, and like Irene, she dies during the narration, for she takes poison. Even the opera comes into it, for Dorian and Lord Henry often attend performances. One of Dorian's ancestors, "Lord Beckenham, the companion of the Prince Regent in his wildest days," is rumored to have been "one of the witnesses at the secret marriage with Mrs. Fitzherbert," just as Holmes acted as witness to the semi-secret marriage of Irene and Godfrey.

Interestingly enough, Wilde mentions the work of the French symbolists in the book, which was published only three years after *A Study in Scarlet*, so associative painting and writing had already achieved some level of the familiar with his English readers.

Doyle's writing is replete with thoughts on social mores between the sexes, and obviously he began these Holmes stories expecting the two investigators to be embroiled, one way or another, with women. In the second narrative Watson becomes involved, and now it is Holmes' turn. This is brought to our attention right from the beginning with the doctor reminding us that the Baker Street flat is the scene of "my wooing" of Mary Morstan. Boswell, by his own admission, was a great ladies' man, having relationships with women seemingly everywhere he traveled, and his travels were extensive. Watson tells us he has knowledge of the women of "many nations and three separate continents," even outdoing the Scot. Neither Samuel Johnson nor Holmes can make any such claim, nor would they if they could, for both despise the softer sentiments and also the expression of them. At one point Boswell confesses that Johnson simply does not know how to enjoy life, comparing Johnson to himself, who at least tries to have a good time. All his life Johnson was afflicted with "morbid melancholy," as was Holmes, and both men had an aversion to regular life. Bachelorhood was to the poet "cheerless celibacy," yet following the death of his wife while he was still young, he failed to remarry. Johnson told his biographer that he had heard it said of himself, "He *appears* not to feel; but when he is *alone*, depend upon it, he *suffers sadly*." Boswell recalls that the poet was laughing heartily when he told the story, but I doubt if Johnson could actually have heard such a thing about himself. Was he trying to tell Boswell something very personal without appearing to be doing so?

In "The Dying Detective," Watson makes the observation that Mrs. Hudson became extremely upset at Holmes' apparent life-threatening illness because she, like most women, was genuinely fond of him. The Great Detective "had a remarkable gentleness and courtesy in his dealings with women," Watson tells us, adding, "He disliked and distrusted the sex, but he was always a chivalrous opponent." Here we have clearly outlined Nietzsche's personal feelings toward "the sex." Personally, I think both Holmes and Nietzsche found women so fascinating as to make it necessary to form a crust of resentment toward them. That happens. Doyle is not going to show us "Sherlock in Love," for a love interest does not reappear in the stories. What Doyle is doing is carrying out Samuel Johnson's depreciation of love as an active ingredient in good dramatic writing. Johnson said somewhere, "love is only one of many passions; and as it has no great influence upon the sum of life, it has little operation in the dramas of a poet who caught his ideas from the living world." Holmes has shown his capacity for love, answering Johnson's dictum, "Want of tenderness, he always alleged, was want of parts, and was no less a proof of stupidity than depravity." If there was absolutely no love interest connected with Holmes, the Canon could be viewed as a series of police stories or Victorian adventure yarns fit only for a boys' magazine.

I have come across the theory that women were responsible for Holmes' quick popularity but I can't believe it since women, until recently, have always been rather indifferent to the character. The first theater production of *Sherlock Holmes* was embraced by the ladies, but William Gillette, the American actor who made it his signature piece, was a handsome man already a favorite with the women. They went to see him, not Sherlock. One idea behind "A Scandal in Bohemia" is to show the women that Holmes is basically a normal, even likable, somewhat odd fellow, with Doyle realizing this character has untapped resources for the future.

Everything in Nietzsche is extravagant, exuberant, and complex, forcing any fictional personality finding foundation in his thoughts to be so as well, and so indeed is Irene Adler, who despite appearing in only one tale, became one of the most analyzed persons in the Holmes literature. A flimsy reading of the philosopher confers an impression of misogyny, but he talks about women too much for one to honestly believe he disliked them, though he always writes as if they are, at the very nearest, in the next room; they are never the audience he is writing for. At one point he makes the observation, "They have always been the delight of every tense and profound male soul," but he seems to forget that no man could be more tense and profound than he, and if you had to delineate Holmes with just two words, tense and profound would do nicely. Like the yogi, these two men view women with suspicion and must constantly be searching for justification of their cynicism. "Women are never to be entirely trusted — not the best of them," are words spoken not by Nietzsche but by Holmes. Some Indian ascetics go so far as to castrate themselves, hoping to drive thoughts of sex from their minds, but even a neutered ascetic would have to mull over Nietzsche's bizarre question: "Is it not better to fall into the hands of a murderer than into the dreams of a lustful woman?" He tells us one can recognize a philosopher by his shunning of "three brilliant and noisy things — fame, princes, and women: which is not to say that they do not come to him." Doyle answers by having all three of these brilliant and noisy things enter Holmes' life in "A Scandal in Bohemia."

Irene is being adopted as a personification of women in general, although Holmes never refers to her except in the singular, as the woman. Nietzsche rarely called the female sex anything except "woman," or often "the woman," even when speaking in the plural. Judge Wendell Holmes often refers to "woman" when dealing in plurality, and Nietzsche may have borrowed it from him, as he in turn took it from his father, who when complimenting a beautiful female singing voice, such as Irene must have had, tells us, "it had so much *woman* in it."

"Two different things wanteth the true man: danger and diversion. Therefore wanteth he woman, as the most dangerous plaything," Nietzsche tells us. This heroine Irene, in a pure spirit of playfulness, has the audacity to tempt detection by the world's greatest detective by bidding him good night by name, as he is about to enter his flat.

One reason Doyle was so opposed to women's suffrage, which I have always felt to be somewhat out of character for him, was the German philosopher's conviction that anything "that pampers, that softens, and that brings the 'people' or 'woman' to the front" operates in favor of the domination of inferior men, and he regarded equal rights as an indication, along with such horrors as the advent of democracy, or arbitration instead of war, as symptoms of declining life. Being against anything that caused weak people to gain power, he despised those who showed mercy to their fellow man. "All that proceeds from power is good, all that springs from weakness is bad," just about sums it up for Nietzsche.

Irene has been, as Nietzsche called it, "defeminized" by dressing as a man, and he considered it laughable for a woman to wear trousers. I suspect Doyle did as well. A real man, the philosopher tells us, will try to "*save the woman* in woman." Both believed they were preserving what was best in women by denying them equality and voting rights. Nietzsche called these defeminizing circumstances of modern society corruption of the instincts, presenting a number of women as examples of his argument, among them George Sand, who often dressed as a man. In the next Holmes story he writes, Doyle will bring up a quote from Gustave Flaubert, taken from a letter to George Sand.

The name Irene has been traced back to its meaning, "peace," and the philosopher tells us that "Ye shall love peace," but only as a means to new wars, for your work is to fight, and your peace should be a victory. Peace is only a means of winning the good war against evil, for peace leads to new wars. "The sexes deceive themselves about each other: the reason is that in reality they honour and love only themselves (or their own ideal, to express it more agreeably). Thus man wishes woman to be peaceable: but in fact woman is *essentially* unpeaceable, like the cat, however well she may have assumed the peaceable demeanour."

In the section of *Thus Spake Zarathustra* in which this information on women is coming to light, one chapter is entitled "The Bite of the Adder," with adder being a weak pun on Adler. If a man falls in love with a woman and she hurts him, that man we often say has been bitten. In the next chapter Nietzsche says, "Bitterness is in the cup even of the best love; thus doth it cause longing for the Superman; thus doth it cause thirst in thee, the creating one!" The only poisonous snake in England is the adder, also called the viper, with the Indian swamp adder identified by Holmes as "the deadliest snake in India." The evil Culverton Smith, a symbol of infection itself, has a name that means adder. Doyle must be going in for some singular humor having the Bohemian nobleman offer to Holmes an emerald snake ring. Is this "a hair of the dog that bit you," perhaps? Irene Adler lives in a villa on Serpentine Avenue, in front of Serpentine-mews. Aside from meaning "of or like a serpent," the word also means "evilly cunning or subtle." The name of her villa, Briony Lodge, is the name of a poisonous vine, a suitable home for a snake.

Nietzsche's Zarathustra lives in a cave with his animal attributes, an eagle and a serpent, which intertwine with each other. These are personifications of his idiosyncrasies for they are "the proudest animal under the sun, and the wisest animal under the sun," and the prophet laments that he is not as wise as his serpent. This however he knows to be impossible. "Therefore do I ask my pride to go always with my wisdom! And if my wisdom should some day forsake me: — alas! it loveth to fly away! — may my pride then fly with my folly!" If he loses his wisdom then he might as well lose his pride, and so Holmes has lost both, for his serpent and his eagle are both gone now. "I love him whose soul is deep even in the wounding," the philosopher tells us.

When Holmes is summoned to act as witness to Irene and Godfrey's wedding, we actually find the Great Detective, however unplanned, taking part in a religious ceremony. "Has it been observed to what extent outward idleness, or semi-idleness, is necessary to a real religious life," Nietzsche asks in *Beyond Good and Evil*. Those who are not idle, the laboring class, do not really have time for religion, but Holmes, disguised as an idle, unemployed horseman, had "lounged down the street" Irene lived on to spy on her, and now "lounged up the side aisle like any other idler who has dropped into a church." Those who are fully occupied do not know nor care whether religion is "a new business, or a new pleasure," the German claims. Holmes gets both for he finds himself "vouching for things of which I knew nothing," which he regards as very amusing, while he as well makes a business of the experience for he is given a sovereign for his assistance. Why does he go along with all this? Like most people Holmes is only doing what is required of the occasion. "State affairs perhaps, require their participation in such customs, they do what is required, as so many things are done — with a patient and unassuming seriousness, and without much curiosity or discomfort; — they live too much apart and outside to feel even the necessity for a *for* or *against* in such matters." Nietzsche claims this is why some people, at least, participate in religious matters. And it is a question of state affairs that has sent Holmes into the church in the first place so he is doing what is required and feels no discomfort in his deception. The philosopher tells us the majority of these indifferent people are Protestants and the scholars, who have "a lofty and almost charitable serenity as regards religion."

Building upon the word Irenic, "A Scandal in Bohemia," becomes an attempt at showing an example of the fostering of peace between the two main branches of Christianity: the Catholic and Protestant. Irene could be Catholic since many Germans are, Godfrey is probably Protestant, while Holmes is Protestant, admitting he knows nothing about the creeds in question since the church is probably Catholic. St. Monica, the church in which the wedding takes place, was St. Augustine's mother, and like Irene a woman remarkable for her strong character and independence. Augustine was a Father of the Church, an African bishop whose writings are mandatory reading for anyone of any religion wishing to understand Christianity. He believed that man could speak directly to God, and therefore has no need for an intercessor such as a priest or minister. This famous thought leads to the belief that structured religion as such is at times nothing but an interference between man and God. Doyle seems to be saying it is not important which branch of Christianity a man follows so long as he leads a moral life, and Augustine himself said much the same thing. What we find here I believe is Doyle's own position as regards organized religion. His second marriage was a Protestant ceremony, although in theory this is not permitted to a Catholic. Doyle cannot take religion, even his own, seriously enough to make a fuss about it, treating it with the respect it deserves, but nothing more. I have no doubt he would have liked to see some new hybrid Christianity come into being, a merging of the different branches, something like his grandiose plan for the amalgamation of Britain and America.

In the chapter "The Friend" Zarathustra ponders the man he calls an anchorite, one who lives alone, apart from a disruptive society where he can practice solitary religious devotions and meditate on life, and of course the philosopher reads himself into this, realizing such a person would be vulnerable and would try to conceal that vulnerability. "'Be at least mine enemy!' — thus speaketh the true reverence, which doth not venture to solicit friendship," describes the anchorite's relationship to others. Holmes can hardly solicit friendship, much less love, from Irene; for he has been hired to thwart her future plans if necessary. He thus settles for being both her enemy and, as we learn from the outcome of the case, her friend. "If one would have a friend, then must one also be willing to wage war for him: and in order to wage war, one must be *capable* of being an enemy." Holmes shows himself more than capable of playing the enemy, even if it is to the friend. Women, Nietzsche tells us, are vengeful, because revenge and rancor belong to weakness. To be able to be an enemy presupposes a strong nature and is bound up with all strong natures. Irene, however, shows no revengeful nature for she, like her friend and enemy Holmes, has a strong, healthy spirit. The King of Bohemia thinks differently, claiming that "Rather than I should marry another woman, there are no lengths to which she would not go — none." This is simply an example of the man's egotism rather than Irene's imagined need for revenge. Holmes has waged war against Irene but his actions show he is also her friend, even if she won the battle, for he cannot be any more vindictive than she; his strong nature will not permit it. "In one's friend one shall have one's best enemy. Thou shalt be closest unto him with thy heart when thou withstandest him."

Now we are getting close to the bottom line as Zarathustra tells us, "Art thou pure air and solitude and bread and medicine to thy friend? Many a one cannot loosen his own fetters, but is nevertheless his friend's emancipator." Through the actions of Holmes, Irene has been freed both from the egotism of the King and from committing a regrettable act of blackmail, which could harm her soul. She experiences no bitterness towards the one who liberated her, with her parting letter to the detective displaying gratitude. She has gained independence with a better man while Nietzsche's dictum "Art thou a tyrant? Then thou canst not have friends," sums it up for the jilted monarch.

We are led to believe Sherlock fell in love with Irene after having seen her from a distance. That's an unusual occurrence. When thinking back, we realize that Watson as well fell in love with Mary Morstan as soon as he met her. We can learn something about our two investigators from this, for love at first sight occurs only in men who are not used to women, who do not often speak with them or associate with them to any marked degree, and such a phenomenon is probably impossible for a man raised in a household of sisters or female cousins.

When Holmes realizes he has lost Irene for good, he asks for and receives her photo, which he obviously places great emotional value in, having shunned proffered wealth for it. In *The Autocrat of the Breakfast-Table*, Dr. Holmes has something to say about all this. A conversation, as usual, takes place with Dr. Holmes telling his audience of fellow lodgers that looking at a woman tells you no more about her than if you were looking at a picture of her. After looking at the picture, you still know nothing about her. He is talking about the miniature portraits so popular in his day, not photographs, but these portraits served the same purpose as photos. "I'll tell you how it is with the pictures of women we fall in love with at first sight." He also says, "all men love all women," and adds, "Well, now, the reason why a man is not desperately in love with ten thousand women at once is just that which prevents all our portraits being distinctly seen upon that wall. They all *are* painted there by reflection from our faces, but because *all* of them are painted on each spot, and each on the same surface, and many other objects at the same time, no one is seen as a picture." We cannot see any one image if we look at them all, at least not at first. "But darken a chamber and let a single pencil of rays in through a key-hole, then you have a picture on the wall. We never fall in love with a woman in distinction from women, until we can get an image of her through a pin-hole; and then we can see nothing else, and nobody but ourselves can see the image in our mental camera-obscura." Irene is the woman among women Holmes has isolated in his mental camera and fallen in love with. Her photo is the personification of this isolation process, and in this case a picture is almost as important as the person herself.

At the very opening of this case we are informed Irene Adler is dead. In "The Grave-Song" from *Thus Spake Zarathustra* we are shown "the grave-island, the silent isle," that contains the graves of the "sights and scenes of my youth! Oh, all ye gleams of love, ye divine fleeting gleams! How could ye perish so soon for me! I think of you to-day as my dead ones." Irene has fled from Holmes, but Nietzsche tells us of his youthful loves, "Yet did ye not flee from me, nor did I flee from you: innocent are we to each other in our faithlessness," for "we were made to remain nigh unto each other." Malice has killed the youthful loves of Zarathustra as he laments, "too early did ye die for me." Malice aimed its arrows at the heart of Zarathustra, "And they hit it! Because ye were always my dearest, my possession and my possessedness: *on that account* had ye to die young, and far too early! At my most vulnerable point did they shoot the arrow — namely, at you, whose skin is like down — or more like the smile that dieth at a glance!" He tells of an attack on him as he slept. "And there came an adder and bit him in the neck, so that Zarathustra screamed with pain." When the serpent realizes whom it has bitten, it tries to flee, but the poet/warrior stops it, for it has not yet received his thanks. "'Thou hast awakened me in time; my journey is yet long.' 'Thy journey is short,' said the adder sadly; 'my poison is fatal.'" Zarathustra smiles at this and asks, "When did ever a dragon die of a serpent's poison? But take thy poison back! Thou art not rich enough to present it to me." The adder then falls upon the prophet's neck and licks his wound. Love those who awaken us to the length and labor of the journey, Nietzsche seems to be saying, even if it is with the bite of an adder. Doyle's young wife is one slated for a lingering, early death by tuberculosis, and he knows it.

CHAPTER SEVEN. WATSON FINDS A TREASURE

The Sign of Four, the second Holmes novel, is yet another account of one coming to London from foreign parts seeking revenge for a wrong. Holmes and Watson are interrupted by Mary Morstan bearing a tale of her father having returned to London and almost immediately disappearing without a trace. The Army Captain had been in charge of the prison on the Andaman Islands in the Indian Ocean. There are no clues to the mystery, but after years of silence Miss Morstan answers a newspaper ad requesting her address and ever since receives, each year through the mail, a large, lustrous pearl. The sender never reveals himself, but she is convinced it has something to do with her father, and when this year's gift is accompanied by instructions to meet her benefactor at a theater, she seeks out Holmes for advice. The two detectives will accompany her; in the meantime Holmes researches what he can of the case, concluding that a Major Sholto, who had known the Captain in India, must be mixed up in it. The three go to the meeting, and from there are taken to the residence of Thaddeus Sholto, who admits his father, the Major, had cheated Morstan out of an ill-gotten treasure years ago in India. Morstan tracked down Sholto in London, dying immediately following a heated argument. The Major in turn dies one night a few years later of a heart attack, after seeing a face at the window. The actual whereabouts of the jewels remains a mystery until the Major's twin sons, Thaddeus and Bartholomew, locate them at their home, Pondicherry Lodge. The group arrives at the Sholto estate just in time to learn of the murder of Bartholomew and the theft of the jewels.

Hawkeye is alluded to twice by this time, for we learn this complicated mystery would be interesting to Holmes since it "would tax his sagacity to the utmost," and when the police show up Holmes says, "But here are the regulars; so the auxiliary forces may beat a retreat."

The miscreants are tracked to the banks of the Thames with the aid of Toby, the bloodhound. Scotland Yard first used dogs for tracking in 1888, just one year before this scene was written. Holmes tells us he would like to explore fully the use of dogs in police work, particularly the relationship of dogs to their masters. Holmes himself is repeatedly compared to a dog, usually a hound, and often enough it is he making the comparison. When the other detectives are stymied by events they come to him hoping he can "put them on the right scent." In *A Study in Scarlet* the maneuvers of the detective are compared so vividly to a canine we can almost hear him bark. "As he spoke he whipped a tape-measure and a large round magnifying glass from his pocket. With these two implements he trotted noiselessly about the room, sometimes stopping, occasionally kneeling, and once lying flat upon his face. So engrossed was he with his occupation that he appeared to have forgotten our presence, for he chattered away to himself under his breath the whole time, keeping up a running fire of exclamations, groans, whistles, and little cries suggestive of encouragement and hope. As I watched him I was irresistibly reminded of a pure-blooded, well-trained foxhound as it dashes backward and forward through the covert, whining in its eagerness, until it comes across the lost scent." When on holiday "this amateur bloodhound," is unexpectedly consulted by the local vicar about a tragic affair, and he "sat up in his chair like an old hound who hears the view-halloa." When questioned by the police about a murder, Holmes will remind them he is "one of the hounds, and not the wolf." The other detectives also compare themselves to dogs, with Gregson, defending his own methods, calling himself "the old hound." Jefferson Hope, on his arduous quest for justifiable vengeance, is compared to "a human bloodhound, with his mind wholly set upon the one object to which he has devoted his life." By way of compliment, Holmes claims that Lestrade is "as tenacious as a bulldog," and adds that this tenacity led to his success in Scotland Yard. The followers of the ancient Zarathustra used dogs to protect their farms and homes, for their keener senses warned of approaching danger.

The forces of evil in the Canon are compared to lions and tigers, traditional enemies of the dog, with Baron Gruner, to pick one good example, being described as "a precise, tidy cat of a man in many of his ways." Hawkeye compares the Indians to tigers and panthers. Holmes has a much easier time keeping up with Toby than Watson, for it is Hawkeye who can follow the hounds all day without tiring while on the hunt. Hawkeye is never without his hound Hector, which he regards as one with himself. When the people of Cooperstown, New York, erected a bronze life-size statue of Hawkeye they included Hector by his side. In one case Holmes uses a bloodhound named Pompey, the name of a Roman king, just as Hector was the name of a Greek king. *The Sign of Four* evolves into an episode of one party tracking another, on land and over water, the situation found in any number of Cooper's tales. Hawkeye, with admiration, tells us one who can track and kill his enemies is "a hound of the true breed."

After much investigation, Holmes learns the killers have chartered a launch, planning to intercept a freighter at sea and make their getaway with the treasure, but Holmes and the Yardmen overtake them in a police boat before they can make their connection. The outlaws turn out to be Jonathan Small, an English soldier, and his accomplice Tonga, an Andaman

Islander. Tonga is killed outright by a shot from Holmes or Watson, while Small is captured. "If his life is threatened, even a Brahmana may use arms," is a teaching of the Aryans, and he may even kill. "In a Purana (it has been declared), that he who slays an assailant does not sin, for (in that case) wrath meets wrath." Wrath meeting wrath is the theme of the revenge tale, as it is of the history of law itself.

In his presentment Small discloses his version of what happened, and why. It is a story of India, the land of the Aryans. During the Sepoy Mutiny, Small finds himself at the besieged Fort Agra in charge of three Sikhs guarding one of the gates. The Sikhs inform Small of their plot to kill a merchant coming to the fort at midnight with a case of jewels, seeking protection. As the price for his silence the Englishman is cut in on the deal and the four thieves lurk in the dark for the ill-fated merchant and his servant to show. Having second thoughts about the deed Small tells us, "but I thought of the treasure, and my heart set as hard as a flint within me." During the actual killing the merchant makes a run for it, "My heart softened to him, but again the thought of his treasure turned me hard and bitter." He trips the man and the Sikhs stab him and his servant to death. One of Hawkeye's most vicious enemies is "Flint Heart," an agent of the French, whom the Indians, who baptized him with his sobriquet, regard as being even crueler than themselves. Flint Heart allies himself with the Iroquois in order to lay waste the settlements of the English, as Small now allies himself with these Indians. The stolen gems are hidden in the Fort to be retrieved after the war as the murderers draw up a written oath of allegiance and autograph it with the sign of the four. The British authorities unearth the plot, arrest and convict the four, and send them to prison on the Andaman Islands where, in an effort to gain his freedom, Small takes Major Sholto and Captain Morstan into his confidence. Sholto goes to India to retrieve the gems but never returns, and Morstan, fearing the worst, goes after him only to discover both he and the treasure are missing. He tracks Sholto to London but dies following an argument over the loot. With the assistance of an Andaman Islander named Tonga, Small escapes and they set out in search of the two double-crossers and the treasure. "From that day I lived only for vengeance. I thought of it by day and I nursed it by night. It became an overpowering, absorbing passion with me," Small tells us. He finds but cannot approach the Major in London, but when learning of his having been taken ill at his estate, goes there and looking in the window, kills Sholto with guilty shock. The Major has paid with his body for his duplicity. Small leaves, but learning the booty may be in Bartholomew Sholto's room he returns and sends Tonga up in search of it. Tonga kills Bartholomew with a poison dart, and then steals the jewels yet again, and the two take off with Holmes in hot pursuit.

Small and Tonga, unquestionably two of the most fantastic characters in literature, actually owe much of their uniqueness to Nietzsche. The German realized that most of the thoughts and actions of mankind are motivated by the spirit of resentment and revenge, and people who have suffered want to see other people suffer, despising them if they do not. The crippled, sickly, and weak spend their lives seeking revenge against the healthy and strong.

Small is a good-sized, powerful man with aggressive features, curly black hair and a beard shot with gray. He also has a wooden stump for a right leg, his own having been bitten off by a crocodile in his early days in the East. He is a cripple, a peg leg, and a living metaphor of Nietzsche's "deformed cripples," these being the resentful, vengeance seeking ones. In "The Sussex Vampire" the unbounded hatred of the crippled boy Jack toward his younger, healthy brother is taken from Nietzsche's thoughts on the matter. Small proudly tells us he lived only for retribution, which the philosopher regarded as belittling, and therefore unworthy of a real man, hence the name "Small," while Tonga is "a little black man," who would be resentful both for his color and his size. These two possess animal instincts and mentality, along with suitably primitive physical features, and we are told they live in a lair. Tonga's inventory of beastly characteristics includes the fact that he "could climb like a cat," is as "proud as a peacock," and in a bad light "looked like a Newfoundland dog." His personage is as nebulous and frightening as the spiteful, revengeful monkey of "Green Tea."

There is a class of individuals Nietzsche calls "nay-sayers," those who strive to stifle the best intentions of mankind in general and of the superman in particular, and he dubs these people "malignant dwarfs," the most abject and contemptible of mankind. We have already met Culverton Smith, a perfect example of the breed. Malignant means evil or malicious, and in the case of the disease cancer, "likely to cause death," and the Andaman Islander certainly is lethal enough. Small informs us Tonga is as venomous as a young snake, comparing him to "a little bloodthirsty imp," who when first found by Small is "sick to death and had gone to a lonely place to die." Small had planned only on getting back the treasure, not on killing anyone, but when they visit the Sholto estate the dwarf kills Bartholomew out of spite, and during the chase on the river he tries to kill Holmes and Watson. Watson tells us, "Never have I seen features so deeply marked with all bestiality and cruelty. His small eyes glowed and burned with a somber light, and his thick lips were writhed back from his teeth, which grinned and chattered at us with a half-animal fury." When they first catch a glimpse of Tonga he is squatting in the back of the boat attempting to escape. In trying to warn us of these people Nietzsche says, "many a mischievous dwarf squatteth in your corners," and Small's lust for another's goods and his need for retaliation has made him as much of a dwarf as Tonga. "Naked have I seen both of them, the greatest man and the smallest man: — All-too-similar are they still to each other," Nietzsche tells us. Doyle finds this an interesting comparison, a large and small man in juxtaposition and uses it twice in the same story. As the thugs await the arrival of the merchant at the gate of Fort Agra, Small sees someone approaching and his lantern reveals the two Indians. Small tells us of the one, "Outside of a show I have never seen so tall a man," while the second is, "a little, fat, round fellow," so small he is compared to a mouse.

When Holmes and Jones question Small and hear his chronicle of killing for personal gain they listen with disgust written on their faces, the same disgust Nietzsche felt for such people, but Small defends himself, claiming the Sikhs would have killed him if he did not abet them, and the other offenses that followed were cases of logical reprisal in his search for "justice."

Several of the Holmes adventures are based somewhat upon Charles Kingsley's *Westward Ho!* in which the English mariner Amyas Leigh pursues the Spanish nobleman Don Guzman de Soto halfway around the world, seeking revenge for the murder of the English beauty Rose Salterne. Rose's father outfits a ship he names *Vengeance* to be used as an instrument of retribution upon the Spanish who have killed his daughter. Small, like Leigh, is a giant of a man with a full black beard who lives only for avengement upon those who have injured him, and like Small, and so many others in Doyle's stories, Leigh endures great hardships to extract it.

Tonga is based upon Queequeg, the untamed South-Sea Islander in *Moby-Dick* who befriends the young Ishmael with a savage protective friendship as fierce as Tonga's for Jonathan Small, or a dog's for its master. Tonga's weapon of choice is a dart shot from a blowgun, while the weapon Queequeg and the other harpooners hurl at the whales, and occasionally each other, is called a dart. When Small and Tonga acquire a skiff to effect their escape from the island, we are told, "Tonga had brought all his earthly possessions with him, his arms and his gods." Believing himself to be on the verge of death, Queequeg has a coffin made in which he will float into the afterlife, taking with him his harpoon, sailcloth for a pillow, his paddle, food, and his little god, Yojo. And both men die at sea, Tonga in the Thames, Queequeg in the Pacific.

Tonga is also fashioned after little Pip, the black slave boy completely devoted to Ahab, even going to his death by his side. All three have only one name: Pip because he is a slave, and Tonga and Queequeg because their single name points out their primitive natures.

Peg leg Small and his black heart brimming with dreams of payback is yet another version of the monomaniacal Ahab sailing the seas nursing a blood feud that cannot be bought off. Small, like Ahab, "never lost sight of my purpose," their quest for satisfaction of a grievance. Ahab's leg has been taken off by a whale, and Small's by a crocodile, and Ahab and Jonathan are *Old Testament* names associated with accounts of bloody reprisals. Both these tales end in a sea chase, the police launch after Captain Smith's *Aurora*, and the *Pequod's* pursuit of the white whale. The *Aurora* is the name of a ship found in Captain Frederick Marryat's novel *Mr. Midshipman Easy*, Marryat being a writer Doyle was extremely fond of.

As Small attempts to run for it following the river chase he jumps onto the mud flats only to end up stuck in the muck. The police must throw a rope over his shoulders "to haul him out, and to drag him, like some evil fish, over our side." He is being roped and brought over the side like a doomed whale to be flensed, as we learn in *Moby-Dick*.

Dickens had spent a few nights with the Thames Police out on the water, writing about the experience in his magazine *Household Words*. He describes scenes of sitting in silence in police boats watching the river and shore for suspicious craft the police would then attempt to overtake. One problem the river police had that the shore police did not, he tells us, was that if the river thieves thought they were about to be arrested, all they had to do was drop the loot overboard and the authorities had no case against them, and that's exactly what Small does with the treasure when he realizes the game is up.

The basic material drawn upon to frame a portrait of Holmes as a yogi or ascetic may have been borrowed from the ancient texts, but Doyle's favorite historian Thomas Macaulay supplied the inspiration. His essay on Lord Clive in Volume Four of *Critical, Historical, and Miscellaneous Essays*, is actually a review of John Malcolm's *The Life of Robert, Lord Clive*, published in 1836. Robert Clive had been sent to Madras, India in 1743, as a clerk for the East India Company, and ended up being regarded as the founder of the British Empire in India. In the bloody struggle between the English and French for influence in India, Clive distinguished himself with his bravery, good judgment, sagacity, and defiance of legitimate authority. In 1755, by now a lieutenant colonel in the British Army, Clive joins with the commander of the British squadron in the Eastern seas, Admiral Watson, in attacking the stronghold of a tribe of Indian pirates on the Arabian Gulf. Clive by land and Watson by sea, after great fighting, succeed in bringing the marauders to justice.

When Calcutta falls to the Nabob Surajah Dowlah, Macaulay describes the atrocity of the killing of one hundred twenty-three civilian prisoners in the chamber known as the Black Hole, for which Clive and Watson are sent to avenge the British. They beat the Indian at his own game of deceit and treachery, for without a major battle the Nabob agrees to restore the East India Company's property and make some amends to the victims, and the pair is instrumental in further developing English domination in India with Clive coming forward as a diplomat and negotiator.

Clive was a boxer at school, as was Doyle and Holmes, Macaulay mentioning this to emphasize that, contrary to the opinion of some, he was a man of honor in his political dealings; a good sport, quite simply, which to the British mentality makes up for any number of sins. This defense of the man comes about when Macaulay is forced to admit Clive was not above pulling tricks such as forging a signature, if he believed he was right.

At one point in the essay we actually come across a four-way pact amazingly similar to that found in Doyle's narrative. The Nabob Dowlah is so overbearing and cruel, not only to the English, but to his own people as well, that they all scheme against him. "A formidable confederacy was formed against him," which included three Indians: the minister of finance, the principal commander of the troops, and the richest banker in India, and when the plot was confided to the English agents they joined the conspirators. If you think of the English as one party you have an equation for the cabal in Doyle's adventure.

Clive had gathered a large fortune in India, converting some of it into jewels that he brought home with him, and just how this treasure had been acquired is still somewhat of a mystery, so it could possibly have been stolen. Since the defense of Arcot by a garrison of English and Sepoy soldiers against a besieging force was the event that gave Clive such distinction, you could say these gems were the treasure of Arcot, just as Doyle's gems could be called the treasure of Agra. We even have Lord Macaulay telling of a rich Indian merchant taking refuge, along with his wealth, among the English to avoid being plundered by an Indian despot. While back in Bengal as an administrator, Clive sent gifts of jewels, including pearls, back to his wife in England.

When things went wrong in one of his campaigns, Clive "retired alone under the shade of some trees, and passed near an hour there in thought." "It was said that he would sometimes, after sitting silent and torpid for hours, rouse himself to the discussion of some great question, would display in full vigour all the talents of the soldier and the statesman, and would then sink back into his melancholy repose." And Holmes as well plays the yogi in *The Sign of Four*, for this aspect of the Great Detective is emphasized here. When Mary Morstan leaves the Baker Street apartment after her invited visit, Watson can't help exclaiming, "What a very attractive woman!" Holmes, with drooping eyelids, mind you, asks, "Is she?" and adds languidly, "I did not observe." This is really playing the holy man, for the true Indian ascetic does not even look at a woman. Watson's wedding plans are answered with the notice that Holmes himself shall never marry, for "love is an emotional thing" and may "bias my judgment," a situation the yogi sternly avoids. We also listen to the detective tell us he is "not a whole-souled admirer of womankind," this term whole-souled being a borrowing from the Hindu religion.

Narcotics, such as Holmes is addicted to, are mentioned in Macaulay; Clive had contracted several painful maladies which he used opium to relieve, "and he was gradually enslaved by this treacherous ally. To the last, however, his genius occasionally flashed through the gloom." Pondicherry Lodge, the name of the Sholto estate, is taken from the city-fortress of Pondicherry, India, the great city fought over by the French and English.

In the summation of the character of Lord Clive we are told, "His name stands high on the roll of conquerors. But it is found in a better list, in the list of those who have done and suffered much for the happiness of mankind." Macaulay admits he had great faults, "But every person who takes a fair and enlightened view of his whole career must admit that our island, so fertile in heroes and statesmen, has scarcely ever produced a man more truly great either in arms or in council." History will not deny "to the reformer a share of that veneration" which he so richly deserves.

When Doyle, as a boy of sixteen, had a stopover in London while on his way to finish his schooling under the Jesuits, the first thing he did in the city was to visit the tomb of Lord Macaulay at Westminster Abbey, telling us, "It was the one great object of interest which London held for me. And so it might well be, when I think of all I owe him."

Deception, and the treasure that brought it to the surface, the stuff of *The Moonstone*, and the very fabric of *The Sign of Four*, is as well the raw material of Stevenson's short story "The Rajah's Diamond," probably the most direct of all the influences on Doyle's narrative. A young bank employee, for no apparent reason, receives through a lawyer an annual allowance of five hundred pounds from an anonymous benefactor. This year the messenger delivers instructions for the young man to attend a certain performance at a Paris theater where he will be contacted. Doyle pays his respects to Stevenson for we read of the contents of the merchant's chest of gems, that it contained "one which has been called, I believe, 'the great Mogul' and is said to be the second largest stone in existence." A mogul is a rajah with both words meaning an Indian ruler. Instead of a chest of jewels, one fantastic stone, the Rajah's Diamond, does the business of corrupting all who come near it, as did Jonathan Small's evil loot. Jewels in all three stories first saw light in India where they fell into the hands of unsavory natives and just as unscrupulous Englishmen, usually military personnel. All three stories also end in marriage: for Watson ends up getting Mary, and not long after the affair of the Rajah's Diamond the bank clerk Francis marries the young lady who became embroiled in his adventure, while *The Moonstone* as well ends with wedding bells.

The Sign of Four has also been linked, with good reason, to Stevenson's *Treasure Island* with Long John Silver, peg leg and all, serving as model for Small, and his ubiquitous parrot replaced by the little animal-like Tonga. In Stevenson's work Jim Hawkins does most of the talking, with Dr. David Livesey adding a few chapters, while in Doyle's piece Watson tells the bulk of the account, with Small adding a lengthy story of his own. The grounds of the Sholto estate, dug up by the twins in their search for their father's spoils stands in nicely for Treasure Island itself, also the scene of much digging for plunder.

It was an American, Joseph Stoddart, editor of *Lippincott's Monthly*, who commissioned *The Sign of Four*, the novella that really fixed Holmes as a character worthy of serious consideration in the public mind. At the same time Stoddart commissioned Oscar Wilde for a piece that turned out to be *The Picture of Dorian Gray*. Doyle was so impressed with the effete, over-aesthete Irishman he crossbred him with his equally bizarre creation Dorian Gray and had the hybrid offspring serve as archetype for Thaddeus Sholto. His having a twin in Bartholomew is a comment on the theme of *Dorian Gray*, for the portrait of Gray is regarded as so realistic an image of the man the artist calls it a "twin."

With the love and respect one great artist feels for another, Sir Arthur let the French writer Jules Verne guide his thoughts and pen throughout his entire career. It may have been *Around the World in Eighty Days* that initially inspired Doyle to write for the simple reason that it was Verne's amazing instant success with this work that he envied and hoped to emulate. *Around the World in Eighty Days* is the story of an Englishman, Phileas Fogg, who accepts a bet that he cannot circle the globe from point to point, that point being his London club, in eighty days. The loyalty agreement written out and signed by the four men in *The Sign of Four* is analogous to the document outlining the wager between Fogg and his fellow clubmen. Verne's story opens and closes in London, with long narratives of action taking place in such locations as India and America, and this plot sets the boundaries for a large number of Holmes' tales. Nations such as the two named, as well as Australia, Canada, or Africa, and so forth, have a place in many of the adventures, and if the foreign country is not dealt with directly, often an individual is from there, or has lived there, or an incident occurred between its borders upon which the plot turns. The first two Holmes sagas are what the French label *Romans de voyage*, with Verne calling his entire output of forty-three years *Voyages;* and *Around the World in Eighty Days* is the mother of all voyages, for the starting point is also the objective, and further than that you cannot go.

Both *A Study in Scarlet* and *Around the World in Eighty Days* open with a broad range of speculations as to exactly who Holmes and Fogg really are, their backgrounds, where they get their money, etc. We know little or nothing about Fogg at the opening of the story, and not much more at the close, and this would have been the case with Sherlock if Doyle had not been encouraged to continue the character. Both men are unmarried, live alone, and have rare mental abilities. Fogg seems to be personally acquainted with foreign parts, while Holmes knows how to find the information he needs about them, though we are never quite sure where Holmes has traveled. Fogg is so severely economical in his gestures, and so regular and cold-blooded as to make some wonder if he has a heart at all, speculations Stamford brings to the surface as he describes Holmes' scientific if somewhat inhuman nature.

Doyle must have been amazed upon reading in Verne's novel that the house Fogg lives in was once the home of the playwright Richard Sheridan, especially in view of the fact that Fogg is a fictional character.

Verne's story takes on the trappings of a mystery when news of the robbery of fifty-five thousand pounds from the Bank of England interrupts the comfortable ease of the Reform Club. Advertising for a servant and companion for the trip, Fogg receives a response from Jean Passepartout, a Frenchman, and like John Watson, a stranger to London looking for a place to live and some peace and quiet. The Englishman addresses his new assistant as John, only to be corrected — but since Jean is French for John, nothing is changed. Passepartout is a name meaning "one who can go anywhere." Like Watson, Passepartout will prove to be far more than simply an assistant, even saving Fogg's life.

Phileas Fogg is a man of experiments, with this voyage being nothing less than one great exploration carried forward by a nature pragmatically equipped. The Yard comes into it, for one of their men, Detective Fix, clever, unscrupulous, and as relentless as his name, believes none other than Phileas to be the bank robber, and sets out after him. Fix is usually dead wrong about most things, being one who deals strictly with appearances, failing to see the importance of thought. He compares himself proudly to a hunting dog when questioned as to how he shall recognize Fogg, claiming his animal instincts will put him on the right scent. We have here a model for Jonathan Small, whom he physically resembles, as he follows a man around the globe for revenge and the recovery of stolen goods. A large section of Verne's novel takes place in India, with the Sepoy Mutiny being mentioned, as well as Fort Agra, and one important character introduced is Sir Francis Cromarty, a British officer who survived the rebellion. Passepartout, observing an elaborate ceremony, commits an offense by entering a temple, an act forbidden to an unbeliever, and with his shoes on to boot. The temple is undoubtedly meant to be a Zoroastrian holy place, for they have very strict laws forbidding such pollution. A practitioner of the ancient religion is introduced, a Parsee, who acts as guide to the travelers during an overland trek by elephant where they stumble upon a suttee ritual. A young Zoroastrian princess is to be burned alive upon the funeral pyre of her husband, but four men, including Fogg, hatch a plot to rescue her. As in *The Sign of Four*, the conspirators remove the bricks from a temple façade, not to hide a treasure, but to free one. Phileas Fogg cannot be dissuaded from his purpose; he is completely unflappable and determined, accepting everything "with coldness, neither his voice nor his manner betraying the slightest emotion." It pays off, for the woman is rescued and flees with them to the nearest port. This exploit is an echo of *The Last of the Mohicans* wherein Hawkeye and his companions liberate Alice Munro from the "Indians," who also plan to burn her alive. In reference to the event Fogg says, "The chance which now seems lost may present itself at the last moment," in a statement reminiscent of the theatrical yet oddly natural speech of the American scout. No people in the world, not even the Americans, had such deep appreciation and respect for Cooper as the French, even in translation, and in spite of the fact that he always portrayed them in a bad light. Honoré de Balzac considered Cooper one of the greatest writers in history. Fogg's initial reaction to the exotic charms of the Princess is cool indifference; he hardly looks at her, like Holmes with Mary Morstan.

A situation similar in spirit and circumstances now emerges for Fogg, Passepartout, and Princess Aouda, who like Holmes, Watson, and Morstan, unwittingly become embroiled in a search and struggle focusing upon stolen loot, one in the form of jewels, the other being the pilfered bank funds, and all parties become involved in journeys by land and sea hoping to bring about a conclusion in their favor. While at sea the Fogg group passes the Andaman Islands, "near the shores, but the savage Papuans, who are in the lowest scale of humanity, but are not, as has been asserted, cannibals, did not make their appearance." A water pursuit evoking the chase on the Thames, or the desperate life and death canoe races in Cooper's works, develops when Fogg, failing to connect with the steamer from China to Japan, commissions a water pilot boat and attempts to overtake it. Eventually they end up in America, have some scrapes in San Francisco, and catch a train East. Like Doyle, the French novelist dwells upon the harsh nature of the plains and desert, "No wild beast appeared on the plain. It was a desert in its vast nakedness." As the train passes through Utah a proselytizing Mormon Elder boards and delivers a lecture concerning the mysteries of the religion of the Latter Day Saints. The missionary is a fanatic who opens his harangue with claims that the U. S. Government is persecuting his religion, citing the armed conflicts between the Mormons and the American authorities. Verne adds details of the imprisoning of Brigham Young on charges of rebellion and polygamy. Elder Hitch, in retelling the story of the Mormons, dwells upon the trek of Young and his followers to the sanctuary offered by the relative isolation and freedom of Utah, the very wagon train Doyle writes of in *A Study in Scarlet*. Fogg and his friends spend some time in Salt Lake City, described as filled with Mormon women "neither well off nor happy," who fill the Europeans with contempt for the practice of polygamy.

While in San Francisco, Fogg had met with atrocious consequences, a character whose singular personality stamps itself on Doyle's mind, influencing indelibly the Sherlock Holmes stories. Fogg and Fix, acting together, get involved in an argument that quickly escalates into a fistfight with an American military officer, Colonel Stamp Proctor. The Colonel proves overbearing, arrogant, and violent to a completely unnecessary degree, features Doyle appropriated for any number of colonels found throughout his writings. Some of these, as we shall see, are Nietzsche's "higher men," who have achieved what they have achieved by catering to the lowest instincts of the people. Proctor is as thick and stupid as the Mormons themselves, and despised the two Englishmen as soon as he laid eyes on them, with his sole purpose being to assault them. He deliberately insults Fogg, but circumstances do not allow an opportunity for satisfaction while in America, yet Fogg vows he will return after he has won his bet to settle the score. There is no doubt but that this man would travel thousands of miles searching for satisfaction, the very theme of any number of Cooper's and Doyle's writings. When the two find they are on the same train they arrange for a duel with pistols, but as they are about to carry out their plans Indians attack the train. The defenders hold the attack off but the engineer is killed, and the train becomes a runaway. When the situation is finally brought under control, Passepartout and two others are missing and presumed captured by the Sioux. "I will find him, living or dead," Fogg tells Aouda, and in his mind he thinks, "It is my duty." We are listening here to the thoughts of Hawkeye as he sets off to attempt the liberation of three prisoners of the Iroquois in *The Last of the Mohicans*. The whites usually tried to get back the dead bodies of their people from the Indians since they mutilated the dead as well as the living, scalping being only one example. Of Fogg we are told, "He had sacrificed his fortune, and was now risking his life, all without hesitation, from duty, in silence." For the second time, someone must be saved from the fires of the Indians. In a borrowing from Cooper, Fix declares that if Fogg fails to return, he will attempt to track him by his footprints, but this proves unnecessary for Fogg effects the release of the prisoners, and the action continues toward New York City, the last staging area before reaching England. "At last the Hudson came into view," Verne tells us, having mentioned the great river a number of times already. This river and its associations seem to have played an important part in his thoughts. Fix, as did Hope and Small, catches up with his quarry in London, arresting Fogg on English soil, after chasing him all over the world, only to learn the real culprits have already been arrested.

The question comes up as to why Fogg undertook the journey at all, since the expense of it ate up any money he won on the bet, and it can't be said he really enjoyed the trip. In Doyle's work the disputed gems are thrown into the Thames, and in Verne's piece the trip cost as much as the wage won, but in each case someone gained the love of a good woman: Fogg marries the Princess Aouda, something he did not seem capable of until now, and Watson has wed Mary Morstan.

Chapter Eight. My Brother's Keeper

Nietzsche's creation Zarathustra is a man of light bemoaning the fact that "it is my lonesomeness to be begirt with light!" He tells us he lives "in mine own light, I drink again into myself the flames that break forth from me." Carlyle views the hero in terms of light, calling a great man "a blessed heaven-sent Bringer of Light," with Jesus being "the light of the world." In the study of the biography of great men, and of history, we could find the hidden and immutable divine truth. "In all epochs of the world's history, we shall find the Great Man to have been the indispensable saviour of his epoch; — the lightning, without which the fuel never would have burnt. The History of the World, I said already, was the Biography of Great Men." Carlyle claims the great man is a "light-fountain," we can gain something from just by studying or being near. Such a man has "enlightened the darkness of the world," with his "native original insight," who makes "all souls feel that it is well with them." The truly intelligent man who reads the actions of his fellow man, by which he means the biographer, he calls "the seeing eye." Biography he regarded as an extension of history, and "history held its divine message secret until perceived by the seeing eye." The expression makes one think of Hawkeye as well, whose very life depends upon his ability to read the actions of his fellow man. The biographer must be a worshipper of heroes, and is almost as important as the hero, for both are seeing eyes, and it is the biographer who is responsible for acknowledging excellence where it exists, demonstrating the lost art of discipleship, a regard for divine wisdom, and himself becoming a witness to the high truth of hero worship. Boswell tells us he worshiped Johnson, and Carlyle may very well have this pair in mind. The aim of biography is "the writing of true scripture," with the greatest biography being the story of Jesus. "Every man that writes is writing a new Bible; or a new Apocrypha; to last for a week, or for a thousand years: he that convinces a man and sets him working is the doer of a *miracle*." Carlyle's hero "can be Poet, Prophet, King, Priest, or what you will, according to the kind of world that he finds himself born into." Because all heroes are perceivers of the emblematic nature of matter, the individual hero resembles heroes of all ages. This is the very heart of the meaning of the Sherlock Holmes stories. Carlyle's heroes are not the beings of myth or anthropology; they are the more perfectly attuned beings in a divine creation and his hypothesis rests upon the conviction that the law of God is the law of life, that "the greatest of all Heroes is One — whom we do not name here!" In the *New Testament* we learn the mission of Jesus is "To enlighten them that sit in darkness, and in the shadow of death: to direct our feet into the way of peace." "Light in the Darkness," is the chapter in *A Study in Scarlet* in which Holmes begins to solve the mystery.

The world is introduced first to John Watson, not to Sherlock Holmes, and what is lost on today's preconditioned readers is the fact that initially those who opened this novel for the first time must have understandably believed they were going to be dealing with a work in which John Watson is the central figure of the story, for nothing leads you to think the wounded doctor, whose memoirs you are supposed to be reading, according to the title, is not going to go on being the protagonist. Only as one proceeds does the character of Holmes emerge as the lead figure. John, as the name of a personality, can be traced, by association, to both John the Baptist, and to John the Apostle/ Evangelist. The Apostles, in their gospels and epistles, tell the world of their master, and of his miraculous deeds, yet only four wrote anything: Luke, Matthew, Mark, and John, with John, a cousin and favorite of Jesus, being distinguished for the extent to which he relates the words of Jesus, and the length he devotes to single incidents and occasions. All four gospels open with numerous statements, not about Jesus, but about John the Baptist, just as in the Holmes fiction nearly each individual story, beginning with this earliest creation, commences with details and thoughts, not of Sherlock, but of John. John the Baptist was such a sagacious prophet many believed him to be the Messiah, but in the course of events the Baptist meets Jesus, whom he acknowledges to be one greater than he, insisting he himself is no prophet at all, since he cannot, like Jesus, foretell what is to happen. According to Luke, John's primary function is as a prophet, not of God the Father, but of Jesus, and he was intended to "go before the face of the Lord, to prepare his ways," adding that John's ambition is "to give knowledge of salvation to his people." Matthew endorses this, believing John must be the one foretold of in the written records as the angel or messenger that, in regard to the Messiah, is to "prepare thy way before thee." The Baptist tells us, "he who is to come after me, is stronger than I, whose shoes I am not worthy to carry," and that as you acquire knowledge of this new man, "He must increase, but I must decrease." Luke is a physician, called by Paul, "the most dear Physician," and John the Baptist can be considered a healer for by his will he restored the speech and hearing of his father, the priest Zachary. The Baptist comes out of the desert to tell the world of Jesus just as Watson, after suffering his own baptism of fire, comes out of the East to tell us of a man with the powers of a prophet. Even the ship Watson sails on to Europe shows his Eastern roots, for the *Orontes* is the name of a river flowing through Syria and Turkey into the Mediterranean, roughly the route of early Christianity. Holmes and Watson meet under the auspices of the *New Testament*, being introduced at Saint Bartholomew's Hospital, an institution named after one of the Apostles. John the Baptist and Jesus are often confused with each other, as when King Herod, upon being informed of the powers of Jesus, claims he believes him to be John returned from the dead. This development comes into operation in "A Scandal in Bohemia," when the King first enters the Baker Street flat, and Watson says, "He looked from one to the other of us, as if uncertain which to address." This type of mix-up takes place a number of times, with Holmes usually pointing out to the visitor which is which.

In *A Study in Scarlet* we are shown that Holmes actually gets little or no credit for his enormous efforts fighting evil, and that he expects to get little. Jesus lived in almost total obscurity for what we read of his life is only a brief record of the few years previous to his death. Carlyle reminds us that great men are "*silent* men!" who usually speak or write only when it is necessary to throw some light on a mystery. Holmes, according to Carlyle's criteria is one of his "noble silent men, scattered here and there, each in his department; silently thinking, silently working; whom no Morning Newspaper makes mention of!" and then he adds, in a deliberate paraphrasing of Jesus, "They are the salt of the Earth." Following the solution of this first case, in which Holmes played the major part, he quotes aloud the summation of the story in a morning newspaper ironically called *The Echo*, "the credit of this smart capture belongs entirely to the well-known Scotland Yard officials, Messrs. Lestrade and Gregson," and that "It is expected that a testimonial of some sort will be presented to the two officers as a fitting recognition of their services." The testimonial in question is no doubt a banquet of the type so popular at the time, at which the two men would be honored. Holmes makes a statement we must now interpret on other levels: "Didn't I tell you so when we started? That's the result of all our Study in Scarlet — to get them a testimonial." One astonishing piece of information this quote provides is that Holmes is actually referring, by title, and as a title, to the novel in which he is to be a character. He is seeing into the future for the book could not possibly have been written yet if the action to be recorded in the novel is only now taking place in front of us. His "Didn't I tell you so," also refers to a prediction that has now come true. The phrase "to get them a testimonial" no longer applies simply to the two Yard Men, but to all mankind, for testimonial in a colloquial sense means, "a copy of the *New Testament*." We have here John the Evangelist "testifying to the facts," and it has nothing to do with a banquet. "I claim no credit in such cases. My name figures in no newspaper. The work itself, the pleasure of finding a field for my peculiar powers, is my highest reward," Holmes tells us elsewhere. Johnson worked for years in relative poverty and obscurity, often signing other people's names to his own work for a few pounds. Boswell published letters in *Gentleman's Magazine* showing Johnson attempted to have his signature poem "London" published anonymously rather than under his own name, and indeed it was published as such in 1738. Jesus, like Holmes and Johnson, receives little recognition or compensation for his services, but all three accept gifts and tribute when it is offered. Jesus was not averse to receiving homage as we see from his triumphant entry into Jerusalem on Palm Sunday, and his insistence on accepting oil, which was costly at the time, from a grateful woman he had cured, adding that he regards himself as more important than the poor.

Holmes, like Descartes and Johnson, tell us little about themselves. Descartes wished to remain hidden without alienating himself from the reader, and although the philosopher insists his writings are autobiographical in nature, and regardless of his promise to the reader of a portrait of himself, little such information actually surfaces by way of content; he wishes to remain a bit mysterious and he succeeds. As we know, Descartes published anonymously fearing reprisals from the Church and others, but he also was apprehensive some would alter and misrepresent his words, saying, at one point, that some of his work had been altered already, and "I could no longer acknowledge them as mine." And just so did Holmes know the newspapers' accounts of what happened would be altered and distorted. Jesus even regards the course of his execution as one gross misunderstanding as to the intentions of his preaching, claiming he did not come to destroy the law, as was charged, but to fulfill it.

In the *Bible*, the title "prophet" is often applied to any man of superior learning or uncommon gifts, whether their knowledge regards divine or secular aspects of life. In the gospel of John we are told that when Jesus meets Nathaniel he says, "Behold an Israelite indeed, in whom there is no guile." Nathaniel asks him how he knew this since they have never met. Jesus answers, "Before that Philip called thee, when thou wast under the fig tree, I saw thee." He is one who knows things that are done in private, in his absence, and here he also seems to be claiming to be able to read minds, since seeing someone, in a vision or otherwise, is hardly the same thing as having knowledge of that person's thoughts. When Jesus is talking at the well to the Samaritan woman, she suddenly realizes he knows her innermost thoughts, and calls him a prophet. Holmes has great knowledge, and the ability to predict the future, as we have seen. Watson tells us, "Here I had heard what he had heard, I had seen what he had seen, and yet from his words it was evident that he saw clearly not only what had happened but what was about to happen, while to me the whole business was still confused and grotesque." This is a reiteration of Jesus' words, "Therefore do I speak to them in parables: because seeing they see not, and hearing they hear not, neither do they understand." This theme is carried forward with the name of one of the two detectives Holmes is so often called upon to assist, Tobias Gregson. Tobias was a pious elder of the Nephthali tribe who was blinded by God to test his patience, therefore to be used as an example of righteous patience. The Lord repents, sending his angel Raphael (the medicine of God), who cures the blindness of Tobias. The elder, thinking surely he will soon die for the Lord has sent an angel to him, in leaving his son his inheritance of faith, admonishes the youth, also named Tobias, to "Seek counsel always of a wise man." One of Jesus' most oft repeated miracles is the granting of sight to those who are blind, and I notice that when he is disgusted, as he so often is, with those who fail to understand his reading of the laws, he calls them blind, or foolish and blind. Gregson and Lestrade, who call upon Holmes for assistance quite often, are like the two blind men quoted in *Matthew* who sought out Jesus in their desperation. "And as Jesus was departing from thence, there followed him two blind men, crying out, and saying: Son of David, have mercy on us. And when he was come to the house the blind men came to him. And Jesus saith to them: Do you believe that I can do this unto you? They said to him: Yea, Lord. Then he touched their eyes, saying: According to your faith, be it done unto you. And their eyes were opened: and Jesus strictly charged them, saying: See that no man know this." Gregson and Lestrade must henceforth be regarded as among the pious for indeed they go out of their way to see "that no man know this." Notice the blind need go to the house of Jesus; he does not go to them. Neither does Sherlock, as a rule, go to the police; they come to his house.

Just as Jesus never doubts his own mission, Holmes, in the role of Christ, and therefore as one even higher than the prophets, expresses little or no doubt as to his own powers. In the scene dealing with Holmes' article "The Book of Life" (an expression often used for the *New Testament* or sometimes the teachings of Jesus) Watson informs us that the piece "attempted to show how much an observant man might learn by an accurate and systematic examination of all that came in his way." This strikes him as being a remarkable mixture of shrewdness and absurdity, which is an apt description of any piece of religious writing. "The writer claimed by a momentary expression, a twitch of a muscle, or a glance of an eye, to fathom a man's inmost thoughts. Deceit, according to him, was an impossibility in the case of one trained to observation and analysis." Supernatural powers are being hinted at here, for such an all-seeing mind would have to be of necessity godlike. Watson complains that the writer's "conclusions were as infallible as so many propositions of Euclid. So startling would his results appear to the uninitiated that, until they learned the process by which he had arrived at them, they might well consider him a necromancer." Now, necromancy makes of one a prophet, for it is the practice of foretelling the future by communication with the dead, with the Hebrew prophets all claiming to be able to do so; indeed this is how they tell the future, the dead acquaint them with it. The writer of the article makes a subtle claim of being more than mortal, telling us, "nor is life long enough to allow any mortal to attain the highest possible perfection," in making true observations and deductions, yet we know the writer himself has reached this level of accomplishment. Watson calls this commentary twaddle, and the work of some armchair lounger living in seclusion, claiming that no one could possibly be intelligent enough to be able to guess the trades of all he meets, saying he would "lay a thousand to one against him" being able to perform this, to which Holmes calmly replies, "You would lose your money." As Watson slowly accepts and acknowledges Holmes for what he is, he comes to regard him as nothing less than the benefactor of his race.

Without guessing the exact nature of Holmes' business, which he is in no hurry to divulge, the doctor observes those who came seeking his help. "One morning a young girl called, fashionably dressed, and stayed for half an hour or more. The same afternoon brought a gray-headed, seedy visitor, looking like a Jew peddler, who appeared to me to be much excited, and who was closely followed by a slip-shod elderly woman. On another occasion an old white-haired gentleman had an interview with my companion, and on another a railway porter in his velveteen uniform." These "nondescript individuals," Holmes tells us, "are my clients." We know Jesus owned a house and was habitually visited by those in need. I can't help thinking of the "Sermon on the Mount," in which Jesus sets forth so much of his message to the motley crowd following him, with his words on that day including the Beatitudes, the backbone of his reflections on the need for compassion in life. "Blessed are they that hunger and thirst after justice: for they shall be filled. Blessed are they that suffer persecution for justice sake: for theirs is the kingdom of heaven." Blessed are the meek, and the poor in spirit, and so forth, all those souls who flock to the house of Holmes in their desperate and anxious hours. Doyle even adds a Jew to make the scene that much more authentic. The history of the Holmes literature is of people in dilemma, people seeking liberation from fear, or those falsely accused of crimes, or in need of protection or advice, which search out the detective for assistance and consultation. Doyle creates an ominous sense of emergency from the very entrance of a visitor to the rooms of Baker Street, and Holmes, like Jesus, is defined by the crises he manages to resolve.

The idea of Holmes personifying Jesus, and Watson portraying John the Baptist, may have been given abstract justification by Carlyle, but concrete example already existed. Emile Gaboriau is credited with the invention of the still popular form of the French police novel. *Monsieur Lecoq* of 1869 introduces us to the young policeman Lecoq and his assistant, a somewhat older alcoholic officer ironically called Father Absinthe. In one episode the two investigate a tavern where three men have just been killed in a brawl. A suspect has been arrested, and Lecoq and Father Absinthe are left at the scene pending the arrival of Inspector General Gevrol, head of the department. Doubting the guilt of the suspect, Lecoq begins a Socratic dialogue with his assistant, and to strengthen his speculations he takes the older man out to the backyard, scene of the killings, to examine the footprint evidence found in the new snow. "Without hesitation, Lecoq threw himself upon his knees in the snow, in order to examine them." Fortunately Holmes and Hawkeye weren't there or the three of them would have banged heads on the way down. The sagacious detective is compared to a hound. "A bloodhound in pursuit of his prey would have been less alert, less discerning, less agile than he. He came and went, turned, came back again, hurried on, or paused without any apparent reason; he scrutinized, he questioned everything: the earth, the logs of wood, the blocks of stone, and even the most insignificant objects; sometimes standing, but oftener on his knees, sometimes flat upon his belly, his face so near the ground that his breath must have melted the snow." One after another the suppositions of Lecoq are proved by deductions made from such assorted evidence as the depth, direction, and spacing of footprints, the impressions made by people resting on a log, or the circle in the snow made by the sweeping skirt of a woman. The young policeman, discovering from these marks many secrets never guessed at by the older man, has raised close attention to detail to a fine art. Absinthe, in a flurry of admiration, the admiration of a man who has spent a lifetime in police work, cries out, "Here *is* a detective if you like!" adding, "And they say Gevrol is shrewd! What has he ever done to compare with this? Ah! Shall I tell you what I think? Very Well. In comparison with you, the general is only John the Baptist." He also says, "You can scarcely blame an old man for being a little like St. Thomas. 'I have touched it with my fingers,' and now I am content to follow you." The reference is to the wound from the spear thrust into the side of Jesus as he hung upon the cross, the touching of which was the only evidence Thomas would accept of the Resurrection. In *A Study in Scarlet* the policeman John Rance plays the role of Father Absinthe, interested only in his gin and retirement, and therefore useless.

Sergeant Cuff, the detective who eventually solves the theft of the Moonstone in Collins' novel is a prophet, even a Christ figure, with the role of the Baptist played by the butler Betteredge, who introduces Cuff and whose name Gabriel means "God is my strength," and whose function is as a "herald of good news." The two conjointly work at the solving of the crime, as do Holmes and Watson. Betteredge constantly reiterates Cuff's astonishing ability to seemingly read minds, and it is he who keeps the plot moving, augmenting our knowledge of how the events are taking shape and telling us of the Sergeant's advances and setbacks.

Cuff is a man of unflappable determination and coolness, never letting the slightest thing deter him from following his clues. He makes three predictions in regard to the case, all of which come true, causing us to realize Holmes also makes prophecies in the course of investigations. Cuff speaks of throwing the "necessary light on the matter," and Betteredge questions, as the solving of the scandal seems close, "Was the darkness going to lift?" John the Apostle tells us the coming of Jesus was a great event "because the darkness is past, and the true light now shineth."

None could be poorer in spirit than James Ryder, found in "The Blue Carbuncle," a case revolving around the blue gem stolen from the Countess of Morcar. The stone turns up in the crop of a freshly killed Christmas goose, and the two detectives set out to find out why. After a good deal of trouble they locate Ryder who worked at the Countess' hotel and force an admission that he and the Countess' maid had swiped the jewel. Ryder suddenly kneels on the rug in front of Holmes, "For God's sake, have mercy!" he shrieked, "Think of my father! of my mother! It would break their hearts. I never went wrong before! I never will again. I swear it. I'll swear it on a *Bible*. Oh, don't bring it into court! For Christ's sake, don't." Then Ryder yells out, "God help me! God help me!" Holmes listens to the story and the pitiful pleas of the criminal laced with allusions to God and Christ, then tells Ryder to arise, get out, he is free to go, and he leaves with a "Heaven bless you!" over his shoulder. Holmes admits that he is probably committing a felony, "but it is just possible that I am saving a soul." Lesser spirits fight only crime, but Holmes, like Jesus, fights evil, being more interested in the soul than in the body. If you send him to jail now you could ruin him for life, and he will not go wrong again, he is so frightened, says Holmes, and adds that it is the season of forgiveness. Holmes plays Christ and a prophet as well, for when he is questioned by Watson as to how he can be so sure Ryder will not go wrong again, he claims, "My name is Sherlock Holmes. It is my business to know what other people don't know." Jesus tells us, "Come to me, all ye that are heavy laden, and I will refresh you; and though your sins be as scarlet, they shall be as white as snow."

This story also deals with Wendell Holmes' realization that unthinking punishment is not the true function of the law, and we must take into consideration whether or not harsh punitive measures will not actually make the man worse. Ryder's plea is actually a presentiment, with the accused explaining why they should not notify the authorities of the details of the case and therefore, "bring it into court." To make Ryder pay with his body by incarcerating him is not the answer to this particular problem.

Here's something very interesting I found in "The Blue Carbuncle." Listen to the last sentence. Holmes is speaking, "If you will have the goodness to touch the bell, Doctor, we will begin another investigation, in which, also, a bird will be the chief feature." What he is talking about? As far as I know, no other case deals with a bird, and since when did Holmes ever ring a bell to begin a new case, and what would such a bell be connected to?

Boswell says Johnson had a "great and illuminated mind," giving to him an intuitive sympathy with the people and their problems, and could always be counted upon to help if he could. Another of Johnson's biographers, a personal friend, Hester Thrale tells us, "Mr. Johnson has more Tenderness for Poverty than any other man I ever knew," describing his flat as a nest of people including "a Blind Woman and her maid, a Blackamoor and his Wife, a Scotch Wench who has her Case as a Pauper depending in some of the Law Courts; a Woman whose Father once lived at Lichfield, and a superannuated Surgeon." This doctor was Robert Levett, an unlicensed but trained physician who had undertaken the care of Johnson's health. He is described as a clever man, though uneducated, who treated the poorest of the poor, often being paid in drink. His heavy drinking habit Doyle possibly transferred to Watson's brother, whom we are told about but never meet. Dr. Levett and Johnson always had breakfast together, with the poet having a high regard for the surgeon, believing the man was doing great good among the London indigent.

Hawkeye is born into the midst of a truly bloody, vicious world of sorrow and strife; he takes part in its warfare, not having much of a choice, but he preaches peace and mercy, and the rule of law, such as it was, in speech and example. Although his society is brutal and violent he never loses his humanity and sense of compassion in his dealings with mankind, even with his enemies.

In *The Prairie* Hawkeye is introduced to the reader through the eyes of a family of settlers who first view the scout as he is standing on the crest of a hill backlit by the setting afternoon sun like the statue of a deity in a sacred grotto. "In the centre of this flood of fiery light a human form appeared, drawn against the gilded background, as distinctly, and seemingly as palpable, as though it would come within the grasp of any extended hand. The figure was colossal; the attitude musing and melancholy, and the situation directly in the route of the travellers. But embedded, as it was, in its setting of garish light, it was impossible to distinguish its just proportions or true character." They view him with "dull interest, that soon quickened into superstitious awe." Before realizing he is human they regard Hawkeye as "the impression of a supernatural agency."

In one episode in this novel his enemies, the Teton Indians, light a prairie fire hoping to kill him, but get caught in it themselves. Studying their tracks the scout realizes what has occurred: "[C]an it be that the Tetons have been caught in their own snares? Such things do happen; and here is an example to all evil-doers." He regards himself as one going about the Lord's work, sometimes calling out following a successful effort against his foes, who he often compares to devils, "Thanks be to the Lord!" The greatest compliment he can pay to a man's sagacity is to say of him he is a prophet.

There are stories written by Doyle focusing on the transition, and the need for this renovation of the "old religion," and its laws, to the "new religion," and its rules, just as Wendell Holmes exhibited the exigency for alterations of the old blood feuds into the neoteric laws of society, and from that to the needs of modern life, and just as Darwin recapitulated the evolution of man from his primordial beginnings to his contemporary persona. Doyle had a great deal to say about the *Old Testament* in his writings, especially when one is scanning his entire output, but the Hebrew religion was hardly an isolated mythology the new wave teachings attempted to replace, with the fecund nature worship of the ancient Greeks, for one, meeting twilight at the hands of the Apostles. Anyone studying the rich diversity of thought, and the intensity of the personalities the fields of religion and philosophy are famous for, cannot fail but to be impressed with the contributions of the Greeks. A somewhat in-depth awareness of Greek philosophy and culture is essential to even a rudimentary comprehension of the existential actuality of modern life. You can live quite well minus such knowledge, but you will never understand yourself, or the fullness of the Western World, without it.

"The Greek Interpreter" revolves around the account of Mr. Melas, an Anglo- Greek who was kidnapped, blindfolded, brought to an unknown location, made to translate the Greek of a bound and gagged countryman, Paul Kratides, and when finally released unharmed, threatened not to reveal what had happened. However, he tells his story to Mycroft Holmes, who calls in his brother. After listening to the story, Sherlock attempts to flush out the facts with the newspaper ad ploy. The ad brings a clue to the whereabouts of the bound victim, and Watson and the Holmes brothers set out for the place, learning in the meantime that Melas has again been abducted. They arrive at the victim's residence but in time only to save the life of Melas, who along with his unfortunate and now dead countryman had been bound and abandoned in a room filling with poison gas. An aborted effort at forcing Paul Kratides to sign papers turning over his and his sister's property to two malefactors was the crime going forward. At the conclusion of the drama we learn the kidnappers and murderers have paid with their bodies for they are found stabbed to death halfway around the world.

Mycroft Holmes is introduced to the world ensconced in the Stranger's Room of the Diogenes Club of London, the only room we are allowed in, not being members. I doubt if all of us would wish for membership anyway, since one thing all affiliates must maintain is a ritualistic silence at all times while on the premises. The members in general, and Mycroft in particular, are wholly content to watch the world go by, observing it but not taking part in it, except perhaps, in Mycroft's case, save for his government job, which seems to be in some intelligence department. Doyle we know did not have a very high opinion of the British Intelligence Service. In the English language those who cannot speak are called "dumb," with a number of other languages following suit. Perhaps it was once assumed the speechless simply had nothing to say. I believe Mycroft to be Doyle's personification of the stolid British government, threatened by the raiders and rovers, and more deadly enemies such as the Germans, as well as vicious enemies within, yet content to watch it all happen, doing little or nothing about it. Sherlock tells us that from time to time his brother "*is* the British government." This defensive and protective stance on the part of our author amounted to a life-long theme with the man.

Phileas Fogg's club, the Reform, is "an imposing edifice in Pall Mall," which happens to be in the same neighborhood as the Diogenes. Fogg can be found there "at hours mathematically fixed," for he lives by the self-imposed rigidity of a silent schedule, as does Mycroft. At his refuge Fogg sits in near silence for fourteen hours a day reading newspapers, a form of recreation equally popular at the Diogenes, whose brothers lounge in absolute quiet reading the periodicals. Fogg enjoys an occasional game of whist, principally because it is a silent contest requiring little or no talking.

The Diogenes Club is a sanctuary for those, some from shyness, some from misanthropy, or other reasons, having no wish for the company of their fellow man. Such men are automatically pessimistic, as are those who seek asylum in Stevenson's Suicide Club. This London club, as we know, was established by those whose cynicism and despondency with existence have brought them together, not for aloof silence or whist, but to provide contingent opportunity and a support structure whereby each member is facilitated in putting an end to his morbid existence, with each affiliate taking a turn to see who will be next. This alliance of morose defeatists and would-be suicides is one inspiration for Mycroft's silent fellow dropouts from the bad game.

Among the ancient Greeks, there was a loose association of philosophers and students centered in Athens known as the Cynics, who held that the world was evil, so in order to live properly and possibly find some happiness, one should not fight the world and its corruption but rather withdraw entirely from participation in it. In essence, here is what the Greek cynic Diogenes was doing, leaving imperfect humankind to itself, living out existence in a pot, depriving himself even of the little luxuries life might have to offer while at the same time rejecting all convention. In a final gesture of contempt laced with bitter humor, Diogenes carried a lit lantern about in daylight, searching for an honest man. Mycroft and his colleagues have come to accept, even, no doubt, appreciate, a few of life's bounties: money, a good club, fine clothes and food, and so forth, but in the philosophy of Cynicism this is quite permissible, provided one faces the actuality that each of these things is precarious, for if we trust our happiness to the possession of them, we may find ourselves betrayed by life and lose them. If a cynic wishes to encounter true contentment and salvation in this life, he must discover it within himself; therefore this negation of worldly pleasures and chattels is what valid virtue consists of. The denunciation of external goods included the rejection of other people. This resulted in a complete indifference to, and lack of feelings for others. This thought and its resultant consequences is diametrically opposed to Doyle's own commitment to the world and its problems. This was possibly one reason he has portrayed Mycroft as a bloated freak, for the man is unbelievably fat, thereby showing his contempt for this way of life. Cynicism is basically a doctrine that is antisocial, the last word in the world you could apply to Doyle, although Sherlock feels comfortable in the role from time to time, for he practices asceticism and Cynicism is regarded as one of the forerunners of this life style.

We learn Mycroft does not have the ability or the energy to work out the many points of a police case, rendering him inefficient for detection, a reflection on the Greek cynics who, in spite of their intelligence were famous for not being practical, and is undoubtedly yet another allusion to the British government. We are told, "Mycroft has his rails and he runs on them," an insinuation that the ultra-conservative stance adopted by the regime on so many issues, merited reform. Fogg could easily be thought of as having a railroad mentality for "He never took one step too many, and always went to his destination by the shortest cut," and "reached his destination at the exact moment."

The mental texture of the Diogenes Club is that of the state of philosophy before the appearance of Descartes, and consequently modern thought, with Mycroft also serving as a denotation of the world of thought prior to the introduction of pragmatism, for he carries with him an atmosphere of all theory and no practice. Here is the philosopher's club mindset the British Utilitarians and American Pragmatists were so eager to replace with a more substantial, hopefully more beneficial guide to thought and action. Dewey and James, the latter in particular, knew it was wrong to regard philosophy as an exclusive club whose rules only a limited membership could understand and enjoy. After the introduction of pragmatism anyone with access to a library or a lab could read philosophy or conduct his own experiments, or at least this was James' hope.

Mycroft Holmes is absolutely corpulent, but it is called to our attention that his face is otherwise as sharp and knowing as that of his brother. Sherlock is as thin as Mycroft is fat. The man is full of contradiction for Diogenes himself practiced asceticism with its rule of self-denial, so it's doubtful if the Greek was anything approaching portly, or how could he have fit into his pot? Cynics, ancient or modern, Nietzsche tells us, are often very silent, some have strange bodies and habits, and he presents Voltaire as an example of their bizarreness. "It happens more frequently, as has been hinted, that a scientific head is placed on an ape's body, a fine exceptional understanding in a base soul, an occurrence by no means rare." Nietzsche confides that the philosopher should use the "so-called cynics, those who simply recognise the animal, the commonplace and 'the rule' in themselves," to be his "suitable auxiliaries who will shorten and lighten his task." By the rule he means the common man, or, as he calls them, "men who are the rule." A cynic who would seek out absolute privacy was not predestined for knowledge, Nietzsche claims. But Sherlock needs rest and recovery time as well, admitting that he has occasionally found his brother's silent haunt to be a very soothing atmosphere. Nietzsche understands, realizing that "Every select man strives instinctively for a citadel and a privacy, where he is *free* from the crowd." William James admits there is an element of the vulgar in pragmatism, and it is this earthiness that Sherlock, but not Mycroft, faces in his daily life. It is "The long and serious study of the *average* man" "that constitutes a necessary part of the life-history of every philosopher," the German puts forth.

The Diogenes group is a reference to the transcendentalists, a low-keyed literary and philosophical movement popular in America just prior to the Civil War, whose followers believed real life was only to be found on a higher plane than everyday existence. Elizabeth Peabody summed up the ideal nature of this in the quote, "Contemplation of Spirit is the first principle of Human Culture." True enough many transcendentalists were high-minded and idealistic, laying stress on individualism, self-reliance, and social reform, active outgoing people such as editors, writers, and teachers like Margaret Fuller, Ralph Waldo Emerson, and Henry David Thoreau, but most were the opposite, keeping to themselves. Listen to what Emerson says of this branch, "But their solitary and fastidious manners not only withdraw them from the conversation, but from the labors of the world; they are not good citizens, not good members of society; unwillingly they bear their part of the public and private burdens; they do not willingly share in the public charities, in the public religious rites, in the enterprises of education, of missions foreign and domestic, in the abolition of the slave-trade, or in the temperance society," Disassociating themselves from life, friends, and even family, like the constituents of Mycroft's club, they were extremists, some going so far as to be hermits, like Thoreau, living in his shack in the woods. Emerson refused to join the utopian commune of Brook Farm because of its exclusiveness, yet he did visit occasionally, just as Sherlock drops in on his brother's refuge, and Emerson was often referred to as their leader, as Mycroft was one of the founders of his club. Emerson warns that people should not live in "ivory towers," and like Sherlock, anchors his creed in practice. Nietzsche says the genuine philosopher, as opposed to the false, who withdraws from life, lives unphilosophically, and "feels the obligation and burden of a hundred attempts and temptations of life — he risks *himself* constantly, he plays *this* bad game," which the false philosopher renounces by living prudently and apart. In "The Adventure of the Bruce-Partington Plans," Sherlock makes the statement, "Jupiter is descending to-day" when Mycroft has come to walk among mere mortals; the father of the ancient gods did not often deign to descend to help mankind, although Mycroft has aided on various cases, always without getting too involved.

The references to Mycroft in conjunction with government leads our thoughts to John Stuart Mill's *Representative Government*, wherein Doyle found many decisive reflections. Proving that a government founded on democratic principles based on utilitarian theories tempered with humanitarianism would probably be the best overall political system was the theme of the essay. In Mycroft we have a character being contrasted against Sherlock. It was clever of Doyle to have developed one who is none other than Sherlock's brother, for the contrast becomes all the more sharper. Sherlock's corpulent sibling has all the resources to be like his famous brother, but he just doesn't wish to. Part of Mill's complex composition deals with the impact different types of people have on their society, for better or worse, asking the all-important question as to what type of individual in a democracy would be best "as regards present well-being; the good management of the affairs of the existing generation," which is after all exactly what Sherlock's assignment is, protecting his generation from the marauders. "This question really depends upon a still more fundamental one, viz., which of two common types of character, for the general good of humanity, it is most desirable should predominate — the active, or the passive type; that which struggles against evils, or that which endures them; that which bends to circumstances, or that which endeavours to make circumstances bend to itself," Mill asks, then answers that it is the active type, bringing about improvement in human affairs, while admitting that the common moralists and the general sympathies of mankind are in favor of the passive type for their passiveness increases our sense of security for they "seem an obstruction the less in our own path." Mycroft and his sedate, quiet approach to life will always be popular with the general run of mankind for this reason, and also because even as energetic a man as the Great Detective requires this lifestyle at intervals, answering Mill's observation that this sort of thing can surely happen for "it is much easier for an active mind to acquire the virtues of patience than for a passive one to assume those of energy." "Enterprise, the desire to keep moving, to be trying and accomplishing new things for our own benefit or that of others, is the parent even of speculative, and much more of practical, talent. The intellectual culture compatible with the other type (passive) is of that feeble and vague description which belongs to a mind that stops at amusement, or at simple contemplation," Mill claims. All intellectual superiority is the fruit of active effort, so Mycroft does not really have a good mind as compared to his brother. Those who improve life are those who take up the struggle for only "practice" is the "test of real and vigorous thinking, the thinking which ascertains truths instead of dreaming dreams." The self-benefiting qualities are all on the side of the active character whose actions are to the advantage of the whole community. Mill drops a comment on the citizen who is privileged, or at least as privileged as others, who never bothers himself, either in feeling or activity, to extend himself for the good of the community. "Their work is a routine; not a labour of love, but of self-interest in the most elementary form, the satisfaction of daily wants; neither the thing done, nor the process of doing it, introduces the mind to thoughts or feelings extending beyond individuals; if instructive books are within their reach, there is no stimulus to read them; and in most cases the individual has no access to any person of cultivation much superior to his own. Giving him something to do for the public, supplies, in a measure, all these deficiencies." What Doyle is doing is giving Mycroft something worthwhile to think about and to actively take part in for a change. In speaking of this contentment of character in an individual, Mill observes that this faculty is not "necessarily or naturally attendant on passivity of character," for Mycroft is a clubman who, if he wishes, can take up the moral burden, as we see him doing in this case. Sir James Damery is another, for remember that when he is trying to help save the life of an innocent girl in "The Illustrious Client," he tells Holmes he can be reached at the Carlton Club. However, one individual who would unquestionably fall into this role of passivity posing as moral virtue category is the banker Merryweather in "The Red-Headed League" who considers his game of whist at his club more important than fighting crime.

The rule of self-imposed silence at this club full of dummies Mill would have considered pure evil, for he emphasizes that speech and dialogue are the very foundational building blocks of any worthwhile community in a number of ways. The development of the different houses of government was brought into being for the purpose of actual spoken dialogue and one must enforce free speech and freedom of the press he points out, reminding us that the greatest men of their age have often been superior orators, using the example of Greeks such as Pericles.

Mill goes off on a slight tangent that Doyle picked up on — "Even among the content and passive when there exists a desire for what you do not have, or think you cannot possess because you do not feel your own efforts to be of any real use in the matter, you are filled with resentment and envy." Nietzsche of course comes to mind and a line could be drawn between the two philosophers. Mill points out that envy can develop itself as a point of national character and that "The most envious of all mankind are the Orientals," and Melas, we are told, is an interpreter for the Orientals. "In real life, he is the terror of all who possess anything desirable," Mill claims, adding, "in Oriental tales, the envious man is remarkably prominent." It is envy that motivated Melas' kidnappers. "Next to Orientals in envy, as in activity, are some of the Southern Europeans," and here Mill gives a few examples, but the Greeks are not among them. Those who are really discontent are happy to take illegitimate means of raising themselves to the level of those who have more than them, and there you have the plot of "The Greek Interpreter."

Upon being introduced to Sherlock, Mr. Melas tells him he is an interpreter and adds, most astonishingly, "I interpret all languages — or nearly all," though he is principally associated with the Grecian tongue. The man would have us believe he can translate nearly all languages, a superhuman feat if ever there was one. We learn in Chapter Two of the *Acts of the Apostles* however, that it is some of the Apostles who have the God-given gift to speak all, or almost all, of the then known languages, supplying a prodigious list of these tongues. The ancients are amazed when they hear this strange speech, accusing the Apostles of being drunk or speaking gibberish. Keeping this thought in mind we must merge it with the knowledge that Melas is based, in part, on Nietzsche, a philologist familiar with a number of ancient and modern languages, but primarily famous for his Greek interpretations. *Melas* is a Modern Greek word for honey, a reference to Nietzsche's gift of knowledge to mankind. Doyle found the etymology of *"melas"* was dealt with at some length by Dr. Holmes in *The Autocrat of the Breakfast-Table.* The partial description of Melas is that of a short, stout man with a black beard, a delineation that could fit the philosopher as well. For seven years the German was a teacher of Greek at Basel with a selection of his writings such as *The Birth of Tragedy* being depictions of Greek social and religious conventions and the insights offered to him by these practices. Nietzsche is not just a reader of the ancients but is trying to understand the thoughts of the Greeks, and this is what Melas is enacting with his "half-spoken, half-written" communications with the Athenian, Kratides.

Melas tells a story of being abducted by an Englishman, taken to the country and forced to translate the speech of Paul Kratides, whose "face was grotesquely criss-crossed with sticking-plaster, and that one large pad of it was fastened over his mouth." These bandages make it necessary for Melas to do the actual writing of the words on a slate. In his *Ecce Homo*, Nietzsche describes the writing of his earlier work, *Human, All-Too-Human*, telling us the book was given its main outline at Sorrento, Italy, where he vacationed, then finished later at Basel while the author suffered from one of the crippling headaches plaguing his later years. "As a matter of fact, it is Peter Gast, at the time a student at the University of Basel, and extremely devoted to me, who is responsible for the book. With my aching head wrapped in bandages, I dictated while he wrote and corrected — actually, he was the real composer, whereas I was merely the author." At one point in the *Acts of the Apostles* we learn of Paul that he could indeed speak Greek, but that he could not write any language for he was illiterate. We are never told Melas' first name for if Doyle put it forward that it was Peter, the combination of Peter and Paul would be a tip-off for many readers. In the *New Testament* we are reading Paul's words, but someone else must have written them, perhaps Peter, so in "The Greek Interpreter" Peter Melas does the writing to Paul Kratides' dictation. The Greek Interpreters is a phrase found in footnotes throughout the *Bible*, and other Christian writings, employed to designate those Church Fathers who translated their original languages into Greek, the intellectual language of the day.

This story becomes yet another re-enactment of historical events, an associative maneuver Doyle is adroit at. The Apostles Peter and Paul in their world travels are constantly being arrested and taken into custody. In St. Petersburg, Russia, there was a prison used primarily for political prisoners named Peter and Paul Fortress, perhaps in recognition of this fact. In Chapter Four of the *Acts* Peter is arrested for the first time, then released with a warning not to tell anyone of it, just as Melas is threatened and freed following his initial abduction. Herod was one of the "kings of the earth," who opposed and imprisoned the two Apostles, and one of the London kidnappers is named Harold. His last name, Latimer, is Latin for "an interpreter," an excellent pun. Mr. Melas acts as translator for "wealthy Orientals who may visit the Northumberland Avenue hotels," a reference to the fact that all the Apostles were Jews, for in the ancient world, right up to the modern era, Jews were called Orientals. The second captor was a small, insignificant-looking man, whose "features were peaky and sallow, and his little pointed beard was thready and ill-nourished," named Wilson Kemp, who is constantly giggling, "and his lips and eyelids were continually twitching like a man with St. Vitus's dance." But this little man, Melas and any others who meet him, view with fear and loathing, and well they should for here is a personification of Pan, the half-goat, half-human demigod of the Greeks who caused "panic" among any unlucky enough to meet him, hear his music, or see him dance. We are told Melas could not even speak of Kemp "save with trembling hands and a blanched cheek," the very picture of a panic attack. Pan is portrayed as a diminutive, merry, ugly individual with horns, beard, and goat's feet, and Holmes knows the history of Kemp, calling him "a man of the foulest antecedents."

At one point in the Biblical accounts Felix, governor of Caesarea, holds Paul the Apostle captive, "hoping also withal, that money would be given him by Paul." Felix means "happy" in Latin, so perhaps this is another reason Kemp is always giggling. Paul Kratides has been beaten and tortured and just so were all the Apostles. When Saul/Paul was suddenly converted to the new religion, he was stricken blind and thrown to the ground where some travelers found him and took him with them to Damascus. "And he was there three days, without sight, and neither ate nor drank," and just so is Paul Kratides blinded with bandages and slowly being starved to death in an effort to force money from him. St. Paul is bound and abused a number of times on his travels for he has been told by Christ, "he must suffer for the sake of my name." We are told Paul spoke with the Gentiles and the Grecians, "but they sought to kill him." Kratides' sister, also being held captive, interrupts the bizarre conversation between the captives Kratides and Melas, and we know his sister accompanied St. Paul on his travels, though we are never told her name. Kratides' sister is named Sophy, short for Sophia, the Greek word for "wisdom." In the form "Hagia Sophia" it is an expression used in Christianity to mean "Holy Wisdom" and is synonymous with the teachings of Jesus. Sophie was the nickname Diderot gave his friend Louise Vollard to show his regard for her great intelligence. Before Melas goes to Mycroft, he tells his story to the police, but they doubt him, believing "such a thing cannot be"..."because they have never heard of it before," the same rebuff the Apostles met with when they initially attempted to spread the story of Jesus.

Construing where the house of the kidnappers is located, Mycroft, Sherlock, Watson, and Gregson set out for it but arrive to find the miscreants have fled, abandoning Melas and Kratides in a room filling with poisonous gas. When King Herod learns St. Peter has escaped prison, he too flees in fear of the consequences. St. Peter's keepers numbered two soldiers, and we learn that two others, the coachman and his wife, abetted the London captors.

An anonymous critic, writing in *The Academy and Literature* in reference to the publication of *The Return of Sherlock Holmes* in 1905, made the following remark: "Our children's children will probably argue that Holmes was a solar myth." He was being sarcastic, of course, for he believed the statement to be absurd and was probably irritated over the character's fantastic popularity; yet that is exactly what I am now going to do: argue the position of Sherlock Holmes as a solar deity. Apollo was the Olympian god of light and the sun, music, poetry, pastoral pursuits, and prophecy; and Holmes is a reincarnation of this bringer of light to mankind, as shown in this and many other stories. Nietzsche describes Apollo as "the god of individuation, the god who sets the boundaries of justice." Holmes asks, "Where is a candle?" before rushing into the gas filled room in which the two victims are bound, and says, "Hold the light at the door." "A dull blue flame which flickered from a small brass tripod in the centre" illuminates the room, and we know the tripod flame was always used in the shrines of the Greek oracles, with a flaming tripod part of the permanent furniture of the temple of Apollo. Braving the gas, Sherlock rushes into the room to save the men, to find that Melas is still alive. He revives, but Kratides has expired. "And behold an angel of the Lord stood by him: and a light shined in the room: and he striking Peter on the side, raised him up, saying: Arise quickly. And the chains fell off from his hands." So we are told of one of the instances in which Peter gained his freedom from prison.

Sophy has been abducted by the pair of kidnappers, who themselves turn up later, stabbed to death. The police believe the men to have attacked and killed each other, but Holmes believes Sophy slew them or had them murdered. Here is a convoluted reference to the legend that when Christ was born, the cry "Great Pan is dead!" was heard throughout Greece, for Christ now replaces Pan. Herod is exterminated by an emissary of God, "And forthwith an angel of the Lord struck him, because he had not given the honour to God: and eaten up by worms, he expired." The worms are a visible judgment from God for Herod's pride, vanity, and cruelty. Of Sophy we are told, "she was tall and graceful, with black hair, and clad in some sort of loose white gown," a depiction of Mary, mother of Jesus, and a symbol of the Church, the institution responsible for bringing about the collapse of many ancient religions and cults. Sophy kills her enemies in Hungary, for the Hungarians regarded themselves as defenders of the faith and it was they who helped save the Church from the onslaught of the Turks and Muslims throughout history.

St. Paul died in a foreign land, being beheaded in Rome by Nero, and St. Peter was killed later the same day. It is because of the martyrdom of men such as Peter and Paul that Christianity eventually triumphed over its persecutors in the ancient world.

Nietzsche had a great deal to say about Socrates, as would any student of Greek culture. It was Socrates who went among the statesmen, orators, workers, and artists of his Athens, questioning them as to their knowledge, and it was he who realized these men were without proper and real insight, even in regard to their own professions. Like the official police of London they did not really know their jobs, while Holmes, like Socrates, does not hesitate to acknowledge his ignorance, but attempts to do something about it. Nietzsche emphasizes, "Wherever Socratism turns its searching eyes it sees lack of insight, it sees the force of illusion; and from this lack it infers the essential perversity and objectionableness of existing conditions. From this point onwards, Socrates conceives it as his duty to correct existence," and he does this "with an air of irreverence and superiority." It is in "The Greek Interpreter" that Holmes tells us, "I cannot agree with those who rank modesty among the virtues." Nietzsche continues, "To penetrate into the depths and to distinguish true perception from error and illusion seemed to the Socratic man the noblest and even the only truly human calling: just as from the time of Socrates onwards the mechanism of making concepts, judgments, and inferences was prized above all other activities as the highest talent and the most admirable gift of nature." This seems a bit extravagant but Socrates did change the way people thought, as did Descartes, or Holmes, coming among the silent cynics of the Diogenes Club showing them a different way of thought and action. St. Paul went among "the Jews and the Greeks," the Epicureans and the Stoics of Athens, preaching his new thoughts. Paul finds the city full of sin and idolatry just as Watson, coming from the East, found London full of sin and crime. "As against this practical pessimism, Socrates is the prototype of the theoretical optimist who with his belief in the explicability of the nature of things, attributes to knowledge and perception the power of a universal panacea, and in error sees evil in itself," the German adds. Socrates believed men are evil simply because they do not know any better. "We behold the eagerness of the insatiate optimistic knowledge, of which Socrates is the typical representative." Mention of the optimistic nature of Holmes comes as a surprise to many of us, but if you think of his lifestyle you realize it is indeed the opposite of fatalism. Nietzsche makes much of this attitude of Socrates, giving as one example of it the fact that he practiced music, and elsewhere he has done the same thing with the German philosopher Schopenhauer, a man most would regard as extremely pessimistic. Nietzsche now tells us Schopenhauer regarded music "as an expression of the world," and "in the highest degree a universal language, which is related indeed to the universality of concepts, much as they are related to the particular things." Socrates encourages himself and others to study music, claiming that no less than the gods have told him to do so. The music of Holmes is far from being simply a pleasant diversion and added abundance to the Great Detective's life, for music is instrumental in reasoning from the general to the particular. "This is so truly the case," Schopenhauer adds, "that whoever gives himself up entirely to the impression of a symphony, seems to see all the possible events of life and the world take place in himself, yet if he reflects, he can find no likeness between the music and the things that passed before his mind." When we practice, or even just listen to music, the hidden things of the world are revealed to us. "This deep relation which music has to the true nature of all things also explains the fact that suitable music played to any scene, action, event, or surrounding seems to disclose to us its most secret meaning, and appears as the most accurate and distinct commentary upon it," Schopenhauer adds. The music of Holmes, his own and that which he goes out of his way to hear, often right in the middle of a case, manifests to him "the inmost soul, as it were, of the phenomenon without the body." Music in the mind of Holmes leads to thoughts that help provide answers to the riddle.

"The Norwood Builder" opens with the two investigators talking over past adventures before the fire, when suddenly in rushes John Hector McFarlane with a frantic story that the police are looking to arrest him for the murder of Mr. Jonas Oldacre, a builder of Norwood who has disappeared without a trace. Evidence at the scene points to the possibility that he was killed by McFarlane, last to see him, and the body was burned on a woodpile, on which some burned organic matter and a few buttons were found, behind Deep Dene House, Oldacre's home. McFarlane, a lawyer, admits the builder had business with him the previous night, but knows nothing of the disappearance. Lestrade arrives to make the arrest, but at Holmes' request he listens to McFarlane's tale.

Oldacre came to McFarlane's city office the day before to have the solicitor make out his will when to his astonishment McFarlane learned that none other than himself is to be the beneficiary. Oldacre is "a man of eccentric habits, secretive and retiring," and McFarlane found him "a strange little ferret-like man, with white eyelashes, and when I looked up at him I found his keen gray eyes fixed upon me with an amused expression." He invites the lawyer to Deep Dene House that very night to work out the details of the will, and McFarlane does so, and leaves without incident.

Holmes goes to Blackheath to interview the attorney's mother, as the "father was away in search of his son." This is a reference to the famous essay "The Doctor Searches for the Captain," written by Oliver Wendell Holmes, Senior when his son the lawyer Wendell was wounded while serving in the Civil War and could not be found, one of the most popular period pieces ever published. The essay chronicles the father's desperate search for his son so he could personally attend to his wounds. Mrs. McFarlane knew Oldacre when they were young and has a very unfavorable opinion of the man. "He was more like a malignant and cunning ape than a human being, and he always was, ever since he was a young man," she says, adding that at one time he mutilated a photo of her and sent it to her in a fit of malice.

When Holmes learns the builder has made bank checks out in the name of a Mr. Cornelius he enlists the aid of the police, having them build a fire in the center of one of the hallways of Deep Dene House. A commotion, with yelling of the word "Fire!" ensues, and the ferret is driven from his hole as a hidden door flies open and out rushes Jonas Oldacre. He searches the room with a "malignant" look, and this word will actually be used twice more to describe the man. A really fascinating scene right out of the *Old Testament* has just been re-enacted. When Holmes realizes Oldacre must still be hiding somewhere in the house he forms his plans, beginning with questioning Lestrade as to the number of constables he has with him. The answer three brings our minds to *The Book of Daniel*, where we read of the three Jews: Sidrach, Misach, and Abdenago, who lived in Babylon during the reign of King Nabuchodonosor. The king has cast a statue of gold, and setting it up on the Plain of Dura, demands all pay homage to it, proclaiming that if any man will not fall down and worship the idol, he shall "be cast into a furnace of burning fire." Some Chaldeans, realizing the three Jews refuse to worship the golden statue, report this to the palace. "Then Nabuchodonosor, in fury and in wrath, commanded that Sidrach, Misach, and Abdenago should be brought: who immediately were brought before the king." Holmes has the three policemen heap straw in the hallway of the top floor. It is Lestrade who plays the part of the King in wrath and fury for when he cannot comprehend what Holmes is up to his "face had begun to grow red and angry." He accuses the detective of playing a game with him just as the king cannot believe these three brought before him would be foolish enough to disobey his command. The three Hebrews tell the king they are not afraid of his fire for their God will deliver them. Holmes tells Watson to set the straw on fire. Nabuchodonosor orders the fires to be lit, the three dissidents to be bound hand and foot, and thrown into the furnace. The Jews see this punishment upon them as a punishment from God and beg forgiveness. "But the angel of the Lord went down with Azarias and his companions into the furnace: and he drove the flame of the fire out of the furnace." Azarias is the real name of one of the Jews who have all adopted Babylonian names while living there. The fire is put out and four men, one of them the angel, walk out of the furnace. The King is astonished and asks where did the extra man come from. The place of the fourth man is taken by Oldacre who causes plenty of astonishment himself when he comes charging out of his secret room. The nobles, magistrates, and judges of Babylon now consider upon what has occurred in their midst, so Lestrade tells Oldacre, "That's for a jury to decide," when asking as to what will happen to him now.

The story also has roots in the book known as *The Prophesy of Jonas*, found at the very end of the *Old Testament*. Jonah is the name of the prophet in the King James Version, but in the Standard Catholic Version it is Jonas, and Doyle used both versions, switching back and forth as it pleased him. Jonas has either committed some sin and is fleeing to Nineveh, "from the face of the Lord," or has been exiled by God as punishment for some sin; I have never been quite sure which. Like Oldacre he is a man of secretive habits and is distrusted by the crew of the ship he seeks passage in. While sailing to Nineveh a storm overtakes them and the mariners cast lots to determine who among them is responsible, for they know the storm was sent by God as punishment, and when the lot falls to Jonas and he is cast overboard the fury of the storm abates immediately. A ship, and possibly the sinking of it, comes into "The Norwood Builder" when Watson, looking over his notes, finds they include "the shocking affair of the Dutch steamship *Friesland*, which so nearly cost us both our lives." A great fish is sent by God, which swallows up Jonas, holding him in his belly three days and three nights, and he cries out to the Lord in his affliction. This is not the first time Jonas finds himself in the inner recess of something, for we are told that when he first entered the ship he "went down into the inner part of the ship, and fell into a deep sleep," almost immediately. Reasoning centered upon justifiable vengeance seems implied by this guilt-ridden rejection of the world. Jonas knows he is leading a life of "corruption," adding, in what the Assyrians called "a wisdom piece," "They that in vain observe vanities, forsake their own mercy." The sin of Jonas is vanity and pride, possibly arrogance, and he knows it. Lestrade, thinking he is so correct in arresting McFarlane now plays the role of the prophet for he is overbearing and chaffing throughout the case, and in regard to Holmes, reluctantly admits, in his vanity, that the detective has aided Scotland Yard, "once or twice." Jonas Oldacre is a "very deep, malicious, vindictive person," with a "wicked, scheming brain, and all his life he has longed for vengeance," just like the prophet, who even God dislikes. The fish vomits out Jonas onto dry land and the Lord hopes he has learned a lesson, ordering him to take up his original mission of preaching to Nineveh, but true to form Jonas predicts the great city will be destroyed within forty days, but he does so out of the spite in his heart and without God's permission. Ancient people believed in the power of any holy man, thus the citizens of the city put on sackcloth in fear and repentance for the coming destruction. The Assyrians even extend the quest for atonement to their animals: oxen, sheep, and so forth, which are now to take part in the fasting. God had obviously been prepared to go along with the terms of Jonas' prediction but he relents and showing mercy spares the city. Jonas is exceedingly troubled and angry over this, as Lestrade is made angry a number of times. Jonas is so arrogant he would rather die than see the city spared so he goes out of the place, yet hopes to see its obliteration from a distance, and for a third time God has him hid from our eyes for Jonas "made himself a booth there, and he sat under it in the shadow, till he might see what would befall the city." Jonas is a builder. God prepares an ivy bush that completely covers the booth hiding the seer from sight. Holmes tells us the advantage of being a builder is that Oldacre "was able to fix up his own little hiding-place." God is angry with the mystic for so readily planning to destroy what he had made: the city and its teeming life; and he sends a worm to destroy the ivy covering the shed of Jonas. "And when the sun was risen, the Lord commanded a hot and burning wind: and the sun beat upon the head of Jonas, and he broiled with the heat: and he desired for his soul that he might die, and said: It is better for me to die than to live." Like Holmes, God sends a wave of heat to punish Jonas for his sins and his twisted vanity. Oldacre's plot was to extract revenge on Mrs. McFarlane, his lost love, who when young had refused him in marriage, hoping to cause blame for his murder to fall on her only child. Holmes claims the builder would probably have gotten away with his scheme had he only known when to stop, for it was in the mass of evidence that the detective realized something was wrong. The prophet made a similar mistake for he pushed God too far in his demands for retribution, thus instigating the Lord to turn against him. God at one point reminds Jonas of the thousands of innocent people of the city who would die, as well as "many beasts." This last phrase is rather amazing for it represents, as far as I can find, the first time in history any compassion is shown toward animals. Doyle sees this as well, and wishing to incorporate it somehow into this case makes mention of some animals. To produce the organic remains found in the wood fire Oldacre burned a number of animals, probably rabbits and dogs. A form of Biblical holocaust is implied, a ritual in which humans and animals were burned alive on a wood fire as an offering to God. At one time Oldacre turned a cat loose in a cage full of birds displaying his brutal cruelty, just as the prophet would gladly kill all the animals in Nineveh. One obvious theme of *The Prophesy of Jonas* is that the Jew, Jonas, has a low regard for the Gentiles of a foreign city, and for all life in general, and would kill them all if he could. St. Peter tells us it is not even permitted for a Jew to talk to a non-Jew, but adds he will attempt to change this attitude, claiming God has shown him "not to call any man common or unclean." Peter says that "God is no respecter of persons. But in every nation, he that feareth him, and worketh justice, is acceptable to him." Malignant is the most appropriate name for both Jonas and Oldacre, and in a touch of irony Doyle places Oldacre on the same footing as the beasts, having characters refer to him at various times as an ape, rabbit, and ferret.

Holmes displays prophetic authority when he mentions that the murder weapon was an oaken stick that is now missing, adding that the bloodstains upon it were slight. If it is missing he could not have seen it, but this is bizarre anyway, in light of the fact that there was no murder. Is Doyle saying Holmes is in this case as false a prophet as Jonas himself? At the very beginning of the story Holmes refers to it as the "Norwood Disappearance Case," so he knows in advance it is not a question of murder. That's very strange; as strange as the tale of the prophet it is taken from. Mrs. McFarlane, in keeping with the spirit of the story is a prophetess of some sort herself for when she meets the detective she tells him, "There is a God in Heaven, Mr. Holmes, and that same God who has punished that wicked man will show, in His own good time, that my son's hands are guiltless of his blood." The "wicked man" referred to must be Jonas of the *Old Testament* since Oldacre has not been punished yet, or else she has seen into the future.

In the Catholic version of *The Prophesy of Jonas*, found in the lengthy subheading, we learn that the Church regards this story as "The most incredible mystery of our religion, and the vocation of the Gentiles, are thus insinuated." Lestrade tells Holmes, "this is the brightest thing that you have done yet, though it is a mystery to me how you did it." This subheading also tells us Jonas "prophesied and prefigured in his own person the death and resurrection of Christ, and was the only one among the prophets who was sent to preach to the Gentiles." The tale is a transition mystery of the old law, "Oldacre," being replaced by the new law, "Holmes." Jesus accents the fact that he has come to fulfill *The Book of Jonas*, repeating this pledge a number of times, and this is the main reason it is being discussed at this point in my study. Cornelius, the new identity Oldacre has established for his new bank accounts points clearly to Doyle's intentions. The story of Cornelius is found in the next chapter of the *Acts of the Apostles* following the adventures of Paul and Peter. Cornelius was not a Jew but rather a Roman Centurion stationed in Caesarea. Although a pagan he believes in one supreme God so the Lord sends him a vision instructing him to convert to Christianity, and to facilitate this Cornelius should send for Simon Peter in order to benefit from his teaching. Holmes adopts the role of Simon Peter, with Lestrade playing the part of Cornelius being converted to his methods, which he acknowledges to be superior to his own. "It was amusing to me to see how the detective's overbearing manner had changed suddenly to that of a child asking questions of its teacher," Watson tells us of Lestrade's manner following the solving of this case. This chapter of the *Acts* goes on to illustrate, rather briefly, the main tenets of the teachings of Jesus, which replaced for some, the prophesies of Jonas, just as Cornelius would replace Oldacre in the "accounts," and the allusion to Judge Wendell Holmes in the story forces one to think of his efforts to replace the old vengeance driven laws with a more pragmatic, thoughtful purpose.

Chapter Nine. Miracles Do Happen

"The Yellow Face," in spite of the fact that it has, as far as I know, never been made into a film or play, and is hardly touched upon by other writers, is one of the most interesting and revealing tales in the Canon. I didn't quite know what to make of it, until I realized how fervently Doyle had taken Thomas Carlyle's injunction to write biography as though it were scripture. The two detectives return to Baker Street only to be informed they have missed one seeking their help, but he shows up a bit later in great excitement and distress. Holmes puts in a performance as lawyer as well as detective here, since the client requires his investigative skills along with his "opinion as a judicious man." In answer to the agonized stranger's "I hope to God you'll be able to tell me," Holmes answers that he and his friend, "have had the good fortune to bring peace to many troubled souls."

Grant Munro claims that after three years of married bliss he suddenly finds himself estranged from his wife Effie, for some secret has arisen between them that must be cleared up. When he met his wife she was the young widow of a lawyer, John Hebron of Atlanta, Georgia. "They had one child, but the yellow fever broke out badly in the place, and both husband and child died of it," so Effie returned to England, her birthplace, and upon meeting Munro they soon marry and move to a small village where they find happiness, "until this accursed affair began." Effie came to her husband Jack, which is Grant's nickname, in need of a large amount of money, and since the funds were actually hers, he gives them to her although she will not tell him the purpose. While out for a stroll Jack notices someone moving into an empty cottage near his house and catches a glimpse of a face in the upper window that "was a livid chalky white, and with something set and rigid about it which was shockingly unnatural." Trying to be friendly he knocks on the door but receives no answer. Munro observes his wife sneaking out early one morning and spies her coming out of the newly rented cottage the next afternoon. Holmes takes the case out of curiosity, telling Munro to return home and try to learn more of the situation. Once again the strange face makes an appearance at the cottage window. Mrs. Munro promises her husband not to go to the bungalow again but she does, and when Munro searches the place he finds it empty, but there is a photo of Effie on the mantelpiece. Holmes and Watson catch a train to Norbury, meet Jack Munro, and walk to the cottage, where they come across Effie outside the cottage. She begs them not to go in. Jack rushes inside only to find a little girl in a red frock and long white gloves. "As she whisked round to us, I gave a cry of surprise and horror," Watson tells us, for "The face which she turned towards us was of the strangest livid tint, and the features were absolutely devoid of any expression." She is dead. We have indeed learned she died of fever in America, and Munro has read her death certificate. Her costume is, appropriately enough, that of a dead child laid out for her wake and burial. "Holmes, with a laugh, passed his hand behind the child's ear, a mask is peeled off from her countenance, and there was a little cole-black negress, with all her white teeth flashing in amusement at our amazed faces." By his touch, Holmes/Jesus has brought the child back to life. Lucy, daughter of Effie and John Hebron, has been living in secret from Grant Munro, and the world, for three years. Hebron was a Negro, and Effie was unsure of her new husband's reaction to the child.

Death is bad enough, but the death of a child is always tragic. We have accounts of Jesus bringing back to life a dead girl in both Luke and Matthew, with Luke's version being the closest in spirit to "The Yellow Face." Luke tells us the father of a recently dead girl came to Jesus begging him to return with him to his house and bring the child back to life. The father's name is Jairus, which helps explain why Effie calls her husband Jack when his name is Grant. Jairus seems much like Jakes, a diminutive of the French name Jacques, which translates to John, bringing us to Jack. When they come to the house, Jesus enters, taking with him Peter, James, John, and the mother and father. "And all wept and mourned for her. But he said: Weep not; the maid is not dead, but sleepeth. And they laughed at him, knowing that she was dead. But he taking her by the hand cried out, saying: Maid, arise. And her spirit returned, and she arose immediately." Her parents and the others are amazed, and Jesus tells them not to tell anyone of what had happened.

Doyle actually seems to experience some guilt over this blatant rendering of his alter ego Holmes as a Jesus figure, so Holmes is made to admit that he believed the face at the window to be that of Effie's first husband, or someone trying to blackmail her. He turns out to be wrong; he is only a man after all, and thus he tells the world he considers this erroneous presupposition to prove his humanity and fallibility.

The name of the town, Norbury, can be interpreted to mean, "not buried," since "nor" means "not," though I think "Norman" was the actual intention of the prefix, in this case, and the area was probably a Norman burial site. Hebron is a city of refuge mentioned a number of times in both *Testaments*, to which one could flee to avoid persecution, in this case Mrs. Hebron and her mulatto daughter, who would not be socially accepted in America. Grant Munro is a reference to two American presidents: Ulysses Grant and James Monroe, who were rulers, just as we are told the dead girl's father who came to Jesus for help was, "a ruler of the synagogue." Munro has symbolically taken Holmes to his own home for Effie Munro was paying rent on the cottage.

The name Effie, slightly altered, was borrowed from George Eliot's work, *Silas Marner*, another tale of a secret hidden away in a rural cottage. This popular English novel is the story of the weaver Silas Marner, turned out of his native village as the result of the deception of a friend, and taking up a poor but honest existence in the hamlet of Raveloe. His disappointment with humanity forces him into isolation and miserliness until the day his hidden gold is stolen, compelling him to make contact with the wider community. That winter the spurned wife of Godfrey Cass dies in the snow within sight of Silas' humble cottage and her two-year-old girl, Eppie, crawls into it, falling asleep on the hearth. The near-sighted weaver, finding the child, mistakes her golden locks for his missing gold coins come home again. Doyle has had to alter the child's name somewhat to keep from being obvious. Doyle adopts these details from Eliot's novel for the poignant opening of the section, "The Country of the Saints" in *A Study in Scarlet*, in which John Ferrier is doing his utmost to save a girl from the slow death suffered by the rest of the travelers. The American child is described as having "towsy golden curls which covered the back of her head," and both she and the child in "The Yellow Face" are named Lucy, but what common source Doyle borrowed this name from I have yet to discover. In both cases the men who rescued the children, Marner and Ferrier, keep them as their own.

The color yellow and its connotations play a role in both novels. The weaver is described at one point as "so withered and yellow," the children fear him. An exchange has taken place in *Silas Marner*; for inflexible gold has been replaced by the yielding gold of a child's love. The real father, Godfrey Cass, will not come forward to acknowledge the dead mother as his wife, or the daughter as his own. In "The Yellow Face" it is the child's father who has died, and the mother who hides knowledge, and Godfrey's new wife, Nancy, like Grant Munro, is unaware of the girl's existence. In both tales the remaining parent lives near the cottage where the daughter lives, but keep their own secrets. These rejected children are a form of salvation, for Eppie's loving presence reconciles Silas with the world, and Lucy Hebron's own joy fills her new father's heart with happiness. Both are better men by realizing their capacity for love through the child, and at the conclusion of each story the marriages seem to be enhanced by the revelation of the secrets: Munro accepts Lucy as evidence of his wife's humanity, for she could not abandon her daughter no matter what, and Nancy accepts and loves Eppie as the daughter she never had.

Divine intervention is a persistent theme in Eliot's novel, for the love Eppie brings is as "miraculous" as her sudden appearance on the miser's hearth, and heavenly intercession is even suspected in the disappearance of his money. It is believed the weaver could work miracles such as cures, with the help of God, or the devil, just as Holmes has done in "The Yellow Face."

"The Adventure of the Blanched Soldier" is one of the few cases Holmes himself writes up, in an easy, direct style not so different from Watson's own. This comes about at this point in time because Watson, whom Holmes addresses as "my old friend and biographer" (a phrase right out of Boswell), "had at that time deserted me for a wife," this being a reference to the fact that during their long friendship Boswell had indeed married, and for a time seemed to have abandoned Johnson. In "The Yellow Face," I believe we meet Mrs. Boswell, for the cottage, which is the scene of the mystery, is secluded in a "little grove of Scotch firs," and maintained by a stern, churlish, Scotch woman, this being Johnson's opinion of Boswell's wife, and Grant Munro resents this woman, and is resented in turn, a commentary on Johnson's relationship with Mrs. Boswell.

"The Blanched Soldier" could be regarded as a companion piece to "The Yellow Face," the stories and themes are so similar. In January of 1903, following the conclusion of the Boer War, Mr. James M. Dodd, "a big, fresh, sunburned, upstanding Briton," visits Holmes and tells of joining the army with his friend, Godfrey Emsworth, son of Colonel Emsworth, and of their getting into the war in Africa. Young Godfrey is wounded out and sent back to England, and when James returns home his inquires after his comrade are ignored, so Dodd traveled to the Emsworth estate searching for an answer to his friend's disappearance. An interview with the Colonel informs him Godfrey has gone abroad and will not be back for at least a year, but when the faithful old butler Ralph speaks of Godfrey as though he were dead, Dodd's suspicions are aroused. Upon being asked directly if he is dead Ralph gives the "terrible and unexpected" answer, "I wish to God he was!" Things become more confused when James looks up only to find Godfrey staring through a window at him. "He was deadly pale — never have I seen a man so white. I reckon ghosts may look like that; but his eyes met mine, and they were the eyes of a living man. He sprang back when he saw that I was looking at him, and he vanished into the darkness." Dodd chases this zombie down the garden path but he loses him among the outbuildings. The next day Dodd comes across a small, bearded man dressed in black coming out of one of the cottages, and that night, playing the spy, James sees this stranger and Godfrey in one of the cottages, but the father finds him and orders him off the property, so he goes with his troubled soul to Baker Street.

Yellow Fever is not the only disease Jesus/Holmes overcomes. He and Dodd make the journey to Bedfordshire to look into the matter, and on the way Holmes has the young man describe the situation to an unnamed stranger he brings with him. At the estate they first encounter Ralph, dressed in black except for the curious fact of wearing leather gloves giving off a strange odor. Next they come across the irritated Colonel who threatens to call the police, but one word Holmes writes upon a piece of paper completely dissipates his resistance, and the party is taken to a cottage where we find Godfrey, suffering from some disease evidenced by the whitish patches against his dark skin. He gives an account of having been severely wounded in action, getting separated from his men, finding a house in the darkness, crawling into an empty bed, and sleeping till dawn. He awakens to find he has fallen asleep in an enemy leper hospital and is being confronted by a true malignant dwarf, a leper, "a small, dwarf-like man with a huge, bulbous head, who was jabbering excitedly in Dutch, waving two horrible hands which looked to me like brown sponges." This hideous, sick individual, uttering cries like a wild beast, drags Godfrey out of bed regardless of the fresh flow of blood from his wound. Nietzsche's sick and deformed one is seeking revenge upon a healthy one, or, in this particular case, a less sick one. George Eliot makes this interesting observation in *Silas Marner*, "It is seldom that the miserable can help regarding their misery as a wrong inflicted by those who are less miserable." A doctor rescues the Englishman, binds his wounds, and sends him to Pretoria where he is exchanged and sent to England, when signs of the dreaded disease appear. Leprosy, grounds for ostracism from society, convinces Godfrey to hide away on his estate and elude Dodd and all others. Holmes has brought along Sir James Saunders, a famous specialist in the field of dermatology who realizes the young man's illness is not the real thing, but rather a form of pseudo-leprosy and quite curable.

In "Matthew," Chapter Eight, we find Jesus descending from the mountain following prayer when he is greeted by a multitude among whom is a leper begging the Lord to make him clean. "And Jesus stretching forth his hand, touched him, saying: I will. Be thou made clean. And immediately his leprosy was cleansed." In "Luke," Jesus actually cures ten lepers at once, only to have but one of them come back to thank him.

James Saunders is certainly an altogether interesting figure whose philosophical last question to the world is roughly the same as that asked by Dr. Hesselius at the conclusion of "Green Tea." He asks, "Are there not subtle forces at work of which we know little?" Saunders finds his prototype in Hesselius, but only his earthly one. Described as "a grave and taciturn gentleman of iron-gray aspect," this silent "austere figure," is Death himself, or some aspect of God, for Holmes seems to need his presence and permission to raise Godfrey from the dead. Doyle refers indirectly to him as "Lord," for he compares him to Lord Roberts. All those present hear Godfrey's story except Saunders, yet he knows of his misadventures nevertheless. When Holmes escorts Saunders back into the group a new characteristic of the man manifests itself. "But for once his sphinx-like features had relaxed and there was a warm humanity in his eyes." The sphinx is a character from Egyptian and Classical Greek mythology usually referred to as a monster since it is composed of assorted body parts both human and animal, such as the head of a man and the body of a lion, or of a ram, and so forth. The Greek word sphinx means "the Strangler," an allusion to the legend that if you could not answer the riddle of the Theban Sphinx you were throttled by it. Saunders does an interesting thing following Godfrey's miraculous cure, for he walks up to the Colonel and shakes his hand. "'It is often my lot to bring ill-tidings and seldom good,' said he. 'This occasion is the more welcome.'" The young man will live and even Death seems pleased with the outcome. Godfrey, we know, means "peace of God," and here we are being shown a good example of it.

Godfrey has risen from the dead before, for he tells us he was wounded in Africa by being shot in the shoulder with a bullet from an elephant gun. Doyle had been a physician in Africa during the Boer War where he no doubt came across cases of men having been hit with a shot from an elephant gun. One cannot be struck in the shoulder with such a high caliber bullet, stay on a horse all night, find a house in the dark, crawl in, go to bed, and awake the next morning. The impact of a round striking you from such a rifle would probably blow away your shoulder, arm and all, the result being you would die of shock and loss of blood. Doyle is simply telling us here, "Miracles do happen."

Their both springing from a common source, *Silas Marner*, further enhances the connection between "The Yellow Face" and "The Blanched Soldier." Godfrey inhabits an isolated cottage nursing his ailment, as Silas lives in equal detachment nurturing resentment towards mankind, and his disease of miserliness. The relationship between Dodd and young Emsworth is based upon the friendship Silas enjoyed with William Dane, who eventually betrayed him, just as James Dodd feels Godfrey is somehow deceiving him. Silas keeps to himself, all but shunned by neighbors male and female, "and it was soon clear to the Raveloe lasses that he would never urge one of them to accept him against her will — quite as if he had heard them declare that they would never marry a dead man come to life again." Silas is disliked for, among other things, his pale face and unexampled eyes, and is actually quite sick for he is subject to cataleptic fits "which, lasting for an hour or more, had been mistaken for death." Godfrey Cass, the Squire's son, doesn't look so good himself from time to time. "There was something wrong, more than common — that was quite clear; for Mr. Godfrey didn't look half so fresh-coloured and open as he used to do." His secret marriage to an opium addicted woman, her death, and his desertion of his daughter Eppie weigh heavily on his mind, encouraging his shunning and distrust of those he loves and those who love him; he even considers, like Godfrey Emsworth, enlisting as a soldier, a desperate step in his day.

Silas Marner is a missing person mystery of sorts with the disappearance of Dunstan Cass, the culprit who stole Silas' gold, but who remained above suspicion. In his summation of "The Blanched Soldier," Holmes lists a number of possibilities he considered as responsible for Godfrey's disappearance, and among them he mentions hidden crime. "If it were some crime not yet discovered, then clearly it would be to the interest of the family to get rid of the delinquent and send him abroad rather than keep him concealed at home." Dunstan Cass has in fact managed to do both, for his body turns up only yards away from the scene of the crime.

The character of Col. Emsworth is based squarely upon the blunt, energetic figure of Theodore Roosevelt, who during that period of his pied career that sheds the most influence upon "The Blanched Soldier," was a colonel in the American Army. For the Boer War you can substitute the Spanish-American War in which Roosevelt played a large part. The years are almost the same: the Boer started in 1899, the Spanish-American one year later. The unit TR commanded was a cavalry group he built from scratch; it consisted of friends and volunteers and was called the Rough Riders. In "The Blanched Soldier," the word rough is used to describe army life a number of times. Colonel Emsworth's time in service is called "a day of rough language," and Dodd tells us he and Godfrey "took the rough and the smooth together for a year of hard fighting." In Africa, Godfrey finds action at Diamond Hill, while Roosevelt and the Rough Riders distinguished themselves with their famous charge up San Juan Hill. Dodd received a letter posted from Southampton, this being also the name of a town on Long Island near Montauk Point, where the Rough Riders had a permanent camp and where they disbanded after the war. Doyle learns they had to be quarantined at Montauk a few weeks before going home to make sure they had brought back no tropical diseases. The description of the Emsworth home as "a great wandering house, standing in a considerable park," and being "of all sorts of ages and styles, starting on a half-timbered Elizabethan foundation and ending in a Victorian portico," answers quite well to a description of Sagamore Hill, the Roosevelt home on Long Island, especially the porch. Theodore Roosevelt's son Quentin had been killed in the First World War, and this may have inspired Doyle to write this story.

A number of men in "The Blanched Soldier," are named James. William James, when a young student, had joined Louis Agassiz and others on a zoological expedition to Brazil in 1865, a voyage Doyle fictionalized in his novel *The Lost World*. James and most of the others were seasick during much of the trip, but it was nothing compared to the illness James experienced in Brazil. Expeditions into the interior began in early May, but William was left at Rio with the task of setting up a marine lab when he came down with a high fever and was rushed to a hospital where the Brazilian doctors diagnosed smallpox. Agassiz returned and after examining William determined his assistant had been attacked by varioloid, a less noxious disease that resembles variola, the deadly smallpox. Like Emsworth, James was infected by one malady that is a false form of another, more grave one. James lay quarantined for nearly three weeks abysmally depressed and anxious, his eyes so inflamed and painful he feared blindness. By June he was up and about, but stayed on in the hospital another week or so before returning to his work, yet he left for the States before the rest of the expedition, so you might say he had been "wounded out." Much of the information we have on all this comes to us from letters William wrote to his mother and father, just as our information on Godfrey's ordeal is given to us by his parents. Agassiz's chief purpose on this trip was to classify hitherto unknown species of fish he believed were to be found in Brazil. Dr. Saunders said Godfrey had a "case of pseudo-leprosy or ichthyosis, a scale-like affection of the skin," with ichthyosis meaning, "of or characteristic of fish." Like Agassiz, he is classifying his fish-like discoveries. This adventure of William James' must have put Doyle in mind of his own youthful journey to West Africa while a medical student. He too became fever ridden, assuring us he almost died.

In his book *The Varieties of Religious Experience*, William James devotes a great deal of time to the then new movement in America and elsewhere, known as "mind-cure," the belief that God, religion, and one's style of living can answer the needs of one's health without the aid of medicine or doctors. James, a physician himself, realized how important such a development could become, and he was quite right for such movements as the Christian

Scientists and the Church of the Nazarene attract millions of followers, none of whom believe in conventional medicine. James' experience taught him it is impossible "not to class mind-cure as primarily a religious movement. Its doctrine of the oneness of our life with God's life is in fact quite indistinguishable from an interpretation of Christ's message." James Dodd, with his concern for his friend, and his willingness to help, finds his archetype in his namesake William James. For the last two pages of this tale we have Holmes, acting as Christ's messenger, explaining just how it was he reached the conclusion Godfrey was suffering from an illness, rather than any other problem being responsible for his isolation. When several explanations present themselves one tries test after test until one or another of them has a convincing amount of support. Now all these tests took place in Holmes' mind, yet this is pragmatism pure and simple, as William James made known to the world. "The Blanched Soldier," is a mystery solved by men like William James, James Saunders (who is filling in for William), Holmes, and Agassiz, working together, science and philosophy solving the problems of the human condition, with some help from God and religion, such thoughts summing up the teachings of William James and Martin Hesselius.

Having a twisted lip is not as devastating as yellow fever or leprosy, but if you are the one whose lip is twisted, it is significant enough. "The Man with the Twisted Lip," opens with Kate Whitney, wife of Isa Whitney, a friend of Watson's, and an opium addict, barging in on Watson and his wife one evening. It is at this point Watson's spouse calls him "James," and we are quite possibly being shown James Boswell at home with his wife. Isa has not been home for two days, and his wife believes him to be in an opium den "breathing in the poison or sleeping off the effects." Watson starts searching for his friend at the Bar of Gold, a despicable den, located in "a vile alley lurking behind the high wharves," "Between a slop-shop and a gin-shop, approached by a steep flight of steps leading down to a black gap like the mouth of a cave." Watson is advancing upon a tomb, a place of the dead. The ancient Jews buried their dead in caves, and Isa Whitney and his brother Elias have Jewish names. Watson enters a long, low room, "terraced with wooden berths," upon which he finds "bodies lying in strange fantastic poses, bowed shoulders, bent knees, heads thrown back, and chins pointing upward, with here and there a dark, lack-lustre eye turned upon the newcomer." The battle between good and evil, the truth and the Drug, has resulted in a few casualties, and many a body has been thrown through the trap door into the Thames. When found in this unholy place Whitney does not even know what day it is, neither does he care. St. John had the power to perform miracles such as raising the dead for Jesus gives the Apostles this ability in his absence. As Watson is helping Isa out of this den of iniquity he runs into none other than Sherlock disguised as an old addict. The detective recommends Watson send a note to his wife saying that he has thrown in his lot with Holmes. This is a re-enactment of the kind of friction that existed between Johnson and Mrs. Boswell, for the woman resented her husband spending so much time with the poet. Watson tells us, "It was difficult to refuse any of Sherlock Holmes's requests, for they were always so exceedingly definite, and put forward with such a quiet air of mastery," adding elsewhere that the man had "his own masterful nature, which loved to dominate and surprise those who were around him." These are direct references to Johnson's manner as reported by Boswell, for this was the way Johnson addressed the world, and because of his great intelligence and large generous nature, most people acceded to his requests.

What Holmes is doing in "the vilest murder-trap on the whole riverside," is imitating Dickens, who as a young journalist went alone to some of the worst areas of London, living and sleeping with the low society he wrote about. J. T. Fields, editor of *The Atlantic Monthly*, wrote that he and Dickens ventured, with the police, into "lock-ups, watch-houses, and opium-eating establishments." Holmes is searching for Neville St. Clair, a missing businessman, and during the case is staying at his residence, The Cedars, in Kent. Watson agrees to help him and they take a dogcart where Holmes takes the reins from an assistant named John, and they proceed to the missing man's home. It seems that Mrs. St. Clair, unexpectedly going to town one day to pick up a package, found herself passing the Bar of Gold and looked up to find herself staring at her husband in the second story window. He appears agitated and excited, is without collar and necktie, and is plucked away from the window "by some irresistible force from behind." She attempts to gain entrance to the hellhole but the lascar scoundrel running the den, aided by another foreigner, a Dane, pushed her out into the street. The distraught woman returns almost immediately with the police but they find none there but the foreigners and "a crippled wretch of hideous aspect, who, it seems, made his home there." The lascar claims to know nothing of Neville St. Clair, and cannot account for the articles of the man's clothing found in the room, and as well claims little knowledge of Hugh Boone, the desolate lodger sitting in the corner. The sober and prosperous man with two children has simply disappeared without a trace. Holmes suspects Boone, who has a disfiguring twisted lip, and is a regular feature in the City, making his living begging near the stock exchange, to know more than he is letting on. The case is under the supervision of Inspector Barton, who by pure chance as it were, happens to have the same name as Captain Barton in Le Fanu's "The Familiar." Low tide reveals St. Clair's coat, the pockets stuffed with small coins, but no body, and Boone is taken into custody awaiting developments. Holmes and Watson journey to The Cedars and encounter Mrs. St. Clair, only to be surprised with the knowledge that she has received a letter from her husband that day. That night Holmes collects pillows and "constructed a sort of Eastern divan, upon which he perched himself cross-legged, with an ounce of shag tobacco and a box of matches," to think out the problem, with morning bringing light to the darkness. Believing he has the answer, the two investigators head back to London and the Bow Street Police Station where Holmes asks to see Boone, then sneaks up on the hobo, and washes his face, thus transforming the cripple and unsightly vagabond into "a pale, sad-faced, refined-looking man, black-haired and smooth-skinned." A miracle has once again taken place right before our disbelieving eyes. Neville St.

Clair had been a writer and actor who, realizing he could never earn enough money in business to support his family in an elegant enough style, resorted to impersonating a pauper to gain easy money begging.

The afflicted in the *New Testament* often call upon the Lord to relieve their suffering, and Neville is no exception. Believing his wife and children will be disgraced by his actions he calls out in sorrow, "God help me, I would not have them ashamed of their father. My God! What an exposure! What can I do?" When Sherlock sits next to the man and pats him upon the shoulder, Boone says devoutly, "God bless you!" for he knows there will be no scandal. With the disclosure of the deception the begging must come to an end for St. Clair, and the man must earn a living some other way.

I can't help thinking of Johnson in all this, for he lived in poverty all his life and although he earned money as a writer, it never amounted to enough to relieve his distress, or the needs of those he helped, while his friends, writers and actors such as Garrick, suffered similar fates. There is of course a bit of Doyle here as well, for he and his family were poverty-ridden for years, especially when he was young, and even later as a doctor, for he tells us there were days when not a single patient called.

The Bar of Gold was near Paul's Wharf, on a lane leading to St. Paul's Pier, on the Thames. Now I have read that Paul's Wharf is far to the west of London Bridge, while Watson locates the Bar of Gold east of the Bridge, but by doing so references to St. Paul are deliberately brought into the story. As Holmes would say, "It is, of course, a trifle, but there is nothing so important as trifles," echoing Johnson's "Life is made up of little things." Mrs. Thrale tells us Johnson had such profound knowledge of the "little things" of human existence, and such appreciation of their value, he often acted as advisor to people on personal, or even business and legal matters.

We have seen Watson, acting the role of an Apostle, raise the dead. St. Paul raised a dead man while preaching in Greece and he also cured a cripple. When Paul and Barnabas were in Lystra they came upon one who had been lame from birth. Paul tells him to stand upright; he does so, and is cured from then on. Peter can also affect cures for in the *Acts* we read, "Now Peter and John went up to the temple at the ninth hour of prayer." Remember a man named John accompanied Holmes and Watson to Kent, and Watson's first name is also John, no matter what his wife thinks. "And a certain man who was lame from his mother's womb, was carried: whom they laid daily at the gate of the temple, which is called the Beautiful, that he might beg alms of them that went into the temple." The cripple begs of the two Apostles, "But Peter said: Silver and gold I have none: but what I have, I give thee: in the name of Jesus Christ, of Nazareth, rise up, and walk." The man does so, "And they knew him, that it was he who sat for alms at the Beautiful gate of the temple: and they were filled with wonder and amazement at that which had happened to him." We are told of the amazement of the police at Bow Street witnessing Boone's transformation, as well as the fact that "they knew him," who had been crippled. "'Great heavens!' cried the inspector, 'it is, indeed, the missing man. I know him from the photograph.'" The London Stock Exchange stands in for the temple of the Biblical account, for it is a temple of commerce. In place of the gold he begged for, Holmes has given Neville St. Clair the peace of God, so we have another chronicle with the same theme as *Silas Marner*. Gold has been exchanged for a new understanding of God's will.

Neville was a dead man, for he writes to his wife from Gravesend, and is kept at Bow Street, the name deriving from the fact that during the Plague the area had been one long bow-shaped mass grave. The "huge ledger upon the table" found at the Bow Street Station signifies the giant merit book St. Peter keeps at the entrance to the other world. Doyle has the New York City prison "The Tombs," in mind here, a place he made a special point to visit while in that city.

The Picture of Dorian Gray seems to have exercised some influence upon this story wherein we learn that Dorian's love of dissipation leads him to spend time "in the sordid room of the little ill-famed tavern near the docks which, under an assumed name and in disguise, it was his habit to frequent." Like St. Clair, Gray has absences he cannot explain, and he brawls with foreign sailors in a low den in Whitechapel, becoming notorious, and a character in London. Visiting his family estate he studies the portraits of his ancestors searching for evidence of the source of his foul nature and discovers a painting of George Willoughby. "How evil he looked! The face was saturnine and swarthy, and the sensual lips seemed to be twisted with disdain." Dorian's own likeness, capturing the buried malevolence and immorality of his soul initially expresses to the world his depravity by a certain sneer upon the lips. Trying to block from his mind his vile existence, Gray finds himself in an opium den on the docks full of Malays and sailors suffering the effects of drink and drugs. Just as Watson discovers Isa Whitney in the den, Dorian comes across his comrade Adrian Singleton, an addict to the drug. St. Clair is much like Dorian Gray in his own way for rather than work at an honest profession he earns his place in the world by presenting to it an image that is not his true nature. He is a Dorian Gray in reverse, but a Dorian Gray nevertheless.

The name St. Clair links Neville and his wife with their namesake, St. Clare. As a girl of eighteen, after hearing the preaching of St. Francis, Clare walked away from her home and joined an order of Benedictine nuns, there to lead a penitential life, wearing only sackcloth and going barefoot. In imitation of Jesus and Francis she took a vow of strict poverty that influenced even the Popes of her day. Her ideal in life was based on this evangelical poverty, and she founded an order of nuns called, after her example, The Poor Clares. Her life was so devout and her example so strong even her mother and sisters put themselves under her rule. She died in 1253 at the age of sixty and was canonized two years later. We are never told Mrs. St. Clair's first name, so once again we are free to use our imagination and construe one. Doyle however, I believe, offers us a strong clue with his persistent use of the feminine name Kate, earlier on in the story. Kate is Mrs. Whitney's first name, and I think Doyle wants to recycle the name for Mrs. St. Clair, who would also then be named after St. Catherine of Bologna, the abbess of a convent of the Poor Clares who had in fact been responsible for adopting the rules of St.

Clare into other institutions. She followed a path of humility and poverty yet was an artist and writer whose works are still studied in religious circles. It is Neville and his wife who are the poor Clairs, but they are a strange model of the saints' examples and teachings, for although he begs his living like a Christian mendicant, Neville rebels against his poverty. I believe Doyle is saying here that this malcontented individual should accept his lot in life and not strike out against what is, after all, God's will. Among some people it is regarded as very bad taste, almost sinful, to complain about one's situation in life. The young Eppie chooses paucity with her adopted father, Silas Marner, whose love she is sure of, rather than the luxury offered by her real father, Godfrey Cass, for his love is not so certain; he has been foolish and selfish in the past, and may be in the future. Doyle has seen real need in his life, and he knows this pseudo hardship of the St. Clairs' is far from the real thing. Let Neville go out and work for his living like the rest of us, Doyle is saying, for the bar of gold is nothing but an opium dream.

"The Disappearance of Lady Frances Carfax" is a complicated business and I can consider dealing with but a small portion of its multifaceted nature. The former governess of Frances Carfax has consulted Holmes over the fact that Lady Frances has broken her custom of writing to her. Lady Frances, the last survivor of an ancient family, is described as part of a dangerous class of woman, for she is single, alone, migratory, and susceptible to every rogue in the world who might be after her money or position, and she is also in the habit of carrying around with her a remarkable collection of jewels. Her last letter was from Lausanne, where she then left after drawing a large check to her maid, Miss Marie Devine. Unable to leave London, Holmes sends Watson to Lausanne to see what he can find out, and he learns that just before Lady Frances left her hotel, a tall, dark bearded man described as a savage Englishman visited her. Watson traces her to Baden where she made the acquaintance of Dr. Shlessinger and his wife, a pair of missionaries from South America. Lady Frances found great comfort and occupation in religion and is deeply affected by the pair. Mr. Shlessinger had contracted a disease in South America and Lady Frances insists upon helping "the convalescent saint," who spends his days on the veranda "preparing a map of the Holy Land, with special reference to the kingdom of the Midianites, upon which he was writing a monograph." We are being given a fat clue with mention of this tribe for the Midianites were a nomadic people who attacked the local Hebrews and lay waste their land, for they were rovers, enemies of the settled people. The three of them: Lady Frances, and the Shlessingers, departs Baden for London, and nothing more is heard of them. Holmes wires Watson with a request for a description of the missionary's left ear, but Watson ignores him.

The savage Englishman, the Hon. Philip Green, who had once loved and lost Lady Frances, and is now stalking her with a view to marriage, has also been making inquiries, and when he and Watson cross paths, questions lead to a brawl. Green is overpowering the doctor when Holmes, disguised as a French workman, interferes and drives him away.

It turns out that Dr. Shlessinger is none other than an unscrupulous Australian grifter, nicknamed "Holy Peters," who preys upon the religious zeal of lonely women, robbing them of everything. "That she is already dead is a very likely supposition," Holmes theorizes. The action shifts back to London where Holmes visits Scotland Yard, but neither they, nor his own small but efficient organization have any leads. Finally Shlessinger pawns one of Lady Frances' jewels, and Holmes starts following the pair and watches as the wife purchases a coffin at the local undertaker and has it sent to her home. "We are, as usual, the irregulars, and we must take our own line of action," is Holmes' line of reasoning as he and Watson barge into the Shlessinger flat where the detective insists upon viewing the coffin and its contents, only to discover it contains a much older woman, a deceased family servant, and the two investigators leave little more enlightened than before. Following a sleepless night the morning brings a possible solution to the Great Detective's mind as he grabs Watson and they rush to stop the funeral. Tearing off the coffin lid they are overpowered by the smell of chloroform. "A body lay within, its head all wreathed in cotton-wool, which had been soaked in the narcotic." Plucking off these wrappings discloses the face of a handsome and spiritual woman of middle age. Holmes reaches into the casket "and raised her to a sitting position," and after a frantic half-hour of work she shows signs "of the slowly returning life."

Jesus performed many miracles but he is reported to have raised the dead but a few times. St. Luke tells of one such incident, "And when he came nigh to the gate of the city, behold a dead man was carried out, the only son of his mother: and she was a widow: and much people of the city was with her. And when the Lord saw her, he had compassion on her, and said to her: Weep not. And he came near and touched the bier. (And they that carried it, stood still.) And he said: Young man, I say to thee, arise. And he that was dead, sat up, and began to speak. And he delivered him to his mother." Holmes and his Apostle John come upon the funeral as it is crossing the gate of the cemetery. The procession is halted and those who carry the body are told to wait. The dead in both instances are told to come back to life, do so, and sit up.

The raising of Lazarus is the most famous miracle ever performed by Jesus, and the most important to Christianity, with the only account of it appearing in "The Gospel of John." When Jesus hears of the illness of his friend Lazarus, he starts immediately for his village, just as Holmes travels to rescue Lady Frances, but Jesus is too late, and the body of Lazarus has already been placed in a cave. The sister of Lazarus berates Jesus, claiming that if he had come sooner her brother would still be alive, but Jesus assures her that her brother will live again. Martha says he will rise only on the last Day of Judgment, but Jesus again insists that although he is dead yet he shall live again. Lazarus' two sisters take Jesus to the tomb where they find a stone laid upon the doorway which Jesus orders to be removed. Martha tells him, "Lord, by this time he stinketh, for he is now of four days." Jesus tells them to believe a little more and cries out, "Father, I give thee thanks that thou hast heard me." "When he had said these things, he cried with a loud voice:

Lazarus, come forth. And presently he that had been dead came forth, bound feet and hands with winding-bands, and his face was bound about with a napkin. Jesus said to them: Loose him, and let him go." We can be sure that somewhere along the line Lady Frances was bound hand and foot and now her face is covered with a cotton bandage saturated with a chemical that indeed stinks. Holmes calls on heaven before attempting to raise the dead, as did Jesus, for as they are rushing to stop the funeral procession he calls out, "Good heavens, Watson, what has become of any brains that God has given me?" This is an acknowledgment of God's role in the miracle. By the way, Lazarus is Hebrew for "God has helped."

Although much has been left out of this analysis, we have addressed a few details coming within the compass of this brief review. Much of what I have to say about some forthcoming assessments can be applied equally well to "Lady Frances Carfax," as the readers will see for themselves.

Chapter Ten. The Method of Tenacity

Zeroing in on Doyle's thoughts in these next two stories is to share with him a truly fascinating aesthetic experience. "The Disappearance of Lady Frances Carfax" is a companion piece to "The Adventure of the Illustrious Client"; they are that close in nature. Ironically enough both open with mention of a Turkish bath, for in "The Illustrious Client" the two detectives enjoy one at the Northumberland Ave. establishment, while in "Lady Frances Carfax," Watson has just returned from one. Doyle has reread the first story, written ten years earlier, before starting on the second. Sir James Damery, possibly helping a friend, calls upon Holmes with an urgent request for assistance in dissuading a young woman from marrying a foreigner, Baron Gruner. The Baron is suspected of having killed at least one previous wife, and it is feared he will kill again if he can marry Violet de Merville. The police are helpless to act, for the only witness to his wife's death has himself mysteriously died. Holmes takes the case, visits the Baron, who refuses to quit his pursuit, threatening the Great Detective with violence. The aid of a thug named Shinwell Johnson and a young artist's model, Kitty Winter, a victim of the man's lechery and brutality, are enlisted in the good fight.

If you thought Lady Frances was naïve, let me introduce you to Miss Violet de Merville, one who makes a clear point of ignoring reason and advice, living in a haze of self-deception. Miss Winter and Holmes pay a visit to Violet, where the former model enlightens the intended victim of the man's malice, which included throwing acid in her face, only to be thrown out amid accusations of slander. Following this visit Holmes is attacked by henchmen of Gruner's, who rough him up, but he uses this incident to fake reports of his calamitous defenselessness, hoping to hoodwink his enemies into underestimating his strength, much as he did in "The Dying Detective."

Baron Gruner is a collector, not just of women, but also of Chinese pottery, so Watson is put to studying this field, intending to pose as a fellow enthusiast of the art form. Under the name Dr. Hill Barton, Watson visits the man, offering to sell a rare piece; but the shrewd bounder sees through the ruse. An argument ensues but is interrupted by a sound outside the French window, for it is Holmes, attempting to steal the man's notebook. The Baron rushes outside to attack whoever is hiding there, only to come across Kitty, also hiding in the bushes, who now evens the score by throwing acid in his face. Holmes succeeds in stealing the Baron's diary of lust, which is presented as evidence of his vicious animalism to Violet, who finally accedes to breaking off the misalliance.

"The Illustrious Client" is an answer to Bram Stoker's wildly popular *Dracula*, but whereas the Transylvanian Count journeyed to London desirous of the blood of young women, Doyle's foreigner is hungry for their bodies and their wealth, using their money to live on, just as the vampire craves their blood to sustain his own murky existence. Stoker probably told his friend Doyle about the Roman practice of older men suckling the milk of young girls, thereby hoping to regain their youth, and he simply substituted riches for milk.

Sir James Damery spends much time at the Carlton Club, for which please read the Metaphysical Club, an informal weekly gathering that met in Boston to discuss philosophical issues and counted among its members William James and Wendell Holmes. Sherlock assumes some aspects of William James for Watson tells us, "When our visitor (James Damery) had left us Holmes sat so long in deep thought that it seemed to me that he had forgotten my presence. At last, however, he came briskly back to earth. 'Well Watson, any views?' he asked." As a teacher James every so often would become lost in his own thoughts and sit in silence oblivious of students and surroundings for a while, suddenly looking up and asking, "What were we talking about?" The name Damery is a corruption of the word "dame," coming from the Latin "*domina*," the feminine form of "*dominus*," which means "a lord." The English word dominate, meaning, among other things, "to tower or rise above others, or the surroundings," comes from this root, and the work of William James, as well as that of his brother, answers to this accolade. Sir James is presented as a diplomatic and sophisticated man of the world with a "large, bluff, honest personality," and so indeed were the James brothers, with his "broad, clean-shaven face," and "pleasant, mellow voice," associated with Henry in particular. "Frankness shone from his gray Irish eyes, and good humour played round his mobile, smiling lips." This is an apt picture of both brothers, although I admit I don't know what color eyes they had. William often made jokes about the Irish, and about his being Irish, and Henry may have as well, although I haven't come across any of his. Sir James is dressed in a top-hat, frock-coat, black satin cravat, and lavender spats over varnished shoes; the manner in which William dressed when lecturing, and the way the dandyish Henry was attired at all times.

Sir James describes the Baron as the most "dangerous man in Europe," and Holmes recognizes him as "the Austrian murderer," adding that from what he has read he could have no doubt of the man's guilt and evil intentions. The Baron lives at Vernon Lodge, near Kingston, and to an American, Vernon usually reminds him of Mount Vernon, the Virginia plantation of George Washington. Violet's father is referred to, as "the General," which in America, used alone, is a title reserved only for George Washington. For a number of years the James family lived on Mount Vernon Street in Boston. In New York State the towns of Kingston and Mount Vernon are found in the Hudson Valley, so we know we are in dangerous waters. Remember Hawkeye believed firmly that it is the function of a good man to warn his friends of danger.

Warning one's friends of menace is not as easy as it sounds. The Baron killed his wife during a climbing trip and claims it was an accident, but Holmes tells us he is as sure the man did it "as if I had seen him do it," which he has, in his role of prophet. Violet de Merville knows of the incident but refuses to regard it as anything more than an accident, for her fiancé could not possibly be guilty of such a crime. William James discusses a murder in his essay "The Dilemma of Determinism," one of his most respected works, which deals with the unending controversy of whether or not man actually has free will. His aim is to induce his readers to join him in assuming the existence of free will using selected examples enforcing his point, these examples taken from human conduct and character. What Doyle is saying is that the Baron has taken away the free will of his young victim, in which case he will be attempting to control her by controlling her future, the means of this being to marry her. James adds, "Do not all the motives that assail us, all the futures that offer themselves to our choice, spring equally from the soil of the past; and would not either one of them, whether realized through chance or through necessity, the moment it was realized, seem to us to fit that past, and in the completest and most continuous manner to interdigitate with the phenomena already there?" The past, in this case the past of the Baron, a past full of wickedness and death, will determine the course of the future, and the future will "fit that past." James does not agree with this, and in a strange footnote to the sentence just quoted adds, "A fantastic argument against free-will is that if it be true, a man's murderer may as probably be his best friend as his worst enemy." Even James, in the same footnote, is forced to admit that sometimes it does happen that, "Persons really tempted often do murder their best friends." This starry-eyed girl actually believes Gruner is her best friend, as anyone would of the person they are planning to marry. He has been "really tempted," by the opportunity placed before him, and can be relied upon to repeat his past behavior. Those who argue against free will would tell us the Baron has no choice himself in the matter; his decisions only appear to be choices, but they have nothing to do with free will, only necessity. The girl is about to make what James calls "judgments of regret," that life is full of, for not being able to foresee the point of view of the end of her choice, she will make her judgment and then regret it. The philosopher tells us it is best to forget our regrets but admits, "some regrets are pretty obstinate and hard to stifle, — regrets for acts of wanton cruelty or treachery, for example, whether performed by others or by ourselves." Violet is in for a hat full of regrets one way or the other. The Baron and his wicked ways leap to mind with the example James gives of wanton treachery, for he makes reference to a newspaper account of a real incident that occurred in Brockton, Mass., not far from Boston. "Hardly any one can remain *entirely* optimistic after reading the confession of the murderer at Brockton the other day: how, to get rid of the wife whose continued existence bored him, he inveigled her into a desert spot, shot her four times, and then, as she lay on the ground and said to him, 'You didn't do it on purpose, did you, dear?' replied, 'No, I didn't do it on purpose,' as he raised a rock and smashed her skull. Such an occurrence, with the mild sentence and self-satisfaction of the prisoner, is a field for a crop of regrets, which one need not take up in detail. We feel that, although a perfect mechanical fit to the rest of the universe, it is a bad moral fit, and that something else would really have been better in its place." The device of a newspaper reporting a crime makes an appearance in "The Illustrious Client," for as Watson is strolling along a London street he catches a headline informing the reader that Sherlock Holmes has been assaulted. This article, though longer than the description of the Brockton murder, does add, "There are no exact details to hand," for James tells us in his essay that the exact details are not necessary when making a generality for the sake of a moral. The Baron's killing of his first wife is the application Doyle has in mind for this Brockton study, and as well the possible upcoming homicide of his next spouse, who, in her abject ignorance of human nature, would no doubt also not suspect her own murderer of having the will to do it on purpose. "If this Brockton murder was called for by the rest of the universe, if it had to come at its preappointed hour, and if nothing else would have been consistent with the sense of the whole, what are we to think of the universe?" James asks. It is Sherlock working under the instigation of William James that shall see this treacherous preappointed hour does not strike again — the point and moral of "The Illustrious Client." The American says the murder was bad, and that something else should be in its place, and here is the function of Holmes and his allies, an attempt at altering the course of the future, putting in its stead something hopefully better.

While "looking down at the rushing stream of life in the Strand," Holmes philosophizes, "Woman's heart and mind are insoluble puzzles to the male. Murder might be condoned or explained, and yet some smaller offence might rankle." Has not the Brockton victim explained away in an instant, and almost condoned as well, her husband's murder of herself, as long as she could tell herself he didn't really mean it? Pessimists such as Schopenhauer say that "the murder is a symptom; and that it is a vicious symptom because it belongs to a vicious whole, which can express its nature no otherwise than by bringing forth just such a symptom as that at this particular spot," James claims. Baron Gruner is an exponent of the pessimism of the German school of philosophy, while his enemies Sir James and Holmes personify American thought, perhaps the most optimistic school of thought in the world. James tells us optimism has been the saving grace of some of the most religious personalities in history. Gruner is German for "green" and James mentions a philosopher he calls simply "Mr. Green," who is Thomas Hill Green, an English disciple of Georg Wilhelm Friedrich Hegel, a staunch German advocate of determinism or lack of free will and one considered pessimistic. I have not read Thomas Green. Also remember that Philip Green is the name of the savage man hounding Lady Frances Carfax.

James has much to say of the nature of good and evil in the "theological form." This issue, what James actually regards as the question of optimism and pessimism, cannot be answered by simply stating that evil is wrong and that good is not wrong. "The world must not be regarded as a machine whose final purpose is the making real of any outward good, but rather as a contrivance for deepening the theoretic consciousness of what goodness and evil in their intrinsic natures are. Not the doing either of good or evil is what nature cares for, but the knowing of them." Violet's father and his helpers are trying to bring knowledge of good and evil to her, even if she doesn't want it. "Life is one long eating of the fruit of the tree of *knowledge*," James claims, and although they have pointed out the tree of knowledge to Violet, she will not eat of it. The Baron is the devil/snake in the drama, for the man is "cool as ice," and "poisonous as a cobra." Called, a "cunning devil," he yet manages to make himself out to be an offended victim; a devil's trick if ever there was one.

The word "dilemma," found in the title of James' essay comes into the story, for when pressed by Holmes to reveal the name of his client, Sir James admits, "You place me in a most serious dilemma." At the conclusion Watson believes he has learned the identity of the illustrious client and is about to state that it is none other than King Edward but Holmes silences him with, "It is a loyal friend and a chivalrous gentleman," an allusion perhaps to the King, but to William James as well, for when James died in 1910, one journalist, speaking for many, called him "the greatest friend mankind has ever had." Doyle may have picked up the idea of introducing thoughts of the King from a reference to the king chess piece as it is used in the game, which James employed as a prop in his discussion of freedom of choice in the closing paragraph of "The Dilemma of Determinism." The spiritual forces of the yogi and the potential forces of the king, combining to combat one who cannot restrain himself from doing evil, is the theme of "The Illustrious Client."

Watson tells us, "September 3, 1902, the day when my narrative begins," and I don't believe any other story starts with this need for such exact dating. I also don't know exactly what date he began them, but in September of 1902, William James was in Edinburgh delivering lectures entitled *The Varieties of Religious Experience*, which proved so popular he brought them out in book form a year later under the same title. The book speaks of the influence religion plays on the lives of individuals, and how different people face the question of their spiritual experiences. The infatuation Violet feels for the Baron acquires overtones of religious adoration, for listen to Holmes' report of his impressions following his visit to the girl: "I don't quite know how to make her clear to you, Watson. Perhaps you may meet her before we are through, and you can use your own gift of words. She is beautiful, but with the ethereal other-world beauty of some fanatic whose thoughts are set on high." Holmes compares her feelings to one who is in a post-hypnotic trance, for she seems like one "living above the earth in some ecstatic dream." James brings up hypnotic suggestion, attempting to explain certain types of religious experience such as fanaticism or conversion in which people do not always seem to exercise complete control over their own minds or emotions. This foreigner has developed this naïve woman into a fanatic with his oily personality, the same trap Lady Frances fell into. Violet has all the capacities of a saint, but not all such qualities are beneficial, in view of the fact that saints often become blind to the real character of those around them. He quotes from the writings of one such saint: "I thought, if I were surrounded by enemies, who were venting their malice and cruelty upon me, in tormenting me, it would still be impossible that I should cherish any feelings towards them but those of love, and pity, and ardent desires for their happiness." These thoughts from the mind of an aspirant for sainthood find a trouble-free fit in the mind of Violet, or Lady Frances, or even the Brockton wife. Many saints love not only their enemies, James claims, but show love to people they know to be personally loathsome or sinful, proving that the love of a saint is as blind as is any other type of love. Violet realizes others despise Gruner, but this only adds to the intensity of her feelings, which adopt an odor of sacrifice that elevates it to a spiritual plane; even knowledge of his sins might cause her to care for him more. She even cherishes the poverty of the man, for poverty is regarded as a truly great thing in many of the world's religions. Ask the Poor Clares. Because of her rigid, austere demeanor and cool beauty, Violet puts Holmes in mind of "a snow image on a mountain." She is like a statue, as the saint is like a statue, living within the will of God, and having no will of their own. Remember Lady Frances, even when half dead, was regarded as "statuesque." They are proud of their inability to rule their own destiny, placing what will they have, "in God's hands." "Each emotion obeys a logic of its own," James says of the psyche of the saint, "and makes deductions which no other logic can draw." Violet's face, with its lack of logic and will, is compared to "such faces in the pictures of the old masters of the Middle Ages," this being the age of the spirit and of the Church, with almost any painting of this period showing scenes depicting the exploits of the saints, usually in their martyrdom, and often in their glory. Violet speaks with Kitty and Sherlock in a room hung with yellow curtains so she is surrounded with golden color, as are the saints when presented to us in medieval art. We saw the same thing with Mrs. St. Clair, another personification of a saint, for when first encountered in the doorway of her house she is outlined by the yellow light of the interior.

The emotional makeup of Miss de Merville contains an "excess of good" that can only force her to commit a terrible error. "We find that error by excess is exemplified by every saintly virtue," James alleges, but, "In the life of saints, technically so called, the spiritual faculties are strong, but what gives the impression of extravagance proves usually on examination to be a relative deficiency of intellect." Such selectivity in human nature is a loss of balance that must be countered by a powerful intellect, but Violet does not have a penetrating intelligence, and any lack of balance can lead the saint, or anyone, astray. The girl is engaged to be married to someone she loves and who she believes loves her; she is happy. "To the man actively happy, from whatever cause, evil simply cannot then and there be believed in. He must ignore it; and to the bystander he may then seem perversely to shut his eyes to it and hush it up." There are people in the world, James says, who are congenitally good and happy, a type of individual who cannot possibly see the unhappiness and evil of others no matter how obvious it is. James adds, "we all have some friend, perhaps more often feminine than masculine, and young than old, whose soul is of this sky-blue tint, whose affinities are rather with flowers and birds and all enchanting innocencies than with dark human passions, who can think no ill of man or God, and in whom religious gladness, being in possession from the outset, needs no deliverance from any antecedent burden." Even Violet's name emphasizes her affinity with these flower people, and notice it is the older men who immediately perceive the Baron for what he is. James tells us in regard to the type of person Violet represents that such persons do not look back into themselves so they are not distressed by their own imperfections, and in fact "they hardly think of themselves *at all*," therefore they never see evil in any other person. They know so little of the world they approach it with complacency and a "romantic sense of excitement." Holmes says of Violet, "there was something indescribably annoying in the calm aloofness and supreme self-complaisance of the woman whom we are trying to save." He is disgusted with her stubborn insistence upon the rigid belief in Gruner's virtuousness, and James as well feels aversion for one who does not have the ability to face reality and admit some simple truths to themselves. He has of course the example of the Brockton wife in the back of his mind.

The philosopher advances his theories with various arguments for self-protection and attitude that could be used to advance my position showing the connections between "The Illustrious Client," and *The Varieties of Religious Experience*, but this will do.

The Medieval Irish philosopher John Scotus Erigena influenced Charles Peirce, and through him, William James. The Medieval world in which Scotus Erigena philosophized believed in the general or universal, as exampled by God, the particular or singular seeming to elude altogether the grasp of their minds. John Scotus Erigena emphasized a more scientific insistence on the concrete nature of reality, just as Sir James is trying to rehabilitate Violet to the concrete nature of the life that surrounds her, but which she fails to understand or even perceive. Scotus Erigena may very well have been the first person to think in terms of "reality," the knowledge that something has existence whether or not you want it to, and he may also have been the first writer to use the word reality, and James hints at this.

One thing Peirce learned from Scotus Erigena is the theory that the will is superior to the reason, and as such is itself reasonable. The will of Violet de Merville is vastly more advanced than her reason, and therefore takes the place of her reason, being reasonable while her reason now becomes unreasonable. Holmes tells us he is aware of Sir James' handling of the Hammerford Will case, a reference to William James' essay "The Will to Believe." Hammerford is a word created for its evocative value, calling to mind iron strength, and we are told of Violet that she "has a will of iron." James argues that some people want to believe in something such as a Supreme Being, whether there is adequate evidence for such or not. The effect of believing for these people can be momentous in their lives, and should not be denigrated just because such believers cannot prove or substantiate what they deem reality. I know Blaise Pascal and Søren Kierkegaard, as well as James, insisted that believing is different from knowing; they are different forms of knowledge and do not affect each other. One gives credence in spite of the lack of knowledge, if believing is of sufficient importance. Peirce realized that belief in anything is not arbitrary, but requires a cause, and although Violet has no real cause, outside of her desire, to love the Baron, it has happened, perhaps in answer to James' statement, somewhere in his writings, that a man can make a woman love him if he simply insists upon her loving him. "There is no more striking characteristic of the dark ages," Peirce claims, "when thought was little developed, than the prevalence of a sentiment that an opinion was a thing to be chosen because one liked it." The young lady in question prefers her own opinion of reality and therefore chooses it above the judgment of others, whose thoughts are less Medieval and thus more developed.

The De Mervilles live at 104 Berkeley Square, an allusion to the Irish philosopher George Berkeley, a thinker James was very impressed with. James had taught for a while at the University of California at Berkeley, a city named after the philosopher, who had visited there. James was nearby when the San Francisco earthquake struck in 1904, a possible numerical pun on the de Merville house number 104. Berkeley alleged that the life within the mind, not the existence outside the psyche, represented the authentic world, much as had Descartes, but if you were to carry this thought too far, you would encompass the mind of Violet de Merville, for only what it is she thinks will she accept as actuality.

James' "The Will to Believe" treats of, obviously, just that topic, and in so doing covers almost every facet of our story. Using terminology applicatory to the case in front of us, the essay harbors thoughts as to why people believe in whatever it is they do believe in, and as well explores the differences of judging with the mind or with the heart. After Kitty disfigures the Baron with acid, Sir James hopes Violet will no longer be devoted to him, but the detective knows a backlash effect must now take place for she will "love him the more as a disfigured martyr," unless he can also be proved morally reprehensible, for no allusion to his physical character could elicit any negative response from her. William James tells us the intellectual side of belief is not as important as the moral side. "The state of things is evidently far from simple," James maintains in regard to whether or not we should believe in anything, "and pure insight and logic, whatever they might do ideally, are not the only things that really do produce our creeds." "*Our passional nature not only lawfully may, but must, decide an option between propositions, whenever it is a genuine option that cannot by its nature be decided on intellectual grounds; for to say, under such circumstances.*" Violet's passions, governable by her morals, must decide an option between propositions, for it cannot by its nature be decided on intellectual foundations. Since it is an affair of the heart, the heart must settle it.

Holmes is willing to commit a crime by breaking into the foreigner's villa and stealing his notebook detailing his past immoral life, and in so doing is embarking upon what the American calls "the quest or hope of truth itself."

Of the truth James maintains we must "pin our faith on its existence," and William James assures Holmes in regard to breaking into Gruner's house that "Not where it comes from but what it leads to is to decide." Deciding his act, though a criminal one, will lead to a greater good, the detective goes ahead with his plans. "It matters not to an empiricist from what quarter an hypothesis may come to him: he may have acquired it by fair means or by foul; passion may have whispered or accident suggested it; but if the total drift of thinking continues to confirm it, that is what he means by its being true." Holmes is an empiricist, and a hypothesis is, in this case, a question that must be answered. The passionate directness of Kitty Winter adds to the total drift of the acquiring of truth, in this case by foul means, and the very appearance of Kitty on the scene at the Baron's villa at this particular moment in time was simply an accident.

For James and Holmes the finding of the truth is almost a religious ritual, for the American tells us our first and great commandments as would-be knowers is that *"We must know the truth; and we must avoid error."* William James objected to the practice of prescribed forms of thought and action in law in place of genuine morality, much in line with his friend Wendell Holmes. Ultimately, man is not tested by such codes but all codes are to be tested by human experience. Sometimes, he realized, genuine goodness involves acting against the letter or spirit of accepted regulations for bona fide morals go beyond the legal system. Genuine morality accords abstract and remote ways of considering individual facts, and it will never completely divorce its generalizations from the human situations out of which they arose, and to which they refer. Behind the lives of James and Wendell Holmes lies the quest for the moral truth of the universe, expressed in rules. In any case it will be maintained by these men that rules and laws do not in themselves carry the full riches of the moral life. If morality be theistic, James claims, it will constantly refer to God as a person and not merely adhere to his commandments, seeing that God is working for man's salvation not only in making rules but also in an endless variety of encounters with mankind. This brings us to the King, God's representative on earth, if he is Holmes' client. Perhaps the illustrious client is "a person," much higher than a king. Salvation means, "to save" and this is just what they are trying to do for Violet. Religious overtones always seem to come into these stories and the same may be said of James' writings, for he incessantly returns to religious themes and examples.

James, like the followers of Zarathustra and like Descartes, believed good as well as evil is introduced into the world by intelligent beings. The Baron is an intelligent being who represents concrete malevolence, which James realizes does exist, but which can be overcome by "extraordinary souls." He believes that the philosopher must recognize the fact that occasionally "some one is born with the right to be original," who will "replace 'old laws of nature' by better ones." The right person will comprehend that the problem of real evil does exist, and it is not a speculative problem, but one that is eminently practical. He will ask not why evil should exist at all, but rather how he can lessen the actual amount of it in this life. James alleged the moral life to be a war, "and the service of the highest is a sort of cosmic patriotism which also calls for volunteers," and thus Sir James asks Holmes to volunteer in the struggle.

It is imperative the Baron be exposed and halted in his plans. He ignores Holmes and the others, and will probably kill Violet if he can marry her, but Kitty Winter will stop him, and make him pay for his past. Like her name she is as innocent as a kitten, but with a heart as cold as winter ice. Like Dracula's victims, Kitty is a zombie, one of the living dead, a piece of damaged goods. "The good which we have wounded returns to plague us with interminable crops of consequential damages, compunctions, and regrets," James warns. Kitty returns like a curse to plague the Baron, giving him what he gave her, and he will now have some regrets of his own to occupy his wicked mind. James calls people "goods," as was common usage in his day, and also employs the word as a pun. "It is the nature of these goods to be cruel to their rivals," and we recall Kitty has even shown a certain amount of cruelty to Violet. These goods "call out all our disposition, and do not easily forgive us if we are so soft-hearted as to shrink from sacrifice in their behalf." Kitty would forgive none who showed soft heartedness toward the object of her retaliation. "The strenuous mood, on the contrary, makes us quite indifferent to present ill, if only the greater ideal be attained," James claims, and so the two detectives, and Kitty for that matter, are indifferent to present danger in going to Gruner's villa. Kitty must now face the stern retribution of the law for she is sent to prison, and although Holmes considers her sentence far too severe he can do nothing about it.

In "The Illustrious Client" we are dealing with a conflict of wills, Gruner versus the community. In "The Moral Philosopher and the Moral Life," an essay James published in 1891, we come across the following: "The presumption in cases of conflict must always be in favor of the conventionally recognized good. The philosopher must be a conservative, and in the construction of his casuistic scale must put the things most in accordance with the customs of the community on top." Green, the philosopher I mentioned before, comes into the argument at this point, for James gives us a quote from his *Prolegomena to Ethics*, "Rules are made for man, not man for rules." Now James is presenting this thought to us with his approval; one must not be too conservative, one must be always open to new ideas, but Doyle seems to be warning us that Gruner (Green) has taken this one sentence and distorted its meaning to suit himself, which would not be difficult for any immoral man. Carry this consideration too far and you achieve a human moral disaster that believes that they can make up any laws, so long as they benefit from them. James tells us there are always "innumerable persons whom it weighs upon, and goods which it represses; and these are always rumbling and grumbling in the background, and ready for any issue by which they may get free." There are always those people looking to free themselves from moral restraints which do not suit them, people such as the Baron. James continues: "See the abuses which the institution of private property covers, so that even to-day it is shamelessly asserted among us that one of the prime functions of the national government is to help the adroiter citizens to grow rich. See the unnamed and unnamable sorrows which the tyranny, on the whole so beneficent, of the marriage-institution brings to so many, both of the married and the unwed." Here is a portion at least of the problem found lurking at the bottom of "The Illustrious Client." The man is adroit at what he does, which is murdering his wives, and if he can marry Violet, the British marriage laws will facilitate his efforts, offering him a field of operations and a modicum of protection. This essay also repeats James' assertion that some individuals have better morals than society in general and therefore have the right to replace old laws with a finer moral code. Such a man "by breaking old moral rules in a certain place, bring in a total condition of things more ideal than would have followed had the rules been kept." By obeying the law and not breaking into the Baron's home ("a certain place") the murder of Violet becomes all but inevitable. Interestingly enough for this particular case, James says moral questions and answers can be found "only through the aid of the experience of other men." A sort of consensus must be taken to determine what should be done to bring about a more ideal condition. A number of men, especially Watson, play an important role in this case, and Sir James, in the beginning, tells us of Watson, "His collaboration may be very necessary." The American equivalent of the king is the statesman, and James says of the moral philosopher, "His function is in fact indistinguishable from that of the best kind of statesman at the present day."

"On a Certain Blindness in Human Beings," William James' most famous piece of writing, as we see from its title, comes close in theme to "The Illustrious Client." If reduced to one sentence, the intention of the essay is to show that you never know what another person is thinking. The young heiress is simple enough to believe she has the ability to read Gruner's mind, but William James, in the persona of James Damery, is attempting to teach her that such a feat is absolutely impossible. William James puts forth examples of errors he made in the arena of life from his own experiences, and uses conditions from the lifestyles and writings of people such as Walt Whitman and Robert Louis Stevenson, to affirm that one person cannot possibly have any idea of the values and motivations found within another person's thoughts. Justice Holmes has already said the same thing briefly, and in legal conversation, in *The Common Law*. This reminds me that James wrote somewhere that he believes one man cannot put a thought into another person's mind. Blindness to each other's intentions and mentality is simply part of our natural inheritance, he claims, and a man (or woman in this case) must strive constantly to overcome it. Doyle also has before him Diderot's famous insight, that it takes the greatest intelligence in the world to see evil.

Did the brothers James know Doyle used their writings as models for his work? I don't think there can be any doubt but that they did. I know William enjoyed mysteries; he wrote his wife from a hotel in Maine that he was reading Gaboriau. It's possible the James brothers and Wendell Holmes, and perhaps other Americans, may even have exchanged thoughts on Doyle's use of their material, and evidence for this may exist, but I have yet to find it.

Sherlock tells us of his two friends among the criminal class: Charlie Peace and Wainwright, one a violin virtuoso and the other an artist. The names are allusions to two American thinkers whose work so sharply foreshadowed and complimented their contemporary William James: Charles S. Peirce and Chauncey Wright. Wainwright and Wright are the same name for both mean "maker or worker," with wainwright being a compound form meaning "wagon maker." The persona of Sir James is a pun, and also a reference to the fact that Peirce often told people his middle initial "S" stood for Santiago, Spanish for St. James. This was his way of expressing appreciation to William James for his having been such a supporter and staunch personal friend. Wright was an early enthusiast of Darwin, whose doctrines appealed to him as a sort of supplement to those of John Stuart Mill. Much that Doyle has to say about the nature of Miss de Merville is abstracted from Peirce. In his essay whose very title "The Fixation of Belief," would work well as a subtitle for "The Illustrious Client," we learn there are people who believe in what they believe in through what Peirce calls "the method of tenacity"; one will hold something as true simply because to do otherwise would make them feel uncomfortable. Peirce comes up with a fictitious quote that best sums up his theory, "Oh, I could not believe so-and-so, because I should be wretched if I did." He affirms, "a steady and immovable faith yields great peace of mind," and the complacent young lady in question expresses every indication of having this peace of mind. Her faith in her betrothed will eventually "give rise to inconveniences, as if a man should resolutely continue to believe that fire would not burn him." Such a person "does not propose to himself to be rational, and, indeed, will often talk with scorn of man's weak and illusive reason," the situation Holmes faces when he visits the girl attempting to dissuade her from marriage, for he is met with scorn, and would have been given the same reception from Lady Frances Carfax. Once again we are shown the low opinion of reason among those whose will to believe rules their lives. Holmes almost gives up in disgust while Peirce as well almost throws in the towel for he tells us, "So let him think as he pleases." The family and friends of the heiress, united in their disapproval of the forthcoming nuptials, personify what he refers to as "the social impulse," those who realize the individual who adopts the method of tenacity, is making a great mistake. This individual "will find that other men think differently from him, and it will be apt to occur to him, in some saner moment, that their opinions are quite as good as his own." The problem however, is that Violet is not able to achieve this saner moment thanks to the machinations of the Baron and her own tenacity. Peirce claims we cannot see a quality for it is a conception and "conceptions which are really products of logical reflection, without being readily seen to be so, mingle with our ordinary thoughts, and are frequently the causes of great confusion." "A quality, as such, is never an object of observation," and "We can see that a thing is blue or green, but the quality of being blue and the quality of being green are not things which we see; they are products of logical reflections." The Baron's name is Green, and Violet can see this Green, but she cannot see the quality that makes Green what he really is. "Few persons care to study logic," Peirce tells us, "because everybody conceives himself to be proficient enough in the art of reasoning already."

Peirce has read, not only Diderot, where he borrowed this thought, but John Stuart Mill as well, and with Mill in mind he goes on to describe how systems of government in which power ends up in a certain class, such as the aristocracy (the Baron's first name, Adelbert, means "nobility"), produces a situation in which their thinking, that is the aristocracy, produces the thought of all. Gruner's simply belonging to a certain class will influence Violet's thinking. "Cruelties always accompany this system; and when it is consistently carried out, they become atrocities of the most horrible kind in the eyes of any rational man." As usual in my trifling monographs, much else in this fine piece of thought could be brought into it, but I must go on.

Why are there two philosophers classed among the criminals? I believe Doyle is trying to show that they (the criminals) are often worthy adversaries for Sherlock. If at least some miscreants were not highly intelligent, we would not need a Sherlock Holmes to turn over the rocks they hide under.

The Baron's noble genealogy can conclusively be traced to John Stuart Mill's work *The Subjection of Women*, written in 1869. The work contains a brief outline of what could be termed a history of the abuse of women by a political system, and some men within it. In the middle ages, Mill asserts, a man such as the Baron, whose very title links him to this era, would have the opportunity to exercise at will arbitrary power, which counted for everything, without restraint, over his serfs, slaves, and wife. The Baron, as are all the nobility, is born into a world of unearned distinctions and privileges not acquired by his own merit, and this made him cruel and vicious, as many of the early nobility were to their vassals. His power will be exercised in a brutal and purely selfish manner, and on top of this he is a Northerner, a German or Austrian, people who practiced the subjection of the female more ardently than in the more enlightened republics of Greece or Rome. Doyle lived in Germany and witnessed how dominant the German male actually is. Mill tells us the viciousness of these noble men, if they find themselves in the modern world, is curbed by the certainty of resistance in their intercourse with other men, their equals, but it breaks out towards all who are in a position to be obliged to tolerate them, and they often revenge themselves on their unfortunate wives. It is only Gruner's equals such as the General, or the King, who can really oppose him.

The Baron could be considered a political tyrant, and as such would have almost absolute power over his subjects. "In domestic as in political tyranny, the case of absolute monsters chiefly illustrates the institution by showing that there is scarcely any horror which may not occur under it if the despot pleases, and thus setting in a strong light what must be the terrible frequency of things only a little less atrocious." Mill adds that marriage to such a person must be terrible. "Absolute fiends are as rare as angels, perhaps rarer: ferocious savages, with occasional touches of humanity, are however very frequent: and in the wide interval which separates these from any worthy representatives of the human species, how many are the forms and gradations of animalism and selfishness, often under an outward varnish of civilization and even cultivation, living at peace with the law, maintaining a creditable appearance to all who are not under their power, yet sufficient often to make the lives of all who are so, a torment and a burthen to them!" The Baron is certainly one such form, and a good one too, a cultured man with a fine collection of delicate pottery which he both understands and appreciates. "Marriage is the only actual bondage known to our law. There remain no legal slaves, except the mistress of every home," Mill claims. We must add to this the worst and strongest bond possible, the fact that Violet actually loves this cruel man, and in spite of everything, will probably continue to love him. All his life Doyle advocated changes in the English divorce laws that would give women more control over their own lives, and no doubt we can trace these convictions directly to this essay. Some of the mental disposition of "The Illustrious Client" is however obviously a refutation of Mill's assertion that young women, even girls, should always be allowed to make all their own decisions regarding the direction of their lives, not being influenced in any capacity by the opinions of their fathers, who, Mill is sure, would only make mistakes in these choices. Doyle asks us to decide which of the two, Violet or her father, is more prone to making a mistake in this case.

"Only that his name is a household word in society," is the answer Watson gives when asked if he knows anything about Sir James. Men such as Voltaire are often called "social philosophers," for their work deals heavily with the relationship of man and society. Hobbes had assumed an active egotism in the mind of man within the state of nature, being more violent and egotistical the more primitive he was, but Jean-Jacques Rousseau believed the opposite; it was society that corrupted "natural man," or for our purposes, man before he entered society. The lusts for domination by violence, and for robbery, both of which are on Gruner's mind, Rousseau held, are unknown to the natural man as such. These can only appear and strike roots after man has entered society and become acquainted with all the artificial desires society fosters. Hawkeye is Cooper's version of uncorrupted man, one morally and ethically better than any society that could have produced him. Man in his natural state would not produce the violent subjection of others, the Frenchman deemed, but would be indifferent to them. Gruner epitomizes artificial man, one completely corrupt, while Holmes actually seems to adopt some characteristics of Rousseau's natural man, and as such is being contrasted with his opposite. Natural man, Rousseau claims, was capable of sympathy with others and has by nature the ability to place himself in their position, to sense their feelings, and therefore to practice empathy, enabling him to a certain degree to feel the sorrows of others as though they were his own. This form of sympathy he believed was the goal of society although he did not view it as the beginning of society. The interests of a man like Gruner are at odds with society in general, and in particular with a sociable clubman like Sir James, who, assuming Holmes to be one such as himself, after informing the detective of his need for assistance, says, "Then you will sympathize with the client in whose interests I am acting." Men such as Gruner regard social laws as a yoke they would put upon others without ever thinking of yielding to them themselves. Society is held together by a "social contract," according to Rousseau, for better or worse, and so Holmes makes a purely social, not a legal contract with Sir James, who has already made his contract with the

General, and with one who remains unknown. Man should enter into such a bond of individual wills out of a genuine moral obligation, for the social contract has moral value only when the individual is not simply subject to it by purely juridical obligation such as the law, but subjects himself to it willingly. Holmes is not being paid for what he does. Sir James wants to see Holmes come to the problem willingly, on his own, and does not press him too hard. The King or ruler, the unknown aristocrat, comes into Rousseau's contract for the philosopher believed no real unity results where the partners to the moral contract continue to act as individuals despite this obligation they now have. Picking an incognito member of the aristocracy to portray the autonomous personality of the general will of society was a stroke of genius on Doyle's part. It is the ruler who is "pledged" to maintain the law within the society. Social moral unity cannot be attained by force, it must be founded on liberty, and this liberty does not exclude submission, in this case to a ruler. The individual, in contract with other individual wills ceases to be individual wills as such, for they all no longer desire and demand for themselves, but exist and will within the framework of the "general will." General de Merville's title is obviously a pun on this thought. This kind of contract is the only moral force, for it is compelled by objective obligation, not force. In the free acknowledgement of law lives the true character of liberty, and that liberty includes empathy with others, and hate for tyrants. In a good society each would obey only himself, but he would be united with others for the good of society thus we would "gain the equivalent of all that we lose," and have "more power to preserve what we have," while such a society would be a bulwark against those who are governed simply by their appetites and passions. It would result in what Rousseau called "the autonomous personality," which is actually everyone in the society who would benefit by being bound by the general will. This society would take primitive man and "transform him from a stupid and ignorant animal into an intelligent being and a man."

An enthusiasm and respect for the force and dignity of the law was characteristic of all of Rousseau's ethical, moral, and political writings. He considers the laws that govern society the most sublime of all human institutions and a real gift from heaven by virtue of which man has learned to imitate in his earthly existence the inviolable commandments of the Deity.

In respect to Thomas Hobbes and his philosophy of society being a contract or covenant between the ruler, "the monarch or sovereign," and "the subject," Doyle presents us with some interesting and elegant thoughts. Hobbes, in talking of certain liberties the subject has, defines those liberties as "the things which, though commanded by the sovereign, he may nevertheless without injustice refuse to do." Remember Holmes has the right to refuse to help. Since the sovereign is created by a contract, the subject retains all those natural rights that cannot be transferred by covenant, and since the subject has entered into the contract to preserve and protect his life, he is entitled to refuse to obey the ruler when to do so would place his life in danger. Holmes almost loses his life working on this case. For instance, the monarch's command to the subject to kill himself, or not to resist those who assault him, can be justly disregarded by the subject, Hobbes tells us. It just so happens Holmes is assaulted while trying to do a favor for the monarch, and he does resist. Hobbes claims that a command for dangerous military duty may be refused if the obvious intention of the ruler in issuing it is not to preserve the peace, but adds that no man can justify objecting to defending his country when a foreign aggressor attacks it. None could be more foreign, or more aggressive, than the Baron, so Holmes, and any other citizen who can, must help out in this situation, just as though an alien army was attacking their country. They, the subjects, have agreed among themselves to abide by certain laws and have appointed the sovereign as the agency for enforcing such laws. Hobbes tells us. "The end of obedience is protection," is the true purpose of the social contract, each one protects the other for everyone's mutual benefit, and he adds that the obligation of the subjects to the ruler lasts only so long as the ruler is able to protect them, so the King is perfectly justified, even obligated by self-interest, in protecting the life of one of his subjects.

Following the execution of King Charles the First, Hobbes published his most important work, *Leviathan*. One purpose of the book was to justify the power of the monarchy and the authority that attached to it. He conceived civil association as a "Commonwealth," arranged in rank and influence around the sovereign power, much as the parts of an organism are arranged around a single active principle of life. The organic analogy was very important to Hobbes, and enabled him both to describe the nature of the sovereign power, and also to separate it intellectually from any particular person, assembly, or constitutional process that might exist for the moment. It is not this person or these people, or this process, that holds power at this particular time, but rather the thought of these that count, for they only embody the thought. The anonymous persona in Doyle's tale is unnamed for he, she, or it, does not need a name, they are "embodiments," of themselves, of what they represent, and the name is of no importance when compared to this embodiment. Hobbes asserted that there could be "no obligation on any man which ariseth not from some act of his own." No man is born into the world encumbered by obligations, and no state has a right of allegiance unless it arises from some act of "consent," however tacit, unreflecting, or spontaneous, on the part of the citizen. Notice Sir James wants Holmes to take his time in thinking over his obligation to help a fellow citizen, although it would not matter whether the decision was spontaneous or not. Doyle is simply bringing it to our attention. When Hobbes speaks of an act, he means an intentional act of a kind that could be seen as bearing within itself the creation and acceptance of an obligation. The King, Holmes, and Sir James, all obligate themselves of their own free will, as it were, by accepting responsibility for Violet de Merville's future. In this sort of thing, Hobbes claims, every citizen, even the sovereign, becomes an equal. The citizen should act in this fashion for he has accepted the benefits his government has to offer and therefore has a certain obligation towards the established order of the Commonwealth. The sovereign, who is nothing but the embodied will of this order, acts with the authority of all those who have sought, one way or another, his protection.

There are other, equally subtle thoughts being escorted into this story with the use of this word society. Lord Shaftesbury, along with a few other English philosophers such as Francis Hutcheson, had a theory of benevolence based on the capacity for one's ability to lead a moral life generated by this capacity for benevolence, arguing that the disposition of men to feel discomfort and pain at the sight of each other's suffering and to rejoice at each other's delights, is, insofar as it exists, the motivating force behind the perception of moral qualities, and the actions which are precipitated by it. This is sympathy of course, and the disposition to sympathize in these and in all the many other ways with which we are familiar, is part of what later philosophers were to call "the social nature of man." The British empiricists deserve credit for this; they so described the moral life as to make it clear there could be no moral theory, whether skeptical or otherwise, which treated individuals as an isolated unit, in only accidental relationship to others. Sir James is asking Sherlock to sympathize with the plight of Violet, so he uses that very word, and also to act according to his moral sense, which is based in Holmes' "rational nature," as Hutcheson believed. It's all founded in society, the laws that govern society, and the moral life of the individuals that constitute it.

Henry James, Senior, William's father, was so sure that society was the key to bringing out the moral nature of man he wrote a book on the subject entitled *Society the Redeemed Form of Man*, which Doyle probably read. I have never come across it however.

Holmes employs the help of a character of dubious reputation, Shinwell Johnson, nicknamed Porky, to fight the evil Baron. Porky was a slang word used in Doyle's day to denote one who was "saucy, cocky, presumptuous, and impertinent," a comment on the man's personality obviously, but also an apt enough description of Samuel Johnson as he was seen through the eyes of his enemies, and even some friends. Samuel himself had the oft-used nickname "Dictionary" bestowed upon him following the publication of his famous *Dictionary of the English Language*. Shinwell's appearance follows that of his namesake for he is "a huge, coarse, red-faced, scorbutic man, with a pair of vivid black eyes which were the only external sign of the very cunning mind within." In *The Hound of the Baskervilles* we hear of a Theophilus Johnson. "Theophilus," means "a lover of God," and this describes Samuel as well. Shinwell itself is surely a name out of the eighteenth century, if it exists at all. The use of any nickname could bear reference to Johnson; for Boswell tells us he gave everyone he knew a nickname, such as his own, "Bozzy." Such bynames were popular in Johnson's day, and many of his female acquaintances had titles like Queeney, and yes, Kitty. Johnson had visited the King, just as Sir James is obviously known to the King, and is of service to him, for Samuel tells us he served just about every adult member of the royal family as a ghostwriter.

Johnson and Boswell were acquainted with a number of army generals, including General Oglethorpe, who had been present at the siege of Belgrade, and an Italian Army General, Paoli, living in England, who was considered a national hero in his own country. Holmes tells us everyone has heard of

General de Merville and Boswell says the same thing of General Paoli. Samuel Johnson loved everyday business, and his ability to operate in real life got him involved with people and their problems, and he had sympathy to offer to many, going far out of his way to help any woman.

Shinwell's first job for Holmes is to locate Kitty Winter. He tells the detective she was easy to find for it only took an hour, and Kitty adds, "I'm easy to find." "Hell, London, gets me every time. Same address for Porky Shinwell." Kitty is speaking not just for herself when she tells us London gets her every time. Boswell's work is replete with quotes of Johnson's such as, "Why, Sir, you find no man, at all intellectual, who is willing to leave London," and "The happiness of London is not to be conceived but by those who have been in it." One of his most oft repeated quotes is, "when a man is tired of London, he is tired of life," and his most thoughtful piece of poetry was "London: A Poem," a spiritual description of the great city. Samuel put up for free anyone, including women, who needed a place to stay for a while, a common practice in the poverty-ridden London of his day. Like Sherlock, Samuel had his vices, and the poet's involved women, but Boswell does not go into details. Johnson was not adverse to meeting women of questionable character, and often did so, sometimes at the law courts where he hung out with his friend, the writer Richard Savage. Johnson was a friend of Sir Joshua Reynolds' model, Kitty Fisher, one of the luminaries of the London demimonde. There is a portrait of her at Petworth by Reynolds. Kitty Fisher died in 1767, according to one source, poisoned by the white lead with which, like many other beauties, she blanched her skin, so she seems to have suffered a fate not unlike her fellow model, Kitty Winter. Oil of vitriol, the fluid that disfigured Kitty and the Baron, was a term employed in the eighteenth century for sulfuric acid, and Boswell tells us Johnson once bought some for a chemical experiment. Boswell fills his book with many such interesting details.

One woman Johnson befriended was "generally slut and drunkard; — occasionally, whore and thief," named Bet Flint who came to him seeking advice on her poetry. The name Flint reminds Doyle of Hawkeye's cruel enemy, Flint Heart, which leads him to the name Kitty Winter, whose last name shows her now cruel nature. Shinwell brings Kitty to Holmes where she relates her corrosive experience with the Baron. "He owned to many of his friends, that he used to take women of the town to taverns, and hear them relate their history," Boswell tells us of his friend.

During the course of "The Illustrious Client," we experience, as the newspapers call it, a "MURDEROUS ATTACK UPON SHERLOCK HOLMES," when two thugs armed with sticks beat him about the head and body, obviously at the command of Gruner. Johnson and his friends occasionally found themselves engaged in street fights with pimps and thugs, and one night Johnson was attacked by no less than "four men, to whom he would not yield, but kept them all at bay, till the watch came up, and carried both him and them to the round-house." Johnson was no doubt aided by his oak walking stick. Boswell assures us he "made his corporal prowess be felt as much as his intellectual," when necessary. On one occasion his friend Giuseppe Baretti stabbed a pimp to death on a London street, and Johnson, among others, went to court to give character testimony for him. Baretti could be used as a model for the Baron, for Mrs. Thrale claims that for some reason he "breathed defiance against all Mankind," and "had a very savage nature," also claiming that he had "great powers of mind," but his poverty left him constantly dependent upon others who he resented because of this. Like Gruner he lives upon others, yet hates them nevertheless, and Mrs. Thrale adds that in spite of this many people considered this Italian pleasant company. Johnson, who had befriended Baretti since his arrival in London, often found him hard to tolerate and "used to oppose and battle him." Baretti lived with the Thrales on their estate, where he acted as tutor to their daughter Queeney, a much younger girl, for whom this foreigner conceived "a violent attachment" that in this case was not reciprocal.

Boswell constantly refers to Johnson as "my illustrious friend," and at one point the two have a discussion about the word illustrious. The conversation is instigated by Lord Monboddo's criticism of Johnson's language as being too rich. Johnson defends himself: "Why, Sir, this criticism would be just, if, in my style, superfluous words, or words too big for the thoughts, could be pointed out; but this I do not believe can be done. For instance; in the passage which Lord Monboddo admires, 'We were now treading that illustrious region,' the word *illustrious*, contributes nothing to the mere narration; for the fact might be told without it: but it is not, therefore, superfluous; for it wakes the mind to peculiar attention, where something of more than usual importance is to be presented." In "The Illustrious Client," Doyle, as we see from the amount of mental labor he put into the piece, is trying to tell us something of more than usual importance.

"James, of title most illustrious" is a line from Christopher Smart's 1765 poem, "Hymn. St. Philip and St. James." In the next line Smart reminds us that James and Jesus were brothers.

Sir James' lavender, nearly effeminate mode of fashion brings us back, once again, to Oscar Wilde and his creation Dorian Gray. The parallels between Gray and Gruner (Gray and Green) are easily spotted: both corrupt everyone they go near, especially the ladies, and both are famous for their manners, elegance, and good looks. Some of Gray's victims seek escape from his evil infection in suicide; he can even be thought of as having killed Miss Vane, for it was his brutal rejection of her that brought about her death as surely as Gruner kills those women who love him. Gray's despicable nature is reflected in a self-portrait which absorbs into itself this vileness, disfiguring the face, while Gruner has acid thrown in his face, which, when absorbed into the flesh, renders it as hideous as his corrupt heart. The Baron kept a record of his wickedness, not on canvas, but in a journal of lust. This painting of Dorian has evolved into a register of his soul's transgressions, "a hideous face," in which we can hardly read the fine features of the handsome man. Watson tells us, following the attack on the Baron, "The features which I had admired a few minutes before were now like some beautiful painting over which the artist has passed a wet and foul sponge. They were blurred, discoloured, inhuman, terrible." Each man now shows the world his true identity; they can no longer secrete their sins but must live in its knowledge, for the acid burning into the face of Gruner is like the "leprosies of sin," that inexorably corrode the attributes of Dorian, and like his portrait, now personifies the incontestable situation of his soul. In a sense the artist Basil adopts the role of Violet, for in spite of the shameful and reprehensible accusations coming to his ears about Dorian, he steadfastly refuses to believe them. A notebook of sorts comes into Wilde's novel, for this painting that contains so much foulness and failings is referred to by Gray as "a diary of my life from day to day," and he adds, "it never leaves the room in which it is written." A murder also occurs in Wilde's story when in a sudden confused rush of fear and loathing, Dorian grabs a knife and stabs Basil to death after confessing to him the transformation his canvas has been undergoing.

The plot of a foreigner, often of the nobility, scheming a young American woman out of her inheritance by marrying her under the pretense of love is a preferred theme of Henry James, while the more universal theme of any suitor hoping to marry wealth amounted to his signature. For the 1908 New York Edition of his works, James wrote Prefaces and notes to many of his stories and two of these Prefaces, those for "A London Life" and *The Reverberator*, are often paired together, and I will also deal with them as a single thought, which they essentially are. James wishes us to understand that his tales of young women being taken advantage of by European men, and by European civilization in general, never deal solely with the evident encounter in which all the positives are in one column and all the negatives are in another. A good writer goes beyond this, developing a theme primarily with his skill, or "attraction of facility," rather than exclusively with a strong story, adding that the plot of these tales were relatively easy to think up for there were copious examples of these women, and "one had but to put forth one's hand and pluck the frequent flower. Add to this that the flower *was*, so often, quite positively a flower — that of the young American innocence transplanted to European air." Violet de Merville, as so many of the young girls found in James' stories has the name of a flower, and Violet, as a name, is lifted from another example found in the Preface to "A London Life." As was common, and still is, a woman was often compared to a flower, as in the pun, "An American Beauty," which, although the name of a species of rose, frequently captions a picture of any handsome American woman. Lucy Ferrier is regarded as "the flower of Utah." Many women in the Canon have the names of flowers, such as Rose, or Flora. Rose was the name of one of Dr. Shlessinger's victims in "Lady Frances Carfax." Doyle took the backbone of this idea from Henry James, who named many of his female characters after flowers, but he could not have overlooked Cooper's use of the thought, for both Hawkeye and the Indians called women "flowers," and James may have borrowed the idea from Cooper, for I know he read the man. James tells us some women we encounter in his stories would act as they do, "whatever her producing clime," meaning the system they grow up in is only partly responsible for their naiveté. One doesn't have to be an American to harbor self-deception James is saying, and so Doyle makes his young victim English, but still the Baron and his chosen remain natives of countries foreign to each other. What Doyle has accomplished is to impel the work to be "an international tale," the very article Henry James loved. In the same essay, the American outlines a general plot he employs frequently that comes close to "The Illustrious Client" in spirit. "It wasn't after all of the prime, the very most prime, intention of the tale in question that the persons concerned in them should have had this, that, of the other land of birth; but that the central situation should really be rendered — that of a charming and decent young thing, from wheresoever proceeding, who has her decision and her action to take, horribly and unexpectedly, in the face of a squalid "scandal" the main agent of which is her nearest relative, and who, at the dreadful crisis, to guard against personal bespattering, is moved, with a miserable want of effect, to a wild vague frantic gesture, an appeal for protection that virtually proves a precipitation of her disgrace." Here are all the ingredients of Doyle's story, especially if we read death for disgrace. James claims these young women "were least of all conscious of deficiencies and dangers; so that, the grace of youth and innocence and freshness aiding, their negatives were converted and became in certain relations lively positives and values." Notice that Henry James is not saying these converted negatives are forms of good, only that they are positives while remaining dangerous to their holders. Violet has great loyalty to the one she loves, certainly a good quality, but still, in her case, very dangerous. He adds that often these people will remain signally unaware of life no matter what happens to them, for some people are too innocent, too pathetic to live, and "too consentingly feeble to be worth saving." Like Sherlock, he asks if there aren't some people who in their unawareness of life are not worth bothering to help. Is he thinking of the Brockton wife here, do you think? They are so ignorant as to be "beyond fishing out," as he calls it, and both Holmes and Kitty are forced to reflect on whether or not Violet is worth fishing out.

Doyle is also making an uncomplimentary observation on the fact that so many women are willing to forgive a man any faults he may have, no matter how glaring or sadistic, so long as he has a title of some kind, an observation shared by Henry James, who tells us his victims are but part of "the general quaint sisterhood," in this respect. We can assume Violet would hardly consider marrying this penniless foreigner without his imposing title.

In the Preface to *The Reverberator*, James includes a story, a true incident, about a young American lady who gets herself involved in a scandal, "The scandal reigned, however, and the commotion lasted, a nine days' wonder; the ingenuous stranger's name became anathema, and all to the high profit of an incorrigible collector of 'cases.'" A collector of cases in this instance would be that type of person who is always searching out examples from life to illustrate a point in what they regard as a moral story. Our collector of cases is Henry James himself, with his case taking the life form of a story. "The Illustrious Client," is to be found in *The Case Book of Sherlock Holmes*, which is replete with tales utilizing the philosophy, fiction, and life, of members of the James family. Doyle amends a lengthy Preface to this collection of tales, the only one to have such, the Preface to *His Last Bow* amounting to a single paragraph. James adds in his Preface, "The finer interest was in the facts that made the incident a case, and the true note of that, I promptly made sure, was just in the extraordinary amount of native innocence that positively *had* to be read into the perpetrated act." The word perpetrated is always used in association with a crime, and although he is not talking of a crime as such, a note of violence, either physical or emotional, it matters not which, is read into it.

The case James is now talking of involved an American family living in England. He implies that one reason for taking this incident as a source for his fiction was so that he might render a certain amount of "miscellaneous justice," to the characters involved. In Doyle's narrative as well, a certain amount of justice must be granted to Kitty, and others the Baron has injured. In Henry James' notebooks (a model for Gruner's notebook?), a collection of essays and random thoughts James put together, Doyle found more information on the event involving the American family James mentioned. He records an infamous scandal of his day involving May Marcy McClellan, daughter of the famous Civil War General. The General had died young, and May lived with her mother, mostly in various places in Europe. May had pretensions to being a journalist, and in November of 1886, published in the *New York World*, an indiscreet, gossipy column about some of the Venetian nobility, whose hospitality she and her mother had been enjoying. To the Americans, James realizes, nothing very shocking resulted from this young lady's making light of these aristocrats in print, but for the old-world nobility, such a thing did not happen, and was unforgivable. James regards the girl as thoughtless for what she did, realizing she has just about committed social suicide. He has a great capacity for sympathy with these indecorous women, explaining that any story he might choose to write using this incident as a case would show "the drama is in the consequences for *her*." Marriage comes into it since the consequences for her include the relevant fact that now she has threatened her attempts to marry well in Europe.

His Last Bow, Doyle's collection of stories published in 1917, takes its title from the Preface to *The Reverberator* when James, in a layered and subtle metaphor dealing with the art of writing, assures us the thoughts of the writer conduct a sort of mental war with the material available to him, which, if it is to be formed into a work of art, must sometimes be approached by the author as a soldier would an action. The word action is here used as a pun on the action of the story to be told, I believe. The soldier or writer may have need, when facing the possibility that "anecdotic grace does break down," of "another string, a second, to my bow," in the event the challenge must be faced in order to place the work in, "that blest drama-light which, really making for intelligibility as nothing else does, orders and regulates, even when but faintly turned on; squares things and keeps them in happy relation to each other." The second string of the bow is used when the thoughts become so complicated, as they often do with Henry James, that he is forced to admit, "I seem so sometimes to be about one set and sometimes about another!" A set is the groups of different people or single individuals, with their divergent attitudes and objectives that always intermix, sometimes in rather complex and surprising ways, in all of James' work, no matter how brief the piece is. In the Preface to *His Last Bow*, Watson wants us to know it is the approach of war with Germany that has instigated Holmes to abandon retirement and once again arm himself to fight evil, and for himself therefore to pick up pen and record it. The writer and the soldier get their bows and bowstrings ready for another struggle.

In the novel *The Reverberator*, we are introduced to Francie Dosson, an American girl with "a weak pipe of a voice and inconceivabilities of ignorance," but so beautiful one character refers to her as "*cette merveille*." The French word *merveille* means "marvel or wonder," and Sir James declares that Violet de Merville is "a wonder-woman in every way." George Flack, a society writer for this American newspaper, the *Reverberator* comes out with an article dealing with Miss Dosson's future in-laws. Flack, "a deep one," as obviously the Baron is a deep one, aided by the all unawares Francie, have caused an international scandal analogous to treachery of the worst kind. A man who knew better has intentionally led a young woman astray. The part of Kitty Winter falls to Delia Dosson, the sister of Francie, who is more conscious of the world and the intentions of some of its inhabitants. "What power, in heaven's name, has he got over you? What spell has he worked?" she asks Francie in regard to her devotion to Flack, who, it becomes obvious, hopes to marry Francie himself.

One Henry James novel exercising a weighty influence on Doyle's artistic life is *Washington Square*, a story of New York, in which the daughter of a prominent doctor, Catherine Sloper, falls in love with Morris Townsend, who is evidently after her fortune. The girl's father knows what Townsend is and forbids the marriage, but Catherine, in spite of her father, or perhaps because of him, wants to marry Morris so passionately she would consider eloping with him, something completely against New York social standards. It is understood that Violet would marry Gruner with or without her father's consent, and just as the General gives up attempting to influence Violet's will, so also does Dr. Sloper ultimately prove unsuccessful in stopping his daughter's upcoming nuptials. Of Morris Townsend himself, we learn from one of the characters in the tale, that he is "still looking for a wife — having had one and got rid of her. I don't know by what means," so he's no better than Gruner. This marriage took place in Europe somewhere, and the bride "died soon afterwards." We are told that Townsend's wife died of natural causes, but we do not know if this is true, and I for one doubt it. Townsend's salient feature is his handsomeness, with some in the novel regarding him as beautiful.

In Henry James' novel *Madame de Mauves*, we come across another young American who adamantly insists that a man who has a noble title could not conceivably be himself anything but noble, and is eager to marry any

European aristocrat regardless of what he is really like. James regards her views on the nobleness of the nobility as "a masterpiece of idealisation," with deception, aided and abetted by self-deception, being the theme of all this. Part of this girl's dream image of her prospective husband is actually that he should be poor, and thus it is to be her fortune upon which they will build their rosy future. Euphemia, for such is her name, meets Madame de Mauves, descended from a long line of baronial ancestors, who realizes she is dealing with an "angel of innocence," and attempts to warn her about life, men in general, and her own grandson in particular. The grandson Richard, twice Euphemia's age, is noble by birth, distinguished, corrupt, and absolutely merciless. Like many, possibly all of the aristocrats in James' works, Richard's interest in people is limited solely to their wealth. This "thoroughly perverse creature," is out "to mend his fortunes by pretending to fall in love," and actually harbors no more actual regard for women than he does his lavender gloves, which he is in the habit of throwing away immediately they become the least bit soiled. Naturally the young American falls hopelessly in love with him for is he not her childish fantasies given flesh and blood. Richard doesn't go too far out of his way to hide his literal disposition, he has no need to, for, "Even after experience had given her a hundred rude hints she found it easier to believe in fables, when they had a certain nobleness of meaning, than in well-attested but sordid facts." Hasn't the thoughtful Baron even sent his intended "a bouquet of violets," to prove his affection. It is the American mother who realizes the girl is committing an irreversible mistake, certain that Richard de Mauves has horrible morals, but Euphemia marries him nevertheless, in spite of warnings. What James is talking about is the death of the spirit; the spirit of a young girl who marries for love, only to realize that the "insolently frivolous Frenchman" she is wedded to is not capable of love. Perhaps Baron de Mauves traveled in the same circles as Baron Gruner, for he had been active in France before he had a run-in with the detective Le Brun. It quickly becomes apparent that the Baron's indifference and indiscretions have produced a truly unhappy woman of Euphemia, but the marvel of it is that she still feels warmth for him and will never leave him. "Was it strength, was it weakness, was it a vulgar fear, was it conviction, conscience, constancy?" James asks of her devotion. Conviction, conscience, and constancy, all positive qualities being used for a wrongful purpose, convertible schemes of thought Henry shared with his brother William. In the end it is Baron de Mauves who dies, and that by his own hand.

Regarded by many as James' most penetrating achievement, *The Portrait of a Lady* develops more fully his lifelong premise of fate playing the dominant function in human existence, for all one's talent, fame, money, education, looks, or what have you, means little when balanced opposite one grain of destiny. Pansy Osmond is young and impressible with a dexterous intelligence, but with little awareness of the potential for hidden iniquity, having been raised in a convent. "Pansy was really a blank page, a pure white surface, successfully kept so; she had neither art, nor guile, nor temper, nor talent." James rounds out her personality: "Yet to be so tender was to be touching withal, and she could be felt as an easy victim of fate. She would have no will, no power to resist, no sense of her own importance; she would easily be mystified, easily crushed: her force would be all in knowing when and where to cling." The question of whether or not Pansy is prepared to face the world at all is actually but one leitmotiv of this rather complex work, for although it surfaces a number of times throughout the tale, it has only a loose parallel development of theme to the actual story, for Pansy is not the "Lady," of the narrative.

The idea of a relationship flowering between an older man and a younger and wealthier woman finds characterization in Pansy's father, Gilbert, and his pursuit of the American heiress Isabel Archer, the lady of the novel. One character, a Madame Merle, married a much older man who proved to be "a positive adventurer," appearing however "originally so plausible, who had taken advantage, years before, of her youth and of an inexperience in which doubtless those who knew her only now would find it difficult to believe."

The problem of how to handle a corruption that presents a smoothly hypocritical surface to the world is a characteristically Jamesian preoccupation, as we see. The young people in his work hardly have the ability to grasp the reality that others they meet with can have altered morals, or none at all, and thus are guided by motivations and emotions different than their own. A friend of Miss Archer's visits her home in Italy attempting to dissuade her from marrying Gilbert, but she will do as she pleases, for reasons of her own. A number of dialogues occur between the heiress and her family and friends as they try to stop her marriage to what her cousin Ralph labels "a villain," which is the very word Sir James used to describe the Baron. One entire chapter of *The Portrait of a Lady* is the record of an argument between Ralph and Isabel similar in spirit to the one that Holmes had with Violet. Ralph realizes his cousin does what she wants simply because she is willful, with reason having nothing to do with the problem. Isabel assumes her family and friends dislike her choice because he is poor, or because they cannot have him for themselves, considering it therefore her duty to please herself, not them. Like Gruner, Osmond is a collector of porcelains whose first wife, also like Gruner, had died in the Alps, and it is more than hinted at that Osmond is quite capable of killing someone to get his own way. The Baron has a dehumanizing love of possessions with his women being merely additions to a collection, and this thought, not quite as strong perhaps, but evident nevertheless, finds voice in a number of Henry James' works.

We learn Isabel's critics have been accurate in their negativism toward Gilbert, for about him there is an air and attitude of pose and purpose, the implication being that Isabel has made a grievous mistake, for she does marry him, and will now pay for it. Gilbert is economically and emotionally far from the indifferent, unconventional, and easy-going man he appeared to be, and their marriage is thoroughly unhappy within the first year as the horrible realization comes to Isabel that her husband has a "faculty for making everything wither that he touched, spoiling everything for her that he looked at." "It was as if he had the evil eye; as if his presence were a blight and his favour a misfortune." Gilbert Osmond seems to loathe all women for some reason, and cannot the same be said of Gruner? In the end, Isabel admits that she knows Gilbert married her only for her money, which is a great step for her to take.

CHAPTER ELEVEN. ENLIGHTENED SELF-INTEREST

The many references to Holmes' gift of light to those adrift in darkness asserts connection not only to Jesus, Nietzsche, and Carlyle, but as well to the doctrines propagated during that unique era in the evolution of human thought known as the Enlightenment. Although England, in addition to some other countries, made their contributions, one cannot estimate fully the overall impact of the movement without emphasizing the French augmentation, for they gave foundation, example, and insistence to the campaign. The eighteenth century was the grand age of individualism and of the personal search for the truth of matters, and if you apply this notion to a single person you have Sherlock Holmes. Voltaire, Rousseau, and Diderot, form the trinity of the movement, with the latter encapsulating in his terse quote "A new world is born," the entire circumstance of the alteration of the human condition. Diderot felt nature had put between all mankind "a bond of fraternity, which links us in a particularly sacred way to those who are unhappy," so he acted as a sort of consultant to those in distress, being famous for his charity and generosity, with self-sacrifice being not only a facet of his philosophy, but a profound need of his emotional life. Scores of people came to see him each year, often from foreign lands, and sometimes of the nobility, to seek his advice on a wide range of subjects such as law and music. Diderot liked to broadcast his good deeds, for he wished people to know of his liberality and intelligence, never worrying for a moment if they considered him vain; indeed, he seemed to be completely unaware of his egotism. Once he wrote of himself, "the highest respect in the memory of man is assured to me," which turned out to be true, so seemingly the French philosopher, not unlike Justice Holmes, alleged humility was an unnatural scorn of self. One critical aftermath of this crusade was the altering of human consciousness into what is commonly referred to as "enlightened self-interest," with its formula of intelligence, optimism, utilitarianism, and theism.

In common with Sherlock, Diderot had served, and received gifts, from a grateful Queen, Catherine the Great of Russia, whom he had visited with in her own country, traveling there by carriage. He accepted numerous gifts and money from her including a red agate ring engraved with her portrait, which he wore everywhere. The Frenchman went out of his way in his quest for knowledge, attending so many courses covering numerous diverse subjects in so many different schools that no one is quite sure what was encompassed. Like Holmes, he would work day and night for days and weeks on end, and then do little or nothing when laziness or the slightest annoyance overtook him.

The *Encyclopédie*, published in twenty-eight volumes between 1751 and 1765, under the direction of Jean d'Alembert and Diderot, is both a program and a symbol of the Enlightenment, being an attempt at supplying curious intellectuals as well as the proliferating middle class with a work of universal knowledge. Many people contributed, but the man most involved, both as writer and editor, was Diderot, with his use of alphabetic arrangement being given its first trial in a work of this class and scope. He acquired, through his constant study, reading, and observations, knowledge of many crafts and trades, visiting workshops, studios, factories, and businesses, and questioning workers and artists, on every level in just about every field. He would have made a great detective himself.

The philosophers showed that the authoritarianism of the *ancien régime* and the privileges of the Church were irrational anachronisms, pleading instead for institutions founded upon reason. Naturally not everyone felt comfortable with self-interest and reason becoming guides to the order of man's thoughts, with the Church and various governments, as well as different individuals, believing themselves menaced by such vain beliefs. These thinkers questioned all authority, and authority saw motivation, in turn, to question them, while commercial interests disliked their trade secrets being depicted in books anyone could read. Two main tenets of the Enlightenment and its property, the *Encyclopedia*, was the great importance attached to making knowledge as comprehensive as possible, and the idea that this knowledge is a sum of items of information to be kept and conveyed in alphabetical order. This brings us to the great file, kept in careful alphabetical organization by Holmes, of any and all information that might be useful to him. "For many years he had adopted a system of docketing all paragraphs concerning men and things, so that it was difficult to name a subject or a person on which he could not at once furnish information," Watson informs us. Holmes' files are not simply a symbol; it is an encyclopedia in itself. Holmes epitomizes one who is referred to as having an encyclopedic mind, being familiar with an extraordinary range of subjects in many fields. Doyle also maintained a sort of personal encyclopedia, for he assembled files filled with clippings from newspapers, magazines, and notes from books on historical events, criminal activities, science, psychology, exploring, etc. French philosophers consistently regarded knowledge in close connection with action, for they wanted comprehension to serve a utile purpose, as did Aristotle. Holmes' thoughts and actions are governed by what his intelligence, and often his intelligence alone, shows him.

Diderot said something that is very close in spirit to the cerebration of Dr. Joseph Bell and Holmes, that Doyle must have found interesting, for in his writings he tells us part of his theory of physiological unity: the blind man, the hunchback, the porter, the pregnant woman, and so on, all bear throughout their entire bodies the signs of their occupation or condition; the body is a unit.

In "The Red-Headed League," Holmes will become engaged in investigating a bank vault robbery plot, unwittingly brought to his attention by Jabez Wilson, "a very stout, florid-faced, elderly gentleman with fiery red hair." Wilson owns a pawnshop, a situation meant to refer to Diderot's materialism, the pawnbroker being a common metaphor for the materialistic nature. This spokesman for skepticism and materialism made the declaration, "It is exciting to be a materialist." Lester Crocker, one of his biographers, claims Diderot was so poor that "visits to the pawnbrokers must have been part of his regular schedule." There is also a grain of coarseness in Jabez Wilson, as there was in Denis Diderot, with the stout florid-faced description being acknowledgment that the philosopher was both a heavy eater and an equally heavy drinker. When Watson is introduced to Wilson he says, "The stout gentleman half rose from his chair and gave a bob of greeting, with a quick little questioning glance from his small, fat-encircled eyes." Here is a physical description of Diderot, especially the fat-encircled eyes, a feature emphasized in all portraits of the man. He is dressed in "baggy gray shepherd's check trousers, a not over-clean black frock-coat, unbuttoned in the front, and a drab waistcoat," the very image of the philosopher that has come down to us, with the famous Garand portrait serving as a good example. Watson assures us that Wilson is "not over-bright," as well as "obese, pompous, and slow," adding that he "bore every mark of being an average commonplace British tradesman." Interestingly enough, for all his powerful genius, many contemporaries looked upon Diderot as a sort of slow-witted clown, giving rise to his appellation, "the great scatterbrain of the Eighteenth Century."

In the course of his presentment Wilson tells of being offered a job "to copy out the Encyclopaedia Britannica" for a sum of money so generous he could not refuse, but which also forces him to question the intentions of his employer, who claims he is to be paid for his services by a rich American who left his estate to benefit redheaded men throughout the world. The copying of these books amounts to a form of plagiarism, and this charge was leveled at Denis Diderot and his staff, somewhat justifiably. The scene of this occupation is Pope's Court, a reference to Alexander Pope, one of Diderot's favorite writers, who he read in English, and a poet popular with all the leaders of the Enlightenment, whose famous quote, "The proper study of mankind is man," gave pregnant impression to the sentiments of the age, becoming a shibboleth for the struggle.

Writing out a book in longhand can be construed as superfluous, which leads us to Diderot's own work, the *Encyclopedia*, where, under the heading "Encyclopedia" we find his prophesy of the books of the future. In the past, before the invention of the printing press, we had a few gifted men who would compose the manuscripts, and a large body of other workers transcribing them, and if you look ahead to the future you will also see a two-fold division of labor. Some people will not do much reading, but will do investigations into the great number of books the printing press has brought into being, without exactly knowing what it is they are reading. "The others, day laborers incapable of producing anything of their own, will be busy night and day leafing through these books, taking out of them the fragments they consider worthy of being collected and preserved. Has not this prediction already begun to be fulfilled? And are not several of our literary men already engaged in reducing all big books to little ones, among which there are still to be found many that are superfluous? Let us assume that their extracts have been competently made, and that these have been arranged in alphabetical order and published in an orderly series of volumes by men of intelligence — you have an encyclopedia!" Doyle brings the printing press into it for Duncan Ross, who engaged the day laborer Wilson to copy out the books, tells him, "There is the first volume of it in that press," this being a pun on the printing press and the upright closet known as a press. The position stipulates that Wilson must do this copying at a location distant from his pawnshop, requiring him to be away a certain number of hours each week. One morning when he reports to Pope's Court he finds Ross has deserted him without explanation, and it is at this point that the perplexed man takes his bizarre story to Baker Street. Wilson has lost nothing by former arrangements, but the details are so strange he just wants "to find out about them." "It is this ambitious curiosity that leads us in spite of ourselves to examine things and thus in the long run dissipates all sorts of falsehoods," is a famous quote of Diderot's. Holmes says he is usually "able to guide myself by the thousands of other similar cases which occur to my memory," when presented with a problem, but now, "I am forced to admit that the facts are, to the best of my belief, unique." If any man in history deserved to be termed unique it is Diderot, with the Enlightenment itself being without precedent.

Wilson is a Freemason, a reference to the fact that when the work on the final volumes of the *Encyclopedia* ran into difficulty with the French government, the members of Freemasonry, finding the book's message coincided with their own liberal doctrines, aided the publishers with their influence.

During Wilson's initial visit to the office of the Red-Headed League, the organization supposedly set up by the wealthy American, Ross, in a fit of skepticism, attempts to yank off his red hair, pretending to believe it is a wig. Diderot's hair comes into his biographies, for at one time his father had him incarcerated in a monastery following his refusal to accept his family's decision concerning his future marriage plans. Diderot was burning with rage and frustration, so his jailers, hoping to prevent his running away, cut off his hair.

Holmes, aided by tobacco and music, comes to the realization that bank robbers, one of them the notorious John Clay, who is working incognito in Wilson's shop, are digging a shaft from the pawnshop to the vault of the

City and Suburban Bank, hoping to steal a shipment of gold coins. Music is emotionally the most effective of all the arts, Diderot stated, stirring the imagination of mankind because of its vagueness. The whole thing is a ruse to get Wilson away from his shop for a while. Diderot's native country comes into it, for the bank vault contains gold napoleons borrowed from the Bank of France, which coins, having been struck in France, are an import, as was Diderot's philosophy; French gold if ever there was. The French Revolution, a product of the mind of Diderot, along with some others of course, generated conditions that gave rise to Napoleon. England is often considered the primary home of the Enlightenment, especially when the efforts of Isaac Newton are factored in, so the sending of gold from France to England may be a metaphor for a sort of obligation returned; a debt repaid. The French originally conceived their *Encyclopedia* as a translation of Ephraim Chamber's *Cyclopedia*, an English work, before it took its own way.

The nonexistent Ezekiah Hopkins, credited with having left his fortune to benefit other redheaded men, was modeled upon the American philosopher Josiah Royce, who also had red hair. Royce had a biblical first name followed by an English second name, as does Jabez Wilson. Hopkins was from Pennsylvania, where C. S. Peirce lived for a number of years, and the pragmatic development of Royce and Peirce is reliant upon the breakthrough thoughts of the French, as is all modern life, so an inventive link is established between all parties. Ironically, the name Wilson itself is interesting here, for Arthur M. Wilson was a philosopher/scholar who wrote extensively on Denis Diderot, but after Doyle's time. In the *Old Testament*, "Book One of Paralipomenon," Jabez is mentioned, but only once, so we know little about him. We read he was more honorable than his brethren, and for some reason not explained he believed himself to be the target of evil. When he asks the Lord to bless and protect him, God does so. Diderot as well realized he was the target of many a reactionary sharpshooter.

Wilson's assistant Vincent Spaulding, practices what was then the revolutionary new art of photography, and uses the basement of the shop as a darkroom. As it turns out he was the major instrument instigating Wilson to apply for, and accept, the lucrative position offered by the League. A German named Johann Joachim Spalding was a member of an early group of theological innovators who were proponents of "neology," a word they made up meaning new science or new learning. They hoped to remove from religious dogma all ingredients that cannot be derived from its definitions, and tried to show by means of investigations into the history of dogma that these ingredients are later and heterogeneous additions to the originally pure faith. Such intellectualism applied to religion is bound to result in a loss of faith, and would be a blow to the power of organized religion, so Spalding would indeed be regarded as a forerunner of the Enlightenment. Vincent is no doubt a reference to yet another real personality, but just whom I do not know. His real name is John Clay, a known criminal, and it is he and his associates that are digging the tunnel. The pawnshop is located on Saxe-Coburg Square, an allusion to the Prince of Saxe-Gotha who had a chateau at

Fontenay-sous-Bois, France, where the philosophers, among them Rousseau and Diderot, were often to be found.

Holmes and Watson visit the shop undercover where they exchange a few words with John Clay. That night the two detectives, a public detective named Peter Jones, and a director of the bank, Merryweather, go into the vault to await and possibly ambush the gang Holmes believes is tunneling toward them. Merryweather's name is a pun on "fair-weather," with the man himself a personification of the smug indifference, complacency, and inertia of the aristocrats, Church, and even intellectuals, prior to the Enlightenment. Merryweather is the epitome of bored self-interest that doesn't wish to be disturbed in its routine, reluctant to join others to fight evil. William James believed that for man this incomplete, imperfect world we live in is well suited to man in the sense that it, far more so than a perfect universe, offers him a challenge and an opportunity for growth and sacrifice. "Will not every one instantly declare a world fitted only for fair-weather human beings susceptible of every passive enjoyment, but without independence, courage, or fortitude, to be from a moral point of view incommensurably inferior to a world framed to elicit from man the very form of triumphant endurance and conquering moral energy." Merryweather's world is like himself, morally indifferent and inferior, lacking in moral energy, or energy of any kind really. James was nominally brought in on the case already when Holmes attended a performance "at St. James's Hall" while thinking things over.

During the vigil in the vault the four men must of necessity sit in a darkness Watson describes as, "an absolute darkness as I have never before experienced," with this utter blackness that Watson finds so overpowering being the darkness of the blind, having association to Diderot's observations found in his book *Letter on the Blind for Those Who Can See*. He claimed the senses actually were handicapped by the fact that there were so many of them, therefore if we lose, let us say, sight, the other senses, such as hearing, would become sharper. What modern research later proved to be true, Diderot learned simply from a few interviews with blind people. Watson suddenly finds his sense of sight is of no value to him, but his other faculties, as the philosopher predicted, have become more accurate. The doctor tells us, "my nerves were worked up to the highest pitch of tension, and my hearing was so acute that I could not only hear the gentle breathing of my companions, but I could distinguish the deeper, heavier in-breath of the bulky Jones from the thin, sighing note of the bank director." He must envision in his mind's eye, and in the mind's eye only, "that the night must have almost gone, and the dawn be breaking above us." Diderot was the first to deal with the problem of the needs of the blind with this much understanding, and also the first to advocate that the blind and other handicapped people be given education and training suitable to their needs. In every sense of the word he was a man of experiments. When Wilson went in search of the headquarters of the League after they quit Pope's Court, he traces them to King Edward Street, near St. Paul's (he who cured the cripple and the blind), but the address turns out to be the location of "a manufactory of artificial knee-caps," just the kind of thing the men of the Enlightenment would have been interested in, for they believed in helping the disadvantaged, and themselves as well, through knowledge. King Edward may have been instrumental in helping the handicapped, but I don't know that.

The depressing and subduing" vault personifies the benighted human condition in its ossified state antecedent to the Enlightenment, as mankind sits in darkness waiting for the freedom that comes with knowledge and reason. "Suddenly my eyes caught the glint of a light," Watson says. "At first it was but a lurid spark upon the stone pavement. Then it lengthened out until it became a yellow line, and then, without any warning or sound, a gash seemed to open and a hand appeared; a white, almost womanly hand, which felt about in the centre of the little area of light." The silent birth of the Enlightenment, aided by a somewhat effeminate hand, is occurring right before our amazed eyes. Gash is still street corner slang for vagina. The hand "was withdrawn as suddenly as it appeared, and all was dark again save the single lurid spark," a nod to the fact that Diderot was imprisoned quite early on during the publishing of the great books, almost extinguishing the work, for many, including the nobility, tried to halt all this questioning of the natural world. "Its disappearance, however, was but momentary. With a rending, tearing sound, one of the broad, white stones turned over upon its side and left a square, gaping hole, through which streamed the light," Watson adds. The Enlightenment is born, with ripping and tearing, into a world of darkness, not unlike the sudden opening of some great light-filled book. John Clay and another rascal called Archie crawl out of the hole where Holmes is waiting for them.

The Enlightenment was an attempt at making a better, more perfect world, and William James believed in this effort, calling it "melioristic," meaning "to make better." When Clay breaks into the underground chamber he at first believes the coast is clear, then suddenly spots Holmes and yells out, "Great Scott! Jump, Archie, jump and I'll swing for it!" The phrase, in order to make realistic sense, should read, "jump or I'll swing for it!" Doyle has altered its sense for some reason. "If we do our best, and the other powers do their best, the world will be perfected," James claims. This was also the ambition of the French philosophers in question, and some other powers, of which Clay is a symbol. James tells us we can, and we may as it were, jump with both feet off the ground into or towards a world in which we trust the other parts to meet our jump. He seems to have some sort of mental acrobatics in mind in which we must put our trust in each other's good intentions in order to, as James calls it, "swing" together, like a circus act. It implies a type of trust, in oneself, and in others, all "jumping" at the right time to be able to perform the noble act of perfection. He appears to be using the word jump as one might use "leap of faith," and I believe he took the one idea from the other. I admit it's a difficult concept to give a concrete example of, and I do not feel comfortable with it myself, but I believe that is the meaning of it all. The Enlightenment is here referred to by this jump, for the crusade is considered a great leap forward in the history of human thought, especially in regard to scientific knowledge.

Diderot's fecund mind shows us his variety of thought in the article "On Beauty," he wrote for the *Encyclopedia* in 1751. Clay "Has a splash of white acid upon his forehead," yet in all else he is extremely good looking with "a clean-cut, boyish face." The thinker deemed that in literature one should describe a scene, or a person, by a few precise, essential facts or traits, for the mind cannot unify a mass of details, cannot portray the whole. The impression of realism should be obtained by use of trivial circumstances that appear necessarily true; the artist need only put a wart or a scar on a beautiful head to make the "ideal model" (Kitty Winter?) an everyday truth. Baron Gottfried Wilhelm Leibniz, Diderot tells us, claimed that no two grains of sand are exactly alike; every being is distinguished by some characteristic details. This is of course a reinterpretation of Francis Bacon's "There is no excellent beauty that hath not some strangeness in the proportion." Clay is "a remarkable man," whose "grandfather was a royal duke, and he himself has been to Eton and Oxford." "He'll crack a crib in Scotland one week, and be raising money to build an orphanage in Cornwall the next."

The most remarkable pun Doyle ever pulled off is found in the fact that John Clay is a personification of Lord Shaftesbury, with Clay digging a *shaft buried* deep within the heart of the world. Lord Anthony Ashley Cooper was the Third Earl of Shaftesbury, and a subtle philosopher. His great-grandson, a politically active individual also named Anthony was a social reformer who introduced legislation in 1826 prohibiting the employment of women and children in coal mines. Wilson's shop employed a fourteen-year-old girl, something the Seventh Earl would have opposed, and may have been illegal in Doyle's day. The presence of a young girl is also a reminder that Diderot enjoyed sex with young girls and even believed in raping them if necessary. Diderot's thoughts and writings are full of paradox and contradictions, none of which he denies nor wishes to change. Shaftesbury the philosopher, like Clay, believed true morality had to be a balance between open egotism and altruism. Balance is made possible between the individual and society, for man has innate instincts, or moral sense, to promote harmony. Lord Shaftesbury greatly impressed and influenced Diderot, who translated his *An Inquiry Concerning Virtue, or Merit* into French in 1745. Clay looks like the Third Earl, for he is small and light, with a pale, hairless, boyish face, and effeminate features, and "a white, almost womanly hand." In the only portrait of Lord Shaftesbury I have ever come across, an etching, he looks like either a nineteen-year-old girl dressed up as a nineteen-year-old boy, or a nineteen-year-old boy dressed up as a nineteen-year-old girl. Take your pick.

Clay has been given a strong education, but it was Diderot's contention that education as we know it does not really change the innate qualities of a human being, for one who inherits an evil will shall always be evil, and this fits the completely unrepentant Clay, whose only lament is that he has been caught. "A wicked man," Diderot assures us, in reference to the question of free will, "is one we must destroy, not punish," for such a man could never be anything other than evil, claiming that neither the good nor the evil man is free; they all must follow unwritten laws of necessity. He diluted this somewhat by claiming modification can take place through rewards and punishment, but his examples, such as sermons and education, seem too lame to alter the original statement. Diderot claims little is gained by simply the loss of the evildoer's goods, or even his life; that doesn't seem to do much good, and he wants the criminal "to be wretched and despised as he contemplates the splendid rewards he has gained by his crimes." Doyle not only agrees, but also uses Clay as a fitting example of why this attitude is proper. Having been arrested by the police, Clay sarcastically commands, "I beg that you will not touch me with your filthy hands," as he is handcuffed, adding, "You may not be aware that I have royal blood in my veins. Have the goodness, also, when you address me always to say 'sir' and 'please.'" His arrogance is so thick you could cut it with a knife. No possible punishment or rehabilitation could make such an individual of any real value to society, or to himself. John Clay has had his ears pierced by the gypsies when young, for he is at heart one of them — a rover and a pillager.

Shaftesbury had formulated a philosophy in which aesthetics not only represents a systematic province, but occupies the central position of the whole intellectual structure. According to him the question of the nature of truth is inseparable from the nature of beauty, for the two questions agree both in their grounds and in their ultimate principle, thoughts much in the strain of Plato. All beauty is truth, just as all truth can be understood basically only through the meaning of form; that is the meaning of beauty. Everything real partakes of this form or beauty although we do not always know it. He believed that in the contemplation of the beautiful, man turns from the world of created things to the world of the creative process, from the universe as a receptacle of the objectively real to the operative forces which have shaped this universe and constitute its inner coherence. Clay is intelligent, for Shaftesbury believed not just the senses had to be involved in the love of beauty but also the intellect, which was a sort of super sensual organ. The objects of its environment can affect any animal; but they are ignorant of all knowledge of beauty. The real center of art is to be found not in the process of enjoyment, but in that of forming and creating, the process of becoming rather than the reality of being. Doyle is saying that the tunnel is a work of creative art, one of the "operative forces which have shaped this universe and constitute its inner coherence." John Clay is an artist ("although we do not always know it") and by Shaftesbury's standards he is close to God in nature for he is a "Creator," and like God he is recreating the natural world itself with his tunneling into the earth. The ability to "immerse" oneself in the artistic process is the real value and mystery of genius the Earl tells us, and therefore Clay is truly an artistic genius, and Holmes as well is a creative genius, for contemplation is a work of art according to Shaftesbury, encapsulated in his quote, "Genius is sublime reason." Genius is the highest sublimation of reason and is the predominant power of all operations of the mind.

We could say however that Clay, for all his birthright and superior education, lacks, as the French aesthetician Dominique Bouhours called it, "good sense." He has been caught robbing a bank, and he is still young, so there is a good chance of his spending many years in prison, perhaps the rest of his life, since he already has a record. Bouhours did not regard genius as the intensification and linear continuation of intelligence, but he assigns to this concept a considerably more complicated function. Genius consists not so much in grasping the simple truth of things, and in expressing this truth as concisely and fully as possible, as rather in the capacity to sense subtle and hidden connections. Holmes has indeed shown a great deal of this form of genius, especially in this case, with its hidden tunnel forming connections between two unrelated points. The thoughts and expressions of the genius depart from the ordinary and lead to new and surprising views of things, oft times unexpected artistic developments, as we see with both Clay and Holmes.

Shaftesbury/Clay is under the street of the city, just as Shaftesbury's philosophy was an underlying factor in the developmental history of the Enlightenment, and the work of the *Encyclopedia* was indeed carried out in secrecy and concealment, as was the subterraneous digging of the shaft. Shaftesbury and a few others were the "foundation of the movement."

Clay's first name was also the name of John Locke, who happened to be a tutor in the household of the First Earl of Shaftesbury, and he as well can be linked to the Enlightenment. "The light of reason," something like the shaft of light from Clay's lantern, was a term initially employed by Locke to imply that reason itself is an aid in discovering reason as a "law of nature" rather than as an "innate law," which man was born with. What reason discovers, Locke believed, is not innate, even though reason itself is natural revelation. He claimed the mind of a newborn child was a *tabula rasa* awaiting the inscription of experience; there was absolutely no *a priori* knowledge although there may be the "power" to acquire it in every one of us, which is not the same thing. The implication here is that most of what the individual becomes has to do with factors such as education, culture, etc., rather than with the accidents of birth, and this brings Locke's philosophy close in spirit to the goals to be set for mankind, if the Enlightenment were to take root. John Clay is also a personification of the Anglo-Irish deist John Toland, with both clay and land meaning essentially the same thing — earth. Tollund is a word used in Ireland to mean a peat bog and I believe it is used, or was, in England to mean a clay or peat bog. (The "Tollund Man" is a desiccated corpse of a Celtic warrior recently dug out of a Danish bog in such excellent condition it is displayed in a museum in Aarhus, Denmark. This was after Doyle's time, however.) John Toland believed that religious knowledge should be subject to the same scrutiny as any other data, and tells us so in his *Christianity not Mysterious* of 1696. The work aims to banish mysteries, miracles, and secrets from religion, and expose it to the light of facts, just as if it were any other field of study. He is regarded as the first full-fledged critical deist, arguing that God had given man a religion worthy of him; a reasonable religion, for man was capable of both reason and religion, but priests hoping to gain power must have later interpolated all the mysteries of Christianity. Critical deism was concerned with attacking and downgrading conventional Christianity, drawing its ammunition from the biblical scholarship of its own day, and from the skepticism about miracles and clerical morality that always exists. The relationship of all this to the Enlightenment is obvious.

In *D'Alembert's Dream*, Diderot pushes his materialistic line of reasoning to its logical conclusion. Borrowing an idea from John Toland, he asserts that flesh can be made from marble, and marble from flesh. All one would have to do is grind up the marble stone so fine it could be added to a liquid and drank, claiming this experience happens continuously in the life cycle. The process of the eventual formation of a man or an animal from inactive and inanimate matter follows, so God was not necessary to make either life or man; it all could have come about through the laws of nature. Toland, like Diderot, had a number of staunch followers.

John Clay's assistant is identified only as Archie. There was an English philosopher, Archibald Alison, quite famous in his own day, who wrote primarily on aesthetics with his best known work being *Essays on the Nature and Principles of Taste* of 1790. His influence on the romantic poets and theorists was considerable and enduring. The basis of Alison's theory of art seems to be that "the qualities of matter are not beautiful or sublime in themselves but as they are, by various means, the signs or expressions of qualities capable of producing emotion." His hypothesis was criticized because it tended to make taste entirely dependent on the imagination to the exclusion of judgment and reason, but it still managed to be very influential. I'm afraid I can't add anything to this brief outline for I can find little on Alison. Lord Shaftesbury is considered the father of modern aesthetics and as such definitely influenced this theorist one way or another.

For someone like Doyle, John Clay epitomized pure evil — the iniquity of doubt and atheism. The trap door of the bank chamber, created by Clay/Toland's efforts out of seemingly solid, impenetrable material, is being laid open like the fissure to a new understanding of the circumstances of human existence, and to the setting of wider bounds to the exploring, by the curiosity of the mind, in all fields of knowledge and perception. The laborious breaching of the vault is the ambitious tearing away of the veils of nature, but only to reveal to Clay and his cohort's surprise, a domain of the universe ruled by law, to which even they are reluctantly subject. Diderot was interested in the discovery and diffusion of truth, the advancement of science, and the moral regeneration of man, holding that a mind was like a piece of wax (an idea borrowed from Locke) that could be molded into anything. If this was accurate, reasoned Diderot, could not a wise education and a well-organized social system make man happy as well as virtuous? "I like a philosophy which lifts up humanity; to degrade it is to encourage men to vice," he once wrote to a friend.

The edition of *Beeton's Christmas Annual* carrying the first Sherlock Holmes story, *A Study in Scarlet*, has on its cover an illustration referring to the story inside. It's not a scene depicting any particular event or interlude in the drama, but rather represents an attempt at capturing the mood and thoughts reflected in the artistic intention of the piece. Holmes is shown in his dressing gown in the process of rising from his desk where he has obviously been working on his studies. The man, in this half raised position, turns sharply as he reaches upward and backwards to raise the flame on his kerosene lamp, hoping to bring more illumination into the room. Since this scene does not appear in the narrative we can assume Doyle dictated to the artist what he thought would be a relevant gesture condensing and epitomizing the character and work of Sherlock Holmes. He is seen bringing light to mankind. Diderot realized all men should take pride in themselves and work toward "enlightened self-interest" and the enlightenment of others. We have here Doyle's own relationship to the Enlightenment, the role of his invention Sherlock, and also Sir Arthur's attempt at being a continuator of the French philosopher's ideas, and in the same format, for the bulk of Diderot's work, like Doyle's, was in the form of stories and novels, plays, and dialogues that read like novels; works of fiction that mingled the problems of aesthetic creation with philosophical speculation. The center of preoccupation of Denis Diderot's existence was all questions relating to the human adventure, and Doyle continued this example in his life and in his writing. Diderot's purpose in much of his fictional efforts was to test the extreme possibilities of character, behavior, moral theory, and judgment. Holmes represents Doyle's most challenging and successful exploration of the utmost limits of character development, for not only is he original, he is extreme, severe, and perhaps improbable.

In this drama in front of us Holmes is combating the disposition of the Enlightenment, and yet I have made the claim that he is the modern animation of this agitation. Add to this my putting forth that Wilson is meant to portray Diderot, the most challenging spirit of the Enlightenment, yet in this mystery the dupe of its deception. I also state that Doyle would regard a personality such as Clay to be an evil entity, although he is a symbol of the early struggles of the movement. What we have here is a major example of the complex and often contradictory temperament of the Holmes Canon. We should not be so eager to take any thought, even thoughts generated by our own investigations, for granted. Sir Arthur was not in comprehensive agreement with the philosophical and theoretical idealism of the Enlightenment in spite of the fact that he lived by its precepts, nor was he conclusively sympathetic to science and its methods and investigations, although he was a scientist and physician. Even his alter ego Holmes was a chemist and investigator of the first rank, and both were authors of scientific research papers.

Emotional needs must be met first with a mentality like that of Arthur Doyle. One justified criticism leveled at the thoughts and application of the *Encyclopedia* was that the books "dared to assert that there was no mystery which Reason could not make plain." Scientific objectivity was the archenemy of spiritualism, a morbid curiosity Doyle entertained, and devoted his thoughts, money, and energy, to propagating, one way or another, almost all of his later life. Any person who believes in spiritualism must automatically have faith in a God of some sort who controls the spirit world. The gold in the strongbox becomes symbolically "reason" and "truth," and the object of a vicious competition for possession by two parties; let us call them "faith" and "science" for the sake of simplicity. The faith people hold the treasure at this point in historical and metaphysical time, so the science or enlightenment crowd realize they must acquire this golden truth by any means, melt it down possibly, and redistribute it as new coin, even if they must undermine the old faith and steal it. The faith men have inherited their defensive positions from past generations and are deeply entrenched, while the newcomers must labor hard, and scheme well, to consolidate their endeavors. The reward of ownership is a golden greatness and well worth fighting over. The battle for control of men's minds takes place right in front of us in the cellar of the bank.

Much of the motive for the Enlightenment was inherent in the innovative reflections of Descartes, especially the realization of the potential of the scientific method. He knew his radical redefinition of philosophical discourse, and his displacement of the focus of where it was man must now search for truth, would cause contention and strife in the world, commenting upon it in his book *Discourse on Method*. Here he alludes to the allegory of the cave found in Plato's *Republic*, to describe the impact his new philosophy might have on humanity. We shall discuss this parable of the cave in more detail later, but for now, let it be enough that the story involves those who sit in darkness within the cave, which becomes our cellar, and they cannot see reality, but nevertheless believe they can, but there is one who can truly see what is real. Descartes is the one who can see this reality. Those who live in the darkness Descartes called "the other philosophers." "In this they (other philosophers) seem to me like blind men who in order to fight on equal terms with one who sees, would have the latter to come into the bottom of a very dark cellar. I may say, too, that it is in the interest of such people that I should abstain from publishing the principles of philosophy of which I make use, for being so simple and evident as they are, I should in publishing them, do the same as though I threw open the widows and caused daylight to enter the cellar into which they have descended to fight." The other philosophers, struggling in obscurity and blind to the truth, do not want Descartes to publish his thoughts and indeed censorship and condemnation dogged the man all his life. Descartes realized that his thoughts were so simple and evident that if he broadcast them he would be throwing light into the dark cellar of the mind, therefore giving himself, the one who could see, all the advantage while the others understood as well that they must keep the battle in a condition of shadows for their strength to be at all equal to these new truths. Descartes views himself as the dispeller of gloom and ignorance, and once again Doyle contradicts himself, for he has Holmes be the one in the bank vault who lights the lantern, even though he then single-handedly engages in a struggle with the Enlightenment men. Holmes is the one who fights the opaqueness of ignorance and yet embraces the forces of the anti-Enlightenment, at one and the same time. With these bizarre conclusions we are witnessing our author's mind being caught up in necessary inconsistency over questions of great importance, making an effort to rationalize and exercise options of thought that will lead to resolutions conforming to both reason and emotional, spiritual needs. The obvious antagonisms conveyed in these considerations haunted Doyle all his life, as they do so many thoughtful people. It was the confronting of these variances in reason and belief that gave the Holmes stories their outstanding three-dimensionality and unequaled originality.

CHAPTER TWELVE. EITHER I — OR THOU

"The Final Problem," perhaps the most interesting and complicated short story in literature, opens with a visit to Watson from a frightened and desperate Holmes. The two have not worked on a case for a few years, and recently Holmes has experienced a number of assaults, and even an attempt upon his life, blaming these attacks on a criminal organization controlled by Professor Moriarty, the leader of a gang so vicious the detective claims he must leave England in order to avoid destruction at their hands, and hopes Watson will go with him. With the assistance of Mycroft the two eventually manage to get to the Continent and settle down at a Swiss inn, but Holmes is sure the gang's leader has followed them. They hide among the glaciers and mountains of the Alps, where during a day trip to Reichenbach Falls, hand-to-hand combat ends with Holmes and Moriarty both tumbling into the abyss.

Since creating Holmes, his author seemingly displayed a genuine desire to rid himself of the character, evidenced by his reluctance to resurrect the detective following his mishap at the falls, not to mention the fact that he pushed him over in the first place. Doyle actually tried to dissolve the friendship between Holmes and Watson after only the second story, with the doctor going off to marry Mary Morstan, while Holmes returned to his drugs. He may even have hoped to bring a halt to his detective's career after the first novel; remember that *The Sign of the Four* was a commission offered at a time when the writer needed money. One reason Sir Arthur may have been pleased to see the end of Holmes, and he seems to have been as delighted about it as Moriarty himself, is because the character's crowd-pleasing effects must have been a source of guilt feelings stemming from his unwanted self-image as a popular hack writer. Doyle considered his historical novels, which are really just admirable replications of Kingsley and Scott, to be solid literature of some value — something he rather doubted, to his dying day, regarding the Holmes work. He claimed these historical pieces contained his "larger thoughts," adding, in reference to the detective stories, that he was tired "of being entirely identified with what I regarded as a lower stratum of literary achievement. Therefore as a sign of my resolution I determined to end the life of my hero." Notice the use of the word hero, a reference to Carlyle. We should keep in mind that artists can be wrong about their own work, and often are. Substantially prior to writing "The Final Problem," he had obviously entertained the ghoulish idea of killing the detective, and one wretched day while vacationing in Switzerland, he took his wife Touie to visit Reichenbach Falls, where he found the sight personally terrifying, yet useful from a literary perspective, for he knew it "would make a worthy tomb for poor Sherlock, even if I buried my banking account along with him." That's a telling statement for he actually appears to be thankful to be rid of the income generated by these lucrative efforts.

I shall treat "The Final Problem" keeping in mind the author's original intentions, for it was planned to be the concluding Holmes tale. However, it did occur to Doyle that he could have included things in this account after it had been published, for instance the actual contest of the two antagonists, which took place offstage, as in a Greek tragedy. When he thought this over as he was working on "The Empty House," he realized he had indeed missed a colorful opportunity by not depicting it, so he does so now, and I'll therefore use what I might need from the story of Holmes' return, and any other narrative; but we should remember the fact of Doyle's original intention. Prof. Moriarty makes his first appearance in "The Final Problem," and it almost turns out to be his last. Regretting this, Doyle rounds out the character in later tales and we can borrow on some of this information. The Professor did not come into the fray until now since technically he was unnecessary, and following the death of Sherlock his purpose for existence will have been fulfilled. The man seems to have descended from an undistinguished family, but it is emphasized that he has a recognized intellect of exceptional degree, has a promising career in mathematics, including a chair in mathematics, and has written a treatise on the binomial theorem, as well as a book called *The Dynamics of an Asteroid*. He eventually went to London and set up as an army coach. Holmes describes him as "an abstract thinker," who usually "sits motionless," just like himself, he could have added. Proof of the importance of Moriarty is evidenced by the complexity of his models, references, and spiritual overtones. "Sometime when you have a year or two to spare I commend to you the study of Professor Moriarty," Holmes entreats us, but I assure you it required longer than two years in order to even begin to understand the man.

Moriarty is regarded as "the Napoleon of crime," and for Nietzsche, Napoleon is as close as any human has come to personifying his superman, so if Holmes is to have a match, it must be with a Napoleon of something, and bear in mind that Doyle held a certain admiration for the French leader, evidenced in his Brigadier Gerard stories. Actually he had an ambiguous attitude toward Napoleon, for in his novel *The Great Shadow*, the persona of Napoleon, the shadow, is a symbol of evil. Take into account that Holmes, who usually echoes his author's thoughts, referred to Moriarty as "this Napoleon-gone-wrong," and you are truly in murky waters.

Nietzsche, the passionate individualist, the believer in the hero, loved Napoleon, making the astonishing observation that "The revolution made Napoleon possible: that is its justification." He looked upon all the suffering, butchery, and mayhem of the French Revolution as legitimized, not for what humanistic hope and precautionary counsel it may hold out as a model to the world, but purely because it functioned as a catalyst in bringing a superman into being. After the Revolution, "there appeared Napoleon, the most unique and violent anachronism that ever existed, and in him the incarnate problem *of the aristocratic ideal in itself* — consider well what a problem it is: — Napoleon, that synthesis of Monster and Superman." This quote is where we get the word "problem," found in the title of our story. The problem the philosopher presents is how does a world that needs law and order, a world of those who wish peace rather than war, and prosperity rather than suffering, deal with one among us, who is, and very much wants to be, this synthesis of monster and superman; an aristocratic ideal that is a law unto itself, and yet finds support among those who fought to suppress just such an ideal, and just such a person. In recapitulating the events of Lord Clive's life, Macaulay reminds us of his magnificent success in the field of battle, for Clive had conquered almost all of India by the age of twenty-five. "The only man, as far as we recollect, who at an equally early age ever gave equal proof of talents for war was Napoleon Bonaparte." Note the expressive application of the word equal.

The Professor's name, a pun on "*mort,*" which means death in French, comes from "*mors* and *mortis,*" Latin words denotative of "the absence of life." Moriarty is also a play on the Sanskrit "*marati,*" which actually means "murder," and is the root for "mortal." Doyle used the pun before when he told us of the shop of Mortimer, the tobacconist, obviously a reference to the lethal effects of the habit. The early Assyrians, and the people they developed into, the Persians, the people of Zarathustra, feared and despised death, one reason being that they had no covenant with their gods, who were an arbitrary bunch. In *The Saga of Gilgamesh*, the ancient Assyrian epic poem depicting the hero's struggle with a persona of death, the noxious creature is referred to as "the evil that is in the land." The great iniquity to the Persians in their violent war torn world was "death that creeps unseen." As Holmes enters Watson's rooms in the opening scene of "The Final Problem," he asks if they can close the shutters, for he is afraid of air-guns. The silent air-gun, which shows up in a number of stories, personifies the hushed death that comes, "like a thief in the night," unseen, unheard, and unwelcome.

Two original Zoroastrian spirits unite in the creation of the good and evil of existence, both actually in the present, and in the principles that have their issue in the future, and that future is now. If there existed a supreme god whose power could undo the very laws of life, no evil could have been known, but the doctrine denies there is any such being. The good and evil in the world limit each other, and there can be no goodness that does not resist evil and sin, accordingly, the evil principle is recognized as so necessary that it is represented by an evil god, and we must acknowledge Professor Moriarty as a god, and one of a pair of gods. He is also the son of a god, for if there is a spiritual son of Zarathustra, born to aid mankind in the future, there must be his opposite, the son of the evil Mainyu. "Everything comes in circles — even Professor Moriarty," Holmes says, adding, "It's all been done before, and will be again." The evil is often called "The Worst Mind," and displays wanton cruelty, and works for dishonest acquisition. He it is who "threatens to take away fullness and increase from the world, and to bring in sickness and death." Holmes is "The Beneficent One," thus making his opposite "The Malignant One." Both are symbolic ardent practitioners in this ancient religion, and it is pointed out to us that the Professor, like his contrary spirit, is "ascetic," in his looks. While in Switzerland the two adversaries travel through the Gemmi Pass, with "Gemmi" being a fortuitous pun on "Gemini," Latin for "twins," an allusion to their roles as mirror reflections. Twin gods and demigods are standard in many of the world's religions, with the Gemini being a personification found in the Greek horoscope, the sign being a representation of the twins Castor and Pollux, known collectively as the *Dioskouroi*. Pollux may be looked upon as the divine potential within each of us; Castor typifies the earth force we cannot deny. Pollux is viewed as immortal while Castor is mortal. They are spoken of as spending alternate days in the heavens and the nether world, while together they express light and dark, manifesting the unending battle between night and day found in nature and depicted in almost all religions.

The idea for using Castor and Pollux was given to Sir Arthur from his constant reading of Diderot. *D'Alembert's Dream* is the minutes of a conceptualized Socratic exchange between: D'Alembert, Mlle. de L'Espinasse, Dr. Bordeu and a servant. The doctor is telling of a set of twins he recently came across. "The fable of Castor and Pollux made actual: two children; when one began to live, the other immediately died: similarly when the first one died, the second began to live." Mlle. de L'Espinasse asks how long did this last. "Their time of life was two days, which they shared equally and in turns, so that each had for its share one day's life and one day's death." Diderot now tells of the case of Siamese twins who, when one dies, both die, for one cannot live without the other. The use of Gemmi Pass is also an endorsement of the knowledge that the Greeks believed that everything in each individual life is governed, not by gods, or laws of nature, but by fate, for the twins' strange fortune is responsible for their existence, and neither god, their father, nor nature can change that. Like Castor and Pollux, Holmes and Moriarty are bound together in the network of threads that is fate, depending upon each other for existence itself.

In the opening sentences of "The Book of Job," God gathers his sons around him, one of whom is Satan. This is the son whose fate it is, in spite of obvious good birth, to fall into evil ways, endeavoring to lead mankind into error. Satan or Lucifer replaces Angra Mainyu in the Hebrew Bible, and the Professor is called a devil, as when Holmes is questioned as to whether or not mankind can ever "get level with this king devil?" "No, I don't say that," Holmes answers, "and his eyes seemed to be looking far into the future. I don't say that he can't be beat. But you must give me time — you must give me time!" Moriarty can naturally be considered Satan for the word means simply "the enemy or the adversary," Moriarty's position in regard to society and to Holmes. Jesus and Lucifer are brothers, and not just brothers, for in keeping with the mythology of many religions they are regarded as twins and equals. Holmes: life, light, and cosmos, rules the upper world, while Moriarty: death, darkness, and chaos, rules the underworld. "The Final Problem," captures that spirit of the time when the everlasting war which is in heaven between the children of light and the children of darkness culminates and ripens into a Day of Judgment, becoming palpable and incarnate; no longer a purely spiritual combat, but one of flesh and blood, wherein single men must choose their side and fight, not merely with pen and prayers, but with weapons and with their bare hands.

Never underestimate the influence Dickens exercised over Doyle. Fagin, one emblematic of the willful corruption of innocence in *Oliver Twist*, also served as prototype for the Professor, beginning with their Irish names. In Doyle's day the Irish exhibited an amazing capacity for crime, especially the well-organized variety, with espionage, a practice of the Professor's, often justifiably put down to them. The Scots and Irish detest crime and the criminal mentality, with Doyle exemplifying such disdain in all his writings. Green is the color used to symbolize the Irish, and Doyle used the color green of the Irish flag to represent the soldiers behind it in the short story "The Green Flag," and then titled a collection of short stories in book form after this tale. Moriarty is alluded to, by association, as being "Black Irish," an expression once commonly used to denote someone Irish who did not follow the law, for when Watson spots him approaching the Swiss falls he tells us, "I could see his black figure clearly outlined against the green behind him."

The name Moriarty has an element of the comic about it. One hardly expects unmitigated malice from a math professor, and possibly the last person you would select to symbolize evil intent would be an Anglo-Irish professor named Jimmy Moriarty; the kind of name found on the bill of a Brighton music hall of the day. Appearing on stage in baggy, patched trousers, rope belt, battered top hat, a merry twinkle in the eye, and of course the mandatory red nose, the straight man would ask with a sly grin, "Tell me Professor, what are you a professor of?" And then the laughs would begin. Fagin also operates from a position of concealment and safety while the members of his gang take all the risks. The devil can, like Angra Mainyu, assume any disguise he wishes, and he loves this kind of thing. In war, invisibility, and the sabotage it permits, is the greatest weapon in your arsenal, and both come under the heading of deceit, the end product of the Drug. Professor Moriarty does not come across as the badge of evil, for unlike, let us say, Iago or Fagin, we are not shown individual examples of his felonious actions, with the exception of the few Holmes outlines to us now, but he certainly brings a formless menacing spirit with him, a strong suspicion of disorder and mystery.

The conversation between Holmes and Watson wherein they discuss the machinations of Moriarty is a reenactment of a three-way conversation involving D'Alembert, Bordeu, and Mlle. de L'Espinasse, found in *D'Alembert's Dream*. The piece is written by Diderot and represents no one's thoughts but his own. The Professor is described by Holmes as a man who does little himself, but only plans, and this with "a brain of the first order." "He sits motionless, like a spider in the centre of its web, but that web has a thousand radiations, and he knows well every quiver of each of them." His agents are numerous and well ordered, and when there is a crime to be carried out, "the word is passed to the professor, the matter is organized and carried out." He is "the central power which uses the agent." Notice that a message is first carried to the Professor. The relationship of the mind or brain to the sense organs, and the sensations the organs produced that affects the function of the mind interested Diderot all his life, as it has many others. Let it be understood that the following is only a small portion of his thoughts on the subject. He visualized all of life, the life of the universe, as well as the life visibly before him, and human life of course, as a vast network comparable to the web of a giant spider, which is sensate to the smallest disturbance on the threads of its web. He also likens the human mind and the organs of the body to a spider and its web. Mlle. de L'Espinasse asks us to "imagine that you see a spider in the center of her web. If you disturb a single thread, you will see how the alert little creature comes running. Well, then, what if the threads which this insect spins out from her body — and can swallow up again whenever she pleases — What if those threads were a sensitive part of her body?" Bordeu answers, "I follow your thoughts. You mean to suggest that inside your own body, in some region of your brain — perhaps in the part known as the meninges — there may be one or more points to which are conveyed all the sensations that are produced anywhere along the threads." The individual is "the origin of the feeling network, that part which constitutes one's self." Diderot tells us that the spider, what he calls "the origin of the will," is the one who gives the commands, after receiving information, to that which becomes his "end," or "ends," and the brain he calls an "absolute despot," which controls the rest of the animal's organs. The origin of the will, if it is the brain one thinks of, leads us to Holmes' assertion that the Professor only plans, for the mind or will itself does no physical work. At one point Bordeu reminds us we actually know little of the mechanics of memory as it relates to the brain, and he is accused by Mlle. of eluding her questions on the subject. "I elude nothing; I tell you what I know, and I should know more if the organization of the origin of the network was as well known to me as that of the end, if I had the same facilities for observing it." Holmes assures us, "the central power which uses the agent is never caught — never so much as suspected. This was the organization which I deduced," in speaking of the control Moriarty exercised over his "ends." Mlle. says, "So that the animal is either being controlled by an absolute despot or else living in anarchy." "An absolute despot, yes," answers Bordeu, "that's very well put. The origin of the bundle gives the orders, and the rest of the organism obeys. The animal is its own master, *mentis compos*." The young lady adds to this, "Or else in a state of anarchy, when all the fibers of the network rise up against their ruler, so that there is no longer any supreme authority." Well there is indeed a state of anarchy, for the Professor's organization has become a "defective network," for one under his authority, a man named Porlock, has revolted against his despotism, informing on him to his archenemy Holmes. Moriarty is losing his supreme authority and is no longer *mentis compos*, but rather *mens rea*, or "guilty mind" or "evil will." It is not Diderot, but Wendell Holmes who talks of *mens rea*; it being that part of the actions in a law case that cannot be measured since it represents the mind of the accused, and none have the ability to read the mind of another. Wendell admits that the actual evil will of a person is impossible to gage; exactly what we have in the case of Professor Moriarty. "A man may have as bad a heart as he chooses, if his conduct is within the rules," the Judge tells us. The Professor has not stayed within the rules of society, but neither the authorities nor the public know anything of his criminal actions, so it comes to much the same thing. The psychological make-up of Doyle's detectives and criminals is not explored in any depth, for the mentality of an individual was only marginally important in a court of law at the time, although lawyers and others did, from time to time, bring it up. Professor Moriarty is a freak, not a physical specimen, as Diderot so often speaks of, but a mental one; a man with the despotic mind of an animal. The brain has been disturbed and the whole "bundle" is now disturbed. "The variations that occur in the bundle of each species give rise to all the malformed variations within the species," Denis Diderot claims.

Another dialogue takes place when Moriarty ventures into Holmes' rooms and the two antagonists face off, with the Professor warning that since he has been "incommoded," and "inconvenienced," by the detective's actions, the situation has been forced to a climax, claiming that if Holmes attempts his destruction he will only bring destruction upon himself as well, but the man already knew this, and seems willing to face the inevitable.

In his book *Letter on the Blind for Those Who Can See*, Diderot discussed the mental effect of blindness, reporting a conversation between the blind English mathematician Nicholas Saunderson, and an English churchman, the Reverend Holmes, with the entire conversation being the creation of the philosopher. It is a piece of fiction involving real historical characters; a reenactment of a nonevent, if such a thing can be. For publishing this piece the author was cast into a dungeon at Vincennes by those who read his atheism in it. Diderot however rejected atheism as incompatible with his views of harmony and virtue, and even more, as a dogmatism that assumes an understanding of the universe we do not have. When Saunderson, who held a chair in mathematics at Oxford, was dying, the Reverend Holmes was summoned to his bedside where the two discuss the existence of God, and what that implies, with Saunderson doing most of the talking. Prof. Saunderson is an atheist, using his own blindness as one proof that a God who permitted this could never exist. He is a mistake of nature, and he like other mistakes of nature, such as Prof. Moriarty, could be exampled as living proof that God could not exist to make such errors, and also that there is no intelligent purpose to existence. The beauty and order of nature is a proof of God's presence only to those who can see, he claims, and therefore he denies God. What Diderot was doing was showing that every deviation in the organic disposition of a person must necessarily result in a complete change in his spiritual life. The Minister tells the Professor to place his hands upon his own body and he will feel there the perfect physical mechanism of animals — proof of order. "Mr. Holmes," Saunderson replies, "I tell you again, nothing of all that can be as beautiful to me as it is to you." Holmes remarks that many great men of science such as Newton believed in God, but the mathematician reminds him that Newton too could see, and his beliefs where based upon the Word of God, while he himself is reduced to taking the word of Newton. We shall see later that the introduction of Newton into this dialogue is of great importance. Saunderson, like Moriarty, admits there is a wonderful order to the universe, but hopes "that you will require no more of me," for he wishes to think as he pleases about the formation of the universe, just as Moriarty, an authority on the paths of heavenly bodies, would think as he pleases about the universe and its formation. "Look well at me, Mr. Holmes," Saunderson says, "I have no eyes. What did we do to God, you and I, that one of us should possess those organs and the other be deprived of them?" At one point Saunderson, in a fit of depression, implies that he himself is a monstrous being, and that mankind is just one more monster race waiting to be exterminated by nature. The exchange between Holmes and Saunderson is amiable enough with both parties being polite and appreciative of each other's views, but beneath the surface a friction and pressure, similar to the tension and anxiety evident during the exchange between Moriarty and Sherlock can be sensed. As Moriarty says, "It has been a duel between you and me, Mr. Holmes." In both sets of disputants there are differences that can never be reconciled. My life has been lived in darkness, Saunderson concludes, and such is the spiritual condition of Moriarty, for when leaving the apartment of Holmes he does not just walk out but goes "peering and blinking out of the room," much in the manner of a visually impaired individual.

In his essay *Philosophic Thoughts*, Diderot gives arguments both for and against the existence of God, once again using the dialogue structure. The speakers are a deist and an atheist with the latter at one point explaining the godless creation of the universe as a simple mathematical necessity. Given space, matter, and motion as eternal entities, and an infinity of time, the proper combination to form a universe becomes a mere matter of patience. In this work the French philosopher probes the incidents of malformed people born into this world, his fascination with this subject stemming from his belief that being malformed affected the organs, which in turn influenced the ability of the mind to experience life as everyone else knows it to be. He hoped to strengthen his theory that in the exceptions to the norm we would find truths applicable to all. Through the conversation Diderot claims that the children of the malformed are themselves not the carriers of "these irregularities," but that "these irregularities do make leaps, one or other of their children's children will eventually revert to the unusual conformation discovered in its great-grandfather." Here is a partial answer to the statement that Moriarty has diabolical antecedents, for his own parents may have been normal, but some irregularities, in this case mental or moral, have been passed down to him. Holmes talks about the master criminal Jonathan Wild, who was active in London around 1750, as though he was perhaps an ancestor of James Moriarty.

At one point in the conversation Moriarty tells Holmes why the two cannot live in the same world, complaining that because of the detective's "continual persecution," he is "in positive danger of losing my liberty." In addressing the problem of political freedom John S. Mill penned his most influential and in some ways his most impressive work, *On Liberty*. Elaborating on issues already introduced by Jeremy Bentham, Mill argued that the problem of political freedom could be resolved once the matter is seen negatively, in terms of the restraints that can legitimately be placed upon the individual. Working from Bentham's theory that happiness lies in the satisfaction of desire, Mill claims that political liberty, which Moriarty has chosen to interpret as pure power, if it is to be a value in accordance with the principle of "utility," must consist in the liberty to satisfy desires, however, one man may desire to do something that impedes the satisfaction of the wishes of another. What principle should be involved in legislating between them? Or should there be no principle, merely the natural struggle for domination? Mill believed this utility should be the determining factor, by which he meant the ability to produce the greatest good for the greatest number of people, or, "the greatest happiness of all those whose interest is in question." It seemed to him that there should be some form of restraint on human actions, but that it could not be founded merely on the principle of utility; for that would lead to no settled law, and no civil allegiance to the established order. Each man after all might differ, as we see with the case of Holmes and Moriarty, in his opinion as to which satisfaction would be the greater or most beneficial in the long run. Professor Moriarty has no compunctions about what he is doing; it must be giving him some satisfaction, and not he alone, for he has a whole crew of like-minded rascals behind him; others have an interest in it, giving to him a certain level of legitimacy in his desires. Hence, Mill says, we need a more straightforward criterion, so he proposed the criterion of "harm," wherein a man is at liberty to pursue whichever of his desires that causes no harm to his fellow human beings. Sherlock must stop his enemy, for as we have seen from his list of offenses against society, Moriarty is doing great harm, both physical and moral, to his fellow man. Under such conditions, Mill tells us, negative restraint must be applied.

In the Introduction to his essay Mill tells us this question is far from new, but rather "in a certain sense, it has divided mankind, almost from the remotest ages, but in the stage of progress into which the more civilized portions of the species have now entered," by which he means for modern man, this question of liberty now "presents itself under new conditions, and requires a different and more fundamental treatment." He observes that "The struggle between Liberty and Authority is the most conspicuous feature in the portions of history with which we are earliest familiar, particularly in that of Greece, Rome, and England." Doyle however, realizes this conflict betwixt authority and liberty reflects back to an era when Greece was little more than a cluster of dirty villages, for it goes back to the time of the struggles of the people of Zarathustra. In defense of his theory Mill adds, "All that makes existence valuable to any one, depends on the enforcement of restraints upon the actions of other people." The very life of any society, or of any individual in that society, would be less valuable if people like the Professor were to acquire more liberty. Rules of law, Mill claims, must be imposed, by a legal system in the first place, and by opinion, on many things which are not fit subjects for the operation of the law. The philosophical importance of the Holmes stories is brought home to us in Mill's next observation: "What these rules should be, is the principal question in human affairs; but if we except a few of the most obvious cases, it is one of those which least progress has been made in resolving. No two ages, and scarcely any two countries, have decided it alike; and the decision of one age or country is a wonder to another." This seems to be part of Doyle's reasoning for his compulsive interest in such literature as *The Common Law* as a basis for these stories. Mill's principle for the imposing of laws on the individual reflects the most important question in human affairs, as well as the needs that forced Zarathustra's people to call him from his farm to be their champion in the struggle against the marauders. "That principle is," says Mill, "that the sole end for which mankind are warranted, individually or collectively in interfering with the liberty of action of any of their number, is self-protection. That the only purpose for which power can be rightfully exercised over any member of a civilized community, against his will, is to prevent harm to others." Mill carried the problem beyond this, and Doyle did as well, but we shall pull up here.

Following the death of his brother, Colonel James Moriarty sends letters to the press defending his memory. This man sees nothing wrong with this action, for he understood the importance of the role the Professor played in the maintaining of power in the universe. He's hardly alone, for Watson tells us the memory of Moriarty is defended by "injudicious champions," implying that there are any number of followers standing behind the man's ideals. The Professor has two brothers: the youngest became an obscure stationmaster in the West of England; the other served his country as a military officer. Colonel Moriarty has the same first name as the Professor, the other brother may be named James as well for all we know, and the situation is so improbable we can see our author wants us to think about it. Part of the answer is no doubt a simple interpretation of the axiom, "For every evil that you kill there are two to take its place." But the question still remains as to why the name James at all? And why use it so often? The use of the same name carries the connotation that there are others who are just as evil as the Professor, whose names are also James, and not just his brothers.

At least one root of the name can be traced back to Robert Louis Stevenson's *The Master of Ballantrae*. The Master, James Durie, is a man who seems to be evil for its own sake, exampled by his hatred for any number of people in the novel, including his younger brother Lord Henry. Like Moriarty he comes of good stock, but cannot control his passion or his hatred, forcing Mackellar, secretary to Henry, to say to the Master, "I do not think you could be so bad a man," "if you had not all the machinery to be a good one." James is an intelligent man with a "love of serious reading," as well as an ardent student of mathematics. One character, university educated, finds among James' belongings a volume of math he describes as being "far beyond where I have studied." The Master makes most of his decisions, even those of great importance, matters of life and death, by tossing a coin, telling us he knows, "no better way," "to express my scorn of human reason." Such a declaration on the efforts of the human intellect amounts to a unique and deadly form of evil.

This is reading the Master on a purely human level, for in a broader zone he is the devil himself, being guilty of "diabolical acts," for "diabolical amusement," and is called by one who knows him well, an "insidious devil." James Durie even conducts a symbolic pact with the devil, and then plays the role himself when he forms a compact with a vicious pirate captain, who refers to him as "Satan." Durie seems to die, one way or another, a number of times, only to reappear more evil, crafty, and deceitful than ever. The devil is often depicted in Scotch literature as a black man, and the Master turns up, uninvited, to torment his family with the assistance of a black servant, Secundra Dass. Doyle's notion of drowning Professor Moriarty in the abyss was inspired by the scene in Stevenson's drama when Durie, Mackellar, and Dass, aboard the ship sailing to America, are overtaken by a hurricane. Mackellar tells us, "At first I was terrified beyond motion, and almost beyond thought, my mind appearing to be frozen. Presently there stole in on me a ray of comfort. If the *Nonesuch* foundered, she would carry down with her into the deeps of that unsounded sea the creature whom we all so feared and hated; there would be no more Master of Ballantrae, the fish would sport among his ribs; his schemes all brought to nothing, his harmless enemies at peace." In Doyle's day the ocean depths were, and often still are, called the abyss. Mackellar, like Holmes, is willing to be drowned if only the evil one goes under with him, even praying to God to bring it about.

The two warring brothers, Henry and James, travel to America, over water and land, the one trying to flee the other, but escape is futile for the New World is to be the scene of their last desperate struggle. The Master goes into the forests of New York and word reaches the outside that he has died a natural death. Traveling to his gravesite, Mackellar asks himself if both brothers are not now dead, for Henry's mind has been killed by his evil half. Dass has buried James Durie although he is not dead, a trick to save him from the buccaneers seeking his treasure. When Henry comprehends that his brother is possibly still alive, he dies of a stroke and is buried in the same hole as James, just as Holmes and Moriarty are buried in the same pit. Doyle took the idea of using Switzerland from this novel in which the combat between good and evil takes place in New York State, for the land is described as a wild mountainous region full of great waterfalls, and at the time was touted as the Switzerland of America or the Switzerland of the New World. A careful reading of *The Master of Ballantrae* shows that Stevenson has been rereading his Cooper, of whom he was very fond.

In English literature, if not world literature, no name is more evocative of deception and evil intent than James, for translated into Spanish it becomes Iago. In Shakespeare's play even Iago's nationality is hidden, for

Othello is set in Italy yet Iago is Spanish, with Doyle having a good deal to say about Spanish trickery in a few of his non-Holmes stories. The theme of *Othello* is close in spirit to the Holmes stories, for the conflict between good and evil in an ostensibly Christian world was the basic element of many of Shakespeare's presentations. Iago is the most conspicuous villain in literature, possessing boundless hate and spite; the very soul of deception, and the epitome of *mens rea*, telling us proudly in the first act, "I am not what I am," and then calmly proceeding to prove it. Throughout the drama, Othello, Desdemona, and the others, address him as "honest Iago," and speak of his "honesty and trust," yet all in the play should have recognized Iago for what he was. We are told of Moriarty that his evil genius controls almost all the crime of London, yet within the city, "no one has heard of him." The people of London are, as Iago's wife Emilia says of Othello, for having been so easily gulled by him, "as ignorant as dirt." Even the police do not believe Holmes as regards Moriarty, yet who has shown them such examples of a penetrating intellect as the Great Detective. We are never given reasons why Moriarty, having had superior beginnings, turns to a life of crime, and Shakespeare, in a sense, never goes into the purpose of Iago's malevolence. The wickedness just exists, it seems natural to him and needs no cause. He hates and destroys, or tries to, just about every person in the drama. Iago despises Othello for every reason under the sun, from his color to his position, but he as well loathes Cassio, with no real motivation. Just as Moriarty is put forth as a sort of divine devil, the playwright does likewise with Iago, for when Iago has the alarm bell rung as Cassio and Montano fight in the street, someone yells from their window, "Who's that which rings the bell? — Diablo, ho!" Notice the use of the Spanish word for devil. Iago calls himself "Divinity of hell!" and calls upon "all the tribe of hell," to aid him in his plans. Finally grasping the full extent of his aide's deception, Othello searches Iago's feet to see if he has cloven hoofs. Stevenson had Iago in mind for his characterization of James Durie for duplicity is the art of both men, with the Master too having an "original genius," for blinding all who come in contact with him as to his literal nature. Much of the plot of Stevenson's novel is based upon the play, with Henry as Othello, James as his namesake Iago, and Henry's wife portraying Desdemona.

"The Suicide Club" is one of a collection of three eccentric short stories Stevenson published in 1882, as part of a group of stories entitled *New Arabian Nights*. This London club, as the name implies, is a gathering of men who for one reason or another, have given up on the world. The common bond of their death wish finds opportunity for fulfillment as each member is selected systematically to be murdered by the others, the whole thing determined by the luck of the cards. The organizer of these lethal proceedings, called simply the President, passes as the soul of respectability yet personifies wickedness, for suicide is the supreme act for which there is chance neither for forgiveness nor repentance. The love of the game, or perhaps a fascination with death, or both, and then some, seems to be his motivation for composing the deadly selection since he is never the one picked to die, or to do the actual killing, for he is never dealt a hand of cards. One of the members of the club, hoping to embrace death, tells us, "For three years he has pursued in London his useful and, I think I may add, his artistic calling; and not so much as a whisper of suspicion has been once aroused." In yet another section of the story we come across a Dr. Noel, who in collusion with Prince Florizel, disposes of a dead body that has been planted in the apartment of an American in an effort to pin a murder on him. Silas, the American, questions Noel as to his background, being astonished that such a gentle and unlikely person would be so adroit at getting rid of a murdered body, but from the good doctor Silas learns a terrible secret. "Know, then, that although I now make so quiet an appearance — frugal, solitary, addicted to study — when I was younger, my name was once a rallying-cry among the most astute and dangerous spirits of London; and while I was outwardly an object for respect and consideration, my true power resided in the most secret, terrible, and criminal relations. It is to one of the persons who then obeyed me that I now address myself to deliver you from your burden. They were men of many different nations and dexterities, all bound together by a formidable oath, and working to the same purposes; the trade of the association was in murder; and I who speak to you, innocent as I appear, was the chieftain of this redoubtable crew." His name Noel means Christmas, personifying the opposite spirit of that which had been his nature. Noel epitomized, as does the President and the Professor, not just evil, but hidden immorality, aided and abetted by tightly controlled and very efficient organizations of malevolence.

With the mention of the brothers James I can't help wondering if Doyle is not thinking of the Americans, Jesse and Frank James, and their gang, the notorious James Gang, who, before they were stopped, had nine train robberies, twelve bank holdups, twenty-three gunfights, and numerous murders to their credit. As unlikely as it sounds, Oscar Wilde was visiting Kansas on April 3, 1882, when Jesse James was murdered by one of his own gang (Porlock?) in nearby St. Joseph, Missouri. In a letter to Helena Sickert from Nebraska, Wilde described how the people of St. Joseph mourned over James' death and bought relics of his house: door-knocker, dust-bin, anything they could lay hands on. Wilde describes two of them having a gunfight over ownership of a hearth-brush. He must have told his friend Arthur of this curious event for both shared an interest in things American, or anything unusual dealing with human behavior or morals.

Another set of James brothers is of course the Americans, Henry and William, and other members of the James family are brought into it for at the time of the writing of the story there were three James brothers still alive: William, Henry, and Robertson. The latter had a drinking problem, and after joining with the fourth brother Garth, in 1867, to develop a plantation in Florida that failed, returned to the family home in Boston. After staying home awhile Robertson went out to Iowa where John Murray Forbes, a wealthy family friend, found him a job as timekeeper in the Burlington Station of the Chicago, Burlington and Quincy Railroad. In 1868 he quit the Iowa situation and secured a clerkship with the Milwaukee and St. Paul Railway. He was in effect a stationmaster, as was Professor Moriarty's younger brother, and both of them were working "in the West." The brothers James are being rendered in charcoal as men who are equipped to fight Holmes because they, and only such as they, are his equals, his twin, or in this case, his twins, for only such equals could hope to have a chance of standing against him.

We shall deal with William's contribution to "The Final Problem" more fully later, but first we must discuss some earlier entities in an effort to avoid oversimplifying, which might harm our ability to understand. Descartes develops in his literature a character he represents as God's double, or "the evil genius," a malignant agency whose sole function and entire project is to deceive him, the philosopher, as a thinking subject. In *Meditations* he does not proceed directly from the problem of deception, which is the opposite of perfection, to conclude that the evil genius (as opposed to God), which embodies deception, actually exists. Rather he acknowledges the existence of this author of deception as a fiction that personifies and dramatizes the argument. Now listen to this interesting mind at work; for although it is admittedly a fictitious entity, the philosopher assures us the evil genius exists as surely as René Descartes exists. He is trying to persuade us to believe, as Holmes must convince those doubters that Moriarty, of necessity, has existence. In *Meditations* the thinker addresses this evil personality as "anonymous," elsewhere admitting "I know not who he is," adding that this agency will be "not less powerful than deceitful," and by being "imposed upon by this arch deceiver," we will not even be able to tell the difference between reality and appearance. He is a secretive deceiver who is "always purposely deceiving me." The key to the understanding of the agency, as far as Doyle's use of it is concerned, from what I can see, is the use of this agent to introduce "skeptical doubt," into the world, and into the nature of things, and the nature of God. Hyperbolic doubt and the evil genius are the terms Descartes uses to dramatize in the tangible the sense of having attained an absolute limit in matters of doubt, this doubt being brought to the subject, the "I" that Descartes constantly talks of and thinks of, by this exterior agency. This doubt is uncounted within the self as a structure of deception embedded in its own representation, for it makes one prey to deception and illusion in such a way as to perfect and complete the subject's own capacities for self-deception. The philosopher puts forth that in extending the thinking subject's capacity for deception the evil genius reduces the subject to a passive object — one reason Holmes goes so willingly to his death. This doubt personified by the evil genius is "metaphysical," insofar as it involves both the possible order of the world and that of reason and truth as well, and Doyle realizes that "the possible order of the world," is now just what the ultimate contest between good and evil is called upon to determine. Descartes creates the possibility that total deception can lead to absolute truth defined as certitude. We could say that the more evil the evil one Moriarty is, the more truth and certitude Holmes has, and this I believe is what our author meant. Certitude can be attained only through the absolute negation and expulsion of all that can be deemed doubtful. We shall see that the focus of "The Final Problem" is centered upon the conflict and opposition separating certitude in life from doubt as to the purpose of life.

The philosopher questions if it is possible God himself could be in on the deception, admitting he has been deceived in small things often, questioning if it is possible God sometimes goes contrary to his own goodness, and "makes me such that I deceive myself." The evil genius he calls "God's double," and the Professor, acting out the Zarathustra legend, is one of a pair of gods; he is an evil god who personifies the Drug, which is deceit, but always remains godhead nevertheless. This situation may be thought of as "dualism," the opposition between the mind and the corporal body, or matter, and Descartes believed dualism must exist. Holmes represents the world of the spirit while Moriarty symbolizes the world of the body, and the two can never be at a peaceful understanding.

The French thinker could be regarded as his own evil entity for he permitted skepticism, and even emphasized doubt as the first step to knowledge, and it was he who first suggested that fideism, the belief that faith alone is the basis of knowledge, so necessary to the medieval mind, rather than reason, may not be the ultimate test of truth, and it was also he who initially employed the division of the world into mind and matter. "Give me matter, and I will build you a world," he asserts in his book of physics, *The World.* With neither God nor spirit, anyone with enough matter could do it.

Descartes believed in delving into the secrets of the universe no matter where the investigation led, and Professor Moriarty hunted for the same skeletons in the same closet. The realm of man, and even God, if the argument were pushed, must be subject to the domination of universal laws, taking nothing into regard except themselves, ignoring the spirit of man, and his God. In *Treatise on Man and the Formation of the Fetus* of 1664, he propounded a theory of the "animal spirit" as being the mechanical principle of motion actuating the lower animals by means of pure mechanism, without feeling or intelligence on their part, that raised a great outcry among his enemies. Every human and animal response is controlled by mere sensation, and even the soul is governed by what he called "the rational soul," a sort of collective intelligence. He is often credited with introducing the mechanical theory of the universe with its implications that man has no free will, and God is not really necessary.

And yet there is another side to the man that takes an almost opposite view of reality, for as did many others, Descartes believed man took part in the divine essence and therefore *a priori* was himself part of the divine. Man bears a certain image and similitude of Deity, having been made in the image of God. Modern science says no; man was created in the mud and returns to the mud, and that's the end of it. Materialism and spiritualism are as far apart as possibility is from actuality, and there can be no reconciliation, in spite of Diderot's cocktail of marble dust and liquid, with the stakes being truly high.

On the other hand, if you were to carry Descartes' philosophy far enough in a certain direction, the direction offered by his first principle, you could quite easily come to the conclusion that there is no universal knowledge since everything is in the mind. If this were so, then we need not trouble ourselves either about pity or repentance, pride or humility, or many other human qualities. There is really ultimately no difference between right or wrong; go a little further and there is no good or evil at all, for everything is the same in the reality of the first principle, "I think, therefore I am." He seems to be telling us we can know nothing of God when he says, "There may be in God an infinity of things that I cannot comprehend, nor perhaps even compass by thought in any way; for it is of the nature of the infinite that it should not be comprehended by the finite." True enough most theologians say much the same thing, but they are usually holding out religion as an alternative to this thought, whereas Descartes has little to say about religion as such.

A number of the wars in which the Frenchman had fought had been struggles over religious or quasi-religious principles, and his own philosophy of strict scientific method and mathematical reasoning may have been a reaction to these slaughters. The authoritarian dogmas of religion, philosophy, ethics, and morals, offered to the blind acceptance of the world, began to take on in his mind the aspect of baseless superstitions. His philosophy is a presentment questioning of the alleged demonstrations and casuistic logic by which religion sought to gain the main aspect of the reasoning faculties of man. Descartes argues for the immortality of the soul, but plants doubt in the thinking mind of those who read him. We are now at the very essence of the struggle put forth in "The Final Problem," with contradiction in general, and these contradictions in particular, being a part of the heart of the matter. The ambiguity of it all, the ambiguity in the mind of Doyle, is the product of a spirit that never ceased learning, thinking, and growing, through its own doubts and thoughts.

The Professor is a genius with "extraordinary mental powers," with a book under his belt on the dynamics of the asteroids, as well as a work on the binomial theorem. The discovery of this theorem is credited to the Persian poet/philosopher Omar Khayyam, and Sir Isaac Newton generalized it. Descartes worked on it heavily, and I have come across the statement that he discovered it, but I must leave that question for others. He wrote an essay with the deceptively simple title "Meteors," which is similar to the subject the Professor explores, and both works are attempts at explaining the workings of the universe.

John Stuart Mill said of Descartes that his body of work "constitutes the greatest single step ever made in the progress of the exact sciences," and a great part of that work was in math, where he discovered the application of algebra to geometry, while in physics he introduced the theory of the evolution of the universe through vortices, and much else. Insisting on the exclusion of metaphysics, final causes, theology, and Providence from physical inquiry, he gave matter a status independent of mind, and his physics showed there was no need of mind to explain the universe. Everything had evolved necessarily from the original chaos of matter and motion, and true enough, motion had been imparted to matter by God, but once given, all proceeded according to law, giving us the universe as it is today. It was an easy step for his followers, among them Moriarty, to place motion inherently in matter such as asteroids, and in matter in general, along with the universe's other laws. The Professor, and others like him, are telling us God is probably dead since he is no longer necessary, thus a good segment of mankind, with Doyle probably among them, would regard Descartes and Moriarty as a pair of truly evil geniuses, and they would throw Newton in to keep them company.

Knowledge of math precedes all other knowledge, Descartes believed. In the Preface to *Discourse on Method* he first expressed his disenchantment with traditional humanist knowledge, which he criticizes because of its lack of a fixed order and the masking of its principles. It is here he announces his project of bringing into being a new kind of science, based upon rules primarily of mathematical derivation. In a famous letter to Marin Mersenne he says, "The knowledge of this order (math) is the key and the foundation of the highest and most perfect science that man can hope to attain, regarding material things; since by its means one can know *a priori* all the diverse shapes and essences of terrestrial bodies." Certitude is what he was after, his success in finding it hinging on the prerequisite of his finding a theory of knowledge based on numbers. Moriarty's knowledge of math will allow him to be equal to his brother/god Holmes, with numbers helping him to make true and certain judgments. Descartes did harbor fears that his new science would be misinterpreted and misapplied, and the Professor is the realization of those fears. Math is looked upon by the French philosopher as a logical order, and that order, or rather the knowledge of it, could easily rule the world, for the theory of "numbers" both precedes and sets-up all other knowledge. The recourse to mathematics involves an accession to a new order whose logical structure escapes the illusions of language and allegory, for it is devoid of its representational character. A person who thinks in terms of numerical arrangement thinks in a more scientific, logical fashion, and therefore is more honest, accurate, and more powerful. The language of math lays claim to absolute truthfulness and as such it presents the possibility of the mastery of the world through symbols and esoteric representations. He is not speaking in allegory here; he means exactly what he says. Even Plato believed a study of mathematics and astronomies would lead men to learn that the gods are not ruled by "human necessities"; human needs and cares, claiming those who can master these fields will learn the "divine necessities," and they may in turn become so much like "gods and demons," as to be "capable of exercising serious supervision over humans." Holmes is the equal of any such being this science could produce, for has not Watson told us he is "a calculating machine," the equivalent at the time to our computers.

Descartes realized math represents far more than it appears to, as do most other disciplines. Although I can't find it in his writings he must have apprehended that numbers are the first step in all science, and it is science that can be used to acquire power over the world. He was familiar with the much repeated and obviously true extract of the Pythagoreans, "Numbers rule the universe," and Nietzsche must have agreed with this for he tells us, "Mathematics is merely the means for general and ultimate knowledge of man." A great deal of irony in that "merely." In his work *Regulae ad directionem ingenii (Rules for the Direction of the Mind)* the Frenchman attempted to develop a generalized logic and a new symbolic language based on math, and Martin

Heidegger, among others, consider this book the first true attempt at formulating modern science, as we know it.

In his *Thoughts on the Interpretation of Nature* Diderot claims nature is so complex, so far beyond our understanding, that at best we shall never know more than small pieces of it, but the fundamental questions will always remain the same. While our understanding is limited, our senses uncertain, and our instruments imperfect, phenomena are infinite, and their causes hidden. "What is our purpose then?" he asks, and answers his own question: "The execution of a work which can never be accomplished and which would be far above human intelligence if it were achieved." Diderot gave science a few centuries before it exhausts its useful potentialities, and like mathematics, is abandoned. It's not important if we disagree with him. Men with the mentality of Moriarty would lay the groundwork for human error and misery, and Diderot and Doyle foresaw things such as the atomic bomb and its consequent amount of evil. Diderot believed religion spared us these errors of thought, and although he is regarded as an enemy of religion this is not true; he was against absolute power and intolerance in any form, but not religion itself. Moriarty would take away man's need for God, indeed would take away God altogether since the knowledge of the laws he is examining, the plotting of the course of a heavenly body, would show the capacity to negate the need for God. His book would rob man of his uniqueness in the universe since the faithful believe that God created man in his own image, and if you take this away, man automatically becomes just another animal. "Always keep in mind that nature is not God; that man is not a machine; that a hypothesis is not a fact; and rest assured that you have not understood me whenever you think you see something contrary to these principles," Diderot puts forth. If the universe is a great organism, he claims, then perhaps it has a soul, and that soul may be God, while a too strict belief in the laws of the universe implies man is machine-like and without a soul.

Let's listen in on a conversation found in *D'Alembert's Dream* before we go any further, for perhaps it will help secure for us the seriousness and depth of the problem in hand. Diderot believed that all we do is determined by our organization, our education, and by the chain of events. One speaker makes the observation that "intelligence allied to very energetic portions of matter," would produce "the possibility of every conceivable sort of prodigy." Dr. Bordeu agrees with this, and then asks, "What is there terrible in this idea? There would be an epidemic of good and evil geniuses: the most constant laws of nature would be interrupted by natural agencies, our general system of physics would become difficult: but there would be no miracles." In *Rameau's Nephew* we have the nephew tell a philosopher, "If I knew history, I could prove to you that evil has always come here below through a few men of genius," adding, "Men of genius are poisonous and that if at birth a child bore the mark of this gift of nature, he should be either smothered or thrown to the dogs." That's a very strong statement, all the more so because we can feel the sincerity in it. The Professor has not been thrown to the dogs, so his energy and intelligence, adding to our general system of physics, will do away with miracles, unless Holmes can stop him. Do away with miracles and you do away with God.

In the entire history of science, Sir Isaac Newton, inventor, scholar, and researcher, stands out as the world's most important figure. The theories he first put forth in light, gravity, motion, optics, and other fields, are still used today in radios, televisions, space shuttles, telescopes, atomic bombs, etc. He was also a great mathematician, perhaps the greatest, with his most important work often regarded as *Mathematical Principles of Natural Philosophy*. The spirit animating this work is Newton's dynamics and his law of universal gravitation, and the application of both to the solar system; what he called "the system of the world," or as it also has been termed, "the dynamical harmony of the heavens." Among much else, the book accounts for "the motions of the planets, the comets, the moon, and the sea." I don't think asteroids could be seen at the time, so they are left out. Newton believed this wondrously complex fabric of stars, planets, and vast empty space, moved with a clock-like predictability that human reason could reduce to a few simple equations, and as such is similar in nature, possibly compatible, with Professor Moriarty's work on heavenly bodies. Kant tells us, "Newton was the first to see order and regularity combined with great simplicity, where hitherto disorder and multiplicity had reigned, and since then comets move in geometric paths."

"The father of modern science," was born is Woolsthorpe, England, on Christmas Day, 1642, which happens to be the year Galileo Galilei, "the father of modern astronomy," died. The year 1642 is important for students of Sherlock Holmes. After a brilliant childhood spent inventing and building things such as water clocks and small windmills, Newton went to Cambridge to begin a lifelong habit of experimentation animated by unceasing curiosity. His interest in optics led him to build a revolutionary telescope that produced a clearer image for its size than any in existence at the time. Descartes believed the telescope (in general) was the most useful invention in history because it increased man's power of sight.

Newton is credited by some to have invented calculus, and then utilizing it to determine much that was previously only guessed at about the solar system. He was a continuator of Descartes' math, Galileo's machines, and Bacon's method, and is thought to have first used the term "experimental method," linking him to the pragmatics. In 1662 he claimed, "I deduced that the forces which keep the planets in their orbs must be reciprocally as the squares of their distances from the centers about which they revolve." This man had truly looked into the secrets of the universe with a range of achievements too long to deal with here, but let us say he was the greatest investigator into the mysteries of God and nature that ever lived, and predictably is, to some minds, an absolute and utter horror; pure evil.

Doyle cannot believe fully in the spirit of Newton; indeed he feels distinctively threatened by it, for he was basically both a religious man and a spiritualist, regarding them as one and the same. Spiritualism pervaded all of Doyle's thoughts, especially in his later life, when he traveled the world carrying its banner. The goal and fundamental presupposition of Newton's research is universal law and order in the material world, not the spiritual world. The materialistic point of view, in reducing or eliminating all spiritual data, all mystery, develops a world that denies man's very rational and balanced desire for a universe invested with genuine significance.

Only one year after finishing at the university, Newton became, as did Moriarty, a Professor of Mathematics. By the age of twenty-three the young Newton had worked out the essentials of calculus, hit upon the crucially important optical law that white light is a mixture of colors (the prism), and grasped the principles of gravitation. Moriarty is a youthful achiever as well, having written his binomial theorem work by the age of twenty-one. Doyle does not claim Moriarty published his book at this young age, since his prototype Newton did not publish until years after having written his work. Newton, like Moriarty, had "come down," as the English say, from Cambridge to London, in Newton's case, to become Master of the Mint, in which capacity he reformed the coinage system of Great Britain.

We are told of Moriarty that while teaching at a university something went wrong for "Dark rumours gathered round him," forcing him to leave. Dark rumors also circulated about Newton while teaching at the university, and he neglected his appearance, health, and friends as gossip abounded over his secret life and ambitions. The dark side of the man came to the surface, prompted possibly by pressure from work and unending conflict with others. He developed an aversion to all food and an almost total inability to sleep, culminating in 1690 when he suffered an alarming mental breakdown characterized by delusions of persecution, forcing him to curtail much of his activities. He accused John Locke, of all people, of trying to embroil him with a woman. Moriarty as well suffers from a persecution complex that hinders his movements, and he blames Holmes for it. Moriarty keeps a dated list of these offenses against himself, for such would be the habit of a mathematician. Even the fact that Moriarty hired others to do his work allies him with Newton, for the man hated all publicity and controversy, so much so that he frequently got friends to publish his papers and conduct his arguments, staying out of the public eye as much as was possible for a man with his degree of celebrity. His conduct was bizarre, but unlike Moriarty, he got rid of his demons and returned to work.

The conflict between Holmes and Moriarty is a reenactment of the contentions Newton found himself involved in during the course of his entire life. A fellow member of the Royal Society, the scientist Robert Hooke, perhaps envious of the attention the much younger man was attracting, was constantly at odds with him over the proper procedures necessary for bringing proof before the Society, and he also attacked Newton's findings on color theory. One of Newton's most vehement opponents was the physician Linus of Liege, who accused him of gross carelessness and of intentionally misrepresenting the results of a number of experiments — a serious charge. Yet another challenge, perhaps the most important one, was the dispute over who discovered calculus, with both the philosopher Leibniz and Newton claiming the uncovering of this system of measuring motion, a question still alive today.

Newton's writings implied that in a sense God had abandoned the world after setting it in motion, something like a cosmic watchmaker making a timepiece and then letting it run by itself. Those who accepted this thought often referred to God as the mechanic of a universe that in turn was mechanical, obeying laws that God, if he existed, could not even change. Once again we are left with no ground for regarding man as a special being; a thought leading to the conclusion that no meaningful moral qualifications are necessary for an act, and man is completely on his own. Pleasure and profit would, or could, become the only criteria for our actions, with this amoral conclusion being the result of the loss of God to man. Moriarty fears that Holmes plans "to bring destruction upon me," death being the only thing he fears since without God there is nothing else to fear. The bleakness of this consideration that human life came into the world as an afterthought speaks for itself.

Movement, such as Moriarty writes about (heavenly bodies are always in motion), is a property of matter, and Newton found that matter, both large and small, attract each other, and with his laws of motion gave an explanation of celestial mechanics. Matter has stress between them that give to the universe a systematic nature, and Newton was so accurate that the discovery of the planet Uranus was facilitated by the use of this theory of gravitation. The linking of matter and energy eliminates the need for God, especially for God as Prime Mover — Aristotle's God. Moriarty and Holmes are contrasting energies being held in rhythmic balance not unlike the world of God, or the world of Newton, for that matter. Newton's thoughts have been interpreted to mean that nature is dead, and therefore aims at nothing. His theories are inconsistent with free will; indeed, they take choice completely away from mankind. The scientific reasoning of Newton presupposes that mental operations have no effect upon nature, while spiritual reasoning emphasizes the belief that thought influences the constitution of the universe, which is why religious people offer prayers for one reason or another. Those, such as the Quakers, believe simply sitting and thinking is communicating with God. William Blake, who fully recognized Newton's genius, but rejected his theories, cried out, "God is not a mathematical diagram!"

Deism is the belief that God may exist, and may have created the world and everything in it, but only according to natural laws he also created, and that God takes no part in the function of the universe or the affairs of man. A deist could, like Moriarty, believe that the only thing that really exists is the law of physics, chemistry, and perhaps math. Another conclusion drawn from deism is that man is an animal, somewhat more advanced, but still an animal, like the others. Newton would have despised the deists, who turned God into a master mechanic, and would have been outraged by the atheists, but Newton could not foresee where his thoughts might lead others who came after him. This devout Christian supplemented his conception of nature by a theism taken straight from the *Bible*, but he seems to have done this more from a sense of guilt than anything else, and he studied the *Bible* so ardently that for a while his friends began to fear his sanity was in the balance. Doyle reads the similarity of this into the situation of the Rev. Jennings, and Newton may have been one inspiration for the character.

Newton helped bring about the Scientific Revolution, in which the uneasy peace between reason and revelation became open warfare, when science (Moriarty) had turned into open rebellion against the faith (Holmes) that had governed Europe, and much of the rest of the world, for thousands of years. All the men of the Enlightenment agreed that Newton's thought was wholly incompatible with divine revelation, believing that where science advanced, religion had to retreat, just as the advance of Moriarty sends Holmes into retreat. This chasing of Holmes across half of Europe is the advance of science upon the coattails of religion. The work of the Enlightenment has often been called a "reckless search for truth," and Moriarty represents "pitiless logic," as Diderot called it, such logic as would reduce a man to an animal motivated solely by self-interest. Professor Moriarty's lantern show found in *The Valley of Fear*, put on for the edification of Inspector MacDonald, is a gesture lifted right out of the history of the Enlightenment when such demonstrations and experiments were popular fare, as well as a means of instruction.

The abyss over which Holmes and the Professor fight are the chasms of logic and attitudes of thought that lie between the devout believing person and the scientific atheist, the philosophical breach existing between mind and matter; those who believe reality adheres only in the mind of God and man, and in the spirit of God and man, represented by Holmes, and those who like Moriarty, believe only in matter, and necessity, and materialism, in a mechanical universe. The questions these two positions raise can be fought over, and constantly are, and the two schools of thought might occasionally find some common ground to stand upon, but the abyss separating them never closes, nor lessens in scope. The whole question of the destiny of man lies in the outcome of the struggle between Holmes and his enemy, and it is not surprising Doyle shows us both personifications of the struggle falling head over heels into the fissure at the falls. It's as though he has become sick of this lifelong battle, tired of trying to locate answers to unending questions, or at least tired of using Holmes as a weapon in the war.

In William Rowan Hamilton, Doyle came across a model for Moriarty nearer to his own time. Hamilton is by long odds the greatest man of science Ireland ever produced. He was born in Dublin in 1805, and when he died there in 1865, he left behind over sixty huge unpublished manuscripts on math giving years of employment to his fellow mathematicians. Young William fell early under the influence of his uncle, Rev. James Hamilton, an accomplished linguist who spoke many languages both ancient and modern. The boy followed suit and became, like Newton, a childhood prodigy, mastering such esoteric subjects as Arabic and Sanskrit before the age of ten. It seems mathematicians, like theologians, are always at each other's throats. One escapade that has come down to us from William's youth was that at one time he challenged a detractor, who had called him a liar, to mortal combat, but the affair was amicably arranged by Hamilton's second, so William cannot be legitimately counted among the great mathematical duelists.

At the age of twelve Hamilton was introduced to an American youth named Zerah Colburn, at the time a student in London who was an unusual character known as the American "calculating boy," for he was capable of doing unbelievable feats of math in his head. William was so impressed and interested, he mastered math in three years, soon writing books on the subject, as well as working on rays in optics. Thus he had begun a career of fundamental discovery, especially in math, as well as the finding of errors in earlier mathematicians' work. He entered Trinity College in 1824, and was soon regarded in the English-speaking world as a second Newton. The young man was later installed as Royal Astronomer of Ireland, Director of the Dunsink Observatory in Ireland where we find him, like Newton and Moriarty, looking into the secrets of the universe, and like these two he is made a professor — a Professor of Astronomy. Hamilton starts working at this time, at the age of twenty-two, on theories of dynamics, and is considered by some to have put that fundamental science into what is perhaps its ultimate, perfect form. E. T. Bell tells us Hamilton's work on optics was found, one hundred years later, to be just what was required in the wave mechanics associated with the modern quantum theory and the theory of atomic structure. Newton also had a hand in this, being Hamilton's forerunner. Hamilton was given every award you could name for his work on optics and math, including a knighthood, but in spite of starting brilliantly, you guessed it, like Newton before him, and Moriarty after him, there are dark rumors at the university. His dark side is evidenced by a disastrous love affair resulting in a bizarre marriage to an invalid, irregular meals or no meals at all, aversion to sleep, and a growing reliance on alcohol. In spite of this Hamilton did what many consider his greatest work in his later life.

The scientists believed the earth traveled around the sun giving us the heliocentric school of thought, while the devout knew the sun revolved around the earth and thus we have the geocentric answer. Doyle introduced this problem in the opening pages of the initial Holmes story, so obviously the history of these opposing theories (ironically enough modern astronomy finds neither one to be absolutely true) had been on his mind for years. He seems to be now attempting to bring some of these thoughts to some sort of aesthetic climax. A man such as Copernicus might have added greatly to our understanding of science, but with his new discovery that the earth was never the center of the universe, mankind was forced to realize he was no longer special, no longer a part of the center, but merely some uninfluential thing on the edge of reality. Before the heliocentric view, man had a more eligible and secure image of himself, thus this scientist can be thought to have aided and abetted the introduction of evil doubt into the world, resulting in a far less eloquent role for mankind, and James Moriarty is one following upon the heels of Copernicus. But up until James Bradley there was always room for doubt. In 1725, Bradley, an English astronomer, discovered what is known as "the aberration of starlight." He recognized that the earth must have always been speeding in an orbit around the sun when he saw that all the stars were tracing little ellipses against the sky. The stars would never be seen to move like this, in this aberration of light, if the earth and the stars were standing stationary, for no movement would be noticeable at all. The light from the stars seemed to move slightly because the earth itself was in motion, and when the earth came back to the point on its orbit where the phenomena was first observed, the line of light tracing the ellipses of the star would be complete. What Bradley proved was that Newton had been justified in his thinking that the sun's position is at the center of our solar system. James Bradley had, like the Rev. Jennings, once been a clergyman, but had resigned his clerical duties to study the secrets of nature. Newton and Bradley delivered a demolishing blow to human pride. Another way available for proving the earth to be in motion is in the events known as eclipses, which could not take place unless the earth and its moon had movement. Inspector MacDonald as we know, paid a visit to Moriarty, and the talk somehow turned to eclipses, with the policeman telling us the Professor explained it all to him.

Moriarty's backbone is built somewhat on William James, as we already noted, with the American philosopher personifying both his being and the being of his enemy, since he is also a model for Sherlock, the spirit of the design being to assert that the agents are corresponding duplicates within the jeopardy balance. The thoughts of Moriarty and William James are comparable in intensity, as well as being the material for James' work, which was the first real attempt to bridge the mind/body gulf; the Cartesian dualism of mind and matter, basic to Western philosophy for three hundred years. He believed neither in a soul nor an all-powerful deity, and his original psychology did abolish soul substance, although he spoke of a neutral stuff, neither matter nor spirit, that could go either way. In this we see the influence of the popular Spiritualist movement of his day, which he studied heavily.

The doctrine that truth is a ready-made reality, which the human mind discovers, was to James a great "*bête noire*," a black beast, so this could be another reason Moriarty is described as being black. James called this view, which is the opposite of pragmatism, at various times, "vicious Intellectualism," "Rationalism," or "Idealism," considering this doctrine the most pernicious and insidious product of the philosophy shop. It should be remembered that the intellectuals, the opponents of the "Churchmen," were just as dogmatic, unyielding, and intolerant as their opposites. The claim that truth was anterior to man, and superior to man, was idolatrous to James, for it demanded that man conform to this truth regardless of his own needs or interests. Such claims were made in the concrete, James saw, in scientific or philosophical determinism, which rejected man's cherished belief in his own moral responsibility. A world of mechanical materialism, he claims, "is ugly, as arithmetic is ugly, and it is non-moral." James compares materialism to a type of horror not unlike a nightmare, adding, "materialism denies reality to the objects of almost all the impulses which we most cherish." The real meaning of the impulses, he says, is something that has no emotional interest for us whatever. "Materialism means simply the denial that the moral order is eternal, and the cutting off of ultimate hopes; spiritualism means the affirmation of an eternal moral order and the letting loose of hope." What he is implying is that whether you believe in matter as the ultimate reality, or

God as the final answer, the world could possibly come to an end, a situation he has just discussed a bit earlier, but only if you believe in God, can the world have a rebirth. The death and rebirth of the world is a fit subject for thought James insists, and Doyle sees it as a fit subject for fiction.

Intellectualism rejected free-will on the grounds of incompatibility with a pre-existing, completely predetermined universe, thus what Moriarty's writings would do is to deny man the assurance his prayers and his powers, such as they are, are relevant to the universe. A belief in God, which the American, in his own way seems to have had, tells us our lives are pertinent, that God in some way recognizes our efforts, however slight the actual recognition is, but keep in mind James is a scientist with great faith in medicine, chemistry, and the scientific method in general. The belief in God might tell man that his actions, like the efforts of Holmes, could be a factor in the destiny of the creation, but fatalism, which follows from the Professor's philosophy, teaches that "All striving is vain," which is in eternal enmity with the pragmatic concept of truth. The world was both a breeding ground and a battleground for good and for evil, James believed, and human contribution is essential in the cosmic struggle; by his participation man's own fate is determined. We seem to be at the very heart of the meaning of "The Final Problem" now, or close to it. For man, life *"feels"* like a real fight — as if there were something really wild in the universe which we, with all our idealities and faithfulnesses, are needed to redeem." The wickedness in the world is to be endured and overcome by human valor, and this is the opposite of fatalism. The Professor would take away man's ability to act, to redeem the world, thus rendering to him a purposeless existence. James believed that "genuine rationality" takes into account aspects of life other than the purely intellectual, which makes of individuals tyrannical dictators, and the tyrannical disposition of Moriarty is established and emphasized at the very opening of the drama.

The misuse of concepts introduces the gravest unintelligibility into our lives, the acceptance of which would make living in the real world impossible. The vicious intellectualists believe "the intelligible order ought to supersede the senses rather than interpret them." The senses, they believed, stood in the way of real knowledge, but James thought knowledge must always remain in contact with sensation, and he shows that conception is not needed for life while sensation is, this because all conceptual concepts originate in the perceptual world. Professor Moriarty personifies falsehood because human concepts falsify reality, almost like a drug. The truly rational will not be discovered by those who test it exclusively by the demands of intellectualism and abstraction, without reference to other equally essential features of knowledge, and without reference to willing and feeling. Now those philosophers who could do away with this kind of thought, James at least once claims, "are those by whom the world is to be saved," the role of Sherlock Holmes, working to bring into being the Redemption. "Those who identify the truly rational with that which is consistent within an abstract scheme of things have been deluded by thinking that their preference for stability and consistency is an objective feature of reality." They judge the facts of nature by their theories instead of judging their theories by the facts, which burst in upon them. The truth does not lie in abstraction James contends; mere abstraction erects a wall against the truth. "True ideas are those that we can assimilate, validate, corroborate, and verify. False ideas are those that we cannot." For him the possession of insight into the truly rational required a 'truth-seeker," and it is Holmes who is this persona. "The absolute things, the last things, the overlapping things, are the truly philosophic concerns; all superior minds feel seriously about them, and the mind with the shortest views is simply the mind of the more shallow man."

Optimism, which is a part of pragmatism, would be the doctrine that thinks the world's salvation inevitable, and James places spiritualism and optimism in the same boat. "But spiritualistic faith in all its forms deals with a world of *promise*, while materialism's sun sets in a sea of disappointment." "If not a blind force but a seeing force runs things, we may reasonably expect better issues." Meliorism is a concept introduced by James as a doctrine rather than a mere attitude. He believed meliorism treats salvation as neither necessary nor impossible. It deals with it as a possibility that "becomes more and more of a probability the more numerous the actual conditions of salvation become." He tells us you may interpret this word salvation in any way you like, a thought that does not go over Doyle's head. The philosopher puts forth that a genuine pragmatist is one who "is willing to live on a scheme of uncertified possibilities which he trusts; willing to pay with his own person, if need be, for the realization of the ideals which he frames." He further claims that by our acts we can make a better world, and we will be given a chance, "a gap that we can spring into," that springing being our act. "Does our act then *create* the world's salvation so far as it makes room for itself, so far as it leaps into the gap?" he asks, and then finds the answer, "*why not?*" This gap for Holmes is to be the abyss of the Reichenbach Falls into which he shall spring to create the world's salvation. He has flung himself into this gap before in "The Red-Headed League," when he sprang into the tunnel of the Enlightenment. James tells us, "In the end it is our faith and not our logic that decides such questions," and that the true philosopher must always be willing to die for what he believes in. Peirce, James' spiritual father, who also seemed to believe in God, a principle or influence which men may call divine, agrees with this. "He who would not sacrifice his own soul to save the whole world, is, as it seems to me, illogical in all his inferences, collectively," he tells us.

If you wish to see it, and it is there to be seen, "The Final Problem" is the duel between the philosophy of Newton, and consequently the universe he holds out to us, based simply on laws such as gravity, and the philosophy of James, and his universe of the spirit. I am simplifying a bit of course. Doyle is right on the money with these philosophical personifications of enemies at each other's throats, for the history of philosophy is to a certain extent that of the clash of human temperaments. Philosophers are men of radical idiosyncrasy who have set a permanent stamp on the history of thought; major figures in the history of mankind. The intensity of the philosopher forms the atmosphere of his times, and his arguments are always severe.

Newton helped introduce the still continuing era of the progress of science, which self-servingly brought about the enlargement of the field, but the diminution of man's importance was carried in his vision. James demands spirit intermixed with his science, confidant that somehow optimism will elevate to the surface. Holmes and Moriarty are abstractions of philosophical systems given character, the character in question adopting human form.

One ultimate intent of the battle between these two elemental spirits: Holmes and Moriarty, is to bring into being, by having cast each other into the abyss, the Great Renovation of the world; the very crux of Zoroastrianism, and many other religions. The Great Renovation results in "the new world," that is to come, under the auspices of Destiny, following the complete collapse of "the old world," and everything that is in it. This renovation occurs immediately upon the conclusion of the combat of the two opposing spirits. The followers of Zarathustra also called this event "the Eternal Recurrence," among other things, for creation was viewed as a turning wheel, with the ultimate termination of the world regarded as "the last turning of the creation in its course." They believe everything comes around again; everything that has been done in the past will happen in the future, an article of faith they share with the Hindus, among others. Holmes bids his adversary Moriarty to take a seat and tell him what is on his mind at the beginning of their only interview, and is answered, "All that I have to say has already crossed your mind." "Then possibly my answer has crossed yours," the detective replies. We have all existed times without number, and all things with us, therefore these two beings have gone through all this before, since the beginning of creation. Holmes remarks, "His appearance was quite familiar to me," yet he also claims that he has never met the man before. Both men know each other well no matter what they say, and Watson plays something of the same game for although we are told that at this point in time he had no knowledge of the Professor and his gang, we learn in *The Valley of Fear* that he knew of this master criminal and his activities years before the dating of "The Final Problem." "There is nothing new under the sun," Holmes told Gregson, "It has all been done before." We are told of Reichenbach Falls that its waters are "roaring forever down," and its "spray hissing forever upward," rendering it the perfect environment for the Eternal Recurrence.

In the *Zend-Avesta* we learn there are certain spiritual and physical battles to be fought between the children of light and the children of darkness. One such conflict lists the one side as being two of Zarathustra's allies, but the commentators tell us one of them may be Zarathustra himself, aligned against one they call "the Dragon," who is assisted by a host of cohorts. Holmes and Watson become "the two foes who meet the Dragon, demon-made; and who are set to meet, to defeat, and to put to flight, that cheat, the *Pairika*, and to contradict the insulting malice of the *Ashemaogha* (the persecuting heretic) and that of the unholy tyrant full of death." There is a good deal of metaphor being thrown around here, but real beings are often thought of, with the enemies of the farmers being unholy, and heretics, and tyrants full of death and malice, just like the Professor. It is thought this particular unholy tyrant was a despot responsible for the arbitrary execution of many of his own subjects. The *Pairika* may refer to a plague of mice, again causing us to realize that real people and real situations are the foes of the farmers. The use of the expression "dragon" reminds us that Moriarty is a being whose head "is forever slowly oscillating from side to side in a curiously reptilian fashion."

But there is only one "great battle," to be fought bringing about the Great Renovation, and in the ancient texts we learn that prior to this encounter Zarathustra and Angra Mainyu held a meeting in which the forces of evil tried to convert Zarathustra to their side. At this assembly each side calls each other names, and just as do Holmes and Moriarty, show each other they are armed with formidable powers, prayers, words, and actual weapons. Zarathustra prays for help from God: "Bendva has ever fought with me; (yea, since he first appeared at hand to threaten, and also to his advantage in strife). He is the most powerful (in brutal might), and (in his predominance) would crush my strength as I seek to win back the disaffected (in my host) through Righteous (Zeal), O Mazda! Come then with gifts of (vengeful) good to (meet) my sorrow. Good Mind, obtain (for me) that Bendva's death." Bendva, the footnotes add, might be a single person or "a band" of men such as the minions of Moriarty. Holmes and his enemy threaten each other with utter destruction, for each knows the death of one spells the fatality of the other.

Just before the actual melee ending the present period of existence, the world will go through an interlude of hostility and confusion brought about when the malevolent spirit lets loose his forces, which is the state of affairs we find as thug after thug tries unsuccessfully to kill Holmes in the early pages of "The Final Problem." They even topple a building on him in their fury, and he is almost killed by a flying brick. In the sacred texts the final clash seems to take place in what can be thought of as a far country, and can be carried out only by two individuals fighting in isolation. "In whose birth and growth Angra Mainyu rushed away from this wide, round earth, whose ends lie afar, and he, the evil-doing Angra Mainyu, who is all death said: 'All the gods together have not been able to smite me down in spite of myself, and Zarathustra alone can reach me in spite of myself.'" "He makes it better for me that I should leave this earth, he, Spitama Zarathustra, the only one who can daunt me." Moriarty told us it is only Holmes who hinders his plans. Interesting that the ancient Persians seem to have regarded the world as being "round."

The fight between the two forces will take place always in the future, and Ahura Mazda is to be aided by "he who would bend his mind (till it attains to) that which is the better and more holy," and this one "must pursue the Daena close in word and action." The pursuing of the evil one takes place when Holmes and Moriarty travel to the falls, for it is actually Holmes who is leading them to their destruction on a mountaintop, as in the *Zend*. The mountains of the mind come into play, for we learn Moriarty is "on a pinnacle," in the annals of crime, and if Holmes can defeat him his career will have "reached its summit." "Never have I risen to such a height," Holmes claims, in justifiable pride at having tracked down the sinful one.

Watson identifies the Swiss falls as the "abyss," and so we do not miss his intentions, repeats this rich word twice in one paragraph in "The Final Problem," linking the struggle to the ancients for it is the only known word we have coming directly from the Assyrian-Babylonian. I actually found a definition for abyss in the *Zend*: "the world of the wicked, into that dark world, made of darkness, the offspring of darkness." The cauldron of the falls "is an immense chasm, lined by glistening coal-black rock," and in imitation of his ancient model, Watson repeats the fact that the place is composed of black rocks. Following this contest the good character is instantly reborn in the new season, and the fiend himself is as long-lived as the world, for as often as he is vanquished he reappears again, just as dark and ferocious as ever. The fact that in the wake of the demise of the twin gods the world still exists exactly as we have always known it to be is proof that everything will go on "forever," a word and reflection expressed repeatedly in "The Final Problem."

Nietzsche considers the doctrine of Eternal Recurrence the "absolute and eternal cyclical repetition of all things," asking "must we not all have already existed?" and "must we not eternally return?" His Zarathustra calls existence a ring remaining eternally true to itself; a world forever turning: "Everything goeth, everything returneth; eternally rolleth the wheel of existence. Everything dieth, everything blossometh forth again; eternally runneth on the year of existence." With his vicious attacks on all that has heretofore been held sacred by European man, Nietzsche attempted, and succeeded, in bringing into being a great renovation of the world of the mind. Professor Moriarty is Nietzsche's malignant dwarf, the epitome of evil; one fashioned to be the contrary of the superman, one who will go out of his way to bring harm to the superman. The dwarf articulates his fear and loathing for Zarathustra in his cry "Either I — or thou!" a sentiment expressed by Moriarty during his interview with Holmes. The two cannot live together or even stand each other's thoughts.

Mankind seems to have an inclination to believe in the history of creation and re-creation as a spiritual confirmation of the oscillations between the two extremes of birth and death. Both Judaism and Christianity borrowed from this archetype religion of the antique Persians, with its certainty in a clash between good and wickedness culminating in the destruction of the universe, followed by its resurrection representing a portion of that legacy. We find it in the Biblical account of the flood, and the salvaging that followed, while Holmes and his adversary as well die in a flood of water. Sir Arthur also knows that this was the aesthetic intention of Melville in *Moby-Dick*, in which the fight between two great forces: Ahab and the whale, culminates in the drowning of their universe. In the original version of *Moby-Dick*, there were absolutely no survivors of the flood, but the publishers made Melville change the ending so there would be someone left alive to tell the story. Doyle knew of this change, as any serious student of literature does. Armageddon, the final definitive encounter of the *Old Testament*, is as well fashioned after this great contest.

Jesus tells us in "Matthew," that he not only believes in "the regeneration," but that he also would witness it himself, and indeed, help bring it into being, for he and his followers never doubted the world would end in their own lifetime, a theme just about every cult since him has taken up, perhaps in imitation of him. Thus we come across this statement by Jesus: "Lo, I am with you always, even unto the end of the world." Mankind improved, will now find itself in a new world corrected, what Jesus called "the Kingdom of God," or "the Kingdom of Heaven." "For the Kingdom of heaven is as a man traveling into a far country," Matthew says, echoing the *Zend*. Jesus knows everything will be the same as it was before, including himself, for he says: "I am the same, yesterday, today, and forever," the beginning and the end at one and the same time: "the Alpha and the Omega." At the moment of Jesus' death we find a scene of this renovation, for the graves were opened and many holy ones came back to life, the temple was rent in two, the earth trembled, and the rocks were blasted. This resurrection of the universe was understood to be, and is called so by the Church Fathers, "the renovation of the human body and of the whole world." We must keep in mind the fact that Watson is writing new scriptures. In "Matthew," Jesus spends a good deal of time explaining who his enemies are, and how they shall torment him in his days of tribulation. "From that time forth Jesus began to show to his disciples, that he must go to Jerusalem, and suffer many things from the ancients and the Scribes, and the chief priests, and be put to death, and the third day rise again." So does Holmes describe to his Apostle John who it is that is assailing him, and tells of the attacks themselves. These are indeed the "Last Days," also known as the "days of tribulation," as announced by the prophets, foreboding the end of the world.

Before Christ will come again to form "the New Order," the *Bible* insists the Devil must be "abyssed." The words dragon and serpent are interchangeable, as in "And the great dragon was cast out, that old serpent, called the Devil, and Satan, which deceiveth the whole world: he was cast out into the earth, and his angels were cast out with him." After this casting out Christ will reign for a period of one thousand years. "And I saw an angel come down from heaven, having the key of the bottomless pit, and a great chain in his hand. And he laid hold on the dragon, the old serpent, which is the devil, and satan, and bound him for a thousand years: And he cast him into the bottomless pit, and shut him up, and set a seal upon him, that he should no more seduce the nations, till the thousand years be finished: and after that, he must be loosed a little time." Notice the evil one's chief trait is deception. To the people of Zarathustra existence was divided into epochs, sometimes called generations, each understood to last one thousand years, as we have already mentioned. The endings of these millennium periods are regarded as emancipation from the reality of existence. Obviously the Hebrew God must obey Destiny, for the Devil would never be let loose unless it was necessary. The law of God shall rule over this new period, which only Holmes can facilitate, his and Arthur Doyle's final gift to their people. In "The Final Problem" the detective claims he has handled "over a thousand cases," a metaphor for this block of time. This new era of God's rule will however be followed by yet again the end of the world as we know it, and the possible triumph of the Devil, probably in the simple belief that an age of light must be pursued by a time of darkness. The Christians borrowed this time frame and made it the dates of the Second Coming; hence many of them expected this occurrence in the years 1000 and 2000. Now Jesus spoke to Satan face to face a number of times, at one point warning him, "Rejoice not against me, Satan, mine enemy, for when I fall I shall arise!" The promise of Christ is that he will redeem mankind at which time, "his foot would bruise the head of the serpent," who had induced Adam and Eve to eat the forbidden fruit of Paradise. Holmes, as Jesus, has made the supreme sacrifice for the atonement of man's sins.

James Boswell took great pains to describe the circumstances surrounding the death of his friend. Johnson had been a sickly man all his life, with one thing or another, and it finally caught up with him in 1784, at the age of seventy-five. He "had now very faint hopes of recovery," Boswell claims, but rather than remain in the comfortable home of a relative, he became filled with "an animated and lofty spirit," that made him restless and excited. His end will be a struggle, for "I will be conquered; I will not capitulate," is how Johnson anticipated his forthcoming end. At this point Boswell reminds us of the great piety of the man, referring to the numerous Prayers and Meditations, he wrote during his lifetime. "It proves with unquestionable authenticity, that amidst all his constitutional infirmities, his earnestness to conform his practice to the precepts of Christianity was unceasing, and that he habitually endeavoured to refer every transaction of his life to the will of the Supreme Being." Thy will be done, becomes the theme of Johnson's death as he accepts his fate. Just before his end Johnson left his beloved London, as did Holmes, and took to traveling, by coach, to such places as his birthplace, and the city of Oxford, where he had friends. Boswell accompanied him on some of these journeys of the soul, journeys in which Johnson knew he was running away from something, once turning to Boswell and asking, "But who can race with death?" The poet/philosopher becomes obsessed at the end with thoughts of the death of Jesus, with his biographer telling us, "For some time before his death all his fears were calmed and absorbed by the prevalence of his faith, and his trust in the merits and *propitiation* of JESUS CHRIST," adding that "He talked often to me about the necessity of faith in the *sacrifice* of Jesus, as necessary beyond all good works whatever, for the salvation of mankind."

In spite of all said about the optimistic attitude of the Great Detective, we observe him traveling to his finish with a pronounced air of fatalism. When the doctor asks where they are going, he is answered with, "Oh, anywhere. It's all the same to me." The final encounter with the lethal force, and its consequences, cannot be avoided; everything has been arranged by Destiny. Going willingly to his death, as Jesus did, is only fulfilling "that which was spoken by the prophets." The Swiss innkeeper, Peter Steiler is a true emissary of Destiny, for he insists upon Holmes visiting the falls, with his words being a study in unyielding fatalism, "We had strict injunctions, however, on no account to pass the falls of Reichenbach, which are about half-way up the hills, without making a small detour to see them." Watson's use of the legal term "injunction" gives to the scene a sense of ultimate judgment. Christ, regardless of knowing he will be betrayed, also by one named Peter, offers no resistance to the performing of his sacrificial role. There is no longer a clear line between will and act, for the two become one as they focus on the necessity of proceeding according to the spirit of the myths. This leads to an interesting development in which Watson, hurrying back to answer a false plea for assistance, encounters a man dressed in black heading toward the falls. "I noted him, and the energy with which he walked, but he passed from my mind again as I hurried on upon my errand." Who did Watson think this man was? He had to have known, at least momentarily, that it was Moriarty, but his mind has been drugged and deceived, something the gods are very good at. Holmes even goes so far as to tell his friend that with the final contest the end will now follow. "Your memoirs will draw to an end, Watson, upon the day that I crown my career by the capture or extinction of the most dangerous and capable criminal in Europe." It will now be a different world, with different memories.

"It has ever been held the highest wisdom for a man not merely to submit to Necessity, — Necessity will make him submit, — but to know and believe well that the stern thing which Necessity had ordered was the wisest, the best, the thing wanted there. To cease his frantic pretension of scanning this great God's-World in his small fraction of a brain; to know that it *had* verily, though deep beyond his soundings, a Just Law, that the soul of it was Good; — that his part in it was to conform to the Law of the Whole, and in devout silence follow that; not questioning it, obeying it as unquestionable," Carlyle tells us, adding that this is "the only true morality known."

Watson says of Holmes, "for all his watchfulness he was never depressed. On the contrary, I can never recollect having seen him in such exuberant spirits. Again and again he recurred to the fact that if he could be assured that society was freed from Professor Moriarty he would cheerfully bring his own career to a conclusion." The word "watchfulness," is a reference to Jesus, who considered his last days, "a watch," asking if none will watch with him when his hour has come. Learning his friend's life is in danger, Watson tells the detective to stay with him for the evening, but Holmes refuses for "he thought he might bring trouble to the roof he was under." Jesus, realizing his enemies are closing in on him, separates himself from his followers so they will not be "scandalized in me this night." Holmes and Watson make plans to meet the following day, and the doctor tells us, "he rose and came out with me into the garden." Here is a reenactment of the "Agony in the Garden," in which Jesus, with Peter, and two sons of Zebedee, one of whom is John the Apostle, go into the garden at Gethsemane to pray and watch. Holmes climbs over the garden wall and leaves in a cab, just as did Jesus go away "a little further," from his followers. In Victoria Station the next morning yet another incident taken from the final days of Jesus is enacted when Watson fails to recognize Holmes disguised as a priest (which Jesus was). It was Peter who "denies" Jesus twice in the morning, claiming not to know the man, hoping to avoid involvement, and this can be thought of as the first denial, while Peter Steiler's insistence upon them visiting the falls can be thought of as the second betrayal. The two investigators travel through England by train, take a boat to Europe, again board a train, and pass through a number of cities before arriving at the Swiss Alps. Starting at Victoria Station, their train stops at Canterbury, travels on to Newhaven, and over to Dieppe. They also stop at stations in such places as Brussels, Strasbourg, and Geneva. Doyle wants us to know that some time has been spent at stations, elaborating on such details as that the pair sat at Strasbourg for a while, spent time at Canterbury and Newhaven, and amazingly enough waited two whole days at the depot in Paris. Every Roman Catholic Church in the world has, running along its two longest sides, sometimes rendered in paint, but usually depicted in small, low relief plaques of wood or plaster, depictions of the fourteen most poignant incidents taken from the last hours of Jesus' Passion, known collectively as the Stations of the Cross, or more commonly, as the Stations, portraying related events of the Crucifixion, such as the Agony in the Garden, Jesus is Stripped, Jesus is Scourged, and so forth. During Holy Week, the week leading to Easter, called the days of tribulation, pious Catholics "do the Stations," meaning they stand in front of each representation for a few moments to pray and reflect upon Jesus' death. Anyone reared in a Catholic home or having attended a Catholic school would be familiar with the ritual, especially in Doyle's day when it was required practice. "The Final Problem" is a reenactment of these Stations; each episode is a halt along the way, eventually leading to a conclusion focused upon death and rebirth. An awareness of the Protestant efforts in the struggle against malevolence emerges in the ploy of the two investigators getting off the train at Canterbury, now a Protestant seat of power, but at one time a Catholic center, as they are being chased by the devil. At Canterbury they "switch" trains, just as the ancestors of today's Protestants switched from Catholicism to the new religion. Having outsmarted the Professor and his minions, they continue their journey.

Stevenson's aristocrat/detective, Prince Florizel is also a Christ figure, even perhaps a godhead, whose function is to rid the world of malice. When the Prince sends a message to Col. Geraldine, having no desire that any but the receiver should know who sent it, he signs it T. Godall. As the Colonel is seeking recruits in the war against evil, in attempting to inform them as to the true nature of the Prince, yet keeping his real identity a secret, he says of the man: "Three days ago the person of whom I speak disappeared suddenly from home; and, until this morning, I received no hint of his situation. You will fancy my alarm when I tell you that he is engaged upon a work of private justice. Bound by an unhappy oath, too lightly sworn, he finds it necessary, without the help of law, to rid the earth of an insidious and bloody villain. Already two of our friends, and one of them my own born brother, have perished in the enterprise. He himself, or I am much deceived, is taken in the same fatal toils. But at least he still lives and still hopes, as this billet sufficiently proves." The Prince has been missing three days, but now "he still lives," and will continue the fight. When the Prince and the President of the Suicide Club finally find each other, they go beyond sight and hearing and fight a sword duel, just as Holmes and the Professor have their duel in our knowledge, but not within our sight. Although the Prince succeeds in killing the President, it is understood evil itself cannot be destroyed for "that hound of hell" is dead, yet Florizel knows that even revenge cannot be attained if the end is deep enough, asking, "The ill he did, who can undo it?" and adds that "a thousand other innocent persons would be none the less dishonored and debauched," regardless of the fact that one evil person has been destroyed. The use of the number one thousand is of the utmost importance here, and may even be the original instigation for "The Final Problem," being written. Remember, "Prince of Peace," is a title used for Jesus.

Belief in the renovation of the world colored all of Doyle's life and art. Halley's Comet was due to approach earth in the year 1904, ten years following the writing of "The Final Problem," and there was already speculation at the time as to the possibility of this being the end of the world. In *The Poison Belt*, a non-Holmes novel, we have a tale of the end of the world due to a celestial event, complete with an "end of the world party," a phenomenon popular with the approach of Halley's Comet. The sense that a great cosmic change is inevitable also permeates all of Doyle's spiritualist writings, and he actually seems to have regarded the First World War as a great Armageddon eventually leading to the renovation, as we read in his *The History of Spiritualism*. Sir Arthur envisioned this clash as one facet of a divine plan that had been prophesied, and would lead to a purer, utopian state, and the man actually seems to have died still believing in this coming Great Renovation.

Entering the railroad cabin at Victoria Station, Watson believes the space to be empty except for a "venerable Italian priest," who it turns out, is Sherlock in disguise. The use of this devise of the Catholic priest points out to us the Catholic Church's constant struggle with evil. It is the "priest of his people," Nietzsche, speaking in semi-metaphor, emphasizes, who has the function of protecting the "herds," meaning both the folk and the cattle, and Jesus as we know, was a priest of his people. The priest fights with "cunning, hardness, and stealth against anarchy, and against the ever imminent break-up inside the herd." "The ascetic priest must be accepted by us as the predestined savior, herdsman, and champion of the sick herd: thereby do we first understand his awful historic mission." Also, "He must be the natural adversary and scorner of every rough, stormy, reinless, hard, violently-predatory health and power." The sick and weak arouses the predatory instincts of the healthy and must protect themselves against their onslaughts. The priest "will not be spared the waging of war with the beasts of prey, a war of guile (of "spirit") rather than of force, as is self-evident." The priest himself becomes "a new type of the beast of prey," who, when necessity demands, will "come on the scene with bearish seriousness, venerable, wise, cold, full of treacherous superiority, as the herald and mouthpiece of mysterious powers." Arthur is a word meaning "bear." Holmes is not just a priest, but also a venerable one. The Catholic and Protestant clergy, according to Nietzsche, "think like the savior, and think of themselves as the savior." Sherlock Holmes becomes an avatar or incarnation of God, who appears periodically to protect his people and the world from disaster during epochs when it is bent upon its own destruction, and evil prevails. The God "descends," as it were, as did Jesus, Buddha, and Vishnu, among others, from "his state of glory," and taking a human form adequate to meet each particular crisis, rescues and renews creation. Nietzsche, ironically enough, has often been accused of hating the Church and the priesthood, in fact all religions, but that does not seem to be true, for he emphasizes that he hates only the outward trappings of the priest, adding that for the ascetic priest he feels only love.

In *Heroes* Carlyle tells us Dante, minus his misery, would have made a good priest or prior. "Dante does not come before us as a large catholic mind; rather as a narrow, and even sectarian mind: it is partly the fruit of his age and position, but partly too of his own nature," adding that Dante's greatness lies in his depth, not in his range or scope, which puts us in mind of Holmes, judging from Watson's list of his intellectual accomplishments and failures. Dante's intense poetry ("I know nothing so intense as Dante.") deals with the war between good and evil, for "It expresses, as in huge world-wide architectural emblems, how the Christian Dante felt Good and Evil to be the two polar elements of this Creation, on which it all turns; that these two differ not by *preferability* of one to the other, but by incompatibility absolute and infinite; that the one is excellent and high as light and Heaven, the other hideous, black as Gehenna and the Pit of Hell! Everlasting Justice, yet with Penitence, with everlasting Pity, — all Christianism, as Dante and the Middle Ages had it, is emblemed here." All of Christianity, not just any one branch, must exercise its prerogatives in the conflict. "Are not all true men that live, or that ever lived, soldiers of the same army; enlisted, under Heaven's captaincy, to do battle against the same enemy, the empire of Darkness and Wrong?" The priest, according to Carlyle, "is a kind of Prophet; in him too there is required to be a light of inspiration, as we must name it. He presides over the worship of the people; is the Uniter of them with the Unseen Holy. He is the spiritual Captain of the people; as the Prophet is their spiritual King with many captains: he guides them heavenward, by wise guidance through this Earth and its work." The priest is the prophet of his people who enlightens the daily life of his parishioners; a sort of prophet for the people who does not overwhelm them, as would a true prophet, and all prophets, as we know, always carry a tall staff, such as the alpine stock Holmes brings with him to Switzerland.

A good priest, Carlyle tells us, is a good reformer who has the ability to see through the mystery of life. "He is a believer in the divine truth of things; a *seer*, seeing through the shews of things; a worshipper, in one way or the other, of the divine truth of things: a Priest, that is. If he be not first a Priest, he will never be good for much as a Reformer." Luther, a Catholic monk for the first half of his life, is chosen by Carlyle as a perfect example of the reformer/priest, claiming "it was his task to get acquainted with *realities*, and keep acquainted with them, at whatever cost: his task was to bring the whole world back to reality, for it had dwelt too long with semblance! A youth nursed up in wintry whirlwinds, in desolate darkness and difficulty, that he may step forth at last from his stormy Scandinavia, strong as a true man, as a god: a Christian Odin, — a right Thor once more, with his thunder-hammer, to smite asunder ugly enough *Jotuns* and Giant monsters!" And of Luther's sufferings, "the deep earnest soul of the man had fallen into all manner of black scruples, dubitations; he believed himself likely to die." The analogy becomes even stronger, "The essential quality of him was, that he could fight and conquer; that he was a right piece of Human Valor. No more valiant man, no mortal heart to be called *braver*, that one has record of, ever lived in that Teutonic Kindred, whose character is valor. His defiance of the 'Devils' in Worms was not a mere boast, as the like might be if now spoken. It was a faith of Luther's that there were Devils, spiritual denizens of the Pit, continually besetting men." We are even offered some justification for the sense of the power of destiny found in the fatalistic death journey of Holmes as Carlyle speaks of Luther's end. "In his latter days, after all triumphs and victories, he expresses himself heartily weary of living; he considers that God alone can and will regulate the course things are taking, and that perhaps the Day of Judgment is not far." The Reformer, we are told, longed for one thing only, "that God would release him from his labour, and let him depart and be at rest." "I will call this Luther a true Great Man; great in intellect, in courage, affection and integrity; one of our most lovable and precious men. Great, not as a hewn obelisk; but as an Alpine mountain, — so simple, honest, spontaneous, not setting up to be great at all; there for quite another purpose than being great!"

Carlyle speaks in general: "Every such man is the born enemy of Disorder; hates to be in it: but what then? Smooth Falsehood is not Order; it is the general sumtotal of *Disorder*. Order is *Truth*, — each thing standing on the basis that belongs to it: Order and Falsehood cannot exist together." It is "the Hero-priest," "who does what is in *him*," "and wears out, in toil, calumny, contradiction," to create "a noble life," and "to make a God's Kingdom of this Earth."

Holmes meets his death with bravery and determinism, like Ahab; both going to their fate in a "mechanical" way, a word used much in the last episodes of *Moby-Dick*. Ahab's harpoon, carried on the last hunt, becomes Holmes' alpine stock. Color symbolism plays a role in *Moby-Dick* for Ahab is described as black, while his enemy the whale is white; they are opposites. In Japan, where Moby Dick was first brought to the knowledge of the world, white is the color of death. Ahab has killed his evil double the white whale with both now plunging together into the abyss intertwined in harpoon ropes; we are told Holmes, and his enemy Moriarty, no doubt died, "locked in each other's arms."

The hero for Carlyle is one who can lead mankind, "out of darkness into light." "Is not such a one a true Hero, and Serpent-queller; worthy of all reverence! The black monster, Falsehood, our one enemy in this world, lies prostrate by his valour: it was he that conquered the world for us!" It is the giant snake the Greeks called Python that lived in a cave on Mount Parnassus and was killed by Apollo, freeing mankind from darkness and fear, who was afterwards called "Apollo Python," and Holmes has already played

Apollo in "The Greek Interpreter," and will be called back for a curtain call in "The Empty House."

Professor Moriarty is black for he is a "shadow," of a good god. He is what the Germans call a "*doppelgänger*," an evil double of a person, often represented as an evil shadow or ghost image that goes everywhere with you. It's something like a pookah, but it is you yourself. The heroic vision forever stresses light and clarity over chaos, annihilation, and ignorance, even while refusing to deny the necessary and challenging role of this shadow or *doppelgänger*, in whatever form.

Holmes fights Moriarty at the town of Meiringen, and no serious student of English literature can see the prefix "meir" without his mind drifting to thoughts of *Beowulf*. Meir recalls "meer," a German word for sea, or arm of the sea, in our case an allusion to the river and its waterfall at Meiringen. Doyle uses the word "mere," its Old and Middle English equivalent, four times in "The Musgrave Ritual" to mean a place of water. The earliest actual manuscript of the saga of *Beowulf*, in Old English, dates from about the year 1000 A.D., but the work undoubtedly reached literary formulation about two centuries earlier. The work was composed to be projected in public performance, to be sung or spoken aloud, and is the first long poem of the Northern world to be transplanted from this oral tradition to a literary mode; it is regarded as the beginning of English literature. As such it would have been of great interest to Doyle.

Beowulf survives in only one version, a manuscript housed in the British Museum. Each generation translates the work differently, putting emphasis on various aspects of the complicated poem to suit its needs, and unfortunately I do not know which version Doyle used— it would make for nicer accuracy of detail.

The action of the poem lies in the Southern Scandinavia of the fifth and sixth centuries and contains no reference to Britain. In the opening of "The Final Problem," Holmes tells us he just finished a case in which he was "of assistance to the royal family of Scandinavia," so he probably just returned from that part of the world. There is no actual royal family of Scandinavia; the area is divided into nations, each with their own government, although some of these states do maintain royal families. Doyle may have wanted us to read this statement in the plural for Beowulf, the hero, assisted a number of families in his own lifetime. The poem opens with the information that what we are about to hear has already happened in the recent past, and in the opening statements of "The Final Problem," Watson serves the identical purpose as the ancient poet, reminding us quite deliberately that what he is about to narrate has also already occurred.

The main story is the account of the adventures of the young, and later mature hero, Beowulf, the ultimate in human achievement in an heroic age. This is the primary theme of all heroic poetry: the prowess, strength, intelligence, and courage of the single man, undismayed and undefeated in the face of all adversaries and in all adventures. Even in brief summary, the parallels to "The Final Problem" are obvious. Beowulf travels by ship and land from one northern country to another to fight evil, just as Holmes journeys from nation to nation, starting in Scandinavia, to battle the Professor. In his youth Beowulf achieves glory in a foreign land by fighting and killing first the monster Grendel, in King Hrothgar's hall, then Grendel's mother in an underwater cave. When he succeeds in this undertaking he is presented with a gift of gold from a queen, with the royalty of the epic being called "givers of treasure." We can be sure the royal families Holmes has just helped rewarded him for his efforts. The poem is essentially a vengeance tale, for the monster Grendel commits outrages upon the people because "the blood-price was unpaid." Perhaps the "blood atonement" aspect of the work is what attracted Oliver Wendell Holmes to the poem for I know he mentioned it at least once, in a speech. One of the allies of Beowulf is Wulfgar, a "Wendel prince," Wendel being another name for the Vandal tribe, and of course Oliver Holmes' middle name. Beowulf's name means "bear," or, as some believe, "bear-wolf," and the name Arthur is Old Anglo-Saxon for bear. For most of his life Doyle kept a bear skull on his desk to remind himself of this fact.

When Holmes meets Moriarty at the falls, he lays aside his staff, although it would make a good weapon, for he must conquer evil using his own power, just as Samson killed the lion with his bare hands, and Hercules is always pictured as having carefully laid aside his bow before attacking and killing the Nemean lion. The lion was the symbol of evil to the ancients, and it must be killed by simple human effort. Beowulf, like Holmes, has weapons, but insists upon fighting alone, and hand-to-hand. One interpreter of Beowulf's name thinks it could be a reference to the fact that he kills his enemies with a bear hug. Beowulf himself is a sort of monster: a twin of this dragon-like monster, and both taken together are referred to as "the terrible ones." The bear and the dragon: one a real being, the other mythological, but just as real to the hearers of the poem, were the two most vicious land animals the Scandinavians could envision.

Although Beowulf and his men may not be Christians (the question is still open), the poet obviously is, and the work is brimming with Christian symbolism and morals, while some students of the work even consider Beowulf a Christ figure. The story is not of a hero's fortunes against three beasts, but of a fighter defending mankind against its enemies, who are "from hell," and live in "the land of monsters," while to fight these beings is "to encompass evil." They are bringers of death, and as in the case of "The Final Problem," the theme of the piece could be thought of as "man against death." Beowulf, since he is king, reserves the prerogative of fighting the evil ones himself, but he shall receive help from God. Grendel, the first one the hero encounters, is much like Moriarty, for he too is almost invisible and unseen in the black night, yet he can strike terrible and bitter blows. When he dies we are told, "Hell received his heathen soul." Grendel and his mother seem to be part human for Grendel has arms, hands, fingers, and fingernails, not unlike a man, and we can assume his mom does as well. Professor Moriarty is human, but animal imagery comes in when he is described as having a "rounded back," not unlike a dragon, and let's not forget his reptilian oscillation.

The clash between Beowulf and Grendel begins much as does the contest between Holmes and his enemy, for the Baker Street apartment has been burned out by the monster, and one act of violence auguring the coming of Grendel is the burning down of "the world's palace," a reference to the hall of Heorot. The fight takes place in the palace hall, the demon is injured but escapes in the night to "the monster's mere-pool," for he seems to live underwater at least part of the time, and he dies there in a seething pool. The mother also inhabits a pool of filthy "dread waters," and now she exists solely to nurse thoughts of revenge against Beowulf. This fiend lives near a waterfall, for "a torrent of water pours down dark cliffs and plunges into the earth, an underground flood," and this terrible place and the vicious whirlpool at its base is vividly described a number of times. She dies in the whirlpool, ripped apart by Beowulf and the current. When this mother/monster is killed in this hand-to-hand combat we are told, "the holy God, gave out the victory; the Ruler of the Heavens rightly settled it."

In his mature years, after having ruled as king for fifty years, Beowulf goes out once more to fight yet a third dragon which has been destroying the farms of his people. This one protects a treasure hidden in a barrow on the moor, has lived "a thousand winters in the womb of earth," and can "vomit flames and burn the bright dwellings" of mankind. Indeed this one burns Beowulf's own hall with his breath, giving us a real personification of Moriarty. This last struggle displays Beowulf's acceptance of his responsibility toward the welfare of his people, for a feeling of the inevitable finds voice in a sense of foreboding as we are reminded that Sigemund, the great mystical dragon-slayer was killed in a fight with just such a creature. The poet realizes these two must fight, but mutually shall die, and also that both combatants are aware of this. The saga contains numerous references to the overwhelming power of fate (everyman's monster), or, as they called it, "wyrd," from which we get our modern word "weird." The emphasis is not upon individual mortality but rather fate itself, the pattern of things as they must be.

Beowulf, like Holmes, has faced many dangers, and both recount them at this point, telling of their endeavors against evil. The detective reminds Watson of his cases: "forgery cases, robberies, murders," adding, "In over a thousand cases I am not aware that I have ever used my powers upon the wrong side." The heroes are resigned to their deaths as bravely as possible, with the king pictured as "death-eager," and interestingly enough he is depicted now as a man, "wandering." The den of this last serpent is filled with a stream of "fire-blast" and "heat" in his "store-house," or like the abyss of Reichenbach Falls, which Watson tells us, had a spray that "rolls up like the smoke from a burning house." A brave soul named Wiglaf, a shield bearer, volunteers to assist the king in his final struggle with this monster who is so ferocious the very ground shakes from his bellowing. Beowulf uses weapons on this one, breaking two swords, and finally killing him with a knife. The hero is fatally wounded but the animal's den is filled with gold, and this the people now have, a gift from their dying lord. The people's needs come first is one meaning of all this; and sacrifices must be made. Both combatants are dead; the poem ends with Beowulf's funeral, and a prophecy of disaster for his people, the Geats, for we are warned the Merovingian Franks and the Swedes will descend upon the Geats now that their champion is gone, so you could say their world has come to an end. Beowulf is buried overlooking the sea on his coast, just as Holmes retires to a farm on his coast, while the dragon is thrown over the cliff into the abyss; "let the waves take him."

Holmes dies like a true Northman, for Carlyle says, "It is doubtless very savage that kind of valour of the old Northmen. Snorro tells us they thought it a shame and misery not to die in battle; and if natural death seemed to be coming on, they would cut wounds in their flesh, that Odin might receive them as warriors slain. Old kings, about to die, had their body laid into a ship; the ship sent forth, with sails set and slow fire burning it; that, once out at sea, it might blaze up in flame, and in such manner bury worthily the old hero, at once in the sky and in the ocean!" The dead now went to live in Valhalla, "the hall of the slain." The old Norse despised death by old age, calling it "a cow's death," rather than one fit for a man. Holmes, in the waters of the abyss, is dying at sea, and in battle, with the hissing vapor of the falls serving symbolically as the smoke of the burning longboat. The one thing that was needful for a Norseman was "*to be brave*," when faced with this "Destiny inexorable, which it is useless trying to bend or soften," and "has appointed who is to be slain." A man must trust himself to "the upper Powers," which controls destiny, if he hoped to ever see Odin. In this drama Sherlock plays the role of Thor, killing the World Serpent, supreme symbol of evil in Norse mythology, and he will portray the character again in "The Empty House." Carlyle talks of, "the *Ragnarok*, Consummation, or *Twilight of the Gods*," a persistent theme in Norse literature, where, "The Gods and Jotuns, the divine Powers and the chaotic brute ones, after long contest and partial victory by the former, meet at last in universal world-embracing wrestle and duel; World-serpent against Thor, strength against strength; mutually extinctive; and ruin, 'twilight' sinking into darkness, swallows the created Universe." The gods are referred to in the phrase, "partial victory by the former," and we are reminded that Moriarty has formerly charged Holmes with nearly winning this war during their meeting in London. "The old Universe with its Gods is sunk; but it is not final death: there is to be a new Heaven and a new Earth; a higher supreme God and Justice to reign among men," Carlyle tells us in words reminiscent of the *Zend-Avesta*, and adds, "Curious: this law of mutation, which also is a law written in man's inmost thought, had been deciphered by these old earnest Thinkers in their rude style; and how, though all dies, and even gods die, yet all death is but a Phoenix fire-death, and new-birth into the Greater and the Better!" Carlyle reminds us, "this old Paganism of our Fathers," "is in *us* yet, that old Faith withal!" and, "To know it consciously, brings us into clearer and clearer relation with the Past, — with our own possessions in the Past. For the whole Past, as I keep repeating, is the possession of the Present; the Past had always something *true*, and is a precious possession. In a different time, in a different place, it is always some other *side* of our common Human Nature that has been developing itself." The old paganism was the religion of our fathers, and is our religion still, whether we know it or not. In the Preface to

The Case Book of Sherlock Holmes, published in 1927, as Doyle laments he must finally let Holmes and Watson pass on, he tells us hopefully, "Perhaps in some humble corner of such a Valhalla, Sherlock and his Watson may for a time find a place..."

We must try to answer the all-important question, why Switzerland? Doyle could have arranged things so that just about any cliff or precipice would have symbolically served his purpose; the crags of Scotland would have done, but immense heights and a great waterfall were necessary for a struggle of this magnitude. Peter Steiler owns the inn the two detectives stay at, with Peter Steiler being a Latin and German combination of words meaning "rock that is steep," or "a cliff." Watson calls him "the elder," which is a religious term, as well as meaning "father." Nietzsche's conception of Zarathustra as being the conveyor of his thoughts to the world took hold of him while he and a friend, Peter Gast, were staying at an inn in the Italian mountains, and he wrote a good deal of *Thus Spake Zarathustra* while in the Swiss Alps where he went for his health. Doyle makes of such a location both the death place of his hero as well as his new birthplace, for Holmes according to the law of Eternal Recurrence, is immediately reborn, although I admit our author probably had not actually intended to bring him back to life. In talking of Peter Gast, Nietzsche assures us that he too is "one who had been born again."

Descartes had visited Switzerland in 1622, and the James brothers, William in particular, had spent a good deal of time there. Both William and Henry received some of their education in the country, and William's children were schooled there as well. William was a mountain climber who often sported in the New York mountains, "the Switzerland of the New World," and it was following one such strenuous climb that he suffered a heart attack which killed him. He had taken a long walking tour of Switzerland in 1892, and Holmes may be recasting this trip.

At the town of Oberammergau in the German Alps, there was located the home theater of the Passion Play, the re-creation by actors and actresses of the last days of Christ, still found there and still popular. Henry James, Jr. attended this play in 1886, after which he made a stopover at Innsbruck coming down through Italy to Venice and ultimately to Florence, Dante's city. Oliver Wendell Holmes had gone mountaineering in the Swiss Alps accompanied by the English writer Leslie Stephen, while on a visit to Europe in 1866, returning with his wife in 1881. Sherlock Holmes is in a sense re-creating all of these trips, and then some.

Doyle's young wife Louisa showed signs of a lung problem as early as 1892, just as the writer was gaining popularity and wealth. The two set off on a series of trips to escape the damp British winters hoping to find a healthier climate for Louisa's illness, just about the only option open to them at the time. They were trying to run away from death, or at least delay its inescapableness. Both New York and Switzerland were popular destinations for those suffering from lung ailments. James Fenimore Cooper had taken his own wife to Switzerland for her health in 1832. It was on their second trip that the Doyles gazed in astonishment at the Reichenbach Falls in Oberland, while Nietzsche and his sister had visited the town in the summer of 1877, and must have visited the falls. Unfortunately Louisa's malady seems to have worsened in the Alps, and the Doyles returned to London, but almost immediately returned, this time to Davos, in search of purer air. All this occurred in 1893, the year Doyle wrote "The Final Problem," in which he used the ploy of luring Watson away from Holmes at the falls with the story of an English lady stopping at an inn, after having visited Davos, in the last stage of consumption, and needing the help of an English doctor. Doyle, the English physician, who cannot help his own wife, tries to write out his fears for the future. In November of 1893, just after his father's bizarre death by swallowing his tongue in an epileptic fit, and facing his wife's forecasted death by TB, which was always fatal, Doyle joined the British Society for Psychical Research, and his life as a believer in Spiritualism began in earnest.

The title "The Final Problem," amounts to a sort of pun on *The Last of the Mohicans*. One famous scene of combat in Cooper's novel is set on a small island of land surrounded by a great waterfall on the upper Hudson River. A struggle to the death between Major Heyward and a Mohawk ensues with the men using guns, then weapons such as swords, tomahawks, and knives. The contest ends with the Indian falling "over the dizzy height into a neighboring cavern of the falls." He would gladly die if he could but take Heyward with him, for we are told that during the height of the fight "Heyward felt the grasp of the other at his throat, and saw the grim smile the savage gave, under the revengeful hope that he hurried his enemy to a fate similar to his own, as he felt his body slowly yielding to a resistless power, and the young man experienced the passing agony of such a moment in all its horrors." As the Englishman realizes he will not also fall over the falls, "his charmed eyes were still riveted on the fierce and disappointed countenance of his foe, who fell sullenly and disappointed down the irrecoverable precipice." The fight between these two men locked in a death struggle on the edge of a watery height is illustrated either on the inside, or more often on the cover, of just about every copy of *The Last of the Mohicans* I have ever come across, and it was thoughts of this fierce duel to the death that led me to discover the associative connection between Cooper and Doyle in the first place.

Hawkeye's archenemy Magua, "Le Renard Subtil" (the Subtle Fox) as the French call him, is treacherous, cruel, filled with hate, and driven by obsessive lust for vengeance. He is "goaded incessantly by those revengeful impulses that in a savage seldom slumber," and his chief methods are deceit and duplicity, examples of which he shows many times. He is an outsider, a renegade, with loyalty to none: not to his own people, not to the white partisans, and certainly not to any code of honor. He is a member of one tribe but in his guile will pass himself off as a member of any tribe if it will suit his purpose. "At such moments it would not have been difficult to have fancied the dusky savage the Prince of Darkness, brooding on his own fancied wrongs, and plotting evil," and Cooper calls his followers "imps," while Hawkeye at one point says of them, "in calling them devils you have scarcely misnamed them." We are told of Professor Moriarty that he has malignant joy, at the contest to come, this unholy happiness reflecting

Magua's love of vengeance and violence. Hawkeye and Magua, at the climax of the story finally face each other in a struggle to the death on the edge of a cliff whose valley lies "a thousand feet below." The scout has been tracking the Indians and their prisoners and overtakes them on the summit of a mountain, but too late, for Magua, in a fit of rage, kills his captives rather than release them, even the women. Even in a war without rules there are limits, and this goes too far, for the captives cannot now be exchanged for prisoners or guns, nor can their scalps be taken. When the scout views the slaughter, he searches out Magua who, rather than face his foe, attempts to flee the summit. Hawkeye's "keen eye took a single look at the victims, and then shot its glances over the difficulties of the ascent in his front. A form stood at the brow of the mountain, on the very edge of the giddy height, with uplifted arms, in an awful attitude of menace." The renegade is on the verge of escaping as he tries to leap over the brow of the mountain, but he succeeds only in securing a handhold on its rim. Holmes' alpine stock is also a symbol of the long rifle Hawkeye is never without. The Huron is about to pull his body over the edge, making good his escape when Hawkeye raises his gun. "The surrounding rocks themselves were not steadier than the piece became, for the single instant that it poured out its contents. The arms of the Huron relaxed, and his body fell back a little, while his knees still kept their position. Turning a relentless look on his enemy, he shook a hand in grim defiance. But his hold loosened, and his dark person was seen cutting the air with its head downwards, for a fleeting instant, until it glided past the fringe of shrubbery which clung to the mountain, in its rapid flight to destruction." Cooper does not use the word "abyss" here, but he does so elsewhere in his novel.

The ancients place the battle between the good and evil spirits on both a mountain summit and on the site of a waterfall. In *Thus Spake Zarathustra*, in the section called "The Wanderer," Nietzsche imitates the ancients by having his philosophical personification lament that his hard ascent and lonesome wanderings have led him to his last summit. The old warrior now stands before "that which hath been longest reserved for me." The spirit of this is as fatalistic as is that of Jesus, or Holmes, and the philosopher is proud of his alter ego's courage at the end. "He, however, who is of my nature doth not avoid such an hour: the hour that saith unto him: Now only dost thou go the way to thy greatness! Summit and abyss — these are now comprised together! Thou goest the way to thy greatness: now hath it become thy last refuge, what was hitherto thy last danger! Thou goest the way to thy greatness: it must now be thy best courage that there is no longer any path behind thee!" "Everything is fate," Nietzsche assures us, "thou shalt, for thou must!" adding that Zarathustra recognizes his destiny and proclaims, "Well! I am ready. Now hath my last lonesomeness begun." Zarathustra speaks of a vision he had of finding himself wandering in the mountains and coming across, "A path which ascended daringly among boulders, an evil, lonesome path, which neither herb nor shrub any longer cheered, a mountain-path, crunched under the daring of my foot." The intention is that he is lost and must strive to reach upwards. "Upwards: — in spite of the spirit that drew it downwards, towards the abyss, the spirit of gravity, my devil and archenemy." Notice it is "the spirit of gravity," Newton's little contribution to science, that is dragging the poet downwards to the abyss.

In the Persian myth the fight between the warring forces, in the form of Atar, a fire-god, and Azhi Dahaka, a dragon, takes place in a sea into which all the waters of the earth fall down with the winds and the clouds. The scene is chaos itself with seas boiling over amid great roaring caused by a rushing volume of water equal to all the rivers of the earth. The followers of the good God worry if they are up to the battle, "And how shall we drive the Demon of the Lie hence from us? Aye, how shall we, the prophets who are yet to serve and save thy people, drive the Drug from hence, so that we, having power over her as being utterly without power, may drive her hence with blows from the seven *Karshvars*, for the dislodgement of the entire world of evil?" The entire world is understood to end now and the ancient texts tell us, "back and forth," the battle raged with the two antagonists fully aware of the outcome. In "The Empty House," our author will describe for us the actual fight, having missed the opportunity here. When Holmes first encounters Moriarty at the falls he finds him "standing upon the narrow pathway which led to safety," and reads "inexorable purpose in his gray eyes." The two come to grips and both go over the cliff into the abyss, perishing in the chaos of creation. The terrified Danes, listening to Beowulf killing Grendel heard, "the sobs of the damned one bewailing his pain," and Moriarty utters "a horrible scream." Doyle must account for the fact that Sherlock is still alive, so we learn later that only one fell into the pit, but we must not think of that at this point in time since this was not the original intention. With the death of the two opposing spirits the Great Renovation of the world now takes place right before our eyes, and the new world seems exactly like it was before, but that is as it should be.

The waterfall is named Reichenbach, with "reich," meaning, in German, "royal," or "right rule," the right rule that now is to be established on the world. Christ and the anti-Christ have perished, but Jesus had left his Apostle John to carry on his work. It is Jesus who in the "Book of Matthew," cures the woman with the hemorrhage whose faith was so strong she correctly believed she would be cured of her "issue of blood," if she would but touch the hem of Jesus' garment. His Apostle John will carry on in his absence, for we are told that Watson is being called to cure a woman with hemorrhage, and we know that the Apostles were given the power to cure illness "in the name of Jesus," but in spite of this it is still a great tragedy, for the world without its Savior is now like an empty house.

CHAPTER THIRTEEN. IMMORTAL AS MAN HIMSELF

The public outcry over the death of their champion Holmes was unmistakably and understandably loud and bitter. Even his mother was outraged that her son Arthur, a mere mortal, had abetted in the commission of this hideous crime, and she was ready to disown him for it, so ten years later, after killing him off, Doyle decides to bring Holmes back and thus in "The Empty House" we find him returning to London as though from the dead to once again take up the challenge of evil. Ostensibly the detective has returned to help solve the singular murder of a young nobleman, Ronald Adair, shot in his locked second story bedroom by an unknown. The case is a "locked room mystery," reminiscent of Poe's "The Murders in the Rue Morgue." Holmes, in disguise, encounters Watson without being recognized, only later revealing himself and explaining how he succeeded in surviving the Swiss abyss. That night they lie in ambush opposite their Baker St. flat hoping to trap the killer who is sure to make an attempt on Holmes' life, but instead he actually enters the very house the two detectives are hiding in. They watch undetected as their prey takes a shot at what he believes to be Holmes sitting at his window, then jump the marksman. A vicious fight ensues but they finally subdue the criminal, a former lieutenant of the late Professor. Holmes and Watson then go across the street to their place to discuss the case and its implications.

If Doyle is going to bring Holmes back he must come up with some plausible explanation, so he has the detective come up with a rather far-fetched tale of pushing his adversary over the cliff, then climbing up the sheer rock wall above the falls to escape Moriarty's henchman, who witnessed the event and now is bent on killing the victor.

The outrage at the death of the detective was not dissimilar to the disappointment many, especially in America, felt when Cooper, in his 1827 novel *The Prairie*, ended the tale with the death of the old trapper. Then in 1840, thirteen years later, Cooper brought Natty back to life in *The Pathfinder*, and he made yet another appearance in *The Deerslayer*, a few years after that.

Pathfinder, one of Hawkeye's titles is a term of honor denoting one who can fallow trails, even disguised ones, through the woods, still regarded as a useful skill in America. In spite of great hardships, and beset by enemies, Holmes, like his literary godfather, the Pathfinder, finds his path to safety following his misadventure at the falls, then emulates the scout, for this humble man often attributed his skills to the intervention of God. Holmes tells us, "I scrambled down on to the path," and "Halfway down I slipped, but, by the blessing of God, I landed, torn and bleeding, upon the path." He has returned to life as a pathfinder, as did Hawkeye before him. Holmes has even grown to resemble the scout more, for when Watson studies his face after this three years absence he observes that "Holmes looked even thinner and keener than of old," adding that he has an "aquiline face."

Hawkeye, with his message of peace and love in a vicious world is a Christ figure, and the role of Holmes as Christ is not only carried forward now but also takes on a new and unexpected depth, and should be dealt with first. At the beginning of the drama Watson, impersonating an Apostle, claims to have taken up the work of the Redeemer, but to no avail. As did four of Jesus' followers, Watson is revealing to the world, with his writings, the story of his master, even claiming that with this tale of the empty house he runs the risk of relating "a twice-told tale," which is also a reference to Hawthorne, who called his subtle, searching stories "twice-told tales," implying he had heard them from someone else. The world of literature is replete with veiled versions of the story of Jesus, and Doyle realizes he is about to give us another one. When the detective finally reveals himself, one of the first comments he makes is that the doctor has written "fairy-tales," on the life of Holmes. St. Luke writes that many who heard of Jesus' exploits, especially of his return from the dead, were filled with wonder and doubt: "And these words seemed to them as idle tales, and they believed them not."

The crime that instigated the detective's return to London was committed on March 30th with the events being depicted probably beginning around the 3rd of April, which places the story at Easter time, probably Easter Eve flowing into Easter Sunday morning. The year of the story, as is pointed out, is 1894, and a check of a calendar for that year would, I think, bear this out. Easter and April is actually the same thing for the ancient British goddess Eastra, from whom we get the name Easter, was always associated with the month of April, with the entire month being an Eastra festival. She is akin to the Greek goddess Eos, or Dawn, the personification of the rising sun. Holmes, like Jesus, is torn and bleeding from his ordeal, but still alive, and both return from the dead on an April day, along with the corn and the buds on the trees. Watson comes upon his friend disguised as an old bookseller he accidentally bumps into and knocks down several books of "the elderly, deformed man." Christ also engaged in a sort of supernatural wandering journey following the Resurrection, before showing himself to his friends, and he as well seems to have been in disguise, what the Apostles called "another form," for they did not recognize him when they met him on the road to Emmaus. One of the purposes of Christ's death was to make the world believe he had died, and then return, thereby fulfilling the prophecies:

"For as Jonas was in the whale's belly three days and three nights; so shall the Son of man be in the heart of the earth three days and three nights." Holmes exclaims that the instant Moriarty disappeared into the screaming cauldron of the abyss he realized, "what a really extraordinarily lucky chance Fate had placed in my way." These thoughts of Holmes reenacting the story of the reappearance of Jesus can be placed alongside those clues that tell us Sherlock is a personification of Saoshyant, son of Zarathustra.

Watson picks up some books dropped during his encounter with the old bookseller with the title of the only one he remembers being, *The Origin of Tree Worship.* The origins of tree worship can be traced back to the people of Zarathustra, and well before that. The *Zend* instructs the pious with the words: "Go towards that tree that is beautiful, high-growing, and mighty amongst the high-growing trees, and say thou these words, 'Hail to thee! O Good, holy tree, made by Mazda!'" Trees were made by the good spirit for the use of the folk and are worthy of worship. Once a year, in parts of rural India, one priest of the Hindus is elected to carry the sacred tree from the underground well to the temple. His prayers and fasting protect the village and its animals, crops, and people, from harm, and one week from the beginning of the ceremony the priest is offered up by being drowned in the underground well. The tree man dies for his people's benefit and then next year is born again in the form of a new priest; he is immortal. Jesus employs plant metaphor for he equates himself to a vine, and he also compares his father to a gardener. In early Christianity, the identification of the cross with Jesus was so close, and so often was this cross idealized as a living tree, that there are many invocations of the cross as "a divine tree, a noble tree, the likeness of which no earthly forest can produce," and in art representations of the cross as a living tree are numerous. Crosses of living vegetation, such as a palm branch, were regarded as the particular symbol of Christ, the divine source of life and rebirth, and throughout the Christian world people made crosses of palm fronds on Palm Sunday. In the ancient world, right up until quite recently actually, it was believed the tree and the vine completely died in the winter and then came back to life in the spring, thus these two plants were regarded as living examples of man's hope for immortality. In the "Book of Job," we read that the tree is immortal and as such it stood in the symbols of Medieval Church art and literature as a denotative of the Resurrection. For this reason Jesus is said to be the son of a carpenter; one who works with wood, which is a pure folk tale. Jesus is a sacrificial victim hung upon a tree as a sin offering of his people. Holmes is bringing word of the Resurrection with him, and he, like Christ, is offering himself as a sacrifice for the welfare of mankind; his blood is atonement for the sins of man, for he has vowed that if his death would rid the world of evil he would gladly die.

Holmes in the role of Zarathustra is immortal although a reference to this in the texts is rare. "His chosen saint," in the following is Zarathustra: "And to this (man, his chosen saint) Ahura Mazda will give both the two (greatest gifts, His) Universal Weal and Immortality, by means of His bountiful Spirit, and with His Best Mind, from (the desire to maintain His) Righteous moral

Order in Word and deed, and by the (strength and wisdom) of His Sovereign Power, (established) in Piety (among His folk)."

Tree worship in Europe probably had its roots in the Norse, who sanctified a tree they called *Igdrasil*, or *Ygdrasil*, a great mythical ash whose roots and branches held together the universe like some vast network of veins and arteries. "The Tree Igdrasil, that has its roots down in the Kingdoms of Hela and Death, and whose boughs overspread the highest Heaven!" is how Carlyle puts it. "It is all a Tree," Carlyle tells us of life itself, "circulation of sap and influences, mutual communication of every minutest leaf with the lowest talon of a root, with every other greatest and minutest portion of the whole." The origin of tree worship is a phrase close in spirit to James Frazer's *The Golden Bough*, a monumental work replete with examples of tree veneration among various people. He was very popular in Doyle's day, and this book could very well be an abridged copy, which is common, for the whole book consists of numerous volumes. Frazer was a fellow Scot, and Doyle would have enjoyed bringing him into it.

Upon gaining entrance to Watson's flat, Holmes, still disguised, tells him, "I am a neighbour of yours, for you'll find my little bookshop at the corner of Church Street." In "The Hero as Man of Letters," a chapter in *Heroes*, Carlyle attempts to pin down the role of the book in modern culture. "The true University of these days is a Collection of Books." He adds, "The Teacher needed not now to gather men personally round him, that he might *speak* to them what he knew: print it in a Book, and all learners far and wide, for a trifle, had it each at his own fireside, much more effectually to learn it!" One such as a collector or seller of books he also considered a hero. Carlyle mulls the effect of printed books on religious thought and institutions in general. "But to the Church itself, as I hinted already, all is changed, in its preaching, in its working, by the introduction of Books. The Church is the working recognised Union of our Priests or Prophets, of those who by wise teaching guide the souls of men. While there was no Writing, even while there was no Easy-writing, or *Printing*, the preaching of the voice was the natural sole method of performing this. But now with Books! — He that can write a true Book, to persuade England, is not he the Bishop and Archbishop, the Primate of England and of all England?" With the intense references to a book written "to persuade England," I can't help thinking of Doyle's short story, "Danger," a cautionary tale of war Doyle hoped would wake up the English to the realization of their potential vulnerability in the face of modern submarine warfare, whose title he used for an entire collection of short stories. "I many a time say, the writers of Newspapers, Pamphlets, Poems, Books, these *are* the real working effective Church of a modern country. Nay, not only our preaching, but even our worship, is not it too accomplished by means of Printed Books?" Literature, Carlyle believed, as a moral discipline, as an opener of new vistas, as the originator of ideals, would gradually assume the functions formerly monopolized by dogmatic religion.

Yet another work the bookseller is touting is The Holy War, possibly meant to be John Bunyan's The Holy War, Made by King Shaddai (Jehovah) upon Diabolus (Satan) for the Regaining of the Metropolis of the World; or,

The Losing and Taking Again of the town of Mansoul (Man's Soul), a work I have not read. This, in a nutshell, is the theme of "The Final Problem," "The Empty House," and actually all of the Holmes Canon, with London standing in as "the Metropolis of the World," which of course it was at the time. In this allegory the earthly champion of virtue is named Emmanuel, an obvious reference to Jesus.

The old man also has a collection of the works of the Roman poet Catullus. Carlyle tells us, "The noble sentiment which a gifted soul has clothed for us in melodious words, which brings melody into our hearts, — is not this essentially, if we will understand it, of the nature of worship?" adding, "He who, in any way, shews us better than we knew before that a lily of the fields is beautiful, does he not shew it us as an effluence of the Fountain of all Beauty; as the *handwriting*, made visible there, of the great Maker of the Universe?" Carlyle uses the Roman poet Gaius Valerius as an example of such a bringer of beauty. Catullus and Gaius Valerius are two names for the same poet, one being a pen name.

British Birds, yet another text Holmes carries about would be a record of the manifesting of "the handwriting of God," as surely as would any work on flowers. "Perhaps there is no worship more authentic," Carlyle adds of the products of the men of letters.

Holmes is revealing a godlike revelation of his persona in this tale and Carlyle assures us that literature is a "'continuous revelation' of the Godlike in the Terrestrial and Common." "The Godlike," Carlyle adds of literature, "is brought out, now in this dialect, now in that, with various degrees of clearness: all true gifted Singers and Speakers are, consciously or unconsciously, doing so." Carlyle gave an address at Edinburgh in 1866 entitled "On the Choice of Books," that must have influenced this story.

Watson is tricked by the old bibliophile into turning his back on him for a few seconds and upon facing each other again the man is discovered to have transformed himself into Sherlock Holmes. Thor was one of the gods worshipped by the Norsemen and Doyle borrowed the name for the title of one on his best tales, "The Problem of Thor Bridge." Thor's properties included the ability to disappear and reappear at will Carlyle tells us, and gives a case in point. "King Olaf, the Christian Reform King, is sailing with fit escort along the shore of Norway, from haven to haven; dispensing justice, or doing other royal work: on leaving a certain haven, it is found that a stranger, of grave eyes and aspect, red beard, of stately robust figure, has stept in. The courtiers address him; his answers surprise by their pertinency and depth: at length he is brought to the King. The stranger's conversation here is not less remarkable, as they sail along the beautiful shore; but after some time, he addresses King Olaf thus: 'Yes, King Olaf, it is all beautiful, with the sun shining on it there; green, fruitful, a right fair home for you; and many a sore day had Thor, many a wild fight with the rock Jotuns, before he could make it so. And now you seem minded to put away Thor. King Olaf, have a care!' said the stranger, drawing down his brows; — and when they looked again, he was nowhere to be found. — This is the last appearance of Thor on the stage of the world!" Thor is making a complaint that the new Christian religion is replacing the old, a tracing of the theme of this story in which we are seeing Jesus bringing a message of rebirth to mankind. Carlyle adds that the pagan god Neptune was once seen in Pindar's time as "a stranger of noble grave aspect," something like the bookseller. At Holmes' appearance the doctor must have fainted for "a gray mist swirled before my eyes." He may not have fainted however for it is one of the powers of the Norse gods, as well as the deities of many other mythologies, to be able to call up a mist to cloak their activities. "The body of all Truth dies; and yet in all, I say, there is a soul which never dies; which in new and ever-nobler embodiment lives immortal as man himself!" Carlyle points out as the moral of the tale. He reminds us that the gods are often personifications of natural events such as thunder and lightning and deals with the Norse sun god: "Balder again, the White God, the beautiful, the just and benignant (whom the early Christian Missionaries found to resemble Christ), is the Sun, — beautifullest of visible things; wondrous too, and divine still, after all our Astronomies and Almanacs!" "A Hero, as I say, in his own rude manner; a wise, gifted, noble-hearted man." In speaking of Odin, the greatest of the gods, Carlyle says, "The rough words he articulated, are they not the rudimental roots of those English words we still use? He worked so, in that obscure element. But he was as a *light* kindled in it; a light of Intellect, rude Nobleness of heart, the only kind of lights we have yet; a Hero, as I say: and he had to shine there, and make his obscure element a little lighter, — as is still the task of us all." The great man, the hero, is as a kind of tree whose roots reach everywhere. "He is as a root of so many great things; the fruit of him is found growing, from deep thousands of years, over the whole field of Teutonic Life."

We must assuredly probe Doyle's persistent use of the thoughts of Descartes, since a comprehensive appreciation of Sherlock Holmes hinges upon our knowledge of his philosophy and his life. Descartes claims that as a young man he would take the title of a book, even a book of science, and from this title alone, try to cerebrally reconstruct what the book contained, adding that this amusement offered him, "the highest intellectual satisfaction," and "a harmless pleasure." This is explicitly the mental situation Doyle is proposing to us with the numerous book titles found scattered throughout his writings, the supreme example being *De Jure inter Gentes*. A book title becomes an invitation for us to exert an attempt at unearthing the contents and theme of the work. The French philosopher returns to this thought in his work *Discourse on Method*, claiming that every book can be reduced to its essence, to a couple of lines, or unifying figures, and finally, simply to its title, for him to be able to understand its context. It is this kind of contemplation that causes Descartes (and Holmes) to be so highly individualistic and original, even though there is a suspicion of intellectual arrogance in some thoughts just discussed. It has been pointed out that the implication is that Descartes felt free to reinvent the content of a book he was thinking about since its expository context in no way bears upon the application of his method. He seems to be saying that no matter what the book says it cannot affect his thoughts, since they are so original. Descartes' method separates its own rationality from any historical context and the success of the method is defined by its implicit reductiveness. He is considered, at least by some observers, to have been a pragmatic thinker, and a case could be made out for this as "the discovery of reasons by my own proper efforts," which is the recurring signature of the Cartesian enterprise, as it is with the Holmesian. Descartes, like Holmes, is not much of a reader, for he believed in finding out things for himself rather than reading about them, but he is far from being a "non-reading philosopher," as he has been called.

This scene of transformation is also a borrowing from Charles Dickens' *Bleak House*, which, although not a straightforward detective novel, has sections containing a tightly constructed murder mystery. Dickens invents the character of Inspector Bucket of the Detective Squad, has him solve the murder offstage, then explain it, helping to introduce one of the most copied elements of the mystery novel, the wrap-up explanation of the chain of deductions that led to the solution. Detective Bucket, attempting to gain admittance to a London house, disguises himself as a physician making a house call. By chance, as he approaches the building he meets the owner Mr. George about to enter with the novel's heroine, Esther. Believing the Inspector to be a real doctor sent for by George's manservant, they admit him with them into the house where Mr. George and Esther witness an amazing scene. "When we had all arrived here, the physician stopped, and, taking off his hat, appeared to vanish by magic, and to leave another and quite a different man in his place." Bucket, like Holmes, has marveled his audience with this instant change. He now serves a warrant against a suspect hidden within the house. Notice the similarities between this scene and the one in "The Empty House": the parties all met outside the house first, and then the inhabitants of the buildings admit the disguised detectives under false impressions of their true selves. The Inspector reveals himself as though by magic, a word that could easily be used to describe Holmes' change of persona.

The title "The Empty House," is also a borrowing from Dickens, for both bleak and empty denote the same thing since bleak means "bare, empty, having nothing in it," such as "a bleak landscape."

In his wrap-up of the case Mr. Bucket goes into some detail as to the great assistance Mrs. Bucket rendered in catching the murderers, for the original speculations and observations Mrs. Bucket made when she went to tea with the suspected murderess, Mademoiselle Hortense, led directly to her capture and conviction. Mrs. Bucket has risked her life to assist the detective, and in no other case does Mrs. Hudson play such an active role as she is seen to in "The Empty House," actually endangering her life to manipulate the wax figure of Holmes, hoping to delude Moran into accepting the thing as live. When Hortense, as the police are snapping handcuffs on her, realizes further denial is useless, the young murderess puts most of the blame for her downfall on the skill and coolness of the detective's wife. Mademoiselle Hortense, when arrested, is "panting tigress-like," and admits she would like to tear the woman "limb from limb." When Col. Moran is finally subdued he springs at Holmes "with a snarl of rage," but the police drag him away.

At this point in the story Holmes is still quite dead for Watson emphasizes that although his face is keen and alert, "there was a dead-white tinge," to it. The dead Holmes/Jesus has visited his old friend and just as the Apostle Thomas doubted the evidence of his eyes, Watson does not truly believe in the existence of his companion until he lays hands upon him. "I gripped him by the arms," and "Again I gripped him by the sleeve, and felt the thin, sinewy arm beneath it." Watson is forced to admit, "Well, you're not a spirit, anyhow." Following the dispelling of Thomas' doubt the Apostle pledges his willingness to follow the Master anywhere, and when Holmes asks Watson if he will come with him on the night's adventure, the doctor answers, "When you like and where you like." Holmes recalls that he thought out all his stratagem of pretending to be dead, and then returning to London, in the time it took Moriarty to hit the bottom of the pit. Only a God could do this; the thoughts were all there from the beginning of time.

The forces of evil, the minions of the Professor, are still alive and well, and will "take liberties," unless he takes up the old fight, runs the detective's rationale for returning. The devil is indeed active in London, and we are even introduced to one of his assistants quite early in the story when Watson, out of a morbid curiosity, goes to view the scene of the murder. While examining the exterior of the mystery house, he encounters, "A tall, thin man with coloured glasses, whom I strongly suspected of being a plain-clothes detective" who "was pointing out some theory of his own" to the crowd. Watson listens until he realizes "his observations seemed to me to be absurd, so I withdrew again in some disgust." This stranger spreading confusion and error with his ideas is doing the devil's work for all sin is the result of error, and Watson is right to feel disgust with the man. This imp, whom I believe to be none other than a certain Colonel Moran, is surrounded by "A group of loafers upon the pavements," and we all know the devil finds work for idle hands.

In the ancient legend as soon as the good spirit has been born into the New World, the evil spirit comes into being, to balance the scales of the universe, and thus Holmes is attacked by a faceless presence on the precipice above him the instant the old evil is overthrown. Holmes correctly reasons that Moriarty is actually not dead either, regardless of the fact that he fell into the void, for Holmes could hear his "voice screaming at me out of the abyss."

That April evening, a Saturday, the two set out "upon the notable adventure of the empty house," with Holmes, in a paraphrasing of Jesus' words to his followers just prior to his death, telling Watson, "You will hear and see enough before morning." They take a hansom cab, getting out at Cavendish Square, the word "Cavendish" incorporating the word "cave," a reference to the tomb of Jesus. "Square," could refer to the oft-used modern renderings of the tomb of Jesus as a square sepulcher. Watson, studying the face of his friend realizes "the adventure was a most grave one." They arrive at Camden House from which we can abstract the word "den," which is in essence a cave, where, finding a "narrow passage" they "passed through a wooden gate into a deserted yard, and then opened with a key the back door of a house." The whole atmosphere is of a graveyard and tomb. There is an empty building, which is "pitch dark," and they enter. "As dark as the grave," was a common expression in Doyle's day. When Jesus died, according to Luke, "there was darkness over all the earth." Proceeding upstairs the two enter a "large, square, empty room, heavily shadowed in the corners," dimly lit by lights from the street and it is in this room that Satan and death will be overcome.

Just as the Romans had appointed armed guards to watch the body, and following his burial, the tomb of Jesus, we have police posted in the street below. Holmes and Watson have become hunters and trappers, as did Hawkeye and Uncas, as they awaited the arrival of their "old enemies." A back-lit wax figure of Holmes has been set up as bait in the window of the Baker Street flat directly across from Camden House, and the intrepid twosome watch for any sign of attack on this manikin, expecting the miscreant to make an appearance in the street below, but time passes with no sign of him. Holmes grows impatient, "as midnight approached and the street gradually cleared, he paced up and down the room in uncontrollable agitation." Excitement is setting in, for Holmes realizes Easter Morning is upon them and something must come to pass quickly or all is lost. One can imagine the anxiety of Jesus, awaking in the black burial place awaiting someone to roll away the great stone from his cave/tomb. Holmes' senses are keener than the doctor's, and he is the first to realize that a presence has entered the house and is slowly working his way toward the very chamber the pair are hiding in. A savage, vicious, devil of an old man enters the room, positions himself at the window, and fires a shot at the wax dummy of Holmes across the street. It was clever of our author to depict this manifestation of evil as an old man, for God is often referred to in theology and philosophy as one who of necessity must be an ancient, self-renewing being, with one of his titles being "Ancient of Days." The evil balance must as well be of great age. Holmes and Watson ambush this demon and following a terrific struggle lay him low. Two policemen and a detective rush into the room as Watson tells us, "We had all risen to our feet, our prisoner breathing hard, with a stalwart constable on either side of him." It is now Easter Day. In Luke's account of the Resurrection there were two angels present at the tomb informing any who sought news, "He is not here; for he is risen." A few loiterers begin to collect on Baker Street and this is just what happened at the empty tomb of Jesus; a number of onlookers and friends gathered. "Lestrade had produced two candles, and the policemen had uncovered their lanterns," so the room and the world is now filled with light. "I am the Resurrection and the Light," Jesus tells us in the Scriptures. Holmes now closes the window and lowers the blinds and just so was the Resurrection kept secret awhile, and once again Sherlock emulates the self-effacing Lord, insisting Lestrade receive credit for the capture of the murderer, keeping his own role in the case quiet. Lestrade and the police play the part of the Centurion and the other soldiers who were given sums of money to state that the body of Jesus had been stolen in the night.

Holmes has been away (has buried himself) from the world for three years, a metaphor for the three days Jesus lay in the tomb. The two detectives now go across to their apartment to examine the dummy, check on Mrs.

Hudson, and talk over the case. Examining the wax bust of himself that had been mounted upon "a small pedestal table," he questions Mrs. Hudson, his faithful follower, as to her part in the evening's events, asking if she observed all precautions with the strange dummy, and she answers, "I went to it on my knees, sir, just as you told me." Following the Resurrection a great change had taken place in the world. The Apostles are stunned when they behold the Lord returned from the dead. "And they came and held him by the feet, and worshipped him." They kneel down in devotion before Jesus, and this is extremely important, for until now there is no mention that Jesus had ever been worshipped as a divine personage. Had Jesus not risen he would never have been considered godlike, but simply another prophet. Holmes, we learn, has not taken Watson into his confidence regarding these maneuvers, and a careful reading of the Passion reveals parallels, for Jesus made arrangements and plans, yet failed to inform some, or in some cases, all of his disciples and friends, who frequently are now filled with amazement at his behavior.

Doyle is so taken up with his studies of these four accounts of the life of Jesus: John, Luke, Matthew, and Mark, he can't resist mentioning one of them, possibly his favorite. Holmes, looking up Col. Moran's name in his files of biographies and crimes, comes across "Mathews, who knocked out my left canine in the waiting-room at Charing Cross." Mention of the cross even brings in the death of Christ. Moriarty as well experiences something of a rebirth, for he appears as an offstage villain in *The Valley of Fear*, published in 1915. True enough the time of the story is earlier but that does not really change anything. Vincent Starrett points out that "whereas Watson in 'The Final Problem,' declares his utter ignorance of even Moriarty's name, in *The Valley of Fear* he speaks of him with some familiarity." The index on Moran tells us he is "The second most dangerous man in London." Holmes has obviously not had time to update his files since Moriarty was disposed of, or he would have been listed as the most dangerous man in London, so Moran has filled his now empty slot, a form of reincarnation in itself.

Moran, a cold and cruelly capable former army officer saw to it that the malicious wishes of his leader, the Professor, were carried out. He is the archenemy of the people of Zarathustra given flesh and blood; he even comes from their region, for the man has spent most of his violent life in India. He is animalized, having lived in the jungle and written a book on it, as well as one entitled *Heavy Game of the Western Himalayas*, which accents his predatory nature, and Moran belongs to the Bagatelle Card Club, bagatelle being an idle game something like billiards, as well as the Tankerville Club, one meaning of tank being "to drink much liquor." Here is a frivolous and corrupt unsettled rover and hunter, of the aggressive type Zarathustra spent a lifetime at war with. He is a ghost of Moriarty, evidenced by the references to death encompassed in his name, for "*mora*," is a Latin word meaning "to reflect or to mourn," and has roots to the Sanskrit "*smarati*," meaning "he remembers," or "to lament the dead." Both the Professor and the Colonel have names that could be forms of the strange Latin word "*morituri*," which seems to mean "we who are about to die." Moran's first name is Sebastian and I cannot hear this name without thinking, however briefly, of St. Sebastian, an esteemed example of sacrifice as evidenced by the numerous depictions of his death in early Christian art. This Roman soldier was martyred for having become a follower of Christ, around AD 288, by being tied to a post by his comrades, who then lined up and filled his body with their arrows. I've never come across a representation of this saint in which he is not in the very act of dying, thus the name Sebastian is synonymous, by association, with death.

Doyle's writings, as we know, are full of arrogant and malicious Colonels, from Moriarty's brother to Lysander Stark, to name a few. Verne's Col. Proctor fathered some of the characters, but I believe there is at least one other model for Moran. Much of his unscrupulous nature is taken from Col. John Herncastle, found in *The Moonstone*. Herncastle, like Moran, served in India acquiring a reputation, not for big game hunting, but for craftiness and vindictiveness. Unlike Moran we learn that when Herncastle returned from India his repute preceded him, and "The men wouldn't let him into their clubs." Ironically Doyle must also have taken the idea of passing Holmes off as an old bibliophile from Herncastle, who resembles the detective when in this disguise, and collected old books as a pastime. Just as Doyle focuses our attention on the face of Moran, Collins does the same with Herncastle, whose face made him look as though he was "possessed by the devil." Col. Herncastle proves himself to be just as malicious in London as he was in India.

Thomas De Quincey's depiction of the real-life London murderer John Williams, featured in his book *On Murder Considered as One of the Fine Arts*, published in 1854, also contributed to the portrait of Moran. Outside of Jack the Ripper, Williams is England's most infamous serial killer, having slaughtered, with a hammer and knife, three entire families in as many weeks. De Quincey studied the case thoroughly from eyewitness accounts and police documents, and begins his narration with an overview of the fear and panic gripping London following the first set of killings. Williams had been a seaman and he too had been in India, chiefly in Bengal and Madras. Williams had a "natural tiger character" with a "tiger's heart," that "was masked by the most insinuating and snaky refinement," and in a fit of fancy, De Quincey adds that he advanced upon his victims "with a tiger roar." Not satisfied with that, De Quincey calls the murderer a "monster," and "one born of hell." The man had strange colored hair, which De Quincey theorized was dyed for some reason, and "his face wore at all times a bloodless ghastly pallor," yet in spite of this, many people, especially the young, trusted and respected the man, and we must remember the youthful Ronald Adair completely trusted Moran for no real reason. "His eyes seemed frozen and glazed, as if their light were all converged upon some victim lurking in the far background," De Quincey claims, and in the case of Moran this is exactly what is going on as he focuses upon the bust of Holmes. Williams always dressed formally for the bloody encounters, as though he planned an evening at the theater or opera, in "black silk stockings and pumps (opera slippers)" and "a long blue frock, of the very finest cloth, and richly lined with silk." Moran's own formal attire answers this description of the murderous fop. The purpose of the crimes seems to have been simply robbery by the way, as was Moran's original criminal acts, for cheating at cards is a form of stealing. Of interest to us is the fact that Williams committed two of the killing sprees over Saturday nights.

De Quincey picks one of the felonies and weaves a piece of fiction around the facts, drawing a scene of the return of the servant girl Mary from an errand, at which time the family had been already slaughtered, and we, but not Mary, know Williams to be still in the house. The girl enters the foyer in the pitch darkness, there being no streetlights, when she realizes something is wrong, for in spite of her ringing and knocking there was no answer from within. From out of the black stillness she "heard at last and most distinctly a sound within the house," and realizes it could be the mass murderer, for all London talks of nothing else. "Yes, now beyond a doubt there is coming an answer to her summons. What was it? On the stairs — not the stairs that led downwards to the kitchen, but the stairs that led upwards to the single storey of bedchambers above — was heard a creaking sound. Next was heard most distinctly a footfall: one, two, three, four, five stairs were slowly and distinctly descended. Then the dreadful footsteps were heard advancing along the little narrow passage to the door. The steps — oh heavens! *whose* steps? — have paused at the door. The very breathing can be heard of that dreadful being who has silenced all breathing except his own in the house. There is but a door between him and Mary. What is he doing on the other side of the door? A cautious step, a stealthy step it was that came down the stairs, then paced along the little narrow passage — narrow as a coffin — till at last the step pauses at the door. How hard the fellow breathes! He, the solitary murderer, is on one side the door; Mary is on the other side." This sense of tension and horror forming a work of art is well captured by Doyle in "The Empty House," and he could have taken the idea of combining crime and the Resurrection from the history of the second killing in which Williams wiped out a family only a few days after the first. On this rampage the maid, realizing Williams was also probably still in the house, cried out, "Lord Jesus Christ! We shall all be murdered!" The author calls our attention to this appeal to Christ twice more in the essay.

William James believed "objective" theories of reality, like those incorporated in Professor Moriarty's scientific works that left out essential human dimensions such as the volitional and emotional aspects of human nature were hopelessly false and vicious. They would make of man an alien in the world without a living unity of his experience, falsely overemphasizing the theoretical and rationalistic facets of knowledge, and having us believe that everything in the universe was "fixed": the past, the present, and the future, and by affirming humanistic truths, James hoped to liberate the human spirit from the distortions of rationalism. Moriarty is symbolic of those who believe in "monism," for whom "the essence of rationality consists in conceiving the universe as a rigid logical system," as James said. The monist believes there is only one ultimate substance or principle, whether mind or matter, or some third thing that is the basis of both. Reality is then an organic whole with no independent parts. Monism leaves no room for the full human person and contradicts those experiences that testify to the existence of real novelties and change.

James believed "pluralism," the opposite of monism was the moralistic view and that the most effective objections to monism are logical and ethical ones. The monistic view would believe vicious crimes are a necessary part of the universe, James claims, and ethically one objects to this analysis. Pluralism says the universe is loosely connected, having connections that are real without being such as to determine "completely the activity of things." Monism creates a problem of evil, while evil, for pluralism, presents only the problem of how to get rid of it. Pluralism, generally speaking, is a revolt against absolutism and an assertion of moral and religious values. The pluralist needs to invent and reinvent an idealistic basis for connections and interaction and in so doing brings his ethics, morals, and human needs into the universe. In the monism world, novelty, chance, and growth, play absolutely no part since all is determined in advance, like the path of a comet. Morals would have no real value since they would simply be the effect of a cause and not a part of human choice, and if man has no choice he has no real morals. James believed that monistic determinism made all the crimes and sins of history inevitable, and thus was the enemy of this genuine novelty, and we must accept the possibility that Holmes may be Doyle's idea of this novelty. He is certainly novel enough, for Holmes possesses a freshness and innovative style of life that was regarded as even more so in his early days as an entity. At one point James equates pluralism with democracy and freedom, and also genuine individuality, believing it would give to the human venture a fruitful outlook, and without using the word, that I know of, would lead to optimism.

William James' thoughts are so imperative to Sir Arthur that the rebirth of Holmes may be traced to his influence. As we know, the American lectured at the University of Edinburgh in 1901-1902, with one of his most essential works, *The Varieties of Religious Experience* being originally prepared for delivery there, as the Gifford Lectures on Natural Religion, and the resulting book was no doubt the instigation for resurrecting the Great Detective. The work can hardly be called a history book, for the examples used are either borrowed for the most part directly from recent sources or invented by James himself. He mentions James Frazer, for much was taken from that writer.

In the chapter "The Value of Saintliness," in an effort to understand our admiration of this type of fighter of evil, the saint, James draws a picture of how the history of mankind influenced the bringing into being of the saintly nature. The wonder we hold the saint in we at one time felt for our primitive tribal leaders, the chiefs who were special men, usually military leaders, and defenders of the people. Col. Moran, a military leader and writer, an unofficial aristocrat, is also a chief, for his title was Moriarty's "chief of the staff." "The chief is the potential, if not the actual tyrant, the masterful, overpowering man of prey," James tells us, calling them "these beaked and taloned graspers of the world." Watson twice puts us in the picture regarding Moran's nature by suggesting he has the nose of a bird of prey: a "fierce, aggressive nose," with "a high, bald forehead," putting forward an image of the bald eagle. The word bald actually means "white," as Doyle knows, so he's making a pun since this bird has a white head. When Watson initially glimpses the man he stares at him in wonder. "We quail under his glance," James assures us, "and are at the same time proud of owning so dangerous a lord." We learn from Moran's stance towards Holmes for interfering with his plans that the man does not in the least consider his actions reprehensible for, "The leaders always had good consciences, for conscience in them coalesced with will, and those who looked on their face were as much smitten with wonder at their freedom from inner restraint as with awe at the energy of their outward performances." James later claims, "The most inimical critic of the saintly impulses whom I know is Nietzsche. He contrasts them with the worldly passions as we find these embodied in the predaceous military character, altogether to the advantage of the latter." The latter here is the predaceous military character as compared to the saint. James adds, "Dislike of the saintly nature seems to be a negative result of the biologically useful instinct of welcoming leadership, and glorifying the chief of the tribe." Moran plays the role of the military leader, the tribal chief, or perhaps, to stretch it a bit, of Nietzsche himself, and Holmes adopts the aspects of the saint, as depicted by William James. We first encounter the reborn Sherlock as an elderly, deformed old man with "white side-whiskers," for the philosopher claims, "There are saints whose beard you may, if you ever care to, pull with impunity. Such a man excites no thrills of wonder veiled in terror; his conscience is full of scruples and returns; he stuns us neither by his inward freedom nor his outward power; and unless he found within us an altogether different faculty of admiration to appeal to, we should pass him by with contempt." Notice the unusual usage of the word "returns," here. One meaning of return is "to reflect, or to throw an image back," and remember Doyle entitled the collection of stories published with "The Empty House" *The Return of Sherlock Holmes.* A mind full of returns would be a mind constantly thinking and reimaging the world. Doyle does not wish to show Watson in a poor light so he turns the tables and has Holmes, who we eventually learn was only playacting a character role, show contempt when he and the doctor collide in the street, for Holmes walks away from the encounter "with a snarl of contempt."

Holmes, as it were, is brought out of retirement to fight evil. "Taking refuge in monasteries was as much an idol of the tribe in the middle ages, as bearing a hand in the world's work is to-day. Saint Francis or Saint Bernard, were they living to-day, would undoubtedly be leading consecrated lives of some sort, but quite as undoubtedly they would not lead them in retirement," James assures us. Nietzsche obviously disliked saints, holding them responsible for much of the evil in the world, and regarding them as another form of sickness, but Doyle differs with him. "Is the saint's type or the strong-man's type the more ideal?" the American philosopher asks. Well, "The Empty House" is the scene of the clash between the two categories, and we see who won. "But the aggressive members of society are always tending to become bullies, robbers, and swindlers; and no one believes that such a state of things as we now live in is the millennium." Moran qualifies as a swindler, since he cheats at cards. The millennium referred to is the reign of

Jesus; a period of great happiness that never came into being despite Holmes' sacrifice, so the detective must postpone his early retirement plans for yet a little while. In an imaginary perfect society, a millennial society, as James calls it, "the saint would be entirely adapted," for "His peaceful modes of appeal would be efficacious over his companions, and there would be no one extant to take advantage of his non-resistance." Col. Moran has come to London's "good society," and "The strong man would immediately tend by his presence to make that society deteriorate."

"Three undetected murders in one year won't do, Lestrade," Holmes complains in reference to the atmosphere of London in his absence. Now we must ask ourselves if three undetected murders in one year is actually an outsized figure for a city the size of London. The answer is naturally in the negative, for in Doyle's day, as now, such a low count would be considered more or less perfection. But almost is not good enough for the saint, for although others would be satisfied with such superior results, the saint lives for perfection itself in order that he may form a perfect union with God. The saint harbors "the ambition of the sinless state," as the Medieval manuscripts term it, and Holmes even speaks of the environment of London, for the saint wishes to create a perfect environment that God will be comfortable in, James tells us. The saint sees things very differently than other people for he often feels he has formed a mysterious union with the Deity and is now known as one who is "twice-born," as indeed Holmes is a "born again Christian," a religious movement James discusses in his book.

In this tale all the important incidents take place on the second story of a house: Ronald Adair is shot to death in the front room of his second story, and Holmes ambushes a master criminal in the second floor room of a building across from the second story of his own house. In *The Varieties of Religious Experience* James claims those who view life so optimistically that they cannot see any wrong have entirely different conceptions of the universe as others experience it, others who perceive that evil is a fact of human affairs, and that this difference in people should always be kept in view. A person or system of thought such as that offered by a religious mentality that does not recognize the existence of malevolence is false and unreal. To such people, "the world is a sort of rectilinear or one-storied affair, whose accounts are kept in one denomination, whose parts have just the values which naturally they appear to have, and of which a simple algebraic sum of pluses and minuses will give the total worth." They believe quite simply that everyone and everything is just as they, or it, appear to be. Adair is this innocent type, and is killed while working on the "sum of pluses and minuses," his winnings at cards. "Peace cannot be reached by the simple addition of pluses and elimination of minuses from life. Natural good is not simply insufficient in amount and transient, there lurks a falsity in its very being," James says. Young Adair actually believes all he needs to do is give back the money and everything will be fine. He has been foolish enough to place his confidence in someone he hardly knew, not being intelligent enough to conceive of any acquaintance being malicious while posing as its opposite. Yet to those who view reality for what it in actuality is, those who understand something of life, James says, "the world is a double-storied mystery." Realities overlap like one floor of a house over another, to build up to a more clearly focused picture of existence, having an essence containing both good and evil.

An incident involving the killing of a human by a tiger in India is presented to our view as a case in point of natural viciousness, in James' book. Moran is an example of natural evil, which would be the opposite of James' natural good, for he is as accepted as the tigers he in turn hunts, and James reminds us that the tigers would pounce upon us and kill us if they could, for it is their nature. In a really intelligent person there is always knowledge that devilry is a part even of the best of us, and must never be ignored. Of evil the philosopher declares, "renunciation and despair of it are our first step in the direction of the truth," and it is pure despair that has brought the Great Detective back to London to solve this double-storied mystery.

Jungle imagery as well as metaphors of the predatory beasts that inhabit those worlds is very pronounced in "The Empty House," with Moran rendered as something of a big cat: a tiger or lion, with his face being "scored with deep, savage lines," as well as his having a "fierce, aggressive nose," and a "threatening, deep-lined brow," with cruel eyes; a face Watson tells us, "was wonderfully like a tiger." The Indian tiger is considered by hunters to be the most dangerous animal in the world. In his novel *The Refugees*, a story of the American frontier, Doyle, in describing the Iroquois, to establish their savage and ferocious personality, tells us they have "bodies of iron and tiger souls." Moran is out for vengeance, the kind exhibited by the Indians, as he sneaks into the empty house, takes up a position at a window, puts together an air-gun from his walking stick, and fires at what he believes to be Holmes. As soon as he does so, Holmes "sprang like a tiger on to the marksman's back, and hurled him flat upon his face." He has brought the fight onto the level of the predators. "The Tigers in India" by William James was an address before the American Psychological Association, later published in the *Psychological Review*, 1895. The essay questions how it is we know a thing exists even though that thing exists primarily in the mind alone, for although we all believe there are tigers in India, very few of us actually have seen this ourselves; they exist principally in the mind alone, the mind of each of us. In itself the essay does not relate, as far as I can see, to "The Empty House," but it does deal in a slight, abstract way with tiger hunting. James mentions that one way we would really know of the existence of the tigers of India is "if we took a voyage to India for the purpose of tiger-hunting and brought back a lot of skins of the striped rascals which we had laid low."

Some thoughts of the philosopher on our perception of good and evil are found in the chapter, "The Divided Self, and the Process of its Unification," in *The Varieties of Religious Experience*, where he tells us there exists people whose essential "character seems to be a certain discordancy or heterogeneity in the native temperament of the subject," adding, that some people are born with great amounts of inconsistency in their natures and if strong enough these inconsistencies can wreak havoc on that person's life. This seems to have been the case with Moriarty and a number of mathematicians we have recently met, and is definitely the problem with Moran, whose personality is captured in his countenance. "It was a tremendously virile and yet sinister face which was turned towards us. With the brow of a philosopher above and the jaw of a sensualist below, the man must have started with great capacities for good or for evil." In Doyle's era, for a man to be considered virile was a great compliment, regarded in itself as indicative of moral virtue, while sensualism was looked upon as symptomatic of incorrigible moral weakness and viciousness. Moran has a completely divided self. "Heterogeneous personality has been explained as the result of inheritance — the traits of character of incompatible and antagonistic ancestors are supposed to be preserved alongside of each other," James says, adding that such people find difficulty "in keeping his spiritual house in order and running his furrow straight, because his feelings and impulses are too keen and too discrepant mutually. In the haunting and insistent ideas, in the irrational impulses, the morbid scruples, dreads, and inhibitions which beset the psychopathic temperament when it is thoroughly pronounced, we have exquisite examples of heterogeneous personality." Moran maintained the career of an honorable soldier and "Up to a certain point he did well. He was always a man of iron nerve, and the story is still told in India how he crawled down a drain after a wounded man-eating tiger. There are some trees, Watson, which grow to a certain height, and then suddenly develop some unsightly eccentricity. You will see it often in humans. I have a theory that the individual represents in his development the whole procession of his ancestors, and that such a sudden turn to good or evil stands for some strong influence which came into the line of his pedigree. The person becomes, as it were, the epitome of the history of his own family." Holmes has been speaking, and Watson answers, "It is surely rather fanciful." Of James' views on psychology, when first published, similar words and sentiments often formed part of the criticism of his writings, especially in regard to the pragmatical side of it.

The Drug, the ultimate deception, is given new material definition when the harmless walking stick of Moran's turns out to be an air-gun, the bringer of sudden, silent death, and to bring home the wicked intentions of the man, Doyle gives him lethal soft-nosed pellets for the thing. This was genius for it reveals, among other things, that the enemy is capable of low tricks, dramatizing the fact that Moran, for all his big game hunting, is not a good sport. Holmes is therefore justified in using any trick necessary to fight him, for to the followers of Zarathustra any subterfuge is acceptable if employed to defend oneself.

The saga of *Beowulf* enjoys a form of continuity in this story, for Ronald Adair was the second son of the Earl of Maynooth, and could himself become an earl, and Beowulf is called, "the earls' defender," with his function as a warrior being to stop "those fell attacks of former times on the lives of your earls." Moran serves as a stand-in for the mother of Grendel, for he is seething with rage against Holmes for having killed the Professor, just as Grendel's mother lives only for revenge following the death of her darling son. Holmes tells us of the fight at the waterfall that Moriarty "rushed at me and threw his long arms around me." Having long powerful arms and fighting by wrapping those limbs, bear hug style, around your opponent, was characteristic of both Grendel and his mother.

Adair's sister is named Hilda, which, like the German "Brunhilde," is related to an old Scandinavian word meaning "fighter in armor." The story of Beowulf is paralleled in this name, for Brunhilde is a character in the Icelandic sagas, a Queen of Iceland whom Gunther, a King of Burgundy, gets as his bride with the help of Siegfried's magic. Following his return Holmes says, "You may have read of the remarkable explorations of a Norwegian named Sigerson, but I am sure that it never occurred to you that you were receiving news of your friend." Sigerson would mean "son of Sigemund," the word son being merged to the father's name in the Norwegian manner. Beowulf is compared to Sigemund, the greatest of the dragon slayers as well as a symbol of the risen Christ.

The English name Adair is a version of the Irish name Ardagh; they are pronounced the same, and we are told Ronald Adair's father is Earl of Maynooth, which is an Irish word. In Joseph Le Fanu's short story "The Fortunes of Sir Robert Ardagh," the young man signs a pact with the Devil to win on the horses, but then one dark night the Devil comes to claim his due. Robert Ardagh dies as the result of his lust for gambling and money, or if you wish, his poor judgment in picking such a partner. Young Adair foolishly befriends Col. Moran and wins a good sum through this unholy alliance playing cards, and in a bit of humor, Doyle claims, "His fortune was a considerable one," a pun on Le Fanu's title.

The depiction of Moran's appearance at Camden House is aesthetically one of the most satisfying as well as most complicated pieces of writing I have ever come across. "But suddenly I was aware of that which his keener senses had already distinguished. A low, stealthy sound came to my ears, not from the direction of Baker Street, but from the back of the very house in which we lay concealed. A door opened and shut. An instant later steps crept down the passage — steps which were meant to be silent, but which reverberated harshly through the empty house. Holmes crouched back against the wall, and I did the same, my hand closing upon the handle of my revolver. Peering through the gloom, I saw the vague outline of a man, a shade blacker than the blackness of the open door. He stood for an instant, and then he crept forward, crouching, menacing, into the room. He was within three yards of us, this sinister figure, and I had braced myself to meet his spring, before I realized that he had no idea of our presence. He passed close beside us, stole over to the window, and very softly and noiselessly raised it for half a foot. As he sank to the level of this opening, the light of the street, no longer dimmed by the dusty glass, fell full upon his face. The man seemed to be beside himself with excitement. His two eyes shone like stars, and his features were working convulsively. He was an elderly man, with a thin, projecting nose, a high, bald forehead, and a huge grizzled moustache."

One of the archetypes for this scene is a typical Le Fanu story, "An Account of Some Strange Disturbances in Aungier Street," in which two medical students, searching for a flat in London, learn of one long left untenanted for fear of its being haunted. Being young and foolish, the students naturally laugh at the superstition and, determined to dispel the myth with example, accept an offer to spend an entire night there. No sooner do they get settled for their lark when, as one of them reports, "I became somehow conscious of a sort of horrid but undefined preparation going forward in some unknown quarter, and by some unknown agency, for my torment; and, after an interval, which always seemed to me of the same length, a picture suddenly flew up to the window, where it remained fixed, as if by an electrical attraction, and my discipline of horror then commenced, to last perhaps for hours. The picture thus mysteriously glued to the window-panes, was the portrait of an old man, in a crimson flowered silk dressing-gown, the folds of which I could now describe, with a countenance embodying a strange mixture of intellect, sensuality, and power, but withal sinister and full of malignant omen. His nose was hooked, like the beak of a vulture; his eyes large, grey, and prominent, and lighted up with a more than mortal cruelty and coldness." Just as in Watson's account of his intruder, the concentration centers upon the face, called a "hellish visage," being brought into our view aided by light from the street shining through a window. These two presences slowly emerging into focus are studies of a malignant and threatening being who has come unbidden among both sets of apprehensive, waiting men.

Holmes and Watson travel to their adventure in a hansom cab, although, since the address is only around the corner, they could just as easily have walked. Here is the scene in "The Adventure of the Hansom Cab," by Stevenson, in which Prince Florizel, Col. Geraldine, and three others, one of which is a doctor, wait in Rochester House, the home of the President of the Suicide Club, for his return. They plan to force him into a duel, hoping the Prince will kill him. It is three in the morning and the room is shrouded in almost complete darkness. "The three officers and the physician hastened to obey, and for nearly ten minutes the only sound in Rochester House was occasioned by the excursions of the rats behind the woodwork. At the end of that period, a loud creak of a hinge broke in with surprising distinctness on the silence; and shortly after, the watchers could distinguish a slow and cautious tread approaching up the kitchen stair. At every second step the intruder seemed to pause and lend an ear, and during these intervals, which seemed of an incalculable duration, a profound disquiet possessed the spirit of the listeners." As in "The Empty House," the suspense is drawn out. "At last a hand was laid upon the door, and the bolt shot back with a slight report. There followed another pause, during which Brackenbury could see the Prince draw himself together noiselessly as if for some unusual exertion. Then the door opened, letting in a little more of the light of the morning; and the figure of a man appeared upon the threshold and stood motionless. He was tall, and carried a knife in his hand. Even in the twilight they could see his upper teeth bare and glistening, for his mouth was open like that of a hound about to leap." That's strange behavior for a man in his own house. Obviously Stevenson has read Le Fanu.

Searching for a myth to base his own myth upon, Doyle once again selects Apollo, Greek god of music and light, slayer of the great reptile, and suppressor of man's lower nature. Like Holmes, Apollo is a maker of music for he plays the lyre, and also like Holmes is often pictured lost in thought as he practices his art. Music is conducive to thinking, Nietzsche emphasizes, being the medium of "the quiet calm of Apollonian contemplation." In *The Birth of Tragedy From the Spirit of Music*, we find his complicated analysis of the differences and dichotomy existing between the Greek cults of Apollo and Dionysus. The shining one Apollo is the soothsaying god with the primary object of the Apollonian culture being "to overthrow some Titanic empire and slay monsters," while Dionysus is the god of darkness, the opposite of light, but ironically enough also a god of music. Both were honored at joint festivals, great events in the Greek world marked by feasting, music, and sacrifices in which the worshippers of both cults came face to face in fierce opposition. The information we have from Watson of the actual meeting between Holmes and Moran is a record of his thoughts, not his speech, for no one is actually saying anything, just like at the pantomime, for song and pantomime played a large part in these encounters between the Greek cultists. Col. Moran having just come from the opera is dressed for the theater, opera hat and all. The opera, like all theater, song, and poetry, began life as an excess of religious emotion, growing more secular over the years. As the old gods began to lose fashion in the Greek world, the pantomimes became desperate contests, often performed on the altars of Dionysus which were covered with the blood of the performers acting out scenes of violent combat between the two gods. We learn from Nietzsche and others that the celebrations were usually orgies of cruelty and sensuality often ending in the death or maiming of some participants. "With what astonishment must the Apollonian Greek have beheld him!" Nietzsche says of these personifications of the dark god. He believes the ancients who worshipped Apollo were guarded and insulated against the more horrible minutes of the festivals by the figure of their strong god, it being his position to protect his people against the onslaught of Dionysus and his minions. "The opposition between Apollo and Dionysus became more hazardous and even impossible, when, from the deepest roots of the Hellenic nature, similar impulses finally burst forth and made a path for themselves: the Delphic god (Apollo), by a seasonably effected reconciliation, now contented himself with taking the destructive weapons from the hands of his powerful antagonist," the German claims. Thus we see Holmes, after a struggle, relieve Moran of his dangerous weapon. "The two antagonists were reconciled," Nietzsche adds, but "the boundary lines thenceforth to be observed by each were sharply defined," and "At bottom, however, the chasm was not bridged over." How could light and darkness be reconciled? "But if we observe how, under the pressure of this treaty of peace, the Dionysian power revealed itself, we shall now recognize in the Dionysian orgies of the Greeks, as compared with the Babylonian Sacaea with their reversion of man to the tiger and the ape, the significance of festivals of world-redemption and days of transfiguration." Moran, god of darkness and debauchery, reverts to his tiger nature in the fulfillment of this nature, in the presence of his old enemy Apollo, on this day of transfiguration and world-redemption. Sensuality and cruelty are blended with music and song in the rites and its practices, and just so is the complex, elusive, opera loving nature of Moran. The votary of Dionysus is understood only by his peers, and interestingly enough this dark persona is not unlike Holmes/ Apollo, for Nietzsche in *Beyond Good and Evil* extols Dionysus for "his courage as investigator and discoverer, his fearless honesty, truthfulness, and love of wisdom," so we are shown that Moran has the features of a philosopher, for the word philosopher means "a lover of wisdom," and like Holmes his iron nerve is unquestioned. In summing up the case we learn Moran is a modern version of the Dionysian rites themselves, representing, "in his development the whole procession of his ancestors," which could be read as a reference to the processions of the cult, infamous for their bizarre climaxes in which celebrants were often torn to pieces in a drunken, bloody frenzy. As with the Professor, this man is an adversary worthy of the Great Detective with this scene of a physical contest meant to personify an equitable meeting of pure evil and pure good.

When Moran realizes he has been tricked and captured, he ignores all present except Sherlock, author of his situation, and mutters, "You clever, clever fiend!" or a variation of it, repeatedly. Holmes is here being addressed with shibboleths the Persians employed in describing their champion Zarathustra for "he is a counter-fiend to the fiends; he is a Drug to the Drug." The *Zend* tells us when the enemies of Zarathustra look at him they are looking into a mirror. Nietzsche, in the German, uses the word, "*der Teufel*," when speaking of the devil, but the phrase actually means both devil and fiend, with fiend itself being a German word sometimes used for adversary or Satan, and in the German military language, fiend is used for "enemy." In *Three of Them*, in emphasizing the prowess of a famous English cricket player named Spofforth, Doyle tells his children Spofforth had the fastest ball in England, adding, "He was a tall, thin man, and they called him the Fiend. That means the Devil, you know." He has obviously been thinking of these words and their interchangeability. This occasion of the detective being called a fiend is also a borrowing from Dickens' *Bleak House*, for when the accused murderess finds herself being cornered by the ruthless questioning of Bucket, she calls him "a devil," and repeats this a number of times. Of himself, Nietzsche tells us sardonically, "my mere existence angers those who have bad blood in their veins." In the combat between these two human adversaries we have a unique reenactment of an imaginary meeting of personifications of Nietzsche's higher man and his Superman; a conflict the philosopher would have loved to have given flesh to, and presented to our intelligence, but failed to. The German maintains that when "a degenerate man arises to the highest rank," he must do so "at the cost of the reverse type, at the expense of the strong man who is certain of life." He regarded those who had risen in the world, but are unable to reach supermanhood, to have done so by pandering to the people, whom he considered a pack of fools. Moran, the higher man, has achieved a certain distinction, what with his rank and books, and has realized this in spite of his vile nature. When such a person shines, "the exceptional man must be degraded to the rank of the evil. When falsehood insists at all costs on claiming the word 'truth' as its world-outlook, the really truthful man must be sought out among those of worst repute." Deceit is being talked about here, the deceit that is just about impossible to fight, and which takes the "exceptional" man even to recognize. This is part of what the philosopher regards as his "Transvaluation of All Values," for he regards those who have heretofore been regarded as good as the truly evil ones, the resentful ones struggling to bring everything down to their level in their resentment. The relatively superhuman type is superhuman particularly as compared with the good man, and "the good and the just" would call his superman "the devil." "So alien are ye in your souls to what is great, that to you the Superman would be *frightful* in his goodness!" Doyle focuses our attention on the "cruel blue eyes" of Moran, telling us they "shone like stars," in their hatred of Holmes. The superman would be hated and feared for he alone conceives "reality as it is," something the simply good man does not have the intellect or courage to grasp. "Ye highest men who have come within my ken! this is my doubt of you, and my secret laughter: I suspect ye would call my Superman — a devil!" The new Superman will have an enemy "worthy of him," as in the ancient legend, and will "not lack his dragon, the superdragon that is worthy of him," a designation that could apply to either Moran or Moriarty. Nietzsche compares the new evil principle to a tiger, stating, "the good hunter shall have a good hunt!" Like his adversary Holmes, the Colonel has recently come from Afghanistan, for we are told he took part in the siege of Sherpur, which is located near the capital, Kabul. Moran's father had been British Minister to Persia, a leader of the people, and undoubtedly yet another higher man. Holmes traveled from Persia to Khartoum, so he must have passed through Afghanistan and India, where Zoroastrianism is still practiced.

Moran is part of the scheme of the Great Renovation, and should be viewed as a compulsory evil Doyle of necessity had to conjure up in order to keep the story line aesthetically and historically credible and flowing, even if he was the sole recognizer of the scheme. Professor Moriarty may have been killed and the gang brought to trial, but Holmes says the police "left two of its most dangerous members, my own most vindictive enemies, at liberty," which is another version of the adage, "For every evil you kill, there are two to take its place." If he can once again rid society of this new manifestation of maliciousness, Holmes claims that "will in itself justify a man's life on this planet." Watson realizes, as they are setting out on this adventure, "It was indeed like old times," and at the conclusion of the account, he adds, looking over the Baker Street rooms for the first time in years, "the old landmarks were all in their place." The New World, by the blessing of God, is exactly like the old one.

For three years the dead Holmes, in a sort of Cook's tour of limbo, wandered around the world. To be understood these solitary rambles must be divided into segments, for our hero obviously had a busy trip given the condition of travel at the time. After returning from his own spiritual journey of the soul, Nietzsche's Zarathustra speaks of having gone through a prolonged period of sea and land travel, and is now, like Sherlock, reborn into the world, for those who knew him thought him to be dead. Holmes at this point claims he is certain "that no one in the world knew what had become of me." The exception to this is his brother Mycroft, his one confidant, the only one who has aided in this plot of his brother's resurrection, for as a farmer he has the most to gain. After Holmes finds himself on the path of rebirth he immediately leaves Switzerland and a week later finds himself in Florence, the center of the Renaissance, or the rebirth of man. Henry James wrote much on this beautiful and impressive city in his travel works and fiction, for he and his family had spent a good deal of time there. Florence is the city of Dante, the city from which he was exiled for backing the wrong political party. In the Medieval world, to be banished, as was Dante, was almost tantamount to a death sentence. While suffering under this condemnation he began his *The Divine Comedy*, bringing it with him to Ravenna, where he lived out his last years, and the homecoming of Holmes recreates this circumstance for he too now has literature, his books, which he wishes to sell and distribute, as Dante did his masterpiece. When initially evicted the poet spent an episode of wandering from city to city in great distress, but Carlyle claims that if he had not suffered so he no doubt would have ended up only mayor of Florence or perhaps a monk, nothing to compare to the writer he became. "A nobler destiny was appointed for this Dante; and he, struggling like a man led towards death and crucifixion, could not help fulfilling it. Give *him* the choice of his happiness! He knew not, more than we do, what was really happy, what was really miserable." "For Dante there was now no home in the world. He wandered from patron to patron, from place to place; proving, in his own bitter words, 'How hard is the path.'" "By degrees, it came to be evident to him that he had no longer any resting place, or hope of benefit, in this earth. The earthly world had cast him forth, to wander; no living heart to love him now; for his sore miseries there was no solace here." Holmes has returned to Florence; something the great poet could not do. "The Poet who could merely sit on a chair, and compose stanzas, would never make a stanza worth much. He could not sing the Heroic warrior, unless he himself were at least a Heroic warrior too. I fancy there is in him the Politician, the Thinker, Legislator, Philosopher; — in one or the other degree, he could have been, he is all these." Carlyle informs us, "Perhaps one would say, *intensity*, with the much that depends on it, is the prevailing character of Dante's genius," and to unintentionally bond the temperaments of Dante and Holmes even more solidly adds, "Poet and Prophet differ greatly in our loose modern notions of them. In some old languages, again, the titles are synonymous; *Vates* means both Prophet and Poet: and indeed at all times, Prophet and Poet, well understood, have much kindred of meaning. Fundamentally indeed they are still the same; in this most important respect especially, That they have penetrated both of them into the sacred mystery of the Universe; what Goethe calls 'the open secret.'" It is the poet and prophet who goes beyond mere appearances to find what is at "the bottom of Appearance," as Carlyle calls it, and is a revealer of mystery, or "That divine mystery, which lies everywhere in all Beings," and "especially the Appearance of Man and his work." The poet and prophet find the truth that "is greatly overlooked," by others.

Our warrior also wanders over to Mecca, an oblique association to Mohammed, a prophet covered extensively in Carlyle's work. In speaking of him, the Scot could easily be describing Sherlock as well. "But, from an early age, he had been remarked as a thoughtful man. His companions named him 'Al Amin, The Faithful.' A man of truth and fidelity; true in what he did, in what he spake and thought. They noted that *he* always meant something. A man rather taciturn in speech; silent when there was nothing to be said; but pertinent, wise, sincere, when he did speak; always throwing light on the matter. This is the only sort of speech *worth* speaking! Through life we find him to have been regarded as an altogether solid, brotherly, genuine man. A serious, sincere character; yet amiable, cordial, companionable, jocose even; — a good laugh in him withal." He has most assuredly the Great Detective's manner of addressing the world around him, especially if we admit of some silent laughter on Sherlock's part. Carlyle adds that Mohammed was full of fire and light and was "all uncultured; working out his life-task in the depths of the Desert there." Holmes has been in the desert as well for he visited Khartoum and Mecca, cities of the desert, and remember, Doyle tried to pass the detective off as a very uncultured man who had never even heard of Carlyle, although he was a household name.

In Tibet, Holmes called in at Lhassa, spending time with the Dalai Lama, a living god, a divinity, who upon dying is reborn instantly into the body of a young boy, and is therefore an immortal presence insuring the everlasting cycle of life and rebirth. Holmes has come out of the East, the land of the rising sun, to return to fight corruption and death. "All prophets come from the East," is an adage as old as history itself. Jesus was even called "Eastern Star," by some of his followers in recognition of this. In the *Zend-Avesta* we learn Saoshyant "will come from the region of the dawn to free the world from death and decay, from corruption and rottenness, ever living and ever thriving, when the dead shall rise and immortality commence." Reincarnation, a Hindu form of resurrection is implied, for Holmes seems to have lived many lives as he wandered.

In *The Moonstone* we meet Mr. Murthwaite, the celebrated Indian traveler, "who, at risk of his life, had penetrated in disguise where no European had ever set foot before." It is understood Sherlock toured in masquerade at least some of the time for he stopped over at Mecca, which is impossible without a costume, for no non-Moslem is allowed into the city. Descartes traveled much of the world of his day for one reason or another and Sherlock's voyaging may be a reference to this.

Some of the detective's experiences seem to be based on the adventures of an actual person famous in Doyle's London who possibly was an acquaintance of the writer. Queen Victoria was interested in all sorts of exotic people, and her world was full of them. In May of 1889 she had to dinner at Windsor Castle a Professor Arminius Vambrey, a Hungarian scholar/gypsy in his fifties who had traveled extensively, even through Central Asia, disguised as a Dervish. He was expert in Moslem lore and fluent in the regional languages, and knew the rulers of Turkey, Persia, and Afghanistan, as well as the local khans and caliphs. The Queen sought his advice on India and its people.

Vambrey is described as a squat, bushy bearded character in whom I can find Professor Challenger as well as the old bookseller who is Holmes.

Many of the thoughts presented to our minds in "The Empty House" refer back to fundamental problems in epistemology, the study of how we acquire knowledge, or to equally basic questions in aesthetics, as it was dealt with by the thinkers of the Enlightenment. Opposition, personified by the two central characters, is the central theme of the tale, at least on one level. The conflict between Holmes and Moran is tantamount in spirit to a clash between two bodies of philosophical knowledge that find themselves so dramatically opposed as to make reconciliation beyond the bounds of possibility. They are opposites as two systems of thought are opposites, or perhaps as is the dissension of reason and imagination, or the discord struck between genius and the rules. It's as though these antagonists required testing in terms of one another before either could locate his own inner standard or even understand his own being.

The real struggle for men's minds began well before the Enlightenment. Descartes did not include a systematic aesthetics in his philosophy, but the broad outline of an aesthetic theory is implied in his system as a whole. The absolute unity in which the nature of knowledge consists, and which is to overcome all its arbitrary and conventional divisions, is extended in the Cartesian system to include the realm of art. He does not hesitate to expand his conception of "universal wisdom," so that it also incorporates, as a universally valid postulate, art as a whole and in all its particular forms. Although he never talked about painting and sculpture, the plastic arts, he did take account, in his discussion of knowledge, of the field of music, which he seemed to regard as a science, and his spirit in general became the basis of forceful new laws in aesthetics. We must realize the pure character and basic principles of all the arts and reduce them to one fundamental standard, based on the design that, as nature in all its manifestations is governed by certain codes, and as it is the highest task and the end mission of the quest for knowledge of nature to be able to formulate these rules clearly and precisely, so also art, the rival of the natural world, is under the same obligation. Art, until quite recently, was regarded as nothing more than imitation of nature, and he who could imitate best was considered the most accomplished artist. All the laws of aesthetics popular in Descartes' day, and most of them in Doyle's day as well, would fit into, and be subordinate to one simple attitude, the quest for imitation in general. This is exactly what Oscar Meunier's wax bust is, a duplicate of Holmes so accurate it could fool people into thinking they were looking at the real thing. Even Newton was utilized as an example of this theory of the imitation of nature, for it was believed the order he had discovered in the intellectual, mathematical, and ethical world might also be located in the aesthetic universe as represented by the term "universal harmony," and so forth. The entire reflection of Descartes' use of beeswax to demonstrate to the world the flow of his thoughts comes into play with the use of wax, a very natural medium in itself. We must keep in mind that the statue of Holmes, and the gun that was employed to kill it, are both works of art. True enough the gun may also be a work of science, but that does not hinder its being also deemed a piece of art, especially to Descartes. Cathedrals were constructed with a religious purpose uppermost in mind, but they can still be viewed as art. Holmes has credited those forces that wish to destroy him as "my old enemies," and one of these old enemies who would also be judged an enemy of Descartes, and whose thoughts would be in conflict with his, is Isaac Newton. The Englishman and his school were opposed to Descartes on many points, especially in the fields of optics and physics. Spiritually, where Descartes had to appeal to the "truthfulness of God," as the copestone of his doctrine of the certainty of knowledge, Newton and the new scientists appealed more to reason and the truth of experience. Those such as Nicolas Boileau wished, in his aesthetics, to elevate art to the rank of an exact science, and hoped to introduce, in the place of merely abstract postulates, concrete applications and special investigations. This parallelism of the arts and science, symbolized by the air rifle, was one of the fundamental proposals of the mentality of the Enlightenment. Part of the idea was simply that both these fields were founded upon reason and should not be further separated; to do anything else is to destroy the real nature of each. There was often inclusive harmony between the scientific and aesthetic ideals in the era of the Enlightenment. The shooting of the wax model of Holmes is an amazing associative pun on the consequences of this new frame of mind for man, and its far-reaching influences, for we are told the dummy was made by Oscar Meunier, an artist, while the gun was crafted by the blind mechanic Von Herder, a scientist. The Enlightenment is regarded by many as the direct root of the Industrial Revolution; the period in which the occupation of the mechanic and the machine he used began to substitute for the vocation of the artisan. Before the Revolution, one man such as Meunier would devote his entire talent and time to crafting a single item in which he could take justifiable pride. Holmes points out to us that the artist "spent some days in doing the moulding," for the exertion of the artist was slow and labor consuming, and not affordable by everyone. With the advent of the Industrial Revolution, a group of people called mechanics, could each make a single part of a consumer item, such as a gun, usually using a machine or some other piece of equipment, and then different workers would assemble the final product. The day of the craftsman was over. Meunier is a pun on *menuisier*, a French word that means "a carpenter or an artisan in wood," and before the Revolution a *menuisier* manually labored in a woodworking studio with a few assistants creating some of the most striking furniture and related articles ever seen. In an age such as ours, craftsmanship of this caliber can usually be found only in art galleries or museums, while in early Europe it was employed to construct a desk or chair, or even a commode. Meunier has the German first name Oscar, for it was in France and Germany that some of the preeminent examples of this kind of thing were fashioned. The Enlightenment period itself ironically enough was one of the greatest epochs of design and workmanship the world has ever seen, but the mechanics like Von Herder put a bullet into the system with their machines. This rifle that Moran must assemble from pieces was made to the specifications of Professor Moriarty from the theories of men like Newton, speculation that led directly to both the advantages and drawbacks of the Industrial Revolution. The fact that Von Herder is blind may partly be a comment on the fact that one did not really need to see in order to take part in the making of an article using the mechanical process. A single person, working on one piece of a larger whole, can be blind, as we find in some controlled situations found in today's industrial society, and yet still turn out a fine product. Oscar Meunier however, could never compose his work of art if he were blind, for he must control the process from first to last and allow for a good deal of training and talent, and vision is necessary for that.

Some of the background for "The Empty House" is a reflection of the aesthetics of the French Enlightenment personality Bouhours, an advocate of the belief that art was not subject to a strict following of the laws of nature, but rather that a good deal of the love we feel as observers of the work rested, not in its correctness and precision, but rather in the opposed ideal of "inexactness." Aesthetic reason, as Bouhours points out, is not tied to the limit of the "clear and distinct." The mind enjoys and is inspired by the indeterminate and unfinished thought and it is not a matter of the simple content of thought and its objective truth that causes the enjoyment, but our witnessing of the process of thinking, of the subtlety, lightness, and swiftness with which it operates. Doyle gives a choice example of his unfinished thought when, following the capture of Moran, Lestrade and the other police rush into the room only to be told by Holmes, "I think you want a little unofficial help. Three undetected murders in one year won't do, Lestrade. But you handled the Molesey Mystery with less than your usual — that's to say, you handled it fairly well." Even though the unspoken thought was closer to the objective truth of the matter, Holmes changed one thought to another, almost immediately, leaving one unfinished, and it was a pleasure watching how quickly he disengaged himself from hurting his friend's feelings. Bouhours believed that aesthetically, a thought is more valuable the more it reflects process and the emergence of unexpected forms. Strictly "linear" thought, which classical aesthetics established as the norm, is insufficient here, for the straight line is the shortest distance between two points only in geometry, not in art, which should startle the mind, and what could be more startling than Holmes' salute to the captured Moran: "Journeys end in lovers' meetings." Nothing could be more false than the thought that these two love each other, so we are dealing here with an obvious falsehood, but a good piece of writing. Bouhours teaches that truth alone by no means makes an epigram good in the artistic sense, for if this were true, any logical proposition, no matter how poor in aesthetic qualities, would have to be considered art. An epigram such as Holmes', if used in a situation wherein its meaning was true, the opposite of what we have in the meeting of Holmes and Moran, would be true enough to meet the situation, but it would not be art. "Thoughts are sometimes trivial because they are true," Bouhours puts forth, and it is the sudden turns of expression, the new use we give to the epigram that gives them their aesthetic value. The real emphasis now falls more on the expression; in this case the sense of irony carried within the expression, than the real content of the thought, which in itself is trivial, even meaningless. Aesthetic reality as such does not originate and flourish in the pure and colorless light of thought; it requires a contrast such as false or true, or as Bouhours calls it, a distribution of light and shade, which we perceive in abundance in "The Empty House." The French philosopher demands for all efforts at making a work of art a certain amount of falsehood, and in the ambiguous he sees the combination of both forming a unity. The stress should not be simply on art that resembles something in nature (such as a representation of a human being, I might add here) but on the specific mode of artistic expression and representation. The bust of Holmes has far more meaning than just representing someone, and it is loaded with falsehood, this actually being its very purpose for having existence; creating a false impression. The image which art draws, since it never resembles or coincides with the object, is not condemned as untrue; it possesses rather its own immanent truth: "The figurative is not false and metaphor has its truth." In Doyle's work all is metaphor, illusion, allegory, association, and contingency.

The new motif discernible in Bouhours' work reaches full development only in René Dubos, another philosopher of the Enlightenment. Dubos no longer proceeds simply from the contemplation and analysis of works of art; he pays attention particularly to their effect, from which he tries to determine the real nature of art. In this analysis of the aesthetic impression of a work of art, subject and object are treated as equally necessary factors, for Dubos believed art was an "experience," an "impression," and I think Doyle has succeeded in giving us an artistic experience in "The Empty House."

In "The Red-Headed League," we have Bouhours: through Doyle's bringing into play the character of John Clay, showing us that genius often does not have "good sense." We could say, that from time to time Holmes himself lacks Bouhours' "good sense," and I think we are being shown an example of it in "The Empty House," although his genius remains unquestioned. After capturing Moran the detective turns to him and admits the Colonel took him by surprise: "I did not anticipate that you would yourself make use of this empty house and this convenient front window. I had imagined you as operating from the street." We have to ask ourselves why it was Holmes did not have the usual sagacity to imagine Moran might possibly utilize the empty house, especially since he realized the front window is convenient for the man's purposes, and certainly more private than Baker Street on a Saturday night. I even thought it rather stupid of Holmes to stand in the dark and let Moran put together his gun and load it. Moran might have sensed someone was in the room with him and quickly turned the gun on his intended night's target in an instant.

We know Holmes often steps outside the law in order to bring into being a more concrete justice, and John Clay as well obviously habitually runs counter to standard principles. Both Dubos and the English philosopher, Anthony Ashley Cooper, Earl of Shaftsbury, although divergent on a number of aesthetic tenets, admit that genius has the right and power to break "the tablets of the law" and to establish new rules by virtue of its own authority. We see in this the associative nature of Doyle's mind, especially if, in "The

Red-Headed League," we regard the stone slabs of the bank vault floor as stone tablets, which they are. Dubos and Shaftsbury also turn against all attempts to comprehend the nature of the beautiful by mere reasoning, by means of analytical distinctions. John Clay we are told was somewhat effeminate looking, a reference to the Earl himself. Doyle is also making an allusion to the expression denoting a good-looking boy as being "as pretty as a girl." Clay partakes of the nature of the beautiful with, and in, his antipodean personality, as well as his astounding contradictory moral measures, which cannot be rationalized by mere reasoning, for reason has nothing to do with Clay's aberrant existence. The character of the attractive in art for Lord Shaftsbury lies in pure creation, and so we have John Clay creating a work of art with his tunnel, for if he is beautiful he is only following his true temperament. Dubos saw beauty in "conception," and the concept of the tunnel can be contemplated as a work of art to satisfy this perception. He believed all aesthetic enjoyment owes its existence to certain reactions called forth in the "spectator" by the presence of the work of art. Dubos realized the value of the spectator in all this, and for our purposes here Holmes and Watson can be thought of as the spectators of Clay's, and Moran's works of art, and Watson in particular becomes the aesthetic observer, watching Moran and Clay in these dark rooms, whose thought and mental participation is equal in artistic weight to Clay's tunnel project and Moran's more subtle semiscientific air-gun project. Dubos put forth that a work of art had a certain "movement," and Clay, shovel in hand, and Moran, with his grave and inopportune concentration on his gun assembly, would have to agree. The spectator feels himself overwhelmed as it were, by the work of art and enraptured by its movement. The stronger the movement, the more intensely the beholder will feel it, and thus the more the artist will have accomplished his goal.

Dubos postulated that the artist should make us feel strong emotions when we look at their paintings or listen to their plays, these emotions being similar to what we feel, for instance, at the execution of a criminal or at gladiatorial combats or bullfights. As spectators we monitor with amazement the movement of Col. Moran as he prepares, like a predatory animal, to kill his victim, as well as Clay's first appearance in the bank vault, and both scenes end in desperate violent combat a gladiator would find familiar. A superior work of art arouses our emotions to a high degree, Dubos claimed, and this intensity is what Doyle hoped to capture in both these stories under discussion, especially in the brutal struggles in the dark between crafty opponents, with such scenes referring back to Descartes, and others. Dubos seeks to examine and survey the reactions of the viewer, the pure feelings, which are occasioned in man by works of fine art and good writings such as classical poetry. The highest requirement that we can make of the artist, the premier rule to which we can subject the artistic genius, one such as Clay, is not that genius follow certain objective norms in its production, but that it, as subject, must always be present in all its creations, again like Clay in his tunnel, and that it (the genius) can communicate and force upon the spectator its own profound emotions, which Clay and Moran have successfully accomplished. Dubos tells us, "Always be passionate and never allow either your spectators or your listeners to languish"; a shortcoming Doyle cannot be accused of. The intensity of the effect is looked upon as its valid aesthetic standard, and the degree of emotion it elicits decides its value.

The "sublime," in a work of art, is "that which moves and pleases," and all of Doyle's writings attempt this. After the middle of the eighteenth century the problem of the sublime rose to the same level as the question of the beautiful, although the concept was acknowledged before then, but Edmund Burke's *A Philosophical Inquiry into the Origin of Our Ideas of the Sublime and Beautiful,* published in London in 1756 constitutes the first essential presentation of the question. This work attempted to identify and decide fully certain aesthetic phenomena. Elements other than those with artistic foundation came into play within a good work of art Burke realized, and such things as distortion or terror that are not governed by rules or accepted standards are often the most important aspects of a work, especially when thought of in a psychological atmosphere. This phenomenon he calls the sublime. Never are we more powerfully moved then when we are confronted with the terrible, and this confrontation presents to our minds pleasure, for we have a sort of delight in the face of terror, a dread that involves our emotions, and it is this alarm that Doyle strives to achieve, especially in these two tales, but elsewhere as well. The horror and panic of an unknown being coming into our area, and that region being so dark we cannot make out clearly its nature, which we know to be malevolent, fills us with consternation and delight. As the features of Moran, satiated with vice, iniquity, and a longing for vengeance, is described for us in minute detail by Watson, himself gawking in astonishment in the half-light, we are being shown Burke's "face of terror." He calls this "a sort of delightful horror, a sort of tranquillity tinged with terror." The entire realm of aesthetics can be, and frequently has been, characterized by the expression "confused perception"; a reference to the truth that all art is a fusing together of elements that cannot be isolated without doing damage to the whole. It is confused perception, the perception of the Colonel in believing he is actually seeing Holmes sitting in a chair in his flat, that is a major philosophical element of "The Empty House." Thoughts of baffled observation reach out in supplementary directions as well, for the tricking of Moran has been brought into being by any number of diverse reasons. The study of what knowledge is, and how we acquire it or fail to acquire it, the field of epistemology, has intrigued philosophers from the beginning of time. The Colonel has been fooled into falling for this ruse, and the instrument of this artifice was his own imagination, and both Descartes and his countryman Nicholas Malebranche had something to say about the human imagination. Descartes believed in intuitive knowledge, as we might expect, but adds that the purely intuitive character of knowledge belongs to geometrical figures, for these are based upon the laws of spatial intuition. The nature of all being, in order to be clearly and distinctly conceived by the mind, and understood in pure concepts, first must be reduced to the laws of spatial intuition, which exists in the mind. However, he did hold that intuition had its limits and that there were obstacles that beset the imagination.

"Space," in Cartesian epistemology is not subject to the conditions of sensory experience or of the imagination, but to the conditions of pure reason, to the circumstances of logic and arithmetic. The discovery of analytical geometry resulted from Descartes' need to unearth a geometrical method by which all intuitive relations among figures can be represented and determined in exact numerical relationships. Now the predicament Moran experiences in telling that the wax figure of Holmes is not the actual man is a question of "space"; he is too far away from it. His "relationship" is flawed for he is being manipulated only by his intuition, not his logic, but his logic could not participate for there is too much space between the two figures. Moran permitted his imagination to run away with him. As part of his reasoning for doubting the reliability of his sense data, which led to the great discovery regarding his confidence that the mind unaccompanied is the seat of knowledge, Descartes emphasized that the sense of sight in particular can easily deceive us, for one may see something at a distance that eventually turns out to be quite otherwise when viewed close up. Since this sometimes happens, he suggests we cannot really be certain we are not always mistaken. Moran cannot clearly see the statue of Holmes; therefore he cannot recognize the truth of what its reality consists of. In *Meditations*, the philosopher says, "clarity and distinctness must be the marks of truth, the distinguishing characteristics by which you can tell the true from the false," adding, "whatever is clearly and distinctly conceived is true," but the Colonel's conception is neither clear nor distinct. Malebranche takes up the position of Descartes, and his major work, *The Search after Truth*, is chiefly devoted to this investigation. Here again the imagination appears not as a corridor to truth but as the source of all the delusions to which the human mind is exposed, in the realm of material science, and in the arena of moral and metaphysical understanding as well. The imagination may perhaps be the preliminary step to awareness, but without logic it can lead to immense confusion, and, as Moran has learned, to huge mistakes. Malebranche endorsed the belief that to keep the imagination in check and to regulate its scope is the highest goal of all philosophical criticism. Imagination must be left behind, especially when dealing with physical objects, for the real essence of these can be determined accurately only by the literal science of math, and not to do so is to permit the senses (which Moran does exercise) to dictate the essential existence of an object, but this nature may not be the real life of the article, but an illusion that does not capture the reality of the "thing in itself." Sift out the totality of sense properties and subjective illusion, and what remains in the sphere of truth is the real nature of the entity, not that which the object offered to direct perception, but what is now known is identified in certain pure relations which can be expressed in terms of exact and universal rules which are the fundamental framework of all being. We are talking here of course of logic and mathematics, and they are the norm from which being itself cannot deviate and which it cannot abandon without sacrificing its real character as being, that is, as objective truth. I believe I just heard Moran mutter under his breath, "Now you tell me!"

Epistemology, the problem of how sense perception is translated into knowledge, is hardly a philosophical abstraction, for just about anyone such as Descartes or Doyle, who has studied optics, either as a science or as a philosophical abstraction, has had to confront the fact that man's real understanding of this field is extremely limited. The fact that we do not really know the nature of light itself proves this. And the profound questions of what it is that affects what we see, and how we see it, is complicated by the issues raised by such questions as how do the various senses aid or interfere with each other. The best minds in history: William Molyneux, Bacon, Voltaire, and Diderot, among many others, worked on these questions, and in fact we have already witnessed some of Diderot's observations taken from his studies on the alteration of the senses of those who are blind, being utilized by Doyle to great effect in "The Red-Headed League." One central question in the field is how do we have the power, or lack of it, to distinguish objects with the visual faculty. How do we judge concerning these forms on the basis of purely optical data? Will we be able to "distinguish," by sight alone what something in actuality is, or is not? Étienne Bonnot de Condillac declared that these questions contain the source and key to all modern psychology, and he seems to be coming close to a great truth here. These questions he believed drew attention to the decisive role of the faculty of judgment in the simplest act of perception, and it is this judgment of perception as practiced by Moran that caused him to be mistaken in his mental act of perceiving the wax image as his enemy Holmes. One reason Moran is mistaken is because he has relied on sight alone in his judgment, and Molyneux and Condillac, just to mention two, question whether sight alone, or even sense as such, can clearly indicate and "produce," the physical world which we find in consciousness, or whether to this end it requires the cooperation of other powers of the mind. Even the element of time enters into it, for Col. Moran does not have enough time to think about what he is doing, for morning is coming, and he acts without the necessary "thought," that may have prevented him from making his costly mistake. Diderot points out that a child must be taught, through means other than vision, to know what it is looking at; one must take time with a child for it to be able to absorb the nature of what it sees. When you play "peekaboo," with an infant, a game children have loved for probably thousands of years, Diderot tells us the child actually believes you and it disappear when you both cover your eyes, not having any rudimentary understanding of the nature of material objects, such as human bodies. Thus the child, relying upon its vision alone, believes in this arbitrary and amusing disappearance and reappearance as reality.

Similar inquiries also occupied the mind of the Irish philosopher George Berkeley, culminating in his works, *An Essay Towards a New Theory of Vision*, and *A Treatise Concerning the Principles of Human Knowledge*, attempts at formulating his ideas on the subject. He had proceeded from the paradox that the only material available for the erection of the structure of our perceptual world consists in what we learn from our simple sense perceptions, but that, on the other hand, these perceptions do not contain the slightest indications of those "forms," in which perceptual reality is given. I believe Berkeley is saying that what we see does not inform us about how what it is we perceive came into being. What we observe could be made of anything: wax for instance, or even flesh and blood. We judge that we envision this reality before us as a solid structure in which every individual element has its assigned place, and in which its relationship to all other parts is exactly determined. The fundamental character of all reality lies in this definite correlation. Sight by itself is not enough however, for without input from the other senses there can be no real objective world, no "nature of things," as Berkeley called it. Ernst Cassirer tells us, "And not even the most determined idealist can deny this nature of things; for he too must postulate an inviolable order among phenomena, or else his phenomenal world will dissolve into mere illusion." The world of experience cannot help Moran for, according to Berkeley, experience shows us the reality of products, not the world of process; experience confronts us with objects having definite shapes, especially in respect to spatial arrangement, without telling us how they acquired these shapes. If Moran witnessed how his target object acquired its shape he would have seen the form of its becoming, not just its being, and would never have fallen for the trick.

Moran observed his target by "the light of the street," which "fell full upon his face." The ray of light that passes from the object to my eye, Berkeley claims, can tell me nothing directly about the object's shape or distance from me, for all the eye knows is the impression the object makes on the retina. This is important, for we know it is basically distance that has kept the Colonel from detecting Holmes' deception. The Irish philosopher has a great deal to say about position, magnitude, and distance, and what applies to our case is that distance between objects, or between perceiver and object, by its very nature is itself imperceptible, and yet it is an element which is absolutely essential to the structure of our conception of the world. Distance is a great, perhaps even the most imperative determinate in what we really see, in what our vision tells us is really there, and not just what we think is there. Berkeley discusses the reciprocal use of the other senses in order to get an accurate picture of reality that causes us to realize Moran could not be fooled if even one other of his senses (with the possible exception of smell, which is weak in the human animal) came into play. The other senses offer clarification that Moran, being as he is at a distance from the wax model, cannot take advantage of.

Every philosopher we have been dealing with, each of them, has been looking into his Aristotle, for the Greek seems to have thought of it all first. The question of vision will come up again when we discuss Baron Leibniz.

When Watson returns to the Baker Street flat the full import of the bust of Holmes as a work of art hits him, for he now sees that it is only a depiction of a small part of the natural man. Most of this personification of the nature of Holmes is simply blank space with a dressing gown covering the space causing one to think a human figure is beneath it. Moran has committed the fallacy of mistaking a part for the whole, which is a reference to Alexander Gottlieb Baumgarten, who regarded this thought as one of the problems of aesthetics, for a true work of art can never show us all of nature, but only a small "symbol" of it.

A good deal of time is spent discussing the "famous air-gun," and the method of its execution. "An admirable and unique weapon," the detective tells us, "noiseless and of tremendous power: I knew Von Herder, the blind German mechanic, who constructed it to the order of the late Professor Moriarty." The symbolic evil of the gun used to kill the Earl's son is part of the legacy of Moriarty himself. Descartes listed the study of mechanics, along with fields such as optics, music, and astronomy, as one of the "true mathematics," so this thing of science, this weapon, is a product of the mathematical mentality, and as such is opposed to the spiritual mentality of Holmes/Jesus. The one who made it was blind therefore he could not recognize the malevolent one he was serving; his blindness is denotative of his ignorance. But be aware that Diderot presented an argument that a blind person has no morals, so perhaps it would not have mattered to Von Herder who it was he was working for. In *Elements of Physiology*, which includes the notes he jotted down while reading the Swiss philosopher Albrecht von Haller, Diderot says, "the blind man who cannot see the outward aspects of a man in pain, is blind to much of life and cannot be expected to possess great compassion or a particularly refined awareness of goodness and beauty or any passionate love of truth." Von Herder could be a pun on Von Haller.

The gun is of German birth, just as is (primarily) the philosophy of materialism, with the German "mechanics," as they are called, believing that everything was matter, and that everything in the world, including the actions of man, were mechanical, thus determined only by laws of cause and effect. These mechanics were interested in penetrating behind the mechanisms, behind the events of nature, not being satisfied with merely beholding the picture of reality. Many thought this outlook reduced the dignity of the universe because such knowledge limits the world and the laws of nature to a sort of clockwork. Doyle displays this awareness of the analogy of the timepiece assessment of the universe when he has Watson tells us, "We have been in this room two hours, and Mrs. Hudson has made some change in that figure eight times, or once in every quarter of an hour." The two men are very conscious of time and can hear the bells of a church clock, for they are aware of the approach of midnight.

Bernard Fontenelle, the French Enlightenment thinker, was proud to be considered a mechanic, writing, "I esteem the universe all the more since I have known that it is like a watch. It is surprising that nature, admirable as it is, is based on such simple things." He can be regarded as an antagonist of Descartes, for he and some other Enlightenment thinkers no longer accepted Descartes' belief of a nature based on the laws of matter and motion alone; they no longer wanted to acknowledge the world as empirically given, setting themselves the task of analyzing the structure of the universe, in fact, of producing this structure with their own resources. Such mechanistic principles are the opposite of the free will advocates and also antagonistic to the ideology of Descartes and William James, both of whom held man's greatest asset to be his spirit; which the dummy of Holmes, the product of human ingenuity, completely lacks. This comes down to bifurcation, the question of soul or body; which of the two is more important. Von Herder is a reference to the German poet and philosopher Johann Gottfried von Herder, who lived from 1744 to 1803. De Quincey, in the essay just discussed, brings up Herder as one who, like himself, would consider murder as a suitable subject for a work of art. Descartes and James would regard Herder, and the other mechanics, as blind to reality for they are completely opposed to Cartesian belief in mind or spirit, and all it represents, and would gladly put a bullet through it if given the opportunity. "Plumb in the middle of the back of the head and smack through the brain," is how Holmes describes Moran's rifle shot. Notice the use of the word plumb, a method and instrument for making exact engineering calculations. Goethe says of Herder, "his significance as an historian and philosopher of history consists in the fact that he concentrates with all his might on the factual, the unique, and the particular, without succumbing to the sheer material power of the factual, to the mere matter of fact." Notice here the complimentary "unique," the very word Sherlock used to praise Von Herder's air-gun. Goethe commends as Herder's fundamental ability his gift to "transform the rubbish of history into a living plant," and the transformation of the walking stick into a gun can be construed as a metamorphosis, a word denoting changes in living organisms and other natural changes, but now being utilized for an inanimate change. Herder used the word "metamorphosis" in his theory of history to mean a process of a series of changes.

Those who do not believe in free will are regarded as mechanistic, and are not necessarily materialists. Diderot, later in life, came to the conclusion that man is "simply a passive mechanism acted upon by the various motives that have set him in motion, that he has not produced even one single purposeful act of his own will." Anyone who in this world is not satisfied with the visible and seeks the invisible cause of visible effects, is no wiser than a peasant who attributes the motion of a clock whose mechanism he does not understand, to a spiritual being concealed inside. The French thinkers in general adhered to a materialistic outlook that gave a clockwork vision to the universe. Some of the Enlightenment theorists went so far as to regard God himself as a mechanic, a sort of cosmic watchmaker who had built a superb machine, given it laws to run by, and then withdrew. From such a view it followed that the only reliable road to knowledge of God's plan was through science, through observations and experiment, not dogma and revelation. As such Diderot would naturally be diametrically opposed to the ideas of Descartes, as we know them. Diderot, in *Elements of Physiology*, tells us of man: "He has thought, he has felt, but he has acted no more freely than an inanimate body, than a wooden automaton made to execute all the same movements as he himself." The wax model is man without free will; man as the materialists view him. In the same essay the theorist claims, "will is always the effect of a cause that sets it in motion and determines its effect," which generates self-evident thoughts paralleling the theme of "The Empty House." After reenacting the Resurrection of Jesus, the two detectives return to their old apartment where Holmes "had thrown off the seedy frockcoat, and now he was the Holmes of old in the mouse-coloured dressing-gown which he took from his effigy." The frockcoat is an apt enough symbol for Diderot, who always wore such a garment, while the dressing gown is an excellent denoter for Descartes, who wore one almost constantly, and even wrote an essay about his comfortable old dressing gown. The effigy that is "Descartes in thought," as it were, sitting motionless in solitary silence, had on this gown, which Holmes now accepts as a mantle cloaking his own symbolic philosophical position.

It was Aristotle who first emphasized the thought that motion or movement is the sign of a soul, and that everything that moved, even plants, had souls. The bust of Holmes has movement, for that was the function of Mrs. Hudson, and she goes out of her way, risks her life even, to bring this motion into being. Mrs. Hudson brings "spirit" to the bust. Julien Offray de La Mettrie, a true materialist, writing in *Natural History of the Soul*, claims he is resigned "to being ignorant of how inert and simple matter (the wax dummy) becomes active and composed of organisms as I am to not being able to look at the sun without a red glass; and I feel the same way about the other incomprehensible wonders of nature, about the emergence of feeling and thought in a being which appeared otherwise to our weak eyes as a mere bit of dust." La Mettrie adds, "One must grant me only that organized matter is endowed with a principle of motion, which alone differentiates it from matter which is not organized, and that all animal life depends on the diversity of this organization." The principle of movement in the image has endowed that image with the ability to appear as a form of animal or organized life, for it is primarily a question of involvement and complication of structure of matter that gives life to higher forms of being. With respect to apes and the other higher types of animals, the behavior of man stands in the same relationship as the planetary clock constructed by Christian Huyghens does to a primitive timepiece, La Mettrie claims. He now introduces us to an actual corporeal mechanic; a mechanical genius famous for constructing lifelike creatures that achieved an amazing degree of animation. " If more instruments, more cogwheels, and more springs are required to register the movements of the planets than to denote the hours; if Vaucanson had to employ more art to produce his flutist than his duck, if he had employed still more energy he might have produced a being with the power of speech." The human body is a clock, La Mettrie insisted, just more intricate and better able to maintain itself, and this thought covers a big chunk of the symbolic intention of the image of wax. Remember Mrs. Hudson's movements were governed by the measurements of a clock. What this theorist did was to reduce everything in the universe to a clockwork mechanism and the question of the relation of the "essences" of body and soul did not disturb the early materialists, for to them the separation of corporeal and psychological phenomena is a mere abstraction without proof or support in experience. Moran is being displayed to us as a pure materialist who cannot tell the difference between the essence of the body, and the essence of the soul. The apparent chasm separating dead matter from vital phenomena, separating motion and sensation, is insignificant for the materialistic, so Moran has been fooled into error of thought leading to error of action. Dogmatic materialism for a thinker such a Doyle, who communicated with ghosts, was no doubt the pinnacle of folly and error. The materialists held we are ignorant of the manner in which sensation arises from motion, and that the same ignorance prevails when we are concerned with matter itself and its basic phenomena, nor can we understand conceptually the process of a mechanical impulse or the transmission of a certain momentum from one mass to another (Mrs. Hudson's to the image). They insisted we must be content to observe them in experience, but ignorance of Mrs. Hudson's transmission of motion has cost Moran the game, although he did indeed observe it in experience, but such experience proved to be a fallacy. La Mettrie wrote a book, *Man a Machine*, but we will leave it here for now. What Doyle has been trying to show is that we cannot rate the mind, or the soul, or any other psychological process higher than anything that has extension: anything that can come out of the mind and be given number, color, size, etc. La Mettrie believed this held true also for our desires, appetites, decisions, and moral acts, which would make him, especially in his incarnation as Col. Moran, the avowed enemy of Holmes/ Descartes.

I have simplified, but hopefully not vulgarized materialism, which should not be judged solely upon the applications our author puts it to in his stories, as clever as it is. Doyle has naturally left out thoughts, the inclusion of which would give a more three-dimensional, even ethical view of these thinkers and their works. The materialists attacked spiritualism and organized religion, even theology, for the same reasons these institutions attacked them; both sides held that they alone knew the formula for human happiness and truth, and they can be judged only by that standard.

The air-gun can be thought of as something organic, like a plant, since it has the capacity to change and grow, and this admission ushers into our study the philosophy of Leibniz, who brought into the world a new intellectual power and way of thinking that altered the content of the prevailing world picture, while empowering thinking in general with a new form and an innovative direction, and as such he can always be thought of as one of those thinkers who helped "kill" Cartesian notions. In many respects Baron Leibniz is simply a continuator of the ideas Descartes formulated, as if his intentions were to free the forces latent in that work in order to augment and enhance them further. His work in math stems directly from the French logician, as well as other aspects of his thought. Leibniz was a great mathematician, declaring there was no cleavage between his math and logic, or his metaphysics, claiming his entire philosophy was mathematical in nature.

It is in the Leibnizian concept of substance that we find the new trend in thought, for his metaphysics differs from Descartes in that it substitutes for his "dualism," a "pluralistic universe," wherein the basic structure of substance was the "monad," a unit whose true correlate is not particularity but infinity. The monad is different from the atom in that the atom is a fundamental substance of things that remains when matter is divided into its ultimate parts, a unit which, so to speak, resists multiplicity and retains its indivisibility despite every attempt to resolve it into subdivisions. The monad, on the other hand, knows no such opposition, for with the monad there is no alternative between unity and multiplicity, but only their inner reciprocity and necessary correlation. It is neither one nor the many, but rather like Moran's walking stick/air-gun, "the expression of multiplicity in unity." The monad is dynamic, a living center of energy, and it is the infinite abundance and diversity of the monads that constitute the unity of the world. "The nature of the monad consists in being fruitful, and in giving birth to an ever new variety," Leibniz claims, and anything that could happen to a monad must lie in the nature of that monad itself, also a reference to the gun, as is the fact that the monad "is," only insofar as it is active, and its activity consists in a continuous transition from one new state to another as it produces these states out of itself in unceasing succession. The reason for any of its states is to be found, initially at least, in the totality which constitutes its whole; a whole that is not the sum of its parts, but, as Leibniz says, is a thing that constantly "unfolds," into multiple aspects. The individuality of the monad (its uniqueness) manifests itself in these progressive acts of individuation, an individuation that is only possible and understandable, under the presupposition that the monad as a whole is self-containing and self-sufficient. Leibniz sums up his concept of the monad by bringing in a concept of "force," which is the present state of being insofar as this force tends toward a future state or contains that state in itself. The walking stick did contain, in itself, the force of the air-gun. Cassirer tells us, "The monad is not an aggregate but a dynamic whole which can only manifest itself in a profusion, in an infinity of different effects." He goes on to call the monad "a living center of force." Holmes declares that the gun is "of tremendous power," and this power or force was present in the walking stick, holding it for a future state. The Baron's theories have often been called a philosophy of "transformation," and indeed it is. The walking stick/air-gun is a monad in the dynamic activity of transformation from one form to another, this form being related and unrelated at one and the same time. "Anything we may find in the monad is to be understood rather as in transition," Cassirer claims, adding, "Its recognizability, its rational determinability is not owing to the fact that we can grasp it by a single characteristic criterion, but that we can grasp the rule of this transition and understand the laws according to which it takes place. Never is one of the elements just like another; never can it be resolved into the same sum of purely static qualities." The gun and its changes, and the laws of those changes, can all be understood for they are laws and functions found in art and science. Every simple element of the monad contains its own past and is pregnant with its future, the Baron insists, and so we are told of the past and future of the gun: where it was made, by whom, working under what conditions, to whose orders, and where it will eventually end up. And all aspects are related and unrelated to each other. This philosophy replaced the analytical identity of Descartes with the principle of "continuity," constancy in change, with the change the stick goes through being symbolic of this aspect of Baron Leibniz's thought.

Doyle seems to be making commentary on the abstruse and rarefied ideas of the Baron, with the concept of the monad uppermost in mind when he has his alter ego Holmes say of this gun, "For years I have been aware of its existence, though I have never before had the opportunity of handling it." Full comprehension of many philosophical concepts is anything but easy, with years of study often necessary before one can handle them, and Doyle is simply being honest. Perhaps this is his first reference to Leibniz in his stories, and that's what he is saying. I myself can understand the monad only as an abstraction, regardless of what Leibniz had in mind. Voltaire regarded Leibniz's ideology as a mass of "confusion," and when a philosopher named Christian Wolff published a fifteen-volume work on him, Voltaire claimed it "more than ever will put German heads to reading much and understanding little."

Leibniz put forth that every person was a monad, and like all substances other than God, each person/monad has both matter and form. The world of the monad also contains all the things of the mind: things such as perception, appetite, and a quality he called, ironically, "confusion." This confusion, which, strictly speaking, is the situation we find the Colonel to be in, for his point of view representing the universe around him, has ensnared him in complete confusion. The more confused the perception, the more "distant," do we represent a monad as being, distance being Moran's great error and the major source of his confusion.

Leibniz called the presupposition of all factual truth, "the Law of Sufficient Reason," and when Moran is finally subdued he complains to the police, in reference to Holmes, "there can be no reason why I should submit to the gibes of this person," for he does not believe he himself is subject to the laws of reason, and possibly has no regard for the truth.

Leibniz dwelt on the problem of the complexity of cause and effect, especially as to their connections, and therefore we have Moran admitting to Holmes, "You may or may not have just cause for arresting me." Notice he has left the question open, as it still is. These thoughts are as interesting, interlocking, overlapping, and convertible as the air-gun itself.

While we are talking about point of view we must bring in the fascinating discovery that the "cave," symbolized by the empty house, is also a reference to the cave of Plato, not just the tomb of Jesus. In the allegory of the cave, as Book Seven of The Republic is often referred to, Plato, through his speaker, Socrates, draws a picture for us of why some people cannot grasp reality. Socrates claims they are like people who only have one prospect in life, like "prisoners" chained to a wall, "from their childhood," whose situation forces them to look in only one direction, and in that direction a screen, something like the drawn shade on Holmes' window, has been raised for them to view, while upon the surface of this screen shadows of objects are thrown. The misguided prisoners would naturally assume these shadows, which represent the world of appearance, is as well the world of reality. Colonel Moran is like the prisoners, and indeed before the night is out becomes a prisoner and is referred to by that very word, due to his unawareness of reality; that the appearance of Holmes on the screen of his shade, is the real "universal, or form," of the man, but not the physical being. The truth of the reality of the dummy lies with Mrs. Hudson, who creates the illusion of self-motivation. She represents actuality but knows this certainty cannot be seen by anyone for, "She works it (the dummy) from the front, so that her shadow may never be seen," like those whose efforts give veracity to the shadows in the cave. Plato is sure that if a prisoner were to be released so that he was free to leave the cave and walk upward out of it, he would do so and encounter the light of the outside world, but this encounter would not be without difficulty for "he will suffer sharp pains; the glare will distress him," and "is he not likely to be pained and irritated," and confused by these new truths; the truths of reality that will now be brought home to him. Moran, as we see, is all of the above, and not the least bit grateful for being shown the light that Holmes now calls for. Leibniz held that the real nature of the world can be given from no single point of view, for everything is simply too complicated and confusing for that, thus for anyone to see through the falsehood to reality would necessitate many points of view. The point of view of each monad, or individual soul (in this case) is merely a matter of representing its internal constitution; it does not represent the universe as it is in itself. The reality of the world, through the principle of "preestablished harmony," will however, appear to be the same to each person Leibniz believed, for anyone strolling down Baker Street would have assumed they also were viewing Holmes sitting in his rooms, but the belief presents to us no knowledge of the real world, only its shadow. He argued that the whole world of common sense belief is no more than an "appearance," for reality is accessible to reason alone, since only reason can rise above the individual point of view. It was Moran's reasoning that was tricked, causing him to receive a false reading.

David Hume's version of all this is in some measure the opposite of Leibniz, for he denies the possibility of knowledge through reason, since reason cannot operate without ideas, and ideas are acquired only through the senses. The only experience that can confirm anything for us, according to Hume, is our experience, for they are as they seem, and seem as they are, for here seeming is all there is, and these sensory "impressions" are what make a belief true. In basing all knowledge on experience Hume reduces my familiarity of the world to my point of view. Moran followed Hume's advice, but his sensory impressions told him a living man was on the other side of the shade, and he was proved wrong to begin with, based upon only impressions, as it were. When I claim to have knowledge of objects externally to my perception, all I can really mean is that those perceptions exhibit a kind of constancy and coherence, which "generate an illusion." Watson says the dummy ruse was so well put together, "the illusion from the street was absolutely perfect." Notice our attention is called to the fact that it all depends on where you are viewing the statue from for the illusion to work. Hume deemed all claims to objectivity became spurious and illusory, and Moran would have to agree. Our reason can inform us as to "relations of ideas," for example it can inform us that the idea of space is included in that of shape, but what space in what shape Doyle is asking. It can all be an illusion. Hume claimed that reason could never lead to knowledge of matters of fact. Stauton tells us, "Hume took his skepticism so far as to cast doubt upon the existence of the self, saying that neither is there a perceivable object that goes by this name, nor is there any experience that would give rise to the idea of it." It is the very selfhood of Sherlock Holmes that is in question. Watson reinforces thoughts of this problem a number of times, as when upon initially seeing the model from across the street he actually must touch Holmes, although he is standing right next to him, to confirm the detective's selfhood, and perhaps more important semantically, when he for the first time enters the Baker Street rooms, and instead of saying that Mrs. Hudson was there alone, says, "There were two occupants of the room," the one being the landlady, the other "the strange dummy." An inanimate thing being called an occupant is tantamount to endowing it with spirit, which causes us to question who is the real Holmes. It was of course also the question of the existence of the self that motivated some chief thoughts of Descartes.

Much of Kant's work is a reflection of these ideas of both Hume and Leibniz, and a comprehension of the one is not really possible without some knowledge of the others. Kant saw this skepticism of Hume as a threat undermining the foundations of scientific thought. He believed neither experience nor reason alone was able to provide knowledge, since the first provides content without form, the second form without content. Only in their synthesis is knowledge possible; hence there is no knowledge that does not bear the marks of reason and experience together, and such knowledge is genuine and objective, transcending the point of view of the one who possesses it. I mention this now because this seems to be close to Holmes' variety of knowledge, reason and experience working together in an atmosphere of almost pure thought.

The wax figure made in Grenoble, France, is a personification, in part, of the thoughts of Descartes, who may have lived in or visited Grenoble, for he traveled much. Both he and the wax figure were French. The shooting of the model by the gun, which is a product of science, represents the distinction Descartes felt to exist between the arts and the sciences. As L. J. Beck in *The Method of Descartes* tells us, "In making his distinction between the sciences and the arts, Descartes explicitly posits a distinction between mind and body, the former depending upon the cognitive exercise of the mind, the latter upon the exercise and disposition of the body." The wax figure represents, one way or another, the body; the human body that is experiencing and therefore learning the arts. The French philosopher's critique of the arts announces his general refusal to confront experience (which comes into the body like a bullet, [my metaphor]) and the instrumental role of the body in the acquisition of knowledge. The abolition of the body as a mediating term between cognition and the world underlies the radical separation of the mind from the body. The bullet "passed right through the head and flattened itself on the wall." Is Doyle trying to say that this missile's effect, as a piece of experience on the body was negligible, and that it fell flat? Maybe he's claiming it had no effect at all, for the wax, as Descartes so carefully showed us, can simply be reworked, leaving the mind of this occupant untouched. The gun comes close to being a work of art itself and we know it is going into a museum, but you can find all sorts of things in museums. Doyle may be calling our attention to the school of thought of Newton/Moriarty, in which the air-gun is the product of a scientific mind that does not involve itself with the end use of its research or development. Von Herder may be blind, but he certainly cannot fail to realize that a weapon such as his would have only one real purpose, to murder people noiselessly. He is an evil genius himself, he would have to be in order to engineer such an instrument in spite of his handicap. Taking an ordinary bullet, as Moran has done, and crafting it into a soft-nose, a dumdum, which spreads out and becomes jagged at the edges before it hits the flesh, is also a good example of scientific principles (ballistics) being used for a malevolent purpose. In "The Adventure of the Mazarin Stone," Holmes also has a wax figure of himself made, whose maker, Tavernier, a French name for landlord, tradesman, or tavern owner, may be a reference to Descartes having discovered his system of thought in which existence is centered in the mind, while staying at a tavern. Jean-Baptiste Tavernier was the name of a famous French jeweler who supplied rare gems to European royalty. The maker of Count Sylvius' air-gun is a German mechanic named Straubenzee; names and thoughts whose meanings I yet hope to explore.

Some of the imagery refers back to the studies in psychology of Condillac, a man held in high esteem even by those who disagreed with his findings. The question of what sensations register on the mind, how the mind utilizes these sensations, etc., has interested philosophers since before Plato. Condillac believed the senses are not the "cause," but the "occasion" of all knowledge, for it is not the senses which perceive, it is rather the mind itself which perceives when modifications of bodily organs take place. Mental operations are transformed sensations. He, like Bacon, assumed we must create the whole human mind anew in order to really understand its structure, how we change and grow mentally. Here is exactly what Holmes has done, fashioned a new being, a whole new human mind, although the mind is implied. The fact that it is made of wax adds to its value philosophically, I think. Condillac is saying we are obligated to carefully observe the initial sensations of which we become aware; we must discover the first operations of the mind, watch them in their development, and pursue them to their extreme limits. In the *Treatise on Sensations*, his most significant work, he does not merely attempt to set forth a list of observations; he follows a rather strict systematic plan, and proceeds from a systematic assumption to which he tries to adhere and which he tries to prove step by step. One illustration he uses to prove his point is that of an inanimate statue which is awakened to life by means of the impressions striking it, and which in this way advances to increasingly rich and differentiated forms of life. When the mind of the statue of Holmes' body is struck by a sensation that is the pellet from the air-gun, it certainly can be said that a modification of a bodily organ has taken place, it has changed, and this alteration was created by the first sensation we are aware of, so observation should be made of it, and this is just what Holmes and Watson do, in some detail.

The conflict that is the theme of this story has not been resolved yet for the antagonism, the struggle between Holmes and Moran, has associations to any number of philosophical historic conflicts as well as the religious and scientific disputes already discussed. One such competition for the minds of man transpired between our old friend Herder and a newcomer, Baron de Montesquieu, a French philosopher and historian, whose most famous work, *The Spirit of the Laws*, was an investigation of that subject plus a good deal more. The volume is a description of the forms and types of state governments and their constitutions, and of the forces that brought these systems into being. Baron de Montesquieu believed the ideal society was a secular society; the subjects of a state should obey the laws for political and legal reasons, not on tribal or religious grounds. In this great treatise, often regarded as the first work that could be labeled sociology, the Baron stated that the laws that govern the shape of human societies are established by institutions, while social and private behavior is conditioned by climate, soil, and religion, and all these things in turn influence politics. His method of study was roughly equivalent to modern comparative sociology; he assembled information on primitive and civilized societies, past and present, and compared their various features. Of interest is that some of the writings of Herder contained an unabashed attack on the thoughts of Baron de Montesquieu, for the German did not agree with his interpretation of the historical reality of history. Herder assailed his methods as well as his premises. The details of the philosophical spat do not really concern us, but rather that it took place at all, for Doyle is recreating the conflict itself as the bullet from Von Herder's gun carries within it the spirit of the assault on the mind of Montesquieu, the firing of the shot into his brain. In philosophy the work of an individual, and usually any others that follow his example in thought is called "a body of knowledge," with the wax image symbolizing Montesquieu's body of knowledge (he had many followers) being attacked by his major critic. The dummy has been struck with a missile designed to do as much damage as possible. Baron de Montesquieu held that in a good government every "force" within the society has a "counterforce" to keep it in check and balance. Many forms of administration familiar to us have taken this message to heart; hence we have two houses of Parliament in England, two different, often opposed "houses" in America, and so forth. The force that is Moran and his allies counterbalances Holmes and his associates, and Doyle shows responsiveness to this thought when we learn from the police that Moran is "The man that the whole force has been seeking." An awareness of the group nature of the actions is evident, for Moran is considered one of the "old enemies," and the police are the "merry men." Baron de Montesquieu, like Herder, is a philosopher of history, one who studies history from a philosophical point of view. Not unlike Sherlock, Montesquieu shows a decided love of detail in his work, which was extensive, and he traveled a great deal in an effort to comprehend his subject, which basically was the history of law, the major field of Sherlock and Wendell Holmes. In his writings his delight in particulars is so evident that at times his illustrative anecdotes overshadow the main lines of thought and threaten to make them unrecognizable. With respect to content however, all this material is dominated by a strictly logical principle.

The face of Moran, that of a philosopher above and a sensualist below, is a reference to Immanuel Kant, a superior thinker having quite a sensual, lusty love of women. Herder, a pupil of Kant, in admiration, described him as a man who "in his most vigorous manhood had the gay liveliness of a youth which will, I believe, accompany him into his old age. His forehead, built for thinking, was the seat of indestructible serenity and joy, talk rich in ideas issued from his lips, joking, humor, and wit, were at his disposal, and his teaching lectures were the most amusing concourse." Herder in a sense became a continuator of his, and they could be thought of as one entity. Kant's influence on the world of thought was wide and deep for his mind ranged over so many fields and illuminated such diverse matters that Goethe, whose own mind was almost as vigorous, claimed that reading Kant was like entering a lighted room.

Kant's investigation into the nature of knowledge was an enterprise in the great tradition of Newton and Hume, and there is reason to believe he wanted to be regarded as the Newton of philosophy, evidenced by his seemingly constant effort to find correspondences connecting his thoughts to Newton's laws, as well as mentioning Newton repeatedly in his writings. In his Preface to *Critique of Pure Reason* Kant claimed, "there is not a single metaphysical problem which has not been solved, or for the solution of which the key at least has not been supplied," and he does indeed, at least here, sound like Newton, who seems to have felt the same way about science. Kant saw in Jean-Jacques Rousseau the Newton of the moral world, and interestingly enough he possessed only one work of art, an engraved portrait of Rousseau. The French thinker is alluded to in a fascinating manner in "The Final Problem," when we are told that an account of Holmes' death appeared in the *Journal de Genève*, although he is actually alive, for this in point of fact happened to Rousseau while he was living in Geneva, when his enemies, hoping to give reality to their desires, placed his obituary notice in German and Swiss newspapers while he was still living. The remarkable archetype for this incident in "The Final Problem" causes me to speculate if Doyle did not, in the back of his mind at least, even now, ten years before writing "The Empty House," have plans for resurrecting his hero one day.

Kant was the author of works on dynamics and math, and at the age of thirty-one published a treatise on the origin of the universe which contained the first formulation of the nebular hypothesis. His writings on religion exhibit one of the first attempts at the demystification of theology, claiming man should not bring God down to simple human understanding through such things as the use of images and anthropomorphism. In this he is obviously going against what Doyle seemed to believe, if we accept Holmes as a Christ figure: wax image, Resurrection, and all. Kant holds we should not accept anyone as a substitute for the reasoned interpretation of God, believing God cannot be experienced through the senses. In *Meditations*, Descartes offered proof of the external world by establishing the existence of an Omniscient God with the universe then validated as an object of

God's awareness, which needs no perspective. The essence of Kant lies in his egocentricity. All the questions of existence, including God, must be asked from the standpoint that is mine: my point of view, my perspective, and a position I find to be an early existential development of thought. Kant proposed one could find the answer to every philosophical question in the presuppositions of the perspective from which it must be asked, a theme developed by William James, among others. The dissension of thought represented by the considerations of Descartes and Kant cannot possibly be reconciled, whereupon Doyle has Moran/Kant fire a pellet through the brain of Holmes/Descartes, immediately followed by hand-to-hand violent combat between the two antagonists.

The major question for the German thinker, as stated in *Critique of Pure Reason*, is the problem of objective knowledge, as this had been posed by Descartes, who believed it was senseless to doubt I exist, for existence is an objective fact, proved by one's doubt itself. Kant called the Frenchman (with a sneer, possibly) the "I think philosopher," at least once. At one point Kant says that no person has the point of view of subjectivity who does not have knowledge of objective truths, for he would belong to a universe of things which can be other than they seem, and which exists independently of his own perspective. The question of what really is, and what may in fact be other than it seems, runs all throughout Kant's writings, in common with "The Empty House." He also questions what has the power to exist when unobserved.

Challenging the truth of Descartes' "I think, therefore I am," Kant claims that "although it expresses the consciousness that accompanies all thought, it does not include any knowledge of the subject, it is idealistic because although it can include itself and is always included in every representation, it does not involve any knowledgeable experience of itself." He also challenges the intuitive character of the *cogito* (I think) argument; holding that it does not have empirical comprehension therefore there is no experience of it. Beyond a logical meaning of the "I" we have no awareness of the subject itself. Kant disagreed with Descartes' first premise and the doctrine of the soul that flowed from it. We cannot be sure of our present mental state Kant claimed, because we cannot extend our skepticism into the subjective sphere, holding that I cannot be immediately certain of what I am, or of whether, indeed, there is an "I" to whom these states belong, asking, "What is the character of this immediate and certain knowledge?" "The distinguishing feature of my present mental states is that they are as they seem to me and seem as they are," he believes, adding, "In the subjective sphere being and seeming collapse into each other," while "In the objective sphere they diverge." Holmes and his image are in the objective sphere, and in fact the mindless dummy may never be in the subjective sphere since it has no thinking "I" and therefore they are diverged, separate, much to Moran's chagrin. He had much to say about "illusion," and even the logic of illusion, and some of his thoughts lead us to the problem of the question of whether the world must be as it appears, asking "how subjective conditions of thought can have objective validity" in oblique reference to the above. A case could be made that this is the theme of "The Empty House."

There can be no judgment without objectivity is his position. Subjective conditions can be thought of as the philosophy of Descartes however, and Doyle could be questioning whether these conditions can be objectified. "The world is objective because it can be other than it seems to me," Kant says, and so he gets just what he deserves and expects, when as the persona of Moran he looks out the window and sees, not the subjective world, but the objective image of Holmes, and accepts it as reality. "So the true question of objective knowledge is: how can I know the world as it is?" This is the question Moran should have asked himself on, let us say, Saturday afternoon. "I can have knowledge of the world as it *seems*, since that is merely knowledge of my present perceptions, memories, thoughts, and feelings. But can I have knowledge of the world that is *not* just knowledge of how it seems?" Kant asks. In the psychodrama unfolding before us, only Holmes and his allies seem to have that. The philosopher states that the character of an object is given by the point of view by which it can be known, and he wonders if we can have knowledge of the universe that is not just knowledge based on my individual point of view. Science, common sense, theology, and personal life all suppose the possibility of objective knowledge, and if this supposition is unwarranted then so are almost all the beliefs that we commonly entertain, Kant realizes.

The final sentence of "The Empty House" assures us, "once again Mr. Sherlock Holmes is free to devote his life to examining those interesting little problems which the complex life of London so plentifully presents." This is Holmes speaking of himself in the third person; speaking in a self-conscious technique bringing our minds to Kant's thoughts which deal with the conditions of self-consciousness and its relationship to time and duration, emphasizing that we endure only if our past explains our future since this gives us genuine duration rather than an infinite sequence of momentary selves. Moran is in on this for he lives on Conduit Street, a conduit being a device for aiding the continuous flow of a liquid for he has continuous duration; his past explains his future perfectly. The statement also relates to Kant's moral attitude towards "duty," moral duty as expressed by Holmes, and is as well the way Kant explained his distinctive moral vision. He believed that duty was the purpose of practical knowledge; you put your knowledge to work in a moral expression. Those little problems Holmes is so modest about are after all actually the all-important effort to fight evil. It was Kant who postulated that man was encumbered by "radical evil," in reference to human nature, a thought that caused Goethe, in spite of his admiration for the man, to say that the elderly philosopher had "slobbered on his philosopher's cloak." According to Kant's famous maxim that "ought implies can," the right action must always be possible; which is to say, we must always be free to perform it. Holmes tells us he is free to solve life's problems and thus is what the German called "a moral agent," who "judges that he can do a certain thing because he is conscious that he ought, and he recognizes that he is free, a fact which, but for the moral law, he would never have known." In other words, the practice of morality forces the idea of freedom upon us. Holmes is free to do his duty, if you wish. Kant admits later in his writings that he finds a contradiction in this, but Doyle ignores this.

I know that Kant is brought into other stories. "Dirty-looking rascals," Holmes observes as he watches shipyard workers heading home after a day's work on the banks of the Thames in *The Sign of Four*, "but I suppose every one has some little immortal spark concealed about him. You would not think it, to look at them. There is no à priori probability about it." The question of *a priori* probability is dealt with, not exclusively of course, but certainly emphasized by Kant, who put more thought into the problem of *a priori* and *a posteriori* concepts and their application to human knowledge and existence than any other theorist I personally know of.

With the conflict involving Kant and Descartes we are witnessing nothing less than a battle of the gods, for in the world of thought evolution that is a justifiable designation for both of these great men. Has Holmes in this wax reincarnation become a *deus ex machina*, a deity brought in to interfere in the action, a god from the machine? Kant, in his famous letter to Markus Herz of Feb. 21, 1772, said, "Plato took an older conception of the divine being as the source of principles as pure concepts of the understanding, while Malebranche took a conception of God which still prevails." Malebranche intensified Descartes' doctrine of innate ideas to the assertion that we see all things in God. There is no true knowledge of things except insofar as we relate our sense perception to ideas of pure reason. In this Kant does not seem to be so different from Plato himself. "But a *deus ex machina* in the determination of the origin and validity of our knowledge is the most preposterous device that one can choose; and, besides the vicious circle in the sequence of influences from it, has the further disadvantage that it fosters every pious or brooding whim," Kant warns us. The wax model of Holmes has indeed led to mistakes in the "determination of the origin and validity of our knowledge" as well as leading to pious thoughts. In this negative, even irreligious statement, the German philosopher reinforces his position as an enemy of Descartes, and it's easy to imagine him wishing to be able to poke holes in the earlier man's thoughts. Kant, with this symbolic killing of Descartes, may be understood as now replacing him as the first truly modern philosopher, as many deemed. But although he blasted a nasty wound into Descartes' body of knowledge, we know that the wax has not really been injured, it's too soft and malleable, and a few minutes work will have it as good as new. Doyle realizes many thinkers have had their shots at Descartes, and have more or less left their marks on him, but his thoughts continue to be read and studied, and argued over, and never fail to find supporters in each new generation, and in many ways he's more popular now than ever.

In his work *Substance and Shadow* of 1863, Henry James, Senior, claims the proper study of philosophy is a demonstration of the Infinite and the Absolute; God. The book is basically a reaction to Kant's beliefs, which James says has reduced existence to its scientific and materialistic aspects that are understood by the senses but not by the mind or through conception. James considers this simply absurd, for the real life is the life of the mind, the conception, especially the conception of God. "You ask Kant a question of creative substance or spirit, and he answers you by an analysis of constitutive surface or body. You ask him what creates things, or gives them absolute being irrespective of our intelligence; he replies by telling you what produces them to sense, or gives them phenomenal existence." Do we not have here Moran's mistake? He does not realize the wax manikin, which Watson tells us Holmes takes pride in as though it were "his own creation," has phenomenal existence, and can be validated by the senses (at a distance, as the case may be) but lacks the things of the spirit that would endow it with life. James accuses Kant of causing philosophy to abandon her true mission, the study of the spiritual world. "A true Philosophy whenever confronted with this grand fact of selfhood, this supreme fact of life or consciousness, cannot help feeling herself on hallowed ground; cannot help feeling herself in the presence, veiled it is true but still most vital, of the Infinite and Absolute: and it is a rare philosopher as philosophers have hitherto been estimated, who is not utterly disconcerted by the apparition." Moran has indeed been disconcerted by his confrontation with the apparition of the Absolute. James goes on to say that Kant was more a man of science (Von Herder?) than a philosopher. "He lent himself with extreme good will to the scientific demolition of religion as a doctrine; but he had no foresight whatever of its philosophic reconstruction as a life. He had no objection to exalt the purely negative scientific research of cause into a positive utterance of Philosophy; but when as here he found it bringing him face to face with the infinitely more august because truly philosophic problem of creation, he felt an instant instinct of disaster to all those cherished interests of skepticism by which his intellectual vision was bounded, and without more ado accordingly he gathered up his coat-tails and fled ignominiously to the uttermost parts of the earth." Kant, Herder, and Newton, not to mention Doyle's creations Moriarty and Moran, among others, represent those modern theorists who seek to explain creation on purely scientific or logical terms, which, according to James, denies creation in any intelligible sense of the word. They know the universe of the wax without its spirit and therefore must account for existing things on scientific principles, or without the allegation of spiritual substance. Holmes has "the true philosophy," which, when one is in its presence, one feels its vitality and truth, even though it may be veiled from us, as the model was from Moran. James claims, "The modern philosopher especially has drunk of the new wine of science till he has become foolishly inebriated and lost the remembrance of higher worlds." He interprets this attitude as a direct assault upon God, or in this case Holmes. James tells us he sees a number of German philosophers performing over the years the same horrible work as Kant and he brings up Johann Fichte and Friedrich Schelling as part of the plot (the old enemies?) of "converting our very faculty of knowledge itself upon which we fondly relied to give us eternal conjunction with God, into a faculty of unlimited self-deception merely: *i. e.* into a guarantee of our eternal and most righteous incorporation in the devil." Self-deception is Moran's great error. What should be a union with God, Kant and his supporters would turn into a pact with the devil. The promoters of Kant's philosophy represent the world of shadows, as Henry James, Senior, says in *Christianity the Logic of Creation*, adding, "The sensible world is purely formal, not essential; it is, and ever will be, the realm of shadow, not of substance; of seeming, not of being." He assures us the world of the spirit casts no shadow and we know Moriarty cast a black shadow upon the earth, for he is a thing of sense and science; a being that can block light and cause shadow. The world of shadows is "a sphere of effects not of ends." James tells us, "evil is only the running away of the fish with the line which binds him to his captor, and is but a surer argument of the skill which is bound eventually to bring him to land." Give evil enough rope and it will hang itself. It is Holmes who, though seeming to flee Moriarty, has actually reeled him in like a hooked fish, bringing about the final meeting, and he as well succeeded in luring Col. Moran into his trap. James equates Kant with death, for he claims the man represents the death of the soul since his scientific logic would kill the soul, and he claims Sir William Hamilton assisted Kant in bringing about this condition of reducing the man of science to a coroner, and the philosopher to an undertaker. Now one of the commentators on Henry James, Senior's writing tells us the William Hamilton referred to is the Scotch philosopher who believed only in using one's common sense to find truth, and not the Irish mathematician, and I am sure Doyle knew this, and he must have seen the irony of it.

From Plato onward the problem of semblances as a producer of illusion and error is recognized. Representation based upon resemblance often gives occasion to error according to Descartes, who tells us in his work *Regulae*, "Whenever men notice some similarity between two things, they are wont to ascribe to each, even in those respects in which the two differ, what they have found to be true of the other." Something that looks like Holmes is Holmes, Moran assumes, since both objects have the same silhouette, but Descartes realized the interpretation of the resemblance was wrong since only the similarities were being dealt with. Much of Descartes' work is built upon Platonic thoughts and metaphors with his mind even acquiring the feel of Plato's rich mental texture, in spite of his claims to originality. Doyle's mind is also based upon Plato, while his alter ego, strangely enough, is based squarely upon Aristotle, if you close your eyes to some, but only some, of Holmes' spiritual aspects. We cannot picture Sherlock Holmes at a spiritualist séance, except perhaps to debunk it, yet his creator attended them with regularity. If you wish to introduce your mind to a mind based on Aristotle, read Oliver Wendell Holmes; if you want to meet a mind with a foundation in Plato, study Descartes. In *Discourse*, Descartes borrows architectural analogies taken from *The Republic*, hoping to bring into focus his thoughts on the composition and organization of his new network of knowledge, his method, comparing it to a new city being built upon empty land. He compares himself to Plato in the fact that they are both founders of novel ground rules for neoteric models: in Plato's case, cities, the Republic, and paths of knowledge, in Descartes' case, the method, for actual men to live better lives; new houses for men's bodies and new schema for their minds. Also in *Discourse*, the philosopher alludes to the Platonic allegory of the cave, already mentioned, to describe his own philosophy, telling us other philosophers seem to him "similar to a blind man who wishes to fight on even terms with one who can see, and brings him to the back of some very dark cave." It is in the interest of such people that he will abstain from publishing his principles, for being so simple and evident as they are, publishing would be like throwing open a window flooding the room with light. His enemies would not stand a chance if he were to publish, for the light from his knowledge would aid only him, who has the vision to use it. Here we see the bond between "The Red-Headed League," and "The Empty House," for both are framed upon this thought, with both using the imagery of men fighting each other's wills in a darkened room.

Descartes, like Plato, saw himself as the only one who could solve the problem of the relationship to appearance, with the modern thinker picturing himself as the one who engineers the abolition of Plato's cave by putting windows in the thing, and then throwing them open. Descartes' new principles are the windows, the luminous difference signifying the displacement of one system of thought by another, creating a new kind of philosopher, based upon the subject, who stands outside of ordinary philosophy. The window now opens to the modern world, which acquires the character of representation; of a picture subtended by the position of the subject. He seems to be saying a new position in philosophy will show us a new concept of representation. A new position in reference to Holmes' window would show some people a completely different appearance also. Holmes, the thinking subject is looking at Holmes, the object, the dummy that cannot think, and therefore has no existence, because Descartes has told us, "I think, therefore I am." It is the ability of the human subject to think that gives it existence, even "humanity," as Descartes said, so Moran has merely killed Holmes as an object. The wax bust is the "form" of Descartes' thought, as Aristotle would call it, given material substance through the wax.

Now here is the point of all this thought, as far as I can make it out. "The Empty House," is one great philosophical metaphor or allegory based on everything we have just been talking about. What Doyle is saying is that as far as he is concerned Descartes is absolutely right. The material world is as nothing. The wax that gives the material universe dynamism can take on any memory and any form you may wish to give it. Each person looking at the mannequin of wax saw it as something different: Moran, as his old enemy given flesh and blood, which blood he now hopes to shed, Mrs. Hudson, as a god to be worshipped, and for whom she would lay down her life in martyrdom. Watson sees a dummy as strange as the rest of the night's adventure, and Holmes as "I am," without "I think," and "therefore" not him in reality, but a thing to be used as bait to lure the devil of the mechanical world into a trap. The physical property of the matter is secondary to the mental image of it. Everyone visualizes something entirely different in the object that is the wax, for the real essence of everything is strictly in the mind of each person, not in the wax, although it is of the wax. We have seen Watson transfer human personality; an anthropomorphic signature, to the icon, saying there were two occupants of the room and the statue is now regarded as a Christ figure fit for worship, for Sherlock Holmes personifies the Second Coming.

Here's something really interesting I would like to share with you before moving on to the next story. In the 1908 short piece "The Jolly Corner," we have a case of Henry James, Jr. borrowing from Doyle, instead of the other way around. Remember, "The Empty House" was written in 1903. In James' story we find Spencer Brydon paying a visit to his childhood home in New York City after spending more than thirty years in Europe. The large house he has inherited is now up for sale and stands empty in the heart of the city. Brydon enters into the habit of visiting the empty rooms in the middle of the night, for he enjoys the sensations and emotional situations it gives rise to. On one such visit he encounters the "ghost" of himself as he would have been had he stayed in crass New York struggling for financial power rather than enjoying a more cultured leisure life in Europe. The ghost, for some reason, perhaps to display wealth, is dressed in "evening-dress, of dangling double eye-glass, of gleaming silk lappet and white linen, of pearl button and gold watch-guard and polished shoe." He has obviously just come from the theater or opera. Spencer christens his alter ego "the fanged or the antlered animal brought at last to bay." The apparition has his face covered with his hands, which he slowly lowers to reveal an expression so hideous, unknown, inconceivable, and awful, that Spencer must turn "away from it in dismay and denial." A bizarre psychological confrontation between two personas: Brydon as he is, and Brydon as he would have been, follows; a staring contest involving the two divergent personalities: one grasping, blatant, and vulgar, the other a man of some culture and refinement. The phantasm vanishes after showing Spencer what greed and ambition may have forced him to become. This scene is some of James' best writing, as is the similar scene by Doyle. The work has much else in common with "The Empty House," including a returning native son coming from foreign lands, allusions to big game hunting, policemen outside in the street, and so forth. Women play a large role in each: Mrs. Hudson in the Doyle piece, Mrs. Muldoon and Alice Staverton in James' work. Doyle must have read this short story and his observations would be invaluable. He realized the experience of Henry James, Sr. having been visited by a malicious presence had not been lost on the son. I wonder if Henry understood fully all that Doyle had taken from him, from his brother William, and even his father. If he did see it all he must have found it unbelievable.

Chapter Fourteen. Let Sleeping Dogs Lie

A Dr. James Mortimer visits Baker Street, asking the two investigators to look into the mysterious death of his neighbor Sir Charles Baskerville, thus beginning one of Sir Arthur's most successful pieces of writing, *The Hound of the Baskervilles*. Three months previous the man was found dead at the foot of a yew alley adjoining Baskerville Hall, having ostensibly died of heart failure, with the coroner's jury returning such a verdict, but Mortimer suspects the death had been deliberately caused by frightening the man, which amounts to murder. An old manuscript in which the curse of the Baskervilles is laid out instigated his speculations, and Dr. Mortimer now reads the document's tale of Sir Charles' randy ancestor Hugo Baskerville's abduction, in days of yore, of the innocent daughter of an honest yeoman. The maid makes her escape into the black night, but Hugo lets slip the hounds as he and his worthless henchmen follow in pursuit. Hugo's rowdy underlings lose their master temporarily, catching up with him just in time to witness a huge, black, nightmare of a hound tearing at his throat, the girl herself lying nearby, dead of fright. Since then it has not been safe for any member of the Baskerville family to walk upon the moor at night for fear the phantom hound will carry out further vengeance upon them.

The latest Baskerville heir, Henry, newly arrived from Canada to claim the estate, joins them in London where it is decided that he, Watson, and Mortimer, will proceed by train to the moorlands of Devonshire, while Holmes reluctantly stops in town on other business. Upon arriving in Devon the group learns of a manhunt being conducted on the moor for an escaped convict named Selden. Watson encounters some neighbors — the naturalist Stapleton, and his wife Beryl, as well as Mr. Frankland and his daughter Laura Lyons.

It becomes increasingly obvious there is some giant, devilish dog hounding the wasteland, and the convict Selden ends up being killed as the result of stumbling upon it. Holmes now comes back into it when he is discovered by Watson to have been hiding in one of the ancient stone huts dotting the landscape, for the Great Detective has kept up with developments and learned much on his own. Having arrived at certain deductions about the affair, Holmes enlists the aid of Watson, Henry, and Lestrade, and they set a trap for the fiendish hound. The ambush works and the dog is killed, but his master Stapleton, an incognito relative of Henry's, and a contender for the estate and title, escapes into the fetid swamp.

The signature theme of Holmes being a bringer of light is heavily reinforced in *The Hound*, extending to the people involved. In a complimentary aside Sherlock accuses Watson of habitually underrating his own achievements and abilities, telling him, "It may be that you are not yourself luminous, but you are a conductor of light. Some people without possessing genius have a remarkable power of stimulating it. I confess, my dear fellow, that I am very much in your debt." Nietzsche assures us there are two kinds of geniuses: "one which above all engenders and seeks to engender, and another which willingly lets itself be fructified and brings forth." When Stapleton meets Watson for the first time, he asks, hoping for a negative reply, if Holmes will be coming himself to investigate the mystery, and upon being informed that the detective cannot leave town, the man replies, "What a pity! He might throw some light on that which is so dark to us." When Stapleton finally meets Holmes he asks, "I hope your visit has cast some light upon those occurrences which have puzzled us?" In discussing the case Holmes claims, "There are several points upon which we still want light — but it is coming, all the same." A false clue throwing them off the trail elicits the lament from Watson, "It seems to leave the darkness rather blacker than before."

The earliest modern fiction writer to influence *The Hound* is probably Cooper, with the tale brimming with random allusions to his work, quite a few actually. Holmes plays Hawkeye when questioning Mortimer about the details of Sir Charles' death, and when the doctor admits that the footprints at the death scene left him confused since he could discern no other tracks than the victim's, Holmes yells out, "If I had only been there!" confident he would have found something the others overlooked. Watson becomes Chingachgook, the scout's constant Indian companion and the only one in the forest as full of expertise as he. At one point Watson claims, "I am certainly developing the wisdom of the serpent," as he successfully dodges an inconvenient question. The wisdom of the serpent was the ideal for the Indian warrior, and Chingachgook, the subtlest of them all, carries proudly a name meaning "Great Serpent." While Holmes, Watson, and Lestrade are lying in ambush, anticipating the arrival of the hound, hoping to kill it, Holmes "dropped on his knees and clapped his ear to the ground." When he hears something he utters, "Thank Heaven, I think that I hear him coming." Listening with one's ear to the ground was common practice for the Indians, especially when searching for prey such as buffalo, or searching for enemies, while the pious expression of gratitude refers back to Hawkeye, who regards himself as God's servant in his work. Holmes is playing the hunter and trapper; two of the scout's occupations, and the scene in which he shoots the hound is borrowed from *The Pioneers* where Hawkeye kills a mountain lion attacking Elizabeth Temple. We are told the hound was "as large as a small lioness," which is roughly the size and appearance of an American mountain lion.

Adding greatly to the fascination of Doyle's novel is the fact that Cooper has been incorporated into the story. By way of comic relief we are introduced to Mr. Frankland of Lafter (laughter) Hall, an elderly man whose passion for the British law (the common law) has cost him a fortune in litigation; fighting for the pleasure of it, equally quick to take up either side of a legal question. "He is learned in old manorial and communal rights, and he applies his knowledge sometimes in favour of the villagers of Fernworthy and sometimes against them, so that he is periodically either carried in triumph down the village street or else burned in effigy, according to his latest exploit." Cooper grew into a crotchety old man constantly engaged in tirades with his neighbors concerning questions of American law (common law). Cooper was a recognized authority on American Constitutional law, and had vast knowledge, from personal experience and reading, of other categories of legislation. Frankland is a witty characterization of Cooper in the midst of his unending, pointless and foolish legal skirmishes, and he is at present engaged in a case entitled "Frankland v. Morland," so obviously the struggle involves someone else as silly as himself. In one suit Frankland successfully "established a right of way through the centre of old Middleton's park, slap across it," and he tells us, "And I've closed the wood where the Fernworthy folk used to picnic." In the village of Cooperstown, New York, Cooper owned a park on the lake that the people of the village used for picnics and for no apparent reason one day he decided to refuse access to the park, taking the case to court when meeting opposition. Frankland boasts that one day the villagers praise him, and the next burn him in effigy, and this is exactly what the citizens of Cooperstown did to their town's most famous son.

Frankland tells of a famous case he won in which he actually lost money, explaining that he started the litigation "entirely from a sense of public duty," and that he "had no interest in the matter," and such words could just have easily been spoken by Justice Holmes, for they epitomize his exacting attitude toward the law. Frankland says, "I mean to teach them in these parts that law is law, and that there is a man here who does not fear to invoke it." Now if you were to carry Wendell Holmes' philosophy of life too far, his seemingly complete indifference to everything except the absolute letter of the law, you would arrive at the ridiculous figure of Mr. Frankland, but remember Justice Holmes never went too far. Cooper and Frankland did. When Watson questions Frankland as to the details of some of his cases, he is told, "Look it up in the books." This advice is a multiparty reference to the citing of the vast number of books quoted and referenced in Wendell's book, *The Common Law*, as well as the fact that the work is constantly referring the reader to other law books and case histories. In his book Justice Holmes makes a comment about such people as Frankland, some of it good, some bad. Frankland declares, "We'll teach these magnates that they cannot ride rough-shod over the rights of the commoners, confound them!" Justice Holmes crusaded to help disband the unfair trusts and cartels run by unscrupulous businessmen, called "magnates" in America, that were crippling fair trade and small enterprise at the turn of the century. *The Common Law* had a good deal to say about what is called "dog law," and the responsibility attached to owning a dog, quite a bit actually. Doyle's thoughts must have been brought around to Wendell by the fact that he was being considered for the U. S. Supreme Court at the time of the writing of *The Hound*, being elected a year later. Interestingly enough Holmes and Cooper may not be the only legal historians mentioned in Doyle's novel for since we are never told the first name of the killer Selden we are free to invent one as we did in "The Greek Interpreter." John Selden (1584-1654) was an English politician and legal historian of some repute whose writings may have had their influence on our author. There is a law club called the Selden Society at Harvard that Doyle may have known about.

While thinking about the son Wendell, Doyle's mind wanders to the father, for in his retelling of an interview with Frankland, Watson mentions that he contradicted the man in regard to a point of observation, and "The least appearance of opposition struck fire out of the old autocrat." I take this to be a reference to Dr. Holmes' popular book, *The Autocrat of the Breakfast-Table.*"

Mr. Frankland is also fashioned somewhat after Ebenezer Balfour of Stevenson's *Kidnapped*, a miserly old man whose name is borrowed from Ebenezer Scrooge, living in a rambling old house complete with towers, not unlike Frankland's dreary place. Balfour is a stickler for the law, who upon learning he has been maligned by the local harridan, grabs his coat and runs out to "see the session clerk," hoping to sue her. Chasing Selden over the moorland is a reenactment of the scene in *Kidnapped* where an ambush takes place on the moors of Scotland when Glenure, an English officer regarded as the scourge of the peasantry, is shot from the crest of a hill, initiating a manhunt by English soldiers that occupies a large part of the novel.

I can't help thinking of *The Prairie* with the map of Devon depicted at the beginning of early editions of *The Hound*, for most early editions of Cooper's novel included a map of the prairie, scene of the action. The American countryside comes into it when Stapleton compares the huts of the prehistoric race that inhabited the moor to "wigwams," for only the plains tribes lived in wigwams, none of the others. The moors themselves are reminiscent of the prairie as Cooper pictures it, and Sir Henry, who lived in the Canadian plains, calls Devon "that prairie." The word moor comes from the same root as the Latin "mare," meaning a sea or swamp. The American landscape, like the Devon wasteland, is constantly being compared to a sea, as in Cooper's "The sun had fallen below the crest of the nearest wave of the prairie," and he even refers to it as "the dark abyss." The thickets of trees dotting the background Cooper calls "islands resting on the waters," and his use of nautical terms such as rolling wave and swells, adds to the imagery, while at one point Hawkeye admits "it is hard to tell the prairies from a sea." The movements of Hawkeye and his friends, as they attempt to elude a party of hostiles is compared to a vessel that "changes her course in fogs and darkness, to escape from the vigilance of her enemies." The prairie is covered with a "standing fog," which is what the Americans call the long grass that covered the plains, and much of the action of Cooper's novel occurs concealed in this fog, just as the mist of the moor hides activities in *The Hound*. We experience the hellish nature of the Grimpen Mire as it drowns another moor pony, and the unforgiving nature of the prairie is evident when Hawkeye comes across a horse killed by a wild grass fire, a constant threat on the plains. The fact of the prairie being a western locale is encased subtly in Doyle's novel, for Devon is west of London, and this is pointed out to us. The group of Londoners head west to the moorlands just as the Bush party, travelers on the plains, head towards the west, "more deeply, if not irretrievably, into the haunts of the barbarous and savage occupants of the country."

At the scout's feet walks his dog Hector, "a tall, gaunt, toothless hound," that growls at any who approaches his master. Is this old mutt the actual prototype for the world's most famous hellhound? I think it is. This hound occupies a place in *The Leather-Stocking Tales* that is far and away more prominent than any other dog in the work of any other author, disregarding pieces that can be termed dog stories. Hector, always nearby his owner throughout his entire life, is actually an embodiment of several different animals, descendants of the original dog; necessary in view of the fact that canines have shorter life spans than humans. The people of Cooperstown were astute for including Hector in their commemorative statue of Hawkeye, and as bizarre as it sounds, this bronze group is probably showing to the world a metaphor for *The Hound of the Baskervilles* as well. Keep in mind the gigantic dog in Doyle's story was only following loyally his master's orders in attacking certain people.

As the scout is talking to Paul Hover, the bee-hunter he encounters on the grasslands, they are "interrupted by a long, loud, and piteous howl from the hound, which rose on the air of the evening, like the wailing of some spirit of the place, and passed off into the prairie, in cadences that rose and fell like its own undulating surface." The bloodcurdling wail of the hound of the moor interrupting the initial conversation between Watson and Stapleton is a reinterpretation of this scene. Stapleton, who collects butterflies, is a bug hunter, as is Hover, just a different type of bug, and for a different reason. The old scout listens intently to his dog's message, telling the others "that evil is nigh, and that wisdom invites us to avoid it." A band of approaching Sioux on horse set the scene for Hugo and his gang of mounted devils. Their movement is described by Hawkeye as, "A band of beings, who resembled demons rather than men, sporting in their nightly revels across the bleak plain, was in truth approaching at a fearful rate." This is a sentence that could have been penned by either Doyle or Le Fanu. "Down into the grass," he adds, "if you prize the young woman or value the gift of life!" The Indians come through "the fog of the autumnal grass," and their approach "was swift and silent; adding to the unearthly appearance of the spectacle." The Sioux, who capture the party, are referred to as imps and devils, as are Hugo and his bunch.

One member of the Bush party is not really one of them at all, but a scientist named Dr. Obed Battius, who has contracted himself to the group as their physician in return for protection. This strange man seems to have served as archetype, if not in physical description, then in character, for Dr. Mortimer, Mr. Frankland, and even Stapleton. Like Mortimer he is a man of science and medicine, and like Frankland never hesitates to parade before us his knowledge of the law, and like Stapleton, collects and identifies rare plants, animals, and insects he comes across on his travels, further showing affinity to Stapleton when he is addressed as "the naturalist." When one character in Cooper's work hints she does not believe "the naturalist" is telling the truth, she says, "There is a drug in every word he utters." That must have interested Doyle. Like Mortimer, Battius no longer practices medicine, and like both he and Frankland, is a bit of a comic figure, too wrapped up in his own preoccupations to be of any practical use, even to himself. He has no more concern for his own safety than does Stapleton, for in the midst of a gunfight, while the others are struggling for life and victory, this man spots a rare plant on the face of a cliff to which he is clinging and "Forgetting, in an instant, everything but the glory of being the first to give this jewel to the catalogues of science, he sprang upward at the prize, with the avidity with which the sparrow darts upon the butterfly." The rocks beneath him give way almost killing him. Just so does Stapleton spy a rare butterfly while talking to Watson in the shadow of the sinister Grimpen Mire, and dashes into the thick of it in pursuit. The idea of the written reports of Watson to Holmes outlining the developments of the investigation is a borrowing from the notebook entries of this prairie physician, right down to the fact that in both correspondences one page is missing. When he realizes he has mistaken his own donkey for a new species of quadruped and reported it as such in his journal, Battius tears the page out, while in Watson's initial report to Holmes he writes, "One page is missing, but otherwise they are exactly as written."

The Bush family is being hunted by "the hounds of the law," for a number of reasons. They haul a small closed wagon rumored to contain some living creature never seen by most of the group, and the different conversations speculating as to the nature of this being sets the stage for the numerous discussions as to the nature of the beast upon the moor in Doyle's tale. In a long flashback by Cooper we hear the story of the kidnapping of Inez by White and Bush, the story Doyle mined for "The Crooked Man," as well as the account of Hugo stealing his tenant's daughter. Cooper is exposing the details of a past criminal act, a kidnapping, adding up to motivation for revenge, which is also the function of the 1742 manuscript record of Hugo's foul deed, with each case setting forth a narrative giving creditability to the present and future behavior of the characters.

The Prairie, like *The Hound*, becomes a murder mystery when Asa, eldest son of Ishmael Bush, is found shot in the back during a hunting foray, and Hawkeye is suspected simply because of his independent nature and the venomous suspicions of the family toward any outsider. One of the subtlest borrowings Doyle ever perpetrated emerges with the death of the convict Selden, by a fall from a rock cliff. When Asa's murder is solved the guilty one turns out to be Mrs. Bush's brother Abiram. The Barrymores are servants at Baskerville Hall and we learn that Selden is Mrs. Barrymore's brother. They bind Abiram's arms and stand him upon a tall rock with a noose around his neck attached to the limb of a tree above him. With the words, "You shall be your own executioner," he is left in the moonlight, it being understood the murderer will pay with his body when he becomes too exhausted to stand, dying by hanging. Doyle also shows, with the death of Stapleton, foolish enough to flee into the Mire, that he has become his own means of death.

The scene of the three detectives being filled with fear and dread at the first sighting of the horrible hound in the fog is modeled after the episode in *The Prairie* when Dr. Battius, acting as scout, walks casually into a thicket and suddenly finds himself face to face with an Indian warrior costumed in leaves and war paint. The doctor recoils in terror and, backing out of the thicket, tells Hawkeye he has just seen "a monster that nature has delighted to form, in order to exhibit her power! Never before have I witnessed such an utter confusion in her laws, or a specimen that so completely bids defiance to the distinctions of *class* and *genera*." The man was indeed bizarre, for he was covered in paint that "exhibited all the hues of the rainbow, intermingled." And he sat motionless, pretending to be a bush, except for "a pair of dark, glaring, and moving eyeballs," which watched every movement made around him. Like the phosphorescence-painted hound, he has been decorated to instill fear in any who behold him. The entire party is filled with terror until Hawkeye identifies the being and defuses the situation.

Author of the first scholarly history of the United States Navy, in which he had served in the War of 1812, James Fenimore Cooper had long hoped to commemorate the Navy by representing its fleets in action in a novel. Since no such fleets existed in 1842, the year *The Two Admirals* was published, Cooper set the scene in the Jacobite War of 1745, fought between England and France, when the great British and Colonial American fleets were one. This is a story of England and Europe, not America, as well as a tale that takes place mainly at sea, or the land washed by the ocean, while *The Hound*, we have seen, could very well be thought of as a story of the sea. We are rarely shown Baskerville Hall from a distance that our attention is not called to its two long, thin towers, the allusion being to a ship at sea surrounded by fog and water, and it works very well once it is spotted. Cooper's novel opens on the coast of Devonshire, in an atmosphere of fog, and while Watson watches Stapleton's house he says the fog "rolled slowly into one dense bank, on which the upper floor and the roof floated like a strange ship upon a shadowy sea," and on the same page calls the fog, "that dense white sea." Such allusions we see are many and varied, with even the sounds of the moor being compared to the "murmur of the sea." The local village in Cooper's Devon is Wychecombe, and in Doyle's the village where Laura Lyons lives is Coombe Tracey. Cooper's area is dominated by the ancient house referred to as the Hall, the seat of Sir Wycherly Wychecombe, a baronet like Sir Henry, and Sir Wycherly's Hall possesses a situation of seclusion and isolation similar to Baskerville Hall. The Wychecombe fortune — title, park, and house — due to premature deaths, is without any known heirs; thus a tale of intrigue and guile is obviously on Cooper's mind. Sir Wycherly has a number of brothers scattered throughout the world, who are believed to have left no legitimate heirs, so the plot thickens, and gets even more complex when we learn the baronet's younger brother Thomas, "an English common-law lawyer," has an illegitimate son, Tom, who could possibly be regarded as an heir. A young American naval officer from Virginia, also named Wycherly Wychecombe, and obviously a relative of some kind, is stationed at Devon and introduced to the baronet.

The opening paragraphs of *The Two Admirals* is both a perfect example of Cooper's love of legal detail and evidence of the lamentable truth that he possessed a disorganized mind that experienced difficulty establishing borders to its wandering nature. Doyle imitates the first chapter of the novel, with its lengthy emphasis on legality, lawsuits, and court cases, in the rambling legal conversation between Watson and Frankland, just mentioned. The outcome of the legal wrangling in Cooper's work is that Tom inherits everything, but the choice does not seem to have been a just one when we learn Tom is not really Judge Wychecombe's son after all. Tom is a fraud, as is Stapleton, although in this case Tom does not fully comprehend the full scope of the complicated matter himself. When the fleet arrives at Devonshire with the two admirals: Gervaise Oakes and Richard Bluewater, they are invited to the Hall by Sir Wycherly, where a heavy dinner followed by a night of heavy drinking kills the baronet by a stroke.

Sir Wycherly had been generous toward the downcast Duttons, a family name we met when discussing "Black Peter," with his benevolence extended in particular toward young Mildred, just as Sir Charles offered help to Laura Lyons. In the opening pages of Cooper's work we have the incident of young Lt. Wycherly, the American, falling from a cliff wall while picking wildflowers for Mildred Dutton, a reminder that the very landscape of Devon is dangerous, as are the swamps and mires in Doyle's locale.

Sir Reginald Wychecombe, the baronet's brother, comes to the Hall under an assumed name, and in disguise, attempting to stir up political favor for the young Pretender, his favorite in the struggle. He must have inspired the character of Stapleton for he is yet another contended for the estate, in spite of the fact that he has his own money and lands. The American finally lays claim to the title, insisting he is the son of Sir Wycherly's younger brother Gregory, who contrary to popular belief had not drowned when his ship went down off America. Cooper now reduces his already confusing novel's plot to the level of a comic operetta when we learn Mildred Dutton is actually not the daughter of Mr. and Mrs. Dutton, but rather the child of Agnes Hedworth and Col. Jack Bluewater, the admiral's brother. Agnes had died delivering Mildred, and the Duttons, poor but honest, raised her as their own.

The mystery begins to unravel in *The Hound* when it is learned one of the paintings at the Hall bears a resemblance to Stapleton. This is taken from an incident in *The Two Admirals* when one of the officers on Bluewater's ship, upon hearing his ancestors accused of being a bunch of civilians, or worse yet, army men, defends their honor by claiming "there is an old picture of one of 'em, with an anchor-button, and that was long before Queen Anne's time — Queen Elizabeth's perhaps." He is informing his messmates that one of his relatives was an admiral, and we know the Baskervilles had an ancestor who had been "Rear-Admiral Baskerville, who served under Rodney in the West Indies."

Tom Wychecombe, like Stapleton, does not meet his just rewards at the hands of the law, but dies of a fever a few weeks after obtaining some of the estate illegally. The new American baronet, like Sir Henry in Doyle's tale, takes a long trip to steady his nerves following these adventures.

The influence of *The Spy*, yet another novel by Cooper, a work predating *The Leather-Stocking Tales*, can be felt throughout all the Holmes stories. Even before one deals with the story itself evidence of its impact is obvious, for *The Spy* is dedicated to an English friend, James Aitchison, but instead of the usual short declaration, Cooper wrote out two paragraphs witnessing his friendship. In *The Hound* Doyle's dedication to "My Dear Robinson," also includes two paragraphs of thought and thanks. True enough each of Doyle's paragraphs is but one sentence, but they remain two paragraphs nevertheless. The scene of *The Spy* is the rolling hills and forests of Westchester County, New York, in the lower Hudson Valley, just to the north of New York City. The area is often blanketed in mist, and Cooper tells us the town of White Plains is named so for the fogs arising out of the surrounding marshes, occasionally shrouding it for days at a time. The season of the year, as in *The Hound*, is autumn, the year is 1780, and the Revolution is in full progress. The British hold the city to the south, while the Americans hold the ground above Westchester, and the separating valley has become common ground, fought over by both sides continually. Many inhabitants of the unhappy valley "affected a neutrality they did not always feel," and violence, sabotage, treachery, and spying, have become the way of life. The farmhouse of the Whartons, the Locusts, although it cannot compare to Baskerville Hall, passes for a manor in the new, raw land. The warfare has made the raising of crops unprofitable in Westchester, while on the moor not much grows anyway, so both districts are barren.

Just as Holmes knows about tobacco ash and its value to detection, Mr. Harper, who is actually George Washington in disguise, knows his tobacco. While he is staying at Wharton's home, the host makes an innocent enough observation to the effect that he can no longer get the usual tobacco for his evening pipe, for the English control the supply. Harper laments that the shops in New York City must furnish the best tobacco in the country, but since the English control the city, his host Wharton, could not go there for it, but Wharton lowers his eyes at Harper's gaze. "The box from which Mr. Wharton had just taken a supply for his pipe was lying open, within a few inches of the elbow of Harper, who took a small quantity from its contents, and applied it to his tongue, in a manner perfectly natural, but one that filled his companion with instant alarm." Harper does not make any comment on the tobacco, but he has learned a lot from the gesture, for like Holmes he observes everything that could be of value to him, and he now knows Wharton is in contact with the British.

Henry Wharton could be a model for Sir Henry Baskerville, for both are young, brash adventurers born in America of British stock. Henry Wharton has chosen to fight for the Crown, and is now stationed in New York City.

Cooper realizes "many an individual has gone down to the tomb, stigmatized as a foe to the rights of his countrymen, while, in secret, he has been the useful agent of the leaders of the Revolution." One such individual is the unlikely Harvey Birch, an itinerant peddler often seen wandering the hills with his pack on his back. Birch can read into situations, truths hidden from others, as when he and a party of Americans spot a fleet of whaleboats heading across Long Island Sound towards them, and they speculate as to which side the soldiers could be on, British or American. The boats are manned by British regulars Birch claims, at which the others are astonished, since, as one of them says, "there is nothing but spots to be seen." Like Hawkeye and Holmes, the peddler knows what is going on around him better than other people, even the other combatants, for he realizes things others overlook, such as the fact that men in various armies row a boat differently.

It is Holmes who plays the spy, choosing not to tell Watson, or anyone else, not even the reader, his true plans, just as Birch's motivations and movements are a mystery to all save Washington. Shrouding their identities and whereabouts, Holmes and Birch live upon the moors as hermits, keeping their eyes on everyone from a distance. The hills of America are dotted with sentinels guarding troops and riding in advance of foot soldiers, some of which are searching for Birch, as the Devon patrols hunt for Selden. Birch, like Holmes, is seen wandering the moors by various people, but few know what he is really up to. As well as his house, Harvey often stays in a rude stone hut built into the side of a hill, something like Sherlock's hut, and Birch has a habit of "sitting on the point of a jutting rock that commanded a bird's-eye view of the valley," and observing everything that is going on around him, as did Holmes.

Another character from *The Spy*, Dr. Sitgreaves, physician for the Americans, served as model for Dr. Mortimer, for Sitgreaves, like his English counterpart, is tall and thin, a sort of walking stepladder. Doyle must have found it interesting that Sitgreaves, like himself, has a medical degree from Edinburgh.

Another modern writer making a small contribution to *The Hound* is Wilkie Collins. The Grimpen Mire obviously has the same nasty geological makeup as the Shivering Sand, a stretch of quicksand on the Yorkshire coast, in whose swampy bosom an important character in *The Moonstone*, rather than face an ugly truth and disgrace, drowns himself. Mention is made a number of times in Collins' book of dogs, including mastiffs and bloodhounds.

As fate would have it, while Stapleton and Watson are discussing the horrors of the Mire, a pony happens along, becomes mired in the muck, and they watch in revulsion as the doomed animal sinks into the soggy soil in agony. In Stevenson's *The Black Arrow*, published some fourteen years before *The Hound*, we have a scene in which a character strolling through the English countryside finds a grey horse, "sunk to its belly in the mud, and still spasmodically struggling." The trapped beast is destined to a slow death as surely as the moor pony, and is in fact killed out of sympathy by the one who came across it.

"The Pavilion on the Links," although not Stevenson's most famous short story, is a first-rate example of his style. Huddlestone, an English banker, aided by his daughter and her future husband, tries to elude a gang of Italians whose money he has stolen, and Italian revenge, a theme in a number of Doyle's stories, was possibly a borrowing from the earlier Scotch writer. The party seeks safety in Northmour, the pavilion of a family friend. "Links" is the Scottish word for sand dunes covered more or less with grass, and they are not all that different from the moors, including a quicksand trap into which one of the Italians stumbles and dies, while in *The Master of Ballantrae*, a pirate attempting to escape through a swamp also falls into quicksand and drowns. Both Stevenson's links and Doyle's moor are solitary places fraught with danger, especially when saturated with water: high tide on the links, autumn rains on the moor.

The scene in which the gang surrounds the Huddlestone family hiding in the pavilion is reminiscent of the situation of the Ferriers and Jefferson Hope being encircled by the Mormons in *A Study in Scarlet*. Interestingly enough, when given the chance to take a shot at the banker, the Italians use an air gun. Beryl Stapleton, mistaking Watson for Sir Henry, tries to persuade him to return to the city and forget about living in the Hall, while in "The Pavilion," a male character is warned away from the area for fear of his life by a woman who is the wife of another. In both cases the woman tells the intended victim her advice is for his own good and in both instances she is ignored.

Throughout *The Hound*, Beryl and Stapleton successfully pass themselves off as something they are not, and in Henry James' *The Portrait of a Lady* we find counterparts in the persons of Gilbert Osmond and Madame Merle, for these four people have hatched deep schemes. While Merle and Osmond pretend to be simply friends, they actually are closer than that, and even have a grown child between them whose identity has been kept secret. These two are in league to gain possession of Miss Archer's inheritance by having Osmond marry her, which he does. Like Stapleton, Osmond is knowing and amiable, but subtle and crafty, and he is very familiar with the region he lives in, as Stapleton knows the moorlands. "One should not attempt to live in Italy without making a friend of Gilbert Osmond, who knew more about the country than any one except two or three German professors." Lord Warburton, who could be thought of as a prototype for Sir Henry, had also contended for Isabel's hand but lost her to Osmond. An attempted, or possibly a successful, murder takes place in *The Portrait*, for Osmond and Merle are endeavoring, with subtle insult and indifference, to kill the spirit of Isabel Archer, and perhaps her body through her spirit, with the reader being left to decide if they accomplish it or not.

Our author makes mention in *The Hound*, a number of times, by association, to the initial Holmes book, *A Study in Scarlet*. It was Stamford who introduced Holmes and his biographer to each other, and the name is now recycled as the name of the firm that made the map of Devonshire. The presence of

Lestrade as well serves its purpose, that purpose being to remind Doyle that he is again writing a vengeance tale centered on an animal as malevolent as the ape in "Green Tea." Sir Charles has died in the same manner as the Rev. Jennings, driven to his death by what he and he alone has seen and heard, and the spiritual consequences of it. Jennings cut his own throat true enough, but it was fright that drove him to it, and Hugo Baskerville had his throat severed by the fangs of a hellhound he brought upon himself. Remember only the Baskervilles fear the pookah that is the hound. Watson, quoting from his memory, and aided by notes, as with the English doctor in "Green Tea," tells the story of *The Hound*. An English physician seeks Holmes out for assistance, just as an English doctor asks Hesselius for help with his crisis. Doyle calls our attention to overindulgence in stimulants with the scene where Watson, having spent the day at his club, leaving Holmes in solitude thinking over the quandary, returns only to find the atmosphere so thick with tobacco smoke he chokes on it. The detective acknowledges that he consumed "two large pots of coffee and an incredible amount of tobacco." Doyle can't help playing with his sources a little for when Sir Henry has his boot stolen in his hotel, he tells the world, "They'll find they've started in to monkey with the wrong man unless they are careful."

CHAPTER FIFTEEN. REIGN OF TERROR

The Valley of Fear has similarities to *A Study in Scarlet*, dealing as it does with a murder committed in England, that murder stemming from incidents that took place years before in America. *The Valley* opens with the two investigators puzzling over a coded message from Porlock, their spy in Moriarty's organization, tipping them off to impending evil. The warning however comes too late, for Inspector Alec MacDonald of the Yard arrives with the news that John Douglas of Birlstone Manor House, subject of the very letter Holmes is decoding, has been horribly murdered in the night. The three head to Birlstone Manor House where they question anyone connected with the dead man, who was killed with a shotgun blast to the face by an intruder. They don't seem to be getting anywhere, and White Mason, the chief Sussex detective is called in. Holmes traces the gun to a Pennsylvania firm, and an American is suspected since Douglas himself was an American, but little else can be unearthed. Douglas' wife and a family friend, Cecil James Barker, act not just indifferent, but almost jovial regarding the tragedy.

Holmes eventually posits the belief that the entire story is a fabrication and after observing the house awhile, leads everybody into the study, scene of the crime, and astonishes all by asking that Mr. Douglas enlighten them in his own words, and no sooner does he say this when Douglas now emerges from a secret hiding place in the wall and explains what actually occurred.

The second part of the novel, "The Scowrers," deals with the adventures, about twenty years previously, of John Douglas, at the time a private detective whose real name is Birdy Edwards, hired to infiltrate and bring to justice an American gang called the Scowrers. Criminals, thugs, and crooked politicians of a kind all too common in America make up the bulk of the organization, which claims to be acting in the interest of local coal miners, while exercising corrupt control over Vermissa Valley, a mining region in Pennsylvania. We are being clued all is not right in the valley, for "Vermissa" is a derivative of the Latin "*vermis*," meaning "a worm," and "*vermis*" is also the root of the English word "vermin." Vermin in Britain is used collectively for birds and animals that kill game on preserves, predators, and in the entire English-speaking world it also means vile, loathsome people. A large section of the narrative centers upon the criminal activities of this band's efforts to extract money and advantages from the mining companies of the valley, ostensibly on behalf of the miners.

A private detective named Birdy Edwards adopts the undercover name John McMurdo, and insinuates himself into this organization becoming a favorite of the leader, Bodymaster John McGinty. The group itself seems to have a number of different names, and as we shall see, is derived from different real organizations. I'm going to make the claim now that the Scowrers are based firmly on the Masons, and attempt to prove it later; the connection must be made at this time since so many of the important sources Doyle used deal with the Masons. Our author was a Mason, and had nothing against them as a particular group, but he also understood that any particular association of men forming such a powerful and often secretive alliance had great potential for evil. Edwards/McMurdo, with the aid of the honest elements in the police, in particular a Captain Teddy Marvin, succeeds in gathering evidence against the group, leads them into a trap, and arrests them. While on the case McMurdo meets and falls in love with his landlord's daughter, Ettie Shafter, who he marries and flees the valley with. Ettie dies in America however, and Edwards moves to England, changes his name to Douglas to avert the vengeance of the Scowrers, and remarries. At Birlstone, his English home, he realizes one of the syndicate, released from prison and working in league with Moriarty, is seeking revenge on him. The man breaks into Birlstone, but Douglas turns the tables on him and blows his face off during a struggle over the shotgun, so he attempts to pass the corpse off as his own, hoping the world will think him dead. Douglas is found to have acted in self-defense, and he and his wife flee England for their safety.

In *The Pioneers* we have Hawkeye being portrayed as an older man, a situation that encouraged Cooper to backtrack, filling in the gaps, with other novels depicting the scout at earlier stages in his life. Doyle actually brings this concurrence into *The Valley of Fear*, for here we have Holmes and Moriarty, who after all both died in an earlier story, as did Hawkeye, being revived, and made to serve, zombie-like, the commands of Doyle. As Doyle got older, these two got younger, at least in this story, which is what happened with Cooper and Hawkeye, for in *The Deerslayer*, the last of the series, we find the hunter at his youngest. The setting of *The Pioneers* is the forests surrounding Otsego Lake, and in the raw, new town on its shore, at the headwaters of the Susquehanna River in Central New York State. The name and location of the lake is real; the town, Templeton, is a fictional name, called so after its equally fictional founding father, but the town occupies the actual location of the real village of Cooperstown. In Doyle's day, as now, the town was named Cooperstown, not in honor of one of America's greatest writers, but after his father, Judge William Cooper, developer of the wilderness, although many people, even today, and even in New York itself, believe Cooperstown to have been named after its most famous son. I think Doyle is trying to identify with Cooper, perhaps capture some of his immortality by association as it were, for himself, since the American section of his novel is set in a region of Pennsylvania in which is located the city of Doylestown. Stylestown, a village in the Gilmerton district of Vermissa Valley is meant to be a pun on Doylestown; notice only the first two letters of the names are different. Cooper's fictional settlement of Templeton is named after Judge Marmaduke Temple, local squire and developer of the land grant, and obviously based upon Cooper's father. The grant is jointly owned by Judge Temple and a Major Effingham, but since the Major supported the British during the Revolution, following the war he disappeared and the Judge lays claim to all the territory for himself.

It is from *The Pioneers* that Sir Arthur learned to capture the sense of the environment of an American country town, and the ability to describe it in some detail, and to show its influence on those who live within it, as he does so well, and with such economy in *The Valley of Fear*. The valley of fear in the case of Cooper's novel is the Mohawk Valley bordering the Mohawk River, the valley Templeton is situated in, and Cooperstown as well of course, a truly bloodstained place in American history. Doyle transfers this aspect of terror to the Susquehanna Valley. In each case the hamlets described are raw frontier towns at the time of the action, which is placed some years before the telling of the stories.

Like most places in Vermissa Valley, the population of Cooper's Templeton is comprised primarily of immigrants from Europe, or other parts of America, plus a few Indians. Doyle makes reference to *The Pioneers* on the second page of "The Scowrers," the American section, when he says, "Little could the first pioneer who had traversed it have ever imagined that the fairest prairies and the most lush water pastures were valueless compared to this gloomy land of black crag and tangled forest." This refers to the fact that coal had been discovered in the valley. It was actually Hawkeye who was the first pioneer to settle in the area of Templeton, for he was the only white man Judge Temple and his settlers found when they arrived at the grant. A tribute to the pioneering spirit is found in two names Doyle used which are taken from famous explorers: Scott and McMurdo. The latter is the name of the explorer who gave his name to McMurdo Sound in Victoria Land, Antarctica, while James Scott, a Bodymaster John McMurdo knew in Chicago, is named after Robert Scott, the British explorer who died in Antarctica in 1912, just before Doyle started writing this novel.

The Pioneers opens with the scene of the hunting of a stag, and "The Scowrers" opens with mention of the town of Stagville. Both begin with the protagonist approaching the village in the light of the setting sun at the close of a cold winter day, followed by vivid descriptions of the valleys. Judge Temple is presented to us as an aristocratic figure, politically and financially all-powerful, as is John McGinty, boss of Vermissa Valley. While shooting at a deer the Judge accidentally wounds a young stranger named Oliver Edwards, while in *The Valley* we learn Edwards is McMurdo's real name, and it should come as no surprise that Edwards in Cooper's work has assumed that name to cover his real one. Right from the beginning of *The Pioneers* we are aware that Mr. Edwards is a capable man — independent, and intelligent enough to make an impression on people who are acquainted with dealing with extreme hardships in a new, violent country where such qualities are common. Edwards displays his cool courage and sagacity when he saves the lives of four men trapped in a sleigh in the snow, as it is about to slide over a cliff. He does not flinch as the bullet is removed from his shoulder any more than does McMurdo as he has the organization's brand burned into his arm during the secret initiation ceremony. Oliver Edwards lives in the cabin of Hawkeye and Chingachgook outside the village, but the Judge insists that he stay at Temple Hall following his wounding of the man, and he acquiesces, yet we sense Edwards harbors some private resentment toward the Judge. The love interest that develops between McMurdo and his landlord's daughter Ettie is modeled after the relationship that blossoms between Oliver and Elizabeth, also the daughter of the man in whose house he is staying. Jack and Ettie, in physical characteristics, could be related to Oliver and Bess.

The role and power of the Masons emerges in *The Pioneers*, for Richard Jones, cousin to Judge Temple, and an architect, builder, and general artisan of sorts, is head of the Masons, and holds the title of master. The Masons run the town more or less to suit themselves, even controlling what the design of the principal building will be since the only hotel in town, still being built, actually has Masonic emblems carved into its façade, and is owned by two Masons. The organization meets at the inn, the "Bold Dragoon," and a sort of Irish influence, so heavy in Doyle's book, enters into *The Pioneers* for an Irish couple named Hollister owns the tavern. Like McGinty, Jones is a jovial, backslapping, good-natured lout who will stop at nothing to get his own way, having a vicious appetite for all life has to offer, no matter what the consequences. Both men know everyone in their valley, including their families and their business. Selfish and spiteful, Jones seems to spend most of his time trying to bring other people "round to his own way of thinking," on any subject he finds. His capacity for overindulgence causes him to hunt pigeons with a cannon, hoping to simply kill as many as possible, even if they can't be eaten; a gesture showing such poor sportsmanship it was understood to be designed to elicit contempt among Cooper's readers.

Early on we learn Jones has been appointed "sheriff of the county," and from the language of his plans he obviously looks forward to being a paragon of corruption. The law of the land as portrayed in Cooper's work is inept at best and corrupt at worst, often without those who administer it even realizing it themselves, for corruption is built into the system since everyone knows everyone else too well to be disinterested in the matter before him. This decadence is more treacherous, possibly with an even greater capacity for viciousness than the open, expected corruption of Vermissa Valley, since it is subtler. We are told, "all opposition to the will of the sheriff would be useless."

An elderly man on the verge of death makes an appearance in Templeton and is revealed to be the missing Major Effingham, while Oliver Edwards it seems, is his grandson. Edward is actually the young man's first name. The sudden revelation of the real identity of Effingham/Edwards at this juncture is as dramatic as McMurdo's sudden divulgence of his true self. Judge Temple did not after all swindle Effingham out of the land, for the man had left the country following the war. As in *The Valley of Fear* the young couple, Bess and Edward, marry and leave the valley.

Mining plays a small but important part in *The Pioneers*, for the Allegheny Mountains, in which Templeton is located, is famous coal country, as is neighboring Pennsylvania, which fact Cooper mentions a number of times. We are led to believe there is coal in the hills around Templeton, and the Judge intends to prospect for it. In *The Valley of Fear* we see what could happen if he found it. Doyle having his undercover detective pose as a counterfeiter of coins came about from the suspicions of Sheriff Jones, who believes Edwards is smelting stolen ore at Hawkeye's remote cabin. Counterfeiting was a common practice in early America and Cooper mentions this. Doyle's story is a continuation of Cooper's, an idea that would have been well understood by the American, and the inspiration for *The Valley* may have occurred to Doyle from a remark found in *The Pioneers*. Hawkeye has broken the law by killing a deer out of season, a serious offense, and it is up to the Judge to bring him to justice and see that he is made to pay for the crime, but this will hardly be easy for Hawkeye has just saved Temple's daughter from a mountain lion attack. When Edwards learns the proceedings are going forward, and Natty will be arrested, he tries to convince Temple to drop the charges claiming that old age, habits, and ignorance, are Hawkeye's only offenses. But the Judge says, these circumstances "may extenuate, but can they acquit? Would any society be tolerable, young man, where the ministers of justice are to be opposed by men armed with rifles?" Here is the exact situation found in Vermissa Valley, an intolerable society run by armed thugs opposing the ministers of justice.

McMurdo among the Scowrers is a spy, thus leading us back to one of Cooper's most interesting works, the full name of which is *The Spy: A Tale of the Neutral Ground*, which amounts to almost a pun on *The Valley of Fear*, for the neutral ground in question is a valley, described as a dangerous and fearful place. A great number of the inhabitants "wore masks," Cooper explains, meaning they did not reveal their true interest or motives, giving a window of opportunity to great deceit and treachery. "The law of the neutral ground is the law of the strongest," becomes the accepted attitude of all in the drama. *The Spy* and *The Valley* open with similar situations as a solitary traveler enters the picture of bloodshed and chaos seeking shelter as evening approaches. In *The Spy* it is October and a storm is gathering, as the visitor, a gentleman of breeding, finds lodging at the farmhouse of the Whartons, passing himself off as Mr. Harper, who we know to be George Washington, himself playing the spy in disputed territory. Even more disguise enters the picture when Mr. Wharton's son, a captain in the British Army, finds his way to his father's farm, this very night, having slipped through the American lines. The rest of the family has remained neutral, or pretends to. As we know, Harper, like Holmes, misses little, and sees through Captain Wharton's disguise immediately. There are in this valley a number of groups of irregulars, as are generated by any war, and one such gang, the Skinners, agents of the Americans, are often guilty of great abuses and violence to obtain their ends, committing crimes "under the pretense of patriotism, and the love of liberty," in order to aid only themselves or inflict revenge on any who they dislike. To emphasize their viciousness we are told they have a "love of cruelty that mocks the Indian ferocity," which is quite a thing to say, for Cooper knew only too well the Indian's sadistic nature. The Skinners are so hated even the American troops hunt and hang them when their violence becomes overbearing. The British themselves use unbridled brutality with the exception that their crimes are committed under a cloak of military authority and are therefore "more systematized." The British civilian partisans are called Cow-boys, or sometimes Refugees, for they find refuge for their acts under the powerful British presence. The Cow-boys are so rapacious they even rob the black slaves, who have little enough worth stealing. It's learned the two rival gangs will sometimes league together to commit some act of plunder against one or another of their own people if enough loot is to be gained. Like the Scowrers of Vermissa Valley, these parties rob, loot, burn out, or kill, any who oppose them. As in Doyle's novel the normal needs of society must be held in abeyance because of the dangerous war brought into their midst.

We learn quickly that *The Spy* is not a tale of any single agent but of many, for a number of people in the narrative are other than they appear to be. The fascinating situation Cooper brought about, and which Doyle reiterated so capably, is that although we realize not only one person, but others as well, must be secret agents, we do not know who they are, or what their motivation is. Even the servants are engaged in espionage in Cooper's strange tale. These writers do not take us into their confidence, at least not until we are well into their stories.

Harvey Birch has also sought refuge in the Wharton farmhouse from the storm on this fateful night, such loose, generous arrangements being common in America at the time. Birch is a shadowy figure that both sides mistrust, and harass or arrest, a situation similar to that of Edwards in *The Valley*. He is also much like Holmes and Hawkeye in that he can tell the significance of trifles that constitute great events when taken in the aggregative. It becomes slowly obvious that the man is a spy solely for Washington, without this knowledge being passed to the other Americans, who regard him with suspicion. We suspect McMurdo to be a policeman of some sort, but don't really know this, and we realize that if he is an agent, some of the other police do not know it, for he is distrusted by everyone, including them, and like Birch is completely on his own. In both books the hanging of prisoners is constantly being eluded to, and often, for one reason or another, put into practice on those who are caught playing the spy. In *The Spy* we are told of Major André, an historical personage, an American caught attempting to slip the plans of West Point, hidden in his boots, to the British, being hung from the nearest tree: no judge, no jury, no trial. The Skinners rob Birch of his money and burn down his house suspecting he works for the British, and just as McMurdo has a hoard of silver, Birch has a cache of gold coins, his profits from his peddling business. Interestingly enough at one point the peddler is suspected of passing counterfeit coins given him by the devil. Birch must play the enemy to those he loves and supports, or his game will be up, consequently he is undeservedly despised by some he loves; he knows this but can do nothing about it, the exact dilemma for McMurdo, mistrusted, even hated by people such as Ettie's father. Birch nevertheless risks his life a number of times to save people and property from raiders, just as McMurdo assisted so many, often without their knowledge.

Since he has some of the physical appearance, and all of the moral and intellectual characteristics of Holmes, it is probable Birch acted as a major archetype for the detective. "In stature he was above the size of ordinary men, though his excessive leanness might contribute in deceiving as to his height," Cooper says of Harvey Birch, and Watson also said Holmes looked taller than he really was due to his thinness. In his travels Birch, like Hawkeye, who will evolve out of this character, and like Holmes, who is a combination of the two, "glided over the ground with enormous strides, and a body bent forward, without appearing to use exertion, or know weariness." Here is the Holmes of *The Sign of the Four*, dogtrotting tirelessly behind his hound after Small and Tonga. Birch is also larger than life and is recognized to be so by his enemies, who consider him, "a spy — artful, delusive, and penetrating, beyond the abilities of any of his class." In one of the most important, and for our purposes, revealing episodes in the story, Birch, in an effort to rescue Captain Wharton, imprisoned by the Americans as a spy, dresses up as a Protestant clergyman and gains admission to his cell. Holmes' ruse of passing himself off as a clergyman in "A Scandal in Bohemia," is borrowed from this, and in one scene, Birch, still in this disguise, is surrounded by a gang of soldiers who mock his piety just as Holmes, in disguise, is molested by a gang in front of Irene Adler's house. Cooper calls Birch a "priest" at this point, and the detective we know also garbed himself as a Catholic priest at least once to facilitate his plans. As with Sherlock, Harvey changes everything about himself when he adopts a disguise: his gait, his voice, and his manner. The peddler/operative sets an example in acting when he disguises himself as a woman in order to escape from an American jail. In "The Yellow Face," we saw the trick of putting a yellow mask over the face of a black girl in an effort to change her appearance. Dressed as a clergyman, Birch and Caesar, a black servant, gain access to Wharton's cell where Birch puts the Captain in the Negro's clothes, adds a wig, and covers his face with a black parchment mask of his own making. The servant then takes the prisoner's place allowing the two others to escape. We are told these articles of disguise "formed together a transformation that would easily escape detection, from any but an extraordinary observer," and in "The Yellow Face," it was Holmes who became this extraordinary observer. When it is discovered by the guards that the servant Caesar has changed places with their prisoner, Doyle sees the extent of the hatred some whites felt for the blacks, and this could have prompted him to write "The Yellow Face."

Outside of Birch himself, it is Jack Lawton who would have been the only one sharp enough to spot Henry Wharton's deception, and Jack McGinty is based to a large degree on this perceptive Captain in the American Army.

We are told of Lawton that he is one "who sees so far," and of McGinty that "every whisper goes back to him." This friend of the Skinners has the same low, cunning and good-natured shrewdness as McGinty, and is one who sees everything in an almost clairvoyant manner, as does Holmes, and he too, never sleeps, and if he does he "always slept with one eye open." Lawton is a rough soldier "whose colossal stature manifested the possession of vast strength," with dark hair and a full beard of whiskers. He is obviously dangerous, for Harvey warns the Whartons to beware of him, and fears him personally, for the man assumes him to be an agent of the British and vows to hang him one day. One observation made on the nature of Lawton describes him as a man who loves to "unnecessarily destroy life," which attitude seems to be what Cooper considered the greatest evil in existence. This Captain however plays the role of bringer of justifiable retribution when he tricks the Skinners into taking him into their confidence and then captures them and has them whipped for their foul deeds. As does McMurdo, Lawton hints that a day will soon come when the enemies of the people will get exactly what is coming to them.

The English police learn that the American trying to kill Douglas stayed at a hotel called the Eagle Commercial, and the Eagle Hotel was a real place that existed in Cooperstown in Cooper's day. An Irish hotel and tavern of sorts, a sutler station named the Hotel Flanagan after its owner serves as camp for Lawton and his troops in Cooper's story.

Some information I dug up relating Cooper's work to Doyle can honestly only be filed under the miscellanea column. In *The Spy*, as in "The Final Problem," we enter a situation where the author has pitted two men against each other: Birch and Lawton, Holmes and Moriarty. All four of these men are brilliant, resourceful, determined, and thoroughly committed to the task before them. This is especially evident when we realize that it is over hills and valleys, and across rivers, that Lawton pursues Birch, just as Moriarty follows Holmes across mountains, valleys, and water. Remember New York was at the time called "the Switzerland of America." At the conclusion of "The Final Problem," *The Spy*, and *The Valley of Fear*, some members of the gangs of thugs mentioned: Moriarty's syndicate, the Skinners, and the Scowrers, meet their deaths, mainly by hanging. Lawton, Birch, Holmes, and Moriarty die in battle, while McGinty is hung, and McMurdo dies at sea. In one scene Birch hides himself in a secret recess of his own hut in order to avoid detection, just as we have Jack Douglas doing at Birlstone. The Singletons, a brother and sister found in *The Spy* become the Stapletons in *The Hound*. These two in Doyle's work are not real siblings but somehow that brings the situation closer in spirit to the blurry doings of *The Spy*.

The strange cryptic messages from Porlock, one in the beginning of *The Valley of Fear*, warning of Moriarty's involvement in the business, and another at the end, telling of Douglas' death, echo *The Spy*, where two messages, just as cryptic and dire, are sent by Birch to Lawton warning him of an ambush. Holmes' grasping of the importance of a wedding ring in *A Study in Scarlet*, which eventually leads to the solving of the crime, is probably influenced by the incident in *The Spy* when Miss Peyton is about to marry a British officer, and it is suddenly realized they have no ring. The ceremony is detained for some time while the servant Caesar rides to a military camp to borrow one for the couple, since we are told the wedding could not possibly take place without it. Cooper devotes an entire chapter to this incident. Bigamy and polygyny, and its consequences, are both dealt with, as in *A Study in Scarlet*, for Sarah Wharton goes mad when she learns she is about to be married to a man who already has a wife. *The Spy* ends at Niagara Falls just as "The Final Problem" ends at Reichenbach Falls, with Cooper calling the fury of the Niagara "the abyss beneath." In a battle during the War of 1812, Birch is killed by the British at the edge of the falls, and a note from Washington found upon his body declares to all that Harvey Birch has always been loyal to his country. Doyle translates this idea into the explanatory note left by Holmes at the edge of Reichenbach Falls. Obviously *The Spy* has left its mark on Doyle's genius.

Robert Barr's *The Measure of the Rule* is a story being told by a man remembering incidents from his youth, as is the American section of *The Valley of Fear*. Tom Prentiss journeyed to a city seeking an education at the university and like McMurdo he has just arrived by rail from the west at an eastern city, and he too stays at a hotel before finding more permanent lodging at a boarding house. *The Measure of the Rule* opens as a train draws up at Union Station, at the close of a winter's day. Before the main plot begins we are given a Prologue poem at the heading of the first chapter, entitled, "Address to an Egyptian Mummy." "Perhaps thou wert a Mason, and forbidden By oath to tell the secrets of thy trade." This quote sets up a theme of secrecy and clandestine organizations, as they are found in *The Valley of Fear*, and to a lesser degree in *The Measure of the Rule*. Barr seems to be saying he is planning to expose secrets such as those the mummy would prefer to keep hidden. The initial chapter of Barr's novel deals with Masonic practice, for Tom Prentiss soon comes across a Masonic Temple, and being a member falls into conversation with the other brothers. He enters the temple where an initiation is going forward. Tom is introduced to "the headmaster" of the university, Dr. Darnell, who is called "Prince of Schoolmasters," and is "this grim man clothed with authority, a man of power, free and untrammelled." This is the capacity of the all powerful and ruthless Bodymaster McGinty, antagonist of McMurdo, who is one fretted with the discipline of the law, which he must uphold even if it hampers justice. Of Darnell we are told, "His features were strongly marked and clean cut, and his eyes, when he raised them from the floor, seemed to scintillate with chilly grey light that penetrated me like X-rays." He also tells us, "the Doctor's face reminded me somehow of cast iron," and when he is roused he views the world with "unholy anger flashing from his eyes." When he regards Tom, the youth feels "that I was instantaneously judged, condemned, and cast aside." Yet another man at this Masonic ritual also acted as inspiration for the character of McGinty, one called "the Senator," who was "a rubicund millionaire, and a power in the political world; stout, it is true, but laughing with the heartiness of a boy as he tossed off his Rhine wine." Another in the group is called simply "the Master." As in the Vermissa Valley lodge meeting, a song goes round during the meeting, singing among men being quite common in Doyle's day. Tom Prentiss, like Jack McMurdo, is an outsider, a sort of spy, for he tells us, "I was with the brethren, but not of them," adding, "I was a stranger within the gates." Prentiss must show evidence of being a Mason, this being supplied by his last lodge, and just so did the men of the Vermissa lodge challenge McMurdo.

Tom falls in with, and finally ends up living with another student, Sam McKurdy, whose character is based upon Billy Kirby of *The Pioneers*. McKurdy has a great deal of Kirby's straightforwardness and rough manner, as well as his physical bulk and strength. A situation becomes apparent on the first day of school when we realize the headmaster Darnell is antagonistic toward McKurdy, and these two protagonists practice a continual warfare of wills while in the classroom. "Every one felt instinctively that here were two antipathetic men at daggers drawn, each wary of the other," and wary would be the best word to describe the relationship between McMurdo and McGinty. At the Normal School, and in the boarding houses licensed by the school, the students "live under a state of tyranny and espionage," and therein lies the major link to *The Valley of Fear*. Darnell is considered by his students to have "omnipresence," or as McKurdy puts it, "I may conceal my misdeeds from my Maker, but never from the chief."

Tom meets and falls in love with a young girl, Aline Arbuthnot, also a student at the Normal School, and subject to its oppressive rules. Aline with her face "beautiful and sweetly serious," served as model for Ettie, and her troubles are somewhat the same, for though she and Tom are drawn to each other, the rigid rules forbid them to even talk. Aline it seems is being married off without her approval or consent to the son of one of her father's friends, a primitive situation reminiscent of *Romeo and Juliet*, where the families and their ambitions play the determining role in the making of a marriage. Mr. Arbuthnot does not know Tom, but we sense that even if they knew each other the situation would not alter much. Tom does not fear Aline's father, telling us, "I should have gone and braved the Douglas in his hall if she had allowed me."

The Measure of the Rule deals with the abuse of power by those who hold it, the same theme as *The Valley of Fear* and *The Pioneers*. Favoritism, one by-product of the wrong use of authority enters into the picture in a negative guise when Dr. Darnell warns Tom he will show none of it to him simply because they are both Masons.

John Brent, the sinister individual in charge of the teaching school, whom we have already had the pleasure of meeting, makes his initial appearance "as if he had materialized out of transparent air," through a door that opened "as if moved by some invisible agency." This morose man is regarded as the best teacher in the country, for whom the pupils would have laid down their very lives, much as McGinty's henchmen loved him and would die for him. The Model School is where the would-be teachers are confronted with the real-life situation of teaching a class of the most unruly boys from the public schools. Brent has great physical strength and is considered a great athlete, eliciting dog-like devotion in these pupils, who, even though they loathe and fear him, will applaud him on the field for his keen judgment, strength, and skill at sporting events. Prentiss sees him in a different light for he knows the hatred within the man's heart. Brent despises just about everyone he meets without anyone seeming to know it except a few like McKurdy and Prentiss, who see what others overlook. In order to maintain discipline Brent uses henchmen who play the spy. "The pupils under his direction were supposed to be the most enthusiastic of spies, subtle as foxes, unscrupulous as Beelzebub, and as mischief-loving as city lads usually are." These mischief-loving kids are little more than thugs that only Brent can control. Brent walks with a predatory cat-like tread especially suited for walking silently up behind people, and of McGinty we are told he is like a bear, and his hair is called "black-maned." Collectively and individually, the lodge members of Vermissa Valley are compared to tigers; one of them even proudly bears the name Tiger Cormac. This constant tension, based on antagonisms between society and organizations, and people within that society ruthlessly bent upon getting their own way at the expense of others, is the armature around which Doyle built, layer by layer, the plot and theme of any number of tales, including *The Valley of Fear.*

The events and characters found within Doyle's novel find foundation, as does just about everything else he wrote, in historical events, organizations, and individuals that can be found in the march of human history, often current events. In Doyle's day there was a large number of secret or semi-secret societies, and actually there still is, and probably always will be. America had its fair share of these associations and our author knew more about America, its people and their triumphs, hopes, and disappointments, than the average American. In respect to the secret societies, *The Valley of Fear* is evocative of *A Study in Scarlet,* with its bands of fanatics persecuting the innocent in the name of their religion, any religion being just another semi-secret institution. In *The Valley,* the Scowrers' real name is the Eminent Order of Freemen, while the actual Masons call themselves Freemasons, almost the same thing. Beyond doubt it is the Masons, above the other institutions, except the Skinners of *The Spy,* which Doyle has in mind here, although we know he did not actually distrust the Masons. The efficient local officer in *The Valley of Fear* is named White Mason, with the word "white" being synonymous with good, or worthwhile, and the loyal servant in "The Sussex Vampire," protecting so ardently the child in her care, is named Mrs. Mason. Within the Masons there was a group called the Level Club, whose members were called the Levelers, and the idea for a splinter organization within the main group may have presented itself to Doyle from this development. He also had the example of Stevenson before him, a citation he never failed to take. Within a year of "The Body-Snatcher," Stevenson brought out the novel *Prince Otto,* in which he makes mention of the Masons, for reasons of their own, plotting against the Prince, and although Stevenson doesn't go into much detail about this, Doyle was quick to spot the potential of such a situation.

The initiation ritual scene at the Vermissa Lodge is borrowed from an interesting factual account. In his *Autobiography,* Charles Darwin, speaking of his father, tells us the man could not stand the sight of blood, in spite of the fact that he was a medical doctor. As a young man the father decided to join the Freemasons, and Charles describes his initiation into the brotherhood. A friend of his father's, who was a Freemason, and who pretended not to know about his strong feeling with respect to blood, remarked casually to him as they walked to the meeting, "I suppose that you do not care about losing a few drops of blood?" When they arrive at the lodge, "his eyes were bandaged and his coat-sleeves turned up. Whether any such ceremony is now performed I know not, but my Father mentioned the case as an excellent instance of the power of imagination, for he distinctly felt the blood trickling down his arm, and could hardly believe his own eyes, when he afterwards could not find the smallest prick on his arm." The Masons were having a practical joke on the doctor, but Doyle shows us what would happen among a bunch of men who lack a sense of humor.

The political machinery of Tammany Hall was started by William Mooney, an upholsterer in New York City, in 1789, and was at the onset just a benevolent Masonic society. A decade later Tammany moved into politics, promoting Thomas Jefferson for President, and the honor of being its first machine boss fell to Aaron Burr. After that successful show of strength the Tammany Hall people organized in army fashion throughout the city wards and slowly took control of the entire metropolis, with the Hall itself, like the Vermissa Valley Union House, becoming the focal point where deals of all kinds where made. Tammany maintained a practice of repeat voting and vote buying, then common in America. These factors made it possible for William Tweed to flourish as the corrupt boss of New York, with McGinty and his gang being a duplicate of this system of corrupt police, bought politicians, and miscellaneous thugs that became notorious as the Tweed Ring. Drawing his strength from his adept manipulation of the lower classes, and new groups with political power, Tweed and his confederates: Mayor A. Oakey Hall, Peter Sweeny, and Richard Connolly, stole, in one way or another, over one hundred million dollars from the public. Doyle's rendering of McGinty as a bearded, bloated, giant of a man hung with jewelry and a cigar stuck in his mouth is a verbal depiction of Thomas Nast's famous cartoon "The Tweed Ring," showing us Boss Tweed and his shady cronies dancing in a circle of self-interest and mutual back scratching. Tweed himself was an affable three hundred twenty pound behemoth who died in prison after he and his ring got caught stealing more than twenty million in New York City funds.

Philadelphia, Pennsylvania, also had the infamous "Republican Gas Ring," that was a copy of the Tweed Ring. So much corruption entered Philadelphia politics that the city was called the "City of Brotherly Loot," a pun on its official title of the "City of Brotherly Love." Vermissa Valley is not far from Philadelphia.

McGinty is the worst of criminals; the blackmailer, but his extortion is the public variety, as practiced by these corrupt "Rings," with the citizens in general terrorized into paying levies into a debased and vicious political/social machine. Those who oppose them are intimidated and menaced into "holding his tongue lest some worse thing befall him," as Doyle realized.

The Ancient Order of Freemen is as well a takeoff on the Ancient Order of Hibernians, an organization of Irish-Americans, which is the ethnic makeup of most of those in the Vermissa Lodge. Like the Masons, the Hibernians are basically a benevolent association, but Doyle dosen't seem to care for any group of this stripe, and has chosen to show us their dreadful side. It's altogether possible he may have joined the Masons just to see what was really going on there for himself. The Molly Maguires were a secret branch of the Hibernians — coal miners in Eastern Pennsylvania, active from about 1865 to 1875, who opposed oppressive industrial and social conditions, sometimes with physical force and terrorism. They named themselves after the original clandestine organization of the same name in Ireland, founded in 1843 to prevent evictions of tenants, by harassing the agents of the landlords, their name coming from the fact that members sometimes dressed as women to avoid identification.

In America the period following the Civil War was an era of greed, fraud, exploitation, violence, political corruption, and new opportunities arising out of instability of one kind or another, not just in the South, but in Northern cities as well. Organized bands of whites regularly and systematically terrorized the black population since the climax of the war. Groups with names such as the Regulators, Jayhawkers, and Black Horse Cavalry committed "the most fiendish and diabolical outrages," with those of any color or political convictions that resisted them being killed or burned out. Often these secret societies were popular among the lower classes of poor whites, as is the Scowrers. When McGinty tells us he has the police on his side, this is a reference to the fact that the authorities often sided with and even aided rioters or lynch mobs in their work, especially in the Deep South, in such places as New Orleans, where General Sheridan, sent by Washington to help maintain the peace, told Congress that even the mayor was in on some of the vicious goings-on in the city.

The Ku Klux Klan was a secret lodge organized in 1865 in Tennessee, which seemed to oppose any advancement made by the freedmen, as the ex-slaves were called, while describing itself as an institution of "Chivalry, Humanity, Mercy, and Patriotism," which is exactly how the Scowrers would delineate themselves. They spread quickly, adopting for themselves the shibboleth of the "Invisible Empire," complete with codes, passwords, hand signs, and clandestine elaborate rituals, with members bearing such ominous titles as "dragons, hydras, titans, furies, and night-hawks." The chief was called the "Grand Wizard," or "Grand Dragon." Doyle may very well have had the Klan in mind when he named the secret bands of Mormons in *A Study in Scarlet*. The Klan went in for ghoulish dress, weird rituals, and violent night raids, all calculated to terrorize the Negroes, or anyone else they deemed their enemy. Scowrers is an Old Scottish word for "scarers," and scaring their adversaries was the real function of all these violent groups. By violence and intimidation, social and business ostracism, and any other means, including murder, they grimly moved to wreck each and every phase of the reconstruction work in the South following the war. The Klan adopted a policy of helping out fellow members in distress, or the widows of those who died doing their work, or for the cause of the Confederacy, and thus we see the Scowrers telling McMurdo they plan to pay a "pension to Jim Carnaway's widow," for "He was struck down doing the work of the lodge." As in *The Valley of Fear*, retribution did eventually catch up with some of the Klansmen, for even the Southerners got fed up with them; following 1870 scores were arrested, and several were hung. Also, as in Doyle's novel, enough survived to seek retribution in return on those who were their enemies. Doyle deals with this vengeance of the Klan in at least one short story, "The Five Orange Pips," when they kill the farmer John Openshaw, whom even Sherlock Holmes could not save.

Many other similarly cloaked groups sprang up with names like the Constitutional Union Guards, the White Brotherhood, and the White League, whose aim was the re-establishment of white supremacy in the South. Notice the Scowrers address each other as "Brother." These bands often defended their actions as a form of self-defense, proceeding on the ancient principle that the best defense was a well-planned offense, a sentiment echoed by McGinty and his followers.

The Northern press followed every incident of the atrocities; hence McMurdo makes up a story about having met a reporter from a Northern newspaper when he finds his actions being questioned by McGinty. The editorial that appeared in the Vermissa *Daily Herald*, and which so upset the Bodymaster, compared the practices of the Scowrers to a "REIGN OF TERROR," which was what the press of America called the riots in Memphis, Tennessee, which resulted in the deaths of many people.

The Scowrers could also be meant to represent the Union League, especially since they met at a hall called the Union House. The Union League was founded in Pennsylvania in 1862, to promote and stimulate support for the Union, and by the end of the Civil War the group was a powerful political arm of the Radical wing of the Republican party, who practiced a policy among the freedmen of sponsoring political education. The League worked closely with the Freedmen's Bureau, a government branch, and some people were members of both groups. Working to organize the ex-slaves into a voting block, this being what they considered their best chance of obtaining status and respect, they would move into a black community and enroll the people in one of its branches with organizers initiating enrollees into the secrets and mysteries of the group, complete with identification cards and passwords; much like the Masons. Teaching them how to vote, especially how to vote the way the League wanted them to, seems to have been the main goal of the association. Criticism of their activities was general and widespread throughout the South where they were accused of urging Negroes, through inflammatory speeches and elaborate oath taking, to support the Republicans and to oppose their enemies, with some chapters of the League being accused of committing acts of violence against any who disagreed with them. This crowd was often the target of the Klan's wrath, as was the Freedmen's Bureau, with the Klan striking many blows at the political structures erected by these organizations. A number of the more important members of the Union Leaguers found roles either in state or national politics, or in other areas, and the brotherhood eventually died out.

The scene in *The Valley of Fear* in which the Scowrers are let off in court because of a lack of evidence following the beating of the newspaper editor is typical of the power of the Klan and was a sorry scene reenacted many times throughout the South in this era. At one point McGinty pretends to question McMurdo as to who would have the power to stand against him and his men. "Is it by the police? Sure, half of them are in our pay and half of them afraid of us. Or is it by the law courts and the Judge?" The latter authority is capitalized as though an individual is in mind, and so it is, for Oliver Wendell Holmes was an influential judge in the Federal system at this time who devoted a great deal of time and energy fighting the KKK. In 1871 Congress passed a resolution establishing a joint committee of twenty-one members "to Inquire into the Condition of Affairs in the Late Insurrectionary States," but their intention was simply to stop the outrages of the Klan. Senator John Scott of Pennsylvania was designated to be chairman, and McMurdo tells us he is from the North, where he was in "Lodge 29, Chicago, Bodymaster J. H. Scott."

This reconstruction period also saw the rise of what was to be the beginning of modern labor unions. The National Labor Union was established in 1866, and the Knights of Labor in 1871, whose head man bore the elaborate title of Grand Master Workman, a designation similar to Bodymaster. Unfavorable publicity resulting from the violent tactics employed by Pennsylvania coal miners and others did more damage than good to these labor causes.

In *The Valley of Fear*, his last novel, it's as though our author were summing up much of his life's work, packing in numerous references to writers used in previous work and this is especially true if we accept the allusions already mentioned, to his own earlier stories. Doyle seems to be pointing things out to himself; for instance Shafter's boarding house is located on Sheridan Street, bringing to mind Sheridan Le Fanu. In "The Familiar," the main character is named Barton, and on the first page of the American section of *The Valley of Fear* we learn one of the towns in the valley is named Bartons Crossing. When Douglas tells the tale of his adventures in America, lamenting that he eventually discovered one of the Scowrers had tracked him to England, he adds that this one "has been after me like a hungry wolf after a caribou all these years." We think not just of "Green Tea" and "The Familiar," but also of Jefferson Hope's quest for retribution, as well as numerous other stories of vengeance in Doyle's work. Holmes and Watson stop at the village inn during the investigation where they discuss the case over tea, and where the detective refers to the town policeman as "the excellent local practitioner," a deliberate reference to a physician. As did Descartes and Hesselius before him, Holmes sits up for hours thinking over the problem "as he stared into the fire," and this effort has an effect, for the truth establishes itself under these circumstances. Descartes definitely surfaces to mind as Watson draws a picture of Holmes in the process of thinking: "Finally he lit his pipe, and sitting in the inglenook of the old village inn he talked slowly and at random about his case, rather as one who thinks aloud than as one who makes a considered statement." Here is both the thinking and the writing style of the French philosopher, who did not hesitate to tell the world he found thought a slow and circuitous chore, and whose personal, textured writing style is a study in thinking out loud. And like Dr. Hesselius, the detective is unable to prevent a horrible death from befalling the troubled individual in the story, for Douglas is eventually killed by his nemesis. We know Watson is writing out the tale from Douglas' "singular and terrible narrative," just as the other English doctor used the notebooks of Hesselius.

The incident of having a gunshot disfigure a face so severely as to make correct identification impossible Doyle probably borrowed from Henry James' short story "The Papers," in which we have the supposed suicide of an English member of Parliament while he was staying in Frankfort, Germany. The MP, Beadel-Muffet, missing a week for no apparent reason, is found dead of a disfiguring gunshot to the face; all believe him dead, yet a few days later he turns up alive and well. We are never told what the disappearance and confusion is all about since it does not affect the story proper. It's a bizarre piece of writing and altogether out of character for its author.

Doyle always enjoyed telling a true incident over again in his own way and he does so now; in fact he utilized a number of historical cases as models. In November of 1909, Mr. George Harry Storrs was murdered in his home, near Stalybridge, England, under circumstances that have never been cleared up. Storrs, his wife, a niece, and three servants lived in a large house named Gorse Hall, and on the night of September 10, 1909, as the family was sitting in the dining room, a shot was fired through the window at Mr. Storrs, but missed the target. Rushing to the window Storrs could just make out a dark figure disappearing into the shrubbery. It was suggested the shooter was deranged, and Storrs insisted he did not know who it could be. Mrs. Storrs went to the police and asked them to keep a special watch upon the house and she had a large alarm bell installed on the roof of the house to summon their help if necessary. On the last Saturday of October, Mr. Storrs called on the police, asked them to be particularly vigilant, and upon being asked why, said that he "wanted to be sure." The alarm bell rang around midnight, but when the police arrived Storrs told them he had rung it as a test. On Monday evening some time after dinner the housemaid passed the scullery door and noticed the gas was on and upon going in she encountered a young man with a revolver who threatened to kill her if she made a sound. She twisted away from him and ran screaming through the house alerting the rest of the household and they came to her assistance. As soon as the man saw Mr. Storrs he yelled, "I've got you at last!" and started to have a fight with him. For some reason he did not use the gun he had but rather took out a knife and stabbed Storrs fifteen times, wounding him seriously. The intruder got away, Storrs died without making a statement, and in spite of a wide search and a few false leads, the murderer was never caught. It's believed he left the country. Mr. Storrs was a popular and well-liked man and no explanation for the crime could be found, however, it was obvious George Storrs knew the man who killed him, but for some reason would not identify him. There was never the slightest indication as to the motive for the murder so Doyle gives free rein to his imagination. This mystery became one of the most famous unsolved murder cases in English history, and is echoed in a number of the Holmes stories, and naturally the similarity of it to "The Familiar" must have intrigued Doyle.

Another incident taken from English history involved the Bow Street Runners of London; a group of men having much in common with present day private detectives. They were a perfect example of what could be called an irregular police force since they were attached to the Bow Street Magistrate, yet neither kept regular hours nor reported in each day. Once they had begun a case they were left to their own devices, simply letting the regular police know how to get in touch with them, and they were often paid fees over and above the official rate. The organization Birdy Edwards worked for, the Pinkerton Detective Agency, operated much like this at the time of our story. In 1820 the Runners became involved in a case of espionage that is known as the Cato Street Conspiracy. A man named Arthur Thistlewood, who had served in France with the Revolutionaries, had returned to his native England a convinced and violent radical, his activities constantly bringing him into conflict with the authorities. Thistlewood had actually been one of the instigators of the Reign of Terror following the French Revolution and McGinty is compared to Georges Jacques Danton, a moderate of the Revolution who was executed by Maximillien Robespierre. Thistlewood managed somehow to gather together a group of around thirty men of similar views and hatched a plot to slaughter all the members of the British Cabinet, and then, in the confusion, hoped to be able to seize the government. The mass murders were planned for a Wednesday evening when Lord Harrowby was having the entire Cabinet to dinner at his home in Grosvenor Square. One of the plotters was to go to Harrowby's house pretending to deliver a parcel, hoping to gain admittance. When the door was opened, the others were to rush in and overpower the servants, killing them if necessary. They would then execute the Cabinet members, taking away the heads of Lord Castlereagh and Lord Sidmouth in a sack. As their headquarters, this gang used a broken down stable with a loft in Cato Street, not far from the Edgeware Road, arranging to meet there on the chosen evening before setting out for Lord Harrowby's house. However, a Runner named George Edwards, who, like Edwards in *The Valley of Fear*, sometimes acted as a free agent on behalf of the government, learning of what was afoot, managed to join the plotters, and learned all their plans. The police knew of the plot quite early on, but waited until the last moment so they could catch the whole crew together at the Cato Street stable. Led by the Bow Street Magistrate, Sir Richard Birnie, the police arrived at Cato Street, but found that the only means of getting into the hayloft where the gang was meeting was through a trap door that would admit only one at a time. Two men, Ruthven and Smithers, went first only to have Thistlewood kill Smithers with a sword. In the loft there was frightful confusion since one of the plotters managed to extinguish the lights, and fourteen of them, including Thistlewood, were able to escape. The informer Edwards knew where the ringleader was probably hiding and arrested him the next day. They were all imprisoned in the Tower of London and brought to trial at the Old Bailey in April 1820. All those who had been captured were found guilty of high treason and sentenced to hang, but some of them succeeded in escaping. This incident was borrowed by our author for use in the scene where Edwards tricks McGinty and his gang into walking into an ambush in which they are captured by him and the police, and the outcome of both events is much the same.

Doyle opts to appropriate from some writings of Diderot that are as unexpected as they are curious and novel. The philosopher was a regular contributor to *Correspondance littéraire*, the private newsletter distributed among the friends of the Enlightenment, in which, from 1759 to 1781, with the exception of 1773, when he was in Russia as adviser to Catherine the Great, Diderot contributed art criticism dealing with the works featured in the exposition in Paris known as *Le Salon*. A few of Diderot's essays on artists such as Boucher, Greuze, and Vernet (the latter a relative of Holmes' on his mother's side) come down to us in various collections of Diderot's writings. Diderot liked Vernet, for "He is like the creator himself for clarity and like nature herself for truth." Many of Vernet's works are seascapes, and scenes of shipwrecks and the heroics these give opportunity to, and Doyle must have been fond of them himself. Vernet, to Diderot, is "always harmonious, vigorous, and wise, like those great poets, those rare men whose natural fire is so well balanced by their judgment that they are never either exaggerated or cold." Could this be the inspiration for Doyle's bringing Vernet into the circle of Holmes' ancestors, this balance and judgment?

In *The Valley of Fear*, right at the beginning, Doyle goes off on a tangent, the details of which owe much to Diderot, for the artist Greuze is brought into things when we learn Professor Moriarty owns one of his works, entitled *La Jeune Fille à l'Agneau* (*Young Girl With a Lamb*). Inspector MacDonald, who has seen the work in the Professor's study, describes its subject as "a young woman with her head on her hands, peering at you sideways." There is obviously also a lamb in the scene. I don't know if a work with this name actually exists, although Greuze did execute one with this scene, but it doesn't really matter, for this is not the painting Doyle has in mind. Holmes is familiar with the painter, and tells us Greuze "was a French artist who flourished between the years 1750 and 1800. I allude, of course, to his working career. Modern criticism has more than indorsed the high opinion formed of him by his contemporaries." Of Greuze, Diderot had a good deal to say since he was at the time extremely popular, as he still is, and the philosopher was both a contemporary and friend. "Here is your painter and mine," Diderot claims in a review of 1765, "the first among us to conceive the notion of endowing art with moral content, of linking events in such a way that it would be easy to make a novel of them." Since Doyle is a novelist we know this statement caught his attention. Every so often Diderot's writings lapsed into beautiful nonsense, and this review on Greuze is a good example of it. The essay opens with a simple identification of the painting to be discussed: *La Jeune Fille Qui Pleure Son Oiseau Mort* (*Young Girl Weeping for Her Dead Bird*). The scene is of a "little girl facing us; her head is resting on her left hand; the dead bird is lying near the top of the cage, its head hanging down, its wings drooping, its feet in the air." It sounds dead all right. Calling the work "a pretty elegy," Diderot attempts to construe the grief of the girl, but his imagination reads into it other things, including the tender emotions generated by the girl's love for a young boy that he pretends exists, and is the real cause of her tears, drawing a picture for us of the love he knows must abide between the two. "That morning, unhappily, your mother was out of the house. He came; you were alone; and he was so handsome, so passionate, so tender, so charming!" Diderot tells us she is worried about her lover becoming distant and ungrateful, hence the sadness. When Birdy Edwards, posing as McMurdo, arrives in the valley he is directed to the boarding house of Ettie Shafter, who tells him her mother is not there, for she is deceased, so she, like Diderot's imaginary mother, is out of the house. It is emphasized to us that McMurdo is handsome, passionate, and charming, and immediately wins the love of Ettie. "He had so much love in his eyes, so much truth in his words! He spoke the sort of words that go straight to your heart!" Thus does Diderot assure us of the affection his apparitional swain feels for the young French girl. "From the first he made it evident, by his open admiration, that the daughter of the house had won his heart from the instant that he had set eyes upon her beauty and her grace," Doyle tells of the romance between Jack and Ettie, in unbounded imitation of the florid, convincing style of the philosopher. Diderot himself apparently is infatuated with his melancholy heroine. "But don't you see how beautiful she is! How interesting she is! I don't enjoy making people sad; and yet, in spite of that, I should not at all mind being the cause of her sorrow." It is McMurdo who is the bringer of sorrow to Ettie for in spite of her feelings for him, when upon learning of his connection with the lodge, her father orders McMurdo out of the house. McMurdo/Edwards is also competition for Ted Baldwin, one of the Scowrers, who courted Ettie first, and who she dare not cross, so her sorrow is real enough. The conversation between the imaginary lovers in the Greuze painting is amazingly close in word and spirit to that held by Jack and Ettie when they must part from each other.

The French girl, in at least one translation of Diderot's works I have read, at this point, calls her dead pet, "my birdy," and it was from this that Doyle took the name "Birdy" for his hero, who's real name is Birdy Edwards. The dead bird being mourned is a canary, and thoughts of a dead canary may actually have led Doyle by association to thoughts of coal mining, for caged canaries were taken underground by miners for use as indicators of the amount of poisonous coal gas in the atmosphere. The more fragile birds died quickly if the coal gas level increased, although the miners themselves might not yet realize the danger. "What if my bird's death were only a forewarning of something else?" runs the fictitious thoughts of the girl.

Yet another work by Greuze is brought into it. On the page preceding the one in which Holmes mentions Greuze, we find the scene of Inspector MacDonald commenting on his talk with Professor Moriarty while in the man's study. The subtle scientist, who talked to him of eclipses, even treating him to a reflector lantern show to clarify his thoughts, has impressed the Inspector. "He'd have made a grand meenister with his thin face and gray hair and solemn-like way of talking," the Inspector tells us. "When he put his hand on my shoulder as we were parting, it was like a father's blessing before you go into the cold, cruel world." The thought expressed is also a borrowing from Diderot's essay under discussion. *La Malédiction paternelle. Le Fils ingrat*, which translates as *The Father's Curse: The Ungrateful Son*, was another work by Greuze that Diderot reviewed. Holmes questions MacDonald as to the lighting in Moriarty's room, "Sun in your eyes and his face in the shadow?" It's obviously difficult to see in the Professor's room, and Diderot, right from the start, tells us the scene in Greuze's painting takes place in "a room into which scarcely any light can penetrate except through the door, when it is open, or, when the door is closed, through a square opening above it." Both the Professor's apartment and the cottage room in the French painting are lit only by the sun, which casts severe shadows within the area. In the painting we find we have interrupted a scene of family crisis, for the son has enlisted as a soldier and we are viewing the picture of his leave taking from the family, which includes his old father. The family has depended upon this son for financial support, and the father now regards his leaving as an act of deceit and treachery. The stern face on the wrathful man would have set well on the shoulders of "a grand meenister." An ungrateful member of the family is deserting them, and the bitter father curses him openly. The crafty Moriarty curses MacDonald silently, but he curses him nevertheless, and we know the Inspector has been deceived by the Drug. The entire inspiration for *The Valley of Fear* must have come from this brilliant piece by Diderot, and how many other selections of Doyle's works may possibly be verbal depictions of paintings, or other works of art, or taken from written descriptions of them, I have no idea.

Diderot's philosophical analogy of the human mind functioning as a type of spider web is also brought back into it after having made a first appearance in "The Final Problem," when the Inspector asks Holmes if he is absolutely sure that Moriarty is really the evil one whose income is earned in such an illegal fashion. Holmes answers, "Exactly. Of course I have other reasons for thinking so, — dozens of exiguous threads which lead vaguely up toward the center of the web where the poisonous, motionless creature is lurking."

My desire to know what Justice Wendell Holmes thought of these Doyle stories we know he read and reread all his life goes double for *The Valley of Fear*, which is full of allusions to his life and his main contribution to the world; *The Common Law*. This book was introduced in the first few pages of the initial Holmes novel and now is being discussed in the last Holmes novel. Both the book and its judicial philosophy obviously influenced just about all the tales in one way or another. A number of different countries are involved, as in *A Study in Scarlet*: America, scene of the conspiracy, and England, venue of the final killing. Perhaps the sea was meant to be considered a nation in itself, for Jack Douglas was finally killed on the ocean; it is also a reference to Oliver Wendell Holmes, who decided and discussed many cases of maritime law. Since he is an American, Douglas, after his part in the killing of Baldwin, another American, is brought to light, asks, "how do I stand by the English law?" He is acknowledging the differences within the uniformity found under the umbrella of the common law. Scotland is brought in when Inspector MacDonald is deliberately referred to as the "Aberdonian," after his city of birth, Aberdeen, in Scotland, and remember, Douglas was born in Ireland. All we need is for a Canadian or Australian to come through the door. The diversity of characters in this novel reminds us of the ancient city of Rome, or the modern Babylon of London. In a reference to the Judge, Watson wants us to know that the Great Detective, for some reason, used language during this case that was "in his most judicial style." The case is considered by Holmes as one of "vendetta," with the stalker of Douglas being entitled "an avenger." Baldwin, the avenger of wrong, died by his own hand if you wish, so he paid with his body, as did Douglas at sea. As in *A Study in Scarlet* we have two Americans fighting for the love of a woman who dies. Ettie is of German descent, her father being an immigrant to America, hence a German blood feud is the reference, and indeed Holmes, playing his namesake the American jurist, calls this whole thing "a very serious feud," and realizes it cannot be bought off with money. This final novel, as was the first, is Doyle answering to the tremendous influence of Wendell Holmes on his life, a shadow whose length must never be underestimated.

William James is actually introduced into the story by name, for listed among the victims of the Scowrers is "little Billy James," killed by the enemies of the people. Billy was the nickname used by the philosopher's son, who was also named William. I admit I'm not fully sure of the meaning of this gesture; Doyle may just be playing with names. It's in this story that we learn Moriarty's "younger brother is a station master in the west of England," by the way.

We must return now to American history, the previous encounters being but a part of the whole. The vicious attacks on the *Vermissa Herald*, and its editor James Stanger, as a result of the newspaper's stand against the Scowrers, is taken from any of a multitude of ugly events dealing with America's struggle for freedom of the press. The incident Doyle had in mind took place in Alton, Illinois, and is probably the most infamous case of an attack on the press in the country's history. It was unique in that from beginning to end it had a highly literate witness in the person of Edward Beecher, who immediately wrote a book, *Narrative of Riots at Alton* that quickly gained world fame. Sometime around ten o'clock on Monday night, the 7th of November 1837, Elijah P. Lovejoy, editor of the *Alton Observer*, was shot to death while defending his newspaper office against a raging mob of townspeople, and after killing him the gang destroyed everything in the place, including the presses, before leaving. Lovejoy had been a prominent abolitionist editor and Presbyterian minister who had used his editorial space to speak out against slavery. Many citizens did not agree with him, and grew to fear and despise him and his editorials, as did the Scowrers with Stanger and his editorials. The town of Alton was run by a "committee" of citizens, actually only one step above a mob, who even more than the police or politicians, were the real power. McGinty boasts that he could put two hundred men on the street to carry out his orders, which is a good size mob. Beecher tells us that "A member of the committee now rose and delivered a speech unequaled by any thing I ever heard for an excited, bitter, vindictive spirit." "He endeavored to represent the public sentiment in the nation in behalf of law and order as expressed by the press, as an outrageous attempt to force an editor on them whom they did not like: and called on them to resist the usurpation." At the meeting of the lodge at which the attack on the *Vermissa Herald* is plotted, McGinty takes a slip of paper from his waistcoat pocket and says, "Law and Order! That's how he heads it," in a reference to Stanger's offensive editorial. The subtitle of the *Herald's* article is "Reign of Terror in the Coal and Iron District," which as we know is a reference to the French Revolution, as well as events in America. On the first page of his book Beecher tells us of the events he is about to relate, that if they had happened "in revolutionary France; or in England, agitated by the consequent convulsion of the nations; there had been less cause for surprise. But it was not. It was in America — the land of free discussion and equal rights."

Some references taken from *Narrative of Riots at Alton* included the fact that Lovejoy, much quoted in the work, refers to God as "my Master," as was common among the pious at the time. Doyle switches this around by having McGinty called "Bodymaster." He also saw the importance in America of the word "Union," which he used for the Union Hotel, for the word is used constantly by Beecher to mean the union of states forming the United States and Doyle utilized heavily the words "brother," and "honorable," found on many pages of Beecher's work. Sherlock Holmes has an etched portrait of the abolitionist, Henry Ward Beecher, Edward's brother, hanging in his rooms.

New Orleans, Louisiana, is another city located in a valley, the Delta Valley of the Mississippi River. In the spring of 1862, at the beginning of the hostilities of the Civil War, New Orleans, then part of the Confederacy, fell to an amphibious Federal force, which until the termination of the war, three years later, occupied the strategically important area and held it against recapture. The situation was unusual for both sides: the occupied citizens, and the occupying enemy army, with both being Americans, having the same language and religions, and even many similar political beliefs; and like their countrymen elsewhere, holding mixed and often contradictory emotions, opinions, and loyalties, over the war issues. Americans were placed under military law by their own army acting as a conquering enemy. I regarded the dramatic situation involved similar to the problems posed by circumstances in New York during the time frame of Cooper's novel *The Spy*, only to learn the comparison had been made before me. And Sir Arthur saw the analogy as well.

In occupied New Orleans, as in Vermissa Valley, a large percentage of the population were immigrants, principally French, Irish, and German, as well as people who had been born in other parts of America, especially New York and Philadelphia. Both these American cities had been trading rivals of New Orleans prior to the war, and in Vermissa Valley the workers express concern about their business trade being lost to these particular cities. This is strange since their only real business is mining, but Doyle lets it stand.

Long before the arrival of Federal troops New Orleans already enjoyed a reputation for lawlessness, with the figures for 1850 showing that half the inmates in the state prison system had been arrested there. The city was infamous for its consumption of alcohol, with prostitution and gambling evident on all social levels. It still is. Political corruption and illegal voting was customary, as was government fraud, violence, and murder. In 1853, *The Illustrated London News* said of New Orleans, because of its location in the middle of a vast swamp, that it had been built "upon a site that only the madness of commercial lust could have ever tempted men to occupy." About half the population of New Orleans was Catholic, as were many of the residents of Vermissa Valley, including Morris, who in a form of confession tells McMurdo he is sick of all the violence. Doyle comes across the fact that the French Catholics of New Orleans were so liberal they became active in Masonic lodges. Conflicts erupted between them and the militant, devout Irish Catholics. The Masons and the Odd Fellows were active in coping with the problems arising from poverty in the city, while volunteers aided the small, underpaid police force.

Immediately following the fall of the city to Federal forces, chaos, confusion, brute force, bluff, and mob rule, by any number of different factions, controlled the place. As in no other time in America's history, the habitual state of flux brought about by the impact of hostilities, the uncertainty of the future, if there was to be one, and the rich variety of greed and moral confusion of so many people, added to the opportunity for the criminal element of all stripes to flourish and grow.

John McGinty is fashioned on no less a character than the Northern General Benjamin Butler, who was commander of the Union troops and placed the city under martial law, with himself in complete control. Butler is described as being gross in body, unscrupulous, clever, incorrigibly corrupt, and political in purpose. Shrewd and ambitious, he never hesitated to overstep his authority or disobey orders to get what he wanted. Butler and his military government actually gained the capacity to influence civilian elections for political offices within New Orleans, grabbing enough power to control the elections of senators, congressmen, even governors. We are told McGinty does what he does out of blind ambition, and here again he is fashioned upon Ben Butler, who actually hoped one day to replace Lincoln as President. Control was placed in the hands of a few, who in turn were under the thumb, one way or another, of Butler, who was free to exercise any force he wished, even to killing any who opposed his policies. The General informed his superiors, when he first took over, that he intended to make the people fear him, and he carried out a policy of bold action backed by force, becoming infamous for his vindictive nature when dealing with any he perceived as his enemy. A model is found for the Scowrers practice of destroying the homes of their enemies in the fact that Butler ordered that if a Union soldier was killed in a building, it would be burned down. Doyle probably received much of his information on all this from Butler's own autobiography, published in Boston in 1892, but there is no shortage of material on the subject. The man made his headquarters in the St. Charles Hotel, the best in town, as McGinty made his command center in his town's best hotel.

Old Brother Morris, who resists and turns against McGinty, is I believe, based upon the personality of the Catholic priest Father James Ignatius Mullon, elder Pastor of St. Patrick's, New Orleans, who openly defied General Butler, and for some reason got away with it. Morris emphasizes to McMurdo that he is a good Catholic, as a priest would be, and he defies the Scowrers, yet somehow manages to be left alone. The Catholic Church, to a large degree, was not bothered by Butler's men, and in turn did not go overboard on their criticism of the Federals.

In *The Valley of Fear* John McMurdo plays the role of John T. Monroe, mayor of New Orleans, a crafty politician and an open antagonist of General Butler. Monroe had been mayor twice, with another occupying the chair in between his terms; a testament to how unsteady the times actually were. Monroe, who was a dockworker before becoming mayor, in order to preserve law and order, which was always about to crumble, hired local thugs to assist his police. He and the General were at odds over just about every issue that came before them, and played a game of power struggle, bluff, and backbiting, for the duration of the occupation. One of the townsmen, a friend of Monroe's involved in all this was a banker named Jacob Barker, a name Doyle borrows for the English friend of Douglas, Cecil James Barker, with Jacob being the Hebrew for James. He also uses the name Jacob for Ettie's father, Jacob Shafter. Barker of New Orleans owned a newspaper, the *National Advocate*, which was temporarily suppressed by General Nathaniel Banks, another Union officer, because of its Confederate sympathies, and when Barker's paper offended Butler personally, Butler suppressed it for good. The man put the newspaper out of business for printing disparaging editorials as surely as did McGinty, the *Vermissa Herald*. The local press of New Orleans was harshly dealt with in general, for divulging military information when they did it, and for expressions of hostility toward the occupation, something they never tired of doing. The editors also had to be bullied by threats and brute force into printing Union proclamations. The press was ordered to submit all copy to military censors and nothing disparaging to the Union or the troops was permitted. Butler even closed down completely the two newspapers whose owners had served in the Confederate Army.

The *True Delta* was essentially the voice of the Irish in the city, and was run by Editor John McGinnis, whose name Doyle took for John McGinty. Butler had seized the presses of the *True Delta* for refusing to set type for his edicts and suppressed publication until McGinnis apologized, which he did, but then offended Butler again in an editorial which must have enraged Butler as much as Stanger's piece upset McGinty, for the General threatened to close the paper altogether, so McGinnis gave in again. Someone on the *New York Herald* must have offended the Federal Army, for in August of 1864 their correspondents were ordered to leave the city. When McMurdo realizes the Scowrers are suspicious of him, he tells McGinty the real spy is a reporter he met who worked for a New York newspaper. A number of New York papers had reporters in the city during the occupation. Butler put into practice a vast secret service that came back with reports of plots against him and his men. When things got nasty he had the mayor and city council thrown out of office. McGinty boasts of controlling the police and judges, for Butler eventually had both a judge and chief of police imprisoned, as well as the mayor and many others. He had one man hung for taking down the American flag over the City Mint, and for this the President of the Confederacy proclaimed him "an outlaw," while the people christened him with the title "Beast Butler," and also, because of his eye problem, "The Cross-Eyed Beast."

In the scene where McGinty claims that when there is trouble brewing there is usually a woman behind it, we have a reference to General Butler's "Woman Order" of May 1862. The women of New Orleans were extremely rude and hostile to Union soldiers, since they knew they could get away with things no man could. Butler called them "she-adders," and issued an order declaring that any woman found guilty of showing contempt towards any officer or soldier would be arrested as a prostitute.

The General, his civilian brother, and many friends and cronies became rich on the black market and on the marginally legal trade of scarce commodities in the beleaguered city. A local treasury agent, George Denison, wrote to his chief that Butler "is such a smart man, that it would, in any case, be difficult to discover what he wished to conceal." In order to stabilize the crime rate, Butler ordered a new, larger police force, including policemen brought in from New York, as well as special agents; in effect turning his government into a "city hall machine," which rewarded the faithful with jobs and favors, and punished the disloyal, exemplifying his civilian counterpart, the political "boss." A group of his supporters, calling themselves the "Union Association," took on all the earmarks of a political party, with rallies, work programs, speeches, etc.

From 1862 until 1866, the city was under military law, not common law, and questions of law of all kinds, including international law, were constantly being discussed since over 40,000 of the inhabitants were foreign aliens and thousands more, almost the majority, were foreign born, not to mention freed slaves, Indians, etc. Many of the foreigners believed the Washington government could not actually have jurisdiction over them, and violent controversy over laws was a hallmark of the occupation. Even President Lincoln, himself a lawyer, got into the fray when the problem looked like it was developing into an international crisis. The armchair lawyer in Doyle must have been fascinated with all this.

Butler's replacement, General Banks, was much like his predecessor. Banks drew his power from Lincoln and the Washington government of course, and when the President realized the population of New Orleans was not yielding to the pressure of his troops on important issues, Lincoln wrote to Banks in December of 1863, saying that he had "supreme and undivided authority" in his department and was "*Master*...in the matter of organizing a state government," something Lincoln believed was needed in the situation. Lincoln underlined the word "Master" and wrote to his other officers that they were not to get in Banks' way.

One major problem in the city was with the many different kinds of currency in use: Federal notes and coins, Confederate monies, city specie, bank notes from private banks, and so forth. Counterfeiters floated large amounts of bogus specie, a practice McMurdo convinces the lodge is his means of income. The making of false money became so commonplace General Banks had to stop the circulation of some types of currency altogether.

Toward the conclusion of the war a federal commission was established to study the level of corruption within the U. S. Army stationed in the Delta Valley. They dug into a number of offenses, such as the sale of trading permits to the enemy, rigging of local elections, bank fraud, and much else. A private detective, Allan Pinkerton, was hired to help in the investigation. It was Pinkerton who founded the organization that during the war acted as a Union spy agency and supplied bodyguards to such men as Lincoln, and McMurdo/Edwards worked for this company. The Pinkertons went on to break up the Molly Maguires and as a result were despised by labor unions. Allan Pinkerton later gave testimony in court in New York in a "Report to the Special Commission," which concluded that the Gulf Department, Butler's and Banks' responsibility, had been riddled with "oppression, peculation, and graft." *The Valley of Fear* is essentially a true story, with much of its material being taken from the files of the Pinkertons, which Doyle had access to as a close friend of the president of the company.

This brings us to one of the most fascinating aspects of *The Valley of Fear*. When Jacob Shafter learns McMurdo is "gettin' set on my Ettie," he warns him that another rival is already courting the girl, and McMurdo answers that he questioned Ettie about this but she would not take him into her confidence on the subject, and in agitation Shafter calls his daughter "baggage!" This single word, being used to illuminate the low esteem a father holds his daughter in, is I think one of the subtlest yet informative revelations of character in all literature, for it is the insulting expression Juliet's father uses when addressing her in *Romeo and Juliet*. The use of this contemptuous incivility directed toward her shows Juliet, and the reader, just how little regard this stern, ill-mannered man has for the girl, and thus explains perhaps why it is she so quickly becomes desperately attached to Romeo, whom she hardly knows, simply because he shows some interest in her. Juliet already had a suitor before Romeo showed up, and he is handsome and well liked, but he shows no great interest in her. A picture is drawn for us of McMurdo being "a regular Romeo," with his good looks, charm, and capacity for verbal persuasiveness, and we even have a situation where Ettie's father is instrumental in keeping the pair apart, echoing Shakespeare's drama. The turbulent, bloody streets of New Orleans, with its loose bands of friends and enemies in close proximity to each other, formed in Doyle's mind a perfect stage set for a reenactment of a new version of the great play. Ted Baldwin, young, arrogant, and hotheaded, searching out the slightest excuse to start a fight, stands in well for Juliet's cousin Tybalt, always on the lookout for a chance to draw his sword, and whose actions eventually lead to Romeo's death. Remember that before *The Valley of Fear* is over, both Jack and Ettie are dead, as are the two lovers in the earlier drama. Doyle has some fun with us when he has one character, upon hearing a suspicious sound, throw out the expression, "Hark to that!" This is right out of Shakespeare, and hardly in ready use among Pennsylvania coal miners, although Doyle did come across the ejaculation "Hark!" used by an American cowboy in his reading of Mark Twain's *Roughing It*.

The American Civil War is one of the most reported conflicts in history, and this particular occupational operation in New Orleans gave rise to a variety of firsthand accounts, offering us contrasting versions of what happened, and why. Julia Ellen Le Grand Waitz, a young lady of the city at the outbreak of hostilities in 1862, kept a journal eventually published as *The Journal of Julia Le Grand, New Orleans, 1862–1863*, which became a mine of information on the events in hand. Doyle probably found the edition published in Richmond, Virginia in 1911, or he may have come across excerpts from the book quoted in other works. There was also another work he may have used, *Beauty and Booty: The Watchword of New Orleans*, by Marion Southwood, published in New York in 1867, which has proven elusive to me. Like most Southern women, Julia Le Grand hated the Yankees in general and Butler and his cohorts in particular. Ettie fears and despises McGinty and his crew as well, but like the ladies of the Delta Valley, there is not much she can do about it. Julia's brother Claude, who had shown promise as a sculptor, was wounded in Virginia early in the war and lost his right arm, so this must have fueled her fire of hate. When General Banks took over for Butler he initially attempted to win over the citizens by encouraging fraternization between the factions with balls, concerts, and receptions, in an effort to "dance the fair creoles to loyalty." Julia must have expressed the sentiments of many when recording in her journal: "There is a difference even among devils, it seems, as some of Banks' people do try to be kind to us, while Butler's were just the reverse." She refused to take the Oath of Allegiance to the United States, and eventually, because of her hatred of the Federals, left the city in May of 1863, a sort of voluntary exile. Romeo was banished from Verona for his part in the feuds, while both the young lovers in Shakespeare's play eventually grew to fear the pressure put upon their love by the city with its unrelenting efforts at involving them in its quarrels, and also felt the need to flee. If Romeo and Juliet are to find happiness they must leave Verona, as Jack and Ettie must flee the valley of fear. The unsuccessful ploy of Juliet's feigning death was so they could both escape and begin a new life elsewhere. When Jack tells Ettie they can face out the rest of their lives together, she says, "It could not be here. Could you take me away?" As in *A Study in Scarlet* the beleaguered couple will flee for their lives. It is Douglas who feigns death in Doyle's novel, also with dire results, for he is eventually killed as a result of his actions.

If the thought of falling in love with a Union soldier ever occurred to Julia Le Grand, she too must have realized they could never show their love to New Orleans. There was enough blood in the streets already. She frowned upon any form of contact with the enemy and sternly lectured two young friends who permitted a Northern Naval officer to call upon them, claiming that had he been a true gentleman, he would never have entered their home, "knowing that true Southerners are compromised by receiving Federals." But Julia's innate kindness led her occasionally to show expressions of sympathy for enemy soldiers, especially for the native born, who she tells us, "have a sad and hopeless look, as if their hearts were aching for home." She admits that once she was moved by the act of a Union officer who stopped at her gate and asked if he could pick some rosebuds to send north to his wife. For expressing such sentiments in this difficult time of war, she tells us her friends looked upon her as "half Yankee." She adds at this point, "I accept a bloody triumph only as the least of two evils," a reference to her hopes the Confederates will retake the city and free the citizens from their captors. Many people who she has come to realize are not as evil as she first thought will be hurt as a result of such a battle, so she finds herself ensnared in a dilemma as surely as did Juliet, who after all loves her family, nurse, friends, and city, but must forgo them all if she accepts the love of Romeo. Had such a woman as Julia Le Grand actually fallen in love with a Northerner, all the ingredients of a drama as intense as Shakespeare's would have been present. Julia includes the following tidbit in her journal: "Men's suffering always excites me, let the men be who they may." Now there's an interesting statement.

The Valley of Fear is primarily an American story, and not surprisingly one source Doyle adopted for it was the life and writings of an individual who personified the American spirit for many in his day; Theodore Roosevelt. Doyle must have felt close to his friend TR, for the two had much in common, even looking alike. It has been pointed out that Roosevelt was not unlike a boy who never grew up, and the same has been said a number of times about Doyle. Aside from his considerable attainments as soldier and statesman, TR was a writer, primarily of travel accounts in such places as Africa and the American West. His *Autobiography* was well received, and in it Sir Arthur found a man who is close in spirit, and even lifestyle, to Hawkeye, for when Roosevelt journeyed to the Dakota Territory he described it as a land of buffalo and buffalo hunters, Indians, soldiers, and trappers, thus Doyle realized Hawkeye, who died on the same prairie, would have found it altered, but only little. Doyle reads with delight that TR owned a horse named Ben Butler, "a big, sulky" animal that enjoyed throwing itself over backwards with Roosevelt on it. He also had something to say about "frontier justice," which was still the law of the land, even at this rather late date. "Certain crimes of revolting baseness and cruelty," he tells us, "were never forgiven," making us think of Jefferson Hope's lust for revenge.

The *Autobiography* establishes connections to *The Valley of Fear* right on the first page when the author tells us some of his ancestors were from Pennsylvania, having settled there with William Penn himself. The book also outlines its author's early attempt at entering politics: "At that day, in 1880, a young man of my bringing up and convictions could join only the Republican party, and join it I accordingly did. It was no simple thing to join it then. That was long before the era of ballot reform and the control of primaries; long before the era when we realized that the Government must take official notice of the deeds and acts of party organizations. The party was still treated as a private corporation, and in each district the organization formed a kind of social and political club. A man had to be regularly proposed for and elected into this club, just as into any other club. As a friend of mine picturesquely phrased it, I 'had to break into the organization with a jimmy.'" What we are seeing with Jack McMurdo's attempt at getting into the lodge is simply representative of the state of American politics at the time. TR adds that when he first told his friends about his plans to join a political club they laughed at him "and told me that politics were 'low'; that the organizations were not controlled by 'gentlemen'; that I would find them run by saloon-keepers, horse-car conductors, and the like, and not by men with any of whom I would come in contact outside; and, moreover, they assured me that the men I met would be rough and brutal and unpleasant to deal with." Many, if not most politicians, were subservient to special interest groups and would do their bidding on bills and legislature before them for considerations of one kind or another, with the shibboleth "one hand washes the other," serving the principles of most American politicians, as it still does. Roosevelt made the observation that about a third of the legislators took direct money bribes. Morton Hall in New York City was where the Republicans hung out at the time and "The big leader was Jake Hess, who treated me with rather distant affability." Doyle realized Hess did not trust TR, and transfers this suspicion to the uneasy relationship between McGinty and McMurdo. "The running of the machine was left to Jake Hess and his captains of tens and of hundreds," Roosevelt says, and goes on to explain that much of the campaigning was actually done in the New York saloons with the candidates going from place to place talking to the voters and buying drinks. He gives vivid examples of the power and corruption of the machine with many such examples focusing on the Irish: the ones who wielded the power, and the ones who were destroyed by it. As is the practice in Vermissa Valley, the New York bosses do not maintain power by dealing in simple black and white issues but instead confuse the question, thus depending upon a certain amount of perplexity in the public mind to get their own way. An "inner circle," composed of "certain big business men, and the politicians, lawyers, and judges who were in alliance with and to a certain extent dependent upon them," ran the country. He adds, "the conception of public office as something to be used primarily for the good of the dominant political party became ingrained in the mind of the average American, and he grew so accustomed to the whole process that it seemed part of the order of nature." This patronage system does nothing but favor the "evil elements in our Government," TR insists, adding, "the most openly crooked measure which during my time (as Governor of New York State) was pushed at Albany," was "introduced by a local saloon-keeper, whose interests, as far as we knew, were wholly remote from the Constitution, or from any form of abstract legal betterment."

For the rest of his life Roosevelt aided in fighting corruption, dishonest government, and the practice of placing in public office only those who would cooperate with the power machine. He advocated what he called "practical common sense," and in this statement Doyle saw the application of the pragmatism of Wendell Holmes, Peirce, James, and others, that he himself, through his character of Sherlock Holmes, had been advocating for so many years. It was Theodore Roosevelt who had appointed Wendell

Holmes to a position on the Supreme Court in December of 1902. When a piece of legislature that he had been trying to pass to protect underpaid workers from exploitation was defeated for legal reasons, Roosevelt went on record as saying, "They knew legalism, but not life." He even realized that there were men of a nature who wanted control of people and events, not for wealth, or to satisfy some vice, but simply for its own sake, for the power of it. In speaking of the machine system we learn of one such boss, Mr. Croker, who ran Tammany Hall in 1898: "Croker was a powerful and truculent man, the autocrat of his organization, and of a domineering nature," who does just about anything he wishes, even going against his own Democratic Party if he feels like it. He has complete power and uses it.

One enlightening insight in the *Autobiography* is when Roosevelt, in emphasizing the need for a strong army and navy, tells us that those who serve in its ranks must be only those willing to die for their country, for "He should pay with his body." Doyle sees immediately that Roosevelt is showing us he has read and thought about, and re-applied the lessons of *The Common Law*.

McMurdo is a rendering of Mike Costello, Tammany Democrat from New York City, who fought to clean up politics, of whom TR said, "He was as fearless as he was honest." Both Costello and Roosevelt had morals of the highest caliber and believed in setting an example for others by defeating bills favoring only the machine and its interests, and while most other men in public life at the time were unconcerned about this problem, Costello stood up to the Democratic machine, as Roosevelt had challenged the Republican.

Captain Teddy Marvin of Vermissa Valley is based upon his namesake. Teddy Roosevelt. Costello and Roosevelt were on opposite sides of the fence to the world at large, as were McMurdo and Marvin, but all were attempting to achieve the same goal, the ridding of politics of its inherent corruption. Like Marvin, who had been a Captain in the Chicago Central Police, and later a member of the Valley Police, Teddy Roosevelt was a policeman at one time or another much of his life. Chicago Central is a pun on Central Park, New York City's great commons, where TR had spent so much of his time while serving as Police Commissioner. In 1895, Roosevelt accepted a post on the police board, a governing body interested in curbing corruption in the NYPD. By the time he resigned from this board the department was more honest and less influenced by politicians than it had ever been before. He became Police Commissioner of the city in 1895, only with the understanding that he would disregard all partisan politics and not allow himself to be influenced by anything except justice. Jack McGinty tells Teddy Marvin that they have their own police and don't need any "imported goods" in the valley; a reference to the fact that although TR was a New Yorker, he went out West and became a deputy sheriff.

Friendship and trust, and the ability to work together under difficult and dangerous situations existed between Roosevelt and Joe Murray, another individual he teamed up with. Murray was a tough, affable New York Irishman who had immigrated to America at an early age, fought with the Union in the war, and ended up a power broker in New York politics. It was Murray who convinced TR, quite correctly, to run for the N. Y. State Assembly in his district, which he won with Murray's help. When TR won the election he told his constituents as he set out for the capital in Albany that he was his own man, "untrammeled and unpledged. I will obey no boss and serve no clique," which amounted to revolution at the time.

The special interest that dominated and corrupted above all others was big business, and in particular Jay Gould, multimillionaire railroad baron, land pirate, and swindler. In a speech before the Assembly in April of 1882, Roosevelt charged that a State Supreme Court Justice, T. R. Westbrook, had used the influence of his judicial position to assist Gould in the stock manipulations that had led to Gould's ending up controlling the Manhattan Elevated Railway. McGinty was right when he said he could control even the judges. TR had obtained a letter from Westbrook to Gould promising the necessary support, and in addition he charged that Westbrook had actually held a session of the court right in Jay Gould's office! Roosevelt called for an investigation and demanded the impeachment of Westbrook. The speech startled everyone and was a truly courageous and daring act for a freshman politician. In one speech he called Jay Gould "the archcrook of Wall Street," archcrook being a perfect sobriquet for Boss McGinty. Westbrook ended up not getting thrown out of office, but Teddy Roosevelt became famous for the attempt, thus establishing for himself a reputation for independence and honesty that led to a sweeping victory in the next election, his return to the state government, and eventually the presidency.

The first time Teddy Marvin and Jack McGinty meet in the Union House is a re-creation of a scene from Roosevelt's *Autobiography*. While living in the Dakotas, where he owned a ranch and herd of cattle, and was also a deputy sheriff, TR was often called upon to uphold the law. Marvin is talking to McGinty when he turns around and spies McMurdo, then pretends to recognize him from Chicago, saying, "Here's an old acquaintance!" McMurdo answers, "I was never a friend to you nor any other cursed copper in my life." New York City was just about the only place they called policemen "coppers," by the way, a reference to the copper badges they wore. The situation is obviously very tense, especially in this era when police had far more power to enforce personal justice, called in New York "curb side justice," and just about everyone at the time carried a gun or a knife, or both. The two engage in a duel of words that almost leads to a fight. Marvin reminds McMurdo that he has committed a murder in Chicago. McMurdo denies shooting anyone, and Marvin tells him he doesn't have to worry for the Chicago police haven't enough evidence to press charges, adding that he has given McMurdo valuable information, and "you're a sulky dog not to thank me for it." McMurdo thanks Marvin for the information and the two pretend to become friends of a sort. In the Dakotas there was a cowboy named Bill Jones, a living legend about whom many stories circulated, including tales of how many men Jones had killed one way or another. Teddy Roosevelt was a bit of a legend himself by this time, and indeed so is Teddy Marvin, for he is well known to McMurdo, and obviously to others, who stay out of his way. Jones was a rough, profane character, and a law unto himself, who had actually been with the Bismarck, North Dakota police until he "beat the Mayor over the head with his gun one day." Jones had followers and they loved to hear him tell stories of his exploits, but TR was in one of Jones' audiences one day and found he could no longer take the stream of profanity. "Bill Jones," he said, "you're the nastiest talking man I ever heard." Silence gripped the room, for Jones had been known to kill for less. Jones however simply said, "Maybe I've been a little too free with my mouth," and from that point on Jones and Roosevelt were the best of friends. Now Jones was also a sheriff, and Roosevelt tells us he served as deputy under him for a while, so that makes it a conversation between two policemen, just as the talk between Marvin and McMurdo is between two detectives. The "relations between policemen and criminals are peculiar in some parts of the States," Doyle informs us, during this particular conversation in *The Valley of Fear.*

The relationship between young Theodore Roosevelt and his first wife Alice Hathaway Lee is reminiscent of the events shared by Jack and Ettie. They were married in America but she died young, and Roosevelt went to London where he married again, not to an English girl but to another American living there at the time.

Jacob Shafter throws Jack out of his boarding house for being a Scowrer, but lets him return for meals, establishing a strained relationship between the two. Doyle also took the name of Ettie's father, Shafter, from TR's writings, where we learn that General William Shafter was in charge of American forces during the Spanish American War, in which Roosevelt played so prominent a role. The two men did not get along with each other and Roosevelt had to go over Shafter's head in order to have his wounded men evacuated from Cuba. Jacob Shafter did not want McMurdo seeing his daughter, but Jack goes over his head, you might say, for he maintains a relationship with her anyway.

Questions broached in *The Valley of Fear* and in Roosevelt's *Autobiography* make matters a lot more complicated however. When Teddy Marvin is talking to McGinty in his saloon he says, "We're looking to you, Councilor, and to the other leading citizens, to help us in upholding law and order in this township." On the surface this seems ridiculous, given who McGinty is, but this brings us back to Roosevelt and his struggle for justice and good government. He was no fool, realizing that even a corrupt order, if it worked, was better than no order at all, and that no man was evil all the time; consequently he did not hesitate to act with others who were not as honest as himself, if the outcome might produce good effects. At one time Thomas Platt was boss of the Republican Party, in the worst sense of the word, and a senator as well. Police Commissioner Roosevelt greatly annoyed Platt by dismissing political appointees of his who were obviously corrupt. In the fall of 1898 the two however formed a truce, and a political marriage of convenience, when Roosevelt was running for high office in New York. Roosevelt's opponents at the time were the entire Tammany machines, and they used his friendship with Platt against him, but he won by a slim margin nevertheless.

In his book TR speaks at great length about a Pennsylvania coal miners' strike and his need to intervene, while President, in order to bring the conflict to an end. He tells us he wanted to put at least one high Catholic ecclesiastic on the commission because most of the miners were Catholic. Although the miners cooperated with the government commission set up by him, the owners of the mines displayed a wall of uncooperation and self-interest, and could not be bargained with. Of the owners' attitude toward the striking miners and the federal commission, TR tells us, "They were curiously ignorant of the popular temper; and when they went away from the interview they, with much pride, gave their own account of it to the papers, exulting in the fact that they had 'turned down' both the miners and the President." He adds that the position and actions of the owners "was utterly silly from their own standpoint, and well-nigh criminal from the standpoint of the people at large." All this helps explain part of what must be regarded as sympathy on Doyle's part with some of the goals, and even some of the actions, of McGinty and his men. Their opponents, the owners of the mines, are not so different from them in temperament and methods, and sometimes worse. Obviously all the angels are not on one side; there is more than one point of view to it all. TR reminds us however that labor is often no better than management, for he says he often had to show "the most emphatic disapproval of unwise or even immoral actions by representatives of labor." It's obvious McGinty and his followers believe they are completely justified in their aggressive and criminal behavior, and at one point McGinty states that "there are times when we have to take our own part. We'd soon be against the wall if we didn't shove back at those that were pushing us." He is fully confident that God is on his side in these struggles, no matter his methods, an attitude adopted by many groups with limited power and unlimited grievances in many countries. Without their cartel, so the Scowrers claim, they would be exploited and misused by the ruling class, who control the only means they have of making a living. Roosevelt would have agreed with them. Notice that one of the most vicious of the gang, the rival of McMurdo for Ettie, the one who tried to kill him in England after searching for him for years, is also named Theodore, this being Baldwin's first name, since he is called Ted. At one point in the narrative Doyle refers to Ted Baldwin as the avenger of wrong. When McGinty and Marvin first meet in the Union House and size each other up, McGinty asks the policeman sarcastically, "What are you but the paid tool of the capitalists, hired by them to club or shoot your poorer fellow citizen?" Amazingly Marvin doesn't disagree with him at all, nor seem to feel the least bit offended. He simply answers, "Well, well, we won't argue about that," and he even does it "good-humoredly." Marvin does not see any reason to deny it, for he tells us, "I expect we all do our duty same as we see it." He realizes there is no simple right or wrong and that everyone has the right to get whatever he can out of the world, like it or not. Roosevelt tells us it was the bosses, the ward captains, the mayors and assistant-mayors, the ones who met in the back rooms of saloons, who really knew the people, not the reformers who had never lived among the working class, and had no idea of what they really needed or wanted. Unquestionably Roosevelt, when he held power as President, became a boss in every sense of the word, although his standards were always higher than the others.

In Theodore Roosevelt, Doyle actually found a man so close in spirit and action to Sherlock Holmes that he realized Sherlock's life could be based upon Roosevelt's, and to a certain extent probably was, as was his own. It makes you wonder how much of TR's life could have been based on Sherlock's, and possibly Doyle's, as well. The use of this *Autobiography* as a source of material for this novel points out to us just how alert to the life around him Doyle really was, for the book was published in 1913, yet our author had internalized and utilized its contents for his own purposes by 1914, the year *The Valley of Fear* saw light.

The expression of the role of Jesus in the character of Holmes occurs a number of times in this story, specifically when Sherlock, acting the necromancer, foresees his own death and the abyssing of the devil in a vision. "But if I am spared by lesser men, our day will surely come," he declares to Watson, in reference to the fact that the future shows him the eventual end of both himself and the Professor. The answer given by Watson to this is truly astonishing, "May I be there to see!" Watson "exclaimed devoutly." This is as close as anything we shall ever find in the Canon to Watson's role as John, the favorite Apostle and the "witness" to Jesus. Holmes actually reenacts once again a scene taken from the *New Testament* in which Jesus raises the dead. In the "Gospel of St. John" we learn of the raising of Jesus' dead friend Lazarus, who, like Douglas has been dead to the world when Jesus/Holmes appears on the scene to perform the miracle, and both men have had to travel a distance to get to the place of entombment. Jesus and Holmes approach the tomb and address he who is deceased as though they were still alive, although everyone present: the sister of Lazarus and his friends, and the wife of Douglas, the other detectives, and all others present, "regard" him as dead, or believe him to be so. In the study at Birlstone Manor, Holmes addresses Mrs. Douglas in regard to her husband as though he were right in the room with them, alive and well. Jesus, after thanking his Father in advance for performing this miracle through his agency, stands in front of the cave tomb and yells out, "Lazarus, come forth." "And presently he that was dead came forth." Holmes, in a loud voice, informs Douglas, hiding in the secret room, that the game is up. Of Douglas we are told by John Watson, "we were aware of a man who seemed to have emerged from the wall, who advanced now from the gloom of the corner in which he had appeared." Both men have emerged out of a wall, for Lazarus was buried in a cave built into a rock wall, and Douglas has been hiding in a clandestine area whose door was built into the wall of the study. We are told of Lazarus that his hands and feet were bound with a winding cloth and Douglas echoes this somewhat, for when he emerges from his place of concealment, "Mrs. Douglas turned, and in an instant her arms were round him. Barker had seized his outstretched hand." His freedom of movement is hampered, as was that of the risen Lazarus bound in his winding sheet. Holmes has raised the dead man out of sympathy for his wife. "'Enough and more than enough,' remarked Sherlock Holmes gravely." That "gravely" is a typical Doyle pun. "I have every sympathy with you," he tells the widow. In the ancient account we are led to the conclusion that Jesus raised Lazarus out of sympathy for his sister Martha.

Douglas himself, in his many manifestations, is a sort of Christ figure. McMurdo had been in the valley of fear three months, just as Jesus descended into limbo for three days before rising from the dead, and Holmes wandered the earth for three years before returning to his battle with evil. McMurdo, as did Jesus, has gone down to the valley of death, offering himself as a sacrifice for the sins of mankind, and at the end we learn his sacrifice has been accepted. We are told of Wilson, the fictitious journalist who was after all just another version of McMurdo, "If he could get on a good trail of the Scowrers, he's ready to follow it into hell." Ettie begs McMurdo to give up his life as a henchman of McGinty, and flee with her, "Give it up, Jack! For my sake, for God's sake, give it up! It was to ask you that I came here today. Oh, Jack, see — I beg it of you on my bended knees! Kneeling here before you I implore you to give it up!" Doyle is here paraphrasing any number of Catholic prayers that include such phrases as "kneeling we implore you," or "we beg of you on bended knee," prayers addressed to Jesus, Mary, and the saints.

EPILOGUE

In hitting a few of the highlights in this summation of Doyle's creativity, I realize I am omitting areas of thought equally important (if such a thing can be measured), but I had to draw the line somewhere. Taken purely on the level of associative writing, as put forth by the Symbolist Manifesto, the products of Doyle's mind are the most thoughtful and thought provoking of their kind that I know of, so any assessing of such convoluted introspections would of necessity be abbreviated, arbitrary, and incomplete. Space and time force me to leave gaps, some of which I hope to fill in at a future date. I have dealt solely with sources such as philosophers, fictional writers, and so forth, that I am familiar with. Like a fisherman who cannot see his lure in such deep water, I have no idea of what may have come up to the bait, but failed to bite.

With the exception of religious authority, the achievements in nonfiction that cultivated the most profound and deep-seated control on Doyle's choice of source material are unquestionably the philosophical concepts, which foster and motivate artistic creation by advocating an external prerogative, forcing purpose on the evolution of abstract thoughts serving as an armature of concrete material dress, and in turn becoming the preeminent factor in the esthetic. They gave the work energy and direction. Arthur Doyle owned one of the largest philosophical libraries in private hands. Any work of art, be it a painting, sculpture, or a piece of writing, is an external display of the quality, maturity, and intentions of the mind that created it; the work itself showing what the creator was thinking at the time, his level of mental development, morals, and so forth. Doyle was no exception to this rule. The philosophical reflections expressed in these stories designate the rich mental texture of the artist, who lifted them boldly from their original context, and adding to them the needs of his individual personality, stamped them as uniquely his own. Arthur Conan Doyle and his creation Sherlock Holmes are two of the most unique people that ever lived. Doyle utilized considerations from just about every field of philosophy, but definitely there developed a stronger sphere of influence expressed by speculations and personalities generated within the period known as the Enlightenment, and the conceptions that came about either by what had sponsored its founding, such as Descartes' thoughts, or by what had resulted from its expansion, such as empiricism, pragmatism, and science; yet these stories do not deal with a solitary dominant point of view emphasizing a system contingent on a philosophical attitude, such as we find in the existential concoctions of Jean-Paul Sartre, or the desperate liberalism of Voltaire. Rather they take as their foundation large, heterogeneous chunks from the world of thought that has preceded them or is contemporary with them, and with these considerations weave a new web: flexible, personal, and highly entertaining, whose abstract energy assimilates into the dynamic personalities found in the Holmes Canon.

The keeping of the law, Holmes' role in life, involved precise yet at the same time malleable methods combining logical and cognitive exercises that borrowed spirit from the mind of authors as diverse as Kant, Descartes, Nietzsche, and Wendell Holmes. The specifiable properties of other thinkers redevelop, and in the mode of their application to Holmes and his world, edge toward a still not fully understood goal, and in that becoming we begin to recognize their new value. Even the narrative thread spun back and forth between Holmes and Watson reminds me of nothing less than Platonic dialogue, with usually Holmes, but sometimes Watson, in the role of Socrates. The philosophical subject is encased in both a biographical and autobiographical context, for the stories are meant to personify a fictionalized re-creation of the Johnson/Boswell relationship, the account of which represented a new plateau in the evolution of literature, as well as being an impersonation of the self-analytical writings and life style of Descartes, in addition to being Doyle's own mental autobiographical vehicle. The subject of Sherlock Holmes is the author of Sherlock Holmes.

It's difficult to attempt a thorough study of Doyle's work, for philosophy is a broad field involving diverse personalities, many subjects and various frames of reference, all presented in an enormous amount of literature. Doyle obviously had a great deal of commitment, for philosophy demands reserves of patience and obligation; you must read it over and over again, and think about it slowly and leisurely, before it even begins to make sense. "In your patience possess ye your souls," Luke tells us in the *New Testament*, and Doyle makes reference to this quote and its background thought no less than three times in the Holmes stories alone. We find it in "The Adventure of Wisteria Lodge" when Holmes and Watson discuss the fact that they have no real clues to the crime, and Holmes says, "Well, we can only possess our souls in patience until this excellent inspector comes back for us." You will also find Luke's advice paraphrased in *The Valley of Fear* and "The Adventure of the Three Garridebs," used in each instance with a parallel meaning, and the thought probably appears elsewhere within the full context of Doyle's work. Luke's message seems to be that patience is necessary in the solving of the mystery of life, and to the saving of one's soul. Doyle is well acquainted with the principle of patience, as evidenced by his complex art. Doyle was fully conscious of the vital energy of philosophical issues; he seems to have felt that all figures in the field of philosophy and literature, regardless of place or date, or creative intentions, were his intellectual contemporaries, usually aiding, but often at odds with him in the settlement of abstract, frequently moral problems. Upon studying him carefully we cannot help coming to the conclusion that no other writer of fiction, before or since, has put into their work so much gray matter, so much pure thought and cerebral vigor, without appearing to do so. Unusual about the Holmes stories, all of Doyle's writing actually, is the consistent and persistent elaboration of profound ideas within the literary context, with his relentless utilization of weighty theoretical premises becoming almost obsessive and desperate at times. And this is said with the understanding that I have hardly traced out all the lines of reasoning since I don't have or even know the same maps Doyle used, plus I acknowledge that a good deal of the ultimate meaning and associations found in this work must have gone over my head. Doyle makes reference to writers such as the philosopher Alexander Bain, and I have never read anything by the man, just to give one example. Now we should keep in mind that philosophy, although it may seem slow and dry to many, to a man such as Doyle, who had the money to acquire without too much trouble the books he wanted, plus the energy, patience, and intelligence to understand them, is a highly interesting, absorbing, even entertaining occupation. And to this we must add the fact that these private, thoughtful explorations which his writings actually are, aided him greatly financially. Doyle however, seems to have such a necessity for a philosophical and religious backdrop for his stories that we must ask ourselves why. The main allegorical vision of Doyle is of Christ, his life, death, and resurrection, which are attained, as Carlyle tells us, through a private perceptual memory to a collective one. Doyle is writing Scripture. One message of Descartes is that what truly makes us have existence is that we can have an idea in our mind, and from that a belief in God, for "it necessarily follows that I am not alone in the world, but that there is also some other entity that exists and is the cause of this idea." In his heart Doyle is a Catholic, and seems to have regarded and equated philosophy to an avenue of salvation, for himself, and through Holmes, for his fellow man as well. This belief in the salvation of one's soul through channels of learning and theology is in no way maladaptable to the teachings of the Catholic Church. One can even reach great distinction within the Church itself this way, for men such as Augustine and Aquinas, among others, became saints because they were thinkers and writers. True enough, a limited number of such saints are regarded as true philosophers by the purely secular historians, but such distinctions are valid if you have only a modest, and perhaps no more than an intelligential, interest in the spiritual world, and Doyle would never fall into this category. We know of his awareness of these philosopher/saints for he names the important church in "A Scandal in Bohemia," the Church of St. Monica, after the mother of St. Augustine, and I'm sure Holmes is meant to be "the introspective man" from *Confessions.*

Interlacement is one key to understanding Sir Arthur's writings; his thoughts intercept his thoughts, fuse them, and push them in new directions. He obviously has the ability to merge theology, philosophy, and religious training in his mind, as he has the ability to amalgamate so many other factors from life and literature into the stories. This is not such an unusual capacity; Medieval Schoolmen felt terrible about not being able to canonize Aristotle and Plato, simply because they lived a few hundred years before Christianity. They actually tried to do it, but the popes refused to go along. Some of the narratives, such as "The Yellow Face," and "The Illustrious Client" are so involved with aspects of religion as to literally read like Scripture. One of the last things Doyle said in the hour of his death was, "I am quite serene and happy, quite prepared to go or stay; for I know that life and love go on forever." You can't get more optimistic, or more devout, than that.

As Doyle's appetite for structured religion waned, his belief in spiritualism ballooned. Even if you held that the physical world was merely the product of time, motion, and chance, you could not possibly regard the spiritual realm, if you believed in its existence at all, as the product of accident. What accident could you conceive as having been necessary to bring it into being? Doyle searched for a new meaning to his life to replace that offered by the rigidity of Catholicism, and this new reality is based squarely upon the old, with the focus resting upon the unending wars between good and evil, between life and death. The innovative philosophical hero Holmes calls in original weapons, allies, and strategies, in the struggle.

One aspect of the Christian faith is that you have a certain moral obligation to your fellow man, while the piety of Doyle's religious belief is reinforced by his sense of a secular moral commitment, and he is hardly alone in this matter. Henry James believed that the major function of a novelist like Balzac for instance, was to record the moral history of his age, which I believe is what James himself attempted to do, as it was also the goal of Doyle, and we have some interesting evidence of this. I submit this letter from Wilde to Doyle dated April 1891, in reference to Wilde's novel *The Picture of Dorian Gray*, which had recently been published. "Between me and life there is a mist of words always. I throw probability out of the window for the sake of a phrase, and the chance of an epigram makes me desert truth. Still I do aim at making a work of art, and I am really delighted that you think my treatment subtle and artistically good. The newspapers seem to me to be written by the prurient for the Philistine. I cannot understand how they can treat *Dorian Gray* as immoral. My difficulty was to keep the inherent moral subordinate to the artistic and dramatic effect, and it still seems to me that the moral is too obvious." Doyle and Wilde had apparently been discussing, either through letters or conversation, the question of moral range in a work of art. Doyle appreciates the novel because of its subtle moral, yet also because its message is subordinate to the aesthetic integrity of the piece, and Wilde agrees with him, and both have disliked one newspaper's naïve criticism of the piece for being immoral. It was always Doyle's position that a work should be restrained and artistically good, as Wilde says, but always carry within itself a message.

In speaking of William James, his biographer Ralph Barton Perry tells us, "He was too sensitive to ignore evil, too moral to tolerate it, and too ardent to accept it as inevitable. Optimism was as impossible for him as pessimism.

No philosophy could possibly suit him that did not candidly recognize the dubious fortunes of mankind, and encourage him as a moral individual to buckle on his armor, and go forth to battle." The influence on Doyle of this philosopher need not be reiterated.

Those writers who attain lasting success in their own lifetime do so because in their original ideas they echo the unconscious presuppositions and morals of the age in which they live, and thus appear to have discovered some aspect of truth. Had Hawkeye met Holmes, either in London, or possibly in his forest, which always attracted visitors from Europe, they would both have recognized something in each other. "Morals never did harm to any living mortal, be it that he was a sojourner in the forest, or a dweller in the midst of glazed windows and smoking chimneys. It is only a few hard words that divide us, friend; for I am of opinion, that with use and freedom we should come to understand one another, and mainly settle down into the same judgments of mankind, and of the ways of the world." Hawkeye tells this to a stranger he meets in the woods.

In the secrets of a peoples' art you will find their soul, and Sherlock Holmes personifies that soul, for he signifies an informal way of understanding the world through its reduction to a set of standards, or, if you wish, morals. The people of Doyle's day understood this when Holmes was first presented to them, and this comprehension marked the level of their ethical depths. In the pages of Doyle's stories the best of modern mankind saw that Sherlock was of like passions with themselves, and interestingly enough Holmes also seems to represent the high-water mark of the morals of today's post-modern man, except that many people today are too self-conscious of the fact to take these standards, or themselves, seriously, as we see by the manner in which people often smile or smirk upon hearing of the commission of some crime, or some piece of dishonesty, or skullduggery, or even treachery. It's fashionable and safer to appear more knowing and shrewd than moral in today's society. Neither Holmes, nor Doyle, nor Hawkeye, would have smiled upon learning of a low action being performed. Holmes represents the highest strength that man can attain, and yet still remain a man; for any more intensity and he would become a demigod or superhero, thereby automatically losing his interest for the thinking, critical person. Holmes is a social force, a far more ethical energy than the official law either can or will ever be; a law unto himself, for the good of all. He has feet of clay; he makes mistakes as he therefore fails to triumph in every endeavor, but his strength, including, and perhaps especially his potential for imagination, his vehement sensibility to all that is unjust and wrong in the world, and his balanced sympathy with the wronged and unavenged, place him among the ranks of the highest types: the prophet, the Christian knight and his squire, the poet, the philosopher, the law-giver, the investigator, the irregular soldier in the war against evil. "For the duty which we owe to the weak overrides all other duties and is superior to all circumstances," Doyle wrote in *Micah Clarke.*

Like Socrates, Holmes forces those around him to question themselves as to the wisdom of their judgments; to ask themselves if they cannot probe just a little deeper, or if they couldn't be more accurate in their observations, or perhaps display a bit more keenness in their search for truth, or self-knowledge.

When one feels a strong moral obligation, and acts on it, one makes many friends of a like mind, but also many enemies, and you can define a person by their enemies, as easily, or maybe more so, than by their friends. One great enemy of Holmes is injustice, which Aristotle admits is so vague a concept as to be just about impossible to define, adding that justice is the most difficult virtue to uphold, but Holmes does not retreat from evil because he cannot define it; he goes out of his way to determine its nature, then fights what it is he has concluded is its personality. The importance of the "presentment" scenes in the Canon must never be underestimated. "It's every man's business to see justice done," Sherlock tells us. He is the "seeing eye," as Carlyle calls him who has the capacity to discern the cosmic struggle between good and evil. Crime, one of the great factual details of our world, represents doubt as to the value of life itself, real confusion and error that must lead to solid inquiry, not just a formless search for truths that marginally touch our lives; for crime makes contact with the existence of everyone in one way or another since it deals directly with every aspect and level of society, and possibly represents the most accurate gage we have of any given civilization's failures, shortcomings, or successes. Crime brings into being a loss of the peace of mind of the community, and the faith of the people as to the value of that community, and this value is in doubt until that peace of mind is restored. I use the word community for it derives from "*communis*," the Latin word for "common," as in common law. These pilgrims to Baker Street are the community of troubled minds hoping to achieve, through the interceding of Holmes, a solution to their problems, that resolution often focusing upon gaining retribution for an unavenged wrong. If the appetite and needs of the artist is the determining factor in his work, then Doyle seems to have had an overwhelming dedication for bringing justifiable retribution; a need that has guided the destiny of many. The true detection of crime rests upon concrete demonstrations that thinkers and men of experiments such as Francis Bacon, Charles Peirce, and Dr. Holmes, brought into being. "The object of reasoning is to find out, from the consideration of what we already know, something else which we do not know," Peirce tells us. Questions of doubt are brought to the attention of the investigators in the same way that questions of philosophy are presented to the mind of society and to the minds of the individuals that make up that culture. The demonstrator is instigated by doubt and it is doubt that is the beginning of the Cartesian system of thought, and is indeed, as Diderot claims, responsible for the birth of philosophy itself. The removal of fear and apprehension from the hearts of the people is the function of Sherlock Holmes. And those crimes are committed by his enemies: murderers, blackmailers, scandalmongers, religious frauds, robbers and thieves of all kinds; men who organize and use others by craft and force, poisoners of body and mind, and those whose hearts are so full of vengeance no other emotion can find room to mature. Holmes stands for truth, or rather the spirit of truth, which means science in the intellectual order, justice in the social order, and morals in the human order.

If the violent are not to bear it away, then they must be kept in check by whatever means it takes, as Doyle has learned from his ancestors the Aryans, their laws, and their magnificent leader. If the violent can be reasoned with, as Holmes attempts to reason with Gruner and Moriarty, so much the better, but if they cannot, then as Hawkeye knows, violence shall meet violence, and they shall fall into their own snares. The best example of this is in "The Speckled Band," when the adder is sent back by Holmes to kill the one who would use it to kill a relative for money. The Holmes stories can be thought of as a book of common law, listing for each person his enemies and his moral obligation to fight them, and the methods to be employed in the struggle.

Not all the cases Holmes is called upon to solve are frantic dramas, for often, lesser predicaments (lesser in the eyes of the law, not in the eyes of the victim) are dealt with, as in "A Case of Identity." This is a noteworthy story for it is one of the first written, and as such would be an attempt at setting a construction on the character of the Great Detective. Mr. Windibank has committed no crime for which he can be officially charged but has deceived his daughter into believing she has been appallingly misused by a man, his rationale prompted by monetary benefit. He has, as Holmes realizes, played "as cruel and selfish and heartless a trick in a petty way as ever came before me." Notice he is speaking here much as a judge sitting in court. Holmes' position as a moral arbitrator sometimes extends further than the giving of advice. When Windibank sneers at this inexcusable description of himself, the detective decides to administer his own brand of prairie justice: "it is not part of my duties to my client, but here's a hunting crop handy, and I think I shall just treat myself to — " Unfortunately the villain rushes off before Holmes can thrash him, but the detective's willingness to undertake this act emphasizes his position as the enforcer of standards of decency in cases that are not covered by the civil or criminal codes.

In "The Blue Carbuncle," the doctor opines that a hat Holmes is holding probably has some "deadly story" attached to it. "No crime," Sherlock says laughing. "Only one of those whimsical little incidents which will happen when you have four million human beings all jostling each other within the space of a few square miles. Amid the action and reaction of so dense a swarm of humanity, every possible combination of events may be expected to take place, and many a little problem will be presented which may be striking and bizarre without being criminal."

We find in Doyle's work a pattern of contempt for secret organizations of any kind, and especially for societies whose major purpose for existence is shady self-promotion or the gaining of irrational privilege. These brotherhoods represented to Doyle the capacity for hidden motives of the kind that forms plots and leagues to satisfy greed for money, women, power, or anything else of value. He understood that some of these bands such as the Masons and political clubs, were not actually pursuing iniquitous ends, but nevertheless had potential for great harm, for they could acquire the capability for unlimited loyalty and concentrated power, carrying immense force because of their huge, sometimes secretive membership, and since they were only human, included within their makeup a faculty for almost unlimited corruption brought about by power.

The paramount evil to the people of Zarathustra was the Drug that is deceit, in all its various guises, the epitome of all that is baneful. Innocence renders one susceptible to deceit, Nietzsche claims, and therefore in itself ranks as the capital vice. Remember it was Diderot who realized that it took the greatest intelligence to see the evil in the world. The perfect combination of innocence and deceit appears in one of the most interesting tales in the Canon, one space limitations forced me to neglect — "His Last Bow." In a really astonishing statement Holmes, in warning of the danger offered to Britain by the Germans, and their representative Von Bork, tells us this threat, which the agent himself personifies, is "manifest" to only "the half-dozen people in the world who were really in touch with the truth." We assuredly are dealing with some rarefied intelligence here, and I have wondered what exactly Doyle meant by this, and who were these half-dozen or so people he obviously considered to be the only ones on Holmes', and perhaps his own level. What Doyle has attempted is to illuminate the good in terms of knowledge; something understood in philosophy, Socrates being one example, as well as by some religious leaders, who of course understand it on their own terms. Nietzsche says, "I love him who liveth in order to know, and seeketh to know in order that the Superman may hereafter live."

In our search for the heavy persuaders on the direction of Doyle's mind a few individuals and mental reservations stand out. Descartes' absorbing conceptions represent an evolutionary thrust in philosophy insuring for him an honored niche both in the history of human thought and in the personal understanding of Arthur Doyle. Like the meditations of the Frenchman, the writings of Sir Arthur are an alliance of philosophy, literature, and personal reference; arguments wrapped in fiction with a fine instrumental autobiographic character fostering new, evolved directions of thought. Both men had a resolute need to communicate with the reader, and both also possessed a secretive mind in spite of this; Doyle was a philosophical writer without a proper audience, and Descartes was so enigmatic as to adopt for his persona, "the masked philosopher." The contradictory disposition of both writers points out to us their complicated mental complexion and convoluted needs. The suppositions of Descartes evolved from an informed yet classic, almost unyielding mental exercise, and blossomed in consummate elaboration into the fictional pragmatism of Sherlock Holmes, just as Doyle predicted with his symbolic ploy of having Oliver Wendell Holmes' *The Common Law* being the property of a seventeenth century pragmatic lawyer. Descartes is the masked philosopher in metaphor, but Doyle is the masked philosopher in reality, hiding behind writings that although never considered metaphysical correspondences, most emphatically are. Holmes wears many masks, but none as effective or disarming as his own shrewd face. He mentions a number of times he has read Watson's writings on himself, which is a bow to the philosopher, who in his works places himself as both the author of this "story," as he called his books, and since they are autobiographical, by his own admission, Descartes considers himself his own best reader. A friend of Descartes, in a letter, said his writings showed "the story of your mind," which no doubt pleased him. Descartes believed we must begin with our own mind as the first premise, so to sit still and think to yourself the thought "I think, therefore I am," and to then have this concept become the foundation for construction of an investigation into the nature and value of reality, would be paralleled by the detective as he sits so quietly, and smokes, and thinks: slowly, painstakingly, as did the philosopher, eliminating what must be eliminated if one is to arrive at the truth. He starts at the beginning: his own mind, and reasons outward to a piece of knowledge that can be proved pragmatically. When Sherlock broadcasts his considerations, and the brainwork used to reach these goals, as he does so often, it brings us into his mind, and this is precisely what Descartes tries to accomplish: sharing with us his intricate abstractions, and the steps of the progress, as well as the mental and physical atmosphere surrounding them, as though he were thinking these things for the first time, and inviting us to share in the discovery. Descartes' purpose is to display to you his introspective process, a description of his mental exercises so fine-tuned and rarefied as to evolve into sentences such as "Now I will shut my eyes," and then to involve the reader in the results of these new mental arrangements. The evolution of thought is what Doyle has his protagonist Holmes display, through his conversation and manner, and through the projected thoughts and conduct of Dr. Watson, acting as the form of another "self" for Holmes and acting for the reader as well. The course of the thinking generates the solution: in the case of Descartes, to questions of philosophy, in the case of Holmes, to questions of morals, law, national security, and honor. They are the same thing to the right mind. These ambitious questionings of Descartes occasioned him to be regarded as the first great modern thinker, and Holmes exteriorized that which can be listed as modern or new, or as Doyle hoped to prove, evolved, and that which had evolved out of the old, since it was now merged with the innovative attributes of reason and science, must be better. Wendell Holmes' *The Common Law* is the product of this thought, for its findings represented to some an ameliorated, more evolved interpretation of laws that had been with us since before recorded time. The overwhelmingly modern moral nature of Doyle's intentions comes through in every story, once we know how to look for it, and often enough it must be searched for on the level of an experiment; a practical application of Wendell Holmes' theories of how new thought must generate diverse adaptations of ancient codes. This attitude creates an energy coupled with a striking, searching intelligence, making of Sherlock Holmes a more effective appreciator of the moral turmoil of his epoch than anyone else around him. His apprehension of right is based, as was that of Wendell Holmes, upon a belief in the role of scientific investigations in the search for new certainty, hoping to replace outdated truths. His active energies are not paralyzed by the possibilities of enfeebling doubt, nor his reason drawn down by apprehension lest his methods should discredit a document, or its inferences clash with a dogma or an outmoded law, or his light flash unseasonably upon a mystery best kept hidden. What he does keep hidden is best kept hidden.

A good deal of Doyle's quest for modernity can be summed up in his persistent use of American models. America was the newest country on the map, and the new has always been the first prerequisite for the cutting-edge, especially the new spirit of experimentation in such diverse fields as law, science, politics, religion, social science, and so forth, evidenced in the new country. One fundamental archetype I located for the experimental nature of Holmes, a primary source for the investigational force of the man is an American, Dr. Sitgreaves, surgeon for the American Army, found in *The Spy*. He is, as Cooper tells us, "a man of experiments." "What do you think is the greatest pleasure in life?" the doctor asks Captain John Lawton one day. "That may be difficult to answer," Lawton replies. The surgeon claims, "it is in witnessing, or rather feeling, the ravages of disease repaired by the lights of science cooperating with nature. I once broke my little finger intentionally, in order that I might reduce the fracture and watch the cure: it was only on a small scale, you know, dear John; still I think the thrilling sensation excited by the knitting of the bone, aided by the contemplation of the art of man thus acting in unison with nature, exceeded any other enjoyment that I have ever experienced. Oh! had it been one of the more important members, such as the leg or arm, how much greater must the pleasure have been!" The doctor is one who will experiment on his own body, if that will bring him closer to the truth, and to knowledge. Now, Sitgreaves has been introduced by Cooper as a figure of comic relief, but isn't there something humorous about Holmes when he is initially introduced to the world, particularly his conversation with Captain John Watson, in which we are shown his experiments with blood, using his own body as an instrument for finding the truth? It should also be remarked that if you take your physical description of Sitgreaves, you have a picture of Holmes. The spirit of Holmes' blood test is based upon Sitgreaves' own, while its format, as we know, is supplied by yet another American, an immigrant from Scotland — Alexander Bell. Doyle elaborates on this exploratory nature of his hero, searching the human record for justification through other examples in his quest for modernity.

Pragmatists such as Wright and Peirce believed that philosophy's proper function was as an expression and instrument of human needs; that new truths are not to be searched for only in the knowledge we already have, "or educable from what is patent to common observation." Holmes is "making us observe what we have entirely overlooked, or search out what has eluded our observation," as Wright puts it. In Wright's essay on Darwin, Doyle came across the following: "The doctrines of the special and prophetic providences and decrees of God, and of the metaphysical isolation of human nature, are based, after all, on barbaric conceptions of dignity, which are restricted in their application by every step forward in the progress of science." Charles Frankel said of Peirce that he "brought the spirit of laboratory science to philosophy, but he also brought the tradition of romantic idealists like Schelling." Here then is Sherlock Holmes, half scientist, half romantic idealist, and all pragmatist.

American philosophy is predominantly the thoughts of men who believed the world was good, but that it needed to be changed, who thought perhaps that it was good, indeed, because it needed to be changed. This idea, and much else of what we have been saying, seems to reach ultimately to William James. The overlapping dates and convertible thoughts of Doyle and James place them figuratively writing side by side; James was even more of a contemporary than Nietzsche. I believe Doyle was instigated to bring Holmes back from the dead after reading *The Varieties of Religious Experience*, thus placing William James light years ahead of any other influence in terms of volume alone, not to mention value. Had James published his work on mankind's religious nature a few years prior to the introduction of Holmes to the world, the detective might have been a somewhat altered character, perhaps an altogether different person than we know. Imagine if Doyle had the authority, intelligence, and sensibility of William James to draw upon all those years. In James' "The Dilemma of Determinism," Doyle came across some overall views of James worth developing. "When the healthy love of life is on one, and all its forms and its appetites seem so unutterably real; when the most brutal and the most spiritual things are lit by the same sun, and each is an integral part of the total richness, — why, then it seems a grudging and sickly way of meeting so robust a universe to shrink from any of its facts and wish them not to be. Rather take the strictly dramatic point of view, and treat the whole thing as a great unending romance which the spirit of the universe, striving to realize its own content, is eternally thinking out and representing to itself." Borrowing the mentality of James he is most familiar with, Doyle constructed strong romances of their essence. In the same piece the philosopher explores the question of determinism: if man has the freedom to determine his acts or if his actions are determined for him by the actions of the universe into which he is born, and determined before he was born. The question of good and evil and its relationship to man comes up, with James implying that evil is necessary for it sets a moral example; evil seems to be a form of truth itself. Without this example "a race of creatures of such unexampled insipidity should succeed," and life would be so banal as to be meaningless. "Regarded as a stable finality, every outward good becomes a mere weariness to the flesh. It must be menaced, be occasionally lost, for its goodness to be fully felt as such. Nay, more than occasionally lost. No one knows the worth of innocence till he knows it is gone forever, and that money cannot buy it back. Not the saint, but the sinner that repenteth, is he to whom the full length and breadth, and height and depth, of life's meaning is revealed. Not the absence of vice, but vice there, and virtue holding her by the throat, seems the ideal human state. And there seems no reason to suppose it not a permanent human state. There is a deep truth in what the school of Schopenhauer insists on, — the illusoriness of the notion of moral progress." The quote goes on to become, for readers of Doyle, more specific. "The more brutal forms of evil that go are replaced by others more subtle and more poisonous. Our moral horizon moves with us as we move, and never do we draw nearer to the far-off line where the black waves and the azure meet. The final purpose of our creation seems most plausibly to be the greatest possible enrichment of our ethical consciousness, through the intensest play of contrasts and the widest diversity of characters. This of course obliges some of us to be vessels of wrath, while it calls others to be vessels of honor. But the subjectivist point of view reduces all these outward distinctions to a common denominator. The wretch languishing in the felon's cell may be drinking draughts of the wine of truth that will never pass the lips of the so-called favorite of fortune. And the peculiar consciousness of each of them is an indispensable note in the great ethical concert which the centuries as they roll are grinding out of the living heart of man." Holmes is both a vessel of wrath and honor for lacking evil upon which to vent his wrath he finds life "banal," and we have seen good and evil at each other's throats at Reichenbach Falls, and so evenly matched that neither could destroy the other without annihilating itself. Eventually evil is conquered for the sake of a new world, at least until Col. Moran, "more subtle and more poisonous," makes an appearance. The "intensest play of contrasts and the widest diversity of characters," is a characterizing feature of the Holmes stories, with the supreme example of thoughtful contrasting repeatedly emphasized; Tonga and Small come to mind, as do Holmes and Watson, Holmes and Moriarty, Moran and Adair, etc., and the stories are replete with character diversity: Negroes, mulattos, Islanders, North and South Americans, Hindus, Australians, Germans; the list goes on.

In Arthur Conan Doyle's stories we are listening, like Holmes to his music, to the "great ethical concert," of life. Doyle endorsed the assessment, with James and others, that man is not to maintain the role of a disinterested spectator; the knower is not the watcher, the observer, rather, he is an actor. In the person of Sir James Damery, found in "The Illustrious Client" and based upon the philosopher William James, with some of his brother Henry thrown in, we meet a man who could not sit by while a terrible moral error was to be committed, and thus becomes the instigator of Holmes' intervention in the problem, and one who is quite capable himself of speaking the approximate biblical injunction that was actually a poetic summing up by William James of his own philosophy: "These, then, are my last words to you: Be not afraid of life. Believe that life is worth living and your belief will help create the fact."

Now I realize I seem to be harping on the religious and moral aspect of these stories to an inordinate degree, but there is justification for this, for essentially, at least on some levels, they *are* religious and moral tales, with some of Doyle's writings bordering on theology, with Holmes a proxy Jesus and a surrogate Zarathustra; like them a man of flesh and blood carrying on the work of God. For Carlyle the great man and God stood in a special relationship; the great man like God made order out of chaos, the chaos that confronts us and causes anxiety in our lives. The work of such a man becomes therefore similar to the work of God, revolving upon the individual problems that the great man found himself facing. This it is that makes the biography of such people a form of modern Scripture. Nietzsche, speaking in metaphor, tells us it is up to the "creating will" to create God, adding that God has now been replaced by the Superman. "Could ye *create* a God?" he asks, realizing the answer to be in the negative. "Then, I pray you, be silent about all gods! But ye could well create the Superman." Doyle, in his admiration for the philosopher, feels himself called upon to create the Superman, and in the shadow of Jesus, whom even Nietzsche loved. The German philosopher placed these particular thoughts in the chapter of *Thus Spake Zarathustra* entitled "In the Happy Isles," which the optimistic Doyle equated with the British Isles, and it is to be his creation Holmes who will bring this dream into a more focused reality.

Jesus is an end product of evolution, a new testament, a new law, evolving from the Mosaic Law, the old law. "Behold, I make all things new," is the message of Jesus. The comparison between Holmes and Jesus is made many times, but nowhere more skillfully than that found in "The Illustrious Client," where we actually find both William James and Doyle telling us why they write as they do, why they believe as they do. Sir James Damery attempts to convince Holmes into handling the Violet de Merville case, but the detective is reluctant to accept the challenge, so Sir James, as he is leaving Baker Street, tells Sherlock, "The Carlton Club will find me. But in case of emergency, there is a private telephone call, 'XX.31.'" That "XX.31" is obviously a numerical reference to the *Bible*, and in the King James Version, Gospel of St. John, Chapter XX, line 31, we find, in reference to the teachings of Jesus, the following: "But these are written, that ye might believe that Jesus is the Christ, the Son of God; and that believing ye might have life through his name." The giving of eternal life, through Christ, is the ultimate theme of the work. Violet personifies all naive mankind whose spiritual life is being jeopardized by the snares of the devil himself.

In "The Moral Philosopher," a later essay, James sets forth the thoughts of Jesus in his own words, then follows these up with his own reasoning, his interpretation, culminating with these words: "See, I have set before thee this day life and good, and death and evil; therefore choose life that thou and thy seed may live." James tells us this paraphrasing brings us the true message of Christ, adding, "when this challenge comes to us, it is simply our total character and personal genius that are on trial; and if we invoke any so-called philosophy, our choice and use of that also are but revelations of our personal aptitude or incapacity for moral life." Holmes will accept this challenge, as Kant tells him he must, with willingness, for it is his character and personal genius. "The solving word, for the learned and the unlearned man alike, lies in the last resort in the dumb willingnesses and unwillingnesses of their interior characters, and nowhere else. It is not in heaven, neither is it beyond the sea; but the word is very nigh unto thee, in thy mouth and in thy heart, that thou mayest do it." Thus does James conclude his thoughts on the moral philosopher and the moral life. In his eulogy upon the death of William James, André Chaumeix, writing in *Revue des Deux-Mondes*, hailed him as one who restored life to the universe.

In his *The Life of Samuel Johnson*, Boswell tells us he found a memorandum Johnson had written just after finishing his *Lives of the Poets* in which he expressed his hopes that his great work of biography had been a moral enterprise, and "Written, I hope, in such a manner as may tend to the promotion of piety." Boswell calls Johnson, "our great Moralist."

"And I choose Piety," the ancient Zarathustra, as though he was reading our minds, emphasizes, as we have noted before, in the *Zend-Avesta*, "the bounteous and the good, mine may she be. And therefore I loudly deprecate all robbery and violence."

We see that Doyle during the course of his lifetime gave up his Catholicism and converted to Protestantism, such an act being considered the decision of one who is truly a believer, secure in his belief in a Deity, and definitely not the action of a skeptic. He found it easy to give up one Christian religion for another, since for one who believes, just about any religion will do. Such a man knows all sorts of ways of worshiping and is always at worship. The old attitude of obligations toward devout service and the Deity do not pass away to leave a vacancy but are transferred into an equally fervid commitment (perhaps more so for being the result of conversion) and service toward one's fellow man and especially toward those who have found equal disillusionment in their society and its ability to protect them from evil and harm. What we miss of the ancient solace and personal protection of a religious order grows into a moral sense of participation in the common good, of our new beliefs having a destination of their own, in this case the ethical code found within all the Holmes stories. The removal of apprehensions and dread from the hearts of his people is the function of Holmes. In this way we do not feel as though we have abandoned that which should not have been abandoned, nor that we have in turn been abandoned. Descartes creates philosophy, Sherlock upholds the common law, and Jesus with his life and thoughts solves questions of morals and faith; all three carry peace to a troubled world. All three set conditions for imitation that have been taken up by uncountable numbers of people. The other writers: William and Henry James, Nietzsche, Cooper, Carlyle, Diderot, and so many others I must pretend to overlook, give splendid aesthetic guidance and judgment, while the heroes, such as Zarathustra, Hawkeye, and Beowulf, set further example if necessary.

The Holmes stories satisfy on various levels with one possibility for the universal acceptance of him as a hero being his author's eclectic borrowing from nearly all the Western and some Eastern systems of thought. Contributions from just about every literate culture, and so many eras, plus great blocks of thought from diverse religions, all add to the cerebral makeup of the tales. Through the character of the Detective, the Doctor, and the Professor, and everyone else found within the pages, and through situations the reader could, and often does recognize as his own brave new world, they bring all literature, no matter how ancient, and philosophies, no matter how seemingly unrelated, into the light of modern society. This was the approximate goal Doyle set out to reach when he used the lab at St. Bart's as a backdrop for his introduction to the world of his man of experiments.

The force of the allegories does not lie in their ideological themes however, since the sources and intentions for these arguments were, for the most part, never guessed at. In Doyle's Holmes and non-Holmes tales alike, there is a great deal of simple wish fulfillment and escapism, both of which are beneficial, possibly essential, to mankind, and both of which the world will always have a genuine need of. The tales, and the very character of the man are cathartic in nature, even, as we have seen, whether or not their true personality and intentions are realized. To borrow a thought from Aristotle, they purge the senses as it were, through an intuitive grasp of their purpose and goals. Even the fact that so many people in such diverse backgrounds worldwide admire and imitate Holmes is revealing. And according to witnesses, Doyle performed much of his work in brief periods of time, and often under unsuitable conditions, such as while in line to purchase a railroad ticket, or standing in the street waiting for a bus. His memory must have been truly superior, as was his ability to organize his notes and thoughts.

Time and space make a more complete examination of the messages within the stories an insurmountable difficulty for me, so I know they are still rife with mystery; there were also plenty I could not figure out. The real meanings of the writings are like objects carried in a glacier, with some rocks on the surface, but most below, and therefore not easily seen, or even surmised. I say this with complete confidence for I know what it is I have had to leave out of this study, and I have also dealt with only the four novels and a small block of short stories, ignoring the majority.

Sherlock Holmes, like the Enlightenment itself, personifies a transformation from fixed and finished forms of thought to that of a philosophical basis being the essential instrument into new investigative methods, that in turn leading to more complete truths. Thoughts leading to thoughts leading to yet more thoughts is the way the great philosophers have written, and it is the method of studying the Holmes stories. Holmes is the restless, contemplative curiosity of the Enlightenment, blended with the later richness of British Empiricism and the "almost" common sense American approach to the world, having found a home in a mind as subtle as Descartes. The common sense aspect here is not spoken of delinquently, for although it is not a necessity for philosophical thought, it is a prerequisite condition for investigations conducted in Holmes' field (a field in which enormous endeavor must combat and outwit the cupidity of those who cannot restrain themselves), that of the law, and the upholding of the common law, on which all government is based, and upon which modern man, as did his ancestors, relies upon to protect his farm and cattle, his family and himself, from the bands of rovers.

Doyle filled the character of Sherlock Holmes with so much doubt, confidence, speculation, and personality, that he seems like any other growing and changing living being, and the growth is not over yet. The thoughts of Arthur Conan Doyle are still rich in potential and at best I have only scratched the surface, believe me.

Some Recommended Readings

You can't go wrong tracing the pathways of Arthur Doyle's mind. Throughout the field of philosophy, practically every piece of writing contributes interesting ways of thinking; here are a few of these books, and others, that I know he read — and some he must have read. Many of these are essays or short stories, and they can often be found in collected works. Where I list a writer without mentioning a particular work, essentially everything he wrote is worth reading — and any edition or translation you find will do.

Aristotle

Barr, Robert

Beowulf

Berkeley, George

Bible, Old and New Testaments

Boswell, *The Life of Samuel Johnson*

Butler, *The Lives of the Saints*

Carlyle, Thomas

Cooper, James Fenimore

Cassirer, Ernest, *The Age of Enlightenment*

Collins, Wilkie

De Montesquieu, *The Spirit of the Law* (10 volumes)

Descartes, René

Diderot, Dennis

Dickens, Charles

Elliot, George

Hawthorne, Nathaniel

Holmes, Oliver Wendell Jr.

Holmes, Oliver Wendell Sr.

James, William
James, Henry
Kant, Immanuel
Le Fanu, Joseph Sheridan
Macaulay, Thomas
Mill, John Stuart
Melville, Herman, *Moby Dick*
Nietzsche, Friedrich
Pierce, Charles Saunders
Plato
Poe, Edgar Allan
Royce, Josiah
Scott, Walter
Sacred Books of the East (25 volumes)
Swedenborg, Emanuel
Thoreau, Henry David
Verne, Jules
Wilde, Oscar
Wright, Chauncey

INDEX

A

Adler, Irene, 30, 123-127, 130-135, 137, 140, 345

Agassiz, Louis, 53, 76, 183, 184

Alison, Archibald, 227

Arbuthnot, Aline, 97, 348

Aristotle, 70, 75, 94, 113, 218, 251, 307, 310, 323, 324, 378, 380, 389

Aryans, 99-102, 104-109, 143, 381

B

Baker Street Irregulars, 36, 105

Barr, Robert, 96, 97, 347

Beecher, Edward, 359, 360

Bell, Alexander Graham, 73, 74, 384

Bell, Dr. Joseph, 2, 12, 20, 74, 99, 119, 219

Beowulf, 267-270, 274, 291, 292, 388

Berkeley, George, 69, 78, 198, 306, 307

Boone, Hugh, 185, 186

Bouhours, Dominique, 225, 226, 301, 302

Brent, John, 96, 97, 348, 349

Brockton Murder, 194

Butler, General Benjamin, 20, 159, 180, 361-366

C

Clay, John, 220-228, 302, 303, 379

Clive, Robert (Lord), 146, 147, 233

Collins, Wilkie, 2, 20, 42, 64, 90, 124, 125, 159, 285, 336

Cuff, Sergeant, 20, 159

D

Damery, Sir James, 166, 191, 192, 201, 386, 387

Darwin, Charles, 36, 51, 70, 79, 99, 128-130, 161, 202, 349, 384

Dante, 130, 265, 271, 297

De Condillac, Etienne, 306

De Montesquieu, Baron, 317

De Quincey, Thomas, 285, 286, 309

Dickens, Charles, 10, 145, 185, 235, 281, 295

Divine Comedy, The, 297

Dubos, René, 302-304

E

Eliot, George, 130, 179, 181

Enlightenment, The, 5, 34, 217-223, 226, 228, 229, 252, 256, 299, 300, 302, 309, 356, 376, 389

Erigena, John Scotus, 197

F

Ferrier, John, 38, 40, 41, 43, 45, 47, 84, 125, 179, 210

Ferrier, Lucy, 38, 41, 45, 47, 84, 125, 210

Fontenelle, Bernard, 308

Printed in the United States
By Bookmasters